THE PEOPLE'S ADVOCATE

THE PEOPLE'S ADVOCATE

—

THE LIFE *and*
LEGAL HISTORY
of AMERICA'S
MOST FEARLESS
PUBLIC INTEREST
LAWYER

—

DANIEL SHEEHAN

COUNTERPOINT

BERKELEY

Library of Congress Cataloging-in-Publication Data

Sheehan, Daniel P.
 People's advocate : the life and legal history of America's most fearless public interest lawyer / Daniel Sheehan.
    pages cm
  ISBN 978-1-61902-172-3
  1. Sheehan, Daniel P. 2. Cause lawyers—United States—Biography. I. Title.

  KF373.S485A3 2013
  340.092—dc23
  [B]

  2013014410

  ISBN 978-1-61902-172-3

Cover design by Faceout Studios
Interior design by meganjonesdesign.com

COUNTERPOINT
1919 Fifth Street
Berkeley, CA 94710
www.counterpointpress.com

Printed in the United States of America
Distributed by Publishers Group West

10 9 8 7 6 5 4 3 2 1

To the courageous people whom I have had the privilege of defending as an attorney over my 45 years of legal service:

From Bill Baird who had the courage to be the first to stand up for the right of every unmarried person to engage in responsible birth control; to Paul Pappas who first stood up for the right of every journalist to protect the identity of his or her confidential news sources; to Daniel Ellsberg and the Editors of The New York Times who had the courage to release The Pentagon Papers to the world; to Karen Silkwood who died to stop the construction of dangerous new private nuclear power plants in our country and to stop the smuggling of bomb-grade plutonium to Israel and Iran by our American C.I.A.; to the members of the American Indian Movement who stood their ground against the power of the the U.S. Government at Wounded Knee; to the journalists who died in the jungles of Central America at the hands of the "Off-The-Shore Enterprise" of Ronald Reagan and George H.W. Bush and to Tony Avirgan who survived that attack to give rise to The Iran/Contra Scandal; to Archbishop John Fitzpatrick and Stacey Lynn Merkt and their co-workers at Casa Romero on the Texas border who struggled in The American Sanctuary Movement to give refuge to the innocents who fled the death squads in Latin America trained and funded by our American government; to the courageous friends of Mayor Eddie Carthan, the first elected Black Mayor in the Deep Delta of Mississippi and to the young men and women who gave their lives on the streets of Greensboro, North Carolina confronting the Ku Klux Klan, who, together, successfully pushed back the night of racism in America; to all of the other lesser-well- known women and men whom I have had the privilege of represented who had the courage to give real meaning to our American Constitution, this work is dedicated. Without these courageous "people", their would be no People's Advocate.

CONTENTS

PART IV

FOREWORD

M Y GENERATION HAS been characterized to a degree of nearly mythi-
cal proportions: "the most-written-about" of all presently living generations; "the largest generation in the history of our human family"; "the
best-educated generation in human history"; the most idealistic of all of the
generations presently alive; the most activist generation in human history.
What has not been so widely acknowledged, however, is that we remain the
most *unfulfilled* generation in all of human history. For we, as a generation,
have set very high goals for ourselves, and we have made certain promises—
each of us to ourselves, and to each other, back during a very special time
that we all shared together: "The '60s."

I consider "The '60s" to have taken place not during the single decade
between 1960 and 1970, as one might reasonably expect, but over the full
twenty-year period that extended from the mid-1950s to the mid-1970s.
This "special period" began with the rise of Elvis Presley and Chuck Berry
and rock-and-roll music in the mid-'50s, which helped weld the still-dispa-
rate members of our generation into a unified entity, distinguishing us from
those who had gone before us and from those who were to come after. This
period progressed through the ascent to stardom of actors like James Dean
and Marlon Brando in their respective generation-defining motion picture
roles in *Rebel without a Cause* and *On the Waterfront*, continuing through
the 1960 election and inauguration of President John F. Kennedy . . . and
his assassination on November 22, 1963. It then carried us into 1968 and
the traumatic assassinations of Dr. Martin Luther King Jr. and Robert
Kennedy, followed by the infamous police riot at the Democratic National
Convention; into 1971 and the public exposure of the illegality of the
Vietnam War with the publication of the Pentagon Papers; through Richard
Nixon's presidential resignation in 1974; and on to the 1975 exposure of the
Cold War crimes of the U.S. central intelligence community exposed by the

1

Senate Select Committee Hearings on Intelligence Abuse, chaired by Senator Frank Church of Idaho. Until that point, we as a generation expected that the wrongs of our nation that had then been publicly exposed would be corrected simply by our having exposed them to the world, just as we had been taught they would be by our parents' generation.

It was, indeed, this twenty-year period that has come to be known as "The '60s."

I feel privileged—and very grateful—for the opportunity to recount the details of a number of the most important legal cases that I personally investigated and tried during that period, as well as some of the cases that I litigated in the immediate aftermath of this period. However, these stories are about more than just these cases. They will tell you the story of an era, and of the generation that lived it.

Harvard and Yale sociologists William Strauss and Neil Howe have observed—correctly, I believe—in their insightful 1991 work *Generations: The History of America's Future* that each generation of our human family is born within a specific twenty-one- to twenty-five-year period. The demarcations of different generations are not necessarily confined to arbitrary twenty-five-year points but rather are generated by the major events in the lives of members of each generation, both in their minds and in their consciousness.

Thus the very first members of *my* 82-million-member generation were born on the morning of February 3, 1943, immediately following the official surrender of the German Fifth Army before the gates of Stalingrad in Russia. That event came just seven months after the destruction of the Japanese Imperial Navy by our U.S. Navy's Sixth Fleet at the famous Battle of Midway on June 7, 1942, which was just six months after Japan's attack on Pearl Harbor. At the Battle of Midway, the U.S. Navy inflicted such irreparable damage on the Japanese fleet that military historians have characterized that specific naval engagement as the most stunning and decisive blow in the history of naval warfare. Therefore, the destruction of the German Fifth Army in Russia has come to be uniformly recognized by historians as the clear turning point of World War II, the point at which the Allied powers of Western civilization saw that they had finally successfully broken the

Axis powers of Germany, Japan, and Italy, causing them to realize that victory for the Allies in World War II was, from that date forward, essentially a forgone conclusion.

For that reason, beginning on the morning of February 3, 1943, every American baby born over the next twenty-one-year period was born into what William Strauss and Neil Howe in their 1991 work entitled *Generations: A History of America's Future* described as "a rising sense of élan": an atmosphere of ever-growing optimism and confidence that all things are possible. Such an atmosphere, according to Strauss and Howe, generated a classic "idealist generation." This idealistic atmosphere pervaded the United States until night fell on November 22, 1963: "the day the music died" for our generation.

Since that tragic day—the date that will stand engraved upon the consciousness of every member of my generation like no other date in our shared history—a plurality of the members of our generation has directed a significant percentage of our collective time, intellect, and emotional attention to trying to determine what went wrong with America that could conceivably have made that terrible day possible. This plurality of our generation has been trying, for fifty years now, to discern exactly what steps we need to take as a generation to make certain that the ideals that we were taught by our fathers and mothers of the World War II generation will be made operative in our country before we, as a generation, pass from the scene of history.

For this reason, while the story that follows is, in one sense, "my story" and the story of my legal career, it is, in a larger and much more important sense, the story of my generation and the unique period in which we came of age. It is the story of the period in which we came to be first inspired, then disillusioned, then consciously unsatisfied . . . but hopefully, in the final analysis, idealistically rededicated to fulfilling the promises that we made to each other and to ourselves, so long ago now, in "The '60s."

The principal dynamic of the real-life drama that unfolds in the work that follows—and remains today—is a profound and unresolved clash of worldviews between, on the one hand, the ideals of our nation and the potential *next* cultural iteration of our nation and, on the other hand, the age-old, cynical values of the World War II generation that coalesced to

generate the American National Security State that still dominates and gov-
erns the conduct of our entire Western civilization.

I no longer harbor any remaining doubt that the creators of this
American National Security State sincerely believe that the principal value
of our American government and culture is to protect and promote our
"national security," even at the direct expense of compromising the abstract
principles on which our nation was founded. They have done so to guard
our nation, initially against the potential encroachment of world communism led by the Soviet Union and more recently, following the events of
September 11, 2001, against so-called terrorists who are (according to these
National Security State champions) fervently dedicated to the total elimination of "our way of life" in the West. Since the United States and our "values" (more candidly, the *economic* and *commercial* interests of those who
control the wealth of our nation) are perceived, by these World War II–generation men, as being so seriously threatened by these "potentially insurgent
communities," they deemed it to be necessary to make certain that virtually
all of our conduct in the field of American foreign *and domestic* policy be
governed by what would be viewed by many to be values and beliefs that are
not only diametrically opposed to the most fundamental founding principles
of our nation but indeed profoundly contradictory to the most deeply professed spiritual beliefs of the majority of our own American people.

On the other hand, a *plurality* of the members of our post–World War II
generation came to believe, during "The 60s," in the primacy of the idealistic
principles on which our nation was purportedly founded: equality; personal
freedom; fairness and openness in government; the guaranteed protection,
by our government, of fundamental individual human rights and civil liberties against government repression and against infringement by other forms
of great accumulated power and wealth; the promotion of genuine competition along with the safeguarding of equality of economic opportunity for
all, regardless of the race, ethnic origin, gender, religious belief, or degree
of personal wealth into which one was born rather than sustaining privilege
and favoritism on behalf of the wealthiest and most politically powerful.

Again, make no mistake about this. These two expressly different and
competing sets of values, though not necessarily contradictory sets of values,

have come to be held as the principal values of our nation by a clear plurality of the two distinct generations that clashed during "The 60s," generating the great drama that distinguished this era.

I was a direct participant in this clash, as the work that follows will set forth in detail.

Just as "The 60s" endured specific challenges, so must our current generation of Americans address three major challenges that present a very real "clear and present danger." I believe there are three distinct challenges. These are (1) the immediate current situation in the Middle East, threatening a possible nuclear exchange between Israel and either Pakistan or Iran; (2) the rushing onset of global warming and major climate change, which will generate the massive inundation of our planet's seacoasts, generating the resultant contamination of one-third of our presently available fresh drinking water supply; and (3) the increasing threat of a major thermonuclear exchange between China and the West.

And, of course, there is the continuing dilemma of our entire global economic system, the effective functioning of which is fundamentally grounded and tied to privately owned, profit-driven transnational business corporations and their continued consumption of massive unsustainable quantities of our planet's natural resources.

These major challenges constitute a very real "crisis" that presently confronts the members of our two generations *right now*. All present generations have an unavoidable responsibility to come together and cooperate in formulating concrete and immediate solutions to these twenty-first-century public policy challenges.

PART I

CHAPTER *one*

I T WAS MARCH 21st of 1963.

I was lying atop Harrison Hill, just a short hawk's flight from the northern shore of Lake George, in the Adirondack Mountains. I was in my front yard, in Warrensburg, in upstate New York. Hands folded behind my head, gazing up into the night sky, I was lying in a bed of fresh green grass.

John Kennedy was in Hyannis Port, Massachusetts, that night. He was alive and well, and he was our president—just as he should have been.

Dr. Martin Luther King Jr. was in Selma, Alabama, that night, leading the Southern Christian Leadership Conference. He was marching for human rights in the South—just as he should have been.

And Bobby Kennedy was alive and well that night as well. He was in his Justice Department office down in Washington, D.C., working late into the night with his tie hanging loosely at his neck, white shirt sleeves rolled up to his elbows, scuffed shoes up on his huge wooden desk. He was our attorney general—just as he should have been.

I would turn eighteen in just twenty days. It was springtime in America—and the springtime of my life.

I began thinking back on my trip, just two weeks earlier, down to New York City, to meet with Senator Jacob Javits, one of New York's two U.S. senators. I had traveled to his Fifth Avenue office by Greyhound bus from my tiny hometown of three thousand people to ask him for his senatorial appointment to the United States Air Force Academy in Colorado. Senator Javits had been very gracious that day. He came out from his luxurious, oak-paneled office, shook my hand warmly, and then personally escorted me, his right arm lightly across my shoulder, into his inner sanctum. He gestured toward an expensive leather couch that ran the entire length of the far wall of his many-pictured office, inviting me to sit with a subtle gesture of his well-manicured right hand. Then he drew up a large matching leather armchair and placed it directly in front of the couch where I was sitting and lowered himself comfortably into it.

He appraised me with calm consideration. Then he asked me, simply and straightforwardly, why I wanted to go to the United States Air Force Academy when, it seemed to him, from the folder resting on his lap, that I could have gone to any college of my choice. Even, perhaps, to Harvard or Yale.

I wondered how many times this smallish, handsome man, with his rather pink complexion, had played out this same scene, or a similar one, with other applicants, or with other U.S. senators—or with men of even greater power. It seemed to me that this role came quite naturally to him.

I was very impressed. But, then, who was I? Just a small-town upstate New York high school senior whose future this powerful man held, so casually, in his manicured hands. I was not nervous. I actually felt happy. I knew that things were going just as they should be going and that I was, therefore, exactly where I was supposed to be that day.

I was proud to be one of the very few (five, I was told) *senatorial* candidates for the United States Air Force Academy that year from New York State—the number 1 state in our nation.

I was looking forward to flying off to the United States Air Force Academy in Colorado Springs, Colorado, in July, immediately following my graduation from high school, right after we claimed another New York State Section II Class D Baseball Championship—just as it should be. That would be my first time on an airplane, the first step on my way to the stars. It all seemed so natural to me, just as natural as my looking forward to winning another high school baseball championship. It was just one more natural step in the progression of my young life as an idealistic young American in that best of all times: "The 60s."

"I want to be an astronaut," I said, without hesitation.

The older man smiled, with more than just a hint of condescension: *Doesn't every young man?* he seemed to be thinking to himself. But he didn't say it. After all, this man was a United States senator; he knew how to keep his own counsel.

After his smile, he asked, "And just *why* is it that you want to be an astronaut . . . Dan?"

His question was tinged with just a trace of sarcasm, something bordering almost on boredom, the product, no doubt, of his anticipation of hearing the same trite answer that virtually *every* red-blooded American boy might have been expected to have given to that question on that March day in 1963. This was, after all, just one year after John Glenn had circled earth in his *Mercury* space capsule, an event that had been broadcast live, over radio, into our classrooms in Warrensburg and into virtually every other classroom across America.

"You don't mind if I call you Dan, do you, son?" he asked.

"Danny will be fine," I replied. "Everyone calls me Danny." I hesitated, for just a moment, then I added, "Actually, that's my name. Danny, not Daniel, not Dan, but Danny. That's what it says on my birth certificate. Danny . . . Daniel . . . Dan. I was named after my father's best friend . . . Danny . . . in the army . . . in the war . . . Danny. He was killed, on the beach, at Salerno, in September of 1943 . . . right next to my father. In fact, he was blown up *all over* my father."

The older man was startled.

I was telling him the simple truth, just as my father had told it to me on a night five years earlier, out in California, through his tears, when he was drunk.

I could see that Senator Javits was profoundly affected by this response to his simple question as to whether or not he could call me Dan. It was apparently more than he had expected. After a long and awkward silence, he began again.

"Ahhhh . . . where is your father now, Dan . . . ahh . . . Danny?"

"I don't know, Senator Javits. I haven't seen my father for five years now, just as I have not seen my mother . . . or my brother Patty . . . or my sister Colleen. You see, my father became an alcoholic during the war. He is a ruined man now, Senator. It was the war. My mother and father are divorced now. Well, not actually divorced . . . *separated* is the word that we use for it. We are Catholics. And Catholics don't get 'divorced.' We get 'separated.' I have been 'separated' from my father . . . and from my mother and brother and sister . . . since I was twelve. I live with my Aunt Gladys and Uncle Jim, up in Warrensburg, just north of Lake George. Aunt Gladys is my mother's older sister. She is the matriarch of the Bidwell family, my mother's side of the family."

I hesitated, then gestured to the pale manila folder in his lap.

"But then, you know all of that. It's all right there . . . in the file."

A look of sudden embarrassment, almost panic, whispered quickly across the older man's features, but for just an instant. Then it disappeared just as quickly, drawn back within him like a silent breath. It occurred to me that his ability to conceal his true feelings had become a well-learned skill for him.

He had clearly not read the file.

I sat there, watching the older man wrestling with some internal ghost. What was it that was going on behind his eyes? Why was he so uncomfortable? Was it something that I had said? I thought that I had better break the awkward silence by telling him a little more about me.

I had taken all the required courses and had passed them all with flying colors; indeed, with straight A's in every one of them. As I was to learn later, I had scored among the three highest grade point averages of any of the applicants in the entire state of New York. And I had scored the very highest of all on all the physical tests—because I had insisted on taking, and passing, the United States Air Force astronaut flight physical, just to let it be known, as early as possible, exactly what it was that I intended to do in the air force. I had run all of the required miles—faster and farther than anyone else in the state. I had done all of the required push-ups at the Plattsburg Air Force Base in northern New York, where I had gone to do the physical. In fact, I had just kept on doing push-ups until they had had to tell me to stop. I had also done all the required sit-ups—again, until they had had to tell me to stop. I had played varsity football, varsity basketball, and varsity baseball for four straight years in my high school, for one of the most demanding coaches in the entire country, so those physical tests had been absolutely nothing for me.

At the physical, I had read all the eye charts perfectly, even from farther distances than any other candidates, because I had worn a patch over my strong left eye for the two previous summers to make my depth perception absolutely perfect. And I had submitted all the right letters from all the "right people" in my county.

All that was left for me to do now was to have this interview with Senator Javits and have him give me his senatorial appointment to the Air Force Academy. And then I would be on my way to Colorado—and to the stars—just as it should have been.

But suddenly there seemed to be something wrong, so I felt that perhaps I should go on, to tell him the *entire* truth, to separate myself from whoever else might be my closest competitor.

"I want to be among the first of our species to travel into outer space . . . so I can take part in our getting to meet the other beings who are out there, waiting for us, the beings from other planets, from other star systems. I want to be part of finding out what it is that they have to tell us, to find out how it is that they made it through." I hesitated, but then plunged ahead, as the older man sat, it seemed to me, a bit perplexed. "To see how it is that they made it through—through *their* Atomic Age; how *they* avoided destroying *them*selves with *their* nuclear technology, which, I am sure, must have threatened to outpace *their* spiritual development too."

Senator Javits jerked visibly upward in his chair, as though he had been punched in the back. His head literally snapped up from his concealed attempt to discreetly speed-read the contents of the folder that lay, now finally opened, on his lap. He lifted his right hand from the file and, with the index finger with which he had been slowly turning the pages in front of him, slid his frameless glasses halfway down his nose and peered over them at me.

I waited, sitting comfortably, looking directly at him.

"So . . . you feel that we are in some kind of . . . danger? Of *what*—of destroying ourselves? With this . . . this . . . what—nuclear technology?" he asked. "Is that what you are saying?"

I smiled cheerfully. This was good. A test! Now I knew what to do. I *loved* tests. I was very good at them.

So I pulled myself up out of the depths of the deep leather couch and slid up onto its edge, closer to him, and said, a little more cheerfully than I had intended to, "Oh, no! Not *anymore*, Senator! There *was* a moment there, last fall, between October 22nd and the 28th, when I wasn't so sure. But now I'm sure that we have passed *our* test. If these test ban treaty talks between President Kennedy and Premier Khrushchev go well . . . well then we can all get back to the business of getting to the moon . . . and beyond. That's the business that I want to be part of."

The older man now looked bemused. "So you think that there are other beings out there, out there in outer space, who are, what—waiting to talk to us, do you?"

Now it was my turn to look bemused. This *had* to be a test. I was delighted. This was turning out to be as sophisticated as I had hoped it would be. Without any hesitation, I said, "Why, certainly, Senator! Don't *you*? I mean, there are over 500 billion star systems just in our Milky Way galaxy alone. And there are over 500 billion *trillion* galaxies. You certainly don't believe that *we* are the only planet in this entire galaxy—in this entire *universe*—on which intelligent and technologically advanced life has evolved?"

The old man was totally taken aback. He had not been prepared to be challenged by a seventeen-year-old boy who had come to him from . . . from *where*? From somewhere up in "the sticks" of northern New York, seeking *his* senatorial appointment to one of the military service academies. This was now the second time—or was it the third?—that this young man had presumed to challenge him in less than ten minutes. *What is going on here?* he must have been thinking to himself.

The look on his face made me wonder if I had somehow offended him. I thought back to what I had just said and then quickly recovered.

"Of course you don't believe that! I didn't mean, Senator, to suggest that you *had* assumed that. I mean, you are a United States senator! You can't possibly believe that we are the *only* intelligent beings in the entire universe. I apologize."

Now he was even more embarrassed. But he hid it very well. Suddenly he moved to the edge of his large leather chair, leaned forward toward me, and adopted a much more serious, almost confidential, tone. His whole demeanor changed. He had made some kind of decision.

"Look, Dan," he said.

"You can call me Danny. Everybody does," I repeated matter-of-factly.

Once again, this seemed to throw him off. He must have been thinking, *What is this young man from the sticks doing, declaring what I should or should not believe about such extraordinary subjects as extraterrestrial intelligence and thermonuclear war?*

Senator Javits gathered himself up, as if preparing to say something out of anger. But, after a seemingly practiced moment of reflection, he settled back into his large leather chair and took a new tack. He decided to tell me the truth—something that a U.S. senator, I would learn much later, does not do lightly . . . or often. He leaned in closer again.

"Dan, ah, I mean, Danny. Look, I am not supposed to tell you this, but I have *already* promised my senatorial appointment to the Air Force Academy to another young man."

I was stunned. He looked embarrassed. I sat staring at him. For the first time, I began to suspect that there was a chance that everything was *not* "just as it was supposed to be" in America.

As it turned out, Jacob Javits had given his 1963 New York State senatorial appointment to the United States Air Force Academy to the son of a major financial contributor to his campaign for the United States Senate. My meeting with the senator was to be a purely "perfunctory" interview, since he was required "by the rules" to grant each of the top five candidates in the state for each of the four services academies the courtesy of a "personal senatorial interview."

"Look . . . ah . . . Danny. I am not supposed to have done that—at least not until *after* I had interviewed all of the candidates. You were the last, and I . . . uh . . . I honestly hadn't anticipated that you were going to be quite so . . . uh . . . so *unusual*. I mean, you *are* from just a tiny upstate high school. There was no way for me to know. I mean, I . . . uh . . . I find myself in a very awkward position. I have already promised my senatorial appointment to another young man . . . to the Air Force Academy, I mean. And I have to keep that promise."

He leaned in closer, almost as if to a colleague in the cloakroom of the Senate, sharing a confidential piece of legislative strategy. "Look, Danny. I have decided to give you my senatorial appointment to the United States *Naval* Academy, down in Annapolis, in Maryland, right outside Washington, D.C.

I stared blankly at the older man. This interview was suddenly not going so well, for him or for me. How could he possibly have already given his senatorial appointment to the Air Force Academy to someone else? That was *my* appointment. I had worked for that appointment from the time I had arrived at Aunt Gladys's in the seventh grade. It was my *right* to be the U.S. senatorial appointee from New York State!

"I don't understand, Senator," I stammered. For the first time in the interview, I was at sea.

Javits was now really embarrassed. But after having temporarily let down his guard, for just a brief moment, he gathered himself up and prepared to defend himself and his decision. He approached this defense as he would with a colleague whom he understood to be sympathetic toward the true nature of politics.

"Look, Danny. This is the way it *is* up here. It was a political decision. I *had* to do it! I don't want to go into the whys and wherefores of this right now. But take my word for it—my *political* word for it—I *had* to do it, politically. The boy's father is one of the most important financial contributors to the party—and to my campaigns." He moved his chair closer to me and spoke to me in an almost fatherly tone. "Look, son, I am very impressed with you. And I am embarrassed. I am very impressed with your record here and by the way that you have conducted yourself in our meeting today. So I am *leveling* with you, son." He leaned back into his chair, now having settled upon his course of action. Almost angrily, he said, "Look, I am offering you my senatorial appointment to the United States Naval Academy at Annapolis. You will be able to become a navy pilot and join the astronaut program from the Naval Academy—just as easily as you would have been able to do that from the Air Force Academy."

He could see, however, that this was somehow not working, so he quickly pressed on, taking a different tack.

"Of course, you could simply go back to your *congressional* district. You're out of the . . . let's see," he quickly glanced down at the dossier in his lap. "Ah, yes, the thirty-first congressional district. That's—that's Carleton King's district! I know Carl. He's a good man. A good Republican! He will understand. Look, Dan, I will give him a personal call. Every congressman is ready to do a personal favor for the United States senator from his state, especially when they are both in the same party." He laughed, a little too loudly.

I didn't.

The older man shifted uncomfortably in his chair.

But the interview was now over.

Javits signaled this by rising from his chair, reaching out for my right hand with his, shaking my hand diplomatically but firmly, and then virtually lifting me up from the couch and ushering me toward the door. He continued talking, a bit too loudly, it seemed to me, as he ushered me toward the door.

"OK, OK, Danny. I understand. You've got your heart set on the Air Force Academy. So the Air Force Academy it will be. I'll talk directly to your congressman, Carleton King. You can count on that. With *this* file," he lifted the folder that he was still carrying in his left hand, "you can be certain that you will be given the appointment from your congressman to the Air Force Academy. I will personally see to that. You've got my word on that. You have nothing to worry about, Dan. And, once you're at the academy, after a few weeks, take my word for it, it won't make a damned bit of difference that you are there on a *congressional* appointment rather than on a *senatorial* appointment!"

Then he leaned over and whispered to me, "But don't tell Carleton King that. I want him to continue to think that *my* senatorial appointment is better than his!" He laughed, again a bit too loudly. And with that, Senator Jacob Javits ushered me past his smiling, but a bit puzzled, receptionist, directly to the outer door and into the wide hallway outside his Fifth Avenue office. Slapping me on the back with pretended affection, he bid me goodbye and closed the heavy oaken door behind him, with a thump.

I thought about the interview as I lay gazing up into the nighttime stars in upstate New York on that spring equinox night of 1963.

But on this starry night of March 21, 1963, those events lay shrouded in the mist of future memories.

On that night, a cold wind blew in mysteriously from the south across the mountaintops of the Adirondacks and my hometown.

Chilled by this sudden wind, I rose from the fresh green grass of the springtime of my upstate New York home and of my life, pulled the collar of my blue-and-gold high school letter jacket up around my then young and muscled shoulders, and walked slowly to the door of the white, green-shuttered home of my Aunt Gladys and Uncle Jim.

I would warm myself, that night, just one last time, beside the fireplace of my boyhood home—one more time before I had to go out into the world.

I turned one final time—indeed, for the last time during my youth—and said to the stars above, "Fall will be coming early this year."

And I was right. Fall would come early that year . . . and it would stay for a long, long time.

CHAPTER *two*

MY FATHER DIED at the age of fifty—of "old age." He had become an alcoholic and a diabetic during World War II. The story of my life, therefore, begins before the actual end of World War II, because my father was wounded in Italy, during America's initial invasion of Europe, and he was returned home early.

On September 9, 1943, the morning of my older sister's second birthday, and nine months before the rest of the Allied forces were to go ashore at Normandy in France on June 6, 1944, far to the north, my father landed on the beach at Salerno, Italy. Along with ten corps of young American men, he was part of the first landing party, the men who led the invasion onto the western beaches of Europe—the men who died. Most of those young men, the whole first wave of them, were violently mowed down and blown apart by hundreds of German .50-caliber machine guns that had been set up above and looking directly down on the beaches, as was later portrayed in *Saving Private Ryan*, Steven Spielberg's and Tom Hanks's 1998 homage to the World War II American soldier. My father was one of the first few who made it off the beach alive that day but who were utterly destroyed by the experience of living through it. He saw and smelled and heard—and even tasted—his closest friends being blown up all around him; indeed, all over him.

He told me of this horrible experience one night when I was eleven. He was very drunk. He sat me down, took from the bottom drawer of his bedroom dresser the Purple Heart that he had been awarded, and told me, through his tears, how it was that I had come to be named after his best friend. Danny had been from my father's hometown of Irishtown. They had grown up together in northern New York, and they had gone away to war together. That morning on the beach at Salerno, my father told me, Danny had been hit with a mortar and literally exploded all over him.

My father lived to make it off that beach that morning, and he had gone inland into Italy. He was made a "forward observer"—a private first class who carried a radio on his back. He was assigned to accompany a young lieutenant who was sent up into the front lines, where the fighting was the most intense and where they therefore needed support from the heavy artillery to the rear and from the battleships that lay anchored off the coast of Italy. He was one of the select team of men who were to observe the forward positions of the enemy guns and strongholds and would then radio in the coordinates of those sites to be shelled by the advancing American army and naval ships.

He was hit by heavy mortar fire on Mount Pantano in Italy on the night of November 30, 1943.

It was never clear whether he had been hit by "friendly fire" or by German mortars. But he was struck in the back with heavy shrapnel and was seriously wounded. In fact, the radio, pieces of which were driven deep into my father's back by the shrapnel, had saved his life. For this he was awarded the Purple Heart. His lieutenant was killed in the same barrage. Because of the seriousness of my father's wounds, he had been shipped out of Italy immediately, back down into North Africa, where he had originally been stationed earlier that year, and was cared for there in an American army field hospital.

It was in that army field hospital that he first began to smoke cigarettes—cigarettes that were provided to him, for free, by the army hospital itself, cigarettes that would eventually be the death of him. And it was there, too, that he first began to drink, which would ultimately be the death of our family and of his dreams.

"Shell shock" is what they called it back then, or "battle fatigue." We now know it as "post-traumatic stress disorder," or PTSD. But, at that time, it was not treated or even acknowledged. One just lived with it—or not. Whatever it was called, my father had it. And he had it bad.

In an attempt to self-medicate and allay his anxiety and trauma, my father, Pat Sheehan, began to drink heavily and to smoke a full pack of army-issued cigarettes every day. This was the fate of tens of thousands of American GIs, as well as German, Italian, Japanese, and other soldiers who suffered from this serious medical disability by the end of the war.

Arriving stateside in April 1944, still in a state of deep post-traumatic stress, Pat Sheehan returned to his wife, Margery, whom he had married in 1939 when he was just twenty and she only seventeen, and to his then two-and-a-half-year-old daughter, Colleen, who had been only three months old when he had enlisted in the United States Army immediately following the attack on Pearl Harbor in December of 1941.

Because Pat Sheehan was among the first of the wounded veterans to be returned home before the end of World War II, his application for employment with the state of New York was given top priority. He was awarded extra points on his New York State job application test because of his status as a wounded veteran. The specific job that he chose, from among the several that were offered to him, was the cushiest of the many state jobs available—a position as a New York State corrections officer at the very upscale Great Meadows State Correctional Facility in Comstock, New York. This white-collar-criminal state prison was located three hundred miles north of New York City, in the beautiful rolling green hills of the Adirondack Mountains, just north of Lake George, a well-known summer resort area where the very wealthiest of New York City's business tycoons and industrialists—such as the Vanderbilts, the Rockefellers, and the Carnegies—kept summer homes. Their ten-thousand-square-foot mansions dotted the shorelines of the largest islands that sprinkled the thirty-two-mile-long, deep-blue crystal waters of scenic Lake George.

Great Meadows State Correctional Facility, in 1943, was home to the "high-class" New York City Mafia gangsters, men like Lucky Luciano, Bugsy Moran, and others. The guards at this upscale, white-collar facility were required to be at least high school graduates and were required to wear starched long-sleeve white shirts, pressed navy blue slacks with matching navy blue ties, and spotlessly polished black shoes with black socks. It was also mandatory for the guards to get monthly haircuts and to remain completely clean-shaven at all times, just like in the military.

My father arrived at the prison less than a year after it had hosted an ultra-secret series of meetings between a representative of then New York State governor Thomas E. Dewey and Lucky Luciano. In those secret meetings, Governor Dewey, the former crusading New York City district attorney who had put away Luciano, struck a deal with Luciano . . . and with the

Mafia. Pursuant to that deal, Luciano was allowed to go free and to return to his native Island of Sicily in exchange for his agreeing to recruit his Mafia associates in Sicily to act as scouts for the U.S. landing forces at Salerno and Anzio, Italy, and to lead General George Patton's Seventh Army to the gates of Rome and then on to Berlin, Germany. However, Luciano also agreed, in those meetings, to cause the American Mafia to infiltrate and take over the American Longshoremen's Union and the American Teamsters' Union to "protect" America's harbors and trucking industry *against* "communist infiltration" during and after World War II, a deal that would lead directly to the clash, twenty years later, between Bobby Kennedy and the mobbed-up Teamsters' Union boss Jimmy Hoffa.

It was at *that* Great Meadows State Correctional Facility that my father was working when I was conceived, only four months after my father had returned from World War II.

I was born on April 9, 1945, three days before the death of President Franklin Delano Roosevelt and just one hundred days before the detonation of the first atomic bomb at White Sands Proving Ground in Alamogordo, New Mexico, making me a child of both the New Deal era and the Atomic Age.

At the time, my mother and father were living with their then three-year-old daughter, Colleen, on Crandall Street in Glens Falls, New York, near Crandall Street Park and the downtown bandstand.

Our new family moved, shortly after I was born, from Glens Falls, which had a population of twenty-five thousand, to the tiny upstate New York rural village of Gansevoort, ten miles due south of the southernmost tip of Lake George, which had a population of less than six thousand.

From 1946 to 1950, we lived in a small white house with green shutters in Gansevoort. It was a tiny house, though it seemed very large to me at the time. My father and mother bought that house for less than $5,000 with a loan through the GI Bill.

I vividly remember lying on my back in the large field that lay behind our house, on warm summer days, looking up, way up, into the deep, robin's-egg-blue sky above our home and discovering there a star-bright dot of silver light soaring high above. That tiny dot seemed to lie at the very farthest reaches of my sight, trailing straight white lines of white vapor behind.

When I asked what that was, I was told that that silver dot of light was a huge, eighty-six-ton Strategic Air Command B-52 bomber that flew out of the Plattsburg Air Force Base up near the Canadian border one hundred miles to the north of us. I remember being totally awestruck upon realizing that *people* were actually way up there walking around *inside* that tiny dot of brilliant light as they flew, faster than the speed of sound, through the sky.

That, I believe, was the very beginning of my fascination with the sky— and with the concept of relative point of view, or perspective. The people who were up there inside that tiny silver dot didn't even know that I was down here watching them. *How strange,* I thought. *How could they possibly not know about me? Couldn't they* feel *me watching them?*

I remember a similar vivid experience that happened when I was four. My sister, Colleen, my little brother, Patty (who had been born just ten months after me), and I were playing under the large maple tree out in our front yard with several of our little friends from the neighborhood. It was fall, and we were raking into a big pile all of the maple leaves that had fallen from the tree, and we were then throwing ourselves into them, tossing the leaves into the air and at each other. I needed to go to the bathroom, so I jumped up and went into the house. I remember going up into the upstairs bathroom and being able to hear the children laughing down below, still playing and jump-ing in the leaves, even though I was no longer there, where I had been only a few seconds earlier. As I was getting ready to leave the bathroom to rejoin my playmates, it occurred to me that I could go to the window and look down and see them, without their even knowing that I was looking. I crossed to the window and stood there looking down on them playing in the leaves below. I was not there, but I had been *right there* only a few minutes before. And if someone else had been standing at this same bathroom window where I was standing, when I had been down there, that person could have looked down at me and my friends, and we would not have been any more aware of it than the children I watched were aware of me then.

Suddenly, I was struck with the same strange feeling that I had gotten when I was gazing up at that B-52. How was it possible that the children down there did not know that I was up here, watching them? Couldn't they *feel* me watching? They were playing as freely and as happily as they had been when I was with them, and this made me think: *What would the world be like if I simply wasn't here anymore? Would life simply go on as if I had never even been here, the way my playmates carried on without me?*

How peculiar! How fleeting was our sense of our own importance. And how relative our own perspective on reality.

But, still today, almost none of us ever looks *up*; nor do we ever think about how we look from way high up above.

It would be three more years before I discovered stars that would bring on that same feeling a hundredfold.

During my family's early years together in Gansevoort, my mother would spend all of her time with we three children when my father was out drinking. She would wait for him to come home drunk and nasty. That infuriated her, waiting alone for all of those hours, with nothing to do except rehearse, in her mind, what hurtful and angry things she would say to him as soon as he showed up in the doorway. And she did exactly that. Virtually the second he came through the door, the fight would start.

Sometimes, perhaps even *most* of the time, my father would come home in a happy-go-lucky but decidedly drunken state. This cheerfulness would not last beyond the first minute of my mother's seething, critical comments. Other times, my father started it with some self-justifying or utterly false statement about where he had been, and my mother would explode. Their arguments sometimes devolved into violent fights and my mother would throw dishes at him. One time, on Thanksgiving afternoon, my mother actually overturned our Thanksgiving dinner table on him, resulting in turkey and gravy and mashed potatoes being strewn all across our living room floor. She was understandably, and justifiably, furious at him for getting drunk like that every weekend and squandering on alcohol so much of what little money our family had. But it was very traumatic for my brother and sister . . . and for me. After all, we were only children.

My father was, for his part, in extreme pain. From every report that I have ever heard about my father, when he was out drinking, he was friends with everyone he met. Everybody loved Pat Sheehan. Before he had gone off to "the war," he was the archetypal hearty, well-met Irish lad. But he had come home a drunk, a ruined man. His friends and family would say that it was "something that had happened to him over there." But everyone with whom he drank loved him. It was his children who feared him, and his wife who would never forgive him.

In 1950, when I was five years old, our family moved from Gansevoort, New York, to Fort Ann, New York, a still-smaller village of less than five thousand people, ten miles due east of the southernmost tip of Lake George. The town's namesake was a small fort that had been constructed by the British during the French and Indian Wars. It was forty miles south of Fort Ticonderoga and ten miles east of Fort William Henry, the largest British fort on Lake George. This is the land made famous by James Fennimore Cooper's classic novel *The Last of the Mohicans*, and it is also the land of the Six Indian Nation Confederacy, known to *washeechews* (white people) as the Iroquois Confederacy.

During the four years that my family lived in Fort Ann, my father continued to work at the Great Meadows State Correctional Facility. He worked nights at the prison from 6:00 PM to 6:00 AM, so we virtually never saw him. He was not yet home from work when we were awakened each weekday morning to go off to school. And he would awaken just in time to have a brief dinner with us before he went back off to work, to be there by 6:00 PM. During dinner, little was said. The tension between my father and my mother over his drinking had, by this time, grown to the level where little was said between them in our presence.

It was in Fort Ann that my mother began taking us to church every Sunday. Saint Ann's, the town's tiny Catholic church, was directly across the main highway that went directly through the middle of town. Inside, there were people singing high up in the back, and there was this really interesting-smelling smoke that they called incense that the priest would kind of fling out over the audience as he sang mysterious-sounding songs. Latin, they called it. Colleen, Patty, and I all took our first communion at Saint Ann's.

We lived on the second floor of a redbrick, two-story house right on Main Street, which ran through the tiny town. A big green grassy yard lay on the immediate northern side of our house, between us and Havelan's Lumber Mill. I remember the smell of fresh-sawn lumber and sawdust in the air all the time. The sky was always blue.

This was where I discovered the stars, above that side yard.

During summer weeknights, when my father was off working at the prison, my mother, Colleen, and Patty would huddle together in front of the tiny black-and-white TV watching *Martin Kane, Private Eye*, starring Lloyd Nolan; *Suspense; Kraft Theatre* (with every Kraft commercial narrated by some man by the name of Ed Herlihy, who for some reason always felt moved to tell us who he was); *Perry Como's Kraft Music Hall; The Dinah Shore Show*; and *The Texaco Star Theatre* with Milton Berle. I would, instead of watching these insipid shows, sneak outdoors and lie in the deep green grass of our lawn, waiting for the stars to come out, one by one.

It was like magic to me. At first there was nothing there. I would scour the sky, trying to catch a star "coming out." Nothing. Then I'd turn my attention somewhere else, and when I turned my eyes back to that first spot, there it was! The first star, just barely visible. That's when the show I liked would begin.

I would lie back in the grass with the fingers of both hands interlaced behind my head and gaze up into the ever-darkening sky, watching, one by one, as my favorite stars would come out. There was one particular huge bright star that appeared each night toward the north. It would pulse, first bright white, then red, then green, then blue, and then crystal white again. It was beautiful—not just because of how it looked but because of how it made me *feel*.

I found it difficult to explain this to others. But, then, I never really *had* to explain it to anyone. It was a totally secret experience, like watching the B-52s flying high above, at the edge of space. As I lay in the deep green grass in our yard in Fort Ann, looking up into the billions of stars, I was filled with the strangest feeling that there were people, up there, looking down at us—at me—not from up there in the B-52s. People, orbiting on a planet around one of those stars, lying up there in the grass of *their* yards, just as I was. It was the most fascinating feeling that I had ever had, and it kept coming back every single night when I gazed up into the sky at the stars.

In the flicker, twinkle, and pulse of those stars, it seemed to me that they were almost trying to communicate something to me, a hidden code that I couldn't quite understand. At that point I was too young even to read, but I remember being told by someone that there was such a thing as Morse code that was made up of different combinations of long and short beeps, just like the pulsing of the stars.

I was eager to get to school—so I could learn to read, so I could find out about things like that. And then someone told me that they had heard on television that there *were* people on the planets orbiting those stars way up there, just as there were people down here on our own planet. That was it again! That peculiar feeling of "perspective." I started to reflect on how "those people" might think about us . . . if they reflected on the kind of things that we did and said to each other "down here." Now I really wanted to go to school to find out about that. I made up my mind that I would become an astronomer so I could study the stars.

So when I reached five, it was off to school I went—to kindergarten in Fort Ann—to become an astronomer.

But my first day of school was a disaster.

The kindergarten teacher at Fort Ann Elementary School handed out these big, rough-paper coloring books. On each page was a large object to be colored and below that picture was the name of the color that most obviously corresponded to that object. A huge apple was on page 1, waiting there to be colored red. At the bottom of the page were three big letters: R-E-D.

But I had no idea what those letters said. For no one had ever spent a single minute trying to teach me anything about reading.

So I began to cry. I cried to myself until the teacher saw that I was crying, and then she came over to ask me why I was crying. Then *everyone* knew that I was crying. It was the worst day that I ever spent in school. But it was the last time that I was ever unprepared for a class.

I was five then, in September of 1950, and my studies—which would prove to be extensive indeed—were then about to begin.

I soon learned that many of those stars that I liked to gaze up at were, in fact, *galaxies*. We lived in the Milky Way galaxy, I discovered, in a virtual highway of stars that I had noticed on my own, spreading from east to west above my home in Fort Ann. I learned that that familiar band of stars was just one of the spiral arms of the Milky Way—and that we were *inside* of it!

I began to learn things outside of school too. I began to follow the news with my mother. I remember hearing on the news that there was a "General Eisenhower" who was running to become the president. I wasn't sure what that was all about. But I soon found out that a man by the name of "Stevenson" (with some strange first name) was running against this General Eisenhower and trying to keep him from becoming the president. It seemed like everyone in Fort Ann was supposed to be in favor of General Eisenhower becoming the president.

In 1952, I remember watching on black-and-white television "the convention" at which General Eisenhower was chosen by people called Republicans to be the president. I remember seeing all the balloons and all the people in funny hats with signs with the names of states on them. Confusingly, there was still this other guy running against General Eisenhower for the presidency. I thought that General Eisenhower had already been chosen to be the president at the convention with all the signs with the names of the states on them.

My confusion was because I never saw the *other* convention where the "other guy" had been picked to run for president by a bunch of other people. Those other people, I would learn later, were called Democrats. In Fort Ann, those people were actually referred to as "*those* Democrats."

When I was seven, my mother started taking us to the movies every Friday night when my father went out "drinking." He would come home from the prison early Friday evening. My mother cooked one of those big cans of Chef Boyardee's canned spaghetti or ravioli with scrambled eggs, and we all ate in silence. My father would eat quickly and nervously, marking time until he would get up and ask my mother to step into the other room. There he would tell her that he wanted to "go out," and she would then ask him for "some money for the movies." He would then take out his wallet from his rear blue jean pocket and give her several dollar bills. She would then ask him for a little more "for popcorn," and he would grudgingly give her a few more dollar bills.

Then he would leave.

The Rialto Theater was in Glens Falls, a nineteen-mile bus ride away. We always watched whatever double feature was playing at the Rialto, usually one drama and one Western or comedy. When we got out of that second movie, my mother would look at the clock in the theater and say, "We don't want to be there waiting for *him* when *he* comes home drunk. Would you like to go to another movie?" We would always shout "yes" and then would quickly head four blocks down the street to watch another double feature at the Paramount Theater.

It would be after 1:00 AM when we caught the last bus home from Glens Falls to Fort Ann. But we would always get home before my father did.

If we were all asleep when my father got home, my mother included, then everything would be OK. But if, for whatever reason, my mother was still awake when my father came home, there would always be a big fight. He was always drunk, and she was always mad. And if she wasn't mad when he got there, he would say or do something that made her mad. It was always the same. And it was always terrible.

They were both trapped. He was locked in his world of pain, guilt, and, of course, alcohol, which only deepened his depression and sped his intellectual and physical deterioration over the years. He coughed constantly, from smoking now two packs of cigarettes every day, and he suffered from acute nicotine addiction and growing emphysema.

And my mother, still then only thirty years old, was alone and isolated with three small children, an alcoholic husband who was never home, and no education or job training beyond high school. She had been effectively ostracized by her Bidwell family for marrying my father so young, and now so irresponsible. So she was alone. She took us to the movies to escape. To escape from my father. To escape from having to talk to us. To escape from her life. To escape from reality.

The lead male characters in the serious dramas and the cowboy heroes in the Westerns I watched at the Rialto and the Paramount theaters became substitutes, in my life, for a father. My father figures were Gary Cooper as Marshal Will Kane in *High Noon*; Gregory Peck as attorney Atticus Finch in *To Kill a Mockingbird*; James Stewart as Jefferson Smith in *Mr. Smith Goes to Washington*; Spencer Tracey as Judge Haywood in *Judgment at Nuremberg*; Kirk Douglas as Colonel "Jiggs" Casey in *Seven Days in May* and as Spartacus; and Henry Fonda as Secretary of State William Russell in *The Best Man* and as the president of the United States in *Fail-Safe*.

But above all it was Burt Lancaster who impressed me more than any other actor, even though he often played "the bad guy," such as he did as Nazi judge Ernst Janning in *Judgment at Nuremberg*. But usually he was the good guy, as he was as Sergeant Milt Warden in *From Here to Eternity*, as Lieutenant Jim Bledsoe in *Run Silent, Run Deep*, or as Wyatt Earp in *Gunfight at the O.K. Corral*. The reason I was so impressed by Burt Lancaster was because all of his movies conveyed a clear, strong, moral message, even when he himself was not portraying the good guy. Burt Lancaster made me realize that the people who played the bad guys in movies must in real life be good guys because they so effectively convinced moviegoers to disagree with the evil characters whom they portrayed on screen. I thought this was very interesting, and it was one of the very first complex ideas that I remember coming to entirely on my own, without anyone explaining it to me. It was the plotlines of these 1950's dramas and Westerns that provided moral direction to my youthful years that was not supplied either by my ever-absent father or by my distracted mother.

The role models for my peers later during that period were actors like Marlon Brando and James Dean—the rebels, the misfits, and the outcasts. But I liked Burt Lancaster as "The Lawman" and as Wyatt Earp, the good guy who had clear moral vision and would courageously stand up for what was right—no matter how cowardly the "regular townspeople" were. One could argue that it was my mother, by taking me to all of those movies, who was the one who taught me those moral lessons, rather than Burt Lancaster, Gregory Peck, or Kirk Douglas. But, in a more sophisticated sense, one might more accurately say that it was the screenwriters and the directors of those 1950's motion pictures—men like Abby Mann, Howard Fast, Dalton Trumbo, Stanley Kubrick, Stanley Kramer, Sidney Lumet, and Sydney Pollack—who molded my early moral character. Many of those men, I would learn only later, had been blacklisted for refusing to name the people whom they knew who had attended meetings of liberal, progressive, socialist, and sometimes even actual communist groups in Hollywood in the late 1940s and early 1950s. They were men who sometimes had to write or work in secret to speak out through their movies against unjust authority and convention.

So, with these men as my moral teachers, it is not surprising—or even really to my credit—that I ended up thinking the way that I do. That is probably why I am so righteous—some might even say *self-righteous*—about everything that I do. I learned it in those late 1950's *movies*. I am someone who takes things very seriously and who stays steadfastly dedicated to achieving what I set out to accomplish, not just because I am steadfast in the abstract but because I am convinced that I am *right*—just like the heroes in all of those movies in the late 1950s.

My mother and father moved us from Fort Ann to Hudson Falls, my mother's hometown of eight thousand people, when I was eight. There, in Hudson Falls, an event that would most profoundly influence my future path took place.

My father was on duty one winter night at Great Meadows State Correctional Facility. It was 1955. I was ten years old. An inmate at my father's prison had wedged his bed up against the inside of his cell door so no one could get into his cell and had somehow gotten his hands on some sharp-edged instrument. With that instrument, he had severed the veins in both of his wrists and had then cut the jugular vein in his neck. When my father found him, the inmate was lying in a pool of his own blood, dying. My father sat on the cold stone floor outside of the young man's cell door, holding the young man's hand through the bars as the young man lay bleeding to death. My father pleaded with him to pull the bed away from the door so my father could get into the cell to save his life.

But he wouldn't. He was crying, whispering, with his life's last breath, that he had been treated like an animal ever since he had been arrested down in New York City. He told my father that he had been held there in "the Tombs" for months with no chance of affording the bail that had been set on his release before he had been convicted by an all-white jury in a one-hour trial—without his ever having ever been given a lawyer. They were merely holding him at Great Meadows State Correctional Facility temporarily before sending him on to Attica Prison, where he was to be imprisoned for the rest of his life. He had decided that he would rather kill himself.

My father had managed to hold the man's hand through the bars, but he was unable to provide any reason to the young man for him to live. So he had let the young man die, soaking my father's white shirt in his blood.

The emotional trauma of that experience triggered my father's PTSD from the war, from which he still suffered. With the man lying dead in a pond of his own blood, my father simply rose up from the blood-soaked floor and walked out of the prison. He never stopped to put on his jacket or even to get into his car, which was parked in the nearby prison parking lot. Instead, he walked home sixteen miles through a blinding winter snowstorm. And he would not go back. My mother had to have a friend of my father's, a New York state trooper, go to the prison with a friend to pick up my father's car and drive it back to our house in Hudson Falls.

My father then began painting houses for some income. But after several weeks of that, he resolved that he was going to go to California, to "God's country," to find a job and a place for us to live out there. When he left for California, we thought that we would never see him again. I think that my mother *hoped* that we wouldn't.

But after several weeks, my father returned to Hudson Falls. He had gotten a job in California spray-painting aircraft bodies at Rohr Aircraft Company, an airplane manufacturer in San Diego. It would be a steady job with good pay. He had rented a small two-bedroom house for us in National City. And he vowed that he was never going to drink again.

So we packed everything we owned into our 1948 blue Dodge sedan and drove all the way across the country to San Diego.

I was ten years old and suddenly I was living in California with no friends and no relatives within three thousand miles.

CHAPTER *three*

LIVED IN CALIFORNIA for two years, between December of 1955 and December of 1957.

We had been there for one year when my father started drinking again. It was Christmas Eve of 1956, and I remember him throwing our Christmas tree through the front picture window of our tiny house in National City. We had to move out after that.

I had spent my entire early life just wanting this all to stop—the alcoholism, the fighting, the resulting poverty, all the moving from one town to another. I had been in four different schools in six years. Bad energy filled our house. So one night, after we had moved to Lincoln Acres from National City and then from Lincoln Acres to Chula Vista, I finally confronted my mother and father during one of their big fights. I stepped directly in between them. I was twelve years old then, and I said, "OK! That's *it!* This has got to stop, both of you—right now! This is making all our lives miserable. Colleen and Pat are always afraid. You've got to stop this. You just have to separate or get a divorce or something. But this has *got* to stop."

Within a few days following my intervention, my mother and father had made a decision. My mother came into my bedroom in our small three-room quarters at the rear of a house that we were renting from a very old woman by the name of Mrs. Ford in Chula Vista, California. I remember that it was at 4:00 AM on a Wednesday morning in December 1957. She came in, woke me, and took me quietly out into the kitchen in my pajamas. My father was sitting at the kitchen table, smoking one cigarette after another. My mother sat me down at the table and then said, solemnly, "Your father and I have decided to try a trial separation. He is going to go back to New York. We will stay here."

"Great," I said. "Fine. When is he leaving?"

She stopped me. "But he has agreed to go only on one condition."

"And what's that?" I asked.

"You have to go with him."

"What?" I said. "I don't even *know* him. He's always drunk. I don't want to go with him."

My father started crying then and saying that he was not going to leave without me.

Panicking, my mother said that I *had* to go with him or else he was not ever going to leave and things would just keep on going on the way they always had. She was becoming hysterical. Her eyes and voice were full of desperation. "You have to go with him, Danny! If you don't go, he won't ever leave. If this is ever going to stop, *he has to leave!*"

So, even though I never agreed to go with him, my mother kept me out of school that Wednesday morning and took me to Woolworth's, where she bought me a pair of brown corduroy pants and a flannel shirt. "Because it's going to be cold back there," she said. I had been in California for only two years—1956 and 1957. But that very evening, just as it was beginning to grow dark, my mother put me on a Greyhound bus with my father at the downtown San Diego bus station, and I was on my way back to New York with a man I hardly knew.

For seven long and boring days and seven even longer and more boring and uncomfortable nights, I rode across the country in a bus seat beside my father, who couldn't think of anything whatsoever to say to me. We crossed long stretches of rolling plains by day and passed through the lights of strange cities by night, stopping at poorly lit bus stop diners with Formica-topped counters at odd times of the early mornings to eat greasy eggs and bacon and toast. Meanwhile, my mother, brother, and sister—the only family that I had ever known—turned their attention to living a life without the pain and anguish of an alcoholic in the house. And without me.

My father and I arrived back in Glens Falls, New York, at 10:30 PM on Christmas Eve of 1957. We pulled into the Greyhound bus station, just two blocks from the Glens Falls City Hospital where I had been born twelve years earlier. My father's older sister, Aunt Agnes, met us at the bus station and took us to her home. She was not happy. My father had called her only from Chicago, when we were halfway there, asking if we could stay with her "just until he got on his feet."

I remember sitting beside the Christmas tree that Christmas Eve while Aunt Agnes and her two children, Jimmy and Ellen Keagan, opened their presents. My father wrapped the flannel shirt and the brown corduroy pants that my mother had bought for me at Woolworth's in some bright red Christmas wrapping paper and gave them back to me. It was my only Christmas present that year . . . and the last that I would ever receive from my father or mother or sister or brother.

In the first week of January 1958, my Aunt Agnes enrolled me in Glens Falls Junior High School. It was the beginning of the second half of my seventh grade. While I went to classes, my father went out "looking for work." Each night he would return home to Aunt Agnes's early in the evening, with no job.

At Glens Falls Junior High School, our homeroom teacher arranged everyone's desk by each student's overall grade point average, which she recalculated *every week*. She was a real libertarian who believed in "healthy competition" and "rewarding individuals *materially* for their hard work." I was definitely not in California anymore. My grades had not yet arrived from California, so my homeroom teacher sat me in the very last seat in the very last row in the class. But, by the end of my third week, I had made it to the First Seat, as our teacher called it. It was the beginning of my compulsion to be first—in *everything*. I was not going to be treated as a "throw-away child."

After three weeks, my father began to come back to Aunt Agnes's every night later and later, still without a job. Then, on a Friday in early February of 1958, Aunt Agnes came into my bedroom and woke me up. It was, once again, four o'clock in the morning. She took me into the kitchen, again in my pajamas, and told me, "Your father did not come home last night, and I am going to tell him that he has to leave." She said that she had expressly warned him that she wouldn't stand for him staying there any longer if he began drinking again. And she was certain that he had been drinking.

"Well, where am I supposed to go?" I asked her, not out of fear so much as genuine curiosity.

"You have an aunt around here somewhere, don't you, over in Hudson Falls? On your mother's side? That is just four miles away."

"Yes, I have an 'Aunt Lizzie' who lives in Hudson Falls."

"Lizzie what?" she asked. "What is her last name?"

"I don't know. I don't know what her last name is. It was just always 'Aunt Lizzie.'"

Aunt Agnes seemed exasperated. How could I not know my own aunt's last name? I explained that I had never really met her because none of the Bidwell family ever came around. Then I thought a moment.

"Wait a second," I said. "Her son, my cousin, is 'Scotty Shaw.' So she may be 'Elizabeth Shaw.'"

Aunt Agnes hunted up the phone book and looked up "Elizabeth Shaw" in Hudson Falls. There she was: Elizabeth Shaw, 11 Coleman Avenue. She wrote down the address on a piece of paper, put the phone number on it, and then called a taxicab. Then she helped me dress and pack my little cardboard suitcase, the one that I had brought with me from California. Then Aunt Agnes gave me a twenty-dollar bill and sent me out into the dark at 4:45 in the morning to wait for the cab.

"Eleven Coleman Avenue in Hudson Falls, please," I said, reading off the address to the driver when the cab arrived. The driver got kind of a wide-eyed look on his face and then turned around and drove me there, looking at me from time to time in the rearview mirror, trying to figure out what was going on.

We drove up to the curb on Coleman Avenue just as it was starting to get light. I gave the cab driver my twenty-dollar bill, hoping that it would be enough, and then I started to climb out of the cab with my little cardboard suitcase. He stopped me and asked me what was going on.

So I told him. I told him exactly what was happening.

This upset him, I could tell. He handed me back my twenty-dollar bill and said, "That's OK, kid. Keep the twenty. You're gonna need it more than me."

So I climbed out of the cab and walked up onto Aunt Lizzie's front porch, lugging my little cardboard suitcase, and sat down on it. It was cold, and I was glad that I had on my corduroy pants and flannel shirt as I watched the yellow cab disappear in a cloud of air-chilled exhaust.

At about five o'clock in the morning, Aunt Lizzie came out of her front door to leave for work. She worked at Union Bag, down by the Hudson River, and had to be there by 6:00 AM. She looked at me sitting there on my cardboard suitcase and then squinted her eyes to make sure that she was seeing correctly.

"Danny? Is that you?"

"Yes. It's me, Aunt Lizzie."

"I thought that you were in California with your mother and father."

"Well, I *was*," I said, and then I told her the story.

"Well, you can't stay *here*. Your grandmother Bidwell lives with me. If your father comes looking for you and he's been drinking . . . why, you know, your grandmother has a weak heart."

She told me that I could stay there only for that one night. "But, in the morning, I will take you up to your Aunt Gladys's and Uncle Jim's in Warrensburg. She will know what to do."

The next morning, my Aunt Lizzie drove me forty miles north in her shiny new purple-and-white 1956 Chevy, up to Warrensburg, New York. There, she, Aunt Gladys, and the other Bidwell relatives who could be assembled on such short notice held a big Bidwell Family Powwow to determine what was to become of me.

The result of that summit conference was that my Aunt Gladys would spend the entire second half of my seventh grade and my entire eighth grade trying to get in touch with my mother while I stayed "temporarily" with my Aunt Gladys and Uncle Jim. Aunt Gladys sent letter after letter to our address in Chula Vista, California, in an attempt to arrange for me to be flown back to California, to be reunited with my mother, brother, and sister. But my mother refused to answer. Finally, a letter came back marked "Addressee has moved and left no forwarding address." So Aunt Gladys invited me to spend the entire four years of my high school living with her and her family in Warrensburg.

I quickly began my new life there. On the very day that my Bidwell relatives were all meeting to discuss what was to become of me, I had been sent, with my cousin Mac (Aunt Gladys's and Uncle Jim's thirteen-year-old son), down to Warrensburg Central School, where Mac played Saturday morning basketball. Mac was ten months older than I—the same number of months that I was older than my younger brother, Patty. It was a good fit. Mac was in the eighth grade. In a year he would be fourteen and, as a freshman, would be eligible to start playing high school basketball, baseball, and football.

That first day, I went with Mac to a training session for junior high school boys from Warrensburg, at which the high school basketball coach was priming his best prospects for the Warrensburg Central School freshman team. That coach turned out to be none other than George Khoury—at that time the winningest high school basketball coach in New York State history. He could also claim the same for the other two varsity sports that he coached at Warrensburg: baseball and football. As only an eighth-grader, Mac was six feet tall, and Coach Khoury was building his new freshman basketball team *around* Mac. We went back to the gym the next afternoon, on Sunday, for the freshman and varsity basketball practices because Coach Khoury had made Mac the varsity basketball team manager so he could teach Mac the team's offense and defense. That was how I met George Khoury—one of the three events that most dramatically changed my life.

Warrensburg Central School, where my Aunt Gladys was the first-grade teacher, was a K–12 regional school, servicing a large rural area at the northern end of Lake George in the Adirondack Mountains. The population of Warrensburg was only three thousand, with an annual high school graduating class of only fifty students. That made us a Class D high school athletic team. But Warrensburg Central School was the perennial New York State Section II Class D high school champion in football, basketball, and baseball. This was due to one thing and one thing only: Coach George Khoury. Known simply as "Coach" to every student who ever attended Warrensburg Central School between 1945 and 1982, George Khoury was a Christian Syrian, a fireplug of a man at only five foot five and weighing over two hundred pounds. He had played guard on the varsity football team at Ithaca State College alongside Allie Sherman, who went on to become head coach of the NFL's New York Football Giants. George Khoury had never married. He had had no children, he had no hobbies, he had no close friends, and he had no interests other than winning high school football, basketball, and baseball games. And that he did better, and more often, than any other coach in the entire history of New York State until he retired in 1982. He was, to state it simply but with affection, an absolute zealot. He loved to quote—actually *plagiarize*—Vince Lombardi, the fabled head coach of the Green Bay Packers, telling his Warrensburg Central ballplayers, "The reason why people lose football games is because they play it as though it were *only a game!*" And he meant it! There is no way to describe how excruciating the idea of losing a high school athletic competition was to George Khoury. It was like losing one's firstborn child. He would literally writhe in agony on those very few tragic occasions. And we would all suffer with him—doing wind sprints, push-ups, and laps until we realized, down to our deepest *cellular* level, just how literally painful losing was.

During my five and a half years at Warrensburg Central High School, I became a very, *very* big frog in a very small pond. But it made me what I am today.

I played football, baseball, and basketball, becoming the defensive captain of our varsity football team *as a sophomore* and the captain of the varsity baseball team by the time that I was a senior. Off the sports fields, I played the lead in four consecutive Warrensburg Central High School senior plays; I served for three years as president of our Warrensburg Central High School Student Council; I was the class vice president all four years; and I was president of the school's chapter of the National Honor Society, as well as our school's representative to New York's American Legion Boys State. I graduated second in my class of 1963, coming in behind Bo Linfors, who went on to win the congressional appointment to the United States Naval Academy in 1963, and later became chief reactor officer aboard the nuclear-powered aircraft carrier USS *Dwight D. Eisenhower* and chief engineer of the USS *Theodore Roosevelt*, another nuclear-powered aircraft carrier.

I was absolutely blessed to have attended that wonderful school, and I was blessed by the generosity of my Aunt Gladys and Uncle Jim. Aunt Gladys was part of the leadership of the school, and Uncle Jim was part of the local political leadership as a member of the Republican County Committee of Warren County. He had been appointed by County Supervisor Charlie Hastings to be director of the Civil Defense Department of Warren County.

Aunt Gladys told me that she and Uncle Jim would not be able to pay for my college, since they had three children of their own to put through college ahead of me. But they provided me with the opportunity to get there on my own. I lived with—and grew up with—Aunt Gladys and Uncle Jim from the time that I was twelve years old until I turned eighteen and was declared, by the Superior Court of Warren County, to be an "emancipated minor."

I spent my entire high school experience devoted to one objective: proving to everyone—most importantly to myself—that I was "of value." My mother, my sister, my brother, and even my father had, in effect, abandoned me and had never seen me play in a single athletic contest or act in a single play during my entire high school career. I was very upset about that at first. But ultimately, my unique situation forced me to learn how to become totally self-reliant and independent. I channeled all of my energy and all of my attention into demonstrating to everyone that I could be the best at anything I did. And I was.

On my eighteenth birthday—April 9, 1963—the letter came in the mail. It arrived in a cream-colored envelope with robin's-egg-blue lettering. I remember it to this day. It was from the office of Congressman Carleton King. Aunt Gladys had laid it on the blue-and-white-checkered oilcloth tablecloth that covered the small table in the sunlit kitchen of our hilltop home overlooking Warrensburg, where the letter waited, unopened, for me until I returned home from baseball practice that April 1963 late afternoon. I knew what it was the second that I saw it lying there with the congressman's return address. This was the letter that I had been waiting for—the letter that would notify me that I had received Congressman Carleton King's congressional appointment to the United States Air Force Academy and that I was on my way to the stars.

In a slow, almost liturgy-like set of motions, I placed my blue-and-gold high school gym bag in its usual place in the corner of the kitchen. I then set my books down in their usual place on the shelf between the kitchen and the living room. Then I removed my high school letter jacket and hung it in the living room closet, just as I did every evening after football, basketball, or baseball practice. I wanted everything to be just as it should have been for that special occasion.

Aunt Gladys sat quietly in her chair in the living room, grading her first-grade papers. She did not look up.

She knew what it was too.

I turned and walked slowly back into the kitchen and sat down at the table, not reaching for the letter right away. Instead, I wanted to savor that moment, looking around, taking in the cupboards, the flowered wallpaper, everything that had become so familiar to me over the past five and a half years.

This would be the last time that I looked upon this familiar setting as a civilian. *This* was the letter that would inform me that I would be spending the next twenty years of my life as an officer in the United States Air Force—first as a cadet at the United States Air Force Academy in Colorado Springs; then at flight school at Edwards Air Force Base in California; then on to the astronaut program in Houston, Texas. And then to the stars.

I reached slowly for the letter, rose, and went to the silverware drawer and took out a sharp kitchen knife. I would open the letter carefully, cleanly. I would want to save it, to show it to my friends and family over the years.

Carefully, I slid the blade of the knife into the envelope and sliced a clean incision in the top of the creamy white envelope. I blew into the envelope to pop it open and then withdrew the precious letter with my right forefinger and thumb. I unfolded it slowly and read:

Dear Master Sheehan:

It is with deep regret that I have to inform you that you have not been selected to receive my congressional appointment from the 31st Congressional District to the United States Air Force Academy for the year 1963. My appointment has been given to A—— of Glens Falls, New York.

AN INVOLUNTARY GASP escaped from me. He had selected the son of the Republican mayor of Glens Falls!

I had no desire, or need, to read the rest of the letter, which informed me that I could reapply again the following year. I let the letter and the envelope drop to the floor.

I rose from the table, turned, retrieved my gym bag and books, and went upstairs to my room. There, I stared out into the growing darkness outside my window.

My mind was simply blank. I couldn't visualize anything. My future was *empty*.

For years I had imagined myself at the United States Air Force Academy in Colorado Springs as soon as I graduated from high school. I was so certain that I was going to the academy that I had not even applied to any other college.

How could this have happened? I asked myself over and over. *How could Carleton King have given his congressional appointment to A——, who was only number seven in the overall ranking of candidates in just our congressional district competition while I had been number one in every category?*

I was one of the top five in the entire state! I began to recite to myself, over and over again, all the awards, titles, and contests that I had won— that I had *fought* to win—just to get them on my résumé so I could get this appointment.

But it had all been for nothing. The decision had been made, out of my control, by someone else.

Just like the decision had been made, back in 1957, that I was to be sent off to live with my father so that my mother and brother and sister would be free of an alcoholic husband and father.

Just like the decision had been made, in 1958, that I would be sent away from Aunt Agnes's home because my father was being asked to leave.

Just as it had been decided, again in 1958, that I would stay with Aunt Gladys and Uncle Jim for my entire high school career.

Here I was again, lying on a bed that was someone else's, having my future decided *for* me by someone else. I was sick of it. It was time for me to decide for myself what it was that I was going to do with my life.

I went downstairs, where Aunt Gladys had set the table for dinner. The letter was back in its envelope, lying on the shelf between the kitchen and the living room.

"Well. I guess you saw what they said?" I said.

Aunt Gladys was well aware that I had not applied to any backup college. She had, in fact, suggested that I apply to at least one other college, but I had stubbornly refused, arguing that such an action would be a sign of weakness . . . of doubt . . . of insecurity on my part. She wiped her wrinkled and blue-veined hands on her flowered apron and moved to a seat next to me. She looked at me, reaching out a strong hand and placing it on my forearm. It made me very uncomfortable. This was not like her at all.

"I'm going to have to become a lawyer," I announced.

Aunt Gladys looked shocked. "I thought that you wanted to be an . . . an astronaut?" She said the word slowly, careful to avoid the usual sarcasm that Uncle Jim always assigned to the word.

"Well, that was then." I nodded toward the envelope. "Now I have to become a lawyer to try to fix this system. What Javits did, what Carleton King did—it's against the rules! It's against the law!"

"There are rules and then there are *rules*," Aunt Gladys said calmly. I just stared at her. "Part of the *real* rules is the political weight that you bring to your application for those political appointments. You knew this, Danny. That's why you had our Republican county supervisor write one of your letters of recommendation. And that's why your Uncle Jim, a member of the Republican County Committee, made all of those phone calls to the 'right people.' You knew about the politics."

I blinked as the truth of what she was saying swept over me.

"Where do you plan to study, to become a lawyer?" she asked.

"Uh, I don't know," I said. I hadn't thought about it.

She slowly rose from the table and disappeared into her bedroom off the living room for a few short minutes. When she returned, she sat down beside me again. Without saying a word, she opened her apron and removed from its folds an envelope. It was addressed to me, but it had already been opened neatly, with a sharp knife, the way that I had opened the letter from the congressman. I was puzzled. She held out the letter and gestured at it with her eyes. Slowly, I reached for it.

Less arrogantly this time, I pushed open the envelope with my fingers and removed the one-page letter.

Dear Master Sheehan:

It is with great pleasure that I wish to inform you that you have been accepted as a member of the freshman class of Northeastern University. It is also with pleasure that I wish to inform you that you have been awarded a full academic scholarship for your first year of studies at Northeastern. You will, of course, in your second, third, fourth, and fifth year, be expected to work at a work-study position at which you will receive important and valuable work experience in a field of employment directly related to your selected field of study. And you will also be paid for your work in that position so as to enable you to pay for your tuition and expenses at school each alternative semester.

Congratulations. I look forward to meeting you in August at Freshman Orientation.

I had never applied to Northeastern University. I had never even *heard of* Northeastern University. I looked at Aunt Gladys, who had been staring into her aproned lap.

"I applied for you," she said, a bit embarrassed. "I knew that you were going to be totally pig-headed, just like your mother. So I applied for you. Northeastern University is a co-op school where you go to school for ten weeks, then you go out to work for ten weeks, enabling you to earn the money to pay for your next ten weeks' tuition." She looked embarrassed again. "Danny, you knew that your Uncle Jim and I were not going to be able to afford to send you to college. That was our agreement when we took you in six years ago, remember?"

I could see that this was very hard for her. And, suddenly, I felt a great deal of compassion for my aunt. Compassion, and a great deal of gratitude. I had never really shown much gratitude in all of the years that I had been with her and Uncle Jim because I thought that Aunt Gladys had simply felt obliged to take me in. I assumed that in her eyes I was the "cast-off waif" of her youngest, irresponsible sister. In return, I had felt nothing more than a commensurate obligation to Aunt Gladys and Uncle Jim to achieve every possible accolade and award that I could garner, to prove to them that I was worthy of the clear "favor" that they were doing for me. Not actually for me even, but for "the family."

But, in fact, it was not for them that I had performed. It was for *me*.

In that moment of awkward embarrassment on the part of my Aunt Gladys, who had taken me in and had taught me, above all, the value of an education and hard work, I experienced my first moment of true gratitude for her. And so, for the first time since I had cried myself to sleep after arriving at that tiny hilltop home overlooking the Adirondack Mountains, I cried. This time, not in self-pity and sorrow but in genuine gratitude and affection for this strong and courageous woman who had given me a home and who, now, had given me her final gift before my leaving for the outside world—a place at which to begin my education *of* the world.

Then I realized that I had no idea where Northeastern University was. I had never even heard of it.

I laughed out loud through my tears and reached out and placed my hand gently on Aunt Gladys's cheek. "Thank you, Aunt Gladys, my dear Aunt Gladys. Thank you for *everything*."

She began to cry too. There we were, two tough and self-reliant Bidwells, for one brief moment together in our mutual appreciation of one another, for what each of us had given to the other.

My Uncle Jim had one final lesson of his own to impart, which he chose to do on the morning that I was leaving home.

It was June 21st of 1963. I had to report to Northeastern University's freshman football camp in Boston (I had finally figured out where Northeastern was located) immediately after the Fourth of July. I was delighted to discover that Northeastern had both a college football program and a college baseball program. So I had contacted Northeastern University's Department of Athletics and had learned that the week of July 4th was "Walk-On Week" at the team's football camp. Ninety-nine percent of the young men who would make Northeastern's college football team that year had been scouted and recruited by Coach Zabilski, the varsity football coach, and by Dick Dukeshire, the freshman football coach. All of those recruits had been awarded full athletic scholarships. The other 1 percent of the team, including me, would be walk-ons. But I had absolutely no doubt about my being able to make the team. I had played for the best high school football coach in the entire history of New York State.

So I packed everything I had into an old used 1959 Chevy Bel Air that I had bought with my summer job money for $500, and I was preparing to drive away from my boyhood home when Uncle Jim approached me and asked me to come with him out into the front yard. There, we stood apart for a long moment, looking off into the distance to the north, toward Canada, across the tops of the evergreen forest of the Adirondack Mountains.

Uncle Jim gestured for me to come closer and to stand next to him. So I did. Uncharacteristically, he put his right arm up around my shoulders, which was not that easy since I was six feet tall and he was only five foot four. But his eyes remained fixed on the far horizon.

After a dramatic pause, he said, "You see out there, Danny?"

I looked. But I didn't see anything that I hadn't seen a thousand times before.

"You see up in that blue sky on the horizon?"

"Yes . . . I see it," I said, not having the slightest idea what he was trying to show to me.

"Someday, Danny, you will look out there along that horizon and you will see Russians . . . Russians parachuting down from that sky into our hometown."

I was taken aback. This was absurd. But then, Uncle Jim had always been a little absurd, with his stomach ulcers and collection of guns. He had pistols, shotguns, deer rifles, rifles with scopes, lever-action rifles, bolt-action rifles, .45 pistols, .38s, and a German Luger. He was especially fond of the German Luger, just as he was especially proud of his German shepherd, Kraulla, a trained police attack dog, whom he took with him everywhere—into restaurants, into meetings of the Republican County Committee, everywhere. He liked to give Kraulla stern commands *in German* to show everyone how this savage attack dog obeyed his every command. Uncle Jim had been an orphan who had been adopted. And he was short. He had never gotten over either of these things.

He hugged me tighter to his side with his uplifted right arm around my shoulders, and he pointed to the horizon with his free left hand.

"Russians!" he repeated. "They will be flown in from Canada by the United Nations. There *may* be Cubans with them too." Suddenly, he turned toward me, and, taking me by both shoulders with his upwardly outstretched hands, he looked up into my eyes. "I want you to promise me, Danny. Promise me that you won't let those *communist* teachers down there in Boston talk you out of fighting for your country—for your hometown— when the time comes." He turned his eyes dramatically back to the northern horizon and looked dreamily up into the blue summer sky. "When you see that sky filled with Russians and Cubans parachuting down into our home-town, I want you to promise me, Danny, *promise* me that you will *fight!*"

I didn't know what to say. So I stammered, "Uh . . . Jim, I . . . uh . . . don't believe that there will ever be Russians or Cubans parachuting down into our town. I just don't think that is ever going to happen."

He seemed ready for this. He dropped his hands from my shoulders and looked up at me.

"I *know* that you think I'm a fool, Dan," he said, with a bit of a question mark at the end of his sentence.

I let the question hang in the air, unanswered. This did not go unnoticed by Jim. But he went on. "I know that you think I'm a fool, Dan. But I want you to promise me that *if* it turns out that I am right and that you are wrong and we *are* invaded by Russia and Cuba, that you *will* fight to protect our home against them."

Jim was right: I *did* think that he was a fool. But he had allowed me to stay in his home for almost six full years and he had participated, at least in part, in providing the income that had provided food and shelter for me all of that time. So I decided that I would not spend these last few moments that we would probably ever spend together criticizing him. So instead I said, "Look, Jim. You know that I don't agree with you on many things. This Russian thing is one of those things. But—" I cut him off before he could interrupt. "Let me say this. If you turn out to be right, and I turn out to be wrong, I promise you that I will be one of the very first to fight the Russians or the Cubans, or anybody else who tries to invade our hometown, or any other part of our country for that matter! And that includes *domestic enemies of our Constitution* as well!"

Uncle Jim looked puzzled at first. He wasn't sure whether I was agreeing with him or not. But then he decided that I was, and he smiled. Then he beamed. It was as if I had finally come around to seeing things his way.

"I *knew* that you would fight. I told them that you would."

I had no idea who "them" was. But it made no difference to me. So I let him hug me goodbye, and I turned and walked away from my hometown front yard for the last time. I climbed into my old used Chevy filled with wastebaskets and pillows and clothes and backed around to pull out of the driveway.

As I put the car into first gear, I glanced off toward the house and saw Aunt Gladys standing in the kitchen window, a shadow behind the flowered curtains. She had tears in her eyes. But she did not wave. At first I thought that I should just pretend that I didn't see her so I wouldn't embarrass her. But at the last moment, I slowed the old Chevy and leaned over in the seat and blew her a final goodbye kiss. It was the least that I could do.

CHAPTER *four*

MY EXPERIENCE AT Northeastern University was formative. I played freshman and varsity football and freshman baseball; I acted in college plays that ranged from *Carnival* to *A Midsummer Night's Dream* to Bertolt Brecht's *A Man's a Man;* and I helped found, with Father Arthur Brown and Cardinal Richard Cushing, the Roxbury Summer Program in the black ghetto of Boston—and thereby established my lifelong link with the American Catholic Church and my passionate commitment to civil rights.

At Northeastern University, in my sophomore year, I fell in love with Esther Smith, the first of only two women I have ever loved. I met Esther just after I had succeeded in persuading Cardinal Cushing of the Archdiocese of Boston to reopen a number of previously closed Catholic high schools in the black ghetto of Roxbury. In those reopened high schools, Father Arthur Brown and I had set up day-care centers, job-training centers, alcohol and drug rehabilitation centers, and after-school tutoring centers for high school and junior high school students. Esther had volunteered as a remedial reading teacher, and she had a wild streak that immediately caught my eye. Matters between us quickly developed into a passionate and almost comically torrid love affair. We made love, wrote poetry, challenged one another intellectually, and took full advantage of the "free love" philosophy of "The '60s."

It was also during my two years at Northeastern University that I was personally confronted by the profound injustice of the Vietnam War. In my freshman year, I had joined the U.S. Army Reserve Officers' Training Corps (ROTC) at Northeastern University and was in training to become a member of the Army Green Berets: Special Forces. Part of that unique training included the serious study of guerrilla warfare. I studied guerrilla warfare's earliest origins with aboriginal people, including Native American warriors who employed it against the invading and occupying European military forces. I studied how guerrilla warfare was practiced later by the American colonial forces against invading and occupying British troops, and by Filipino natives against invading and occupying Japanese forces in the Pacific. And I studied how guerrilla warfare had been employed by the Free French underground against the invading and occupying German forces of the Third Reich. Indeed, as a result of these intensive studies, it became abundantly clear to me that in virtually every case of genuinely effective guerrilla warfare, the guerrillas were "the good guys" and the forces that opposed them were, virtually always, would-be occupiers invading indigenous territory. I learned that a principal tenet of the doctrine of successful guerrilla warfare was that to succeed, guerrilla forces had to retain widespread popular support of their actions among the indigenous population. These self-evident truths became more and more apparent to me as I consumed one book after another on the tactics of successful guerrilla warfare.

When I was deployed into the field alongside my second-year cadet comrades for war games at Fort Devens in Massachusetts in the spring of 1965, I found myself assigned to lead a mock guerrilla force. My squad of guerrilla fighters was always able to successfully ambush and wipe out full companies of regular U.S. Army forces deployed in the field against us. I knew how to beat them because I always knew exactly what it was they were going to try to do—and we never did what we were supposed to do. That is why we were called "guerrillas."

My insistence on employing unpredictable tactics as a squad leader led to repeated clashes between me and Sergeant Dunderdale, the regular army sergeant who was assigned to be our immediate superior, and then later between me and Captain Campbell, a U.S. Army brigade commander. These confrontations occurred each time I refused to obey Sergeant Dunderdale's order to "lie down" for the trainees at Fort Devens. These running conflicts came to a head in the spring of my sophomore year.

We were just beginning training for HALO (high-altitude, low-opening) parachute jumps, which involved skydiving from forty thousand feet into the pitch-black night behind enemy lines, in black camouflage jumpsuits and camouflage face paint. Our instructor was a five-foot-four black man, a regular Army Special Forces captain who was built like the proverbial brick shit house. He was mean. He was smart. But, above all, he was totally ruthless. Indeed, he thought it essential to make perfectly clear to us that our *hearts* would get "little preppy college shits like you killed in 'The Nam.'" I thought he had seen too many Clint Eastwood movies.

It was that instructor who told us that, during our second year in the program, we would each be issued a small puppy, which we would have to tend to and keep happy and healthy for the first two weeks of summer camp. Then, in the third week of camp, we would be ordered to break all four of that puppy's legs—all of them with our bare hands. Then we would be instructed as to how to "field brace" that puppy's legs and how to care for the puppy, taking it with us everywhere for a full week to keep it alive—only to be asked to re-break its legs in the fifth week.

This was pitched to us as "medical training," training that we would need to know in order to know how to keep our buddies alive in the jungles of Vietnam. But it was clear to me that this program was equally designed to harden our hearts and to dumb down our very souls in preparation for what was waiting for us in "The Nam."

I was certain of this when that Green Beret captain informed us, "The first man whose fucking puppy dies on him will have to kill all of the rest of the puppies at the end of the exercise—with his field shovel!"

At the end of my sophomore year, during spring training camp, this same Green Beret captain instructed us that when we HALO-ed in behind enemy lines in Vietnam, it was essential that we understand that we were required *immediately* to kill *anyone* who might happen to see us land in the night, even if that "someone" happened to be an entirely innocent civilian woman or a child, and that we were to immediately bury the body of that "someone" with our chute. I was stunned. I had never imagined that an American military officer would give me an order to murder an innocent woman or child.

Dick Bronstein, to my immediate left, was also stunned, as was "Sully" to my immediate right, with whom I had played freshman football the fall before. We all looked at each other when we heard that order.

Then suddenly it hit me. *We were "the Russians" from Uncle Jim's bad dream.* We were the ones parachuting into *their* hometowns with orders to murder *their* innocent women and children.

At first I couldn't breathe. Then I got a grip on myself and sat in stunned silence through the rest of that lesson.

However, on the very next day, we were ordered to go to the gymnasium there at Fort Devens, where "the brick shit house" was to instruct us on how to use the C-string, or carborundum piano wire garrote, that we each wore sewn into the collar of our shirts. The wire had a small wooden peg attached to each end, in each collar point. He demonstrated how we could chew through the point of the shirt collar, remove the wooden peg, and then slide the C-string piano wire out of the collar. The wooden pegs could then be inserted into loops at the opposite ends of the wire so that the C-string could be used as a garrote to strangle the enemy, whom the instructor referred to as Charlie. "But," he warned us, "you must remember that this C-string garrote is not—I repeat *not*—a class 1 killer." With a demonic look on his face that I will never forget, he then proceeded to demonstrate that when you approach from behind and throw the loop over Charlie's head, and then turn and immediately draw, with all your power, the two wooden pegs to your opposite shoulders, this will cut Charlie's head clean off, even cutting directly through the spinal column that holds his head to his body. "But when Charlie's head comes off," he ghoulishly announced, "it will hit the ground, and when it does, it will make a sound. The C-string garrote is therefore not a class 1 killer. It is *not* totally silent, like a knife. *That* is a class 1 killer. He glowered at us, swiftly removing his Ka-Bar, and then scanned the audience of clean-cut young American men before him on the bleacher seats in the gymnasium.

Then he turned toward us with that demonic expression and said, "You have *got* to remember to immediately wash your shirt and pants out in the nearest source of water, because when you cut off Charlie's head, the gore that will pour out of his severed neck will pour all over your shirt and pants. And when you are lying out in the weeds, hiding, with Charlie all around you, looking for you, all of that gore will start to rot, and Charlie will *smell* you."

Immediately, a picture appeared in my mind of me lying there, eight thousand miles from home, in a field that had belonged for ten generations to the family of a man whose innocent wife and child I had just killed the night before and buried with my chute. *For what?* I asked myself. *To defend democracy?*

This was insane.

I immediately rose from my seat in the second row of the partially rolled-out bleachers and walked directly past the brick shit house. I was moving toward the gymnasium door when I heard Captain Campbell scream my name.

"Shee—haaan, you stupid son of a bitch! Where the hell do you think you are going?"

I turned and looked directly at the Green Beret captain, then at Captain Campbell. Finally, I looked at each and every one of the young innocent faces of my peers. Everyone's eyes were fixed on me.

"Someone here is fucking *nuts*. And it sure as hell *ain't* me!" I said.

And with that, I turned and punched the gymnasium doors open with the butts of both of my hands and walked out. I went directly back to the barracks, where I took off my army field clothes, packed them into my khaki army duffel bag, put on my civilian blue jeans and T-shirt, and walked right off the grounds of Fort Devens. I had to hitchhike back to Boston.

After that, I refused to go back to a single ROTC class. I was given a C for ROTC that spring. It would be the grade that drove my overall Northeastern University GPA down to a 3.96.

The previous year, 1964, was a pivotal one for me. I was starting to question things. I wasn't sure what I believed. In November of 1963, President Kennedy had been assassinated, and immediately afterward came the televised murder of Lee Harvey Oswald, right before our very eyes. What had actually happened there? I knew that *something* here was terribly wrong. Then the bizarre report of the Warren Commission came out, suggesting that President Kennedy and Governor John Connally of Texas had both been shot by the very same "single bullet," and that a mysterious "Dallas nightclub owner" by the name of Jack Ruby had simply walked into a Dallas police station and had murdered Lee Harvey Oswald, right in front of a dozen police security guards, simply "because he felt so sorry for Jacqueline Kennedy." It was clear to me that we were not being told the actual truth about what had happened in Dallas by the people in authority.

Things were suddenly not "just as they should have been" in America anymore.

Then I was reminded of the old Irish aphorism that my godfather, Uncle Jack Sheehan, used to repeat to me. He told me that Irishmen always used to refer to Ireland as "the Ole Sod." And he told me an old Irish saying that I should remember: "Ahhh, the Ole Sod! It's not what it used to be . . . but then it never was."

In the summer of 1964, I worked my first ten-week "co-op" work assignment at Goodwin, Proctor & Hoar, the Boston silk-stocking corporate law firm of the famous Massachusetts governor Samuel Hoar. I approached my work assignments with the same degree of enthusiasm and commitment with which I approached my classes.

I was always at the office before any of the other office assistants, and I was always willing to take on whatever necessary tasks the other office assistants were unwilling to do. I fetched coffee and stayed on late to Xerox and collate copies of emergency legal filings. Typically, I would arrive at 6:00 AM to sort and deliver all of the incoming mail for the partners and associates. That way I got to meet all of the early birds who came into the office before 9:00 AM.

One of these early birds was Donald J. Hurley, the senior partner of the firm and the president of the Boston Chamber of Commerce. He was also a former chairman of the Massachusetts Democratic Party and had been chairman of the 1960 John F. Kennedy-for-President campaign in Massachusetts.

One early Friday morning during a much later co-op work period, in May of 1965, I was contacted by Winnie, Mr. Hurley's executive secretary, and was summoned to his office. To my surprise, Winnie ushered me directly into the presence of Donald J. Hurley himself.

Mr. Hurley came out from behind his large desk and picked up a beautiful leather briefcase with solid gold combination locks. He told me that he had been informed by a number of partners that if he had some really important task that needed to be done right away—and done right—he should have "that new young office assistant from Northeastern" do it. When he had inquired of Winnie who it was that they were all talking about, she told him that that *had* to be me.

I was flattered. But I still didn't know what it was that he wanted.

As it turned out, Mr. Hurley was scheduled to fly off to Europe that very evening for two weeks of important meetings with a European client, and his favorite legal briefcase had broken. He had tried everything to get it repaired, but no one was able to fix it. They all said that it needed to be sent back to the manufacturer, which would take at least a month.

What Mr. Hurley wanted to know was whether there was any way that I might possibly get his favorite briefcase repaired in time for him to take it on his trip to Europe that afternoon.

"Leave it to me, Mr. Hurley. I will have it back to you by five o'clock, as good as new."

With that, I took the magic briefcase under my arm and walked deliberately from his office.

As soon as I was out of sight, I dashed to my little cubbyhole and began burning up the telephone, trying to find some luggage repair service that could fix it. When I described the briefcase to each shop I got on the line, they each told me that it could not be done. So I grabbed the briefcase and set out into the world to get it fixed. I went from shop to shop, dropping every name I could think of: the Goodwin-Proctor firm, Donald J. Hurley, Senator Hoar, even the late President Kennedy—all to no avail.

I finally ended up, at four o'clock in the afternoon, in some little hole-in-the-wall jewelry shop in South Boston, miles from the office.

But it worked. The wonderful jeweler *loved* President Kennedy, so he loved Mr. Hurley for being Kennedy's presidential campaign chairman in Massachusetts. He carefully removed the sensitive golden combination locks and repaired them, using a jeweler's eyepiece and his tiny tools. He even polished the briefcase.

When I asked him how much it would be, he told me to consider it a favor to Mr. Hurley. "Tell him thank you from me for helping the president."

I dashed for a cab to return to the office. I ran from the cab to the elevator and asked Jackson, the building's elevator operator, to step on it. I sprinted down the carpeted hallway on the fourteenth floor and then walked, slowly and confidently, past Winnie, into Mr. Hurley's office.

He was just getting up from his desk to pack his legal papers into an old worn-out briefcase when I presented him with the fully repaired briefcase, allowing it to catch the waning sunlight to show off its new polish. It was perfect.

"A piece of cake, Mr. Hurley," I said casually. I turned to walk out.

"Ah, Danny. How much did it cost?"

I turned. This was all perfect.

"It was free, Mr. Hurley. The jeweler did it as a return favor to you, for your having helped President Kennedy the way I told him you had." With that, I walked out of the office and looked at the antique grandfather clock in the hallway. It was five o'clock on the nose.

Two weeks later, I had almost forgotten about this great feat when I received a telephone call at my little cubby from Winnie. Could I please come to speak with Mr. Hurley? He was just back and wished to speak with me. I went directly up to the fourteenth floor and approached Winnie's desk.

"Mr. Hurley is expecting you," she said with a special smile.

When I entered, Mr. Hurley immediately rose from behind his huge desk and rushed across the room to greet me with a warm hand pump. Unexpectedly, he guided me over to the large soft leather sofa in his office and asked me to sit down. I did. He returned to his desk and retrieved a manila folder. Then he sat in a large matching leather chair that he'd turned to face the sofa. He then laid the manila folder in his lap.

I began to get a very strange sense of déjà vu of my interview with Senator Jacob Javits two years earlier.

After Mr. Hurley had settled into the chair and taken a comfortable moment, he said, "I can't tell you how impressed I was at the way that you accomplished that little task that I asked you to do for me before my recent trip to Europe."

"I hope it was successful, Mr. Hurley. I was pleased to do whatever I could to make it more pleasant for you."

Mr. Hurley sat and stared. He was quite beside himself.

"I, uh, I hope that you don't mind, Danny, but I took the liberty of contacting Northeastern University, where I understand you are a sophomore this year. Is that correct?"

I was puzzled. But I replied that it was.

He consulted the open manila folder in his lap. "It says here that you are taking seven full courses this year, just as you did last year, even though only four are required for full credit. Is that correct?"

I was impressed that he'd gone to such lengths. *If only Senator Javits had been as responsible as Donald J. Hurley, I would be flying F-102s right now,* I thought to myself.

"That is correct, Mr. Hurley."

"Why is that, Danny, exactly?"

"Well, Mr. Hurley," I said, "I am the very first man in our Sheehan family ever to have gotten a chance to go to college. So although Northeastern is not exactly a bastion of intellectual achievement, I wanted to take as full advantage as I possibly could, to learn as much as I possibly could while I am getting to go to college. I didn't want to disappoint all of the people who have helped me get here."

Again, he simply sat and stared. Then he looked back down into the folder.

"It says here that you have a 3.96 grade point average, out of a possible perfect 4.0, while you are carrying seven full courses each quarter. Is that true?"

"Well, Mr. Hurley, that .04 grade point deduction came as a result of my having refused to return to the army ROTC program after a certain incident at Fort Devens this spring, Sir."

"No. No," he said with great emotion. "I wasn't asking you to explain the .04 grade point deduction. I was interested in how you maintained an almost perfect grade point average while taking seven full courses?"

"Oh. Well, Mr. Hurley, while I am really grateful to get to go to Northeastern University, with all due respect to the university, I have found that, in getting to take classes for only a short ten-week period at a time, one can virtually *memorize* the limited classroom readings and assignments that one receives in this short of a period and simply repeat it back to the professors at the school."

This earned another straight stare.

"Well, that is exactly the purpose of my having asked you to come to speak with me today. What I am asking, Danny, is why on earth did a young man like you ever choose to attend a place like Northeastern University when it is clear from your records here that you could have gone to any college of your choice? Didn't you ever want to go to a college like Harvard or Yale or one of the other finer schools in the country?"

Again I was struck by the déjà vu of my interview with Senator Javits two years earlier.

Without further prompting, I launched into my Air Force Academy story, explaining how I had been denied the senatorial appointment and had thus ended up at Northeastern. I even included the information about my Aunt Gladys's and Uncle Jim's inability to pay for my college education.

"Would you like to go to Harvard College, son?" Mr. Hurley asked me. "If you were given the chance?"

"Oh, Mr. Hurley," I said. "I would never be able to pay for an education at Harvard. I have no money, and my parents are separated. I have no one to help me pay for college."

It was as though a lance had pierced his heart. Tears came into his eyes. "That is why Harvard College has the generous endowment that it has, son, so that young men like you can get the chance to go to school there." He leaned forward in his chair and looked me straight in the eye. "Would you like to go to Harvard, son?"

I told him that I absolutely would, if there was any way that I could afford it.

With that, he rose from his chair and went around behind his desk. He opened a drawer and withdrew a piece of white writing paper. As he wrote, he spoke to me without looking up. "I am writing a personal note to Fred Glimp, the dean of admissions at Harvard College. I am going to have you hand deliver this to Fred, this afternoon. Winnie will call the car for you. I will give him a call and let him know that you are coming over. I hope you like it, son. It will make all the difference in your life."

With that, he finished writing the short note, quickly read through it, and then added a short footnote before signing it and slipping it into an envelope. He came out from behind his desk and handed it to me. When I shook his hand, he seized me and embraced me, with tears in his eyes, like a proud grandfather.

As I walked past Winnie, I heard Mr. Hurley saying over the intercom to her, "Winnie, please call the limousine and charge it to Recruiting. Mr. Sheehan is going over to Harvard."

I walked to the elevator—and into another world.

I received my acceptance to Harvard College—with a full academic scholarship—at the end of that very month and immediately transferred from Northeastern University. It was a transition that would take me from the archetypal working-class American college, at which three-fourths of the students probably could not have told you the name of the American secretary of state, to one of the premier centers of learning in all of Western civilization, at which three-quarters of the students enrolled were probably related *by blood* to at least one American secretary of state.

Because of my heavy course load at Northeastern, I had accumulated too many course credits to transfer into Harvard College as a sophomore. So I had to enter as a full junior into the class of 1967—the last all-male class to graduate from Harvard College after 325 years.

At that time, in 1965, the National Collegiate Athletic Association (NCAA) had a rule prohibiting any undergraduate who had lettered in a varsity-level intercollegiate sport from transferring to another college and then competing in the same sport until one full year had elapsed. This meant that I could play neither varsity football nor varsity baseball at Harvard College until my senior year. But, in preparation for my playing both varsity sports once I was eligible, I was placed in Kirkland House, the "jock house." Out of ten upperclassman houses at Harvard in 1965, Kirkland House had graduated more Rhodes Scholars than any other *entire college* had graduated. I felt like my new life was off to a running start.

I pulled up to Kirkland House in September 1965 in my old used '59 Chevy Bel Air. I was assigned to suite L-42, with three Harvard Varsity football players: Bruce Corker, Robert Buritz, and John Jamison. Across the hall from us were a couple of varsity baseball players, and another varsity football player was down the hall. They had all graduated in the top two—in both academics and athletics—of their respective high schools, and they all seemed to have fathers who had graduated from Harvard College as well. That's when I began to see what a change this was from anywhere else I had ever been. All of these guys had been student council presidents and varsity team captains as well as valedictorians or salutatorians of their high schools or private prep schools. Up to that point in my life, I had always found myself capable of doing virtually anything better than anybody else around me. Now here I was in a place where *everyone* was just like that too.

I started at Harvard College as a government studies major, and one of the first books I had to read was *Design of Water-Resource Systems* by Arthur Maass. At the time, Maass was the chairman of the Government Department at Harvard University. I viewed his book as a 350-page apologetic for our then politically and financially corrupt American public policy system. The core of the book was a case study in which the citizenry of America's Southwest was in clear need of a freshwater supply, but no public interest groups provided adequate political leverage to acquire that water system for them. Maass's proposed solution to this public policy problem was to engage individuals who had a direct *personal* financial interest, such as people who owned private construction corporations, concrete corporations, and large agribusiness corporations that might profit from the water. These private representatives would then use their ample funds to lobby U.S. senators and congressmen so they could secure contracts that would allow them to make millions in profits off a public need.

I was totally offended. This sounded to me like a ploy to convince Harvard underclassman that the only way to get things done "in the real world" was to help the rich get richer

So I wrote my junior honors essay emphatically condemning Arthur Maass's point of view. My junior government adviser was beside himself. "If you are going to do something like this," he told me, "you had better cross all of your t's and dot all of your i's. Or else they will kill you here." By "they" I assumed that he meant the reigning authority whose opinion I was challenging, and by "kill you" I assumed that he meant they would refuse to pass me.

But I was so grateful at having been given this unique opportunity to study with—and debate with—"the greatest minds of the era" that I did not want to flinch in the face of the strong genuine feeling I had when I encountered the very first example of what I viewed to be a "temptation to corruption."

But my junior government adviser was right. One member of the three-professor team that was assigned to grade my junior honors essay went ballistic and threatened to flunk me. But, after seeing that I had straight A's in all my other courses—and the fact that the other two graders distinctly disagreed with him—he was persuaded to relent. He would not have anything to do with assigning a passing grade to my essay, however, which he considered to be a "broadside against the department chairman's principal piece of writing," so he let my junior honors tutor act as the third grader, who gave me an A.

Harvard College had what we called "Shopping Week." It was a week in which we were accorded the right to "shop" various courses by attending the first few lectures without having to commit to a course. It was a way to see if one liked the professor and wanted to read the materials on the course reading list.

I remember going into my first Government 180 class, the top class in American foreign policy, which was to be taught by Henry Kissinger. Kissinger would of course soon thereafter go on to become both the national security adviser and the secretary of state for Richard Nixon. But at the time, in 1965, he was just the top teacher of American foreign policy at Harvard.

The class was held in Harvard Hall, one of the oldest buildings on the campus—and that is saying something, since Harvard College was founded in 1640. Kissinger came out, took the lectern, and then proceeded, in that gravelly voice for which he later became famous to the world, to serve notice on us that

> If there is anyone present here among you who believes that a nation-state, such as our United States, is *not* authorized to lie, cheat, steal, and kill to gain access to the strategic raw materials that belong to other nations that our leaders have determined to be necessary to advance the national security of our nation and to promote the economic interests of our nation and our nation's businesses, then that person should *not* enroll in this class.

I was flabbergasted. But, then, I was a working-class kid from the north woods of New York.

I looked around at what I presumed to be the predominantly prep school–educated Harvard undergraduates in the class, and not one of them seemed to be in any way disturbed by this admonition.

So I resolved to stay in the class to learn how they saw the world—and how Harvard planned to have them "run it" after they graduated.

As had been the case with Arthur Maass's class, I was determined to answer all of the essay questions and write all of my papers in Kissinger's Government 180 course in a manner that aimed to prove that there *was* a way to conduct American foreign policy without lying, cheating, or killing to steal the resources of other nations through the exercise of our military superiority. This led to a series of handwritten notes in the margins of my papers, written by Kissinger's teaching assistants, each one of whom was striving more diligently than the other to demonstrate to Kissinger how hard-nosed he was. It was a very valuable class for me, because it both gave me insight into how Henry Kissinger thought and reasoned, and it enabled me to focus my attention on concrete ways to direct American foreign policy in a less domineering and selfish manner.

CHAPTER *five*

A S I BEGAN my second semester at Harvard College in the spring of
1966, I was just beginning to feel at home within the Harvard community. Out of the dozen incidents that had begun to shape my new worldview
during that first full year at Harvard, two stand out in what was otherwise
a very positive experience.

I had been rushed by the only fraternity at Harvard, Sigma Alpha
Epsilon (SAE), and by springtime of 1966, I had been elected to be the fraternity's social chairman. That spring semester, I nominated for membership
in SAE Tommy Davis, a defensive safety on the varsity football team who
also lived in Kirkland House. He was the first black man ever to receive a
nomination for membership in SAE in the entire history of that old, traditional southern fraternity.

We gathered when it came time to vote for our new members. As social
chairman, I set it up so that Tommy Davis was the first name we voted on.
After the first ballot was taken, there were three "black balls" in the ballot box. A black ball is an old fraternity tradition that allows any member
to veto a nominee without having to provide any reason whatsoever for
his veto. And the tradition was that no one was allowed to ask who had
"thrown the black ball."

As soon as the black balls were recorded, I stood up and announced
that I was going to black ball every single other nominee until whoever had
thrown the black balls against Tommy Davis fessed up and gave us their
reasons.

Everybody was pissed. But I didn't flinch. I black balled each of the ten
following nominees. Some members complained that it was unfair to exclude
all these worthy guys just to make a point. I told them that I was not black

balling these guys "just to make a point." I was black balling them to get whoever was black balling Tommy Davis to tell us why they were doing it.

On the fifth ballot, deep into the night, only one black ball was thrown against Tommy Davis. When I promised to black ball everyone else on the sixth ballot, finally someone fessed up to being the holdout on Tommy. A guy named Gary Beck, from Cleveland, Ohio, stood up. When I asked him why he was throwing a black ball against Tommy Davis, he said that he had heard that Tommy Davis dated white women. "If he were ever to show up at one of our SAE social gatherings with a white date, why, I just don't know what I would do!"

I sat staring at him. There was one of "them"—a simple straightforward racist.

"Gary," I said, "He is on the dean's list. And he is one of the nicest guys that I have ever met at Harvard. And, besides, I understand that he presses twice his weight in the varsity weight room. So exactly what *would* you do if he came to one of our social functions with a white date?"

The room was silent for a long time. Then Gary Beck said, "Well, I guess that I would just *leave*."

"Leave that specific event? Or leave SAE?" I asked.

Gary Beck looked surprised. "No! I mean that I would just leave that specific event. I wouldn't leave SAE!"

"Good," I said. "Then it's settled. Tommy Davis gets in, and Gary Beck will be supported by everyone if he finds it necessary to personally leave any fraternity event at which Tommy shows up with a white date! Let's take another ballot to make it official."

We took the sixth ballot . . . and someone threw another black ball.

I jumped up and confronted Gary Beck, who insisted that he had abstained. We all looked around at everyone else. Finally, one of Gary Beck's friends sheepishly stood up and admitted that it was he who had thrown the black ball. "I did it for Gary. I know that he wanted to, but you all intimidated him into not doing it."

"Well, do you plan to keep doing it? Because if you do, I am going to keep black balling the other ten nominees, and we aren't going to have any new members this semester, or next semester, or the semester after that. Not as long as I am a voting member of SAE!"

So, on the seventh ballot, Tommy Davis, our Harvard Ivy League defensive safety, became the very first black man ever elected as a member of Sigma Alpha Epsilon.

When I explained to Tommy that he had been elected to SAE and I explained to him how this had taken place, he declined the invitation. I knew that he wanted to join our fraternity, but he wouldn't under those circumstances.

The second less-than-pleasant experience I had at Harvard in my first year there was more dramatic. And it taught me a great deal about institutions in general.

One of my spring semester classes included the Advanced Drama course taught by Professor Robert Chapman, with sections led by Arthur Friedman and another man. The objective of the course was to teach Harvard and Radcliffe upperclassmen the important role that drama played in critiquing social mores and government policies. Professor Chapman informed us at the beginning of the course that he strove to quote George Bernard Shaw at least once in every lecture because Shaw had said, "If, in your play, you do not offend at least one social more or government policy, then your play has been a waste of the audience's time . . . and yours."

Professor Chapman also informed us that our final exam was going to be an essay on why the film of Jean Anhoui's play *Un Chant d'Amour* (*A Song of Love*) had been banned, not only in every European country but also in the United States. He and all the "section men" took great pride in letting us know that they were going to sneak a copy of the film into the country so we could watch it.

At a Kirkland House dinner before finals week, one of my drama classmates pulled me aside and informed me that "the film" had arrived. Robert Chapman and the section men were going to have a preview showing at Arthur Friedman's apartment that very evening, and I was invited. I declined because I wanted to wait and see the film in the theater at Boylston Hall with the rest of the class, so I could get the full experience of seeing it only once and then writing my essay with it fresh in my mind.

The following morning, my friend confirmed that he had indeed seen the film the night before, but I stopped him before he could tell me any details. I wanted to form my own opinion after seeing the movie for myself.

On the day we were scheduled to view the banned film, Arthur Friedman came to the podium in our morning lecture and made a brief announcement: "I am sorry to announce that, due to an addressing error, the movie *Un Chant d'Amour* did not arrive. There will be an alternative question presented for our essay tomorrow for the final exam, a question relating to one of the other plays that you read this semester."

With that, he abruptly left the podium and moved to take his usual seat at the back of the lecture room.

That didn't make sense to me, so I rose to my feet and called to Arthur. I saw terror in his eyes the instant his eyes met mine.

"I think you should tell the class the truth," I said.

"Are you calling me a liar?" he said. "Someone mistakenly put the return address on the mailing instructions in the space for the delivery address. As soon as the film arrived here at the Boston post office, it was immediately returned, back to France."

I was stunned.

"Arthur, I *know* what happened," I said.

He told me to drop it. But I explained that I was aware that he'd screened the film at his apartment over the weekend.

"OK, OK. So I lied to you," he said.

A gasp went up from the class. "Look, I did it for Professor Chapman! His tenure could be set aside if someone were to lodge a morals charge against him." This explanation did not satisfy the class. Arthur admitted that he'd received the film, but this time he tried a new tack, claiming that the film was of too poor a physical quality to screen for us. He suggested that he'd lied out of fear that it would look like he had an ulterior motive for not showing it to us.

"What utter bullshit!" I stated. "If you returned the film because of its poor quality, then what was all that about the morals clause in Professor Chapman's employment contract with Harvard?"

Arthur was caught now, and he knew it. Then the bell rang, signaling the end of class. My classmates grumbled a little, but they started leaving the room.

"Hey!" I shouted after them. "Are you going to just leave this like this?" But they all just kept filing out of the room. I was furious.

That afternoon I had section with Arthur along with half of our class. When I arrived fifteen minutes early, the room was already overflowing with my classmates *from both sections.* They had all come for the confrontation they knew was coming. I took my usual place in the front row of the class.

We waited past the time when class is officially canceled if a professor doesn't show. The film had originally been scheduled to screen right after the section, so we had no other classes in the meantime.

Then, thirty minutes late, Arthur finally showed up. He was unpleasantly surprised to see the entire class waiting for him. He walked up to the podium, a little too casually, and started to read a prepared lecture, never lifting his eyes from his notes.

I rose and called out to Arthur, stopping him. He lifted his eyes from his notes and glared at me. Then he took a prepared note from his inside jacket pocket and read: "Mr. Sheehan, I have been authorized by the dean of Harvard College to inform you that you are officially disrupting a scheduled class at Harvard University . . . and that, if you do not desist immediately, you will be expelled from Harvard University."

"What bullshit!" someone yelled. And then the whole class started repeating it, chanting, "What bullshit! What bullshit! What bullshit!"

Arthur stood before the class, totally humiliated. Finally, he raised his hands in surrender. Then he said, "OK, OK. I am going to level with you. When we saw what was in the film, we realized that if we showed it to a mixed class of Harvard and Radcliffe undergraduates, Professor Chapman might be subject to a morals complaint from one of the Radcliffe parents."

The class exploded into another round of "What bullshit!" led by the Radcliffe students. When things died down, I asked the question on everyone's mind.

"Well, what was in it?"

One of the other students spoke up. "Isn't that what this whole course was supposed to have been about—why this film was banned in Europe and the U.S.?"

After a few long seconds, Arthur reluctantly bowed to our pressure.

"Look," he said. "In this movie, the protagonist is in prison in France. After the protagonist has spent many days in his cell, he hears someone knocking on the other side of the wall. The older man has dug a tiny hole through his cell wall using pieces of straw from his mattress, to get to the other person on the other side of the wall."

Arthur hesitated for an uncomfortable moment. Finally, one of the students prodded him. "And?"

Arthur swallowed hard before he went on. "So the older inmate pushes a piece of straw through the tiny hole that he has made in the wall, and he blows through it. Then the prisoner in the other cell blows back." Arthur shifted.

"And then?" a student asked.

"And then . . ." Arthur swallowed hard again. "And then, there is this long scene in which the two men are breathing through the straw into each other's mouths, and then the protagonist kind of swoons, and he gets up and goes over to the urinal in his cell, with his back to the camera, and he drops his pants . . . and masturbates into the toilet!"

There was a long silence in the room. Then one of the Radcliffe students said, "Yeah, and then what happens?"

Arthur was shocked.

"Then what happens? *That's* what happens!"

"I thought that you said he had his back to the camera."

"Yes, but you can tell!" Arthur said. "You can tell what he is doing even though his back is to the camera."

"Only if you had already done something like that yourself," the Radcliffe student said, and everyone laughed out loud. Arthur was shame-faced. The Radcliffe student continued. "That was all? That's why you decided to send the film back without allowing us to see it? After all of that pitching that you and Chapman did about being such brave guys, that you would dare to show us this banned film?"

But Arthur, glancing nervously at his watch, declared the class over. "This matter is totally moot. The film has already been sent back, and I take full responsibility for that decision. Now let's clear this room so I can get to my next class."

He was making his way to the door at the back of the room when suddenly he stopped. I followed his gaze to the door at the back of the room. There, coming into the room, was the second section man. He was carrying a large film can under his arm. Every one of the students saw this and froze.

Then something occurred to me. Arthur and Professor Chapman had set the whole thing up. It had been a test! It was wonderful, I thought, better than anything I could have imagined when I transferred from Northeastern University.

But when I called Arthur on his charade, he only looked confused. As other students grew audibly excited about this possibility, Arthur could only hang his head in shame. He and the section man, who was carrying the film canister, began to move toward Boylston Hall, where the film had originally been scheduled to be shown. Were they going to show us the film after all?

When I stopped Arthur to ask, he began to cry. I knew then that it was over.

"Look, Danny," Arthur said. "What if *Time* magazine ever got ahold of this? They would crucify Harvard. It's Henry Luce—he hates Harvard! We can't show it to a class of mixed undergraduates. But we've got the film here, so we're showing it to a group of advanced graduate students."

When I turned away, he took me by the arm and whispered, "Look, *you* can come in to see it. We just can't let them all in. So don't tell them. If anybody finds out that we showed it to you, we would have to show it to everyone, and we can't do that."

I pulled my arm away from him and walked back over to the gathered students. I told them what Arthur had just told me, and he immediately denied it. I told him I was walking into that theater to see the film—unless Robert Chapman himself stood in the doorway and formally turned me away.

Arthur was visibly relieved. He went away, and we all waited. When he came back, he had Professor Chapman with him. He positioned himself in the central doorway and read a prepared statement: "I, Dr. Robert Chapman, the Harvard University–authorized professor of Advanced Drama 306, hereby formally inform you that you, as undergraduate students at Harvard University, will not be allowed to enter Boylston Hall to view a certain film that has been secured by the Harvard faculty to show exclusively to a select group of graduate students."

OFF TO OUR left, a scuffle broke out. One of the section men was holding a member of our undergraduate class by the scruff of the shirt. The smallish boy was struggling against the larger man. Suddenly, the boy saw Professor Chapman and his face lit up.

"There he is!" the boy shouted. "He will tell you. I am supposed to see this film for our final exam. I *have* to see it!" The boy struggled over to where Robert Chapman was standing in the doorway. He pulled loose from the hold of the larger section man and gathered his breath. He gasped, "Tell him, Dr. Chapman!"

Robert Chapman hung his head.

"I *can't!*" Chapman whispered to the boy.

The boy's head snapped back. "What? Whaddaya mean, you can't?"

"I can't," Chapman repeated, this time loudly, so all the students gathered in the hall could hear. "I would be fired."

The boy stood to his full five-foot-five height, looked his teacher squarely in the eye, and said, "George Bernard Shaw would never have said anything like that."

Robert Chapman folded and collapsed to the floor, sobbing uncontrollably, his face buried in his hands.

I resolved to go to *The Crimson*, Harvard's daily newspaper, first thing the next morning, to tell them everything that had happened with the class and the banned film.

As soon as I walked in the front door of *The Crimson* office, one of the staffers recognized me and tracked down Ellen Lake from Radcliffe, the first female student ever elected to be the paper's editor in chief. I waited in her office. Within fifteen minutes, she arrived out of breath, obviously having been called out of class somewhere. She swept into the office, tossed her books into a pile, and grabbed her notepad and pencil.

"OK, shoot," she said, throwing herself into a plastic chair that she pulled up in front of me.

I laid out every detail I could remember, and I could remember a lot.

"Holy shit! This is extraordinary!" she said. Then she asked me to go over "that stuff about *Time* magazine." "What was *that?*" she wanted to know.

I repeated what Arthur had said to me while she took notes furiously.

"Look," she said. "These are extraordinary charges that you are making here."

"Charges? What the hell do you mean *charges*? This is what happened! You think that I am making all of this shit up?"

"No, no," she protested. "I don't doubt what you're saying for a minute. We all heard that something big had happened in Boylston Hall yesterday." She got up, pushed her bright orange plastic chair away with her leg, and got professional. "But I need to have all the facts . . . *all* of them. You've got to write down all of the details—dates, names, places, names of witnesses—everything. This is going to be explosive!" She explained that there would be one final issue of the paper published before the end of the semester and that it would be distributed to all the alumni arriving for graduation. The implications of this seemed to hit her as she spoke.

I got up and looked her square in the eyes. "Do you give me your word, as a journalist, that you will print this story? You *know* what it could mean to your career."

She gasped. "I do, I *do*."

That afternoon I got out my typewriter and blue carbon paper and sat down to write up the whole dreadful story. I wrote for the remainder of the day, deep into the night, and then the following morning.

I had two copies. One for *The Crimson*, which I dropped off in person, and a second that I mailed to Professor Robert Chapman at his Harvard office.

The next morning I received a call from the dean of students at Harvard, "Booze" Watson. He demanded that I come immediately to his office in University Hall. When I walked in it was like a tomb. All of the secretaries and personnel sat silently, watching me enter. Dean Watson's secretary gestured silently, with a pointed finger, to the closed door of his office.

I knocked and then opened the door. Watson sat there waiting for me.

When I was seated, he opened a manila envelope and removed a sheaf of papers. He tossed them in front of me. I could see immediately that it was the report I had prepared for *The Crimson*, not the copy I had sent to Robert Chapman.

Dean Watson looked at me. "Did you write this and send it to *The Crimson*?"

"Yes," I said. "And every word of it is true."

"*True?*" he roared, actually raising himself out of his seat. "True? That's not the point! Did you or did you not threaten to go to *Time* magazine with your story if *The Crimson* refused to publish it?"

I picked up the report again, just to make sure that I had said that in this copy and not in the Chapman copy. It was there.

"It was a conditional threat," I said.

"*Conditional?* What the hell difference does it make that it was conditional? The fact is that you threatened *The Crimson*—in writing—and you threatened to go to *Time*. Jesus H. Christ, Sheehan, don't you know that *Time* magazine *hates* Harvard?"

"Why is that, Dean Watson?" I asked.

"What the hell difference does that make why they goddamned hate us? They do! That's all you've got to know!"

"Well, it makes a difference to me," I said.

"And just who the hell do you think you are, Mr. Sheehan, to think that you can march on in here to my office and demand of me to explain to you why *Time* magazine hates Harvard University?"

"I'm the Harvard College undergraduate that you have to persuade not to take this story to *Time* magazine if *The Crimson* refuses to print it."

Saying this was a mistake. A *big* mistake. Booze Watson rose up out of his chair, pushed it away with the back of his knees, and leaned over the desk at me.

"Well, you're going to be the Harvard College undergraduate that gets your little ass expelled if you breathe a single word of this story," he said, lifting up the sheaf of papers on the desk between us. "How's that for an answer to your question, Mr. Sheehan? Now get your ass out of my office. And if you ever want to get a degree from this university, you goddamned better keep your mouth shut about this matter. It ends right here!" he said, slamming the sheaf of papers into the trash can behind his desk.

I turned and walked out of his office.

I had never dreamed that they would really threaten to expel me for doing exactly what they were purporting to train me to do. I was, for the first time, genuinely frightened. What if they did expel me? I loved it at Harvard. It was more than I ever could have dreamed for in my life.

The Crimson printed a short interview with Arthur Friedman, but there was not a single mention of my report. *The Crimson* quoted Arthur as saying, "The Graduate School of Drama had secured a special film to be shown exclusively to graduate students. A young undergraduate—who shall remain nameless—apparently had some 'prurient interest' in getting to see what he thought would be some nudity in the film. When he was turned away at the door to the theater at Boylston Hall, he had gone into a high state of dudgeon over being excluded. But everything was resolved peacefully and amicably."

I never heard another thing about Ellen Lake, the editor in chief of *The Crimson*. I guess she learned all she needed to know about the world of journalism in that one incident.

Later that week, I was sitting in my room, up in L-42, when I heard a din outside of my window. I looked out—and there was *Robert McNamara* standing on top of a stretch limousine with an electric bullhorn in his right hand, shouting at about one hundred Harvard underclassmen who had him cornered in the cul-de-sac between Kirkland House and Elliot House. They were rocking his limousine back and forth. He held on with one hand, the bullhorn in his other hand, shouting responses to their insults and epithets. I wandered out of my room and stood there watching this strange show. And this was Harvard University!

What a strange first year.

I wrote my senior honors thesis on the groundbreaking United States Supreme Court Case *Miranda v. Arizona*, the case in which the Supreme

Court declared that it would be, thereafter, constitutionally required that all state, county, and municipal law enforcement officers, upon arresting any person, inform that person that he or she had the right to an attorney and had the right to remain silent in the face of any police interrogation designed to solicit evidence incriminating that person of any crime. Since, in my junior year at Harvard, I had received an A+ in Constitutional Law from Professor Paul Freund, the principal constitutional law professor at Harvard Law School, I was able to persuade him to be my senior honors thesis adviser—because no one teaching at the undergraduate level was academically equipped to advise me in the preparation of such a thesis. So, in a manner of speaking, my law school career was launched while I was still an undergraduate.

In my senior year, Harvard awarded me with its Rhodes Scholarship nomination for New York State.

I went down to New York City and participated in the first-round interviews and made it to the finals. However, because I had been reclassified by the New York State Draft Board as 1-A, the Rhodes Scholarship Committee informed me that before I could proceed to the final-round interview, I would be required to get a graduate school deferral letter from my draft board.

My draft board took the position that there had been a few days between my having officially withdrawn from Northeastern and my having officially enrolled in Harvard College. My draft board said that it was during that short few-day window that it had drafted me, which was an absolute lie; I had been accepted and had officially enrolled in Harvard College before I even told Northeastern University that I was leaving. And I hadn't withdrawn from Northeastern until a full week after I was already officially enrolled at Harvard. It was a simple bald-faced lie. The draft board said that my 2-S deferment had been revoked when I withdrew from Northeastern, and it had changed my official draft status to 1-A during my two years at Harvard College as a retaliation for my having dropped out of ROTC after two years. It took me two full months of wrangling with the draft board to reinstate my 2-S student draft deferral. But the board informed me that the reissued 2-S student draft deferment was only temporary, just until I graduated from Harvard College.

So when I contacted my draft board in April of 1967 and requested a graduate school student deferment to potentially receive a Rhodes Scholarship to go to Oxford University in England, the board drafted me for a *second* time. Needless to say, it refused to forward the deferment letter to the Rhodes Committee, and the Rhodes Scholarship from New York in 1967 went to a third-string tennis player from the University of Long Island.

The draft board and I thereupon began an exchange of letters in which I informed it that if it wanted to press this second draft notice, I would publicly name the people who had instructed me and my fellow U.S. Army Green Beret ROTC cadets to kill innocent women and children. I knew who had been in all of those classes with me. I knew the names of the officers who had been present, the dates, and the potential consequences.

My draft board finally sent me a notice that I had been reclassified as 1-Y because I had had water on the knee during one football season at Northeastern. This meant that I was still unable to leave the country. So, since I could not receive the Rhodes Scholarship, I accepted a full scholarship to attend Harvard Law School, which I had acquired with the support of a personal letter of recommendation from Harvard Law School's constitutional law professor Paul Freund. I then began my law school career in September of 1967 as an official U.S. Army draftee under the threat of being sent to Vietnam.

PART II

CHAPTER *six*

THAT WAS JUST before The Big Year: 1968. Things were heating up in the country concerning the Vietnam War. Major protests had begun to erupt in college towns all across the land. I was having a personal war with my draft board from northern New York State, and I knew that I wasn't going to go to Vietnam. The board had directly screwed me out of getting the Rhodes Scholarship, so I was taking it all very personally. But I had not yet started participating in any of the big demonstrations. I hadn't joined any anti–Vietnam War groups. I wasn't marching. I was just affronted, morally and politically, at what our government leaders were doing. So I wouldn't go.

Moreover, I *refused* to apply for a conscientious objector deferment, as the board proposed, because I refused to sign an affidavit swearing that I would not fight in the Vietnam War "because I believed in a supreme being." I told the draft board exactly why I wouldn't go fight in the Vietnam War, and it had nothing whatsoever to do with whether I did or did not believe in a supreme being. It was none of their business what I believed about any supreme being.

I remember vividly my very first day at Harvard Law School. One of my favorite Sigma Alpha Epsilon fraternity brothers, John Lesche, who had graduated the year before me from the college and had gone up to the law school, had warned me that Professor W. Barton Leach, the first-year property professor at Harvard Law School, had a specific idiosyncratic action that he performed for every first-year (1-L) law class. Before the first class, he would post a small public notice on the bulletin board outside of Langdell Middle, the central classroom building at Harvard Law School, announcing an assignment for the very first class. "Pappy Leach," as he was known, waited until everyone in his section had arrived in Langdell South and had taken his or her preassigned seat. Then he would mention the assignment posted on the bulletin board outside and say that he assumed that everyone had carefully read the material and was prepared to discuss the issues raised in the reading.

Immediately, 95 percent of the class would be seized with terror. They had succeeded in getting into Harvard Law School, after years of toil and sacrifice, and they had arrived determined to stay on top of every assignment and to never be caught unprepared for class. And here they were, on their very first day at Harvard Law School, totally unprepared, while W. Barton Leach, one of the "great gods" of Harvard Law School lore, loomed over them, eyeing his infamous "name chart."

Then Leach would say,

> Now, you all know the facts of the case. They are simple. Farmer A and Farmer B, longtime friends and neighbors, have adjoining farms. They have lived in perfect harmony, side by side, for over thirty years, each tilling his respective fields and producing the farm goods that have made each of them perfectly happy for a lifetime. Then, suddenly and unexpectedly, Farmer B dies. His children decide to sell the family farm and move to the city. And in order to prepare for the sale, they, in the normal course of business affairs, have a routine survey conducted of the land. To everyone's utter surprise, they are informed by the professional surveyor that Farmer A, unbeknownst to anyone, had, erroneously, thirty years earlier, built his fence, meant to separate the two farms, ten feet *onto* Farmer B's property. So, for thirty years, Farmer A has been tending that additional ten feet of farmland: paying taxes on it; cultivating it; fertilizing it; and harvesting the foodstuffs produced on that extra ten feet of land, the entire length of both of their farms. Now, suddenly, the children of Farmer B insist that Farmer A move his several-hundred-foot-long fence off *their* property and return *their* ten-feet-wide, several-hundred-feet-long portion of Farm B to them. The question before us is, whose property is that portion of land? Farmer A's or Farmer B's?

When this happened, 95 percent of the class would sit stunned and paralyzed with fear, seeing their Harvard Law School careers passing before them on their very first day. Of the 5 percent of the class fortunate enough to have either somehow noticed the posted assignment or been notified about it by a friend, as I had been, all but a very few of them labored under the entirely false notion that W. Barton Leach—like all of the other Harvard Law School professors about whom they had heard—wanted them to respond to his question by "laying out the equities on each side of the issue," thereby demonstrating to this "great god" of Harvard Law School that they were perfectly prepared to argue the case on either side. But, unfortunately for these daring few, nothing could have been further from the truth.

Barton Leach's first choice was to target one of those unfortunate first-year law students who had obviously not heard about the assignment, so he could shame and humiliate that person, thereby striking terror—the terror of not being thoroughly prepared for each and every class—deep into the heart of every member of the first-year class. "It will be a terror that will drive them to their very highest possible level of performance," Barton Leach used to brag, "first as a Harvard Law School student and then as an attorney."

Pappy Leach viewed the imparting of this painful lesson to every entering Harvard Law School student to be his special mission.

His second choice was to humiliate a member of the tiny group of budding law students who had somehow become aware of the assignment. If the student he picked tried to impress him with a careful explication of both sides of the issue rather than answer his simple question as to "Whose property is it?", that student would suffer a fate as painful as if he or she had not been prepared at all.

Moreover, Pappy Leach hated the fact that women were now being admitted to Harvard Law School in larger and larger numbers. He considered this to be a complete waste of valuable positions at the law school because he believed that these women would practice law for just a few years before becoming married and then pregnant and quitting the valuable profession as attorneys to raise their children. He was very clear about his position on this issue. So, by the fall of 1967, as Harvard Law School began to slowly admit upward of 10 percent women, Barton Leach began to focus more and more on women as the victims of his first-class "lesson."

John Lesche had informed me, in detail, the previous year, how Leach had taken the podium and begun his annual ritual of terrifying the incoming class. First he surveyed the room to identify a woman who had that terrified look on her face that revealed to him that she had not heard about or read the assignment. After excoriating that woman and threatening never to call on her again as punishment for her not having read the assignment, he turned his sights on another young woman sitting in the front row: "Miss Smith! Farmer A or Farmer B?" he had demanded.

Miss Smith, who had fortunately seen the notice and had read the material, immediately lowered her head and plunged into her notes, laying out cogent arguments on each side of this difficult issue. She still had her head down, reading her notes aloud, when Barton Leach reached down and slid open the bottom drawer of his desk and took out a bedsheet. As poor Miss Smith continued her head-down account of her notes, Professor Leach rose from behind the podium and walked silently down to where Miss Smith was seated, flung open the bedsheet, and pulled it over her.

"This woman is dead! She is dead!" he proclaimed in a loud and sonorous voice. "When a judge asks you a question, you *have to* answer *that* question. You cannot just prattle on and start listing all of the considerations on both sides of an issue. You will be hired to argue *just one* side of an issue! I don't care which side you argue. But don't *ever*, in my class, do what this woman has just done. This woman is dead! And I am not going to call on her again for the rest of the entire year."

Naturally, I came prepared for that first class. And, since I had written my undergraduate honors thesis in government on the *Miranda* case before the United States Supreme Court, I had experience doing legal research at the law school. So I was very prepared, and I was not intimidated when I found myself assigned to the very first row. Besides, I assumed that he would call on a woman.

The class began, and true to form, Pappy Leach began his ritual. But when it came to selecting his first victim, he looked down at his infamous name chart and announced, "Mr. Sheehan! Farmer A or Farmer B?"

I did not hesitate for a second. "Farmer A," I said.

He waited, hoping that I would go on to explain why I had chosen Farmer A or, better yet, to explain all of the good arguments for selecting Farmer B as well.

But I did not. I had been warned. So I sat and said absolutely nothing more.

Finally, after what seemed to be an eternity of silence, he said simply, "And why is that, Mr. Sheehan?"

> Actually, Professor Leach, as you know, in the original case on which this hypothetical case is based, the King's Bench of England, in 1620, ruled in favor of Farmer B. But that ruling generated such consternation among the landed aristocracy, who preferred a legal principle that provided greater stability to their claims of title to land, that they rose up in the British Parliament and enacted a specific piece of legislation designated as the Adverse Possession Statute in 1623. That statute expressly overturned that specific King's Bench decision and allocated the property to Farmer A, citing evidence demonstrating that Farmer A had exercised all of the indicia of ownership of the parcel of property at issue adverse to all other potential contrary claims for over thirty years. And that specific piece of British legislation has been uniformly adopted by American state courts and federal courts as the common law of England, since that statute was enacted prior to the creation of the United States. So, pursuant to *that* common law English principle, the answer to your specific question is Farmer A.

There was a long solemn silence. Barton Leach had not been provided an opening to pursue either of his two potential objectives. Since he could think of no way around his dilemma, he rather sadly announced, "Well. *Somebody* around here has been doing his homework."

I responded immediately. "That's right, Professor Leach. You will find our class to be very serious students. We live in very difficult times. And we have come here to Harvard Law School to learn the law so we can more effectively address and solve these problems. You will find that we will be doing our work diligently while we are here."

He was literally struck dumb. He did not know what to say.

Suddenly, a loud voice boomed out from the very back of the room. "And we don't want to waste our time learning how to lay claim to no fucking wild animals either! We want to learn about landlord and tenant law. And, while we are at it, here is a first-class assignment for *you!*" And with that, a tall handsome black man in a colorful dashiki with a huge Afro haircut pulled out of his backpack a well-worn paperback copy of *Soul on Ice* by black activist Eldridge Cleaver and tossed it over the heads of the students in all two dozen rows of seats. It landed with a resounding thud, directly on the floor in front of Pappy Leach's podium.

The whole class waited to see what Leach would do.

Pappy Leach began to realize that control of his class was in danger of slipping totally from his grasp. So he slowly descended from his pedestal and bent over and picked up the book. Then he straightened up and announced, "I accept the assignment."

And the class applauded—not for him but for the book thrower, our classmate Ron Brown.

That following Friday morning, Professor Leach announced that he had invited "a very special guest" to address our Saturday morning class. On Saturday, all four sections of our first-year class were asked to gather in Lowell Hall on the college campus. All 540 members of our class were present. Pappy Leach came out and informed the gathered studentry that "an incident" had occurred in one of his sections that had caused him to invite this special guest. He did not say what that "incident" had been. But we all knew. For word of "Leach's debacle" had spread like wildfire.

He then simply turned to stage right and welcomed his guest.

Out from stage right came Supreme Court justice John Harlan, led by his "seeing-eye clerk," who guided him to center stage and pointed him in the direction of the assembled class. Justice Harlan, who had been legally blind since September of 1966, spoke with a gravelly voice that was aged and cracked.

"Good morning, gentlemen!" he began, ignoring the fifty-four women who sat before him, probably because he simply couldn't see them. "My friend Bart tells me that he thinks that there is something mighty peculiar about this class. He thinks that it might have something to do with 'this war' (obviously referring to the Vietnam War, which was raging in the Far East and generating raging demonstrations on college campuses across the nation). So I have come here today to tell you that wars will come and wars will go, gentlemen. But your profession shall endure."

He paused, as though *that* was somehow sufficient to calm the stormy sea on which the Good Ship Harvard was being buffeted at the opening of the 1967 school year. But, as Justice Harlan was waiting for his dramatic message to be sufficiently absorbed by what he had erroneously presumed to be the normally "malleable" collection of first-year Harvard Law School students who sat before him, a member of our section (who shall remain nameless in this account) cupped his hands around his mouth and stood up and shouted down at Harlan, "Fuck you!"

A long pregnant silence filled the room.

Then a second member of our section stood up and shouted, "Kiss my ass!" and he immediately tore a sheet of paper from his notebook, rolled it into a ball, and threw it down onto the stage, it landing just a few short feet from Justice Harlan.

Within seconds, a hail of wadded-up pages of Harvard Law School notebooks began to literally rain down upon the stage all around Justice Harlan and his seeing-eye clerk. They scurried for cover, bobbing and weaving to avoid being pummeled with snowball-sized paper wads. We then simply rose and filed out, not allowing Pappy Leach any opportunity to save face or to chastise us. Most members of our class consciously chose to not remember who threw paper wads and who did not. But I remembered, carefully noting their identities, because those were the people who could be organized into the core of a new student government—young budding lawyers who could be expected to stand up against the kind of tyranny that W. Barton Leach had represented at Harvard Law School for three decades . . . and the kind of blind allegiance to tradition that John Harlan represented and had come to our class to preach to us.

We immediately organized and established the Joint Student-Faculty Committee at Harvard Law School and held an official election in each of the four sections of each of the three Harvard Law School classes.

It was an important lesson. Everyone did not participate, but those who did took and held the initiative. Our twelve elected representatives drafted an official invitation to members of the Harvard Law School faculty, asking them to select an equal number of faculty members to sit on the Joint Student-Faculty Committee. But only Lawrence Tribe, Alan Dershowitz, and Alan Stone showed up at the first committee meeting. Undeterred, we convened weekly meetings of the Joint Student-Faculty Committee with twelve student representatives present and whichever faculty members deigned to attend each such meeting. But a quorum of twelve was authorized to conduct business. So we proceeded without the faculty.

The first matter we resolved was to demand that Harvard Law School award letter grades to its students rather than the numerical grades that had, for the 150 years of Harvard Law School's existence, allowed the administration to compute a class rank down to the *fourth decimal place* for every Harvard Law School student. The administration at Harvard Law School actually computed everyone's GPA and then publicly posted everyone's relative ranking in the class on the public bulletin board in Langdell Middle. We declared this to be a completely noncollegial policy that generated an atmosphere of cutthroat competition at the law school. We wanted to be a generation that had a greater sense of solidarity. So the Joint Student-Faculty Committee voted twelve to zero to have the administration shift to letter grades, and we circulated a petition among the 540 members of our first-year class, soliciting their consensus in support of this demand. The support was overwhelming. Then we did the same for the three other classes. There was a descending percentage of support in each higher class, but even the third-year class approved of the demand by a majority.

As the first semester progressed, some professors insisted on continuing to give numerical grades in defiance of the committee resolution (and, of course, in defiance of the committee's authority itself). Some gave both a letter grade and a corresponding numerical grade, and others gave straight letter grades, thereby acknowledging the authority of the student body.

With the end of the first semester approaching, the Joint Student-Faculty Committee convened and voted to excuse any student from having to take any midterm exam unless the professor who taught that course posted a signed notice *before the exam* agreeing to give letter grades for the exam. The faculty apparently met and agreed not to do that. So our first-year class went on strike and refused to take *any* of the midterm exams at Harvard Law School in January of 1968. Less than a dozen Harvard Law School students out of the 540 students in our class appeared for exams that first semester.

After that "strike," the acting dean James Casner issued a policy directive directing all professors to give both a letter grade (for public posting) and a numerical grade (for internal purposes) to each student on each exam henceforth. That was more than half a victory.

The year 1968 was a watershed year for my generation. That spring, I had become involved in Bobby Kennedy's presidential campaign. Many of us at the law school were trying to get Bobby to run against Lyndon Johnson, who had been elected president in 1964 after finishing the first term of the late president John F. Kennedy. Everybody thought it was more or less inevitable that Johnson would win the Democratic Party presidential nomination. That distressed a large number of us at the law school because of Johnson's hawkish stance on the Vietnam War.

I had a number of conversations with two of our professors, Abe Chayes and Adam Yarmolinsky, who were both close to Bobby. Chayes had actually approached Bobby about running against Johnson and making an issue of the war, but Bobby said he wasn't going to do this; he thought it would be political suicide to challenge Lyndon Johnson, a sitting president in his own party. Bobby had been elected as the new U.S. senator from New York and believed that to be his best launching pad for a presidential campaign in 1972.

So Bobby wasn't going to run in 1968. But in January of that year, Lyndon Johnson was nearly beaten in the New Hampshire Democratic primary by Eugene McCarthy, a senator from Minnesota, who had made his campaign against Johnson all about the war. Lyndon Johnson was so traumatized by this that in March of 1968 he went on national television and shocked the nation—and the world—by announcing that, because he was devoting all his attention to figuring out how to end the war in Vietnam with a victory, he would neither seek nor accept the nomination of his party for the presidency. That immediately opened the field for Bobby, so Abe Chayes and Adam Yarmolinsky went back to Bobby and persuaded him to consider running. This time he agreed, even though he had already missed both the New Hampshire and the Iowa Democratic primaries. This was only five years after the assassination of his brother John Kennedy, so we believed that Bobby's getting into the race was a terrific thing because it promised to bring back those halcyon days of the Kennedy administration. It would be a chance to move past the assassination and the war and get back to a more idealistic development of policies in the United States, as had been promised by John Kennedy immediately before his death.

My first final exam in the spring of my first year of law school was for Jack Dawson's course: The Development of Legal Institutions. It was scheduled for the morning of June 5, 1968, at 9:00 AM. The 3-Ls and the 2-Ls had all completed their final exams, and just we 1-Ls were remaining in residence to take our finals.

I was on my way out the door of my apartment across the street from the law school to go take that exam when I had a sudden strong urge to turn on the television to get a look at the morning's news. This was totally peculiar for me because, as a matter of habit, I typically refrained from cluttering my mind with anything just before an exam. But I turned on the TV and saw the bulletin announcing that Bobby Kennedy had been shot just after midnight, California time, and that he lay mortally wounded in a Los Angeles hospital. I suddenly got the exact same feeling as when I had been told by Sergeant Dunderdale on the drill field that President Kennedy had been shot. I admit that the feeling had been different when I had heard that Dr. Martin Luther King Jr. had been shot. When Dr. King was assassinated, I was shocked and upset, but riots across the country broke out so soon afterward that an emotional confusion was cast over that event. When I saw that Bobby had been shot, though, it was totally surreal, just like when John had been shot back in 1963.

I went straight to the office of Acting Dean Bruce at the law school. When I found him, he had not yet heard that Senator Kennedy had been shot, since it had happened only five hours earlier. He asked me, since the first-year students had already prepared and were now arriving, if I thought they would rather postpone that day's final exam or just go ahead and take it. I said that I didn't know, so we had better simply go and ask them. So Acting Dean Bruce and I went into Langdell Middle, where everyone was getting ready to take the exam, and I made the announcement. Everyone gasped. None of us had looked up from our studying to see the extremely recent news. When I asked the class whether they wanted to postpone their final exam until they knew more about Senator Kennedy's condition or whether they wanted to go ahead and take the exam, the whole class booed. Acting Dean Bruce totally misinterpreted that to mean they wanted to *take* the exam. I tried to explain to him that that was not correct, but he wanted them to take the exam. So we did. But because I knew that he was incorrect, I announced to the class that at the conclusion of this exam I would be passing out a typed petition asking that all the rest of our final exams be postponed until we knew whether Senator Kennedy was going to live or die. Immediately after the conclusion of that exam, I went to Professor Abe Chayes's office and typed up the petition. I Xeroxed a hundred copies so we could circulate them all at once and get all 540 of our class members to sign as rapidly as possible. Over 95 percent of our class signed, requesting that the administration at Harvard Law School postpone the rest of our first-year final exams until we knew what was going to happen to Senator Kennedy. I then submitted the signed copies of the petition to Acting Dean Bruce, right there on the spot.

This put him in a very difficult predicament because postponing final exams was not something he could do on his own; a vote of the entire faculty was required for that. Most Harvard Law School professors did not stay around to proctor their own final exams. They had already left for the summer. They would have to be recalled to vote on this issue. All that day, cars and taxicabs carrying these professors could be seen driving into the front yard of the Harvard Law School.

As the professors' meeting to discuss our petition was getting under way inside, I was in a group standing on the marble steps at the front of Langdell Middle. We had been there for a few hours when a large group of young men from Students for a Democratic Society (SDS) came marching into the yard and gathered at the bottom of the steps. Their leader shouted to the crowd of people in the yard that the professors were just trying to play politics with the exams. He started demanding that the crowd of students and onlookers "crash the meeting." Then the leader turned and started running up the stairs—alone, because the rest of the young people didn't quite know whether to come or not.

Just as he reached the top step, I leaned back and punched him square on the jaw. The blow knocked him flat on his ass, and he tumbled down the steps and fell in a heap at the bottom of the stairs. He was still conscious, but he didn't quite know where he was, and he was bleeding like mad. I had busted his lip and maybe loosened a few of his front teeth. All of the SDS guys who had come with him just stood there, not knowing what to do.

"You guys stay out of this thing," I said. "They have our petition in front of them, and they are going to decide this pursuant to a due process."

They all backed off.

Soon after that, Professor Clark Byce came out to the front steps and asked me to join him in the hall, since I'd been the person who had submitted the petition. I stepped inside, and he asked me why—after Harvard had taught its students for 150 years to put one foot in front of the other and to march forward into the face of all adversity, even through a civil war, depression, and two world wars—the school should postpone these first-year final exams for the first time in Harvard's history?

I looked at him and told him that, as a freshman in college, I had stood on a military drill field in full army uniform and had listened over U.S. Army Radio as it was announced that President Kennedy had been shot; that Martin Luther King Jr. had been shot and killed in Tennessee just that past April of our first year of law school; and that now, on the eve of our very first law school final exam, Bobby Kennedy—our hope for a better future—had been gunned down by an assassin on the very night he had won the California primary. "There are plenty of times," I said, "when it is perfectly appropriate to put one foot in front of the other and to march into the face of adversity, and those of us who have made it here to Harvard Law School have certainly shown that we know how to do that. But there comes a point in time when one ought to stand with one's feet together and come to attention and look around one to see what is going on in one's country. This is one of those times!" I said it to him just like that. And Professor Byce studied me with this big long look, and he started to cry. And then I started to cry— to cry for our country, to cry for our generation, to cry for our world. He immediately turned around and walked back into the meeting.

I had just returned to my place at the top of the marble steps outside of Langdell Middle when Adam Yarmolinsky and Abe Chayes pulled into the Harvard Law School Yard in a yellow taxicab, got out, and walked straight up the stairs into Langdell Hall. Abe Chayes was Bobby's foreign policy adviser, and he was going to be Bobby's secretary of state. Adam Yarmolinsky was the man you can see holding Bobby's head up in that iconic photograph with the bright light shining on Bobby as he lay dying on the floor of the hotel kitchen with his eyes open and looking up. I saw Bobby's blood on Adam Yarmolinsky's left jacket sleeve as he brushed past me. He turned and gave me the saddest look I had ever seen. I knew that Bobby was going to die. He nodded to me—one of his students, who had urged him so strongly to talk Bobby into running. And then he swept past me into Langdell Hall, followed by Abe Chayes, who reached out and squeezed my arm as he passed into the building.

They were in the meeting for no more than five minutes before they came out and announced that the faculty of Harvard Law School had voted to cancel all of the first-year law school final exams.

So in my first year at Harvard Law School in that extraordinary year of 1968, for the first and only time in the 150-year history of the law school, we had no final exams and no midterm exams.

Bobby died the following morning, on June 6, 1968, at 4:44 AM Eastern Time. The dream was over.

I spent that summer of 1968 as Professor Jerome Cohen's chief research assistant. Professor Cohen, chairman of the International Law Department at Harvard Law School, was writing a book on the illegality of the war in Vietnam, and I was helping him edit the chapters. I was still engaged in my battle with my draft board from New York State, and each time I had a draft chapter from Professor Cohen, I sent a copy to my draft board as a reminder of the war's illegality and of my willingness—and ability—to take the board to court over this issue.

That summer I was also heavily involved in putting together the delivery of food to starving Biafrans in Nigeria, whose government had blockaded the food supply to that embattled province after it had seceded from the country. I established an organization named the Nigerian/Biafran Relief Commission, and I secured food, planes, and pilots. After conducting a telephone-in-each-ear negotiation between Nigerian commanding general Otue and secessionist military leader Chukwuemeka Ojukwu, I flew them into Biafra and broke the blockade.

I came back to Harvard Law School for my second year in the fall of 1968. Because we had not taken any midterm exams and only one final exam the previous year, the administration was having trouble determining how to rank us for the *Harvard Law Review*. I was fortunate enough to have gotten an A+ in my Development of Legal Institutions class, and I had been named by several professors as one of the top students in the class. This meant I was asked to write for a position on the *Harvard Law Review*. The assignment was to write a *Law Review* article on how to set up a foreign subsidiary of an American business corporation. I told the editor that I didn't have the slightest interest in learning how to set up a foreign subsidiary for an American business corporation—and I had no desire to instruct anyone else how to do that either. He was shocked. I told him that I wanted to work on civil rights issues, human rights issues, and constitutional law matters. The editor explained that those kinds of assignments arose only when a major constitutional case was decided by the U.S. Supreme Court—and those were few and far between. He told me that a classmate of mine, Mark Green, had said something to him virtually identical to what I had said upon being asked to write the same article. The editor said that this Mark Green had also expressed an interest in working on civil rights issues for the *Law Review*. The editor suggested that I get together with Mark.

I tracked Mark down, and we met and ultimately decided to assemble the *Harvard Civil Rights Law Review* as the founding coeditors. I wanted the *Harvard Civil Rights Law Review* not to be just a vehicle for abstract, academic discussions of theoretical legal points and esoteric constitutional concepts but to have an operational dimension as well—a more immediately *functional* dimension. In short, I wanted it to help young lawyers, fresh out of law school, all around the country, learn how to do civil rights cases. Mark was not opposed to this; he simply thought we ought to have the *Harvard Civil Rights Law Review* be as much like the *Harvard Law Review* as possible, but with an emphasis on civil rights, civil liberties, and constitutional legal issues. We decided that Mark would be the editor of the "regular" part of the review and that I would send out letters to lawyers all across the country, inviting them to contact us if they encountered a challenging constitutional, civil rights, or human rights issue they needed help with. The idea was that our Harvard "eager beaver" law students would draft civil rights complaints, motions, briefs, and other legal memoranda for them. We would then write special articles and notes on those cases and publish them in the *Harvard Civil Rights Law Review*.

Ironically, the first call I received was from none other than F. Lee Bailey, the most famous criminal defense attorney in the country—hell, in the world! I was in the office reading legal cases one afternoon when the phone rang. "Hello. This is F. Lee Bailey. And I've got a major constitutional problem here," he said. He then explained to me the details of the famous Plymouth mail robbery, one of the Brink's armored car robbery cases.

This was a classic case in which a gang put up a fake detour sign on the public highway, diverting an armored truck onto an old road leading into some woods. Then gang members simply took down the sign to let the rest of the traffic pass. The Brink's truck driver then came across a helpless-looking female member of the gang with her car pulled across the road and smoke coming out from under the hood. The truck driver stopped, and the guard unlocked the door to get out of the truck to help her. Suddenly, with the armored door wide open, men in rubber Halloween masks jumped out of the woods and robbed the truck. One would think the Brink's drivers would have seen that coming from Highway Robbery 101, but apparently they didn't. The gang took $1.5 million in cash and sped away in the car that had been sitting across the road, with dry ice under its hood, leaving the Brink's driver and guard tied up beside the road.

The problem was that the gang had not taken down the fake detour sign quite fast enough. After the Brink's truck had been successfully diverted from the main highway, a completely innocent civilian saw the detour sign and had turned down the detour road into the woods. When she came upon the scene, the "damsel in distress" was standing beside the smoking car—wearing no mask of any kind. The Brink's truck driver and guard were tied up and lying on the ground, and there were all the gang members in their masks. The innocent civilian simply drove by, but not before she got a full facial view of the fake damsel in distress.

Bailey wanted me to prepare a motion to suppress on behalf of what turned out to be the *actual* Plymouth mail robbery perpetrators. It seems that, in the near hysteria to arrest somebody for this widely publicized spectacular crime before the expiration of the federal statute of limitations, federal postal inspectors had frantically targeted an entirely different set of suspects.

Facing the impending expiration of the federal statute of limitations on this crime, and suffering the sting of their very public loss of the federal civil rights case filed against them by F. Lee Bailey on behalf of a well-known armed robber who had not been involved, the federal postal inspectors went and fetched Miss Innocent Witness and took her out to dinner at a fine restaurant in the Boston area, where a specific woman just happened to be dining. It was a woman postal inspectors knew to be the female member of a different gang of known armed robbers.

During dinner, Postal Inspector A casually asked Miss Innocent Witness whether there was anyone in the restaurant she recognized from the day of the robbery. Miss Innocent Witness carefully examined the faces of the patrons gathered in the restaurant and then said, "No. No one."

They led her with further questions and hints until finally pointing out the specific woman they wanted her to identify as the damsel in distress from the Plymouth mail robbery. Miss Innocent Witness spent an entire minute examining the woman. Then she turned to the postal inspectors at her table and sadly announced, "I am sorry, guys. But I don't recognize her."

After that, the exasperated postal inspectors turned their attention to every other known armed robbery gang in that region of the country with a female member, attempting to develop any evidence they possibly could. But that did not work.

With just days remaining before the expiration of the federal statute of limitations, the postal inspectors picked up the suspected damsel in distress "for questioning." While she was in custody at the federal postal inspectors' office in Boston, they placed her in a lineup and invited Miss Innocent Witness to have a look. She squinted intensely at all seven people in the lineup and then slowly brightened. "The woman second from the left! I recognize her! I have seen her someplace!"

"That's it!" exclaimed a postal inspector, who then turned to the suspected damsel in distress's astonished attorney. "Your client is under arrest for the August 14, 1962, armed robbery of the U.S. mail truck in Plymouth, Massachusetts."

Based on that eyewitness identification, U.S. postal inspectors who had been standing by to arrest the other seven members of the damsel in distress's gang swooped down and secured federal search warrants to search the homes and premises of all eight members of the gang.

In the attic of the first house searched, postal inspectors found a full-head rubber mask and a U.S. Postal Service bag containing some of the stolen $1.5 million. The robber in whose home the mask and the mail bag had been found immediately retained F. Lee Bailey. And Bailey called me.

It took me less than two days to draft the motion to suppress the fruit of the unlawful lineup with a complete, iron-clad legal brief in support of the motion. It was granted by a federal judge after a fifteen-minute hearing, and all the evidence was order suppressed. At trial, F. Lee Bailey mopped the floor with the U.S. attorney, and all the defendants were summarily acquitted by a unanimous federal jury. This really wasn't what I had imagined as my entry into the legal profession, but Bailey was paid $1 million for his defense—all in crisp twenty-dollar bills.

F. Lee Bailey immediately offered me a permanent position with his law firm in Boston as soon as I graduated. But he wanted to hire me strictly to prepare constitutional law briefs for his clients, not to do trials. When I told him I wanted to do trials, he said that he and Gerald L. Alch did all the trials. He wanted me to just do legal briefs.

"No," I said. "I don't want to do that. I'm going to do trials."

Bailey was surprised. "Look, kid. I am F. Lee Bailey. And I am asking you to come work in my firm. This is the most famous criminal law firm in the country—in the whole fucking world! Are you actually turning me down?"

"Yes. Yes, I am. I am turning you down. I'm not going to just ride some desk. I am going to do trials!"

I was twenty-three years old, and I wasn't about to compromise.

"OK, kid," he said. "Call me if you change your mind."

"Call me if you change *yours*," I said.

And he hung up.

CHAPTER *seven*

THE SECOND CASE that came to the *Harvard Civil Rights Law Review* arrived in late September 1968. It involved the Black Panther Party in Boston. The Black Panthers were an extremely radical black nationalist organization of young, predominantly urban black men and a smaller number of black women—many of whom had been to college and/or prison. By the mid-1960s, the young men and women of the Black Panther Party had concluded that white America was not going to voluntarily make significant changes in its racially segregated social and political institutions. These young black men and women were therefore determined to take up arms to defend themselves and their fellow black citizens against the institutional violence to which the members of their entire race had been subjected since the early seventeenth century, as well as against the blatant police violence to which they and their friends and neighbors had been subjected. The Black Panthers in the Boston area began publishing the *Black Panther,* a weekly newspaper that adopted a fairly abrasive and radical editorial position against the Boston Police Department. Their newspaper included graphic drawings, right on its front pages, that depicted eight- and ten-year-old black ghetto children shooting pigs dressed in Boston Police uniforms.

Provoked in part by these front-page drawings, but no doubt in larger part by intense racism on the part of the overwhelmingly white officers and patrolmen in its ranks, the Boston Police Department began, in 1967, a program of systematically rounding up and arresting young black men who were selling the *Black Panther* newspaper on Boston street corners. Whenever the Boston Police received a call reporting an armed robbery, an armed assault, a shooting, or any other violent crime in which the suspect was described as a young black male, officers would arrest every young black man selling copies of the *Black Panther* at that time. These young black men would then

94

be held in police precincts throughout the Boston area all day long and into the night and were forced to stand in lineup after lineup, the police hoping that someone would mistakenly identify one or more of these young Black Panther Party members as the perpetrator of any given crime. The young black men would be held for as long as the law allowed before the police and the district attorney's office were compelled by law to present probable cause to a judge as to why they had been arrested and were being held in custody. At that point, they would be released. Of course, by then, all copies of the *Black Panther* that had been in their possession at the time that they were arrested would have "gone missing."

The Black Panther Party in Boston called one John Flymm, a young, recently licensed white attorney who had volunteered to provide pro bono legal assistance to help the Panthers stop this practice. Flymm called our *Harvard Civil Rights Law Review* for help.

I was more than willing to assist this enterprising young Boston attorney who was standing up for the rights of young black activists whose fundamental American constitutional rights were being very seriously violated by this practice by one of our nation's preeminent police departments. I drafted a federal civil rights complaint, asking the United States District Court in Boston to declare the Boston Police Department's ongoing program to be an unconstitutional conspiracy forbidden by Title 18, Section 241 of the United States Criminal Code and to issue a federal civil injunction expressly prohibiting the Boston Police from engaging in any such practice or policy in the future.

I worked with John Flymm to prepare this civil complaint, a motion for the issuance of a federal declaratory judgment, a motion for the issuance of a federal civil injunction, and supporting sworn affidavits to be signed by Black Panther Party officials—and by subscribers to the newspaper—to establish, by direct sworn testimony, that the Boston Police Department was substantially interfering with the ability of the newspaper to communicate ideas and news to its readership.

John Flymm took the case before the United States District Court in Boston—and won.

Some of the more conservative members of the *Harvard Civil Rights Law Review*'s board of editors questioned my representing a newspaper that ran drawings that so openly advocated the killing of innocent Boston Police officers. At the same time, I received harsh criticism from some of the more radical members of the Black Panther Party for not "suing the pigs for money damages" and "getting the bastards criminally prosecuted for their crimes." Reflecting on the latter, I became deeply troubled by the specific reason I had decided not to pursue money damages or penalties against individual members of the Boston Police Department who had authorized and/or participated in that obviously criminal enterprise. I had refrained from doing that because I believed that the judges who sat on the federal district court in Boston—all of whom were white—harbored deeply rooted racial prejudices that would have likely motivated them to look for some purely technical legal reason to deny any request favoring the Black Panthers. Suddenly I realized that, like all of those white judges, I had grown up in a totally racially segregated community. None of the major law firms in Boston had a single black attorney on staff. For that matter, none of the major law firms *in the country* to which I was planning to apply employed a single black attorney. Although I had helped found a project to reopen a number of previously closed Catholic high schools in Roxbury (the black ghetto of Boston) to serve the community. I had never been to the home of a black person. I had never dated a black woman. I had never had a black team member or become close friends with a single black person. Even my successful effort to invite Tommy Davis to become the first black SAE inductee had not resulted in any meaningfully close friendship with him. I realized that my actions thus far had been more of an abstract exercise in pursuing "the right thing" than the result of any personal pain or suffering in the face of what was actually being experienced by black victims.

So I resolved, then and there, to come to grips with this reality—first about myself, then about my personal family members, then, most importantly, about my country. I needed to acknowledge this flaw in our state and federal governments, our laws, and all our legal institutions. That shocking realization prompted me to attend meetings of the Black Harvard Law School Society, and I became its only white member. I then actively sought out and became friends with Ron Brown and Bob Holmes, two of the most impressive black men in our class. This was one of the wisest and most profoundly influential decisions I have ever made in my life, for it was through my friendship with Ron and Bob—and with other friends I made through being befriended by them—that I overcame my instinct to view every black person *first* as black and then only *secondly* as another person like myself or any of my family members. I know that this sounds peculiar, but be assured that every black person knows exactly what I am talking about here. It's a reaction that every white person must overcome before we can achieve full racial equality and racial justice in our country.

I returned to Donald Hurley's law firm in the summer of 1969, law clerking between my second year and third year at Harvard Law School. For my first actual physical appearance in court as an almost lawyer, I was sent to a motion session before the Middlesex Superior Court. I was sitting there proudly "inside the bar" that separated lawyers from the civilian population, waiting to notify the court that our Goodwin, Proctor & Hoar law firm and the opposing firm had stipulated the postponement of a specific hearing date, when, all of a sudden, there was a commotion in the back of the courtroom. Well-known Boston criminal defense attorney Joe Ballero rushed into the courtroom and approached the bench. After a hushed exchange, the judge explained to the court that an unusual matter had come up and that the morning's session would need to be adjourned until after lunch.

Given the stir caused by Joe Ballero's sudden appearance in this otherwise boring courtroom, many of the gray-suited civil attorneys who had been gathered before the court sat down to wait and see what all the fuss was about.

Joe Ballero rose and, very awkwardly, began to present a petition for certification of a question of constitutional moment to the Massachusetts Supreme Judicial Court. As fate would have it, I had, in our most recent issue of the *Harvard Civil Rights Law Review*, edited a note on this very unique civil procedure available in Massachusetts. Unlike the state supreme courts of virtually every other state in the Union, if a party in Massachusetts can convince a lower state court in the commonwealth to certify a specific question of constitutional law as "a question of constitutional moment," then the Massachusetts Supreme Court can voluntarily consider that question and issue an "advisory opinion" answering that specific constitutional question.

That action on the part of Massachusetts's Supreme Court thereupon renders the constitutional question ripe for consideration by the United States Supreme Court.

Of course, the United States Supreme Court has complete discretion to either grant or withhold its review of that state supreme court ruling. On very rare occasions, it exercises such review.

I sat there in the motions session of the Middlesex County Superior Court in Boston, watching Joe Ballero and his law partner stumbling around with this petition. Although they were not intimately familiar with this arcane feature of Massachusetts constitutional law, they managed to communicate why they had come before the court. A man by the name of William (Bill) Baird, who was the vice president of the Emco Contraceptive Foam Company and a major advocate of artificial birth control, had been officially invited by the president and faculty of Boston University to make a formal presentation to incoming freshmen on the wisdom of practicing birth control during their undergraduate years at BU. Baird was in the middle of his presentation when he reached for a can of Emco contraceptive foam and held it up to the assembled students. He then invited a young female from the entering class to come up to the stage, and he gave her the can of Emco foam. Before he could turn back to the audience and continue his remarks, four uniformed Middlesex County deputy sheriffs pushed open the twin doors at the back of the auditorium and proceeded to the stage, where they arrested Bill Baird. He was charged with "publically displaying an artificial birth control device" in violation of an 1896 Massachusetts state statute.

Bill Baird had found his way to Joe Ballero, who was now in front of the court, fumbling with this motion. The magistrate judge had never had such a motion made to him before. Indeed, he had never even heard about this particular arcane procedure. Seeing this and knowing everything there was to know about the procedure in question, I approached the counsel table, where Ballero's associate, Chet Paris, was sitting. I tugged Paris by the coattails and whispered to him.

"He's *dying* up there. I think I can help you." I introduced myself and explained that I'd just published a *Law Review* note on this very procedure. "If you ask the magistrate to adjourn the hearing until the end of the upcoming lunch break, I think we could go back to your office and I could work this thing out for you."

Chet Paris looked up at me as if I were a Saint Bernard that had appeared in a blinding blizzard with a quart of rum tied to my collar. "Thank God," he whispered. "We certainly couldn't be doing any worse!" Paris leaned over and tugged Joe Ballero by the coattails and whispered to him. Then Ballero got the magistrate to adjourn until after the scheduled lunch break. You could almost hear the relief in the magistrate's voice as well.

Joe Ballero's penthouse office was on Beacon Hill, not far from the courthouse. There, I tore into volumes of the Massachusetts Code of Civil Procedure, case books, and law reviews available in Ballero's office. They did not have a subscription to our *Harvard Civil Rights Law Review*—yet—but I remembered most of the specific provisions of the act we were working with. With three legal secretaries typing away like mad, I dictated a redraft of the petition to certify a brief in support of the petition and a draft sworn deposition for Bill Baird to sign and get notarized by the end of the lunch break. With a final rush to the Middlesex County Jail, where Bill Baird was still being held, we dashed into the motion session of the Middlesex Superior Court with all the documents in order. As I distributed a copy to the attorney general of the Commonwealth of Massachusetts, he smiled, held out his well-manicured right hand, and gave me a quizzical look as our eyes met. I smiled and whispered, "I'll get my contact information to you after the hearing."

Long minutes passed as everyone read all the documents. When the attorney general finished, he looked up, slowly removed his reading glasses, and then slid back into his chair. It was at that moment the magistrate said, "He seems to *have you* here, Mr. Attorney General."

Attorney General Robert Quinn looked up at the magistrate and smiled. "I believe he does, Your Honor."

"We will see you before the state supreme judicial court, Mr. Attorney General," I could not help myself from saying.

Joe Ballero didn't know whether to be embarrassed or delighted.

Attorney General Quinn approached me and shook my hand. He reached into the small pocket of his blue pinstriped vest, gracefully withdrew one of his gold-emblazoned business cards, and handed it to me.

"I'll be looking forward to that contact information, Mr. . . . ?"

"Sheehan," I said. "Daniel Sheehan. But you can call me Danny. All my friends do."

"Who the hell *are* you, anyhow?" Joe Ballero asked when Attorney General Quinn had gone.

"Danny Sheehan," I said. "Let's get cracking. We have got a lot of work to do before we are up there in front of that court."

Outside, a reporter from the *Boston Globe* took our photograph and started peppering Ballero with questions about the case, which had hit the news immediately after Baird had been arrested right off the stage at BU in the middle of his presentation. As Ballero swaggered in the limelight, I quietly slipped away.

The *Boston Globe* ran a photo of Joe Ballero and Chet Paris the very next morning—and I was in it. Within an hour of my arriving at the office that morning, I got a call from Winnie, Mr. Hurley's secretary when I'd fixed his briefcase back in 1965. She was now the private secretary to Roger Stokey, the firm's senior partner in charge of litigation. Roger Stokey was the partner who had sent me to present the consent motion for a continuance at the courthouse, where I became involved with Ballero on the Baird case. Winnie told me that Stokey wanted to see me first thing the next morning.

Thinking this must mean bad news, I worked up how I was going to defend my actions, including by showing Stokey a copy of our *Harvard Civil Rights Law Review* issue containing the note that related to the Baird case.

I arrived at Stokey's office at 7:30 the next morning. No one was there yet, not even Winnie. So I went into his office and waited for him. I was sitting there, in Stokey's "power seat," going over in my mind the various ways I might respond to his criticism of what I had done, when he walked in. He did not see me at first. He went through his ritual of removing his hat and heavy overcoat and placing them on the standing coatrack. When he finally turned, his eyes fell on me. Before he could say anything, I jumped up from his chair and launched into my defense.

"Look, Mr. Stokey, I didn't have any idea that that matter was going to be presented to the motion session yesterday when you sent me over there. But I've got to tell you, I'm not the least bit sorry that I did what I did. I'd do

it again! I am not going to Harvard Law School to sit around all day presenting consent motions. I want to do civil rights cases, and there was one right
in front of me. So I don't care if you fire me."

"Are you through?" Roger Stokey asked me.

I was a bit taken aback at how casual he had become.

"Actually, I am *not*," I said. And I started to take out a copy of the
Harvard Civil Rights Law Review, but then I stopped. Perhaps it was no
use. "OK. If you want to fire me, go ahead. I am only sorry that I may have
hurt the feelings of Mr. Hurley. He is the one responsible for getting me
into Harvard College and into Harvard Law School. And I wanted to make
him proud. That's the reason I came here to do my summer law clerking. I
thought I owed it to Mr. Hurley."

"You don't owe anybody anything, Danny," he said. "What you did
on Monday was one of the most amazing fucking things that I have seen in
my entire life! I was delighted to see what you had done when I opened the
paper yesterday. I am the twenty-year general counsel for the Massachusetts
Planned Parenthood League, and we have been trying to figure out how to
get that goddamned anti–birth control statute up in front of the supreme
judicial court for the last fifteen years! How the hell did you do that?"

Roger Stokey, the thirty-year senior partner in charge of litigation of the
silk-stocking Boston Brahman State Street law firm of Goodwin, Proctor &
Hoar, sat and excitedly reviewed with me how I had done what I had done.
Then he took an old key he wore on the watch chain that hung between
the two tiny pockets of the vest he always wore. He inserted the key into
a tiny lock on the lower drawer of his desk and—reverently, it seemed to
me—removed an old leather-bound book. He placed it on the desk between
us. As he looked down at this well-worn book, I could see tears begin to fill
his eyes.

"Danny, whatever it is that you have, don't ever lose it. This is an original edition of *Clarence Darrow: Attorney for the Damned*. This," he said,
"is the reason I went to law school." Then he looked slowly, and sadly,
around his office. "And look at me now: filing one meaningless motion after
another. And all of this," he picked up the book again, "all of this is now
just a dream."

He looked at me.

"But it is not too late for you, Danny."

He rose from behind his desk and picked up the leather book and held it out to me.

"I want you to have this. Keep this so that I will always know there is someone out there who will do the kind of things that I dreamed of doing in my life. The kind of things that Darrow did. I think that that man is you, Danny."

My eyes were filled with tears as I reached up and took Roger Stokey's most treasured possession, which I have kept with me all these years.

"But," he said, whirling back toward his desk. "I've got at least one more good fight in me. And I want you at my side when I do it. I am going to write and file a special motion asking the Supreme Judicial Court of the Commonwealth of Massachusetts to grant special authorization for you to present the oral argument before the court on behalf of the Massachusetts Planned Parenthood League. And I hope that you will do me the honor of allowing me to second chair your first oral argument in court, my son."

"It will be my honor, Mr. Stokey. My honor!"

And with that, we briefed—and I argued—the William Baird matter, which became the landmark case of *Eisenstadt v. Baird,* which declared the actions of the state of Massachusetts taken against Baird to be a violation of his First Amendment right to freedom of expression and a violation of the Fourth and Ninth Amendment rights of unmarried citizens of the Commonwealth of Massachusetts to obtain and use medically approved, safe, and effective means of artificial birth control. This judgment ultimately became a hallmark step in the beginning of the Sexual Revolution.

When my name was announced before the assembled members of the Massachusetts Supreme Judicial Court, the chief justice, an ardent Catholic, asked me, "Daniel Peter Sheehan? What is a good Irish Catholic boy like you doing arguing a case like this before this court?"

I responded, "I am here today, Your Honor, to protect the Constitution of the United States. And I hope that you are here to do the same."

In that office, on that day, my legal career took the turn that I have followed every day of my life since.

THE MATTER OF Paul Pappas was the fourth case that came to me through the *Harvard Civil Rights Law Review* and the fifth case that I helped litigate while I was still a student at Harvard Law School. Prior to my contact with Paul Pappas and NBC News, I'd had no personal contact with the professional news media world. The Pappas case (which became known to the world as *In re: Pappas*) ushered me into the world of news media law expertise. *In re: Pappas* began with the urban riots that tore through the ghettos of our nation in the wake of the assassination of Martin Luther King Jr. One of those riots broke out in the black ghetto of New Bedford, Massachusetts, in the late spring of 1970. That city's white mayor had issued an order to "shoot all looters on sight" to the overwhelmingly white New Bedford Police Department. In response, the New Bedford chapter of the Black Panther Party erected makeshift barricades on every street leading into the ghetto and manned those barricades with guns to keep the white police officers out of areas where much of the rioting and looting was taking place. This action, needless to say, attracted numerous local and state police cars, swarms of police SWAT teams, sharpshooters, police dogs, riot vehicles, and sundry armored personnel carriers. Predictably, it also attracted a hoard of local, state, and national news media.

One of those local news media persons was Paul Pappas, a young WTEV-TV New Bedford television reporter based out of that station's East Providence, Rhode Island, office. Pappas endeavored, for days, to persuade the Black Panther Party "soldiers" manning the barricades to give him an on-camera statement or interview. However, every time the Panthers saw Paul directing his team of photographers into place to record what the Panthers were saying or doing, they would immediately give him the finger or shout epithets such as "Fuck you, honky!" at the cameras. Needless to say, that footage was then deemed unsuitable for the six o'clock news.

After days of this, Black Panther Party leaders finally invited Paul Pappas to cross the barricade and interview members. This invitation came with very specific conditions, however. First, Pappas was required to video and file with his station a preprepared official statement by the leader of the New Bedford chapter of the Black Panther Party. He was told that if he did this—and his station agreed to broadcast this statement—he would be invited back through the barricades to film and broadcast a report on a police attack on the New Bedford Black Panther headquarters that the Panthers expected to take place the following morning at dawn. Second, Pappas would be allowed to interview anyone who was willing to speak with him, either on camera or off camera, but he would not be allowed to film anyone, or anything, for which he had not been given express permission. Thirdly, if there was no police attack, Pappas was to treat all the interviews and video footage he had gathered inside Panther headquarters on a "deep background only" basis, and he could never share that information with anyone.

Pappas filmed the required prepared statement and then crossed back through the barricades and took the filmed statement to his station. His superiors aired it on the six o'clock news that evening, as requested. Pappas then presented the offer from the Black Panther leaders to his WTEV-TV superiors, along with its attendant conditions, and his superiors at the NBC News affiliate in East Providence agreed to those conditions. So Pappas returned to New Bedford and, at nine o'clock that evening, was allowed, with his film crew, to pass back through the barricades and be taken to the Panther headquarters.

There Pappas interviewed several Black Panther Party members as they cleaned their weapons, stacked ammunition near windows, and prepared to fend off the expected police attack.

But dawn of the following morning came and went, and no attack came from the New Bedford Police. So Paul Pappas and his film crew packed up their gear—and all their footage—and departed.

Paul Pappas was soon thereafter served with a grand jury subpoena by the Bristol County district attorney, who had called into session a special grand jury to investigate the potential connection between the New Bedford riots and the Black Panther Party. In that grand jury subpoena, Pappas was commanded by the state to surrender all his footage concerning the Black Panther Party—not only the footage that was publicly broadcast but also outtakes and audio recordings of his interviews. He was also commanded to testify as to what he had personally seen and heard during his night inside Panther headquarters.

Pappas did not want to testify or to turn over any of his footage or recordings because he felt that would violate the agreement he had entered into with the Black Panthers. So, upon receipt of his grand jury subpoena, Pappas sought legal support from the management of his NBC local affiliate. The station, in turn, contacted its local lawyers in Rhode Island. But the NBC lawyers in Rhode Island could think of no legal precedent to argue in support of Pappas's refusal to comply with his grand jury subpoena. All they could cite was an internal station policy that allowed news reporters to have "confidential sources." These "confidential sources" were sometimes revealed to editors or to the publisher as a condition of a reporter airing his or her story. But at other times reporters were not required to reveal their confidential sources to anyone. Reporters, editors, and the publisher viewed this as essential in securing certain stories, especially those pertaining to government wrongdoing. Nevertheless, the NBC lawyers could think of no existing legal argument to support withholding such confidential information from a state grand jury once the reporter had been officially subpoenaed. That legal opinion was confirmed by the national legal counsel for NBC News in New York City, the well-known and highly respected Wall Street law firm of Cahill, Gordon, Sonnett, Reindel & Ohl. And with that, the management at WTEV-TV declined to support Pappas's refusal to accommodate the grand jury.

So Paul Pappas immediately called Black Panther Party leaders in New Bedford. He said he wanted to abide by his agreement with them but was running out of options because his station and its lawyers, both in Rhode Island and in New York City, would not support him. Pappas then asked the Black Panther leaders in New Bedford if they could recommend a lawyer who would stand up for his right to refuse to turn over the materials and testify before the grand jury.

Having heard about the successful protection of the *Black Panther* newspaper distributors in Boston, the New Bedford leaders got in contact with John Flymm. Flymm, of course, immediately called the *Harvard Civil Rights Law Review* and asked for me, even though the end of our school year was imminent.

Flymm asked me to draft a motion for the issuance of a federal protective order and a supporting legal brief. In this motion, I asserted that professional news journalists had a constitutional right, under the First

Amendment's guarantee of freedom of the press, to protect the identities of their confidential sources against compelled disclosure to state law enforcement authorities and/or grand juries. This protected information, I argued in my brief, also included any information that would lead to the identification of that reporter's confidential news source.

John Flymm submitted this motion and my legal brief to the superior court judge in Bristol County charged with overseeing the grand jury that had subpoenaed Paul Pappas. We requested that the judge issue a protective order authorizing NBC journalist Pappas to withhold the materials sought from the New Bedford grand jury and to refuse giving testimony. The local superior court judge denied that motion, declaring that he had never heard of any such constitutional right and that there was no support for it in any legal journals or case records.

Once again, I invoked the special procedure pursuant to which attorneys in Massachusetts are authorized to seek an immediate direct appeal to the state supreme court for a vital "constitutional question" without first having to go through the time-consuming process of a mid-level appeal to the state court of appeals. I succeeded in securing the state supreme court review on an "emergency basis" and was, therefore, in possession of a state supreme court ruling *against* our constitutional claim within just a few days' time. In response to that ruling, I was therefore authorized to directly petition the United States Supreme Court to have it voluntarily decide whether to review this state supreme court ruling adverse to a claimed constitutional right.

My petition was granted by the United States Supreme Court. Suddenly, the Wall Street firm of Cahill, Gordon, Sonnett, Reindel & Ohl, which represented NBC News nationally and which had previously refused to assist Pappas in any way, wanted to argue the case—now that it was before the United States Supreme Court. The case also promised a legal fee upward of one million dollars.

Paul Pappas, however, declined. He wanted "those young kids from Harvard Law School" to represent him before the United States Supreme Court. "They were the ones who believed in my right to protect my confidential news sources in the first place, and they were the ones who researched and briefed this issue so convincingly that the United States Supreme Court itself has voted to consider it. Why should I trust a bunch of lawyers who didn't even believe that this right existed?"

So, at the age of twenty-five, prior to the end of my law school career, I had my first case in front of the United States Supreme Court. This case would determine, for decades to come, the degree to which professional news journalists all across our country were protected, under the First Amendment, from compulsion to divulge the identity of confidential news sources to a grand jury or to law enforcement officials.

The idea that Pappas chose a bunch of young law students to brief and argue such a vital First Amendment case before the United States Supreme Court was a serious blow to the professional ego of Cahill-Gordon. The Cahill-Gordon executive committee immediately dispatched a young junior litigation partner by the name of Michael Armstrong to find "The Harvard kids" and to make sure that Cahill-Gordon hired as many of them as was necessary to assure that the firm had the ability to litigate this case before the U.S. Supreme Court.

This "bunch of young law students at Harvard," Armstrong soon discovered, turned out to be just me. Initially, Armstrong was encouraged when he learned that my name was Danny Sheehan, for Cahill, Gordon, Sonnett, Reindel & Ohl had a long-established (but publicly unacknowledged) policy of hiring only Irish Catholics and Jews. The partners half joked, "The Jews are the smartest members of the country's top law reviews, so they can research and write the best possible legal briefs in support of our clients, and the Micks will break a bar stool over their own brother to win a fight." On the other hand, Armstrong discovered that the Danny Sheehan the firm now wanted was a member of the Black Harvard Law School Society. "Could a guy with an Irish name like Danny Sheehan be *black?*"

Michael Armstrong flew to Cambridge, as he explained it to me later, "to get a look at you and to hire you."

I was surprised when I received a call from Dean Derrick Boc's office telling me that a partner from one of the major New York Wall Street law firms was on campus and wanted to interview me.

So I suited up and walked down to Dean Derrick Boc's office, which had been turned over for the purposes of the interview. Puzzled, I opened the door and walked in. There was Michael Armstrong, bright and handsome, about forty and charismatic, waiting for me in a three-piece blue pinstriped suit and wing tip shoes—and obviously Irish.

I caught a fleeting expression on Michael Armstrong's face the moment I walked through the door. It took me the better part of thirty minutes to realize it had been a look of *relief*, because Michael had feared, with the two Black Panther cases I'd been involved in, that I might be black. That would have confronted the Cahill-Gordon firm with a very serious dilemma: Would it be worth hiring a black attorney simply to gain a $1 million legal fee and goodwill from the media world by arguing this crucial case before the United States Supreme Court?

Since I had figured out what was going on as soon as I realized that Cahill-Gordon had come to interview me, I knew I had some real chips at the bargaining table. So, despite the fact that virtually every one of the other 539 members of my Harvard Law School class would have given up a federal judicial clerkship, a Fulbright Scholarship, or even a Marshall Fellowship for the opportunity to become a first-year trial attorney at Cahill-Gordon, I drove a very hard bargain and insisted on several very important conditions. First, I insisted that I be assigned to work directly under the partner in charge of the NBC News account (whom I knew was Floyd Abrams), not only on the Pappas case but on all other First Amendment cases that might be undertaken by the firm while I was a trial lawyer there. Second, I insisted that I be allowed to draft my own "original position" legal briefs in the Pappas case and that those briefed positions would be given active consideration by the firm in its discussions of each legal point raised in the case. Finally, I insisted that I be expressly authorized to devote a number of hours every month to public interest cases of my own selection, equal to the number of billable hours I had logged the *previous* month working directly for paying clients. The executive committee agreed to these stipulations after insisting upon one condition of its own: that I not litigate any public interest cases directly against any of Cahill-Gordon's corporate clients. I thought that was a reasonable request.

So, with all these conditions agreed upon, the deal was sealed in May 1970, just before I graduated from Harvard Law School. I was on my way to

Wall Street, to join the Number One litigation firm in the world, and I would be able to *potentially* establish a virtual public interest law department there at the age of twenty-five.

I would be happy to do this, and they were happy to have me.

CHAPTER *eight*

SOON AFTER I began working at Cahill-Gordon on the Pappas case, I learned of a case that had arisen in California that presented virtually identical legal issues to those presented by *Pappas*. The client was *The New York Times*, and the reporter at issue was one Earl Caldwell. Caldwell was one of a number of young black reporters hired in the late 1960s by mainstream newspapers and television media to cover race relations, particularly urban rioting, which white reporters were not able to cover as effectively. Until those riots, only thirty black reporters in the entire country worked on major newspapers. In the fall of 1968 (just when I was doing the *Black Panther* case), *The New York Times* assigned Caldwell to cover the Black Panther Party in Oakland, California. That particular chapter was under the leadership of the charismatic Huey Newton. Caldwell successfully developed a confidential relationship with Newton and other Black Panther leaders in California, which enabled him to write a unique and widely read series of background stories on the Black Panther Party. Throughout 1969, various FBI agents contacted Caldwell, insisting that he essentially spy on the Black Panther Party for the FBI. Caldwell refused to cooperate, and, on the advice of Wallace Turner, San Francisco bureau chief for *The New York Times*, he even stopped accepting telephone calls from FBI agents. They then began leaving telephone messages, threatening to force Caldwell to testify before a grand jury.

In the late spring of 1970, right when Paul Pappas was having his run-in with the Bristol County district attorney and the Massachusetts grand jury, a member of the Oakland Black Panther Party was delivering a public speech in San Francisco. Referring to President Richard Nixon, the speaker asked, "Lee Harvey Oswald, where are you now that we need you?"

FBI agents, who had been secretly taping the speech, interpreted this comment as a threat against the life of the president, in violation of a federal criminal statute passed by Congress after the assassination of President John Kennedy. In response to this comment, two FBI agents immediately mounted the stage and arrested the Black Panther Party member. The United States attorney for the Northern District of California in San Francisco then impaneled a special federal grand jury and used its powers to investigate the Black Panther Party in California for conspiring to assassinate President Nixon. The first person subpoenaed by the U.S. attorney was Earl Caldwell. The subpoena demanded that Caldwell appear before the federal grand jury in San Francisco with all his notes, recordings, photographs, memos, and other materials containing information from or about the Black Panther Party and any of its members or supporters. The subpoena also commanded Caldwell to reveal the identities of anyone in the party he had ever seen or spoken with and to testify as to anything and everything he had heard them say. Caldwell was certain that FBI agents had broken into his office and tapped the telephones of *The New York Times* bureau in San Francisco because the subpoena included names of specific Black Panthers whom Caldwell had never written about.

At the direction of Lord, Day & Lord in New York City, *The New York Times's* corporate legal counsel, Caldwell's superiors at the San Francisco bureau retained the San Francisco law firm of Pillsbury, Madison & Sutro to represent Caldwell. But when Caldwell met with John Bates, the senior partner of Pillsbury-Madison, Bates told Caldwell, "We have a tremendous problem with law and order out here. Some of your material probably *should* be shared with the FBI." Bates then instructed Caldwell to bring all his subpoenaed material to the Pillsbury-Madison office for a meeting with *New York Times* executive vice president Harding Bancroft so that Pillsbury-Madison could decide which portions of Caldwell's materials to turn over to the Northern District grand jury.

Because Pillsbury-Madison refused to submit Caldwell's demanded motion for a protective order to the federal district court, Caldwell decided to hire his own attorney. He sought help from the New York Association of Black Journalists, which directed him to Tony Amsterdam, who had helped in the appeal of Black Panther Bobby Seal in 1969. At that time, Tony was teaching constitutional law at Stanford Law School. He agreed to represent Caldwell *for free.*

Tony Amsterdam then called Paul Pappas, who put Tony in touch with me. Tony and I exchanged several long telephone calls, during which I explicated the various constitutional positions being taken by NBC News, CBS News, ABC News, *The New York Times,* and *The Washington Post* as amici curiae (friends of the court) in the Supreme Court case of *In re: Pappas*—and, of course, by Cahill-Gordon. I was in an ideal position to explain these positions to Tony because Floyd Abrams, Gene Scheiman, and I were drafting *all* these various amicus briefs.

Tony Amsterdam thereupon decided that he was going to take the most extreme constitutional position possible on the issue. He asserted before the district court in San Francisco that such a subpoena was void ab initio: void because it was an unconstitutional act in and of itself, and therefore it could be deemed to impose absolutely no obligation whatsoever on any newspaper or its reporters to respond to such a grand jury subpoena. This was a very radical position indeed.

By contrast, I had taken the constitutional position in *In re: Pappas* that a news journalist served with such a state criminal grand jury subpoena should invoke his or her First Amendment right to freedom of the press by filing with the state court a petition for a judicial protective order prohibiting the state prosecutor from using a grand jury to try to extract the identity of the journalist's confidential news sources. At Cahill-Gordon, we were arguing that there were no circumstances under which any state or federal prosecutor could be legally authorized by a court, in effect, to transform a journalist into an "investigative agent" for a state or federal prosecutor.

However, Earl Caldwell, pursuant to the advice given to him by Tony Amsterdam, simply refused to appear before the federal grand jury *without filing any motion for a protective order,* and the federal district court then held Caldwell in contempt of court. Caldwell had then (through Tony Amsterdam) immediately appealed the finding to the Ninth Circuit Court of Appeals.

Lord, Day & Lord was furious at Caldwell and Amsterdam for "stiffing" the federal grand jury like that. So Louis Loeb and Herb Brownell, Lord, Day & Lord's senior partners, instructed *The New York Times* to order Caldwell to fly to New York City to discuss the matter directly with *New York Times* general counsel Jim Goodale.

However, the Ninth Circuit Court of Appeals reversed the District Court for the Northern District of California on November 16, 1970, and ordered the contempt judgment against Caldwell to be vacated, holding that "where it has been shown that the public's First Amendment right to be informed would be jeopardized by requiring a journalist to submit to secret Grand Jury interrogation, the Government must respond by demonstrating a compelling need for the witness's presence *before* the judicial process properly can issue an order requiring attendance." The United States attorney for the Northern District of California, of course, immediately petitioned the United States Supreme Court for the issuance of a writ of certiorari, which was granted on May 3, 1971, so Earl Caldwell's and Tony Amsterdam's case was immediately joined with our *In re: Pappas* case to be heard together by the U.S. Supreme Court.

Pillsbury-Madison and Lord, Day & Lord were, of course, totally humiliated. They had committed the worst possible sin that can be committed by any lawyer or law firm: they had failed to present an argument to a court that had demonstrated a perfect willingness to affirm.

A third similar case then arose very quickly out of Kentucky. There, a newspaper reporter, one Paul Branzburg with the *Louisville Courier-Journal*, wrote a series of stories detailing the rise of marijuana growing in Kentucky. One of his stories featured an "anonymous marijuana grower" whose activities the *Courier-Journal* reported in detail. Paul Branzburg and the *Courier-Journal* were both immediately subpoenaed by the county district attorney to appear before a specially convened county grand jury, to which they were ordered to produce all the documents, recordings, and photographs pertaining to the identity, location, and activities of the specific marijuana grower featured in the paper's news stories. Paul Branzburg was further commanded by the subpoena to testify to the grand jury as to anything and everything he had seen or heard while preparing the stories. This was, of course, the pure case: a full-scale effort on the part of a county district attorney to transform a grand jury into a mere investigative arm of the state prosecutor's office and thereby to transform a professional news reporter into an investigative agent of the state prosecutor. As is usually true in a First Amendment case, the "source" was not a particularly appealing person. After all, he was growing marijuana in violation of the law.

The *Louisville Courier-Journal* and Paul Branzburg both sought a protective order from the county superior court that was supervising the grand jury. The order was predictably denied. They appealed to the Kentucky Court of Appeals and then to the Kentucky Supreme Court, both of which affirmed the lower county superior court ruling. The *Louisville Courier-Journal* and Branzburg then both petitioned the U.S. Supreme Court to issue a writ of certiorari to review the Kentucky State Supreme Court's ruling. And given the fact that the U.S. Supreme Court had two virtually legally identical cases already before it, the High Court granted that petition, thereby bringing a third variation of the same constitutional question before the Court. The U.S. Supreme Court then had a range of positions being advocated before it, both by the parties and by various amici news organizations, civil rights organizations, and law enforcement organizations.

The process of preparing the principal brief in *In re: Pappas* and all of the amicus briefs before the U.S. Supreme Court then began in earnest, spearheaded by Floyd Abrams, Gene Scheiman, and myself.

Shortly after I had arrived at Cahill-Gordon, I registered with the New York City office of the American Civil Liberties Union and made myself available to take case assignments as an ACLU cooperating attorney. Once I was officially admitted to the New York State Bar Association, I was immediately called by the ACLU and was asked to take a case that involved a civilian complaint of police brutality on the part of the New York City Police Department.

The victim in this case was a twenty-two-year-old Hispanic young man by the name of Alberto Flores. Alberto lived in Coney Island, in the Bronx, with his father, several blocks from the home of his mother, who was divorced from his father. On a Friday evening in April 1971, Alberto was walking home from his mother's home to his and his father's when he came upon a flurry of activity on the street near his home. New York City police had responded en masse to a call requesting immediate assistance from a police officer. The police were in the process of withdrawing their last men from the block after having learned that the call was a false alarm. When Alberto came upon the scene, only two police cruisers were still there. Unable to get any meaningful information from bystanders, Alberto leaned over one of the few remaining strands of yellow crime-scene tape, which was being taken down, and asked a police officer what had happened.

Almost immediately, Alberto was violently tackled from behind by a very large and muscular NYPD officer, who then jumped up and began clubbing Alberto with his nightstick and kicking Alberto viciously in the kidneys and the head. The officer to whom Alberto had addressed his question was horrified at what he saw. He leaped onto the assaulting officer and struggled to restrain him. This rescuing officer was immediately joined by another officer, and the two of them finally succeeded in dragging the assaulting officer off Alberto—but not before Alberto had suffered significant head injuries, a broken nose, a broken jaw, a broken rib, and a broken collarbone. Instead of calling for an ambulance, however, the two rescuing officers put Alberto into one of the two police cruisers still on the scene and drove him away.

At some point between the scene of the attack and the nearby hospital, it dawned on the rescuing officers that their fellow New York City police officer who had so violently assaulted Alberto could get into serious trouble if Alberto were taken directly to a hospital for emergency treatment. So the two rescuing officers drove Alberto to their local police precinct and began to administer first aid. While they were attending to Alberto's face and lacerations and assessing whether he had suffered any serious internal injuries, the assaulting officer arrived at the precinct and began to insist loudly that all three officers involved sign a formal criminal complaint against Alberto for "interfering with a law enforcement officer in the course of the performance of his administrative duties." The assaulting officer demanded that the two rescuing officers write up Alberto for these charges "because it would look better on the record if the report came from them." The two rescuing officers refused to do this, however. All that they would agree to do was not to contradict the assaulting officer's official report of the incident in their reports.

Alberto was eventually transported to the nearby hospital, where he was given further medical treatment and where hospital personnel took photographs and X-rays of his injuries.

Immediately after being discharged from the hospital, Alberto called the ACLU and asked them to file a civilian complaint against the assaulting

NYPD officer for police brutality. The ACLU filed this civilian complaint and then called me to take over Alberto's case defending Alberto against the criminal charge of interfering with a law enforcement officer.

I took a cab out to Alberto's father's home in Coney Island. It was my first time in that part of the city. All that I knew about Coney Island was that it had a famous roller coaster and amusement park and that it had great hot dogs. Alberto was only five foot six and weighed no more than 140 pounds. He showed me his injuries, the photographs of his face and head, and the X-rays of his broken bones.

When it came time for Alberto's arraignment on the criminal charge lodged against him by the NYPD assaulting officer, I went with Alberto to the Bronx County Superior Courthouse. The assaulting officer lied, testifying under oath that he and his fellow officers had been called to a shooting scene and that while the investigation was still actively being conducted, Alberto had started screaming obscenities at him and his fellow officers, calling them racists and pigs. "Then," the assaulting officer said, "he leaped on me and tried to remove my sidearm from its holster." He swore that he had used only the absolutely minimal amount of force necessary to protect himself and to subdue Alberto.

I was shocked. Alberto, who was sitting next to me at the counsel table, kept saying out loud, "That's not true! That's not true!"

There were no other officers present at the arraignment to bolster this preposterous testimony. So, violating all the rules of a typical criminal defense attorney at an arraignment, I put Alberto himself on the stand to testify. The magistrate judge was so surprised when I told him that I wanted to call the defendant to testify that he actually told the court stenographer to go "off the record" and advised me not to do that.

I thanked the magistrate for his advice, but I insisted.

Alberto then took the stand and recounted exactly what had happened the night on which he had been beaten by the NYPD officer. His testimony was totally convincing, and I had no doubt that the magistrate believed him. Along with the photographs of Alberto and the X-rays that had been taken by the hospital staff, I introduced as evidence the official civilian complaint filed by Alberto through the ACLU.

Because the assistant district attorney had been so caught off guard by my decision to put Alberto on the stand to testify at his own arraignment, he hadn't prepared any cross-examination. Alberto's testimony, therefore, stood unchallenged, except of course for the assaulting officer's rather transparently perjured self-serving testimony.

Before the magistrate ruled, he called both the assistant district attorney and me to the bench and said, "Mr. Sheehan, I appreciate what it is that you are trying to do here. I have reason to believe that, if you were to persuade your client to withdraw his civilian complaint against this officer, the district attorney's office, in light of the comparative credibility of the two witnesses presented here today, might be willing to move to dismiss all charges against Mr. Flores."

To my amazement, the assistant district attorney agreed that he would do that.

I said, "Absolutely not, Your Honor. I think that what is happening here is a total outrage—to have a New York City police officer come before this court and present such transparently perjured testimony, and to then have the city district attorney's office threaten, in effect, to knowingly prosecute a totally innocent man unless that man agrees to withdraw his entirely legitimate civilian complaint against the officer who publicly beat him in front of a dozen witnesses."

The magistrate explained his view as if I were a novice. "Well, Mr. Sheehan, what you are doing may well be the *right* thing to do. But I am not sure that it is the *wise* thing to do in this case. I'm afraid that both you and your client are about to get a lesson on how this system really works here in New York City."

And with that, the magistrate ruled, based solely on the sworn testimony of the assaulting officer, in favor of the district attorney. He bound Alberto over for trial, setting a trial date just two weeks from then, since I refused to waive Alberto's right to a speedy trial.

Furious, I returned to Cahill-Gordon and went directly to Michael Armstrong's office to tell him what was happening. In addition to his recently having been made a partner at the Cahill-Gordon firm, Armstrong had just been appointed by Republican New York City mayor John Lindsay as chief counsel to the New York City Knapp Commission, a powerful independent commission created by Mayor Lindsay to investigate and prosecute police corruption in New York City. This commission had supervised the investigation and public testimony of Frank Serpico, the NYPD detective whose story was later told in the 1973 motion picture *Serpico,* starring Al Pacino. Indeed, since my office at Cahill-Gordon was immediately next door to Michael's office, I had often seen Frank Serpico coming and going with his big shaggy English sheepdog as Michael and Frank prepared his now-famous testimony before the Knapp Commission.

I asked for Armstrong's advice in the Flores case. After a long discussion of my options, I asked Armstrong if he would call the Coney Island precinct headquarters and get permission from its Internal Affairs Division for me to go over and listen to the Internal Affairs Division interviews of the two rescuing officers and any others who had witnessed what had happened on the night of Alberto's beating. Armstrong lit up at this idea. He made that call for me—and it worked!

So I took a cab to the Coney Island police precinct headquarters and introduced myself as one of Mike Armstrong's associates—which was true. But I assume that that introduction caused the officer who met me at the watch officer's desk to think that I was an attorney for Mike Armstrong's feared Knapp Commission. So he immediately showed me to a small institution-green-painted room with a plain wooden table and six wooden chairs on a hardwood floor, directly off the squad room. Then he brought in a box stamped "I.A.D. Evidence" that contained four tape recordings.

"You can listen to them, but you can't take any notes," the big, burly Internal Affairs Division detective announced to me as he tossed the box of tapes onto the table in front of me and then placed a small tape player next to them. Then he turned and lumbered out of the room.

When he had gone, I waited a full two minutes to see if anyone was going to be popping in and out to keep an eye on me. Convinced that I was not being closely watched, I slowly lifted my briefcase from the floor and laid it on the table directly in front of me beside the tape player. I then put the first of the four tapes into the tape player and turned it on. Then, slowly and unself-consciously, I opened my briefcase, just halfway. I had positioned the opening in my briefcase so that it faced me and away from the view of anyone passing by the open office door. Then I turned on the Cahill-Gordon professional tape recorder that I had brought with me in my briefcase, and I recorded all four of the Internal Affairs Division investigative interviews conducted with the assaulting officer's fellow officers.

To my great pleasure, they all told the exact same story that Alberto Flores had provided in his direct sworn testimony in the magistrate hearing at his arraignment. When I was finished recording all four of the taped interviews, I shut off the Internal Affairs Division tape player, placed each of the four interview tapes back into its respective box, and casually reached into my briefcase and shut off the Cahill-Gordon tape recorder. As I walked out, I thanked the scowling and oblivious Internal Affairs Division detective.

On the day of Alberto's jury trial at the Bronx County Criminal Courthouse, Alberto and I arrived to find the courtroom packed with Bronx police officers. The presiding judge was one John Fury. According to Mike Armstrong, Fury was an extremely reactionary "hanging judge," dreaded by all criminal defense attorneys in the city and loved by prosecutors. After picking our jury, I waived my opening statement, allowing the assistant district attorney to assert the assaulting officer's arraignment testimony as "the facts of this case."

As I had hoped, the assistant district attorney then opened with his "star witness"—indeed his *only* witness—the assaulting officer himself. The assaulting officer took the stand in full uniform, including his loaded sidearm, and took the oath. He then proceeded to recount, virtually verbatim, what he had falsely asserted in his perjured sworn testimony at the arraignment.

When he had finished, I rose for my cross-examination. I first asked the officer if he clearly understood that he was under oath. Judge Fury immediately interrupted.

"Mr. Sheehan, the officer certainly knows that he is under oath. There is no need for you to try to play games with this jury. This is not an episode of *Perry Mason*."

The jury laughed.

I laughed too. "Thank you, Your Honor. I understand that. And I would assume, equally, that the jury does not expect this witness to be broken on the stand and then suddenly and dramatically confess to the crime, as might be expected in a *Perry Mason* episode."

The jury laughed again. Judge Fury did not. He simply scowled down at me from the bench.

"Officer, despite Judge Fury's admonition, I want you to tell me . . . and the jury . . . that you are fully aware of the consequences if it is established, by clear and convincing evidence, that you have committed perjury before this jury."

"Mr. Sheehan," Judge Fury said, interrupting again. "I have already warned you that this line of questioning is not appropriate and that it will not be tolerated in this court. You either ask this witness a question that goes directly to the evidence in this case, or else I will allow him to step down."

I then turned back to the assaulting officer, who was now smiling smugly at me. There must have been thirty of his fellow police officers in the courtroom, and they were all smiling at each other too. They knew John Fury, and they knew that he wasn't going to let me get away with anything.

"OK, OK, Your Honor. I just wanted to make certain that there was nothing that this witness wanted to change about his testimony before I ask him my next question."

"Well, then go ahead and ask him that question, Mr. Sheehan, and let's get on with this."

"Yes, Your Honor," I said. And I turned and walked back to the defense table. I opened my briefcase and removed the battery-operated Cahill-Gordon tape recorder. It was cued up to play the Internal Affairs Division interview of the assaulting officer's partner. I carried the tape recorder over to the witness stand and placed it up on the flat rail directly between the assaulting officer and the jury. "Officer, I am going to play for you a recording. If, during the course of this recording, there comes a point in time at which what you are hearing refreshes your recollection as to what actually happened that night, please just stop me at any time."

Before Judge Fury could stop me, I punched the "play" button, and the sound of the assaulting officer's partner's voice suddenly filled the courtroom.

Q: Is your name X—— ?

A: Yes.

Q: Are you presently a police officer of the city of New York?

A: Yes. Yes, I am.

Q: Are you the patrol car partner of New York City police officer Y—— [the assaulting officer] in this case?

A: Yes. Yes, I am.

Q: Were you with Officer Y—— on the night of April 15 of 1971?

A: Yes. Yes, we had been called to a [the code number for an "officer down" call] out Coney Island. But it had been a false alarm.

Q: And, at that time, did you have occasion to witness Officer Y—— engage a person by the name of Alberto Flores in the 1200 block of Fourteenth Street?

A: Yes. Yes, I did.

It was clear to me that the assaulting officer, Judge Fury, and all thirty of the Bronx NYPD officers in the courtroom fully expected the partner's interview to back up the assaulting officer's account of the incident. So they let it play on. But, instead, the partner began to recount, on tape, the same version of events that Alberto Flores had testified to at his arraignment.

The courtroom—and the jury—listened to a full minute and a half of this sworn, tape-recorded testimony, which directly contradicted everything that the assaulting officer had just sworn to under oath, before the officer on the stand exploded. "Where the hell did you get that?" he roared.

"It doesn't make any difference where I got it, Officer Y——. That's your own partner, swearing under oath to your own precinct's Internal Affairs Division that you are an out-and-out liar and that you have been lying to this jury to try to put a totally innocent man in prison simply to cover up for your own, completely unjustified beating of this young man on the streets of our city."

Judge Fury exploded. "Mr. Sheehan! Turn that damned thing off. This is an outrage! You have absolutely no right to play such a tape before this jury without first securing the permission of this court to do so. You will cease this line of questioning immediately. You are attempting to impugn the integrity of a law enforcement officer of the city of New York! And I will not have that in my courtroom."

"You are absolutely right, Your Honor," I responded, within the full hearing of the jury. "And I thought that I was doing a pretty damned good job of it too."

The jury broke out in open laughter, which only made Judge Fury even angrier.

"You are doing nothing here but trying to get this man off!" he shouted.

"And I thought that I was doing a pretty damn good job of *that* too, Your Honor!"

Again, the jury broke out in open laughter. The crowd of police officers in the courtroom was in pandemonium. Judge Fury then rose up and was standing behind the bench, pounding his gavel as hard as he could, calling for order. Standing in front of the jury, I turned directly to the judge.

"Your Honor. I am not here, as you say, 'just to get this man off.' The jury is about to do that. I am here at the direct request of the American Civil Liberties Union of this city, representing this man to secure justice for him—and I am doing this entirely for free."

Judge Fury's face and neck turned a deep scarlet. He growled down at me from behind his bench.

"Mr. Sheehan! I have been a trial judge in this city for over forty years. Don't you try to intimidate me by telling me where you come from!"

It was such a peculiar thing for him to say that I didn't quite know how to reply. This was getting entirely personal. The jury fell silent. All thirty of the NYPD officers in the courtroom fell silent too and turned and stared at me.

"Well, Your Honor. Let's be perfectly clear here. If you have been a trial judge in this city for over forty years and you don't know any more about the law than you seem to, well, then you certainly don't intimidate *me*."

The court stenographer, who had been frantically transcribing everything that was being said, was so shocked at what she had heard that she actually stopped typing, thinking perhaps that she hadn't heard me correctly.

"Mr. Sheehan! We will deal with this after this case is over."

"As far as I can tell, Your Honor, this case is already over," I calmly replied—and I turned to the jury.

And it was. The jury unanimously acquitted Alberto Flores in less than fifteen minutes.

When they announced their verdict, Judge Fury rose from the bench, pounded his gavel angrily, and left the courtroom without uttering another word.

After Alberto's acquittal, I immediately ordered an expedited transcript of the assaulting officer's sworn testimony, and I marched straight upstairs to the county district attorney's office with the tapes of the directly contradictory sworn testimony of his NYPD patrol car partner and the other three officers. I went straight into the district attorney's office and told him what had happened, tossing a duplicate set of the tape recordings on his desk and demanding that the assaulting officer be criminally indicted for perjury. The district attorney simply looked at me and gestured over his shoulder with his thumb to the wall directly behind his desk. There, on the wall above him, was a four-foot-wide bright yellow circle with bright blue letters in it that said, COPS ARE TOPS! He shrugged and said, "Hey! What am I gonna do? I've gotta work with these guys every day." And he then pushed the four tapes back at me and got up and walked out of his office, leaving me standing there.

What a bummer!

I had been swept up into the currents of history straight out of law school, but I was in no way going to be overwhelmed or daunted by the nature of the events in which I found myself embroiled. If I could move from being an abandoned son of an alcoholic father at the age of twelve to being a high school student council president and football captain by the age of sixteen, then I felt that I could take on a faulty law enforcement system in New York City. In fact, I could do more than that—I could represent the freedom of the press before the United States Supreme Court to protect the

First Amendment rights of all news journalists in the country in a specifically effective way for the first time in history, even if I was just twenty-five years old. But I couldn't have done that without my upbringing in Warrensburg. And I couldn't have done it without my experiences and training at Harvard College and Harvard Law School. Now all of that had come together to make it possible for me to put that training to work.

At Cahill-Gordon, I was very fortunate to be a First Amendment associate directly under Floyd Abrams, considered by most of the legal world to be the premier First Amendment attorney in the country, and to be partnered with Gene Scheiman, a great legal mind and a great guy. I lived in a great apartment on the edge of Greenwich Village, directly across the Avenue of the Americas from the New School for Social Research and just two blocks from the heart of Greenwich Village and the Actors Studio. I felt that I had finally arrived.

CHAPTER *nine*

THE TUESDAY MORNING following Easter Sunday of 1971 slid silently in across the East River into New York City. The sun splayed gold and pink atop the pinnacles of the Brooklyn Bridge and crept slowly down the structure, then leaped to the topmost portions of the cold and darkened towers, which stood like silent sentinels of commerce in the waiting dawn overlooking the financial canyons of Wall Street. This golden light came through a high corner office window and fell across the figure of a young attorney with curly black hair as he sat, rocked back, in a high-topped expensive leather chair. That was me, with my Harvard Law School tie untied and hanging loosely at the open neck of a blue oxford shirt, my feet crossed up on my cluttered desk, and my freshly polished Dingo boots protruding incongruously from the legs of a neatly pressed $300 blue pin-stripe suit.

I would turn twenty-six in just seven days, but the upcoming event was approaching unheralded. A yellow wooden pencil was locked firmly between my teeth as I reread for the fourth time the final draft of the brief that Cahill-Gordon would be submitting to the United States Supreme Court the following Friday morning. In it, we would be demanding that the High Court recognize for the first time in history the constitutional right of news reporters to refuse to disclose to criminal grand juries the identity of their confidential news sources obtained in the course of their news reporting. I finished reading the legal brief and then tossed it casually atop the debris of legal books and yellow legal pads that lay strewn across my desk.

I then leaned back and stretched my arms to the ceiling, still unaware that the birthday present of a lifetime would be presented to me shortly after this Tuesday morning sunrise.

I checked my watch, a dark-black, rubber-encased Pulsar that I had purchased as a twentieth birthday gift for myself at the end of my second year of training as an army Green Beret officer. The watch reflected no light, and it would function perfectly down to one hundred meters beneath the sea or deep in jungle swamps. But I would never need that kind of timepiece for duty here on Wall Street. The enemies that I faced here marked their time on walnut-paneled relics that registered the passing minutes in the swaying rhythm of billable hours.

The Pulsar read 6:00 AM, Tuesday, April 2nd, 1971.

From my window on the twenty-fourth floor of the Cahill Tower overlooking Wall Street, I watched the water of the East River flowing silently to the sea below, reflecting on the fact that this same water had, just a few days before, traveled silently through upstate New York, past the hospital where I had been born in Glens Falls almost twenty-six years before. There it had flowed past the forever-silent grave of my fifty-year-old father, who had died, a hopeless and abandoned alcoholic, just two years earlier on Veterans Day in that same hospital. Life had now come full circle. And the torch had been passed to a new generation.

The phone suddenly rang, jarring me from my reflections. *Who was calling my office at 6:00 AM on the first day of work after Easter?*

Snatching up the receiver, I said, "Sheehan here." I immediately recognized the voice of Lawrence McElroy, the stalwart Irishman who manned the night desk and the nighttime telephones at the Cahill-Gordon firm.

"Top o' the mornin' ta ya, Danny, m'lad." McElroy and I had grown quite close during my short time with the firm, due to the long nights that I spent in the Cahill library and at my desk. "'Tis a Mr. Jim Goodale who is wantin' ta speak with ya."

That would be Jim Goodale, the general counsel and executive vice president of The New York Times Corporation. I had been working with Goodale on the amicus brief for *The New York Times* in the case of Earl Caldwell, the "confidential source" case that was now a companion case to *In re: Pappas* before the Supreme Court. So it was not unusual to have Jim Goodale on the phone. *But why at 6:00 AM on the Tuesday morning after Easter weekend?*

Warily, I told McElroy to put him through. I would take the call.

"Good morning, Dan," I heard Goodale say moments later. "I'm glad to find you on the job so bright and early."

Adopting the mock-formal tone of a first-year associate, I assured Jim Goodale that nothing was too good for *The Times*. Goodale laughed, then grew serious.

"Look, Dan, ahhh, a 'certain matter' has come up. I'd like to speak with you and Floyd about it . . . right away, if you don't mind."

I offered to get Floyd Abrams, who at that hour would still be at home, on the line. But Goodale said he didn't think that it was something that we should discuss on the phone. He wanted to know how early we could meet with him.

I laughed. "Hell, I'm already here. It's you guys that're sleeping in for the long weekend."

Goodale laughed out loud on the other end of the line. He loved this kind of banter with a young Irish Harvard Law School grad who had hit the ground running. And I knew that banter like this had made me more like a peer of the older attorneys such as Goodale.

Goodale was not comfortable saying what this was all about on the phone, but I suggested that if it involved the First Amendment (which I assumed that it did), we had better get Gene Scheiman in here too. Goodale agreed and thanked me for arranging everything so quickly. "I wish that the firm that we normally deal with was as responsive as you guys are."

"Well, if they were, then you wouldn't be calling Cahill-Gordon this early in the morning, Mr. Goodale. And in that case, I wouldn't be here at Cahill—I'd be there at that firm."

Goodale laughed again, and with that he rang off and the line went dead—with the exception of a strange hollow echo that I had never heard before. I held the telephone receiver away from my ear and looked at it, as if I might be able to place the strange echo simply by staring at the phone hard enough. Then I moved the receiver to my ear again, but now the sound was gone.

I placed the receiver back in its cradle and tried to shake off the strange feeling that had suddenly come over me.

Next I called Floyd Abrams and quickly filled him in on what I knew and let him know that Goodale would be calling him in a few minutes. Before I placed the receiver back on the hook, I hesitated for just the briefest moment.

There! There it was again—that strange hollow echo.

I still had to call Goodale back, and call Gene Scheiman. But I decided to make those calls from a public phone outside the office. I grabbed a small notebook from my desk and slipped it into my back pocket.

I found a pay phone in the back of a small coffee shop, where a few Wall Street types were securing their morning fix of caffeine and nicotine, and I dialed Gene Scheiman's home number. Gene was the Jewish associate Floyd and Mike Armstrong had chosen to pair me up with to help Floyd tackle the firm's First Amendment assignments. There it was again: the Jew and the Mick.

If it had not been the end of the weekend of the High Holy Day, it would have been a risky proposition to try to reach Gene Scheiman there at his home. Unlike Floyd Abrams, Gene Scheiman was a man of, shall we say, "other interests" besides being at home on weekends. Those "other interests" ran to very pretty legal secretaries; female legal associates from competing law firms; female law clerks of judges; female court stenographers; female news reporters; and, on occasion, female law school summer interns, if they were mature enough. It was not that Gene actually went looking for these young women; they just happened to "cross his path" as he went about his daily business of being a major powerhouse litigation attorney for the most powerful trial law firm in the world. These women simply *loved* Gene Scheiman . . . just as everyone did. He was smart, handsome, funny as hell . . . and not at all shy about letting it be subtly known to any beautiful woman who showed an active interest in him first that he was . . . shall we say . . . "available for consultation" late on weeknights or weekends—at least on a part-time basis.

The excuses that Gene provided to his wife, Madeline, as to where he *had* to be other than at home late on weekday nights or on weekends were as varied and as truly masterful as the legal briefs that Gene wrote to support all possible reasonable extensions of the First Amendment. He was a "free speech," "free love" kind of a guy. So, as a rule, I exercised a great deal of caution before calling Gene at home.

The phone at Gene's expensive Brooklyn Heights condominium rang only twice before Madeline picked it up.

"Yeah, right!" she growled suspiciously after I explained that Gene was needed in the office for a very important early morning meeting. I felt genuinely sorry for Madeline Scheiman, but I did not have time that morning to try to assuage her suspicions. Besides, in this *specific* instance, her suspicions were totally unfounded. If Gene had any chance of making this meeting, I had to speak with him right away. Finally, Madeline handed over the phone to her husband.

"Howdy, pardner," Gene said, his traditional greeting for me since we had, indeed, been "partnered up" by the firm. "Whatcha got for me this morning that justifies you draggin' my sorry ass out of the sack this early in the morning?"

"I just got a call from Jim Goodale."

The conversation shifted immediately to more serious matters, and I told Gene that *The Times* had something new for us and that we were meeting at 7:30 that morning.

"Holy shit!" Scheiman exclaimed. I heard the bedcovers fly on the other end of the line. And he hung up.

I was shaved and in a freshly pressed courtroom suit and shirt, sitting on the sofa in Floyd's office with a glass of freshly squeezed orange juice from a pitcher, when Gene and then Floyd arrived shortly after seven. Floyd was smiling that childlike smile that always lit up his face when the three of us came together in his private office to wrestle with an important First Amendment issue. That was what the practice of constitutional law was all about for Floyd Abrams, and it was what kept him from returning to the quieter Halls of Ivy at Yale Law School to teach constitutional law to an amphitheater full of bright young Yale law students. It was Gene Scheiman who analyzed, case by case, the present justice-by-justice balance of the High Court. It was I who pressed the principles that underlay each provision of the Constitution to their fullest reasonable extension—some would say beyond their fullest *reasonable* extension.

When the intercom buzzed, Lawrence McElroy announced the arrival of "Your 7:30, Mr. Abrams." This heightened our anxiety even more, since Jim Goodale had apparently not even given McElroy his name at the front desk, or else McElroy would surely have used it.

Jim Goodale's six-foot-three-inch bulk soon filled the doorway. His 230-plus pounds looked a bit out of place in his custom-tailored suit. We all exchanged familiar greetings, and Goodale thanked us again for meeting on such short notice, and so early. I was immediately struck again by the fact that so many of the most powerful trial lawyers in America were such huge men: Percy Foreman, Gerry Spence, Edward Bennett Williams, Al Kreiger. There are exceptions, of course—attorneys like F. Lee Bailey, who is only five foot six, and Lenny Weinglass, who is also not especially tall or big. And Clarence Darrow, the greatest of them all, I confidently reminded myself, was of only average height. That fact comforted me every time I found myself dwarfed by the sheer physical size of men like Jim Goodale. Nevertheless, most of the great trial lawyers seemed to be giants, like this gorilla of a man who now gracefully slid into the ancient Louis XIV seat centered in front of Floyd Abrams's desk and carefully placed his $1,000 leather briefcase on the floor beside his size 12 feet.

Gene and I sat on either side of Goodale, all three of us facing Floyd's large oak desk. Floyd took up "the power position" behind his desk.

Then "the dance" began.

Floyd opened. "Well, Jim, I hope that you had a pleasant weekend."

"Yes. Thank you, Floyd. It was, uh, a little busier than I had planned on. We'd planned to go out to the island, but, you know, the best laid plans and all that."

"Yes. I certainly know," Floyd said, waiting for Goodale to broach the point of the meeting that he had been so eager to be granted.

But Goodale drew out the moment further. He wanted to know how things were going with the Pappas and Caldwell briefs that we were preparing for the Supreme Court. "No unexpected problems, I hope, about 'the issues'?"

Floyd was bewildered. He had not expected to be examined on "the issues" in the Caldwell and Pappas cases, much less to be confronted with the prospect that *The Times* harbored any concern whatsoever that some problem might exist with either of those briefs.

"What problems? Do you mean 'the issues' in general, Jim, or on one of the briefs in particular?" Floyd asked.

Goodale said that he meant "the issues" only in general—the issue of keeping secret from government officials the identity of one's confidential source as well as which procedure would provide the most effective means by which to secure that right before a grand jury. Floyd measured his words carefully when he answered.

"As you know, Jim, this area is a little new to all of us. Even Pillsbury-Madison has taken the position that no such First Amendment right even exists."

"Yes. Pillsbury-Madison did have a bit of a 'measured response' to Dan's case presented to the Massachusetts Supreme Court."

I jumped in here. "And I suppose that Lord, Day & Lord did too," I said, referring to the Wall Street firm that handled most of the legal matters for *The Times*. Floyd was certain to perceive this as disrespectful, but matters were moving too slowly for my comfort.

"Of course, the operative question is what position the Supreme Court will take on this issue," Floyd insisted, rushing to regain control after my comment.

"Yes. The Supreme Court," Goodale acknowledged. "How are you feeling about this issue, Floyd, now that it is before the High Court? Do you think we're going to get Potter Stewart or Whizzer White to go our way?"

Before Floyd could answer, I interrupted from my seat on Goodale's immediate left and Floyd's right. "I think that we all believe that Hugo Black, Thurgood Marshall, and of course Bill Douglas are solid. And we feel pretty good about Bill Brennan. But the fact that the Black Panther Party is the only real 'party in interest' in both of the cases that we are handling makes both Potter Stewart and Whizzer White a little iffy. We were kind of hoping that you might have some other threatened subpoena in the offing to make the issue a little more to the taste of the former Harvard running back on the Court."

Floyd drew an audible breath at my lack of subtlety. But big Jim Goodale leaned back in the tiny Louis XIV chair and let out a loud belly laugh that filled the room and broke the tension—which also threatened to break the Louis XIV chair.

"I like you guys. I really do. You have really got balls. You're not like those pussies out at Pillsbury-Madison in California."

"Or like Loeb and Brownell over at Lord, Day & Lord for that matter," I said. This was now entering extraordinarily dangerous territory. If Goodale himself had been the one who had made the error of designating Pillsbury-Madison to represent *The Times*'s interests in the Caldwell case in California, then I would have just made a serious mistake.

A sudden silence filled the room.

Then Goodale leaned forward ominously.

"You're goddamned right! It was those no good sons of bitches over at Lord-Day who *fucked* us in the Caldwell case. And now they're getting ready to fuck us again!"

There it was. It *was* Lord, Day & Lord at which he was pissed.

At this, I stretched out my arms as if I had just awakened in the morning, and I leaned back comfortably in my chair. The first half of my job in this meeting was now over. But what was this about Lord, Day & Lord "fucking *The Times* . . . again"?

Jim Goodale suddenly rose from his chair, moved across the room, and closed the door—despite the fact that there was no one else in the office yet. Rather than sit down again, he immediately began to pace, as all veteran trial lawyers do when they begin to warm to their presentation.

"I didn't want to talk about this on the telephone. You'll understand why when I am done telling you what has happened."

All three of us looked quickly at each other. Electricity filled the air. I had been right. This *was* something big, and it was definitely going to involve Cahill-Gordon getting one up on Lord, Day & Lord.

"It started this past February with one of our reporters, Neil Sheehan— you'll appreciate the irony, Dan. Neil Sheehan was contacted, by phone, by one of his sources inside the Pentagon. The source asked to meet with Neil up at the Treadwell in Cambridge. He had something that he wanted to show to Sheehan. So Sheehan got a room at the Treadwell—he had actually brought with him his wife and charged it all to *The Times*—and he went up to the room with the source." Goodale explained that the source had opened a briefcase and had taken out a huge stack of documents that he had then spread out on the bed in the hotel room.

Goodale then sat down slowly in the chair, leaned forward, laid his massive forearms on Floyd's desk, and looked straight into Floyd's eyes.

"It was a Xeroxed copy of the official summary of an "*above* top-secret" forty-seven-volume, executive branch–ordered, United States Pentagon study of the *actual* origins and objectives of the Vietnam War, prepared by the Rand Corporation in California—at the demand of Bob McNamara. The source had copies of the original classified cable traffic setting forth the entire, detailed secret conduct of the war in Vietnam, including the forbidden campaigns in Cambodia, Laos, and Thailand, as well as in North Vietnam."

"Jesus H. Christ!" Gene exclaimed.

"Holy shit!" I exclaimed.

Floyd just sat there stunned. A deep and heavy silence filled the room.

It was Gene who eventually broke the silence.

"The forty-seven volumes . . . where are they now?"

"I *do* like you guys," Goodale laughed. "Neil Sheehan is presently in possession of a full Xeroxed copy of each and every page of the entire forty-seven volumes, which he, at this moment, has spread out all across the beds and tables and nightstands and the goddamned toilet seats of *two* fucking entire suites at the Plaza Hotel here in town. He's been reading them and preparing drafts of specific articles for a week now."

"And just what do the documents say?" Floyd asked.

Goodale chuckled. "It's the goddamnedest set of documents that I've ever laid my eyes on. I can't figure out how those stupid bastards ever had the balls to put such a report in writing, in light of all of the accusations that have been made about the 'criminal nature' of this war. It's a goddamned *confession*!"

"Are we certain that they're genuine?" Floyd asked.

"I can't tell you who the source is. But if you knew who it was, then you would know goddamned well that they are genuine."

Goodale explained that Herb Brownell, one of the two seniormost part-ners at Lord, Day & Lord, was a powerful figure in the Republican Party and a close friend of Richard Nixon. He had been the attorney general under Eisenhower, and, in that capacity, he had drafted the classification guidelines that were still in effect in 1971.

"That being the case," Goodale said, "he didn't feel that he could attack the statute as being unconstitutional." What Goodale was referring to as "the statute" was actually Executive Order 10501, which had been issued under Eisenhower and amended by Kennedy. It provided three levels of classification: confidential, secret, and top secret. I argued that, because it was just an executive order and not a statute enacted by Congress, it had no force of law on anyone who was not in government service or who had not signed a security oath, and that that executive order, therefore, provided no legal support whatsoever for Lord, Day & Lord's refusal to support the right of *The Times* to print the Pentagon Papers. However, Louis Loeb, Lord, Day & Lord's other seniormost partner, had insisted that "*The Times* was in possession of 'stolen goods' that were officially classified as top secret." He argued that "*The Times* should not only refrain from publishing them but should also return the documents to the government." Herb Brownell had even threatened to turn in *The Times* to the FBI if it did not return the documents to the government. Jim Goodale had strongly disagreed with Lord, Day & Lord—he thought it was the duty of the law firm retained by *The Times* to defend the First Amendment, not the executive branch–created system of classification.

"Well. That's good enough for us!" I said, rising from my chair and starting to pace. "So, let's get on with this thing. What shape are the draft articles in?" I looked at Goodale and could see that he didn't know what I meant. "The drafts of Sheehan's articles! Do you want them vetted? Do you want us to meet with Sheehan, to brief him on the steps to take when he's subpoenaed? What's the next step that you want us to do for you?"

Goodale looked a bit bewildered. He got up and joined me in pacing around the room. "Well. First of all, we wanted to get legal advice from your firm about the *legality* of what to do with them. Damn, about the goddamned legality of even *having* them!"

"Publish them!" I said. "Right on the front page—above the center fold. The only question that you should have should be what *size* of typeface to use."

Goodale looked shocked.

"So you, the Cahill-Gordon law firm, are advising us to publish them? All of them?" Goodale asked.

"Absolutely. Positively. Right on the front page. No mealy-mouthing around. Stick it right to them," Gene added.

Goodale lit up. A huge smile spread across his face. But Floyd, who had been sitting quietly, suddenly rose to his feet. "Hold it. This isn't the official opinion of the firm. This is a pretty serious legal decision that we're making here."

"And what exactly does Cahill-Gordon believe that the Mitchell Justice Department will do if *The Times* starts publishing the content of an above top-secret internal government study across the front pages of *The New York Times?*" Goodale had directed the question to me, not to Floyd, who became suddenly silent because he could tell that the chemistry between Goodale and me was working.

I thought deeply but quickly about all of the possible legal and political ramifications of publishing these above top-secret documents. I couldn't recall any case that was exactly like this one. It was obvious to me that Goodale had put this exact question to Lord, Day & Lord and that the answer over there had not been satisfactory.

Then, suddenly, I knew exactly what the Mitchell Justice Department's response would be. I told Goodale that the Mitchell Justice Department would probably threaten to prosecute both Neil Sheehan and Punch Sulzberger.

"Prosecute them for *what?*" Goodale wanted to know.

I reflected for a brief second on exactly how straightforward I should be and then decided that we had better get right to it.

"For espionage," I said. "If we're lucky!"

"Lucky? *Espionage?*" Goodale looked at me as if I were crazy.

I could see it all now. It had suddenly clicked into focus.

"Don't you see? These unmitigated assholes over at Justice around John Mitchell are just a pack of *bond* lawyers like Mitchell. They can be relied upon to overreact. If we do this thing with enough chutzpah, they'll come after you with what they view to be the biggest weapon that they think they have. And, since Mitchell is nothing more than a fucking securities lawyer, he'll go right straight to the Espionage Act. That's what any first-year law student would immediately think of in this situation—if he didn't see the trap."

"What trap is that?"

"*Gorin,*" I said. "*U.S. v. Gorin,* 312 U.S. 19 (1941)." None of them knew what I was talking about. So I began to lay out the facts of the case as though I were presenting the case to a constitutional law class at law school.

In the year 1941, just after the beginning of the World War II, one Lieutenant JG Edwin G. Gorin—a young naval officer in the United States Navy, based in Pearl Harbor, Hawaii—was discovered to be communicating the schedule of the departures of U.S. warships from Pearl Harbor to our British allies to assist them in coordinating our activities with those of the British navy. For this action, Lieutenant JG Gorin was court-martialed for the federal crime of espionage.

Arguing that he was not aware that the communication of such "national security information" *to our own American allies,* for entirely good faith purposes, was prohibited by the Espionage Act, Gorin insisted that the legal definition of "national security information"—which included "information that could be used by another nation to the detriment of United States interests"—was either constitutionally "overbroad" or "inherently vague," since it failed to clearly communicate to a person of average intelligence precisely what the specific conduct was that was forbidden by the statute.

In rejoinder to this argument, the United States attorney general argued, and the United States Supreme Court agreed, that the challenge of "inherent vagueness" directed against the federal Espionage Act could be overcome by the government if . . . but only if . . . the federal Espionage Act were read by courts to require an explicit finding, on the part of a jury, of an express and actual criminal intent on the part of the defendant charged with espionage to commit espionage against the United States. In short, the government would be *constitutionally* required to both plead and prove, *beyond a reasonable doubt,* that any person charged with a violation of the federal Espionage Act had *expressly intended* to give military or intelligence information to an enemy for the express purpose of damaging the United States.

"That's right!" Scheiman boomed, rising out of his chair. I could see then that they all got it now.

Unless the United States attorney for the Southern District of New York was willing to plead—and was able to expressly prove—that Neil Sheehan and Punch Sulzberger and anyone else he wished to charge with a violation of the Espionage Act had published the information contained in the secret report with the explicit and actual criminal intent of giving U.S. military or intelligence information to the enemy, for the express purpose of enabling that foreign nation to damage the United States, then any such "espionage" indictment against them would *have* to fail as a clear matter of constitutional law. I also pointed out that there was no civil statute on which to base any federal civil injunction action to try to stop the publication of these documents. So the government would probably resort to trying to employ the Espionage Act to achieve that end—to secure a prior restraint on the *further* publication of any *additional* portions of the documents—and then we would have them. With that, the fate of the Pentagon Papers case was sealed.

CHAPTER *ten*

$\mathbf{T}$HE *NEW YORK TIMES* went to press with the Pentagon Papers on Sunday morning, June 13, 1971. On June 13, 14, and 15, the inside account of the planning and execution of the Vietnam War would fill the front page, and numerous inside pages, of *The Times*.

It was on the morning of June 14 that I received the expected telephone call at my office from Whitney North Seymour.

"Whitney North Seymour . . . Whitney North Seymour?" I asked. "Am I supposed to recognize that name?" knowing full well who he was.

There was an immediate explosion on the other end of the phone line. "I am *the* Whitney North Seymour! The United States attorney for the Southern District of New York."

"Oh . . . *that* Whitney North Seymour?" I said. "What can I do for you, Mr. Seymour?"

When he calmed down and returned to his professional voice, he said that he was calling to formally request that our firm instruct our client, *The New York Times*, to cease and desist from any further publication of the forty-seven volumes of the Pentagon Papers.

"Well, Mr. Seymour, let me say first that our client does not admit that it is even in possession of any such report. And, second, it was our firm—indeed it was me personally—who advised *The New York Times* to print its analysis of any such report that might conceivably fall into its hands." I told him that it was my understanding that the report made perfectly clear that our United States executive branch, under four different administrations, had been self-consciously lying to the American people and to the Congress of the United States. I made it clear that Cahill-Gordon was not about to advise our client to cease and desist from performing the very important

138

First Amendment public function that *The Times* was founded to carry out. "Is there anything else, Mr. Seymour?"

I knew that there was. Seymour then said that he had been instructed by the attorney general of the United States, John Mitchell, to inform our office that Seymour would be bringing on a motion, the following afternoon of June 15, seeking the issuance of a preliminary injunction restraining *The New York Times* from further publishing or disseminating any of the content of the secret documents in its possession.

"You mean a prior restraint upon *The New York Times*?" I said.

"I did not call to dispute the merits of this matter with you over the telephone, Mr. Sheehan."

"I just want to make sure I understand what it is you are saying here. You are going to be asking for a 'prior restraint' to be issued against *The New York Times*, is that correct?"

"You can call it whatever you like, Mr. Sheehan. We prefer to call it by its official name: an emergency restraining order."

"Well, I prefer to call it what it has been called in every constitutional law treatise written since the founding of our country: a prior restraint on the press," I said matter-of-factly.

"Mr. Sheehan, as I said, I did not call you to argue over the substance of our motion. I was simply offering your office the courtesy of notifying you of the fact that this motion will be coming on for argument tomorrow, if your office wishes to attend."

"We are rather busy over here at Cahill-Gordon, Mr. Seymour, as I am sure you can appreciate, given the nature, number, and importance of our clients. We usually expect a bit more notice than . . . let's see . . . twenty-eight hours."

There was a long pause.

"Well, under the circumstances," Seymour said. "You can understand why we found it necessary to proceed with all due dispatch, given the gravity of the situation that your client has created by going forth with the publication of these documents without consulting with the appropriate officials."

I smiled on the other end of the line. "Oh? And just who might *that* be, Mr. Seymour? I wasn't aware of there being any office of the censor to which *The New York Times* was required to bring their articles for prior clearance before publishing them."

Another long pause. Then Seymour repeated that he did not intend to argue the merits of his motion over the phone. I told him that I wasn't sure whether our firm would make the court appearance on such short notice but that I would talk to my partners and see if it could be fit into our busy schedule.

"Suit yourself," he said. And he hung up.

I got Gene and we went immediately up to Floyd's office, where I recounted to them my exact conversation with Whitney North Seymour. Despite what I had said to Seymour, we never entertained the slightest thought of *not* showing up for the emergency motion hearing. We decided, however, against having Jim Goodale (or any of the other principals from *The New York Times*) attend that first hearing because we did not want to establish any *in personem* jurisdiction over any officers of *The Times*. That way, the court could not order any one of them to do or not to do any particular act and then threaten that person personally with a citation of direct criminal contempt of court if he or she did not obey. So we decided that only the three of us would attend, since this matter was squarely within the wheelhouse of our constitutional expertise.

Later that day, Punch Sulzberger received a telegram directly from Attorney General John Mitchell, a copy of which was forwarded to our office. It stated,

I HAVE BEEN ADVISED BY THE SECRETARY OF DEFENSE THAT THE MATERIAL PUBLISHED IN THE NEW YORK TIMES ON JUNE 13, 14, 1971 CAPTIONED "KEY TEXTS FROM PENTAGON'S VIETNAM STUDY" CONTAINS INFORMATION RELATING TO THE NATIONAL DEFENSE OF THE UNITED STATES AND BEARS A TOP SECRET CLASSIFICATION.

AS SUCH, PUBLICATION OF THIS INFORMATION IS
DIRECTLY PROHIBITED BY THE PROVISIONS OF THE ESPIO-
NAGE LAW, TITLE 18, UNITED STATES CODE, SECTION 793.
MOREOVER, FURTHER PUBLICATION OF INFORMATION
OF THIS CHARACTER WILL CAUSE IRREPARABLE INJURY
TO THE DEFENSE INTERESTS OF THE UNITED STATES.

ACCORDINGLY, I RESPECTFULLY REQUEST THAT YOU
PUBLISH NO FURTHER INFORMATION OF THIS CHARAC-
TER AND ADVISE ME THAT YOU HAVE MADE ARRANGE-
MENTS FOR THE RETURN OF THESE DOCUMENTS TO
THE DEPARTMENT OF DEFENSE.

JOHN N. MITCHELL
ATTORNEY GENERAL
ACK PLS

We all, of course, simply ignored the telegram.

The following day, on June 15, 1971, Floyd Abrams, Gene Scheiman, and I took the Cahill-Gordon limousine over to the United States District Court for the Southern District of New York in Foley Square. We disembarked and paraded up the impressive marble steps of the courthouse to attend the first attempt in the history of the United States on the part of the federal government to secure a prior restraint against an American newspaper. The front steps were awash with media of every sort. Inside, we took the old-time metal-gate elevator up to the third floor, where Judge Murray Gurfein had his office.

Representing the other side was Whitney North Seymour, the Nixon-appointed United States attorney for the Southern District of New York, with his $300 razor-cut and blow-dried white hair and his freshly pressed Pierre Cardin suit. Seymour had brought with him Michael Hess, the chief of the Civil Division of the United States Attorney's Office in New York.

When we entered Judge Gurfein's chambers, Judge Gurfein was already seated behind his desk. But, unlike most in-chambers meetings, he was in his full judicial robes. This was the man New York State governor Thomas E. Dewey had chosen, back in 1943, to serve as his "personal emissary" to conduct Dewey's ultra-secret negotiations with Lucky Luciano and the Italian Mafia at Great Meadows State Correctional Facility in Comstock, New York, the very prison where my father went to work in 1944.

We all took our seats. There was no shaking of hands. This was not going to be a friendly meeting. Judge Gurfein welcomed us and commented on the historic nature of the gathering. He then asked Whitney North Seymour to proceed.

I believe that there was an official court stenographer present to transcribe the proceedings of that historic first meeting. However, I have never seen an official transcript of that hearing. This is very peculiar, because there exist official transcripts of all of the later proceedings in the historic Pentagon Papers case, including all of the later in camera proceedings.

It is worth noting that I was the attorney officially assigned by the Cahill-Gordon law firm to write the official Cahill-Gordon history of the Pentagon Papers case. To my knowledge, there exist only two copies of this official history. One is locked in the safe of the senior partner of the Cahill-Gordon law firm, and the other was provided to Punch Sulzberger of *The New York Times*. The following account of what transpired in that first historic closed-door hearing is set forth in those two volumes. Until this present writing, however, no one in the outside world has been made privy to what transpired in that historic hearing or why it was so pivotal in the outcome of the Pentagon Papers case.

In that closed-door hearing before Judge Gurfein on the afternoon of June 15, 1971, U.S. Attorney Whitney North Seymour first demanded that Judge Gurfein order *The New York Times* to produce whatever documents that it possessed that had been "stolen" from the United States government, claiming that *The Times* and its law firm were unlawfully in possession of "stolen property" belonging to the United States government and that we had not responded to Attorney General Mitchell's telegraphed demand for the return of those documents.

Judge Gurfein, rather naively, then asked Floyd to acknowledge that *The New York Times* had these "stolen" documents in its possession, saying that he wanted to get "this technicality" out of the way before we went any further. Both Gene and I immediately objected, trying to keep Floyd from being drawn into Judge Gurfein's much-too-casual manner of discussing such crucial constitutional matters. Floyd took our caution seriously, but he seemed very uncomfortable at the prospect of being perceived by Judge Gurfein to be acting "ungentlemanly." Nevertheless, Floyd declined to admit or deny that either *The Times* or our firm was in possession of the documents at issue.

Whitney North Seymour then reiterated the content of the telegram that had been forwarded to *The Times* and our office by John Mitchell the evening before, once again asserting that *The New York Times* was in unlawful possession of documents that bore a top-secret classification and contained "information relating to the national defense of the United States." He maintained that publication of this information was directly prohibited by the provisions of the Espionage Act. Moreover, he insisted that publication of this information would cause "irreparable injury to the defense interests of the United States."

That was great! Whitney North Seymour and the Mitchell Justice Department had walked directly into the trap. When Seymour was finished, Floyd stated that publication of this information was *not* prohibited by the Espionage Act, which was clearly and expressly designed to apply only to persons employed by the United States government who had been issued security clearances, not to *The New York Times*. Floyd then laid out the precedent set forth in *U.S. v. Gorin*, which made it perfectly clear that the Espionage Act could be *constitutionally* applied only to a person who could be shown to have had the express and actual criminal intent, or scienter, to commit an act of actual espionage.

"The government's invocation of the Espionage Act, Your Honor, is entirely inapt in this case," Floyd said. He continued by pointing out that the Espionage Act was unconstitutionally overbroad and too inherently vague to serve as a standard on which to demand a potential prior restraint against *The New York Times*, thereby banning *The New York Times* from publishing information of such a historic nature and so critical to the citizenry of the United States.

"What is the government's response to Mr. Abrams's point, Mr. Seymour?" Judge Gurfein asked.

"Your Honor, the government represents that the publication of the information in those classified documents will irreparably injure the national security of the United States."

"Oh, yeah? Like what?" I interjected from my seat beside Floyd.

Seymour seemed to be thrown off balance by such a straightforward challenge. "The government is not prepared to specify what particular information that is contained in the papers will, if published, cause what specific irreparable damage to the national security of the United States—because neither you, Mr. Sheehan, nor any of the other attorneys in the Cahill-Gordon law firm, with all due respect, possess the requisite security clearances to be provided such information."

This was rich! I was delighted.

"Are we through here, then, Your Honor?" I asked Judge Gurfein. "The government surely bears the burden of proof as to its assertion that the publication of some *specific* piece of information contained in forty-seven volumes of documents would irreparably injure some *specific* national security interest of the United States in some *specific* manner. But if Mr. Seymour is going to refuse to reveal to the court or to counsel such specifics, then I assume that we can all agree that the government has failed to meet its requisite burden of proof on its motion."

Judge Gurfein did, indeed, appear to be troubled by the position that was being taken by the government. He acknowledged that he understood why the government might possibly be reluctant to divulge classified information to counsel for *The Times,* who did, indeed, lack security clearances. "But am I to assume that the government will be unwilling to divulge such information even to this court in support of its motion? Otherwise, I believe that Mr. Sheehan would be entirely correct: The court *would,* indeed, simply have no information whatsoever before it on the basis of which to support the government's motion. The government surely cannot be taking *that* position?"

Seymour had apparently not anticipated this obvious conundrum and was forced to admit that that was exactly the position the government was taking in this case. As far as the U.S. attorney was concerned, neither *The New York Times's* attorneys nor the court possessed the requisite security clearances to be provided information that would support the essential *factual* claim that was being made by Seymour. In short, Whitney North Seymour was asking Judge Gurfein to simply accept Seymour's *personal* word that the evidence supporting the very *factual* essence of his motion, *as a matter of fact,* existed—*without making any "showing" of that evidence to the court.*

In fact, he actually *said* that.

"Your Honor, I am giving you my personal word that those documents *do,* indeed, contain information which, if it were published, would, in fact, injure the national security of the United States."

"Your *word*, Mr. Seymour?" I intervened. "After what has been revealed already about the lies that have been told to the American people to start this illegal war and to keep it going, by men *just like you?* That is asking an awful lot of this court, and of this country."

It was immediately clear that this intervention on my part acutely embarrassed all of the "gentlemen" in the chambers. My statement was tantamount to having called Whitney North Seymour a liar—directly to his face. That was, of course, exactly what Whitney North Seymour had bet that no one who would have been allowed into that kind of high-level hearing would do.

However, Judge Gurfein was not impressed by my observation. Indeed, that intervention on my part was to cost me my place in Judge Gurfein's chambers for all of the remaining in camera proceedings that would take place in this case over the following two days. But I certainly had put the issue squarely before the court.

As history would prove, that hearing—and my specific intervention in it—was to be a pivotal moment in the history of the Pentagon Papers case, because instead of allowing Judge Gurfein to focus solely on the purely legal question at issue in the case, which clearly favored *The Times*, my "throw down" against the government and Whitney North Seymour caused Judge Gurfein to focus on the *purely factual* question as to whether or not there was, *as a matter of fact,* any specific piece of information contained in the documents that would clearly, if published, "irreparably injure some specific national security interest of the United States." The purely legal question, on the other hand, was whether the federal government had the constitutional authority to secure *any* prior restraint against *The New York Times*—even if the documents *did* contain such information.

I was the last person in the whole world who cared in the slightest whether or not there was, in fact, any such specific piece of information in those documents. It was my position that our United States Constitution simply did not allow any court to impose a prior restraint upon *The New York Times* or any other newspaper—even if that newspaper was going to publish such a piece of information.

However, because of that specific intervention on my part, we were now in a position to be able to win this case *on the facts*—so long as Whitney North Seymour stuck to his guns and refused to allow either us *or the court* to have any access to the content of the secret papers. However, if we allowed the argument to degenerate into an argument as to the facts in this particular case, then we were going to be sacrificing a golden opportunity to win this case based squarely on the all-important principle of law—that no set of facts, no matter how damaging they might prove to be to the "national security interests of United States," could *constituionally* authorize the executive branch of the United States government to secure a judicial prior restraint upon the press—because the Constitution expressly prohibited such prior restraints.

It was in that other direction—the *factual* direction rather than in the purely legal direction—that the Pentagon Papers case veered from that moment on. However, I could never have imagined what was going to happen next.

Instead of summarily dismissing the government's motion when Whitney North Seymour flatly refused to disclose, either to counsel or to the court, the specific information in the Pentagon Papers whose publication would "irreparably injure the national security of the United States," Judge Murray Gurfein asked Floyd Abrams whether he would, "as a courtesy to the court," provide a copy of the Pentagon Papers to the court so that Judge Gurfein could determine, *for himself*, whether *he* believed that any information in the documents would "irreparably injure the national security of the United States" if it were published by *The Times*.

And Floyd Abrams agreed to provide to Judge Murray Gurfein a copy of the documents.

I was entirely unable to understand what conceivable reason there was for Floyd Abrams to have done that. It was my judgment that if Floyd had simply politely refused Judge Gurfein's request, Judge Gurfein would have had absolutely no legal or factual basis on which to have then proceeded against *The Times*, and there would have been no prior restraint ever imposed on *The Times*.

Worse yet, after Floyd agreed to provide a copy of the Pentagon Papers to Judge Gurfein, Gurfein thereupon immediately asked Floyd to grant the court the "further courtesy" of asking our client, *The New York Times*, to *voluntarily* refrain from publishing any further installments of the Pentagon Papers until after he and his law clerks had had an adequate opportunity to review the documents and make a ruling.

This was absolutely too much for me.

"Absolutely not," I declared, and Floyd did not object.

But, to my utter shock, Judge Gurfein thereupon immediately entered a temporary restraining order (that is, a prior restraint) against *The New York Times*, barring *The Times* from publishing any further installments of the Pentagon Papers until after he had completed his personal review of the papers and had entered his ruling.

In the intense discussion that followed later that day back at our office, I held down the "absolutist" view of the Constitution. My position was that no executive branch official and no judicial branch official—and not even the Congress of the United States itself—had the *constitutional* authority to authorize the imposition of a prior restraint on the press, even if *The Times* chose to print a piece of information that *did* "irreparably injure the national security of the United States."

I did not believe that *The Times* would ever actually do that, but I insisted that it had to be left up to the editors of *The Times*—not to some government official, or even a court—to decide whether the publication of any specific piece of information would so "irreparably injure the national security of the United States" that it ought to be priorly restrained. I argued that executive branch agents would always make that exact argument in favor of secrecy, if for no other reason than to conceal executive branch mistakes and misjudgments. And I argued that almost every judge was a former member of the executive branch; that's how they got to be judges. Moreover, I insisted that this legal principle had to be the case simply as a matter of constitutional law—not because I thought that our government ought to be "irreparably injured" with regard to its criminal policies in Vietnam. This principle is set forth in the First Amendment to our Constitution: "Congress shall make no law . . . abridging the freedom . . . of the press." I was not alone in taking this "absolutist position." This position had been taken repeatedly by U.S. Supreme Court justices Hugo Black and William Douglas.

Within the Cahill-Gordon firm, I perceived it to be my duty on the team to hold to this purist position on the First Amendment. Floyd, of course, agreed with me in principle and believed that it should be our *initial* position. However, he was convinced that neither Judge Murray Gurfein nor a majority of the judges on the Second Circuit Court of Appeals nor, for that matter, a majority of the sitting justices on the United States Supreme Court would agree with us if we took *only* that "absolute" position. So Floyd wanted the firm, for practical reasons, to have a "fallback position" to place before the court in our briefs.

I opposed doing that. I argued that if we, on behalf of *The New York Times,* actively tendered to the court such a fallback position as constitutionally acceptable to us, then Judge Gurfein and any judge or justice above him would certainly seize upon that conceded fallback position and would impose it upon *The Times*—pointing out that we ourselves had conceded that it was a reasonable position to be taken—and then we would lose the most important legal principle the First Amendment had stood for for 180 years: that no law or government action could be undertaken to limit the freedom of the press.

The only fallback or supplemental position I agreed to research and brief came to me during a short break we took after litigating this case for nearly forty-eight straight hours throughout June 14 and 15.

On the afternoon of June 16, Floyd ordered both Gene Scheiman and me to go home and get a few hours of sleep before returning to the office. I went to my apartment, at 101 West Twelfth Street on the edge of Greenwich Village, which I shared with Marlene Montanaga, Sumie Tanaka, and Patty Hein. I began to pace around the apartment, trying to explain to my three very bright but nonlawyer roommates exactly what was going on in this case, which was generating such an intense amount of national publicity.

I was in the middle of explaining the legal intricacies of the case to my roommates when Marlene asked, "Who the hell do these people think they are anyhow? Did Congress ever give them the right to do this?"

Then it struck me. "*Youngstown Sheet & Tube!* Holy shit! That's it!"

In our case, the Nixon administration executive branch had originally cited the Espionage Act, just as I had thought it would, as the source of juris-dictional authority that allegedly gave it the congressional authority to seek such a ruling from the court, and we had successfully shot that theory down on the basis of the U.S. Supreme Court ruling in *U.S. v. Gorin.* But then U.S. Attorney Seymour had invoked the "inherent authority" of the federal government argument, citing a horrible 1942 U.S. Supreme Court decision that had centered on one Gordon Hirabayashi, a young third-generation Japanese American civilian.

Gordon Hirabayashi had been arrested in his own front yard in Washington State for violating a mere "public proclamation" that had been issued by Lieutenant General John L. DeWitt shortly after the Japanese inva-sion of Pearl Harbor. That proclamation had ordered all Japanese Americans (both citizens and noncitizens alike) to be off the streets and in their homes between 8:00 PM and 6:00 AM every night. Hirabayashi had been outside grilling hamburgers after 8:00 PM.

After the Japanese attack on Pearl Harbor, on February 19, 1942, President Franklin Delano Roosevelt had issued a presidential executive order purporting to authorize U.S. military commanders to issue military commands that would have the authority of law within their military dis-tricts. General DeWitt had issued his curfew order pursuant to the author-ity vested in him by President Roosevelt's executive order, and Gordon Hirabayashi was arrested by military police, incarcerated in a military stockade, tried and convicted before a military tribunal, and then sentenced to a military prison. Hirabayashi, a *civilian* American citizen, immediately petitioned the Washington State federal district court for the issuance of a federal writ of habeas corpus challenging the constitutionality of his arrest, prosecution, and detention by military authorities. He also challenged the constitutional authority of President Roosevelt to issue a presidential executive order of that nature *without any express authority to do so ever having been enacted by Congress.* The case quickly found its way to the United States Supreme Court.

One of my constitutional law professors at Harvard Law School, Albert Sacks, had been a law clerk for United States Supreme Court justice Felix Frankfurter, who had explained to Professor Sacks what had happened behind the scenes in the Hirabayashi case.

Upon the arrival of the case at the United States Supreme Court, Chief Justice Harlan Fiske Stone had found President Roosevelt's action, undertaken without any authority from Congress, to be of highly questionable constitutionality. Since the question presented by that case was not one that Chief Justice Stone wanted the Court to have to address while the war was still under way, Stone *himself* drafted and then sent to Congress (by way of his law clerk) a statute that should have been in place *before* President Roosevelt had issued such an executive order if it were to be adjudged constitutional. He had his law clerk deliver a copy of the draft statute directly to the majority leader of the United States Senate and to the Speaker of the House. That draft statute expressly delegated to the president of the United States congressional authority to issue the relevant executive order in the event that the territory of the United States were subjected to a direct military attack by a foreign power. The U.S. House and the U.S. Senate enacted that statute the very next day and forwarded it to President Roosevelt, who immediately signed it into law.

Only then did the U.S. Supreme Court schedule Hirabayashi's case for oral argument, and Hirabayashi lost the case because the law was then in effect. However, Chief Justice Stone stated in his opinion that the specific question that Gordon Hirabayshi had raised as to whether or not the president of the United States possessed any "inherent authority" beyond that expressly granted to him in the Constitution or by Congress was an extremely important constitutional question, but because Congress had in fact enacted a specific statute giving the president the express authority to act in the manner in which he had in this case, this "extremely important constitutional question" would have to be "saved" for another case in which no such statute existed. So the Supreme Court ordered Hirabayashi to be returned to military detention until the end of the war. This was, of course, a classic ex post facto law. But Chief Justice Stone, after raising this point himself from the bench, noted that Hirabayashi's briefs did not address the issue of the congressional enactment in question having been an ex post facto law. And, of course, they could not have, since the statute to which the Court was referring in its opinion had been passed only *after* the case had been fully briefed to the Court.

Thus this question as to whether or not the president of the United States (or the executive branch of the federal government) possesses the "inherent authority" to act in a particular manner, under a given set of factual circumstances, *without* the express authorization of the United States Constitution or an express act of Congress authorizing him to do so, has come to be referred to within constitutional circles as "the question saved in Hirabayashi." It is, indeed, one of the most profound and troubling questions in the entire field of constitutional law.

However, ten years after the U.S. Supreme Court decision in the Hirabayashi case, the High Court was confronted by the exact same "question saved in Hirabayshi" in the case of *Youngstown Sheet & Tube Co. v. Sawyer*. That case arose when President Harry S. Truman ordered U.S. military forces to seize and operate U.S. steel mills when the Steelworkers' Union went on strike and shut down the mills at the height of the Korean War. Truman, citing his "inherent authority to protect the national security of the nation," had ordered National Guard troops into the steel mills to first try to break the strike and, that failing, to operate the steel mills themselves in the stead of union workers. This time, however, "the question saved in Hirabayashi" was expressly answered—and it was answered plainly in the negative. In the Youngstown case, justices William Douglas and Hugo Black expressly stated the position that I was taking on this critical issue in the Pentagon Papers case—that "emergency does not create power; it merely marks an occasion when power *should be* exercised. ... The Executive, except for recommendation and veto, has no legislative power."

The very opposite position on "the inherent power of the executive" was expressed—and aggressively argued—in the Youngstown case by Chief

Justice Fred M. Vinson, with whom two additional justices had agreed, generating a classic split on the Court.

Justice Robert H. Jackson, in his written opinion concurring in the judgment and opinion of the Court, then set forth what has come to be accepted as "the operational test" in determining whether any specific assertion of purported "inherent authority" on the part of the president or his executive branch can withstand the constitutional scrutiny of the federal courts. Justice Jackson ruled: "Emergency powers are consistent with free government only when their control is lodged elsewhere than in the Executive who exercises them. That is the safeguard that would be nullified by our adoption of the inherent powers formula."

He went on to say, "Nothing in my experience convinces me that such risks are warranted by any real necessity, although such powers would, of course, be an executive convenience."

From a reading of just these brief samples of pronouncements made by U.S. Supreme Court justices on this critical issue of the alleged "inherent authority" residing in the president of the United States or within the executive branch of our federal government, one can see the profound importance of this issue to both the resolution of the Pentagon Papers case and to the disposition of power within the constitutional framework of our representative constitutional republic.

So, when my roommate Marlene asked her simple, point-blank question, I realized that we simply had to get the *Youngstown Sheet & Tube* principle inserted into this case. I rushed back to the office, not yet having slept, and worked late into that night of June 16, researching and writing a long memorandum to Floyd and to the partners of Cahill-Gordon, arguing that we *needed* to supplement our strict First Amendment arguments with this important additional "separation of powers" argument, which nullified the executive branch's assertion of inherent authority in this case.

I argued that *Youngstown Sheet & Tube* stood for the legal proposition that "the government" is *not* the executive branch of our federal government but, rather, "the government" is Congress, because it is Congress to whom the task of making laws has been expressly delegated by "the people" in the United States Constitution. The task of the executive branch is simply to "execute" laws enacted by Congress. Therefore, I argued, the fundamental constitutional principle expressly recognized and affirmed by a majority of the U.S. Supreme Court justices in 1952 in the case of *Youngstown Sheet & Tube Co. v. Sawyer* was that the executive branch is simply not endowed, by our Constitution, with the "inherent authority" that was being asserted in this case by the Nixon administration to stop the publication of the information in the Pentagon Papers.

I argued that this had to be the number 1—and *only*—fallback position that Cahill-Gordon and *The Times* could posit to the Court, arguing that *Youngstown Sheet & Tube Co. v. Sawyer* might implicitly suggest that Congress *might* have the *conceivable* authority to enact legislation that might create some censoring authority over the press but that such authority could not be deemed to reside within the executive branch, even with the participation and support of the *judicial* branch of the government.

But Cahill-Gordon insisted upon being prepared to proffer four *additional* fallback positions to the court. These were:

- NUMBER 2: That the Espionage Act upon which the Nixon Justice Department was predicating its petition for a permanent injunction was not applicable to our case because it was clearly intended to apply only to cases in which a person either took or attempted to communicate classified military information for the express and intended purpose of conveying that information to an enemy nation—with the specific intent of causing serious damage to the national security of the United States at the hands of such an enemy—and that those constitutionally requited facts did not exist in this case.

- NUMBER 3: That explicit legislative history demonstrated that Congress had been expressly asked by the executive branch to grant it the statutory authority to stop an American newspaper or other public media from publishing classified military information or other information "related to the military defense of the United States" but that Congress had expressly refused to enact such a statute, explicitly citing the First Amendment ban prohibiting any prior restraint on the Free Press.

- NUMBER 4: That the executive branch, at an absolute minimum, had "the burden of going forward" to establish, as a matter of preliminary prima facie fact, that the publication of whatever specific piece of information that it sought to have restrained would, in fact, "irreparably injure the national security of the United States" in some specific and demonstrable manner.

- NUMBER 5: That the executive branch bore "the burden of proof" beyond any reasonable doubt that the publication of a specific piece of information would certainly "irreparably injure" an identified national security interest of the United States in a specific way and to a specific degree.

I argued that our firm and *The Times* should *not* broach—and certainly not concede under any circumstances—the constitutional acceptability of arguments 4 or 5 that any set of *facts* would authorize the federal executive branch to obtain a prior restraint on the press.

U.S. Attorney Seymour argued a number 6 position: that all the government had to show to a court in order to secure a judicial injunction against the publication of a given document was that the document contained "information related to the national defense" and that the court should then simply act as an agent for the executive branch and ban the publication of that document by an American newspaper.

He went even further to argue a number 7 position: that to secure an injunction from the judicial branch of the government, the executive branch had only to come before the court and assert that a given document that a newspaper planned to publish "contained information related to the national defense" and merely had to *assert* that the publication of that document would "irreparably damage the national security of the United States"—and that the court should simply take the government's word that this was true.

Seymour's other assertion (position number 8) was that in order for the executive branch to secure a judicial injunction against the publication of a given document, it had to demonstrate nothing more than that the document at issue had been designated by the executive branch as "classified"—and that a court must, thereupon, enjoin the publication of that document.

Since Floyd Abrams had agreed to hand over a full set of the Pentagon Papers to the court, arguments 7 and 8 were off the table, because Floyd's action had put Judge Gurfein into a position in which he could insist that the executive branch meet the factual standard that some information contained in the Pentagon Papers would, in fact, generate irreparable injury to the United States. Seymour, therefore, spent two additional in camera hearings (from which I was excluded) presenting various specific documents contained in the Pentagon Papers, arguing that their publication by *The New York Times* would in fact "irreparably damage the national security of the United States." To do this, Seymour somehow secured immediate security clearances for Judge Gurfein (and, one must assume, his law clerks) and for the Cahill-Gordon attorneys representing *The Times* in those two hearings. That obviously did not include me.

In the first of those two additional in camera hearings, I was replaced by Larry McKay, the senior partner at Cahill-Gordon. So, on June 17, Floyd Abrams, Gene Scheiman, and Larry McKay appeared before Judge Gurfein to argue against *The Times* and our firm being compelled by Judge Gurfein to return our copies of the Pentagon Papers to the government.

But the real mistake, in my judgment, was that on the following day, on June 18, Gene Scheiman was replaced by Alexander Bickel. Bickel was a constitutional law professor at Yale Law School. As the world's foremost constitutional scholar when it came to "balancing competing fundamental interests" on the part of the state against the fundamental rights of citizens, Bickel had been asked by Floyd Abrams to serve as a consultant ("of counsel") to Cahill-Gordon in the preparation of our confidential news sources case, which was then before the United States Supreme Court. Bickel was, however, the very worst of all possible advocates when a news media client was confronted with a situation that required its attorneys to assert an absolute First Amendment right—as was the case in this instance, when the federal government was seeking a prior restraint on the press.

In short, and with all due respect, it was my judgment that Professor Bickel should have been left at the office when we went to federal court to argue the First Amendment right of *The New York Times* to publish the Pentagon Papers.

Yet when Cahill-Gordon appeared in the chambers of Judge Murray Gurfein on June 18, 1971, to argue to him the historic case of *United States v. The New York Times*, it was Alexander Bickel who was allowed to argue the case.

The argument did not begin well. Professor Bickel opened by saying, "Your Honor, we are not in this court because we came to court seeking its approval of our publishing enterprise. We are in this court today because the government brought us into this court. The government obtained from Your Honor a temporary restraining order on the basis that there was relatively no damage, no injury, to *The Times* in imposing a temporary restraint on publication and, on the other hand, that there was serious damage impending to the government."

Judge Gurfein's response was very peculiar and did not bode well for the outcome of the case before him from a First Amendment point of view:

> It seems to me that a free and independent press ought to be willing to sit down with the Department of Justice and screen these documents that you have, as a matter of simple patriotism, to determine whether the publication of any of them is or is not dangerous to the national security. If you disagree, then surely you have the right—and the government has the equal right—to go into a court and ask a court to make that decision. I am concerned about materials sent by foreign governments which do not belong to the United States under the rules of international law as I know them (they are merely in our custody) and a few other limited categories of that type, or perhaps the revelation of methods of intelligence gathering, all of which, as patriotic citizens, I think the [. . .] press

as well as anybody else agrees should be kept sacrosanct—not to deprive anybody of a right to express opinion, mind you, but in order to protect what is dear to all of us: the national security of the country.

Shortly thereafter, Judge Gurfein went straight to the Achilles heel of Alexander Bickel when he said, "I want to test you. You are claiming, apparently, that there is an absolute quality to the First Amendment."

"No, Sir, I did not," Alexander Bickel replied predictably. "I say 'as applied to this case.' I am not claiming, for example, that if, in a time of war or national emergency, a troopship leaves New York Harbor and *The New York Times* takes it into its head to publish the date of departure and the date of arrival and the probable course, that is protected by the First Amendment. I am not claiming that."

"Why isn't it?" Judge Gurfein inquired.

Then Alexander Bickel "gave away the store" with his reply.

"I am not claiming that even the prior restraint element in the First Amendment is absolute. I've spent some years of scholarship, if I may say so, resisting the idea of absolutes, and I am not now turning around and embracing it."

Professor Bickel went even further, expressly acknowledging that it would be constitutional to impose a prior restraint upon the press to stop it from publishing any piece of information that presented a "clear and present danger" of damaging the national security of the United States, so long as the burden of proof as to the "factuality" of that danger was placed on the government.

Since Judge Gurfein already had a full copy of the Pentagon Papers from Floyd Abrams, Whitney North Seymour thereupon agreed to provide examples of specific sections of the documents that, if published, he was willing to assert would "irreparably injure the national security of the United States." With Marine Corps brigadier general Jacob Glick of the Joint Chiefs of Staff dramatically brought into Judge Gurfein's chambers to act as the "security officer" over those portions of the Pentagon Papers, Seymour's tendered examples were then examined by the court.

Though Gene and I had been expressly excluded from that hearing, we were both invited back, by Floyd, for the announcement of Judge Gurfein's decision on the following day, June 19, 1971.

Judge Gurfein ruled that, upon his personal review of the documents at issue, he was personally unable to determine that any irreparable injury to the national security of the United States would follow if the documents were published. *The Times*, and our firm, had therefore prevailed in this specific case . . . but exclusively on these specific *facts*.

However, Judge Gurfein went on to assert a very dangerous principle. He said, "There seems little doubt that the government may ask a federal district court for injunctive relief even in the absence of a specific statute authorizing such relief. Accordingly, even in the absence of a statute, the government's inherent right to protect itself from breaches of security is clear."

And he based this constitutional assertion squarely on Alexander Bickel's concession of this point. He then concluded where my discussion with Jim Goodale, Floyd Abrams, and Gene Scheiman had first begun:

> If the statute [the Espionage Act] were applicable, it is doubtful that it could be applied to the activities of *The New York Times*. It would be necessary to find, as an element of the violation, a willful belief that the information to be published "could be used to the injury of the United States or to the advantage of any foreign nation." That this is an essential element of the offense is clear. This has been an effort on the part of *The Times* to vindicate the right of the public to know. It is not a case involving an intent to communicate vital secrets for the benefit of a foreign government to the detriment of the United States.

It was, therefore, a victory for *The New York Times* and for Cahill-Gordon *on the facts of our case*. However, in winning the case in this specific manner, we had missed the golden opportunity to advance the vital principle that our constitutional community had won in *Youngstown Sheet & Tube Co. V Sawyer* with regard to the issue of "inherent authority" on the part of the executive branch—and we had lost serious ground with regard to the crucial issue of the First Amendment's all-important principle of prohibiting any prior restraint on a free press.

The result was that Judge Gurfein had asserted that there did indeed exist *some* degree of "inherent authority" that could be exercised jointly by the executive branch acting in conjunction with the judicial branch of the federal government that authorized a court, upon the application of the executive branch, to impose a prior restraint upon the press in order to provide to that court the opportunity to review any "controversial" document before its publication, and authorizing a court to permanently enjoin the publication of any such document if *the court* came to the conclusion that the publication of that document would "injure the national security interests" of the United States.

Because of these very damaging constitutional rulings by Judge Gurfein, there existed a serious question as to whether or not *The Times* should appeal. However, because Professor Bickel had expressly conceded our absolutist position in his own oral argument to Judge Gurfein, because Floyd Abrams had voluntarily provided a copy of the Pentagon Papers to Judge Gurfein for his factual review, and because I had "thrown down" on Whitney North Seymour, challenging him to "put up or shut up" concerning his *factual* allegations about the damaging nature of the information in the documents, our ability to effectively appeal Judge Gurfein's refusal to recognize our absolutist position on this issue of no prior restraint had been seriously compromised.

Judge Gurfein seemed to recognize that we had relinquished our right to appeal his failure to recognize this absolutist position regarding the First Amendment when he extended his temporary restraining order to the end of the day of his ruling on June 19, 1971, "to allow *the government* the opportunity to go before the Second Circuit Court of Appeals to seek a review of this order."

CHAPTER *eleven*

IMMEDIATELY AFTER JUDGE Gurfein's ruling, Floyd Abrams, Gene Scheiman, Alexander Bickel, and I followed Whitney North Seymour and Michael Hess directly upstairs in the federal courthouse on Foley Square in New York City to the chambers of the Second Circuit Court of Appeals. Seymour made a beeline directly for the chambers of Judge Irving Kaufman and requested an immediate *second* temporary restraining order, this one to give the Second Circuit Court of Appeals time to convene an emergency three-judge panel to review Judge Gurfein's order.

Judge Kaufman had the unmitigated gall to announce to us, "You know, gentleman, it was twenty-five years *to the day* that I was asked to enter an emergency restraining order in another case. I did not enter it on that day, and I have often wondered whether I acted correctly in denying that requested restraining order. So I am going to grant the requested restraining order in this case." And with that he issued the *second* prior restraint on the press ever granted in the history of the United States.

Judge Kaufman was talking about the Rosenberg case, in which Ethel and Julius Rosenberg had been charged with espionage for allegedly transferring atomic secrets to Russia. On June 19, 1946, exactly twenty-five years earlier, Judge Irving Kaufman had denied the Rosenbergs' final plea for a temporary restraining order to delay their execution long enough to give them time to appeal their conviction and death sentences to the United States Supreme Court. Judge Kaufman had thus, in both cases, done exactly what the executive branch had asked him to do.

We went before the emergency three-judge panel of the Second Circuit Court of Appeals two days later, on June 21, 1971. The panel consisted of Judge Henry J. Friendly, the chief judge of the Second Circuit; Judge J. Joseph Smith; and Judge Paul R. Hays. The hearing ended as soon as it began, however, because Chief Judge Friendly declared, "This appeal raises questions of such extraordinary importance that it should be heard by all of the judges." With that, all eight judges of the Second Circuit Court of Appeals agreed to gather en banc the following day, despite the fact that it was June 22, past time for them to have dispersed for their summer break. The three-judge panel of the Second Circuit Court of Appeals, however, *extended* the second prior restraint already imposed on *The Times* by Judge Kaufman.

Meanwhile, the law clerks of the justices of the United States Supreme Court, which had ended its session on June 21, were dispatched, on an emergency basis, to hunt down and bring back to Washington, D.C., all nine of the justices of the United States Supreme Court, including Justice William Douglas, who was halfway up a mountain in the state of Washington and totally out of telephone communication. Everyone knew that this case was on the fast track directly to the High Court, no matter which way the Second Circuit ruled on the case.

When we entered the ceremonial courtroom of the Second Circuit Court of Appeals in New York City for this extraordinary en banc session on the afternoon of June 22, 1971, the gallery was overflowing with federal judges and their law clerks from throughout the land, because they had been given priority seating in the courtroom. It looked like a gathering of all of the editors in chief of all of the law reviews of the top five law schools in the nation. It also looked like a reunion of my Harvard Law School class; there must have been fifty of my classmates present. And there I was, seated at the counsel table, between Floyd Abrams and Jim Goodale, with Gene Scheiman at the far end of the counsel table. Neither Gene nor I had slept in four days.

Once again, however, Floyd allowed Alexander Bickel to conduct the oral argument for *The Times*. Bickel was therefore standing there before the Second Circuit Court of Appeals, willing and able to defend only Judge Gurfein's *factual* finding that the particular documents at issue in this case had been properly "cleared" for publication by *The Times* by the lower court— not the larger principle as to whether the judicial branch had any authority whatsoever to engage in such a "prior review" of any publisher's documents merely because the federal executive branch had been willing to come before the court and allege that the publication of those documents would cause "irreparable injury to national security interests of the United States."

This was outrageous. And it was dangerous—constitutionally.

Although Alexander Bickel first stated that neither the judicial branch nor the executive branch possessed any "inherent authority" to tell *The Times* not to publish the documents at issue, he immediately shrank back from asserting the proper principle of law. "You say the courts have no power to do anything?" Judge Friendly asked.

Bickel replied:

> Oh, no, Sir. That is not my position at all. I know that the government's brief charges that position to us. I must say, it seems to me that only a failure to read our brief would cause them to say that. Our position is, by no means, that this court has no power to do anything. If either [of our positions] can be characterized that way, it is more nearly the government's. Our position is that it isn't true that the "classification" stamp on a document concludes the matter, that it isn't true that the government's mere statement that national security is involved concludes the matter. Our position is that, in a First Amendment area, it is for this court to (a) decide the applicable law, (b) apply that law to the facts, and (c) make a full judgment.

There it was: Alexander Bickel's express acknowledgment that a *factual* determination would have to be made by a court . . . in every instance in which an American news outlet wished to publish a document that contained "information relating to the defense of the nation," so long as the federal executive branch was willing to go before that court and make the mere *assertion* that the publication of information contained in that document would "irreparably injure the national security interests of the United States." I was furious. What the hell kind of "representation" of the First Amendment was this? Alexander Bickel had instantly retreated to "fallback position 5."

Therefore, it was not surprising that, the next day, on June 23, 1971, a five-judge majority of the eight judges of the Second Circuit Court of Appeals (1) voted to set aside Judge Gurfein's order denying the executive branch's petition for a permanent injunction; (2) remanded the case back to Judge Gurfein, with instructions that he allow the federal executive branch two *additional days* to "supplement" its previous offerings as to specific documents or pieces of information that it demanded be enjoined from publication by *The Times*; and (3) extended the prior restraining order against *The Times* until a final disposition by the district court had been made on the government's assertions, with no time limit or expiration date whatsoever set on the time period of that prior restraint.

That was a constitutional disaster.

However, the Second Circuit Court of Appeals took one extremely important action and vacated the Second Circuit's prior restraining order with respect to any and all documents or pieces of information contained in the forty-seven volumes of the Pentagon Papers that the federal executive branch did *not* explicitly "specify," within that two-day period granted to the executive branch by the court of appeals, to be "documents containing information that posed such grave danger to the security of the United States as to warrant their publication being enjoined." This ruling, therefore, freed the vast majority of the forty-seven volumes of the Pentagon Papers for publication by *The Times* within just two days. However, this peculiar order also implicitly authorized the federal executive branch (if it simply chose to do so) to designate all forty-seven volumes of the Pentagon Papers to be "documents containing information that posed such grave danger to the security of the United States as to warrant their publication being enjoined." That was a sub silentio extraordinary grant of discretionary authority to the federal executive branch by the Second Circuit Court of Appeals—especially in light of the fact that the court of appeals had placed absolutely no deadline whatsoever on how much time the executive branch was to be given to construct and present its arguments in support of the suppression of any and all such documents it chose to so designate in the proceedings to be undertaken before Judge Gurfein on remand of the case to him. And, throughout that entire time—whatever that turned out to be—the prior restraint against *The Times* would have remained in effect.

This was an absolutely extraordinary order on the part of the Second Circuit Court of Appeals. And it—and its implications—have gone virtually unnoticed and entirely uncommented on by the legal and political community because we immediately notified the United States Supreme Court that we would be filing, the very next day, June 24, an emergency petition for the issuance of a writ of certiorari by the United States Supreme Court to review that court of appeals ruling.

By then, Gene, Floyd, and I were really starting to feel the pressure, in between each of these rulings, to prepare and file all of the necessary petitions and filings required to perfect the *next* appeal of this case, as it literally "soared" up to the Supreme Court. Still, on the morning of June 24, we managed to file that petition, and the U.S. Supreme Court immediately agreed to hear our appeal.

However, the U.S. Supreme Court justices, by telephone conference call, voted five to four to continue the prior restraining order issued by the Second Circuit Court of Appeals against *The New York Times,* pending the scheduled June 26 oral argument of the case before the full United States Supreme Court.

Alexander Bickel was once again held forth by Cahill-Gordon as "the attorney for petitioner" to argue the case before the United States Supreme Court. However, Floyd Abrams insisted upon bringing Gene Scheiman and me with him to Washington, D.C., to help prepare the case for its historic argument before the High Court. Little did I know that Floyd had an additional reason for bringing me to Washington.

At the hotel, Floyd secured a two-bedroom suite for Gene Scheiman and me in between the two one-bedroom suites that he had secured for himself and Alexander Bickel. Senior partner Larry McKay and partner William Hegarty each had two two-bedroom suite, directly across the hall.

On Friday morning, the morning before our scheduled Saturday oral argument before the High Court, Floyd telephoned and asked me to come next door to his suite for "an important conversation."

When I arrived, Floyd was very nervous. We sat down across a white-table-clothed table at which breakfast had been laid out. Floyd first told me how deeply he appreciated the work that I had performed on the case so far. Then he started coming around to his point.

"You, above everyone else in the firm, have held fast to the position that the firm should never, under any set of factual circumstances, allow the executive branch, or even any court in conjunction with the executive branch—or even the Congress itself—to impose a prior restraint on a newspaper . . . even if that newspaper intends to publish a piece of information that might indeed irreparably injure the national security of our country.

"I honestly don't know anyone else who actually believes in that position. And, frankly, if you had not been the editor of the *Harvard Civil Rights Law Review*, I'm not sure that I would have thought that that position could be responsibly held by anyone. So I want you to explain to me, as best you can, exactly how and why you hold this belief—since I am convinced that you are a loyal American . . . no matter what anyone else in the firm believes."

There it was. Floyd had just revealed the sense on the part of at least some of the partners of Cahill-Gordon that I was, somehow, not *really* "a loyal American" and for that reason simply did not care whether the national security of the United States was irreparably injured or not. So the moment of truth had finally arrived: in the confrontation between me and the Cahill-Gordon partners; between the Nixon administration and *The New York Times*; between the American executive branch and the American news media; between our baby boomer generation and the World War II generation; and, ultimately, between the natural law theory of fundamental rights and the pragmatic (or utilitarian) theory of individual rights.

That "pragmatic" or "utilitarian" understanding of our constitutional rights, I argued to Floyd, was rooted in a fundamental misconception as to the nature of the *ultimate source* of our rights. That misconception therefore carries with it an implicit constraint on the exercise of each and every one of those rights by our people. That misconception, I explained to Floyd that morning, is that such fundamental rights, such as freedom of speech, freedom of religion, and freedom of the press, were in effect somehow "donated" to American citizens by an intelligent "governing class" made up of the founding fathers and fellow members of their elite company for the "utilitarian" purpose of forwarding specific "practical" interests of government. The constraint on such rights implicit in this misconception as to the source of these fundamental rights, I argued, is that those rights need be recognized and given effect by the governing class (members of which are appointed to our federal courts and appellate courts) *only to the degree* to which a given proposed exercise of those rights on the part of the common people constructively serves the utilitarian practical objectives or interests of government, for which purpose that specific right was "donated" to the common people by the members of the governing class who founded our government. This theory of fundamental rights is known, within constitutional law circles, as the donative theory of human rights. Pursuant to *that* theory of human rights, such rights have their source and origin only in the "positive laws" affirmatively enacted by bodies such as our American Constitutional Convention and our Congress. Pursuant to that theory, such rights can therefore be taken away *by* such legislative bodies or refused to be given recognition or effect by the governing structures that were created by our Constitution (such as our federal courts) whenever any given attempted exercise of one of those rights does not appear, to the governing class members who staff the judicial branch of our government, to serve the originally intended utilitarian ends or purposes of practical government.

I explained to Floyd that, pursuant to the natural law theory of human rights, however, the specific fundamental rights identified in our Constitution were *already possessed* by each American at the time our founding fathers drafted the Constitution, and that those preexisting fundamental rights were simply acknowledged to exist by the framers; those fundamental rights were not created by the Constitution, nor were they in any way *donated* to us by the founding fathers or by the governing class that they represented. I explained to Floyd that it was my ardent conviction that these fundamental rights flow from a decidedly different source pursuant to the natural law theory of fundamental rights, a theory that has obtained in Western civilization since the earliest days of Jewish, Christian, and Greek cultures and theologies, and that it was *this* theory of human rights that was adopted and enshrined in our American Constitution during the Scottish Enlightenment in the eighteenth century. This specific natural law theory, I reiterated to Floyd, postulates that every human being is endowed by the Creator, not by the founding fathers, and not by some governing class, with "certain inalienable rights," rights that we possess as an *inherent* aspect of our very nature as human beings with consciousness and consciences.

I told Floyd that it was my firm and very carefully considered conviction as to the validity of this specific theory of human rights that distinguished me from the other attorneys in the Cahill-Gordon law firm. But, most importantly, I told him that this was what distinguished me, on that specific morning before our historic oral argument before the United States Supreme Court in the Pentagon Papers case, from Alexander Bickel.

After I had explained my views to Floyd, he said to me, "I want you to go down the hall and sit down with Professor Bickel and explain that exact perspective to him. Make sure that he fully understands it and appreciates it. Because if he does not, I am not going to allow him to present the oral argument before the Supreme Court tomorrow. I will do it myself. Do you understand what I am asking of you?"

I did. And I was deeply moved by Floyd's trust in me and in my beliefs.

So I walked down the hall to meet with Professor Alexander Bickel. I did not hesitate. I knocked and was invited in by Professor Bickel. He seemed to be expecting someone else—Floyd, I think. He had not expected Floyd to send me to deliver the message. Bickel and I had crossed swords on a number of occasions, and he viewed me to be "extreme" in my views. He was genuinely surprised to see Cahill-Gordon approach him with what he now expected to be the "extremist position" that he believed me to represent.

I asked him if he knew why I was there.

"You've come to deliver the firm's 'ultimatum' that unless I am willing to drop my insistence upon conceding the troopship analogy to the Court, I am not going to be allowed to present the oral argument tomorrow."

I could hear—even feel—the sorrow that underlay his tone. Suddenly I felt an unexpected degree of compassion for him that I had not felt earlier when he had held the upper hand over me.

"Actually, professor, I came here today to explain why I feel as strongly as I do that we must avoid allowing the argument before the Court tomorrow to devolve into a mere *factual* question as to whether the Pentagon Papers do or do not contain any specific piece of information that might be felt by the judicial branch of the government to threaten to injure some national security interest of the United States if it is published. I am also here to explain to you how I believe that *you* can keep that from happening."

His demeanor changed immediately, and he asked me to continue.

I repeated everything that I had explained to Floyd, and then I explained how I thought he could present the "separation of powers" argument set forth in the majority's opinion in *Youngstown Sheet & Tube* as the *only* "fallback position" that *The Times* would agree to have tendered to the Court—halfway between my "absolutist" position of principle and his position of "pragmatism." With such an explicit compromise in place between us, I would be willing, I told him, to trust that he would do everything in his considerable scholastic ability not to allow the Court to draw him into accepting—much less affirming—any procedure by which the executive branch, simply with the consent and partici-pation of the judicial branch, could *constitutionally* engage in the creation of a system of prior restraint upon the press, at the very least not without our United States Congress having first enacted a specific statute expressly authorizing this.

When I had completed my presentation, he paused, reflected, and then rose and held out his hand to me. "We have a deal, counsel. You have won your point. The line in the sand will be *Youngstown Sheet & Tube*."

I extended my hand, and we sealed the deal.

When I walked back down the hallway, Floyd was genuinely surprised—and relieved. He had dreaded the prospect of having to tell his mentor from Yale Law School that he was going to be banned from presenting the oral argument to the U.S. Supreme Court.

The next day, June 26, 1971, Alexander Bickel presented our case on behalf of *The New York Times,* and he effectively held the line at the *Youngstown Sheet & Tube* "separation of powers" principle, several times turning away sallies from Chief Justice Warren E. Burger and justices John Harlan and Harry Blackmun, each of whom thought, like the five judges on the Second Circuit Court of Appeals, that the case ought to be remanded back down to Judge Murray Gurfein with the prior restraint against *The New York Times* still in place.

The decision was rendered by the Supreme Court four days later, on June 30, 1971, in *New York Times Co. v. United States.* It was the first and only instance in the entire history of the nine-person United States Supreme Court in which *ten* written opinions were published. There was one per curiam opinion, with which six of the justices concurred, stating simply:

Any system of prior restraints of expression comes to this Court bearing a heavy presumption against its constitutional validity. The Government thus carries a heavy burden of showing justification for the imposition of such a restraint. The District Court for the Southern District of New York, in the *New York Times* case, and the District Court for the District of Columbia and the Court of Appeals for the District of Columbia Circuit, in the *Washington Post* case, held that the Government had not met that burden. We agree.

The judgment of the Court of Appeals for the District of Columbia Circuit is therefore affirmed. The order of the Court of Appeals for the Second Circuit is reversed, and the case is remanded with directions to enter a judgment affirming the judgment of the District Court for the Southern District of New York. The stays entered June 25, 1971, by the Court are vacated. The judgments shall issue forthwith. So ordered.

It was clear that, of the six justices who had ruled in favor of *The New York Times* in the Pentagon Papers case, justices William Douglas and Hugo Black were willing to support *The Times's* argument that no prior restraint of any kind should ever be imposed against any publication. But the other four justices who had ruled in favor of *The Times* had relied upon, instead, the fallback position that I had persuaded Professor Bickel to proffer as our only alternative position: asserting the principle of "separation of powers" set forth by the majority of the justices in the *Youngstown Sheet & Tube* case.

Three justices—Warren E. Burger, Harry Blackmun, and John Harlan—dissented, arguing that the five-judge majority of the Second Circuit Court of Appeals was correct in ruling that the case should be remanded back to Judge Gurfein at the district court level to allow the executive branch more time to present additional arguments and portions of the Pentagon Papers to support its contention that at least those portions should be suppressed and permanently prohibited from being published by *The Times*. But they were overruled by the six-justice majority of the Court.

While Cahill-Gordon was pleased that we had "won," my and Gene Scheiman's response to the "victory" was more muted. We had won 75 percent of what we wanted. But neither of us was used to celebrating a 75 percent performance on a test of this importance. In fact, we were both so exhausted by that time that we each "celebrated" only by going to our respective homes and sleeping for two straight days.

In the final analysis, in my judgment, the overall success that *The New York Times*, Cahill-Gordon, and the American news media as a whole achieved in the Pentagon Papers case was only partial. But this success was due to synergy among four specific interrelated factors that are virtually unknown to the outside world. I am revealing them, for the first time, in this work.

The first factor was the degree to which we were able to convey to United States Attorney Whitney North Seymour the radical light in which *The New York Times* and Cahill-Gordon were going to view—and respond to—the executive branch's effort to secure a prior restraint against *The New York Times*. I believe that I personally convinced Whitney North Seymour, in that very first telephone call on June 14, 1971, that *The New York Times* and the Cahill-Gordon firm were going to take a rigidly absolutist, "no prior restraint under any circumstances" position right out of the starting gate. This, I believe, caused Seymour, in our very first in camera hearing before Judge Gurfein on June 15, to make the very serious tactical miscalculation of thinking that he could get away with asserting that neither counsel for *The Times* nor the court itself possessed the required security clearances necessary to be shown the Pentagon Papers. Seymour mistakenly believed that Judge Murray Gurfein—when confronted by such an absolutist position on the part of *The Times* and Cahill-Gordon—would simply, for the sake of the strictly *legal* argument, take the executive branch's word for it when Seymour asserted to him that the papers, as a matter of fact, contained information that, if published, would "irreparably damage the national security of the United States," and that that argument, once initially accepted by Judge Gurfein *simply for the sake of a hypothetical legal argument,* would be taken by Judge Gurfein to be "the fact of the case."

The second factor in our ultimate success, I believe, was Floyd Abrams's instinctive decision—with which I originally intensely disagreed—to provide Judge Gurfein with a full set of the Pentagon Papers to enable Judge Gurfein to see *for himself* that there were, *in fact,* no traditionally accepted categories of "national security secrets" in the documents *of the nature that Judge Gurfein had himself enumerated at the very beginning of that first in camera hearing.* It was entirely likely that Judge Gurfein might well have sided with the executive branch and made the factual assumption that there were indeed "irreparably damaging" documents contained within the Pentagon Papers—if Floyd had refused his request to see the papers for himself. Such a factual assumption on the part of Judge Gurfein would have compelled *The Times* and Cahill-Gordon to go all the way up to the United States Supreme Court defending an absolutist or purist position against prior restraints on the press alone. And, given even that entirely *hypothetical* assumption *of fact* that the Pentagon Papers did in fact contain information that if published would have indeed "irreparably damaged a national security interest of the United States," we would have lost at the U.S. Supreme Court level, five to four, with both Potter Stewart and Byron White having joined Chief Justice Warren E. Burger, Justice Harry Blackmun, and Justice John Harlan. Instead, because of Floyd's instant instinctive decision—which had shocked both Gene and me at the time—Judge Gurfein was able to review the Pentagon Papers and give *The Times* the benefit of any *factual* doubt pertaining to the alleged damaging nature of the documents . . . which he most assuredly did. So because of Floyd's "graciousness" toward the court, Judge Gurfein's operating presumption, while reviewing the documents, had been that the information would *not* "irreparably damage the national security of the United States" unless he came across one of the "specific categories of information" that he had initially informed us that he believed would cause such damage. When he did not come across such information in the papers— and the executive branch attorneys did not point out any such information to him—Judge Gurfein was then able to rule in favor of *The Times as a matter of fact and law* (even though he did not do the latter very well).

The third factor in our success, I believe, was Alexander Bickel's personal prestige in the eyes of Judge Gurfein, in the eyes of all of the judges on the Second Circuit Court of Appeals, and in the eyes of all of the justices on the U.S. Supreme Court. Alexander Bickel was therefore able to grant to the majority of the judges and justices the abstract principle of there being *some* theoretical degree of "inherent authority" on the part of the federal government as a whole, but was also able to successfully draw a line in the sand and hold that line, insisting that any such system of prior restraint could be crafted only by Congress, which had expressly declined to do so.

Finally, I believe that Floyd Abrams's personal judgment and courage in sending me over to explain the substantive content of my absolutist First Amendment position to Professor Alexander Bickel—and thereby allowing me the opportunity to "surprise" Professor Bickel by providing a way for him to successfully argue his one last, and perhaps finest, case before the United States Supreme Court, when he truly expected me to exercise the power that Floyd had delegated to me to deprive him of that one last opportunity as "punishment" for his years of defying my absolutist convictions about our Constitution—constituted the fourth, and perhaps the most important, factor in our ultimate success in the Pentagon Papers case. Because of the trust that Floyd Abrams put in me that morning before our final appearance before the Supreme Court, I sincerely believe that Professor Bickel modified his longtime personal emotional attachment to his long-held and widely publicized personal belief in the existence of some "inherent authority" residing within the executive branch. Because of that genuine compromise on Professor Bickel's part, Floyd trusted Bickel to successfully navigate his way through to a winning argument before the Supreme Court by "drawing a line in the sand" at *Youngstown Sheet & Tube* and convincing a six-man majority of the justices of the U.S. Supreme Court to make affirmative statements in their written opinions, confirming the legal principle of "no prior restraints against a free press," while at the same time setting forth the most extremely restricted set of principles one could possibly imagine (short of an absolutist position prohibiting any and all prior restraints on the press), constitutionally confining even any future acts *on the part of the United States Congress* that it might conceivably try to establish any congressionally authorized prior restraint system in the United States. In short, the tactic that we collectively adopted at the Cahill-Gordon firm caused the majority of the justices on the United States Supreme Court to issue nothing less than an "advisory opinion" setting forth the very narrowest of conceivable parameters within which any system of "national security," even congressionally enacted prior restraints, would have to fall to avoid being struck down by the Supreme Court.

The Pentagon Papers case represented the high-water mark of the post–World War II effort on the part of advocates of a strong National Security State in the United States to establish their long-advocated principles: (a) that the executive branch is the preeminent branch of our federal government, and (b) that the executive branch of our federal government possesses the same "inherent authority" once claimed by kings to take actions restricting the exercise of fundamental rights on the part of our citizens without any express authority having ever been granted to that executive to act in that manner by any constitutional provision and without the government's legislature having ever granted to that executive any such authority to act in that manner. However, because of the combined efforts of such courageous men as Jim Goodale, Punch Sulzburger, Floyd Abrams—and, yes, even Alexander Bickel—with more than just a little bit of help from their friends like Gene Scheiman, Tony Amsterdam, Michael Tierney, and, yes, Marlene Montanaga, those men were able to affirm the principle that until such time as a popularly elected representative federal legislature has expressly granted to the executive branch and to the judicial branch of our federal government the express joint authority to review, before publication, any public release of information to our people, *no* such system of prior restraint on the press shall be tolerated—and even if and when such a popularly elected representative federal legislature has in fact undertaken to expressly grant to the executive branch and to the judicial branch of our federal government the express joint authority to review, before publication, any public release of information to our people by a professional American news outlet, any such *even Congressionally enacted* system of prior review will have to be expressly confined to information that will absolutely and *clearly* irreparably injure some truly vital aspect of our national security. Outside of meeting those standards, no system of prior restraint shall be approved or participated in by our federal courts.

Since a majority of the justices on the United States Supreme Court proclaimed that principle back in June of 1971, the federal executive branch has not deigned to attempt, through Congress, to secure any such even narrowly confined system of prior restraint. So we, the champions of fundamental human rights, have, to date, successfully held the line against the champions of asserted executive "inherent authority."

However, even the instrumental role that I played for Cahill-Gordon in the Pentagon Papers case did not ensure my survival at the firm.

One of the corporate clients that Cahill represented was A&P: the Great Atlantic & Pacific Tea Company, a well-known and historically respected East Coast grocery store chain. A&P had many stores in the ghetto areas of New York City, up in Harlem and all through the Bedford-Stuyvesant area. However, A&P charged upward of 20 percent more for its food and pharmaceutical products in the ghetto areas than it did in white areas of the city, simply because the management of A&P had come to the conclusion (after undertaking specific "surveys") that the poor black people who lived in those poorer areas in the cities did not have access to public transportation systems that would enable them to engage in comparative shopping. Those poor people would, therefore, simply pay whatever the demanded price was for what they needed, such as food and pharmaceuticals. A&P therefore consciously adopted a policy of discriminatory pricing in ghetto areas. This policy became a subject of some controversy in the summer of 1972.

The Reverend Jesse Jackson founded an organization in Chicago named Operation Breadbasket to protest A&P's (and other food chains') discriminatory pricing. Jackson himself telephoned the office of the president of A&P in New York City and asked to meet with him. An admiring secretary in the office of the president of A&P told Jackson that the company's president had an opening the following Thursday afternoon. But after checking with her boss, the embarrassed secretary told Jackson flat out, "He says that he won't meet with you." Jackson asked her to keep the time period open anyway and said that representatives of Operation Breadbasket would show up regardless.

The following Thursday, at two o'clock, into the office of the president of A&P marched five people: two black Protestant ministers, a black Catholic nun, a white Catholic nun, and a black Catholic priest. They walked in and sat down in the waiting room, waiting to meet with the president.

The president's executive secretary, knowing who they were, went into the president's office and informed him that they were there to meet with him. The president went out into the hall and told them that he wasn't going to meet with them and then went back into his office.

The five members of Operation Breadbasket simply sat there and waited. They waited until five o'clock, at which time the president of A&P came out of his office and uncharacteristically announced to the staff that the workday was over and that it was time for everyone to leave. As he went back into his office to prepare to leave, the activists continued to sit there, waiting. And they went on waiting and waiting. Eventually the president walked past them and left the office. And still they remained there, waiting to meet with him. Two hours later, the president returned to find them still sitting in his waiting room. This time he told them that they were trespassing. But they did not leave. They told him that they had come to meet with him about the company's policy of discriminatory pricing of foodstuffs and pharmaceutical supplies in the ghetto areas of the country. Instead of agreeing to talk, however, the president of A&P called the police. About twenty uniformed New York City police officers showed up, physically picked up the group of nuns and ministers, carried them down the stairs, and then sat them down on the public sidewalk.

When the secretary unlocked the offices at 8:00 AM the following morning, these same two nuns, two ministers, and a priest walked in and resumed their places in the waiting room.

When the president arrived later that morning, he became livid and said, "Get those niggers out of my office!" The president's own secretary, as well as the representatives from Operation Breadbasket, all confirmed that that was exactly what he said. But they still refused to leave until he met with them.

The president then telephoned Larry McKay, the senior partner in charge of litigation at Cahill-Gordon. The president of A&P was furious at these people interfering with his business and holding a "sit-in" in his lobby. He wanted a federal or state court order ordering them to leave his office under the pains of being held in criminal contempt of court and jailed if they refused. The word went out like wildfire, all around Cahill-Gordon, that this troglodyte had asked the firm to do this for him.

Later that morning, I received a call from one of the senior associates, asking me to come up to his office. I didn't know him, and I wasn't used to dealing with associates at his low level; I dealt directly with Floyd Abrams and with the seniormost partners. This bald, cherubic man invited me in, sat down behind his desk, and said, "Well, Dan, I suppose you've heard that the president of A&P has called and has asked Mr. McKay to have us file a motion for a protective order to get the people from Operation Breadbasket to leave his office."

I said that I had heard that and asked him what the firm intended to do about it.

He said, "The executive committee has been meeting all morning about this, and they sort of thought that maybe *you* would do it . . . because, you know, 'You know those kind of people,' and you know all about demonstrations and things like that, about civil rights actions. So the executive committee . . . they thought that it would be good for you to do this for A&P . . . for the firm."

I genuinely thought that he was joking. It didn't even cross my mind that anybody had ever *actually* suggested that. I thought that this was some kind of prank being pulled by Gene and Artie Burns, my other best friend at the firm.

So I said to him, "Yeah, right! What are they *really* going to do about this?"

The young bald man became totally flustered. He didn't know what to say. Here he had been given what I am sure he perceived to be a very important assignment, directly from the executive committee itself, and I hadn't even placed an ounce of credence in what he had said to me.

"Look, this makes me feel really awkward, you know, that they asked *me* to ask you to do this."

Then, suddenly, I realized for the first time that he was *serious*. I looked at him and said, "The absolute most that you could possibly ever expect is for me not to question your personal moral integrity for having anything to do with a thing like this."

He muttered something that at first I couldn't understand. Then I began to make out what he was saying. He was saying that this feeling that had suddenly come over him made him feel exactly like an experience that he had had with his brother, back in the mid-1950s. His brother was going to graduate school at Columbia University and had been writing his PhD thesis on the Rosenberg case—about Julius and Ethel Rosenberg being executed in New York and how Judge Irving Kaufman had refused to give them a stay that would have allowed them time to appeal their execution order to the United States Supreme Court. One afternoon, back then in the 1950s, two FBI agents had come to the door of their family's New York apartment, asking if his brother was there. He told them no, that his brother was out, that he was probably at Columbia University because that is where he went to school. The agents said that they knew that. They said that they had received reports that his brother had been checking books out of the library at Columbia University that had to do with communism and the Rosenberg case. They wanted to know what his brother was doing with these books. A couple hours later, his older brother returned home, and the younger brother told him what had happened. His brother became terrified, ran into his bedroom, and started tearing his room apart, gathering together all of his notes for the thesis that he had been working on for months. He was crying as he gathered up every scrap of paper that contained notes about his thesis and brought them all out into the living room. There, he started putting them into the fireplace and burning them, crying the entire time.

I just sat there and listened to this senior associate telling me this strange story.

"I had this terrible feeling as I stood there watching my brother doing this," the senior associate said to me. "And I have that very same feeling right now."

To this day, I have never been able to figure out exactly what caused that senior associate at Cahill-Gordon to tell me that story. But he didn't seem to have anything more to say to me when he had finished telling me of that experience. So, after a few long seconds of silence, I simply got up and walked out.

I wasn't going to do that case. And, as far as I know, Cahill-Gordon didn't do the case either.

But two weeks later, that same senior associate, whose name I honestly don't even remember, called me on the phone again and asked me to come up to his office. When I was sitting in the same chair in front of his desk, he said, "Look, Dan."

"You can call me Danny," I said.

"What?" he asked, a bit bewildered. This wasn't going to be easy for him.

"I said you can call me Danny. All of my friends do."

"Right. Look, Dan," he said uncertainly. "The partners were very upset at your refusal to do the A&P case for them. And they . . . they've come to the conclusion that you would probably be happier somewhere else, in some other firm or in some other line of legal work."

I said to him simply, "No. I'm fine here. I get to do First Amendment litigation with Floyd and Gene. And we have *The Times* account now, so we'll have plenty of First Amendment work. And I have a specific agreement in place with the partners that says that I can spend half of my billable hours doing pro bono work. They knew when I agreed to come here that I wouldn't perform immoral assignments. I bill more commercial hours here for corporate clients than virtually any other associate, so I'm not interested in going anywhere else. You can tell them that if they don't want to speak with me directly."

With that, I got up and walked out of his office. I'm sure that he didn't know what to do. As I understand it, he must have gone back and reported to the executive committee and communicated our exchange.

A few days later, the same senior associate called me back up to his office again and told me that he didn't think I was ever going to be made a partner at the Cahill-Gordon firm.

I told him that I wasn't the slightest bit worried about that. "I am perfectly happy doing the cases that I do. And I am being paid more money than I have ever seen in my life—more than anybody in the entire history of my family has ever made." I reminded him that because of my billable hours with corporate clients such as *The New York Times* and NBC News, the partners were making a substantial profit by keeping me there.

I continued working on the various matters on which I had been working for several more weeks, doing just what I had always done for the two full years that I had been with the firm. Finally, that same senior associate called me to his office for a fourth time and said, "Look, Dan. This is very embarrassing for me. But I've been instructed by the executive committee to tell you that you have been 'terminated' by the firm."

"Terminated?" I asked. "Does that mean that I am going to be rubbed out, like in the Mafia or something? Or is that like I'm being 'fired'?"

"Oh, no!" he said. "I was specifically told that we at Cahill-Gordon never *fire* an attorney. The executive committee has simply voted to terminate your contract with the firm. They are terminating you."

It turned out that it wasn't quite true that Cahill-Gordon had never fired anyone else before. I was actually the second attorney in the firm's history to be terminated. The other was Alger Hiss, who had been a senior associate at the firm when he went to the State Department in the 1950s. There, while officially on leave from Cahill-Gordon, Hiss had been publicly accused by Whittaker Chambers of being a communist. Chambers testified that Hiss had placed secret State Department documents inside an empty pumpkin, out in a garden in New Jersey, for some "communist agent" to pick up. So Cahill-Gordon had immediately "terminated" him. Moreover, the firm's executive committee had then gone through every single memo Hiss had ever written for the firm and every other document in its files that bore his name and had physically purged his name from every such record.

"I don't think they are going to do *that* to you," the senior associate said. "But you *have* been terminated. They are going to give you two months' severance pay. But you have to leave *now*. You have to leave the office."

Neither Floyd Abrams nor Gene Scheiman ever explained to me what, if anything, they were told about my termination from the firm. They both simply accepted what had been done and never spoke to me about it. Gene has continued to be a close, dear friend of mine, as has Artie Burns. But neither of them ever speaks about my termination from Cahill-Gordon. Indeed, when Cahill-Gordon failed to offer Gene a partnership the first year that he was eligible for partner, he left the firm and became the senior partner in charge of litigation at another major Wall Street corporate law firm. Because all but a very few of the entering junior associates at Cahill-Gordon—or any other of the major Wall Street law firms—ever end up being offered a partner position, my termination was viewed, I believe, simply as an "early notice" that I wasn't going to be made a partner, similar to a professional athlete moving to another professional team because he "wasn't getting enough playing time" where he was. When I next spoke with Floyd after my termination, I was in the midst of the Iran-Contra case, so he viewed me as having done very well after having been terminated by Cahill-Gordon.

Moreover, because I had gone directly to the federal unemployment office and signed up for unemployment, Cahill-Gordon was put in the position of having to go on record as to whether I had been let go for some reason that did not involve any fault on my part or had been "terminated for cause" (fired), because the latter would have disqualified me from receiving unemployment benefits. Larry McKay, as the campaign director, wrote the official Cahill-Gordon letter to the federal unemployment office stating that my employment with the firm had ended as a result of "no misconduct or fault of any kind on the part of Attorney Sheehan." The letter stated that the firm's executive committee had simply come to the conclusion that "The interests of Mr. Sheehan and the interests of the firm's clients are not the same." With the important exception of NBC News and *The New York Times,* which were both clients of Cahill-Gordon, the letter was correct.

So I was awarded full unemployment benefits, which, when added to my two months of severance pay, enabled me to go to work, for free, first as campaign director in the Fourteenth Congressional District in Brooklyn for George McGovern's Democratic presidential primary race (which we won), and then for the national Democratic Party, directing all voter registration for the party in the state of New York until voter registration closed in the first week of October preceding the 1972 presidential election.

As luck would have it, just as those when those two tasks were completed, I received a telephone call from famed Boston criminal defense attorney F. Lee Bailey.

CHAPTER *twelve*

I T WAS THE first week of October 1972, and Lee was clearly looking for something.

"It looks like I am going to be indicted," he said, "by the U.S. postal inspectors . . . for alleged federal mail fraud."

I couldn't help but laugh. "I figured that they would try to do something to you for what you did to them in the Brink's case."

After a few minutes, Bailey got down to business. "Dan, you remember that discussion we had a couple of years ago, about your being willing to come to work for me if you could be one of our three trial attorneys?"

"Sure I do," I replied.

"Well. I've been keeping an eye on what you've been doing since you left law school, and I must say that I am impressed. I'm ready to agree that you can do trials if you'll come join the firm."

"What is it that you want me to do?" I asked.

"Well, the first thing I want you to do is to defend me! I'm going to be indicted for mail fraud along with a guy by the name of Glenn W. Turner. He's the founder of a company down in Florida called Dare to Be Great. I've been his lawyer for a couple of years now, and the feds are charging that I got so deeply involved in helping this guy plan his multilevel marketing plan for his cosmetics and other products that I had become a coconspirator with him. That's a load of bullshit, Dan. They just wanted to cut me away from defending him by putting me in a conflict situation." Bailey said that he wanted me to come on to represent Glenn W. Turner. We'd approach the case by making a Sixth Amendment argument that the feds, by falsely indicting Bailey, were in fact depriving Turner of his Sixth Amendment right to an attorney of his choice.

I was impressed, and I said so. "That's very good, Lee. Maybe it's not true what they say about you: that to you the Constitution is just a ship that sits in the harbor in Boston."

I laughed. Lee didn't.

"Who said that about me?" he demanded.

Surprised that he was so upset about this, I told him that it was one of the people on the *Harvard Civil Rights Law Review*. The truth was that it had been me. If he had cross-examined me on it, I would have confessed. But he didn't.

Apropos of nothing in particular, he said, "You know, I was accepted at Harvard College back in 1950. I was there for two years. I could have stayed, but I left to join the Marine Corps and became a fighter pilot." I didn't know it then, but this was a refrain I would hear over and over again, about how Lee could have stayed at Harvard and been a Harvard man too. "You pricks are so goddamned arrogant about your having gone there. I just couldn't stand it. So I went to BU Law School instead as soon as I got out of the Corps."

I said nothing.

Then he added, "As I recall, you did two years in Army Special Forces. Is that right?" I don't know how he knew that. I had never told him that. When I asked how he knew that, he said, "See! You Harvard smart asses don't know everything."

I could see exactly what was going on here. Lee was genuinely bitter at having been referred to in a number of legal publications as "a second-rate legal mind," which he suspected would never have been said about him if he had a Harvard credential. I had no interest in becoming his whipping boy for all of the "Harvard types" who had disparaged his skills as a legal scholar. I said, "You must have learned of my Army Special Forces years from your famous investigators."

"OK, yes. My investigators. They tell me that you did two years in the Green Berets but that you refused to go to Vietnam. Is that true?"

He was trying to lead me into dangerous territory here. I knew that everyone in Lee's firm was a former U.S. Marine. And Marines were unusually patriotic. But if I backed down now, right at the very beginning of our professional relationship, it would have been much more difficult for me to stand up to him later when other differences of opinion arose. So since I felt I was in the strongest bargaining position that I would probably ever be in with Lee, I decided to step directly into the curveball he had thrown me.

"Absolutely!" I said. "And anybody who really knew the first thing about the foreign policy history behind our entrance into that war, right on the heels of the colonial French, would have refused to go there too."

There was a long silence. I knew he'd taken my comment as a push back against him. But since his objective in this conversation was to persuade me to join his firm as one of his only three criminal defense attorneys—not to get me to agree with him about the legitimacy of the Vietnam War—Lee let the matter drop and turned the discussion back to the matter at hand.

"I want you to join my firm, Dan. And I want you to defend me in this upcoming federal indictment. Will you do that for me, Dan?"

I reflected for only a second or two. Then I said, "Sure. I'll do that for you, Lee. But I want it made clear to everyone at your firm that I am a trial attorney, along with you and Gerry Alch. I am not going to be treated like some kind of desk jockey like John Truman, who you've got in there just because he's Harry Truman's grandson."

"Oh! That's mean . . . but I like that," Lee said. "You just might make a great trial lawyer yet. But remember, I am the only partner in the Bailey firm—even though the name of the firm is Bailey, Alch & Gillis. Gillis is the firm's managing attorney, and Gerry Alch is my senior associate. I am the only partner. You will be my junior associate. Is that OK with you?"

I said that it was. "I'm not big into titles. I just want my function to be made clear to everyone at the firm. That's all. I don't want people mistaking me for some law review geek."

"I don't think there's going to be much of a risk of that happening," Lee said, laughing.

So I accepted the position as the third criminal defense trial attorney and junior associate in the firm of F. Lee Bailey, effective October 1, 1972.

The next morning, I took the Sixth Avenue IRT uptown from my apartment to Democratic Party headquarters on Fifth Avenue and told Pierre Salinger and Joe Grandmaison that I was leaving the McGovern campaign.

I'd started to make arrangements for a commercial flight up to Boston to meet with Lee in person, but then I found out that Lee was sending his Learjet down to New York City to pick me up at Kennedy Airport and fly me to Philadelphia to meet with him there. Lee was concluding a trial for the city comptroller of Philadelphia, who had been accused of embezzling over $5 million from the city.

I packed a week's worth of clothes and took a bus out to Butler Aviation, the private air service that handled Learjets at JFK. "Good Andy," Lee Bailey's personal Learjet pilot (and copilot when Lee was piloting the Lear), was waiting for me. He took my bag and escorted me to the jet, which sat waiting on the tarmac, warmed up and ready to fly. It was smaller inside than I expected, but it was expensively appointed. It had one long, light-brown, soft-leather seat in the rear and three individual brown leather seats lining each side of the cabin.

Lee and his entourage arrived within a couple of hours in a large, heavy, black limo with tinted windows. They were jubilant. He had just won a not guilty verdict on behalf of the newly wealthy former city comptroller (who was $1 million *less* wealthy after paying Lee's legal fee for securing his freedom). His entourage on this specific occasion consisted of "Bad Andy" Tunney, the chief investigator of F. Lee Bailey's wholly owned subsidiary private investigation firm, Delaney & Associates; Al Johnson, Lee's "administrative associate"; and Lynda Bailey, Lee's third wife. As Lee whirlwinded into Butler Aviation, his black suit bag over his shoulder, he quickly shook my hand and welcomed me to the firm. When we were all on the plane, he told us to buckle up, and then he ducked into the pilot's cabin and threw himself into the pilot's seat for takeoff.

I was on the rear seat next to Bad Andy, Lee's big teddy bear chief investigator, who gave me an elbow in the ribs and whispered, "Hold on to your hat, kid. And put on your shoulder straps."

Lee suddenly gave the Learjet full throttle. We were thrown back into our seats as we exploded down the runway. The jet leaped off the ground, and Lee pushed the Lear into an almost vertical ascent. It was what I had imagined a ride atop an Atlas rocket would have been like had I become an astronaut. And the excitement was only just starting. At the very top of the climb, Bailey suddenly nosed the Lear over and did a "victory roll"—a complete 360-degree barrel roll. Then he shot away at the top speed he could pull from the Lear.

I was stunned. Bad Andy and the others broke out in laughter

"Welcome aboard!" he shouted. "Forty thousand feet, here we come!" They had all known that the barrel roll was coming. Apparently this was part of the initiation for new people in the firm.

When we reached forty thousand feet, Bad Andy reached up behind me and pushed a button. A full bar mechanically opened above and behind me. Each liquor bottle was firmly secured in place with a small leather strap. Bad Andy unbuckled and leaped to his feet. He reached up, unsnapped a bottle of vodka and a bottle of Jack Daniel's, took a couple glasses from their firm beds in the bar wall, and shouted to me, "Whatta ya drinkin', lad? I'm a vodka man myself. But Lee and Al are Jack Daniel's men!"

I had never had a drink of either. In fact, I had never had anything more than one sip of beer in my entire life. I could tell from the expectant looks on their faces, though, that this was part of the initiation as well. So I said, "I'll do the Jack Daniel's."

Bad Andy looked a bit crestfallen. But Al Johnson leaped to his feet and shouted, "Gotcha! That'll be twenty bucks!"

Struggling with the bottles and glasses in his hands, Bad Andy melodramatically reached into his sports jacket pocket and pulled out his wallet. With a flourish, he produced a crisp twenty-dollar bill for Al Johnson. He glowered down at me in mock anger. "You owe me one, kid! I bet a twenty that you'd be a vodka man!"

Everyone burst out in laughter.

"What was it? Vodka or Jack Daniel's?" Lee shouted through the open pilot's cabin door. When Al Johnson relayed the news, a whoop went up from the cockpit.

Bad Andy pulled out a silver bucket, filled it with crushed ice, and put some in an eight-ounce tumbler. Then he filled it with Jack Daniel's. As he ceremoniously handed me the glass, he looked seriously into my eyes and whispered, "The test, kid, is to finish the whole glass before we land in Boston."

Everyone laughed again—and I took my first sip of Jack Daniel's.

Bad Andy poured himself a full tumbler of Smirnoff and then poured drinks for Al Johnson and Lynda.

Halfway through his first of two full tumblers of Smirnoff, Bad Andy launched into a story about how Lee had gotten this Learjet to replace the smaller Lear he had purchased only a year earlier. At the center of the story was Glenn W. Turner, the man Bailey wanted me to represent in his mail fraud case.

Turner was the founder, president, CEO, and chairman of the board of Turner Enterprises, based in Orlando, Florida. And Turner was a total character. He was a Tennessee boy, born with a harelip, a cleft palate, and a clubfoot, and he was—and probably still is—the best damned door-to-door salesman who ever lived. When selling Hoover vacuum cleaners, he would come to the door of a home and knock. Even if the home had a doorbell, he would knock on the door. When "the lady of the house" opened the door, Glenn would immediately stick his clubfoot into the door, preventing the woman from closing it. He would then announce in a booming voice, "Hello! My name is Glenn W. Turner, and I'm here to sell you a vacuum cleaner!" He would literally push his way into the house and throw a huge bag of dirt on the woman's carpet. Then he'd vacuum it up, "clean as a whistle!" He would then proceed to sell the woman of the house the very vacuum cleaner that had done this miraculous job. He did this, he told everyone, by selling himself.

After becoming the number 1 Hoover vacuum salesman in the history of that vaunted company, Glenn W. Turner went on to originate the pyramid sales structure, which combined two of his very considerable skills: door-to-door selling and conceiving new schemes through which to make himself rich while enriching others all around him. He founded his school, Dare to Be Great, to train "other down-and-outers like me" to become confident door-to-door salesmen. In 1972, however, this new pyramid sales scheme was viewed by most law enforcement officials and by all business regulators as precisely that—a scheme. They perceived this sales system to be nothing more than a modified Ponzi scheme, designed by Turner to swindle people on the bottom of the pyramid out of their hard-earned money.

Attorneys general from all around the country began hounding Turner with threats of civil lawsuits and even with criminal prosecutions. Glenn called around and started asking people, "Who is the best criminal defense attorney in the whole world?" And many of those people said, "Well, I guess that that would be F. Lee Bailey up in Boston." So Turner decided that he was going to get Bailey to be his lawyer. People warned him that it might be very difficult to persuade F. Lee Bailey to be his lawyer, since he had so many wealthy clients. He was very busy and almost certainly all booked up.

Glenn learned that Lee had been a Marine Corps fighter pilot and that Lee loved to fly. Moreover, Glenn learned that Lee had recently purchased a private Learjet, but only the very smallest and least expensive model available. Lee was, at that time, in and out of Philadelphia, engaged in pretrial hearings, preparing to defend the comptroller of the city on that embezzling charge. So Glenn flew directly up to Philadelphia, intent on purchasing the biggest and most expensive Learjet on the market and parking it right next to F. Lee Bailey's little Learjet. He told the people at Butler Aviation, "F. Lee Bailey is going to be coming in here and asking you whose Learjet that is that is sitting out there next to mine. And I want you to tell him, 'Why, that's Glenn W. Turner's jet, and he's sitting right in the next office, waiting for you.'"

Sure enough, Lee came back from court that day, along with his entourage, and when he saw the huge, expensive Learjet parked next to his, he sent his copilot, Good Andy, inside to find out whose jet it was.

The Butler Aviation exec smiled and said it was Glenn W. Turner's. "He's in the office of the manager waiting to meet Attorney F. Lee Bailey. He wants to talk to him." Good Andy relayed to Lee what he had been told, and Lee walked right into Butler Aviation and introduced himself to Glenn W. Turner.

"So you're the famous F. Lee Bailey?" Turner said. "People tell me that you're the greatest criminal defense attorney in the whole world. Well, I'm the greatest salesman in the whole world. And I want you to be my lawyer. To prove what I'm saying, I'm going to give you one million dollars in cash for just fifteen minutes of your time." He placed his briefcase on a desk and opened it. And there was $1 million in cash. "In just fifteen minutes, I'm going to tell you what it is that I want you to do for me—and you don't have to do it. You get to keep the million dollars. Period. But if you decide that you want to be my lawyer, I'm gonna give you that big Learjet out there, just as a retainer. And I'll pay you whatever it is you want me to pay you to be my attorney—in cash, at the beginning of every week. And you can quit whenever you want to."

So Bailey took the $1 million in cash, gave it to Good Andy to put in the smaller Learjet, and then sat down and listened to Turner. Turner explained how he had gotten into all this trouble—that all these DAs were after him and why. And, of course, Lee agreed to be Turner's lawyer—and he acquired the largest and most expensive Learjet on the market.

Just as Bad Andy was wrapping up his story about Turner and the jet, Lee's voice came over the PA system. "OK, boys and girls. Buckle up. Here we go!"

On cue, Bad Andy started gathering up the glasses to close down the bar. I had finished only half my Jack Daniel's. But not wanting to fail the initiation, I gulped down the last half-tumbler of Jack Daniel's and glided to a landing in Boston. As we touched down and the smoke from the wheels puffed up in the windows on each side of the Lear, Bad Andy shouted, "Ah! Cheated the old Grim Reaper again!" And everybody cheered.

I walked off the plane through the fog of eight ounces of Jack Daniel's that followed me to my meeting with the rest of the staff. I vaguely remember being introduced as "the new trial lawyer in the office," but the introduction didn't have quite the zip I had thought it would because of the whiskey-induced daze I was in.

Lee was officially notified the following Monday morning that he had been criminally indicted with Turner. I prepared and filed a motion challenging the indictment with Judge Gerald Tjoflat, the federal judge on the case in Jacksonville. I also drafted, for Lee to file pro se, a motion to dismiss predicated upon the much more sophisticated theory of discriminatory enforcement. Judge Tjoflat denied both motions to dismiss the indictment, and we appealed it to the Eleventh Circuit Court of Appeals.

While that appeal process was under way, and as I turned my attention to helping Turner with his defense on the substance of the charge of federal mail fraud, we got a call at the office in Boston telling us that Glenn W. Turner had just been indicted by the Orlando County district attorney on the charge of allegedly selling an interest in the profits of his company to the students at his school, which the Orlando DA deemed to be the constructive sale of a security by a person not licensed to sell securities. This trumped-up charge was a direct result of Turner's having refused to pay a bribe demanded by that district attorney. When Glenn showed up for the arraignment on that charge (represented by local lawyer Jim Russ), he was then charged with contempt of court for allegedly organizing "a demonstration intended to intimidate the court" that was taking place in front of the courthouse.

Turner was arrested right off the stand when he pleaded his Fifth Amendment right against compelled self-incrimination, which county judge B. J. Driver took to be a confession of guilt. He had Glenn thrown directly into the Pinellas County Jail. So Bailey's golden goose was now out of operation. He called me into his office and shouted, "You've got to get down there and get him out!"

I was flown immediately down to Orlando by Good Andy on the big Lear, and I immediately filed a federal writ of habeas corpus with the federal district court in Orlando. I argued that the arrest was a transparent violation of Turner's Fifth Amendment rights—which it clearly was. I presented the emergency motion to the federal court and argued the case. Within fifteen minutes, the federal district court judge had issued a written order ordering Turner's release—and ordering the summary dismissal of all charges against him.

I took the federal court order with me from federal court and drove down to the Pinellas County Courthouse. I walked in, went into the jail downstairs, and handed a copy of the court order to the county sheriff, who was a friend of the county court judge who had sentenced Glenn to thirty days in jail for criminal contempt of court. He was also a close friend of the county district attorney who had brought the bogus charges against Glenn. The sheriff said, "Well, I think that it's goin' to take quite some time to do the proper paperwork on this." I told him that was bullshit.

I marched directly downstairs into the lockup and ordered the turnkey to open the cell door, showing him a copy of the federal court order. And there was Glenn W. Turner, crouching in a corner of the tiny cell, in one of those terrible bright-orange jail suits. I grabbed him under the arms, lifted him up, walked him straight out the front door of the courthouse, and drove him back to his home, which was in fact a castle Glenn had built next to his Dare to Be Great school. He was totally at sea—unshaven, unshowered, and unhinged. I told him to take a shower and that I would see him first thing in the morning. And then I left. I must have seemed to him like the avenging angel.

The next morning, when I walked into his Dare to Be Great school for the first time and ascended the glass staircase to Glenn's office on the second floor, there was Glenn W. Turner, in full array. He had on a bright-red Turner-Wear suit coat, matching slacks, white patent leather half boots, and a huge rhinestone American flag pin in his lapel. And he was wearing a dark-black wig.

"You are the greatest lawyer I've ever seen in the whole wide world!" he said, jumping right up on top of his huge marble desk. "You are better than F. Lee Bailey. He would never have come right into that jail and picked me up and carried me out of there. I have never seen anything like that in my whole life! You are my *hero*. You've got to be my lawyer!"

I stammered in the face of this spectacle. "Look, Glenn. I can't be your lawyer. I actually represent Lee Bailey. And, even though the case against him is almost certain to be dismissed, I have to remain available to represent him in his case, in case it is not dismissed. That is what I agreed to do."

Lee retained another attorney to represent Glenn, a young man by the name of Kenneth Michael Robinson, who later wrote a book about Glenn's case, *The Great American Mail-Fraud Trial*.

Soon after, Lee called me from Boston, ecstatic. "Look, if you're going to be representing me down there in Florida, you have to look and act the part." He leased for me a high-end condominium at the Catalina Lodge, the "swinging-est singles condominium complex in Central Florida." It came complete with bare-breasted, bikini-bottomed beauties lounging around the swimming pool at almost any hour of the day . . . or night, and racy-looking, expensive sports cars parked in front of every condo. This meant that Lee had to get me a racy-looking sports car too, which turned out to be a six-speed, racing green 1972 MG GT. Directly across the hallway from me was a condominium occupied by three strikingly beautiful sisters whose brother was a professional jockey at nearby Tampa Bay Downs. They were in Florida "to have a good time" after graduating from high school.

The next thing on Lee Bailey's agenda, as it turned out, was to get me a haircut. Three months out of Cahill-Gordon, I had a pretty well-developed Irish Afro head of hair, though not quite so tightly curled as those of my African brothers and sisters. This was too much for Lee, a former "squared-away" Marine, to bear. So, on the Saturday morning of my first weekend at the Catalina Lodge, I heard a knock on my door. When I opened it, a huge man was standing there. He was my age but 225 pounds, with shoulders bulging under an expensive and obviously specially tailored, light-colored sports jacket. He was wearing sharply pressed dark-blue slacks (the pleats of which you could have cut yourself on if you were not careful) and a pair of Marine Corps spit-polished black half boots in which I could see my own reflection out of the bottom of my range of vision. On the left lapel of his sports jacket was the distinctive Marine Corps pin; on his right lapel, the equally distinctive battle ribbon pin of a Marine Corps Vietnam veteran. I could see my stunned reflection in the mirrored sunglasses he wore. Fixing me with a stare from behind those mirrored lenses, he extended his huge right hand to me.

I carefully extended my own right hand, which he immediately seized and crushed in a vice-like handshake. Glaring directly into my eyes from his mirrored world, he said, "Taylor. Bill Taylor. I've been assigned by Mr. Bailey to be your personal investigator."

Withdrawing my throbbing right hand from his, I managed to say, "That's terrific," and invited him in.

He moved into the living room of my condominium with the wariness of a cat, surveying the surroundings like a well-trained security officer— which, as it turned out, he was. He removed his mirrored sunglasses and began, a little self-consciously, to look around for a chair. I didn't have any furniture in the place yet. All I had were two borrowed tomato-red beanbag chairs from the Jockey Sisters across the hall. So I gestured to one of them and invited him to sit down and take a load off.

"Marines don't sit in beanbag chairs!" he said.

I kept myself from laughing, in the interest of getting our relationship off to a good start, and said, "OK, suit yourself." I threw myself down into the other beanbag chair, letting all the air gush out of it. From that vantage four feet below him, I looked up and said, "I see there that you were in the crotch," which is military lingo for serving in the Marine Corps.

He sort of jerked to attention at this remark, apparently unaware that I had spent time around the military. "Yeah, a few years," he said awkwardly.

"And I see you did a couple of tours in The Nam."

"Three tours," he said.

"Three tours?" I shouted, struggling to get up out of the beanbag. I finally regained my footing and exclaimed, "Holy shit! Stand right there. I'll be right back."

With this, I left Bill Taylor standing in the middle of the living room of my condo as I dashed across the hall to the Jockey Sisters, touched them up for a couple of joints, and then quickly dashed back into my condo. Taylor was still standing there, trying to pretend he wasn't totally confused by what was going on around him.

I returned holding up a joint and said, "Let's burn one—for the Corps! For The Nam!" I lit the joint with a bright-red Bic lighter I had also borrowed from the Jockey Sisters.

A look of horror immediately filled his features. He suddenly backed away from the poorly rolled joint, saying, "Ah, no, I don't do drugs."

"Who the fuck do you think you're bullshitting, Marine? You did three tours in The Nam, and you're standing there tryin' ta tell me that you don't smoke reefer? What the fuck kind of a fool do you take me for?"

I took a big long drag and, holding my breath, held the joint out toward him. After a full six seconds of conflicted resistance, Bill Taylor expelled a huge and explosive laugh. With the experienced touch that had become a virtual handshake between most members of our generation, he expertly plucked it from my outstretched fingers and dragged down a hit that would have felled a full-grown water buffalo in Vietnam. He held it until I released a smoke-filled billow of laughter that caused him to expel his own lungful of smoke into the air. We both almost fell over laughing.

And that's how I met William Taylor, the three-tour Vietnam Marine Corps combat veteran and Marine Corps criminal investigator who was to become my chief investigator for the next forty years.

Midway through our second joint, Taylor confided to me that he had been assigned by Lee Bailey "to get that kid a fucking haircut!" We rolled in laughter again.

Then we set about telling each other our stories. Taylor went first. As a precocious sixteen-year-old from South Boston, he had started working undercover for Detective Sergeant Andrew J. Tunney of the Boston Police Department. Bill would go into bars over on the North End and get served, enabling the Boston Police to shut down bars for serving alcohol to under-aged kids in Boston. It had been Andy Tunney who had later persuaded Bill to join the Marine Corps at the age of only seventeen. In the Corps, Bill had become the initial military source for *New York Times* investigative reporter Seymour Hersh, revealing to Hersh the My Lai Massacre. After three tours in Vietnam, Bill had been reassigned out of Vietnam by the Corps for arresting two CIA operatives who were part of an ultra-secret CIA program known as the Phoenix Project. Bill had personally witnessed them blowing up a downtown Saigon restaurant to assassinate a merely suspected South Vietnamese spy. The devastating collateral damage from the explosion included the death of twenty-two Marines. Bill's trouble began when he refused to release the two assassins after he was directly ordered to do so by his Marine Corps superior. That was how he ended up back in Boston working under Andy Tunney as an investigator for F. Lee Bailey.

I then told Taylor my story, tying it off with my knowledge about the Phoenix Project from what I had read in the top-secret, classified Pentagon Papers. We ended that discussion, the first of what would become hundreds of such debriefings, by vowing to work together to track down and put out of business the dreaded Phoenix Project that had effectively ended Bill Taylor's planned career in the Marine Corps.

In that restaurant bombing case, Bill had eventually tracked down Gunney Mack, a gunnery sergeant who had snuck him out of the Marine Corps brig in Saigon after his detainment for having rearrested the two Phoenix Project operatives, who had been released by his superiors. Gunney had told Bill that one of the men was a regular CIA Covert Operations Directorate agent and the other was a former Miami-based anti-Castro Cuban exile who had been assigned by the CIA to Vietnam. According to

Gunney Mack, the two CIA men had been assigned to blow up that restaurant to kill a South Vietnamese CIA operative who was merely suspected of having been compromised because he was having a sexual affair with a Vietnamese woman, whom the CIA thought might be a source of information for the Viet Cong. The two men's CIA superior wasn't even sure that was true, but he wanted the man killed anyway. And he wanted him killed in a manner that would not generate any suspicion that superiors at the CIA had penetrated their opponent's intelligence network. So the two men ended up blowing up this guy in a public restaurant and killing twenty-two Marines to make it look like the Viet Cong had committed the bombing. Indeed, that bombing was widely reported in newspapers in Saigon and back here in the States as a Viet Cong terrorist attack directed against a restaurant where U.S. Marines congregated. Although Bill had been able to resolve the details of the matter, nobody from the CIA was ever formally charged—and twenty-two Marines were dead.

In many ways, that meeting with Bill Taylor began my career as the hunter, trying to uncover and shut down illegal, clandestine "black operations" of the United States government that I deemed to constitute a "clear and present danger" to our constitutional democracy.

While I was in Florida after getting Glenn W. Turner out of jail in Pinellas County, Lee flew down to Orlando from Boston to make sure that Glenn was OK. He then met with me and said, "I'm going to get somebody else to help defend Turner, and then I'll defend him as well, as soon as you get this indictment set aside. There's something more important I need you to attend to for me." But before starting that project, Lee said I should take a short vacation. I found this strange, but I used the time to help out an old friend from Harvard Law School.

CHAPTER *thirteen*

I took Bailey's offer of a short vacation and flew out to Colorado to help Joe des Raismes, my good friend and law school classmate. Joe had gone to Denver to practice law after graduating from Harvard Law School when I had gone to Cahill-Gordon in New York City. Joe had married Esther Smith, the first of the two women I have loved in my life. Joe had followed Esther to Colorado, where Esther had been offered a position teaching creative writing at the University of Colorado at Boulder. As of January 1973, Joe was working at Holland & Hart, the top corporate law firm in Denver, and he'd volunteered to fill the firm's pro bono position, serving as general counsel for the Rocky Mountain states regional office of the American Civil Liberties Union. This office provided ACLU services for all ten Rocky Mountain states.

Joe des Raismes had been contacted by the ACLU's national office in Washington, D.C., to provide legal assistance to members of the American Indian Movement (AIM) in South Dakota. Joe called me because, in his two previous years with Holland & Hart, he had never been in a courtroom. The Republican attorney general of South Dakota, William "Wild Bill" Janklow, had asked the Nixon administration to send federal troops into the tiny village of Wounded Knee on the Pine Ridge Reservation in South Dakota to suppress a full-scale "Indian uprising." So I flew from Boston to Denver. Joe picked me up and drove me to the ACLU office in Boulder, Colorado.

Joe and I flew almost immediately up to Rapid City, South Dakota, and then we drove out to the village of Pine Ridge at the heart of the reservation. It was an "armed camp." U.S. military vehicles and FBI teams were everywhere. It was almost impossible to get physically close to the occupation site because it was surrounded by FBI and ATF SWAT teams, snipers, and helicopters.

We met there with Ramon Roubideaux, Ken Tilsen, Mario Gonzales, Bruce Ellison, and other attorneys who were holed up in the village, as close as they could get to the fighting going on a few miles north at Wounded Knee. We joined them in trying to determine what we could possibly do in the courts to defuse matters. But matters had gone well beyond that. Roving bands of heavily armed gun thugs, known locally as goons, roamed the reservation in the back of dust-covered pickup trucks, randomly shooting into the homes of people they suspected of being supporters of AIM.

Ignoring this, the FBI and other federal law enforcement officials were there to stop only members of AIM who tried to resist U.S. government "authority" on the reservation.

During the short time I was able to spend away from Lee Bailey's firm that spring, Joe des Raismes and I worked to familiarize ourselves with the political dynamics surrounding the occupation, both national and local. Other attorneys there tried to reach out to representatives of the FBI, ATF, and National Guard, who were on the scene to try to get food, water, and medical supplies to the people besieged inside the village. We made some progress in both areas, though Joe and I were primarily involved in gathering potential evidence for the future defense of these people in state and federal courts. This involved making contacts among the lawyers and members of the Wounded Knee Legal Defense/Offense Committee (WKLDOC, pronounced Wickeldoc) and gathering statements and evidence from AIM supporters who had been assaulted, beaten, and shot at by the goons.

The first case I had to deal with involved federal criminal charges lodged against twelve Colorado State University students who had been charged with "interstate travel to aid and abet those engaged in a civil disturbance," a violation of the Rap Brown Act. That case flowed out of the following facts.

The occupation of Wounded Knee by two hundred members of the American Indian Movement had begun on February 27, 1973. It was to last for seventy-one days. On April 26, 1973, Lawrence "Buddy" Lamont, a longtime AIM activist, was shot in the head by an FBI sniper and killed. AIM leaders sent a message out of the encampment to the FBI asking for a temporary ceasefire during which they could conduct a funeral for Buddy Lamont. While this request was being processed, on the night of April 27, several AIM leaders snuck out through the cordon of armed federal and state law enforcement officials and local goons working for Oglala Tribal Council chairman Dick Wilson. On April 29, the AIM leaders went on a speaking tour of Rocky Mountain–area college campuses, inviting college students from the region to come to Wounded Knee on May 1 to attend the funeral of Buddy Lamont to demonstrate their support for the AIM occupation at Wounded Knee. We had firmly instructed the AIM leaders, including Clyde and Vernon Bellecourt, to make it absolutely clear in their public speeches that the plan was to hold the funeral of Buddy Lamont at Wounded Knee on May 1 but that if federal authorities refused to allow that because of the state of siege they had declared around Wounded Knee, the Buddy Lamont funeral would be conducted instead on the nearby Rosebud Reservation. Despite this clear instruction, South Dakota and federal law enforcement authorities viewed any effort on the part of college students to travel to South Dakota to participate in the funeral to be an act undertaken to "aid and abet those engaged in a civil disturbance" (the operative language of the Rap Brown Act), even though the planned action was to be entirely peaceful. So in the two days leading up to the planned May Day funeral, FBI agents monitored the public speeches of AIM leaders and sent out official FBI communiqués to state and local law enforcement agencies in the Rocky Mountain states, warning authorities to be on the lookout for students attempting to travel to South Dakota to attend the funeral.

On April 30, a dozen students departed from Colorado State University to make their way to South Dakota to attend the funeral of Buddy Lamont. Their planned route took them through Nebraska; they were stopped by state police and arrested in Valentine, Nebraska. Joe and I were contacted immediately by the ACLU and were asked to go to Valentine to appear at the federal arraignment of these dozen CSU students. We were informed that William Janklow, the South Dakota state attorney general who had called in the feds against AIM in South Dakota, was going to make a personal appearance at the arraignment in Nebraska. So Joe and I packed up Ole Bullwinkle (a 1970 Volkswagen camper bus used as an ACLU "official vehicle") and drove down from the Pine Ridge Reservation in South Dakota to Valentine, Nebraska, "The Heart of America."

On the morning of May 1—a day on which activists, labor union members, and anti-fascists around the world celebrate liberation movements—Joe and I went to the federal courthouse in Valentine to represent "the Valentine Twelve" at their federal arraignment. Federal marshals brought the twelve young Colorado State University students into the courtroom in leg irons, handcuffs, and chains. Their belts and shoestrings had been taken from them "so they would not hang themselves out of fear and despair in the face of the serious charges that had been lodged against them," as the marshals explained. Over the admonitions of Joe des Raismes that I not say anything, I approached one of the U.S. marshals and instructed him to release the students from their restraints. Since I was the only "authority" in the courtroom at the time, in a suit and tie and with a legal briefcase, the U.S. marshal obeyed and unlocked the students. I then greeted them, giving them all a hug, and instructed them to take their seats in the jury box. They did, with their shoes flopping on their feet and holding onto their pants so they wouldn't fall down around their knees.

When the United States attorney for Nebraska arrived, along with the state attorney general of Nebraska and South Dakota state attorney general William "Wild Bill" Janklow, escorted by an array of uniformed Nebraska state police, U.S. marshals, and FBI agents decked out in blue blazers, gray slacks, and mirrored sunglasses, they found that Joe des Raismes and I and all the defendants had already taken possession of the courtroom. The defendants were sitting in the jury box, and Joe and I were sitting at the prosecution table, immediately adjacent to the jury box.

It was a moment of truth. The U.S. attorney blinked—and without a protest he took the defense table, farther from the jury box.

The federal magistrate was then announced by the court clerk, and the arraignment hearing was called into session. The U.S. attorney from Nebraska led off by putting his first two witnesses on the stand to testify to the facts to establish that a legally qualified civil disturbance was indeed under way in South Dakota on the Pine Ridge Reservation. Since I had no disagreement with that, I passed on any cross-examination. I was waiting for the arresting officer to take the stand. I noticed, however, that both of the first two witnesses, an FBI agent and a U.S. marshal, had identical manila packets in their laps when they were testifying. I looked around and saw that, indeed, each prospective federal witness had on his lap what looked like an identical manila packet. The third witness to take the stand, a very young-looking man who was also an FBI agent, had had a manila envelope with him, but he did not bring it to the stand. He testified that he had personally attended the rally at the Colorado State University Student Center on April 29 and that he had personally heard Vernon Bellecourt invite as many students as possible to travel to South Dakota to demonstrate against the government. He testified further that Vernon Bellecourt had expressly told students to come to the town of Wounded Knee, even though it was a federally restricted area in which a state of emergency had been officially declared by the United States Justice Department.

Joe looked worried. He whispered that, as he understood it, all the U.S. attorney had to establish to bind over the defendants to trial was probable cause to believe that they had traveled from Colorado to Nebraska to "aid and abet" the occupiers.

"Watch this," I told Joe.

I rose and asked the FBI agent if he had been dressed in his blue blazer with the gold-embroidered FBI insignia on its left breast and gray pressed slacks, mirrored sunglasses, and highly polished shoes when he attended the April 29 rally at CSU. He laughed and said, "No. No, I was not."

I asked him to describe how he was dressed when he attended the rally. He said he had been wearing a pair of blue jeans, a flannel shirt, and a pair of sneakers. I asked him if that was similar to the way most of the students who attended the rally were dressed. He laughed and said, "Just the male students." Everyone in the courtroom laughed.

Then I asked, "So, would it be fair to say that you intentionally dressed to look like a student at CSU when you attended the rally?"

He looked puzzled, as if he had not been instructed what to say about that. He looked over at the U.S. attorney for a sign as to what to do. I noticed this and stepped to one side, saying, "Oh, I'm sorry. I didn't mean to be blocking you from being able to see your lawyer over there. Did you need to consult with him before you can answer that question?"

He got a bit angry and said, "No! No, I don't need to consult with him to answer that. Yes! I was dressed to look like a student. Yes!"

"So, is it fair to say then that you attended that student rally to spy on what you thought was going to be a political speech given by Vernon Bellecourt to a group of CSU college students?" I stepped back in between him and the U.S. attorney so he could not see his lawyer. He grew uneasy and attempted to look around me to get some sign from his lawyer.

"No! That would not be fair to say. I was there to determine whether Mr. Bellecourt was going to be instigating those students to engage in interstate travel to aid and abet those engaged in a civil disturbance in South Dakota on the Pine Ridge Indian Reservation." He seemed quite self-satisfied with that answer. I turned and saw that the U.S. attorney was equally satisfied. I then turned back to the young FBI agent.

"Really? And did you hear Mr. Bellecourt expressly inform the students at that rally that it was not the intention of Mr. Bellecourt or any of the leaders of the American Indian Movement to have students who were being invited to come to Wounded Knee commit any unlawful act of any kind, and that indeed the leaders of the American Indian Movement had expressly asked the U.S. government authorities at Wounded Knee for government permission to hold the funeral of Mr. Lawrence Lamont at Wounded Knee, and that if such express permission were not granted, Mr. Lamont's funeral was going to be held on the Rosebud Reservation, many miles away from the site on which your colleagues have testified that there was a civil disturbance under way? Did you hear him tell them that?"

There was a long silence. He looked genuinely concerned at this question. But, after only a moment or two of hesitation, he said, "No! I never heard him say anything like that!"

I turned to Joe des Raismes, who looked shocked and concerned. I was, of course, delighted. So I turned back to the young FBI agent and asked, "Is this the first time you have been asked to lie under oath as an FBI agent?"

The U.S. attorney for Nebraska erupted. "Your Honor! That is outrageous! He has no basis whatsoever for asking a question like that!"

The federal magistrate, who was a very young man, not much older than Joe des Raismes and I, had been sitting on the bench quite relaxed throughout the testimony up to that point. He leaned forward and said to me, "Mr. Sheehan, is it?"

"Yes, Your Honor. Danny Sheehan from the national office of the American Civil Liberties Union."

He smiled. "Well, Mr. Sheehan, I think you might want to rephrase that question. Or at least precede it with a few preliminary questions attempting to lay a foundation for a question of that nature."

"Certainly, Your Honor." And I turned back to the agent on the stand. "Were you or were you not wearing a body mic at the time you attended the rally in question?"

He looked shocked, like I wasn't supposed to ask a question like that.

The U.S. attorney leaped to his feet. "Your Honor, that question is beyond the scope of this arraignment. Moreover, this question is inquiring into the investigative techniques potentially employed by a federal law enforcement agency engaged in attempting to address a state of lawlessness on a federal reserve! And I object to that question. The government has made no attempt to introduce into evidence at this hearing any such electronically recorded evidence. So that question is beyond the scope of this hearing. The government feels that we have met our very limited burden of proof that we are required to meet at this stage of these proceedings. And I protest Mr. Sheehan's attempt to turn this arraignment into some kind of a trial!"

The magistrate looked down on the U.S. attorney from Nebraska, and I could see him turning over in his mind which side he thought might better further his future career as a potential federal district court judge. Then he said, "Mr. Sheehan, I will allow you just a bit more leeway on your questioning of this witness. But if the witness testifies that he was not wearing a body mic when he attended the rally in question, I am afraid that we are going to have to take his word on what he says he heard Mr. Bellecourt say at that rally. The U.S. attorney is correct in that this hearing is not a trial. It is merely designed to determine whether the government is able to present evidence which, if believed by a jury, could reasonably support a belief that it was more probable than not that these defendants were in fact engaged in interstate travel to aid and abet those engaged in a civil disturbance. You may ask your next question."

I repeated my question. "Were you or were you not wearing a body mic capable of electronically recording the statements that Mr. Vernon Bellecourt made to these students on April 29th of 1973?"

The young FBI agent looked at me for a long moment, and then he said, "No. No, I was not."

I turned to Joe des Raismes, who looked crestfallen. Then I turned back to the witness. "No more questions."

The next witness to take the stand was the Nebraska state highway patrolman who had arrested the twelve CSU students.

The U.S. attorney from Nebraska, now smelling victory, took the officer carefully through his paces, describing how the state highway patrolman was supposedly undertaking a set of "routine safety inspections" on Interstate 80 when he just happened to encounter these defendants on their way to South Dakota to demonstrate their support for the people occupying Wounded Knee, which he said they readily admitted to him. So he arrested them.

I rose to cross-examine him and noticed that the state highway patrolman had his manila envelope on his lap. The young FBI agent who I had just questioned now also had his identical manila envelope on his lap again.

I asked the Nebraska state highway patrolman to describe exactly how and why he was conducting a set of "routine safety inspections" on that particular portion of the interstate on that particular day on which he just happened to encounter these defendants. He explained that he had pulled his patrol car across the thruway, causing vehicles to have to slow down and go around his vehicle, driving onto the edge of the grass.

I was intrigued. "Well, were you, for example, measuring the depth of the tire treads on the tires of these vehicles?" He said he was not. I asked him if he was stopping each vehicle and checking to make sure that its headlights and taillights were working properly. Again, he said that he wasn't. I asked if he was checking each vehicle's brakes to make sure they were working. No, he said. So I asked him, "Exactly what were you doing to conduct this set of safety inspections if you weren't doing any of these logical things?"

He said that he had simply positioned his patrol car so that each vehicle would have to slow down and go around him and that he could then check their license plates to see if they were local and look into the vehicles and see whether he recognized the drivers as being "from around there." And if he didn't recognize the driver, he would "stop them and ask them where they were going and why."

Now I was getting somewhere. I made certain to keep myself directly between the state highway patrol officer and the U.S. attorney so that the U.S. attorney could not signal him to stop his line of answers. Then I turned and gestured to the twelve CSU students sitting in the jury box. "Well, officer. Can you tell me why, exactly, you happened to stop these particular defendants?"

He looked at me quizzically and then said, "Well, they were driving a Datsun!" He did not say that they were driving an out-of-state vehicle or that he hadn't recognized them, as might have been suggested by his prior testimony. He said that he had stopped them simply because "they were driving a Datsun." I couldn't for the life of me figure out what this meant.

"Exactly why did the fact that they were driving a Datsun cause you to stop them?"

"Well, it was a Datsun, one of them foreign cars. They all drive them foreign cars!"

I was baffled. I couldn't figure out where this was going. "Who? Who 'all drive them foreign cars'?"

He looked at me as if it should have been obvious. "Students! White hippie-type students. They all drive them foreign cars!"

Then it came to me. "That term, *white, hippie-type students,* that sounds a bit like some kind of a term of art. Can you tell me . . . where did you get that particular phrase?"

He beamed at me. "It was right there . . . in the communiqué!"

I didn't hesitate. "What communiqué was that?" I asked.

"The FBI communiqué—from Omaha!"

Bingo. There it was. "The FBI communiqué from Omaha? Then I assume that you read that communiqué?"

"Sure. Sure, I read it," he replied.

"And, is it safe for me to assume that you also reread that particular communiqué prior to your coming here today to testify?"

He looked a bit puzzled. But then he said, "Yes. Yes, I did."

"And would it be fair to say that you reread that particular communiqué today before coming here to testify in order to refresh your recollection as to exactly what that communiqué said so you could testify accurately about it here today to this magistrate?"

Again, he looked a bit puzzled, and then he said, "Well, yes. Yes, that's why I reread it."

He looked a little baffled, but then he looked directly down at the manila packet that he had on his lap and then back up at me and said, "Yeah, sure, I read it again today."

"And that was so that you would be sure to get it exactly right . . . what it had said in that communiqué. Isn't that right, officer?"

"Well, yeah," he said, still puzzled as to where I was going with this.

"Would I be correct in assuming that that communiqué is right there in that manila envelope that's sitting there on your lap right now, as you are testifying today?"

He looked back down onto his lap at the manila envelope lying there, just as it was lying on the lap of every witness the U.S. attorney planned to call to the stand that day. And then he said, "Yeah. Sure. There is a copy of it in there."

As soon as those words cleared his lips, I immediately stepped forward, leaned into the witness box, physically snatched the manila envelope off his lap, and turned with it in my hands toward Joe des Raismes, who was sitting at the counsel table paralyzed with shock at what I had done. I tore open the clasp on the envelope and poured out all the contents onto the table in front of Joe. And there it was—the tape of the young FBI agent's body mic recording of Vernon Bellecourt's speech at the CSU rally! It was even labeled.

The U.S. attorney from Nebraska leaped to his feet and began screaming. "Give that back! Give that back!" He turned to the federal magistrate. "Your Honor! Your Honor! Make him give that back! That is sensitive federal investigative information! That is classified information!"

The federal magistrate had stood up from behind the bench and was shouting at me. "Mr. Sheehan! Mr. Sheehan!"

I turned and held up the tape cassette in my right hand. It was clearly labeled as the agent's April 29 recording of the Vernon Bellecourt speech at CSU.

"Your Honor! I wish to introduce into evidence defendants' exhibit A, the electronic body mic recording of the speech of Vernon Bellecourt delivered to these defendants, attesting to the fact that FBI agent X—— has committed perjury before this court and that the United States government itself is in possession of absolute dispositive proof that these defendants traveled to this state, on their way to South Dakota, with the express intent of not violating any state or federal law. And every one of those men sitting there before you today knew this to be the truth, and they just sat here before you and suborned that perjury of this young FBI agent in order to cause you to unjustly imprison twelve innocent college students. I move that this court secure a tape recorder and play this tape in open court to prove, beyond any reasonable doubt, that my clients are totally innocent of the charge leveled against them in this courtroom today! Surely, Your Honor would agree that this fact is determinative of this case, even here at the arraignment stage of this case."

I handed the cassette tape directly to the federal magistrate and awaited his decision. Joe des Raismes sat stunned at the counsel table. The U.S. attorney was spitting in fury.

South Dakota attorney general William Janklow jumped to his feet and shouted, "Your Honor! Your Honor! I object!"

The magistrate stood and glared down at the assembled government attorneys and law enforcement officers, the cassette tape recording held high in his hand.

"Gentlemen!" He waited for the din to die down. Then he turned to his law clerk and asked for the tape recorder he kept in his chambers. "Gentlemen. We are going to get to the bottom of this crucial question of fact as to whether these defendants were personally told by Mr. Bellecourt that they would be violating no law and that Mr. Lamont's funeral would in fact be held on the Rosebud Reservation if permission were not granted by the United States government to hold his funeral at Wounded Knee."

The law clerk set up the recorder on the witness stand. When he pressed "play," the voice came out loud and clear. It was Vernon Bellecourt explaining in full detail exactly what we had represented to be the true facts to the court. When the recording stopped, the magistrate announced that he would take final arguments from both sides.

Because the U.S. attorney from Nebraska was in direct jeopardy of being criminally convicted of suborning perjury before the court, South Dakota attorney general William Janklow rose to present the closing argument for the government. Janklow started by insisting that the information on the tape recording be rejected by the court as being "beyond the scope of an arraignment." He argued that the government, through the young FBI agent, had presented credible evidence that, if believed by a jury, would support a reasonable belief that the defendants had engaged in interstate travel to aid and abet those engaged in a civil disturbance—so long as the information on the tape recording was disregarded by the court. Janklow also insisted that the court ignore the information on the tape because of the unorthodox manner in which the tape had been obtained and presented to the court. His conclusion was dramatic: "Based upon all of the information available, it is clear that any mongoloid idiot would conclude that these defendants were on their way to Wounded Knee to aid and abet those engaged in a civil disturbance." And he sat down.

"Mr. Sheehan, your reply?" the magistrate asked.

I rose and said, "I agree with South Dakota State Attorney General Janklow, Your Honor." And I turned and sat down.

A surprised hush fell over the court. The magistrate looked bewildered. "You agree with Mr. Janklow?" he asked.

I stood back up. "Yes, Your Honor. I agree with Mr. Janklow that, based upon all the information available to this court—which of course would include the government's own official tape recording of Mr. Bellecourt's exact statements made to these defendants—that 'any mongoloid idiot' would, indeed, based on this information, conclude that these defendants were on their way to Wounded Knee to aid and abet persons engaged in a civil disturbance."

Then I sat down again.

A silence filled the room. After a long moment, it suddenly began to dawn on the federal magistrate exactly what I had said. He slowly broke into a broad grin, then a chuckle, and finally into a loud laugh.

I rose and repeated my statement.

"Mr. Janklow is right, Your Honor. After listening to that tape recording, one would have to be a mongoloid idiot to have concluded that these defendants were on their way to Wounded Knee to aid and abet persons engaged in a civil disturbance."

Everybody in the courtroom then broke out into laughter. Everyone except for William Janklow, that is. He leaped from his chair and dashed across the courtroom at me, shouting, "Are you calling *me* a mongoloid idiot?" He actually tried to leap across the counsel table after me. I rose up and stepped back, allowing him to fall prostrate on the table.

I laughed and said in a loud voice to the magistrate, "The defense rests, Your Honor! I move that all charges be dismissed against these defendants!"

The magistrate, almost unable to contain himself in laughter, banged his gavel repeatedly and proclaimed, "Motion granted! Motion granted! This case is dismissed against all of the defendants. The U.S. attorney, FBI Agent X——, and Mr. Janklow—if someone will get him up off the prosecution's table—will report to me in my chambers immediately." And, turning to the defendants, he said, "Gentleman, you are free to go. And you can travel to South Dakota if you wish. This is the United States of America, and you are free to go where you wish." He banged his gavel down, bringing the hearing, and the case, to a close.

With that, it was time for me to return from my "short vacation" and fly back to the Bailey firm in Boston. When I had first agreed to join the firm in October 1972, I did not realize that it had been the Bailey firm that had been retained to represent Watergate burglar James McCord. I, of course, knew there was a major scandal swirling around the burglary, but I was so deeply enmeshed in other work that I knew no more about the details surrounding that event and case than those that had been reported in the media. However, very quickly I was informed that "the Watergate burglary case is in the office; we are representing James McCord." *Wow,* I thought to myself. But because Lee had asked me to work exclusively on his case and Glenn W. Turner's case, I was simply following events surrounding that case that were reported in the news. I was not "online" inside the office on the Watergate case. Those activities were all taking place up in the Boston office while I was in Florida.

James McCord was an allegedly retired CIA wiretapping specialist who had been arrested with four anti-Castro exile types including Bernard Barker and Frank Sturgis, inside Democratic National Committee headquarters in the Watergate Hotel on the night of June 17, 1972. While I was in Florida working on the Turner and Bailey case in March of 1973, I heard on the news that McCord had written an explosive letter to Judge John Sirica, the federal judge to whom the criminal case of McCord and his codefendant Watergate burglars had been assigned, blowing the whistle on Richard Nixon and a team of burglars working for Nixon out of the White House. But I had been told nothing about the rift that had apparently developed between McCord and Gerry Alch, Bailey's senior associate.

In May 1973, when I returned from Wounded Knee, Lee asked me to turn my attention to the Watergate burglary case. I was surprised, because Lee had not said anything to me about the case prior to that request. Lee asked me to first monitor the live hearings of the Senate Select Watergate Committee investigating the Watergate burglary and to report directly to him any important information generated during those hearings.

Therefore, on May 23 and 24 of 1973, I was listening to live sworn testimony on television from a motel room in Orlando until I could be flown to Washington, D.C., to attend the hearings in person. Bill Taylor was sitting in the room with me.

On that morning of May 23, Gerry Alch testified before the Senate Select Watergate Committee. He first read a prepared statement outlining his representation of Watergate defendant James McCord. In his prepared statement, Alch denied McCord's claim that Alch had tried to "pressure him" into remaining silent concerning who in the White House had authorized him and his fellow Watergate burglars to burglarize Democratic headquarters and to wiretap the telephones of DNC chairman Lawrence O'Brien in exchange for a promised grant of clemency from President Richard Nixon. The following morning, Bill Taylor and I were seated at the feet of the two beds in the hotel room, preparing to monitor Alch's continued testimony. Lee came into the room and stood directly behind us as we all intently watched the live coverage of the hearing on TV, awaiting Gerry Alch's cross-examination by the senators and their staff counsel.

Senator Sam Ervin of North Carolina, the chairman of the Watergate Committee, and Senator Daniel Inouye of Hawaii started grilling Gerry Alch about McCord's accusation. From their questions, it became clear immediately that senators Ervin and Inouye both believed that Gerry Alch had had a closed-door meeting with Watergate burglar E. Howard Hunt's attorney, after which Alch had indeed communicated to James McCord that "someone from the White House was going to be contacting him about a possible offer of clemency from the White House if he agreed to remain silent about who, in the White House, had authorized the burglary." Both senators emphasized that they knew that Jack Caulfield, a member of Richard Nixon's White House staff, had in fact contacted McCord shortly after Alch had spoken with McCord and had indeed discussed with McCord the possibility of executive clemency—if he refrained from revealing the fact that Attorney General John Mitchell and other high-level White House personnel had known about and had expressly authorized the Watergate break-in. Then Senator Inouye started grilling Alch about the fact that James McCord had contacted F. Lee Bailey's firm, originally to get Lee Bailey himself to defend McCord. Senator Inouye pointedly started interrogating Alch about his status as "an employee" of Bailey and about the fact that Lee Bailey was, at that time, under federal criminal indictment in the Glenn W. Turner case in Florida. His questioning strongly suggested that one might reasonably conclude that F. Lee Bailey might have been involved in "doing a favor for someone very high up in the White House" in exchange for more favorable treatment in connection to his federal indictment.

At the moment that question was asked, Lee rushed out of the room. Bill and I could hear him depositing quarters into a public pay phone out in the hallway. This struck both Bill Taylor and me as very peculiar, because Lee made quite a show of always carrying a special briefcase that contained a large portable telephone, a military-style walkie-talkie with an antenna and a battery pack. Bill Taylor had told me that the phone was scrambled and that Lee used to speak regularly to someone, always out of earshot of everyone else in the firm. Why hadn't Lee used this "field phone" to telephone whomever it was he was talking to?

"What the hell was all *that* about?" I asked Bill. Bill looked at me and kind of shrugged and said he didn't know. Through the closed hotel room door, we could hear Lee's low and intense voice. "Well, find out!" I said, more than a bit irritated.

Lee said nothing to either one of us when he came back into the room. Instead, he simply picked up his briefcase and left. We both shrugged, and Bill said he would look into it.

It took Bill two days to get back to me. I was in the conference room at the Gold Key Motel, at a briefing of Kenneth Michael Robinson, the new attorney Lee had retained to represent Glenn W. Turner so I could work on the Watergate case. Bill came quietly into the back of the room and worked his way over to me. He asked me to step outside to speak with him.

Bill told me that he had spoken the night before with Andy Tunney to get Andy to tell us what was going on behind the scenes in our Watergate burglary case. Andy had said to Bill, "You two boys are nice boys. You don't want to get involved in something like this."

Bill had pushed back, insisting that we really wanted to know what was going on—that we *needed* to know—because Lee had assigned us to work on the case.

But Andy had refused to budge. "You two boys should just get out of Dodge," he said, even going so far as to suggest that Bill and I should consider leaving Bailey's firm entirely, to avoid becoming involved in "something like this." But he wouldn't tell Bill what the "this" was all about.

Bill persisted and finally got Andy to go out for a few drinks with him, knowing that that would loosen Andy up. They went to a bar far enough away that neither of them would be recognized, and Bill began buying Andy drinks. Then he started asking Andy, again, to tell him what he knew about the Watergate case. Bill told me that Andy was on the brink of tears, pleading for Bill to stop asking him what was really going on in the case. But after another couple of drinks, Andy finally began to open up.

Andrew J. Tunney, the former commander of the Massachusetts State Police Special Task Force on the Boston Strangler, told Bill Taylor, on the night of May 26, 1973, that F. Lee Bailey was on "Index 4." Bill and I had never heard of Index 4 before. Andy explained to Bill that Index 4 was a highly classified list of four accomplished American criminal defense attorneys who had been covertly retained by the Central Intelligence Agency to defend active agents of the CIA if they were ever arrested in the midst of conducting a CIA covert operation *inside the United States*. Two of the other attorneys on Index 4 were Edward Bennett Williams and Henry Rothblatt. Rothblatt in fact ended up representing Watergate burglary coconspirators Frank Sturgis, Virgilio Gonzales, Eugenio Martinez, and Bernard Barker— all of whom had histories of working directly for the CIA.

I was shocked because it was—and still is—totally illegal for agents of the Central Intelligence Agency to engage in any form of covert operation inside the United States. Such action is expressly prohibited by the National Security Act of 1947, pursuant to which the CIA was created on July 26, 1947. I was also shocked that Lee would have agreed to this without inform- ing any of his associates in the firm. And finally, I was shocked to be con- fronted by the very real possibility that our firm's representation of James McCord might therefore, indeed, be some kind of covert operation itself, and that we were unknowingly being dragged into such a covert operation without ever having been informed of this fact by Lee.

Andy then told Bill that when Lee had been contacted to represent James McCord, he had reached out to Santo Trafficante, the don of the Mafia in southern Florida, who was also the don in Cuba. As I would later learn, Trafficante was also a CIA asset, so Lee was convinced that Trafficante would be able to brief him on what was actually going on behind the scenes in the Watergate case. I remember being especially surprised when Bill told me this because neither Bill nor I had any idea that Lee had a line of com- munication to Santo Trafficante. We also had no idea why Lee had reason to expect that Trafficante, an organized crime figure of that magnitude, would know anything about the Watergate break-in, or that Trafficante would, in any event, have had any reason to agree to brief Lee Bailey about what- ever he did know. Bill had asked Andy about this and was told that Lee Bailey was, in fact, Santo Trafficante's principal criminal defense attorney. Henry "Hank" Gonzales of Florida, who held himself out to the public to be Trafficante's principal criminal defense attorney, was nothing more than a front, disguising the fact that Bailey was the real attorney for Trafficante— and therefore for the Mafia.

Both Bill and I knew that Lee was the attorney for the Angiulo Brothers, a major Italian Mafia family in the North End of Boston. But this was the first time either of us had heard anything of this magnitude about Lee.

Andy explained to Bill that, in fact, he was the person Lee had assigned to debrief Santo Trafficante about the Watergate burglary. This was surprising because I thought, at the time, that Lee would have wanted as few people as possible to know whatever it was Trafficante was willing to say about that. I remember wondering why Lee would not have wanted to debrief Trafficante himself. We later learned the reason: Andy had lived in Henry Gonzales's guesthouse in Miami for months and had become personally familiar with Trafficante during that time. Andy had kept this a secret, for obvious reasons. He didn't want anybody to know that he even knew Santo Trafficante.

All these revelations were a total surprise to me, but that wasn't the most important or alarming information that Andy told Bill that night. The following is a summary of what Trafficante told Andy in 1972 about the Watergate break-in.

Santo Trafficante, Andy said, knew all about what had happened in the Watergate burglary because the anti-Castro Cuban types involved in the burglary—Bernard Barker and Frank Sturgis were both direct former mob associates of Trafficante in his capacity as the don of the Mafia in Havana. Trafficante had remained very close to these men after they had fled Cuba together when Castro took control in January of 1959. Trafficante's close relationship with these anti-Castro Cubans had continued even when these men became operatives of the CIA in Miami, working on a secret project code-named Operation 40, designed by the CIA to undermine the stability of the new Cuban revolutionary government. Trafficante had maintained contact with the anti-Castro Cubans who had fled with him, particularly with Bernard Barker when he went to work for E. Howard Hunt in 1971, when Hunt operating directly out of the White House.

Santo Trafficante had told Andy, during this debriefing in 1972 following the burglary, that two of the Watergate codefendants, Frank Sturgis and E. Howard Hunt, who had helped plan and supervise the Watergate break-ins, were former CIA "case officers" for Barker, Gonzales, Martinez, and dozens of other former Trafficante Cuban Mafia associates from Havana who had fled Cuba with Trafficante in January 1959. Some of these former Trafficante associates had become covert operatives in that same Operation 40.

However, Trafficante then told Andy that he had personally recruited a dozen former anti-Castro Cuban Mafia associates, who had earlier been recruited as members of Operation 40 by the CIA, to become members of a team to assassinate Fidel Castro, Raúl Castro, Che Guevara, and five other leaders of the Cuban revolutionary government. This select group was code-named the S-Force by Trafficante. He told Andy that the S-Force had been organized in July 1960 by then Vice President Richard Nixon.

During his eight years as vice president, Nixon had been the chairman of the 5412 Committee of the National Security Council, which oversaw all covert operations of the U.S. government. As chairman of the 5412 Committee, Nixon had developed a close personal relationship with billionaire Howard Hughes, who had become a "special consultant" to the National Security Council. Hughes created a business called the Summa Corporation that produced clandestine technology, such as the Glomar Explorer for the NSC, which could pick crashed Russian submarines off the bottom of the ocean so that Russian technology could be analyzed and the all-important codebooks in any such Russian submarine could be recovered from the submarine. According to Trafficante, once Nixon was confident he was going to secure the Republican Party nomination for the presidency in July 1960, he called Howard Hughes on the ultra-secure phone through which Nixon and Hughes communicated and said that he wanted Hughes to set up a team to assassinate Fidel Castro and other leaders of the new Cuban government. Nixon solicited Hughes's help to get this done in a manner that would keep the responsibility for such an operation completely away from the White House.

Trafficante informed Andy that Hughes turned that task over to one of his new attorneys, a former FBI agent by the name of Robert Maheu. Maheu then reached out to Johnny Roselli, the liaison in Las Vegas for Mafia boss Sam Giancana of Chicago. Johnny Roselli was Giancana's "bag man" in Vegas for Giancana's casinos. Maheu explained to Rosselli that it was Richard Nixon who wanted this done, but Maheu raised the fact that Castro had shut down all the Mafia's gambling casinos and prostitution houses in Cuba and had shut off the all-important supply of heroin coming through Cuba from Southeast Asia. So the Mafia had its own reasons for wanting to get rid of Castro. After hearing Maheu's proposal for the creation of this assassination team, Roselli had flown back to Chicago and set forth this request from Nixon to Sam Giancana.

Giancana said that any decision like that was within Santo Trafficante's jurisdiction within the Familia. Even though Trafficante had left Cuba, he was still the Mafia boss of Havana, so Trafficante had to be the one to make such a decision. So Giancana, Roselli, and Maheu all flew down to Miami and had three strategic meetings with Santo Trafficante in July 1960 at the Fontainebleau Hotel. During the second of these three meetings, they agreed in principle that they were open to doing "this thing," but Trafficante wanted to be absolutely certain that the direction was coming from Nixon himself and that a decision of this magnitude was not simply some pipe-dream on the part of Maheu or Howard Hughes. So Trafficante had insisted on receiving some kind of direct signal from Nixon himself for confirmation.

So, when they convened their third meeting, a man who used the nom de guerre of Mr. Ed joined them. This man, according to Trafficante, was Sheffield Edwards, the chief of security of the Central Intelligence Agency under Richard Nixon. Trafficante told Andy that Sheffield Edwards person-ally gave him the green light to go forward with this project, which satisfied Trafficante, who agreed to move forward and do what Nixon had asked.

However, Trafficante, being the wise guy that he was, wanted to use his old gunmen who had now been recruited to work for the Central Intelligence Agency to make up this special assassination team. That way, if his gunmen were caught, the trail would lead straight back to the CIA, and the agency would then have to step in and help cover up the involvement of the team. So Trafficante selected fifteen men from among his former Cuban gunmen who were then working for the CIA in Operation 40. To finance that team, Trafficante and the Mafia skimmed cash off casinos in Las Vegas. They drove the cash all the way to Miami, where it was deposited into the Miami National Bank, owned by Meyer Lansky.

The fifteen men were periodically picked up by a private plane from paramilitary bases throughout the Southeast and flown directly to Fort Huachuca in Arizona. They would "sign in" there but then would immedi-ately disappear. Trafficante said these fifteen men were flown directly from

Fort Huachuca down to Oaxaca, Mexico, to a large private ranch owned by Clint Murchison Jr., who owned the Dallas Texans professional football team. At the ranch in Oaxaca, these men were trained in triangular fire team assassination techniques using high-powered rifles. Funds from the Las Vegas skim that had been deposited into the Miami National Bank were wired from the Miami National Bank to the International Credit Bank in Geneva, Switzerland, and from there to Banco Internationale in Mexico City. The account in Mexico City was handled by an attorney named Manuel Ogarrio, and money drawn from that account financed the private planes, equipment, and additional expenses of the S-Force.

However, Richard Nixon had not been elected in November of 1960, as he and all of his associates in this assassination enterprise had assumed he would be. Instead, John F. Kennedy had been elected. But the S-Force was continued, since it had now been established to run independently from the White House—or from any other official government agency. It did, however, have CIA "handlers" made up of its former CIA trainers.

By the spring of 1972, Howard Hughes had become a veritable vegetable, with long fingernails and hair down his back, and a power struggle for control broke out inside his empire. Lawrence O'Brien, his longtime D.C. lobbyist, evidently lost this power struggle. Within weeks of leaving the Hughes organization, O'Brien was named head of the Democratic National Committee. Nixon became terrified that Larry O'Brien, in his capacity as chief lobbyist for Howard Hughes for so many years, might have come to know about Nixon's direct involvement in putting together the S-Force assassination team, which essentially combined elements of organized crime, the anti-Castro Cuban exile community in Miami, and the CIA. Nixon felt that the public revelation of his direct involvement with that team was the only thing that could generate any conceivable possibility that he might lose the upcoming presidential election to George McGovern, and he wanted to find out what Larry O'Brien knew about this very sensitive issue.

Barker, Gonzales, Martinez, and Sturgis were therefore personally selected by Nixon to burglarize the Democratic national headquarters, because they already knew about Nixon's involvement. The Watergate burglary operation was to be run by E. Howard Hunt because he had been the CIA liaison officers who had overseen and coordinated the activities of the S-Force—so they too knew about Nixon's involvement in that sensitive operation. To put in the wiretaps, however, they had had to secure the expertise of a former CIA specialist in that field: James McCord. Nixon then ordered the Watergate burglars to go into Larry O'Brien's office in the Watergate building, wiretap his telephones, and search for documents that might reveal the fact that O'Brien knew about Nixon's involvement in creating the S-Force.

DNC headquarters in the Watergate Hotel had in fact been burglarized more than once by that team. The wiretaps and bugs were first placed in late May. But one of those wiretaps had stopped working, so on June 17, when the team went in to replace that wiretap and to photograph documents, they were caught red-handed by a night watchman. Hunt and one G. Gordon Liddy (a high-risk-taking former FBI agent who had become part of the White House "Plumbers' Unit"), who were outside on radios, were arrested later.

On June 23rd, within one week of the break-in, Nixon got word that Patrick L. Gray, the new director of the FBI, was being pressured by other high-level FBI officials to investigate the origins of a check found in Bernard Barker's sports jacket pocket when he was arrested inside the Watergate headquarters of the DNC. The check had been cleared through the very same bank account in Mexico City where funds had been previously directed to the S-Force. Gray was calling to find out whether an investigation of that bank account was going to cause any trouble for the White House. When Nixon learned of Gray's inquiry, he ordered his White House chief of staff, H. R. (Bob) Haldeman, to go with John Ehrlichman over to the CIA and to tell Richard Helms and Vernon A. Walters, the director and deputy director of the agency, that if they didn't get the FBI out of that particular investigation immediately, all "the Mexico stuff about the Bay of Pigs guys" could come out. That was the famous "smoking gun conversation" that resulted in the House Judiciary Committee's returning an article of impeachment against Richard Nixon for obstruction of justice.

However, when Bob Haldeman and John Ehrlichman went over to the CIA and personally delivered that message, Richard Helms became furious.

Still, he called Patrick L. Gray that very afternoon and ordered the FBI to stand down from that part of the investigation. Pat Gray then refused to authorize FBI deputy director Mark Felt to go down to Mexico City to investigate the Ogarrio bank account.

After Bill Taylor's meeting with Andy Tunney, in which Andy conveyed all the politics and corruption behind the Watergate scandal, neither I nor Bill Taylor had any difficulty in deciding that Lee Bailey's firm was not the place for us.

However, I still had to return to Bailey's office in Boston. As soon as I arrived, Lee called me in to see him.

When I stepped into his office, he was all smiles.

"I understand you were out in South Dakota for your short vacation, at that occupation thing going on out there. Is that right?"

"Yes, I was," I replied.

"Well, which side of it were you on?"

I was puzzled by Lee's question. "Well, actually, I wasn't on either side." I told him that I was there on behalf of the ACLU and one of my good law school friends.

Lee wrinkled his brow. "Well, like what, for example, were you doing for them?"

Trying to put a moderate spin on what Joe and I were doing for the ACLU and AIM, I explained some of the negotiations that had been conducted with FBI and ATF officers on the site near Wounded Knee about getting food and medical supplies to the natives occupying the village.

After a few additional exchanges, during which Lee seemed to grow more and more frustrated with my answers, he finally said, "Jesus! Why weren't you more directly involved in helping the FBI or the Justice Department officials out there? At least that way you could have been earning some goodwill for our office there that we could translate later into helping get a better plea bargain or other deal for one of our clients."

We were like two ships passing in the night. Here I was, trying to get F. Lee Bailey, the most famous and most accomplished criminal defense attorney in our country, to open himself up to doing something in the public interest realm. And there was Lee Bailey, trying to see how he could extract from a historical tragedy and from an avalanche of personal suffering being heaped upon the Native American people of our country some short-term advantage that might enable him to make a further hundred grand getting some gangster a lighter sentence.

That was it for me. I proceeded to press Lee on why he was a lawyer at all. What was it he hoped to accomplish by doing what he did, and why didn't he seem to be more interested in justice or truth? But when I asked him these questions, he was genuinely puzzled. It was hard to believe, but he didn't seem to understand what I was even talking about.

He then launched into what seemed to me to be an almost rehearsed rant about why it wasn't up to us, as lawyers, to determine what was true or not true. That was up to a jury. "My job," he said, "my *responsibility* is to do everything I possibly can—everything that I can get away with—to get my guy off. That's my job. That's what I get paid to do. And I am paid pretty goddamned well too," he pointed out. "And I do it pretty goddamned well—better than anybody else, to hear some people tell it."

There it was—the absolute relativist! I knew I was done working for F. Lee Bailey.

CHAPTER *fourteen*

T HE WEEKEND FOLLOWING my big debate with Lee over his view of "ethics" and the law, I was staying at his townhouse on Beacon Hill. I went to Sunday Mass, as usual when I was in Boston, at Saint Cecilia's. And I stopped into a bookstore on my way home from church, as I often did during that period on Sundays on the way home from church. I was just kind of rummaging around, looking at the newly published books, when I came across a recently published book by John Rawls, chairman of the Department of Philosophy at Harvard University. The book was titled *A Theory of Justice*, and as I began to look through it, I was completely drawn into it. I bought the book, brought it home, and read through the whole thing in a day.

On Monday morning, I called over to the campus and set up a meeting with John Rawls. I told him I'd seen his book, explained how it related to the ethical confrontation I was having with Lee Bailey, and explained the similar difficulty I'd had with Cahill-Gordon in New York. It was supposed to be only a twenty-minute meeting, but Professor Rawls canceled his next appointment, and we continued on for another twenty minutes. Then he canceled another meeting, and we ended up talking for another three hours. Rawls was struck by the fact that a practicing trial attorney of my experience and caliber would care at all about an abstract discussion like the one we were having, about what specific mode of ethical reasoning was being primarily utilized in Western civilization. By the end of that meeting, Professor Rawls was suggesting that I come back to the university and write a PhD thesis in the field of comparative social ethics, comparing and contrasting the worldviews of utilitarianism and intuitionism, concepts from his book that had intrigued me.

I applied and was accepted. And so, in the fall of 1973, I returned to Harvard to seek the answer to three different but interrelated questions:

1. What were the concepts and vocabulary through which I could more effectively convey to persons who did not believe in the sacredness of constitutional rights and human liberties why they should, and why I did?

2. How could I either convince myself or disabuse myself of the conviction that the application of my talents to the cause of human liberty and to the protection and fostering of American constitutional rights was deserving of my absolute commitment?

3. How could I account for—and determine what degree of value to attribute to—apparently fervently held beliefs of others that were so utterly different from mine?

When I returned to Harvard that September, I assumed I would be enrolled in the Graduate School of Philosophy. However, because Dr. Rawls wanted me to research and write my thesis under the supervision of Dr. Ralph Potter, the chairman of the Department of Comparative Ethics at Harvard, I found myself enrolled in the Harvard *Divinity* School, first in the master's degree program and then in the PhD program, because Potter was also the chairman of the Department of Christian Social Ethics, which was housed in the divinity school. I actually laughed out loud when I discovered I had been enrolled in the divinity school, because I remembered numerous times when I had asked particular questions to professors at Harvard Law School, offered certain kinds of observations, or criticized a specific judicial decision, and the law school professor had said, "Mr. Sheehan, if you wish to discuss that issue, perhaps you should transfer over to the divinity school instead of remaining here at the law school." And here I finally was!

I had returned to Harvard to grapple with issues that had troubled me throughout my young legal career. From the Goodwin-Proctor firm to the Cahill-Gordon firm to the Bailey firm, my superiors did not seem to be guided by any kind of moral referent for what they were doing. They appeared to be pursuing, instead, only self-serving, short-term career objectives or doing whatever their wealthy clients asked them to do. They seemed to have no interest in doing anything on behalf of poor people or about social justice issues. I was twenty-eight years old, and in the fall of 1973, I felt the need to better understand these issues.

Having officially enrolled in the divinity school, I was required to take certain courses to obtain first my master's degree in comparative social ethics and then my PhD. These courses included Theology and The Philosophy of Religion, as well as Christian Social Ethics. Professors at the divinity school, in response to my asking certain kinds of question or making certain kinds of observations, did *not* suggest that I transfer to the law school. They would ask, instead, "Are you Catholic?" I would proudly answer that question by saying, "Well, my name is Danny Sheehan, and I have a sister Colleen and a brother Patty. Is the pope Catholic?" This earned me a certain place in the various conversations held in the classes and seminars I attended in my first year at divinity school.

However, it was in my thesis tutorial class with Dr. Ralph Potter that I began to really appreciate why I had ended up at the divinity school while seeking answers to the seemingly *legal* questions I had been asking.

For example, I discovered there that James Madison, the principal author of our American Constitution; thirty-seven district court judges assigned to the federal bench immediately after ratification of the Constitution; ten members of the first three executive branch cabinets; three of the original justices on the United States Supreme Court; twelve members of the original Continental Congress; twenty-one United States senators; thirty-nine United States congressmen; four signers of the Declaration of Independence; and Aaron Burr had all taken the same college course in Moral Philosophy at Princeton University between 1768 and 1794, from the same professor, the Reverend John Witherspoon.

I learned at the divinity school that the Reverend John Witherspoon was indeed the *source* of the natural law worldview that underlay and shot through our entire United States Constitution. The specific genre of natural law moral philosophy that John Witherspoon taught to all of these founders was that of the Scottish Enlightenment.

Spurred on by this discovery, I began an intense study of "natural law."

The focus of my studies concentrated on natural law and worldviews. A rudimentary understanding of these two subjects is crucial in the field of constitutional law for a number of reasons.

The *Encyclopedia of Philosophy*, published by Macmillan, says of natural law,

> There is a view, attributed with differing degrees of reliability to certain Sophists and to [Thomas] Hobbes, that, in any society, the criterion of justice is provided [strictly] by what the laws decree and that to ask of these laws whether they are "just" or "unjust" is an absurdity. "No law can be unjust," Hobbes asserted in chapter 30 of his work *Leviathan*. It is a necessary condition of any "Natural Law" doctrine that this view be rejected.

There are, of course, more conditions to explore in natural law, but the most basic of these, according to the *Encyclopedia of Philosophy,* is this:

> The Physical Laws of the Universe must govern human conduct. The oldest and simplest account of the "naturalness" of justice is to be found in a conception of the universe that originated with the Stoics Zeno and Chrysippus. But it is also found in thinkers as recent as Montesquieu and Blackstone. The whole universe, on this view, is governed by laws that exhibit rationality. Inanimate things and brutes invariably obey these laws, the first out of necessity, the second out of instinct. Men, however, have the capacity of choice and are, therefore, able, at will, either to obey or disobey these laws of nature. Nevertheless, owing to the character of these laws, it is only insofar as men obey them that we act in accord with "right reason." "Follow nature" is therefore, on this view, the principle to be adhered to in order for human beings to act "morally." However, the "natural laws" that apply to men and which men should and can obey are not identical in content with those that apply to, for example, planets or birds or bees, laws which these objects cannot but obey. Nevertheless, because the universe is a rational whole,

governed by a unitary principle of rationality, the analogy between the laws that govern nonhuman behavior and those of human morality are very strong—and can be readily penetrated by the rational faculty of man, a faculty with which every man is endowed.

The concept of "worldview," stated most simply, revolves around the notion that one's reality is entirely derivative of the answers one provides to four essentially *non*definitively answerable questions of ultimate fact. These four questions are:

1. The Cosmological Question: How did our physical universe come into being, and what are all of the physical laws that govern its past, present, and future functioning?

2. The Teleological Question: Is there a specific direction in which our physical universe is unfolding, and if there is, what is the role of our human species, if any, in this unfolding?

3. The Ontological Question: How did sentient consciousness (especially human consciousness) come into being?

4. The Epistemological Question: What are the means by which we, as human beings, are capable of discerning the facts that constitute answers to such ultimate cosmic questions as these?

Any set of *internally self-consistent* answers one provides to these four critical questions of ultimate fact determines that person's worldview. I concluded that I was in agreement with what Dr. Ralph Potter had taught us: that no matter what factual information one might communicate to an adherent to a categorically different worldview from one's own, one is never going to convince such a person to adopt one's own view of any particular matter—unless and until one addresses, and alters, that person's a priori assumed answers regarding these four fundamental questions of ultimate fact—because we believe only "facts" that are "derivatively consistent" with those a priori "answers" we have provided to the four pillar questions concerning ultimate fact.

After discovering the pertinence of this broad framework in under-standing how different people could come up with entirely different ways of responding to the same ethical question, I turned my attention to trying to understand, as well as I could, the specific beliefs of each of the various *holistic* belief systems (or worldviews), especially those that were different from my own. These studies helped explain to me why so many law part-ners, district attorneys, and other lawyers and I were like ships passing in the night, within shouting distance of each other but unable to see or hear where the other person was coming from. We had utterly different worldviews. That is, we held fundamentally different beliefs about the *facts* as to the very nature of ultimate reality itself.

At the conclusion of my first semester as a master's degree graduate student at Harvard Divinity School, I received an emergency telephone call from Joe des Raismes. The AIM leadership criminal trial had been suddenly scheduled to begin in February of 1974. Des Raismes was in immediate need of my assistance. He asked me to take a one-semester leave of absence from divinity school and to fly out to Colorado and South Dakota to help him serve as amicus curiae counsel to the American Indian Movement in that major criminal case. I was pleasantly surprised to find that the administra-tion at the divinity school—all the way up to Dean Krister Stendahl him-self—was completely enthusiastic about my going out to help in this defense.

So I went.

I flew from Boston to Boulder, Colorado, and became chief of litigation for the Rocky Mountain national ACLU office. I also became cocounsel, with Joe des Raismes, to the Native American Rights Committee of ACLU National, which was based in that office. I then flew to South Dakota and drove with Joe to Wounded Knee. There I met, for the first time, Russell Means and Clyde and Vernon Bellecourt. Dennis Banks, at that time, was already in California, in effect in protective custody of California gover-nor Jerry Brown. I then became deeply involved in working for the Native American movement with the ACLU.

However, several weeks later, the federal district court judge postponed the trial of the leadership of AIM in response to a flurry of pretrial motions we filed demanding that all federal charges against the leadership of AIM be summarily dismissed due to prosecutorial misconduct. Those charges that we filed in those motions included planting spies inside the legal defense team, wiretapping the telephones of defense counsel, and fabricating physical evidence, as well as blatant perjury on the part of numerous federal law enforcement officers. However, since I had already officially taken a full semester leave of absence from Harvard Divinity School, I served as chief trial counsel for the Rocky Mountain ACLU for the rest of 1974, until it was time to return to school that September. In that capacity, I served as chief trial counsel in all trials for ACLU National in North Dakota, South Dakota, Montana, Idaho, Nebraska, Nevada, Colorado, Wyoming, Utah, and Arizona. During that time, I litigated a number of cases.

The first case that came to me at the ACLU during my one-semester sabbatical from Harvard Divinity School, other than the Wounded Knee case, involved Professor Rufus A. Lyman, president of the Idaho chapter of the American Federation of Teachers and the tenured chairman of the Life Sciences Department at Idaho State University in Pocatello. We were called into the case in March 1974, but it had actually started earlier, when the president of Idaho State University, Dr. Donald E. Walker, had died in office and when, at an emergency meeting, the Idaho State Board of Education had decided to appoint William "Bud" Davis, the popular varsity football coach of ISU, to replace President Walker.

The problem began when Coach Davis, exercising his newfound power as the president of ISU, began to transfer funds from the academic side of the university budget to the athletic side. The funds he transferred were to be put toward design and construction of a mini-domed stadium for the ISU football team, which had not won more than three games in any given football season in the previous ten years. A major movement immediately arose within the ISU faculty to stop Coach Davis, now President Davis, from accomplishing his goal. Special faculty meetings were convened and led by Professor Rufus A. Lyman, the seniormost member of the ISU faculty and the president of the Idaho state chapter of the American Federation of Teachers. In the *Pocatello Journal*, Professor Lyman was quoted in one of those meetings as saying, "Coach Davis has played too much football without a helmet!"

This, and Professor Lyman's organizing of the special faculty meetings to oppose Coach Davis's efforts, outraged Davis. So Davis had asked the Idaho State Board of Education to convene a special emergency session to discuss "the Rufus Lyman situation." The chairman of the state board of education, one Dr. John Swartley, agreed to convene the requested emergency session, and at 6:30 on the evening of that meeting—after the six o'clock evening news shows—he exited that emergency session and issued a press statement announcing the formation of a "special select committee to investigate Professor Rufus Lyman." The members of this select committee, authorized by the Idaho State Board of Education, were to be appointed from the ISU faculty directly *by ISU president Bud Davis himself.* Board chairman Swartley's press statement invited anyone who had a complaint of any kind against Professor Rufus A. Lyman, including members of the ISU administration, members of the faculty, students, alumni, or parents and relatives of students, to send it to the committee via the office of President Davis.

Since this announcement was made after the evening news cycle on the day of the board of education meeting, however, representatives of the news media had time to contact Professor Lyman and solicit a response from him before the eleven o'clock news shows that same evening and before the morning newspapers went to print. So the lead story across the state that evening on the eleven o'clock news, on all three statewide television networks and in all the newspapers the following morning, was "ISU Professor Brands Special Select Committee a Star Chamber!" That was, of course, exactly what it was. Coach/President Davis was furious. Dr. Swartley was furious. And a majority of the members of the Idaho State Board of Education were adequately angry at Professor Lyman that they voted to terminate his tenure at Idaho State University "for insubordination" during a hastily arranged telephone conference call organized by Chairman Swartley.

Professor Lyman telephoned the national office of the American Federation of Teachers in Washington, D.C., which in turn telephoned the national office of the American Civil Liberties Union. The ACLU in Washington, D.C., telephoned our Rocky Mountain regional office in

Boulder. And Joe des Raismes and I climbed into Bullwinkle and headed for Pocatello, Idaho—and a showdown between the American Federation of Teachers and the Idaho State Board of Education.

On our way to the federal district courthouse in Pocatello, I asked Joe to make a quick stop at the office of Wayne L. Kidwell, the attorney general of the state of Idaho. I announced to the Attorney General's secretary who we were and that I wanted to speak immediately with Attorney General Kidwell personally before I filed our federal Civil Rights Act civil complaint against Dr. Swartley and each member of the Idaho State Board of Education. Kidwell came right out of his office and invited us in to speak with him. Joe was, of course, his natural, gentlemanly self, being as he was an actual French count—Count Joseph Napoleon des Raismes III de Bourgeon—complete with an always-lit pipe and a tailored waistcoat. I was, of course, my typical Irish bar fighter self. When the attorney general asked what schedule we might want to agree upon pursuant to taking this question to the court, I interrupted to inform him that if he so much as showed his face in a courtroom to support what the board had done to Professor Lyman, I would personally include him as a named codefendant in our federal Civil Rights Act civil suit for having joined in a criminal conspiracy to deprive Professor Lyman of his constitutionally guaranteed right to freedom of speech and freedom of the press. I demanded that Kidwell immediately contact Dr. Swartley and personally inform him that neither Kidwell nor any other member of his staff would defend Swartley or any member of his state board of education for what they had done to Professor Lyman, and that they were going to have to personally hire private outside counsel to defend them in this action.

Attorney General Kidwell was not only "personally insulted as a fellow member of the bar," as he pointed out to me, but he was totally terrified in the face of this threat—because he knew I meant it.

Dr. John Swartley and the other members of the Idaho State Board of Education therefore hired Jess B. Hawley III to represent them immediately after Joe and I filed our federal Civil Rights Act civil complaint against them in the federal court in Pocatello, Idaho. We retained a local ACLU cooperating attorney by the name of Byron Johnson to serve as our local counsel.

I included with our civil complaint an emergency motion for leave to take immediate sworn depositions from all members of the state board of education and from Dr. Swartley's personal executive secretary, on whom I sought special leave of the court to serve a subpoena duces tecum demanding that she produce, forthwith, the official tape recording of the special session. Our motion was grounded on the high probability of the ultimate success of our lawsuit as well as on the fact that what the state board of education had done was a serious and ongoing "chilling" of Professor Lyman's First Amendment right to freedom of speech, which required immediate relief.

The court granted our motion.

We scheduled the immediate sworn deposition of the executive secretary, Miss X, to be taken in the Pocatello Public Library conference room at 9:00 AM on the following Monday morning. Professor Lyman's wife of thirty-five years, Doris, was the city librarian, and she made the city library available to us for the deposition. We scheduled Dr. Swartley's sworn deposition for one o'clock on that same Monday afternoon. But it was to be held in the main courtroom of the federal district court, the courtroom in which any trial would take place in our case. Joe and I stayed at Professor Lyman's home and ate dinner with him and Doris and their two grown children. It was there that Rufus A. Lyman explained to us that Jess B. Hawley III was the grandson of Jess Hawley Sr., the attorney general of Idaho when Governor Frank Steunenberg had called in the United States military to oust the Western Federation of Miners from the mines during the famous mine workers' strike of 1899. Professor Lyman, who turned out to be a regular Wobbly, went on to explain that it was Jess Hawley Sr. who had organized and led the team of "deputies" who went down into Colorado and kidnapped Big Bill Haywood, president of the Western Federation of Miners, and transported him, in shackles and chains, under armed guard, back up to Idaho, where Hawley then prosecuted Big Bill Haywood for the 1905 assassination of Governor Steunenberg on the word of "that dirty rat Harry Orchard," the confessed murderer of Governor Steunenberg. It had been Clarence Darrow, the greatest trial attorney of the nineteenth century, who had come into Idaho to defend Big Bill Haywood *in the very courtroom* in which I was scheduled to take the sworn deposition of Dr. John Swartley the next day.

On Monday morning, we arrived at the Pocatello Public Library and set up the conference room for the deposition. Joe and I were sitting in place, with the court stenographer ready to go, when Miss X arrived—without an attorney. She was about sixty-five years old, very neat, and demure. I had her sworn in, got her to give her name and official position on the record, and then immediately asked her to produce the official recording of the special session of the state board of education that I had subpoenaed. She said she didn't have it. I asked her whether she understood that it was legally required that all such meetings be officially tape-recorded. She said that she did. When I asked her whether she had indeed tape-recorded the special session, she said that she had. I then asked her why she had not brought this tape recording to the deposition.

"It has been destroyed," she said.

"Really?" I asked. "And who destroyed it?"

"I did," she replied.

"And why did you do that?"

"I was instructed to."

"Who instructed you to do that?"

"Dr. Swartley," she said.

There was a long silence in the room. Then something suddenly occurred to me. I suspected that Miss X had been the secretary of the state board of education for some time.

So I asked her about this.

"I have been Dr. Swartley's personal secretary for thirty years," she said.

"And how long has Dr. Swartley been chairman of the state board of education?"

"Dr. Swartley has been chairman of the state board of education for twenty-four years."

"And have you been the secretary of the state board of education for that entire time?" I asked.

"Yes, I have," she said.

"And I'll bet that you were the secretary of the board even before it was required to tape-record those meetings, weren't you?"

She paused, a bit perplexed by the question, but then answered, "Yes . . . yes, I was."

"You know, I'll bet that you used to take handwritten notes at those meetings before it was required to officially tape-record them, didn't you?"

Again, she looked a bit puzzled, but then she answered. "Why, yes . . . I did."

"And I'll bet that you *still* take handwritten notes during those meetings, even today, don't you?"

She looked at me for a long time. I sat and waited. Then she smiled and said, "Yes. I actually do."

Everyone in the room looked shocked, especially Joe des Raismes. "That *never* would have occurred to me to ask," he told me later.

"And where are those notes that you took during this special session of the board, Miss X?"

She hesitated before she said, "They are at my home."

"And how far away is your home from here, Miss X?"

"Oh, it's only about fifteen minutes away from here."

"Good," I said. "Miss X, what we are going to do is, we are going to keep this deposition in session while you go home and get those notes for us. And remember, Miss X, you are still under oath, so you are not allowed to speak with anyone while you go and get those notes." I then turned to everyone else. "And everyone who is here in this deposition will remain here while Miss X is retrieving her notes. And no one will contact anyone to tell them what is transpiring in this deposition or I will move to have them held in direct contempt of court. Does everyone understand that?" Silence reigned in the room. "You can go now, Miss X, and bring those notes back to us. Remember, you are not allowed to speak with anyone about what is transpiring in this deposition. You do understand that, don't you?"

"Yes . . . I understand that," she said. And she got up and left.

We all remained in place for thirty minutes while she was gone. No one got up and left the room.

No one said a word. A heavy silence filled the room. Any sudden sound could have broken the spell.

But it was working.

When Miss X returned to the deposition room, she had with her four small eight-by-four-inch notebooks. I gestured for her to resume her place next to me at the deposition table and asked if she would please identify the documents she had retrieved from her home.

"These are the four eight-inch by four-inch professional notepads in which I took handwritten notes of the March 1974 special session of the Idaho State Board of Education."

"Miss X? Were you functioning in your capacity as the official recording secretary of the Idaho State Department of Education at that March meeting in 1974 when you took those notes?"

She said that she was, and she held up the notepads. "These are the notes that I took during that meeting. I don't know if you could say that I was taking these notes in my official capacity as the official recording secretary of the board of education. I was taking them simply as a matter of habit. But they have been tape-recording all our meetings of the Idaho State Board of Education for the last fifteen years, so I guess you could say that I was taking these handwritten notes of the meeting more or less in my purely private capacity."

"But, Miss X, you certainly would not have been allowed in that meeting unless you were Dr. Swartley's personal secretary. And you certainly would not have been allowed to take handwritten notes of that meeting unless you were the secretary of that organization, would you have, Miss X?"

She waited a long time before answering. "I guess you're right," she said finally. "I would not have been."

"Did you ever tell Dr. Swartley that you were taking handwritten notes of the proceedings of that meeting?"

"Well, I don't remember having to do that. I always did it. I don't think he even noticed."

I then asked Miss X if she could read the notes aloud so that they would be in the record, and she did. When this process was completed, I reminded her that she was still under oath and that she could not discuss with anyone what she had told us until after Dr. Swartley had testified later that after-noon. "Because if you do," I said, "that could be considered witness tamper-ing, which is a federal crime. Do you understand that?"

She was genuinely frightened. "Yes . . . I understand that."

"Good. Now thank you, Miss X, for being so honest and forthright with us in this matter. No one wants to get you into trouble. You are free to leave now. I will contact you if we need to question you further tomorrow. But I am hoping that that will not be necessary."

With that, Miss X got up and left, and we asked the court stenographer to prepare a "rapid transcript" of the portion of her deposition in which she read her notes of the meeting.

We then went straight to the federal courthouse and persuaded the clerk of the court to allow us to set up Dr. Swartley's deposition to be taken directly on the witness stand, as if he were in a trial.

Joe des Raismes, Byron Johnson, and I were in place at the prosecution table nearest to the jury box and directly in front of the witness stand when Dr. Swartley entered, led by a bejeweled Jess B. Hawley III, who wore two large gold rings on each hand, gold bracelets on both wrists, and a huge gold Rolex wristwatch. He had a $200 haircut with hairspray to hold his quaffed hair in place, a sharp suit, and $300 shoes.

Ignoring Hawley, I went directly to Dr. Swartley and told him to get up on the stand so we could get started. "I think that you had better get ready for what's about to happen to you," I said to him under my breath as I helped him up onto the stand.

He looked startled. I told the court stenographer to "swear the wit-ness." It was ten minutes before 1:00 PM, but I was ready to go. Swartley nervously climbed onto the witness stand before Hawley really knew what was happening.

"Dr. Swartley," I began right away. "Please raise your right hand and swear to tell the truth, the whole truth, and nothing but the truth. This is going to be very important in this case."

Jess B. Hawley III, who had just gotten set up at the defense table, which was the only place left for him to set up, tried to raise some objection. But I interrupted him. "Please, Mr. Hawley. Be quiet! The witness is being sworn."

He sat down, and the deposition was under way.

I asked Dr. Swartley to give his full name, home address, telephone number, and full title. He did this, looking questioningly at Hawley about his having to give his home address and telephone number. But Hawley was too confused to raise an objection.

"OK, Dr. Swartley, now let's get right down to it. Can you tell me why you personally voted to terminate Professor Rufus Lyman, a tenured professor at Idaho State University?"

Dr. Swartley and Hawley were taken totally off guard. They had expected me to work up to that question. But I had gone directly to it as my very first question.

"I . . . well, we were asked to convene a special session of the state board of education to discuss some of Professor Lyman's recent conduct—"

I cut him off. "Dr. Swartley, I didn't ask you why you convened the special session. I asked you why you personally voted to terminate Professor Rufus Lyman, whom you knew to be a tenured professor at Idaho State University."

"Well . . . he defied the board. We set up a committee to look into his recent conduct, and he publicly called that committee a star chamber!"

"So, you would have us believe that you voted to fire Professor Lyman because he had given a statement to a local newspaper?"

Dr. Swartley realized the full constitutional import of his potential answer to this, so he hesitated. Before he could think of how to answer this constitutionally loaded question, I said, "Let me withdraw that question for the moment, Dr. Swartley, and ask you something else."

I turned and walked to my briefcase and withdrew a copy of the expedited transcription of that morning's deposition of Miss X. I then approached the witness stand with the transcript in my hand, so Dr. Swartley could see it, though he would not have been able to tell exactly what it was. I paged through the transcript until I came to the appropriate page and then, clearly reading directly from the transcript, I asked him, "Did you or did you not, Dr. Swartley, say, during the course of the special session that the state board of education convened to discuss the Professor Rufus Lyman matter, 'How are we going to fire this son of a bitch? He's got tenure!'"

A look of horror suddenly fell upon the old man like a heavy snow from the roof of his cabin after a blizzard, and his face flushed. Jess B. Hawley III leaped from behind the defense table and tried to approach me to see what it was that I was reading from. I turned on him menacingly and ordered him to sit down. "I am taking this deposition. You can ask your client anything you want to after I am through with him."

Hawley stopped in his tracks, and I turned back to the defense table.

"Dr. Swartley, I want to remind you that you are under oath here today. And if you perjure yourself here, I swear to you that I will seek a criminal indictment against you for criminal perjury and I will do everything in my power—which I might add is considerable—to see to it that you go to federal prison. Do you understand me?"

He said nothing. He simply sat there with that same look of terror on his face. So I repeated my question.

Hawley rose up and, trying to look around me to establish eye contact with Dr. Swartley, said, "We can stipulate that Dr. Swartley is aware of the law of perjury."

I turned on him. "It is not you, Hawley, who will be going to federal prison if this man lies one more time on this witness stand." I turned back to Dr. Swartley and said, "It will be you, Dr. Swartley! So I want *you* to answer my question so I will not have to wonder whether you fully understood the consequences of your action if you lie to me one more time from that witness stand."

Swartley stared at me in continued terror and said nothing.

"OK then, Dr. Swartley. Let me put the question to you one more time. Did you or did you not say, during the special session convened by the state board of education to discuss Professor Rufus Lyman, 'How are we going to fire this son of a bitch? He's got tenure?' Didn't you say that, Dr. Swartley?"

He stared at me for another full thirty seconds. Then, after apparently weighing all the risks, he looked squarely at me and said, "I did not!"

I was, frankly, shocked. I thought that I had adequately frightened him into telling the truth. But it was clear that it was going to take another charge of dynamite to shake him loose. So I leafed through the transcript of Miss X's transcribed notes until I found another set of quotes.

"Dr. Swartley, once again—and for the final time—I am going to warn you that you are under oath in a federal sworn deposition, and if you lie to me in your answer to the next question that I am going to put to you, you will go to federal prison for up to two full years. Now I am going to ask you: Did you or did you not also say . . ." I looked down conspicuously at the transcript in my hand and read, "'President Davis wants this son of a bitch out, and we need to find some way to do this, even though Lyman has tenure.' Did you or did you not say *that*, Dr. Swartley?"

Dr. Swartley's previous look of terror turned into something more like agony. It was a look that seemed to expand out from Dr. Swartley's face down through his entire body. He tried to move his lips, but only air came out. His eyes pleaded with me to stop, to somehow let him off from having to answer that. Then suddenly his face began to turn red, and he clutched at his chest. He slid sideways in his chair on the witness stand and slumped over.

Hawley jumped to his feet. "We need to take a break! We need to take a break!" He started to dash toward Dr. Swartley on the stand.

But I turned on Hawley and snarled at him. "Get back! Get away from him! He has to answer my question!"

"There's something wrong with him!" Hawley was pleading now.

"Certainly there is," I shouted. "He's lying! That's what's wrong with him." I turned back to John Swartley on the stand. "You have to answer my question, Dr. Swartley! Did you or did you not say that as well?"

Swartley looked up at me desperately and then literally slid out of the chair onto the floor.

"There is something wrong with him! Can't you see that?" Hawley shouted out again.

I was a bit concerned now myself. So I said, "OK, OK. I will give you five minutes—and not one minute more. If he is not back in that witness chair in five minutes, I am going to go to the judge and have him held in contempt of court. And nobody is to talk to him during this five-minute break about the questions I have put to him, or else they will be held in contempt of court too!"

With that, I turned on my heel, angrily tossing my yellow pad and the transcript of Miss X's transcribed notes down onto our counsel table, totally pissed that I had let him off the hook. I kicked the air as I left the courtroom and walked out into the public hallway of the courthouse. After a minute or so of stewing, I decided to take advantage of the short break to go to the men's room.

As soon as I entered, I saw John Swartley, all alone, standing in the men's room. As soon as he saw me, he recoiled and backed up against the smooth tiled bathroom wall. I continued toward him, forgetting for the moment my reason for going in there. Swartley stood, backed up against the bathroom wall, as if he expected me to physically throttle him.

"Look, Dr. Swartley, all you have to do is tell the truth," I told him. "Answer the question. You know that I know what you said. I don't want to have to send you to federal prison for perjury. But I will if you lie under oath one more time. If you refuse to tell the truth, I am still going to win the case. And when I do, I am going to ask that you and your entire board—and Davis too—be criminally prosecuted for a federal criminal conspiracy to violate the constitutional rights of Professor Lyman *unless you tell the truth!*"

He started moaning. "No, I can't go to prison . . . I can't!" He was already flush up against the bathroom wall, but he kept pushing himself backward, causing his feet to start to slide out from under him. Suddenly that look of agony filled his features again. His eyes rolled up, and he sagged down the bathroom wall into a sitting position and slumped sideways onto the floor.

I realized that something really *was* wrong with him now, so I turned and walked out of the men's room back out into the public hallway and found Hawley, who was huddling with two of his other lawyers.

I approached him and described Swartley's condition and said that he should probably call a doctor.

Pandemonium broke out. Everybody started calling 911 and asking to have an ambulance sent to the courthouse to take Dr. Swartley to the hospital.

As they were rolling Dr. Swartley away, strapped onto an ambulance gurney, I leaned over him and said to Hawley, "You had better have him back here, in that seat, by 10:00 AM tomorrow, or I will move to have him—and you—held in contempt of court."

Hawley looked shocked.

When I went back into the courtroom to gather up our papers, I told Joe des Raismes and Byron Johnson that I wanted one of them to contact the hospital to find out if anything was really wrong with Swartley.

Byron called me at Professor Lyman's home later that afternoon and told me that Dr. Swartley had in fact undergone triple bypass heart surgery. I told Byron to serve the remaining five deposition subpoenas on the remaining members of the state board of education, ordering them to appear at the federal courthouse for their sworn depositions within forty-eight hours.

I know it is hard to believe, but within forty-eight hours, three of the remaining five members of the Idaho State Board of Education filed motions to continue their scheduled depositions on the grounds that they were *all* entering the hospital to have elective open-heart surgery during that very week. So I filed a motion for an immediate order of summary judgment based on the sworn deposition of Miss X. The federal judge put the motion on for oral argument for that very Friday morning, citing the outstanding "chilling effect" of the state action taken by the board of education against Professor Lyman.

When we arrived Friday morning for oral argument in the federal courtroom, the judge took the bench and, before we began, looked down over his glasses at Jess B. Hawley III, his battery of lawyers, and the two remaining undeposed members of the state board of education and asked, "How are we this morning, gentlemen? No more heart problems, I hope, before we start?"

Hawley rose and informed the court that the defendants were not going to oppose the plaintiff's motion for summary judgment.

The judge then asked what relief the plaintiff was seeking. I informed him that Professor Lyman wanted

1. to be reinstated by federal court order to his position as a tenured professor and as chairman of the Life Sciences Department at Idaho State University;

2. to have the court enter a federal declaratory judgment declaring that Professor Lyman's dismissal had been a "transparent

violation of his First Amendment right to free speech and to the freedom of the press";

3. to have the court enter a permanent federal civil injunction prohibiting ISU acting president Davis and the Idaho State Board of Education from convening the announced special select committee to solicit complaints against Professor Lyman, and declaring the attempted convening of such a committee to be a violation of the due process of law required regarding a tenured professor at a state university;

4. to have the court order the state of Idaho to pay Professor Lyman his full back salary, plus interest; and

5. to have the court refer this case to the United States Justice Department's Civil Rights Division for the criminal prosecution, under Title 26 U.S.C. 248; of the federal civil rights conspiracy proven through Miss X's sworn deposition.

The federal judge had been nodding and smiling at each proposed piece of relief requested by Professor Lyman—up to that final request. As soon as the judge heard that, he scowled at me.

"Well, Mr. Sheehan, the court has no problem providing to Professor Lyman the first four forms of relief that Professor Lyman has requested. But, as to the fifth form of relief requested, the court would ask that the plaintiff reconsider this request of the court. This court takes judicial notice of the fact that four of the six members of the state board of education have entered the hospital for open-heart surgery just this week during the course of your depositions. It is the opinion of this court that you and the ACLU have made your point very emphatically to this state agency, and it is very unlikely that anything like what we have seen in this case will be repeated by these people—or by any other state officials in this state similarly situated."

At that, Byron Johnson, our local Idaho counsel, rose and agreed to drop the fifth request and thanked the court for the relief granted on the other four matters. We then packed up all our papers and returned to Professor Lyman's home for a celebratory picnic.

Byron Johnson later contacted the national office of the ACLU, told them what I had done, and asked that the ACLU's national board vote to direct me not to make any application to the Justice Department to criminally prosecute any members of the state board of education in Idaho. The national board did this, so I did not ask the Justice Department to prosecute those men, or Coach Davis. But I was not happy about that.

On our way back to Boulder in Bullwinkle, Joe des Raismes asked me how I felt about what I had done to Dr. John Swartley. I remember not being the least bit contrite about what I had done. But, upon reflection, motivated by Joe's concern over what I had done, I remember feeling that I *should have* felt something in light of what had happened to those men.

But I didn't. And *that* began to bother me.

CHAPTER *fifteen*

D UE TO OUR success in representing Professor Rufus A. Lyman in what was perceived by the ACLU as a teacher's First Amendment rights case, our office was contacted later in 1974 to represent a twenty-six-year-old high school English teacher in North Dakota. That young teacher had assigned to his sophomore Advanced English class the book *Slaughterhouse-Five*, the 1969 award-winning novel by Kurt Vonnegut. A week into this assignment, a parent of one of the students had picked up the book and discovered the word fuck in it. Outraged, this parent contacted the school's principal to complain vociferously.

The principal convened a meeting of the school board, which recommended that *Slaughterhouse-Five* be replaced with a "more appropriate" book. However, the board also recommended to the principal that he gather the copies of *Slaughterhouse-Five* from the students and have them destroyed. In response to this instruction, the principal instructed the janitor of the high school to use a confidential list of locker combinations, kept in the principal's office, to enter the students' lockers, remove any copies of *Slaughterhouse-Five* that were discovered, and destroy them. The janitor did this pursuant to the instructions from the principal. But he chose to do this by burning all the books retrieved in the school's furnace in the basement.

When the English teacher was notified by the principal of what had been done and was asked to assign "more appropriate reading," he replaced *Slaughterhouse-Five* with Ray Bradbury's *Fahrenheit 451*, a novel about a fictional future in which "firemen" are assigned by a Big Brother government to search citizens' homes and seize and burn "unauthorized books and readings." When the principal and the school board realized what *Fahrenheit 451* was all about, they immediately conducted a telephone conference call and ordered the principal to fire the teacher for insubordination. This, of course, was almost an exact replay of what had been done to Professor Rufus A. Lyman in Idaho, at the college level, earlier that school year.

Joe and I reboarded Bullwinkle and drove up to the Red River Valley of North Dakota. As usual, we enlisted a registered ACLU cooperating attorney from the area as our local counsel, and we filed an immediate federal civil rights civil complaint against the high school principal and every member of the school board. Then we presented the county district attorney with a copy of the complaint, instructing him to order the school board to withdraw its order to the high school principal and to direct him to rehire the teacher. Joe and I then went to meet directly with the chairman of the school board and told him the details of the Professor Rufus A. Lyman case. He immediately convened a special meeting of the school board, and the board voted unanimously to instruct the principal to immediately reinstate the teacher with full back pay.

Once reinstated, the English teacher assigned both *Slaughterhouse-Five* and *Fahrenheit 451* to his high school class and asked students to write their term papers on lessons learned in their reading of *Slaughterhouse-Five* and *Fahrenheit 451*. He went on to win the Teacher of the Year award in North Dakota the following year.

Shortly after returning from North Dakota, we received a call from the ACLU's national office about a case in western Idaho. The owner and manager of the only large movie theater in Idaho Falls had contacted the national office about the following issue.

In early June of 1974, United Artists had distributed a copy of its multi–Academy Award–nominated motion picture *Last Tango in Paris*, directed by Bernardo Bertolucci and starring Marlon Brando, to the main movie theater in Idaho Falls. Idaho Falls was on "the western side of the lava flow" in Idaho, placing it squarely in Mormon territory. On the Friday evening on which *Last Tango in Paris* opened at this movie theater, the district attorney of Idaho Falls, who was a member of the Church of Latter-day Saints, sent his assistant district attorney and two uniformed Idaho Falls police officers (all Mormons) to view the initial showing of the film at 7:00 PM. Three additional uniformed armed police officers stood in front of the ticket window of the theater, taking photographs of every person who approached to purchase a ticket and then demanding to see the official identification of each person. The officers then copied down people's names and addresses. As soon as the first showing of *Last Tango in Paris* was completed, the assistant district attorney and the uniformed police officers who had watched the movie left the theater and went directly to the district attorney's office, where the district attorney sat waiting for them with a set of three identical already-drafted affidavits, each stating that the signing party had "witnessed the showing of the film *Last Tango in Paris*" at the local Idaho Falls movie theater and that, in the affiant's opinion, *Last Tango in Paris* "was contrary to the standards of this community."

Armed with these three signed sworn affidavits, the Idaho Falls district attorney, accompanied by his assistant district attorney and all five uniformed and armed police officers, returned to the theater and marched right in without purchasing tickets. They went upstairs and entered the projection booth, physically seized the film from the projector, took it with them, and locked it in the safe in the district attorney's office. The theater then closed for the night.

The owner and manager of the movie theater was outraged and called United Artists the following Monday morning and reported what had happened. That very morning, representatives of United Artists in Los Angeles telephoned Louie Nizer, the chief counsel for United Artists, in New York City. Nizer said, "Fuck Idaho! It ain't worth it. It'll cost you more to litigate this than you're ever going to make on that film in Idaho. So just let it go."

The theater owner was doubly outraged that United Artists was not going to do anything about this. So he called the national office of the ACLU, and they called us at the Rocky Mountain regional office in Boulder. We, of course, were delighted to take on such a classic case. We loaded up Bullwinkle, and off to Idaho we went again, this time to "the western side of the lava flow."

We rolled into Idaho Falls in our ACLU Volkswagen bus and went directly to the law office of our local cooperating ACLU attorney. Armed with local counsel, we then drove directly to the local state courthouse, went into the clerk of the court's office, filed a rule 41 motion for return of property, and asked the state court judge Thomas for an immediate emergency hearing on the motion.

Judge Thomas came out into the courtroom, took the bench, and read the motion. Then he announced, "Well, gentlemen, I am going to deny your motion. You may not be aware of it, but our city council has recently passed an ordinance granting our district attorney the right to bring a civil action to enjoin a potential public nuisance, and I am assuming that our district attorney will be holding this here film in his safe for evidence, so it will be there if he ever decides to bring such an action before this court." With that, he rose from behind the bench and started to leave the courtroom.

Standing at counsel table, I announced, in a voice that was probably louder than was necessary, "Your Honor, I don't think that you adequately appreciate the gravity of this matter. This action on the part of the district attorney of your city constitutes nothing less than a prior restraint on the freedom of expression of our client, Mr. Y. And, for that reason, I must insist that you order the district attorney to return this copy of *Last Tango in Paris* to Mr. Y until and unless he has obtained a legitimate court order declaring the showing of this film to be a public nuisance. Any such order would, of course, then be subject to immediate appeal to the state court of appeals and then to the state supreme court if that becomes necessary."

Judge Thomas stopped and moved back behind the bench. "No. I think not. I think that our district attorney ought to be given a reasonable amount of time to decide whether he wishes to bring such an action to declare the further showing of this film to be a public nuisance. And, if he does, then we will deal with this matter in that context. But, in the meantime, we are going to let that film sit right where it is so it can't be shown again in this town." He turned to leave again.

"Your Honor. Let me put it this way," I said, stopping him. I then opened my briefcase and removed a copy of a federal civil complaint that I had drafted. "Your Honor, I have here a drafted federal civil rights complaint naming your city's district attorney, his assistant district attorney, and all five 'John Doe' Idaho Falls city police officers who participated in this outrage as defendants in a federal civil rights lawsuit, which I am prepared at this time to file with the United States District Court for the Western District of Idaho. If you will not agree to order your city's district attorney to return that film to Mr. Y immediately, I am prepared to include your name in this complaint as a coconspirator with these men, and I assure you that I will be forwarding a copy of this complaint to the Criminal Division of the United States Justice Department in Washington, D.C."

Judge Thomas stopped, turned slowly, and glowered down at me. He then returned behind the bench. "Well, Mr. Sheehan, is it? I think that, in that case, I can personally assure you that our city's district attorney will be bringing a state *criminal* proceeding against your client before this court for criminal obscenity on Monday morning. And we'll see who's going to be going to prison around here. Isn't that so, Mr. District Attorney?" he said, turning directly to the DA, who was standing there in a state of shock.

"Why, of course, Your Honor," the district attorney said in a voice that could barely be heard. "Yes, Your Honor. Of course. Monday morning."

We spent the weekend researching U.S. Supreme Court cases and Idaho state cases on obscenity, as well as the legislative history of the civil nuisance statute that the Idaho Falls City Council had enacted just weeks earlier. We also sent our local counsel out on a scouting mission to ascertain what other movies had been screened in Idaho Falls in the previous two years and what magazines were available for sale in local stores.

We were in court bright and early on Monday morning when Judge Thomas mounted the bench and called for the clerk to show the voir dire panel into the courtroom. From the jury room entered fifty elderly white citizens of Idaho Falls. It took me no more than two minutes of preliminary questions to realize that they were all members of the Church of Latter-day Saints—Mormons. We had been informed over the weekend that Judge Thomas was, in fact, the president of the Mormon stake that comprised the entire western portion of Idaho Falls.

The first individual voir dire panel member I questioned was a Mrs. Frank G. Thompson. Mrs. Thompson was eighty-six years old. When I informed Mrs. Thompson that she was going to have to see one or more motion pictures during the course of this case if she were selected to sit on the jury, Judge Thomas immediately interrupted me.

"I have made no such ruling in this case. It may be that the content of the film at issue in this case will be deemed by this court to be of such a nature that it would be more appropriate to have its contents simply *described* for the jury in this case. I have not decided that issue yet. So do not make any such assumptions, Mr. Sheehan, when you are voir diring these jurors, please." He smiled at me.

"Well, Your Honor," I responded. "It is perfectly clear to me that, as a matter of law, these jurors will be required to view not only the film at issue in this case but more likely a number of other films as well in order to make a determination as to what the standards of candor are in this community with regard to depicting sexual matters, as is plainly required by the United States Supreme Court in *Miller v. California,* decided just last year. I am attempting to determine Mrs. Thompson's ability to make such a determination, if you will allow me to continue."

"You may continue," he said.

"Now, Mrs. Thompson, can you tell us, approximately how many times a year you go to the movies?"

She smiled at me. "I haven't been to a motion picture show since 1934."

I was shocked. "Really?" I asked. "And why, may I ask, is that?"

"They are un-Christian!"

Now I was really concerned. I asked what she meant by that.

"Well," she said, pleasantly enough. "The women in those movies wear skirts that show their knees—and they don't even have stockings on!"

This was real trouble. I turned to Judge Thomas, and he smiled at me. I turned back to Mrs. Thompson. "Mrs. Thompson, can you tell us why you think that it is un-Christian for a woman not to wear stockings?"

"That's it!" Judge Thomas thundered from the bench. "We will adjourn with Mrs. Thompson to my chambers for any further questioning."

We then adjourned to Judge Thomas's chambers. With Joe des Raismes and I sitting on one side of the chambers and the district attorney sitting on the other, Judge Thomas pulled his chair directly up in front of Mrs. Thompson, who was sitting demurely in a big chair, his knees virtually touching hers. Staring directly into her eyes from no more than two feet away, he then said, "Now, Mrs. Thompson, you know that your friends and neighbors in our community have asked you to sit on this jury, don't you?"

"Well, I guess so," she said, picking up on what he clearly wanted her to say.

"And you do not believe, do you, Mrs. Thompson, that if you are asked to sit on this jury, you will one day have to look your maker in the eye, as you are me now, and answer for that to him? Now do you, Mrs. Thompson?"

Almost hypnotized by the intensity of his directness, she stammered, "Well, no, I guess not."

"Good!" he said, pulling his chair back from her and rising. "This juror will be allowed to sit on this jury. And there will be no more questions of this juror." And then he ushered us all out of his office, back into the courtroom.

Needless to say, we were forced to exercise a preemptory challenge to remove Mrs. Frank G. Thompson from the jury. It went like that until we had used up all our preemptory challenges and seated an all-Mormon jury.

The state's first witness was the president of the city council of Idaho Falls, whom the district attorney attempted to qualify as an expert witness capable of providing to the jury conclusive evidence as to what "the standards of the community" were. I let the DA have the president of the city council say whatever it was the DA wanted him to say, including his "expert opinion" that *Last Tango in Paris* was "contrary to this community's standards." Then I rose to cross-examine him.

I asked him whether, by his assertion that *Last Tango in Paris* was "contrary to this community's standards," he meant to say that it was his judgment that *Last Tango in Paris* was obscene.

"What do you mean by that?" he asked, looking at me quizzically.

"That's precisely my point, Mr. Z——. What do *you* mean by that?"

"By what?" he asked. "Do you mean what is contrary to this community's standards or what is obscene?"

I waited a moment for the jury to catch up with him. Then I said, "Either one. Which one would you rather take first?"

He just sat and looked at me. So I asked him another question. "Are you trying to tell this jury that you think the movie is obscene?"

"Yes! That's what I said. It's obscene."

"Well, actually, Mr. Z——, that's not what you said. You said that that movie was contrary to this community's standards."

"That's right," he said. "It is."

"And what I asked you is whether, by saying that that movie is contrary to this community's standards, you meant to tell this jury that the movie is obscene?"

"That's what I am saying, yes," he said.

I waited a moment and then said, "Let's start over, Mr. Z——. What do you mean when you say that a motion picture is obscene?"

Judge Thomas interrupted. "This man is not a lawyer. He doesn't have to know what the technical definition of obscene is in order to tell this jury that he thinks that that movie was obscene."

"Well, Your Honor. With all due respect, that's not what he was saying. He was professing to be offering an expert opinion asserting that the movie at issue in this case is obscene. And I am just trying to get him to tell us what he means by that—that a movie is obscene. We have a right to know what he means by that."

"Well, then ask him some other question about that. He's already told you that he thought the movie was obscene. So go on to something else."

"Well, Mr. Z——, can you tell me whether or not you think that the movie that you saw in this case was, let us say, utterly without any redemptive artistic value?"

He just sat and stared at me. After about twenty seconds, he asked me what I meant by that.

"Mr. Z——, can you tell me whether or not you have ever attended any classes on art, say, in college or perhaps in junior college? Any classes having to do with art or art appreciation?"

Judge Thomas jumped in again. "He doesn't have to answer a question like that! What are you trying to get at by this line of questioning anyhow, Mr. Sheehan?"

"Your Honor, I am exploring this witness's credibility as an alleged expert witness."

"Are you questioning the credibility of the president of our city council? Are you calling the president of our city council a liar?" Judge Thomas demanded, fury seeping into his tone.

"No, Your Honor. No. A person's credibility, as you know, consists of a number of different factors. One of those factors is the witness's *willingness* to tell the truth. But another factor is that witness's *ability* to tell the truth about a specific issue. For example," I said, turning to the jury to explain, "a specific person might be called to the stand to testify as to whether he personally knows whether a particular person did or did not rob a particular bank in a particular town on a particular day at a particular hour. However, if it could be clearly established that that witness was not even in that town on that day, then that particular witness would lack the *ability* to testify that he personally witnessed the defendant in question rob that particular bank in that particular town on that particular day."

Judge Thomas mulled this over for a moment and then asked, "Well, what if this witness had taken a lot of courses in college in art appreciation and all of that and he *still* testified that this movie was without any redemptive artistic value? Would you call him a liar then?"

"Well, in that case, he would be a liar, Your Honor," I said rather matter-of-factly.

"That's it! You are out of here! Get out of my courtroom!"

I turned and looked at him, not quite believing what he was saying. So I just stood there, more or less ignoring what he had said. I then turned back to the witness and started to formulate my next question for him.

"Out!" shouted Judge Thomas, rising up from his chair behind the bench and leaning over it. "Get out of my courtroom! Nobody comes into my courtroom and calls the president of our city council a liar! Bailiff, take Mr. Sheehan out of this courtroom!"

The bailiff, a mere waif of an old man, looked at me plaintively and shrugged his shoulders. I ignored him entirely and merely walked back over to the counsel table and sat down next to Joe des Raismes, on whom it was just beginning to dawn that he might have to continue this trial instead of me. He had never done a trial, and here I was, apparently being thrown out of this case, which would require him to try it instead of me.

"No! Not there!" raged Judge Thomas when he saw me merely sit down at the counsel table. "I said out!"

I shrugged, slowly rose, and opened the swinging gate that allowed one inside "the bar." I stepped out into the audience area and then took a seat in the front row so that I would be able to confer with Joe.

But this was not good enough for Judge Thomas either. "I said *out!* Bailiff, I said remove Mr. Sheehan from my courtroom . . . *physically* if you have to. I do not want to see him in here ever again!"

The bailiff came over to where I was sitting and again looked at me plaintively. I sat there for a few long seconds and then decided what I would do. I got up and walked straight out, down the center aisle of the courtroom, pushed the swinging back doors open with the butts of both hands, and walked out into the public hallway. A swarm of newspaper reporters came pouring out of the courtroom after me, and TV cameramen dashed for cameras they'd laid down against the back wall of the courtroom. When Judge Thomas saw the TV cameramen picking up their television cameras, he pulled himself up to his full height and announced from the bench, in a booming voice, "I see a lot of TV cameramen and reporters in here, and I want to warn you, right now, on the record, that you had better exercise extreme caution in reporting anything that you have seen go on here in my courtroom!"

A stunned silence fell across the courtroom as it dawned on everyone what the implications were of what Judge Thomas had just said. He was, in effect, ordering First Amendment news media not to report events that had taken place in a public courtroom in an American trial. Everyone was aghast—except, of course, Judge Thomas.

I waited for all the journalists to come out into the hallway, gather around me, and get their cameras and lights all set up. Then I started holding a public press conference, right outside the courtroom. I told the evening news on all three statewide television networks exactly what Judge Thomas had done—to me and with Mrs. Frank G. Thompson in chambers. I spoke about the fact that all the members of the voir dire panel had been members of the Church of Latter-day Saints. But rather than castigating Judge Thomas for that, because I knew that a very high percentage of the television viewing audience was also members of his church, I pointed out that I was confident that this jury would take all the steps necessary to protect the First Amendment right of Mr. Y to screen *Last Tango in Paris,* because members of the Church of Latter-day Saints knew that our United States Constitution, of which the First Amendment right to freedom of speech was a central pillar, was a "divinely inspired document," and that our Constitution was what made our nation the "exceptional nation" of the entire world, destined to lead the other nations to freedom and democracy.

It was a great hit. By the very next afternoon, the United States District Court for the Western District of Idaho had granted our emergency motion for the issuance of a federal writ of mandamus commanding Judge Thomas to readmit me to the case, declaring that his ejection of me from his court was a clear violation of Mr. Y's Sixth Amendment right to counsel of his choice in a criminal case. Joe des Raismes was grateful, as was Mr. Y, to see me back in the courtroom the next afternoon.

However, before recommencing that afternoon session of the court, Judge Thomas ordered me to take the witness stand and placed me under oath. Then he asked me if I understood why he had ejected me from his court the day before.

"As far as I could tell, Your Honor, you felt I was violating your view of this community's standards of candor with regard to matters of Constitutional rights."

He stared at me for a few long seconds and then said, "You're doing it again, Mr. Sheehan! You are doing it *again!*"

But everything went comparatively smoothly thereafter, because Judge Thomas knew that the federal district court was closely monitoring his every step for the remainder of the case. Judge Thomas therefore recanted his original determination not to let members of the jury see *Last Tango in Paris.* However, when we attempted to enter into evidence a dozen copies of *Playboy, Hustler,* and *Gallery* magazines as examples of the community standard of candor with regard to depicting sexual matters, Judge Thomas drew the line. He insisted upon wrapping each magazine in brown opaque paper so that members of the jury could not *see* what was in any one of them. "This is simply for purposes of any appeal," Judge Thomas ruled. "We will preserve, for the record, what you *would have* presented to the jury if I had let you do so."

When we came to the our closing argument, I reviewed all the evidence for the jury and told them that I had absolutely no doubt they would take all necessary steps to protect Mr. Y's First Amendment right to freedom of speech, since the First Amendment was the central pillar of our American

Constitution. I also told them that I knew they would move heaven and earth to protect our United States Constitution because we all agreed that our Constitution was a "divinely inspired document" and that, if they violated the First Amendment Right of Mr. Y by convicting him, they each knew that every one of them would go straight to hell when they died!

Judge Thomas exploded—and ordered me thrown out of his courtroom again. But my work was done.

The jury acquitted Mr. Y in less than thirty minutes, thereby avoiding eternal damnation.

I asked Mr. Y to open his theater for *free* showings of *Last Tango in Paris* for everyone in Idaho Falls for the full two-week scheduled run of the movie in that city, and he agreed to do it. But United Artists headquarters in Hollywood scotched that idea. I thought it was a wonderful idea—the perfect touch. But then I wasn't in the movie business. So *Last Tango in Paris* played to sold-out showings for two full weeks in Idaho Falls, Idaho, one of the most lucrative venues, per capita, of its entire run in the United States.

The ACLU dubbed that case the Last Tango in Idaho.

IN MY WORK on the Wounded Knee occupation case, I had immediately recognized a distinct pattern on the part of FBI and federal Justice Department agents, who I believed were systematically violating a broad range of basic liberties and constitutional rights of members of AIM. These violations ranged from the illegal stopping and searching of AIM members' vehicles to conducting blatantly unlawful searches of their homes without warrants to the infiltration into their legal defense team of agents, provocateurs, and spies. This led me to conclude that FBI and federal Justice Department agents in South Dakota, and in Washington, D.C., viewed themselves to be, in effect, at war against AIM, not simply engaged in a normal domestic law enforcement project. I suspected there was almost certainly a covert campaign of illegal wiretapping and electronic surveillance being conducted by federal agents against AIM members—and that that campaign would almost certainly extend to their lawyers—whom federal agents clearly perceived to be "active coconspirators" with the AIM leadership.

They were, of course, close to being right—at least in the sense that many progressive attorneys, between 1967 and 1974, had become conscious allies with members of the Black Panther Party, Vietnam Veterans Against the War, Greenpeace, Earth First, and even the Weather Underground, groups engaged in aggressive and sometimes overtly violent actions against United States policies. It was clear that the FBI and Richard Nixon's Justice Department viewed some members of our generation as "terrorists" who had "taken up arms" to physically defend themselves and their communities against the historic armed and violent activities that had been perpetrated against those communities for decades. The overt support being provided to the goons on the Pine Ridge Reservation by FBI agents and armed Justice Department agents was just one example of the Nixon administration's violent reaction to this development in America in the late 1960s and early 1970s, clear evidence that an *actual* state of war did in fact exist in South Dakota between members of AIM and the armed and violent agents of the administration of Richard Nixon.

This is what I had walked into in South Dakota. And it was this direct, weaponized assault against racial minority members of my own generation that radicalized me more than any other experience. I instinctively sympathized with the decision of these young activists to take up arms to defend themselves against the armed goons of the National Security State. So I decided to defend them, using all the nonviolent tools of the law that I had been taught. I had crossed over from believing that my proper place was among the rich and powerful, the men who financed Harvard College and Harvard Law School—the men who had in fact paid for my Harvard education. I had decided instead to become counsel to the poor and the oppressed, to try to persuade them to abide by the ideals of our revolutionary forefathers and the ideals of the spiritual radicals of the historical Jewish and Christian religious communities who found themselves confronted with the unjust assertion of power on the part of Egypt and Rome. This was a liberating theology for me, and it was a theology that many of my friends actively espoused and advocated. It struck me at times that both the Democratic Johnson administration and the Republican Nixon administration were not merely like the Russians my Uncle Jim had wanted me to defend our nation against, and that they were not merely the domestic enemies I had pledged an oath to guard our constitutional values against. They were, indeed, very much like *the Romans and the Egyptians,* against whom the prophets themselves had inveighed, calling us as believers to struggle against nonviolently.

Thus it was on the snow-laden fields of the village of Wounded Knee, in the winter of 1974, that I finally came to see who my true clients were to be—and what the true nature of their adversaries was.

It was at that time that I had the privilege of meeting, through mutual friends, Pir Nassar Allah Shah, one of the then five living Sufi masters. As soon as I met him, I realized he was the type of person the scriptures speak about. He was, in short, an "elevated consciousness." Realizing, for the first time, that what I had been taught by religious people was *literally* true, not just metaphorically true—that there were indeed spiritual masters who "saw" reality more clearly than did the most intellectually advanced Harvard scholars—I began to read the poetry, lyrical essays, short stories, and longer treatises of the Sufis. I thereby became convinced that these people, whom I deemed to be as intelligent as I, had had some kind of direct, unitive *experience* that enabled them to see or perceive things in our world differently than those of us who had been trained to conceive of everything going on around us in strictly linear and material terms. And I could tell from the various materials I then began to read that "meditation" was the key to potentially accessing this unique experience for oneself. So, while I was living with Joe des Raismes, Esther, and their Sufi friends in Boulder, in a beautiful little shuttered home in the middle of an apple orchard at the base of the eastern slopes of the Rocky Mountains, I began to read the Sufis . . . and to meditate.

Every day I would meditate for twenty minutes as the sun rose, for twenty minutes at noon when the sun was directly above, and then for twenty minutes as the sun set. I would then meditate for an additional twenty minutes immediately before retiring for the night. I did so by chanting a simple mantra given to me by Baba Muktananda, a Hindu saint whose retreat I once attended north of New York City in 1971. I developed a method of breathing and chanting that brought me to "a place of quiet consciousness" midway through each such session.

Then, one afternoon, Esther put an LSD tab into a cup of herbal tea that she offered me, and I came to see what Maharaja Neem Kardi Baba (Baba Ram Dass's guru) meant when he said, "This could be helpful." That experience provided me with an *experiential* goal toward which I could evolve in my meditation. It required only one such direct experience to understand: *THIS is what they have been talking about.*

It was in this dual context of the violent confrontation between our federal administration and the activist elements of our generation, and my reading of the Sufis and the beginning of an earnest practice of meditation, that I redirected my attention to supplementing our earlier motion to dismiss charges against the AIM leaders predicated on the prosecutorial misconduct of the federal agents of the Nixon administration against the leaders of the American Indian Movement and their lawyers.

Our efforts proved to be successful. The United States District Court for South Dakota dismissed all the charges against the leaders of the American Indian Movement arising out of the Wounded Knee occupation based squarely on the "prosecutorial misconduct" that we had evinced and briefed to the court. And this action was expressly affirmed by the Eighth Circuit Court of Appeals (in *United States v. Russell Means et al.*), citing "grossly negligent conduct" if not "deliberate deception" on the part of prosecutors and the unlawful military involvement with federal civilian law enforcement at Wounded Knee, among other things.

As soon as that order of dismissal of the Wounded Knee leadership case was entered and that case was over, on September 16, 1974, I immediately flew back to Boston and commenced my second semester of graduate school at the Harvard Divinity School.

PART III

CHAPTER *sixteen*

Duri NG MY SECOND and third semesters at Harvard Divinity School, between September 16, of 1974 and June of 1975, I continued to study Christian social ethics and comparative social ethics under Dr. Ralph Potter. In my third semester, in the spring of 1975, I took a course entitled The Theological Underpinnings of Human Rights from Father Roger Couture, a Catholic oblate priest at the Episcopal Theology School in Cambridge.

It is important to make clear how significant this "detour" to Harvard Divinity School was in my career. I only briefly touched upon my Catholic upbringing in the early pages of this memoir. It was pretty standard fare for a young Irish Catholic boy in the 1950s and early '60s in America. I was baptized as a baby and attended weekly Mass throughout my childhood after moving to Fort Ann when I was four. What was less normal was that I continued to attend weekly Sunday Mass at Northeastern University and that I ended up working with Father Arthur Brown, the young pastor of Saint Cecilia's in Boston. But between 1965, when I transferred over to Harvard College, and the fall of 1973, when I started at Harvard Divinity School, I did not attend a single Catholic Mass—with the exception of the wedding of my college sweetheart Esther Smith and Joe des Raismes, which was held at the Yale Cathedral in the spring of 1970.

However, after meeting Sufi master Pir Nassar Allah Shah, reading the writings of other Sufis, and undertaking a more dedicated meditative practice—to say nothing of my one unsolicited LSD experience, "gifted" to me by Esther—my Harvard Divinity School studies took on a much deeper and more substantive dimension. I returned to Harvard Divinity School much more eager to delve into the realm of intuitionist social ethics.

During my first semester of those graduate studies, I had focused on natural law, worldview studies, and the purely secular "sociological" ideas of

Professor Talcott Parsons, who had concluded that whenever a human community is confronted with a particular public policy problem, that human community will invariably divide itself into five different and distinct "factions," with each one arriving at and advocating a categorically different solution. These factions, identified by Talcott Parsons, are indeed the source of the now famous designations "right wing" and "left wing" within our public discourse about things political, because Professor Parsons splayed these factions out along a linear sociological bar graph ranging from right to left.

Among the more significant things I discerned during my second and third semesters at Harvard Divinity School was that "liberals" and "conservatives" had been functionally left out of Professor Parsons's previous spectrum of sociological factions. That discernment was to become the subject of my master's degree thesis at Harvard.

A second all-important realization that came to me while I was studying these issues at Harvard was that Professor Crane Brinton, the chairman of Harvard's Department of Intellectual History, had been correct when he had said in his final lecture at Harvard University in December of 1967 that our human species is presently in the process of the very next step in our *biological* evolution. This step, he had argued, would be as momentous for our human family as had been our leap from *Homo erectus* to *Homo sapiens*—but that this leap in our evolutionary advancement would *not* be in our intellect. It would be in our intuition.

In May 1975, after completing my last third-semester final examination in Father Couture's course The Theological Underpinnings of Human Rights, Father Couture telephoned and asked me to come to his office to meet with him. He expressed a high degree of interest in my discussions with Professor John Rawls, chairman of the Department of Philosophy at Harvard (about which I had written in a paper I had submitted to Father Couture in his course), as well as in the wide range of actual case experiences I had had and the practical experience I had gained in the field of law. After Father Couture and I had talked for a while, he broached the subject of the Jesuits (the Society of Jesus of the Catholic Church), and he inquired as to whether I knew what Father Pedro Arrupe, the superior general of the

Jesuits, was doing at that very moment in Rome. I told him that I did not. So he explained it to me in detail.

Father Roger Couture, in that one-hour meeting in his office, in May of 1975, explained to me that Pedro Arrupe, a medical doctor and a surgeon in 1920s' Spain, had become a Jesuit priest in 1927 and had immediately begun speaking out publicly, from the pulpits of Catholic churches throughout Spain, against the rise of fascism in Europe. In 1932, Francisco Franco, the dictator of the fascist government of Spain, had secretly ordered the assassination of Arrupe. But one of the assigned assassins had confessed to his local Catholic priest that he felt guilty about having been ordered to murder a Catholic priest. So Arrupe had been immediately transferred by his Jesuit superior from Spain to Japan, where he was secreted in a monastery. It was during that time, in Japan, that Arrupe studied—and began to practice— Buddhist meditation. And it was there, on August 6, 1945, in the city of Hiroshima, Japan, where the monastery was located, that Pedro Arrupe personally experienced the atomic bomb that our nation dropped on that city.

Father Pedro Arrupe was the famous doctor reported around the world to have led more than two hundred people out from under the looming mushroom cloud over that city and to then have cared for the many injured and dying in his monastery, which he converted into a hospital, saving hundreds of lives. Because of that experience, Father Arrupe thereafter had dedicated his life, and his priesthood, to eliminating nuclear weapons from our world, as well as to seeking to eliminate "the structural and institutional sources of injustice in our world,"[2] in both our Eastern and our Western cultures, that made a coming Third World War likely. Because of his direct expertise with Buddhist meditation, Father Arrupe had been selected by Pope John XXIII, in 1962, to chair the Committee on Ecumenicism (interfaith dialogue) at Vatican II in Rome. In Rome, Father Arrupe became a close friend of Pope John XXIII and was nominated by Pope John to become the new superior general of the Jesuit order when the previous superior general passed away in 1962. As the new superior general of the worldwide Jesuit order, Pedro Arrupe immediately set about radically transforming the historical order from an elite corps of handsome, socially polished, young intellectuals, who were traditionally assigned to the courts of the rich and powerful, into a cadre of even more excellently educated men who were then assigned by the order to "go out and live among the poor and the oppressed, the least among us, and learn from them what must be done." This experience led them to espouse what was later to become known as liberation theology. They were social, economic, cultural, and political radicals, in the true sense of that word, which derives from the Latin *radicus*, meaning "root." In the early 1960s, therefore, Father Pedro Arrupe started sending his young Jesuit priests out to live among the poor and the oppressed, to work among them, taking guidance from those people and empowering poor and oppressed people to rise up and lift from their own shoulders the yolk of oppression that had been imposed upon them through "the structural and institutional sources of sin"[3] in our world. For the older and more traditional Jesuit priests, he ordered annual forty-day directed spiritual retreats, usually requiring many days of absolute silence and mystical readings.

At the moment I was meeting with Father Couture in May of 1975, Father Pedro Arrupe had already summoned all one hundred provincials of the Society of Jesus from throughout the world to come to Rome for the first general congregation of Jesuit provincials in the entire 435-year history of the order for any purpose other than selecting a new superior general upon the death of the previous general. That unprecedented general congregation of Jesuits was to remain in session in Rome until a majority of the one hundred Jesuit provincials agreed to the specific provisions set forth in a set of Thirty-second General Congregation documents on social justice. Father Couture explained that word had leaked out that the documents being drafted called for a radical revision of the entire mission of the Society of Jesus, calling upon the men of the Jesuit order to become "men for others."

Roger Couture thought I might be interested in talking to the Jesuits and that they might be interested in talking to me. The Society of Jesus was planning to establish a new national Jesuit headquarters in Washington, D.C., and was looking for a general counsel among its ranks to head up a new Social Ministry Office to help save the world.

I had just turned thirty. I decided to take the train down to New York City and meet there with the formation director of the Society of Jesus for the New York province. He turned out to be a close personal friend of

Father Daniel Berrigan, whom the Boston Archdiocese had tried to retain me to defend when I was at Cahill-Gordon in New York back in 1971. Our meeting went well, so I was then interviewed by Father William J. Davis, the prospective director of the new Office of Social Ministry—the true "tip of the spear" of the social justice movement within the Roman Catholic Church in the United States. Father Bill Davis traveled all the way up to the Canadian border to interview me.

I had been dispatched there by the Native American Rights Committee of ACLU National to mediate a dispute between the Six Indian Nations and the state of New York concerning the state's attempt to lease to the New York–based lumber company Finch & Pryne a large tract of timberland that, in fact, was part of the thousand-year-old territory of the People of Flint (the Mohawk Nation). Father Davis was sitting there, waiting for me, when I emerged from a twenty-four-hour sweat with the six medicine men of the Six Indian Nations, undertaken to determine what steps should be taken to peacefully resolve that dispute. As soon as Father Davis saw me emerge from that sweat with those spiritual leaders, my "interview" was complete. At that moment, he became my Jesuit superior as a candidate for the Jesuit priesthood in the Catholic Church. I became the chief legal counsel to Jesuit headquarters in the United States in Washington, D.C., a position I held for the full ten years of my training.

After I completed my work for the Six Indian Nations, I took the train from northern New York State down to Washington, D.C., and was met by Father Davis at Union Station at the foot of Capitol Hill. He picked me up in "the Blue Flame," his faded-blue standard-shift 1962 Ford Falcon, and drove me directly to my new office at Jesuit national headquarters, located at 1717 Massachusetts Avenue on Embassy Row, just off Dupont Circle. The headquarters was immediately next door to the Brookings Institution and directly across Massachusetts Avenue from the Chilean Consulate. Prior to my arrival that day in 1975, I had only been in Washington, D.C., twice before, and for only a few days on each trip.

Father William J. Davis was forty years old and had been a member of the Society of Jesus for twenty-two years, ever since his graduation from high school at the age of eighteen. He had attended the Jesuit novitiate (the

Jesuit seminary) with Daniel Berrigan, a poet and professor of literature and poetry at Cornell University. Father Daniel Berrigan, his brother Philip (a Josephite Catholic priest), and Elizabeth McAlister (a founder of Jonah House, a major American peace center) had begun entering American draft boards and destroying records in those offices to prevent thousands of young American men from being drafted to fight in Vietnam. The Berrigan Brothers Gang (as they had come to be referred to, first by federal authorities and then proudly by the American peace movement) would sneak one of its members into a draft board during daylight business hours and that person would hide in the office. Later, in the middle of the night, that person would unlock the door, and in would come the rest of the gang. They would then gather together all the files in the draft board, take them out into the parking lot, and either set them afire or pour their own blood over them, rendering them unusable and freeing the young men listed in those files from future military duty in Vietnam. Both Daniel and Philip Berrigan spent three years atop the FBI's Ten Most Wanted list. Elizabeth McAlister soon joined them there, becoming only the third woman in history to make it onto the list. During those three years, both Catholic priests repeatedly showed up in Catholic churches across the country—in Los Angeles, New York City, San Francisco, Chicago, and Buffalo—delivering powerful sermons against war and nuclear weapons. This drove state and federal law enforcement officials ballistic.

Father Davis (code-named Dubber by his Jesuit brothers for his lack of golfing skills) drove the getaway car (the Blue Flame) for the Berrigan Brothers Gang, taking them to and from their draft board raids. Father Davis had a sign on the wall behind his desk at Jesuit headquarters that read, "If they made being a Christian illegal again, would there be enough evidence to indict you?" There was a certain consciousness in our office about the Nixon–Ford administration being completely criminal and engaged in a criminal war, and that it was therefore "a matter of Catholic conscience" that we oppose that war . . . and that administration. It wasn't "political"; it was "spiritual." When I arrived at the office, I found a very welcoming atmosphere, especially after being at Cahill-Gordon and at F. Lee Bailey's office.

Shortly after I arrived at headquarters, the new Thirty-second General Congregation documents came in over the teletype machine from the JA-ZU (Jesuit international headquarters in Rome, located immediately adjacent to Saint Peter's Basilica and the Vatican). The documents were entirely in Latin, so Bill Davis and I spent a full week and a half translating them into English. Then we immediately mailed a translated copy to every member of the Society of Jesus in the American apostolate. On the very day we sent out our last copies, Pope John Paul II issued an order of impoundment, declaring that these documents had not been cleared by the Vatican's Congregation for the Doctrine of the Faith, headed up by the dreaded Cardinal Joseph Ratzinger, and that those documents were therefore banned from distribution to members of the Jesuit order. But it was too late. We had already put copies into the hands of all the Jesuits in the United States before they had been ordered impounded. The Vatican couldn't unring that bell.

To those of us at U.S. Jesuit headquarters, the documents amounted to a "new constitution" for the Society of Jesus, a set of new founding principles that had been generated by all one hundred Jesuit provincials from throughout the world. We began advocating directly from those documents, taking them as "official authorization" to say the same things we had been saying before. All of the provincials in the United States were thereby "under authority" to articulate the positions set forth in those documents. I was now among men who stood directly under authority to go out into the world and to set about "deconstructing the structural sources of injustice in the United States."

The United States has ten Jesuit provinces. I sat down with Father Bill Davis and suggested that we call all ten provincials into Washington, D.C., and impress upon them the "social ministry" importance of these new Thirty-second General Congregation documents. I also advocated that we ask each of the provincials to appoint a new assistant provincial in charge of social ministry, focused solely on the issue of social justice and on getting members of the society in their provinces to comply with the mandate of these documents. We then assembled these ten assistant provincials to constitute the board of directors for our national Social Ministry Office. We would thereafter present to them every public policy position our office proposed taking on both international and domestic issues and would get this board to either sign off on or amend these proposed positions as necessary. This way, the whole organization would, together, speak for the American apostolate of Jesuits.

That was the kind of counsel I began to provide to the Jesuit order in the United States.

I provided to them my skills as a lawyer, an understanding of corporate law, and an understanding of how one goes about professionally setting up an institution or a governing structure that is actually able to get something done rather than simply convening meeting after meeting, conducting internal discussions, and wrangling about procedures. In effect, I redesigned the national Social Ministry Office of Jesuit headquarters so it could function as an authoritative arm of the Jesuit order.

Once we had structured the office, we needed to develop a set of policy positions for each cabinet-level position in the federal government of the United States. There were fifteen cabinet-level departments in the executive branch and six additional agencies whose directors regularly attended cabinet meetings. I was therefore tasked by Father Davis to draft twenty-one separate white papers to correspond with these cabinet-level positions. I drafted these positions with the aim of deconstructing "the structural sources of injustice in Western civilization." In short, it was my assignment to reformulate the structural processes by which adequate and just government services were to be provided to the people of our country—and to the world—by our United States government. I chose to do this in the same format in which papal encyclicals had been historically issued. Through the centuries, popes have issued papal encyclicals on such issues as the right of workers to organize labor unions, the redistribution of wealth by government to gradually relieve gross economic disparity, and opposition to unjust wars. I took those Catholic Church documents, along with the Thirty-second General Congregation documents of the Jesuits, as basic "legal directives" from my "client" and used them to fill in the details of a public policy program that would carry into effect those objectives. It was a systematic and scholastic undertaking.

However, because we didn't want to have to lobby on behalf of these progressive positions all by ourselves—we wanted as many churches and synagogues in the country behind us as possible—I went to talk with Father Robert Drinan, a Jesuit priest who in 1975 was the congressional representative from Brookline, Massachusetts, and the chairman of the House Judiciary Committee. I explained to Father Drinan what we were doing at Jesuit headquarters and asked him, "The Sierra Club is the big lobbyist on all the environmental issues; the National Organization for Women lobbies on behalf of women's rights; and there are hundreds of lobbyists in town advocating the interests of major defense contractors and agricultural conglomerates. Where is the lobby group for genuine spiritual values and the social justice positions dictated by those spiritual values?"

"There aren't any," Father Drinan said. "The doctrine of separation of church and state runs very deep here in Washington, D.C."

I pointed out that the doctrine of separation of church and state set forth in the Constitution does *not* require people of faith to refrain from organizing ourselves into effective lobbying groups. I argued that people in the faith community were allowed to speak out on behalf of what they thought ought to be done. I was talking about having all people, not just Jesuits—not even just Catholics or even just Christians—effectively articulate their positions on specific issues publicly, including speaking to their congresspeople and senators. I pointed out that reactionary church people were doing this. Why weren't we progressive members of the spiritual community doing this?

Father Drinan admitted that there wasn't anything like that in Washington, D.C., at that time. The closest thing to that, he said, was the National Council of Churches. "But it's all Protestant. And it is just a very loose coalition of about fifty different major Protestant denominations: the Baptists, the Southern Baptist Convention, the United Methodists, the Disciples of Christ, the Lutherans, the Episcopalians, the United Church of Christ, and so on." The National Council of Churches had offices directly across First Street from the United States Congress.

I wanted to go over to the National Council of Churches to talk about setting up a collegial process through which we could discuss our various public policy positions together. But before that, I wanted to get the U.S. Catholic bishops on board with the idea. So I went to the U.S. Conference of Catholic Bishops and spoke with Thomas Quigley, the civilian nonpriest, who headed the organization's peace and justice office. He was a big tough Irishman. In the old days, he would have chewed a cigar—except in the old days there wouldn't have been any laymen on the bishops' staff. And there wasn't any Peace and Justice Office either. Quigley and I, a couple of Micks, hit it off right away. I told him I wanted to get the U.S. Conference of Catholic Bishops to agree to authorize me to speak to the National Council of Churches. He said that the bishops were going to meet in just one month. He would put my proposal on the agenda and put in a good word for it.

We were successful. After I was given permission by the U.S. Catholic bishops, I went over to the United Methodist Building, armed with the authority of both the Jesuit order, the largest order within the Catholic Church, and all the bishops of the Catholic Church in the United States. I persuaded the heads of all fifty-four offices of the Protestant denominations to meet with us. Then I went to the Reformed Judaism group, which included many of the most liberal members of the Jewish community in Washington, D.C. There I met with Rabbi David Saperstein and discovered that he was my age, about thirty, and that he was an aspiring attorney as well. I explained to him, lawyer to lawyer, why I thought the organization we were trying to create was so important from a public policy perspective. He agreed to bring his organization on board, as long as we did not attempt to bring up any issue that was critical of the state of Israel.

So we had our new organization—except it suddenly dawned on me that we had left out the Unitarians, one of the most progressive and active of all religious denominations. So I got on the agenda at the national conference of the Unitarian Church. I got up in front of the group and was talking about our common Christian beliefs, but I wasn't getting the kind of response I was used to getting when I talked to Christian groups about these matters. Then I realized that Unitarians didn't consider themselves to be "Christians." So I said,

> Gee, I've got to apologize. During the whole first three minutes
> of my presentation, I could tell that I was not getting the kind of
> response that I had expected. Then I remembered what Father

Bill Davis had told me when I asked him about the Unitarians. He said, "Unitarians are people who believe in the fatherhood of God, the brotherhood of man, in the neighborhood of Boston! But they don't consider themselves to be uniquely Christian." [They all laughed because they knew that it was true.] Now I realize that I've been talking to you as if you considered yourselves to be Christians but that you have an entirely different attitude about Christ and who he was than most Christians do—which I guess puts you guys pretty much in the same boat as most Jesuits I know.

That was a big hit with the Unitarian crowd, so I continued presenting what was basically a comedy routine about the Jesuits and the Catholics. That was a tremendous hit with the Unitarians. So I succeeded in persuading them to join our new coalition.

We named ourselves the Washington Interreligious Staff Council (WISC), since we were made up of the directors of the national offices of all the major religious denominations in the United States. At the first meeting of our seven-person board of directors, in the main conference room of the United Methodist Building at 110 Maryland Avenue—looking directly across First Street at the porticos of the U.S. Capitol—I presented the twenty-one white papers I had drafted on policy positions, which had been approved by the national board of directors of the Jesuit Office of Social Ministry, and I suggested that the WISC board establish permanent task forces to address the seven most important of them. I proposed that we take the issue of abortion off the table to keep from alienating the Catholic bishops. I had drafted a position for the Jesuit order that was completely compatible with the U.S. Supreme Court decision in *Roe v. Wade*. I told the WISC board that this proposal would have its best chance of being implemented if it were left to be advocated within the Catholic Church.

Secondly, I proposed that the WISC board take off the table all issues relating to the state of Israel, because we didn't want to have potentially disruptive disputes about those issues and potentially lose support of the Union of American Hebrew Congregations. This proposal generated a great sigh of relief on the part of the new board members.

I recommended that we then consider establishing seven joint task forces: one on military spending; one on nuclear weapons and nuclear energy policy; one on health and human services; one on economic and tax policy; one on criminal justice; one on civil rights and human rights; and one more to be chosen among the remaining fifteen topics on which I had drafted white papers for the national Jesuit headquarters.

I proposed that each of the seven board members agree to chair one of those seven task forces. I emphasized that I had no investment in the board adopting any one of the recommendations I had made to the Jesuit order. I merely wanted to provide the new organization with a certain forward thrust. So the WISC board could either amend or reject entirely any of the twenty-one proposed policies I had recommended to the Jesuit order in favor of some totally different concrete, specific resolution; I merely wanted to help the board *do* something rather than simply *discuss* matters. That action helped provide leadership that was sensitive to the political realities that each Washington office had to deal with in its own denomination while providing the forward movement that had been lacking for so long in each denomination because each had been fearful of offending one or more of the other denominations.

Father Bill Davis chaired the Permanent Task Force on Economic Policy, which eventually helped prepare and publicly issue a policy on economic justice that adopted virtually every position taken by the United States Conference of Catholic Bishops and the United Methodist Board of Homeland Ministries, chaired by the Reverend Joe Eldridge, in their virtually identical "Pastoral Letter on Economic Justice." The policy was a blazer! It radically criticized the capitalist structure of Western civilization for being "inherently unjust"—because such an economic system was entirely motivated by private greed and avarice, appealing to "the very lowest angels of our human nature." However, the letter also excoriated the communist system, condemning it for its violations of human rights and for its lack of respect for and acknowledgment of individual liberties, as well as for its betrayal of the original ideals of the worldwide socialist movement of the early twentieth century. The Ford administration and the Republicans in Congress went berserk over how critical the "Pastoral Letter on Economic

Justice" was of the capitalist structures of Western culture, while they of course praised the letter's "meritorious" criticisms of the shortfalls of the communist system.

In October 1975, a one-year amnesty offer that Republican president Gerald Ford had publicly tendered to all young American men who had refused to participate in the draft for the Vietnam War was scheduled to expire. I was contacted by Brian Barger, the young president of the student body of the University of Maryland, who wanted to "turn himself in" at the White House in a big demonstration against the Vietnam War. Instead, Brian and I developed a plan to stage a major "Trial of the Vietnam War"— not a mock trial at which sympathetic lawyers would play the role of judges and totally biased citizens would sit as "jurors" to whom evidence of war crimes would then be presented, but instead a *real* trial.

I arranged for Brian (who had refused to register for the draft when he turned eighteen) to write a letter to the White House. I actually wrote the letter for him, to make certain that it set up the White House, legally, for what we were planning to do. In the letter, "Brian" informed President Ford that he was interested in coming in to talk about the amnesty offer and that he "might be able to persuade 'several friends' to come in with him."

During the entire year that Gerald Ford's amnesty offer had been outstanding, not one single young American man had so much as even inquired about this offer. So, as expected, the White House virtually leaped at this ray of hope. It thought it might have a "poster boy" for Gerald Ford's amnesty program, proving that Ford, who had pardoned Richard Nixon, was willing to be "evenhanded" by granting amnesty to deserving young Americans who had made a purportedly "similar" mistake in judgment by refusing to serve their country in Vietnam but who were now willing to come forward and apologize for that action. The White House political appointee in charge of the program invited Brian Barger and "his friends" to come to the White House to meet with him. The date was set—and the hook had been swallowed.

At the same time, everyone was starting to hear about this new guy, Jimmy Carter, the former governor of Georgia, who was an openly professed Christian and a candidate in the primaries for the Democratic Party nomination for president. I wanted to find out about him. I learned that he had a major office in Washington, D.C., right over on Dupont Circle, just two blocks from our Jesuit headquarters. So I went over to the office and spoke with Stuart Eizenstat, Carter's policy director. Eizenstat and I had a long discussion about various issues, and it occurred to me that our Jesuit Social Ministry Office, and perhaps even our new Washington Interreligious Staff Council, might propose a policy position to Jimmy Carter to see if he would agree to promote it as part of his campaign. After a second meeting with Stuart Eizenstat, we agreed to have the candidate meet with the directors of the Washington offices of every major denomination in the United States. Carter was delighted by this prospect. I met with WISC members and proposed that we focus on a single issue and tell Carter that if he would support and advocate this particular issue as a candidate for president, we would tell people in our respective congregations and parishes throughout the country that he supported that particular policy. We would not agree to ask our members to vote for him, but we would tell them that Carter had agreed to implement this particular policy if he were to become the nominee.

Father Philip Wheaton, from the Episcopal Church, a committed human rights organizer in Latin America, recommended that we ask Jimmy Carter to announce, as an integral aspect of his campaign, that he would, as president, cut off all military financing from the United States to any foreign dictator who systematically violated the human rights of his own citizens. We went right after that commitment in our meeting with Carter and eventually succeeded in persuading him to agree to this. We wouldn't let him wiggle out of the agreement. First he said that he would consider it. But that wasn't good enough for us. We told him that we were not going to say a single thing to anyone in our congregations about him unless and until he publically announced that he would promulgate this policy if he were elected president. He finally agreed to do that.

Ultimately, Jimmy Carter was elected president of the United States in November 1976, and the second executive order he issued cut off all military financing from the United States to any foreign dictator who was found to be systematically violating the human rights of his own citizens. Pursuant to that executive order, President Carter, in February of 1978, cut off all military funding to Anastasio Somoza of Nicaragua, causing Somoza to fall from power in just over one year, in July of 1979. Carter later cut off all military funding to the shah of Iran. The shah fell from power in December 1979. Both of those dictatorial regimes collapsed because of President Carter's cutting off U.S. military aid to them pursuant to the very executive order that we had persuaded him to promulgate.

While Gerald Ford was still president, however, filling out the remaining period of Richard Nixon's second term after Nixon's resignation, Brian Barger and "his friends" accepted the written invitation extended to them by the White House regarding Ford's Vietnam War–protester amnesty program.

On the appointed date, Brian Barger showed up with twenty "friends" and took his place in the White House tour line. When Brian reached the front of the line, he and his twenty friends entered the White House and were shown around the public portion of the building. It was not long, however, before one or more of the Secret Service personnel stationed around the inside of the White House recognized Father Daniel Berrigan and Father Philip Berrigan—since they had spent over three years on the FBI's Ten Most Wanted list. The Secret Service members also recognized Dr. Benjamin Spock, the baby doctor; Ralph David Abernathy, the president of the Southern Christian Leadership Conference, who had ascended to that position upon the assassination of Dr. Martin Luther King Jr.; and the well-known black comedian Dick Gregory; as well as a dozen more antiwar-looking types.

Frantically talking up their sleeves to one another and holding their earpieces with their other hands, the Secret Service guards quickly encircled the group of twenty and locked arms to keep the "intruders" from fleeing. The White House was ordered onto emergency shutdown status, which meant that everyone but the "intruders" were evacuated from the premises.

After only a brief delay, the director of the White House Secret Service detail and the chief of the White House Executive Protective Service detail arrived at the scene and announced over an electronic megaphone, "The White House is now closed to all outside persons and has been placed on emergency shutdown status. You are hereby instructed to leave the White House premises immediately—or you will be charged with the federal offense of failure to quit!"

"Failure to quit? Failure to quit?" a number of the Barger "friends" exclaimed aloud. "I want *that* charge on my yellow sheet!" And they all immediately reached under their jackets and removed previously rolled-up bed sheets bearing antiwar slogans such as "Nix-On War!"; "Out of Vietnam NOW!"; "Too Many Have Died!", and "Bring Our Troops Home." Then they all sat down on the floor of the White House and locked arms. Up rushed a battery of White House cameramen, who began taking live video footage of what was transpiring. Then the chief of the White House Executive Protective Service informed the "intruders" that he was going to order them to leave the White House premises three times, allowing a three-minute interval between each warning, and that if the occupiers did not immediately disperse and leave the premises after the third warning, anyone who remained would be arrested and criminally prosecuted for the federal offense of failure to quit.

"Failure to quit! Failure to quit!" Up went the chant again, and a loud cheer went up from the occupiers, followed by exclamations of "Take me! Charge me with failure to quit!" After a few moments, shouts of "I am Spartacus!" started breaking out from the circle of occupiers. And then the group sat and sang renditions of "We Shall Overcome," "Study War No More," and other antiwar favorites. After all, these were "the veterans." The fathers Berrigan sat silently, Daniel simply watching, smiling, and turning his head from side to side, observing what was transpiring around him, perhaps silently constructing a poem to commemorate the occasion.

After the third and final reading of the videotaped bullhorn warning, a dozen fully armed, riot-shield-carrying members of the federal protective service surrounded "the occupiers" and began to yank them apart. As the members of the gendarmerie moved in, I rose from the circle and announced that I was the group's attorney and that we had come to attend a meeting with the man the White House had assigned the unenviable job of political appointee in charge of the amnesty program. But it was too late. The Executive Protective Service personnel had their blood up and would not take that as a reason to stop making arrests. I made it a point to make the announcement *three times* on the official video recording. I made it a point to obtain the cameraman's name and White House ID number for purposes of subpoenaing him and his film for the trial that was sure to follow.

That is how I ended up becoming the attorney for Father Daniel Berrigan, Father Philip Berrigan, Elizabeth McAlister, Dr. Benjamin Spock, the Reverend Ralph David Abernathy, the Gold Star Mothers, University of Maryland student body president Brian Barger, and nine other "friends" of Barger who came to the White House that day to meet with the director of Gerald Ford's amnesty program.

The first thing I had to do was to go over to the D.C. jail and bail them all out. Then I prepared to file an immediate motion for the issuance of a federal writ of habeas corpus demanding an immediate emergency hearing at which to establish the innocence of my clients. Before I filed it, however, I stopped and reconsidered that tactic. If that motion were granted—which I was sure it would have been—that would have meant that only the federal magistrate would have heard our testimony, and he would then immediately release everyone from all charges. Then we wouldn't have gotten the big trial of the Vietnam War that we wanted. So instead I filed a motion for an immediate trial with the District of Columbia Superior Court. We waived the right of every defendant to a preliminary hearing, and I invoked each defendant's right to a speedy trial.

So the case moved quickly to a trial. When we were asked to help pick a jury, we announced that we would take the first twelve jurors who came in off the street. The Ford administration district attorney agreed to seat the first twelve potential jurors, and we proceeded immediately. The government prosecutor presented his witnesses first. They included the head of the Secret Service and other witnesses in uniforms with insignias, sunglasses, and sidearms. They went through "all the gory details" of this "assault on the White House." They explained to the jury how all the defendants had the audacity to sit down on the White House floor and how they had "failed to quit" when they were told to do so. Every time any one of the government's witnesses used the term failure to quit, a number of our defendants would leap to their feet and start to chant, "Failure to quit! Failure to quit!"

When the prosecutor was done presenting his witnesses, he played the White House videotape of "the intrusion." Our defendants cheered each time there was a close-up of any one of them, cheering for that person's bravery.

Then it was our turn to put on our case. Seeing what was coming, the judge asked us whether we wanted to make a motion for a judgment of acquittal at the close of the prosecutor's case. I said, "No, thank you, Your Honor. We are perfectly prepared to put on our case." The judge sighed and told us to go forward.

It was the most spectacular thing I had ever seen in a courtroom. We opened with Father Daniel Berrigan, twenty-two years a Jesuit priest, who gave a detailed account of everything that had happened leading up to the war in Vietnam. He outlined the revelations set forth in the Pentagon Papers, and he reviewed the Watergate scandal and how that had led to the impeachment resolution of Congress and the resignation of Richard Nixon in the face of ever-mounting public opposition to the war. He then detailed the implications of Gerald Ford's pardoning of Richard Nixon. He went on to explain how Brian Barger had been invited to the White House to meet with the man in charge of President Gerald Ford's amnesty program and how Brian had obtained express permission to bring with him to this meeting "a number of his friends." Then he began to lay out the details of the atrocities committed by both the French and the American militaries and by the CIA in South Vietnam.

The government prosecutor protested vigorously, insisting that none of that detail was relevant to the charges in this case.

The judge ruled that it was, because we had asserted the affirmative defense of "necessity." That common law/criminal law doctrine exempts a person from guilt in the commission of a less serious legal violation if that violation is necessary to prevent or stop a much more serious wrong. This would apply, for example, if a small child wandered into a busy lane of traffic on a busy thoroughfare and a responsible citizen found it necessary to violate the lesser ordinance prohibiting jaywalking to rush out into the busy thoroughfare to rescue that endangered child. In that case, when charged by the public prosecutor with the crime of jaywalking, Ms. Responsible Citizen would be entitled, as a matter of common law, to assert—and *affirmatively* prove—all the elements of the necessity defense.

So the D.C. Superior Court judge was forced to allow us to have every defendant take the stand to set forth his or her full "state of mind" when he or she came into the White House. Father Daniel Berrigan, in Catholic priest attire, explained to the jury his genuine desire to personally ask the man in charge of the White House amnesty program whether it was really true that our American servicemen in Vietnam were being ordered to drop "butterfly bombs" into the neighborhoods of Vietnamese children—with the intention that those bombs would lie partially embedded in the earth, looking exactly like brightly painted butterflies, until Vietnamese children would pick them up. The bombs were designed to blow off only hands and arms, and to blind and disfigure people—but to not kill them, so the children would have to be taken care of every minute of every hour of every day of the rest of their lives by their grieving parents and family. Father Berrigan told the jury that he absolutely *refused* to believe that a White House aide could possibly know that was true—and still ask an American boy who had refused to participate in such a war to apologize to Gerald Ford for his conduct after Gerald Ford had granted amnesty to Richard M. Nixon, the man who personally oversaw and authorized the use of those butterfly bombs, when Richard Nixon was never asked by President Ford to apologize for anything as the price for *his* grant of amnesty from Ford.

It was excruciating. And it continued like this. Dr. Benjamin Spock testified about all the young Vietnamese children who had been burned alive beneath tons of napalm that our young American servicemen had been ordered—under the pains of court-martial if they refused—to drop on the homes of innocent Vietnamese women and children. His testimony was followed by that of five Gold Star Mothers, each of whom had a son who had been awarded the United States Medal of Honor *posthumously*. One of the Gold Star Mothers testified that she had come to the White House to meet with people who were offering amnesty to young men because her son couldn't come in to apologize for what he had done—because he was dead! Two other Gold Star Mothers read letters from their sons, written before their deaths, in which they confessed to some of the things they had been ordered to do and of which they were ashamed. One soldier even suggested that he was going to undertake more and more dangerous actions, hoping that he would be killed by a Vietnamese man defending his homeland against the American invasion, thus casting a serious shadow over his death suffered in the action for which he had been awarded "the highest honor our nation can bestow upon a fellow American." At the end of her testimony, she turned and placed her son's Medal of Honor on the judge's bench and asked him to return it to the president on behalf of her son. "He wouldn't have wanted it." She left it lying there as she got up and walked off the witness stand.

Finally, we closed our defense by calling to the stand "the man of the hour," Brian Barger, the twenty-one-year-old president of the University of Maryland student body who had refused to come in to register for the draft when he turned eighteen. I took him, step by step, through the process by which he had become thoroughly disenchanted, not with his country but with our leaders and with the war. Brian spoke eloquently for our entire generation. When he completed his testimony, he introduced into evidence the long-awaited "letter of invitation" expressly inviting him and "as many of your friends as you can persuade to come with you" to come to the White House and meet with the director of the amnesty program at the very moment when Brian and his "friends" had been arrested and dragged from the White House.

I calculated that it would take the jury maybe five or six minutes to come in with a verdict of not guilty by reason of necessity. The jury did reach a unanimous verdict in our favor, but as they retired to deliberate briefly, Brian Barger came over and sat down at the counsel table.

"That was absolutely amazing," he said. "I have never seen anything like that. It was just like being in a movie—better than being in a movie, because we got to write all our own lines! You could do some really important things doing cases like these."

He told me that, after he graduated from the University of Maryland, he was going to become a stringer for the Associated Press. He had studied Latin American affairs at the university and was going to investigate and write stories about "all of the same things that we just told this jury about." Then, almost immediately, he started to tell me about a very good friend of his, Patti Neighmond, who worked for National Public Radio (NPR). She was the public health reporter for NPR. "Perhaps you have heard her on the radio?" he asked.

"Yeah. I think I have," I said.

"Well, my friend Patti Neighmond is a member of the Washington, D.C., chapter of the National Organization for Women. You know, NOW. And they are looking for a lawyer to represent the Karen Silkwood family out in Oklahoma."

"Karen Silkwood?" I exclaimed. "Wait a second. Isn't that that woman who was killed out at that nuclear plant out in Oklahoma last year?"

He said it was, and that her family was looking for a lawyer.

CHAPTER *seventeen*

ORTY MINUTES LATE, Sara Nelson came sweeping into the amphitheater at the Institute for Policy Studies, a few short blocks from our
national Jesuit headquarters building. She was thirty years old, slim, and tall
at five foot nine, with soft brown hair cut short in a feathered cut. She was
wearing a floor-length blue jean skirt that had been converted from a pair
of old faded blue jeans, the cut pants legs of which had been sewn together
with a brightly colored red-flowered cotton fabric. She also wore a green and
turquoise roll-neck sweater. With a doe-colored tan complexion and bright
hazel-blue eyes, she was, simply stated, the most gorgeous human being I
had ever seen. All the men in the meeting who already knew her turned subtly to observe my reaction to first seeing her. I tried to remain inscrutable.

When she came whirling into the room, she was hugging an armful of
congressional reports and political flyers tightly to her chest. She launched
straight into a fervent speech about how we might have to file a federal
civil rights lawsuit on behalf of Karen Silkwood's three infant children and
her family as a follow-up to the planned congressional hearings. She was
inspiring. She spoke about Karen Silkwood being "one of us" and how "if
we don't do anything about their killing one of our own, then we could not
expect anyone to help us when our turn came to be martyred." She actually
used that term: *martyred*. She said, "These people in the FBI aren't going to
do anything, so *we have* to get a joint hearing in the Senate and the House."
She spoke of this with the naive confidence of a person untutored in the
complex ways of Washington, D.C. But I could tell that she was going to
make that happen. We were going to mobilize people all across the country
to demand justice in the Karen Silkwood case. She was absolutely fabulous!

Then she turned and swept out of the room, leaving us all to discuss
without her. She was, as I would learn later, forty minutes late to her next

meeting. The moment after she disappeared, Steve Wodka, a strikingly hand-some, muscled, thirty-year-old, big-mustached national organizer for the Oil, Chemical and Atomic Workers Union, turned around to me and, fold-ing his arms on the back of his seat, said definitively, "*That* is Sara Nelson!"

I was in. How could we lose with an organizer like that! Certain that I was going to be the lawyer for the Karen Silkwood case now, I agreed to go to the next meeting of SOS (Supporters of Silkwood), which was scheduled for later that month at the offices of the Environmental Policy Institute in Washington. Maybe Sara would be there. I returned to my office at Jesuit headquarters to tell Father Davis that I was inclined to undertake this case for the Silkwood family.

The next week I visited the three different women I had been seeing and explained that I would no longer be dating them. I'm sure they all concluded that my decision was governed by my candidacy for the Jesuit priesthood . . . but it wasn't.

After Father Davis and the board of directors of the national Jesuit Office of Social Ministry officially gave me their consent to undertake the Karen Silkwood case, I explained to Bill Davis what I had felt the instant I first saw Sara. Prior to that point, Father Davis had not been troubled by the fact that I was still dating a number of women. After all, I was only a candidate for the Jesuit priesthood. I was not yet an official novice (similar to a seminarian in other Catholic orders) and had therefore not yet taken any vows of chastity or poverty. I lived with Bill Davis and four other Jesuit priests in Arrupe House, a three-story, one-hundred-year-old former Catholic convent on the eighty-acre grounds of the National Franciscan Monastery. The convent had stood abandoned for more than twenty years before Bill Davis heard about it from Sister Carol Cosner, director of NETWORK, an organizational member of the Leadership Conference of Women Religious. The rest of the national Jesuit headquarters staff used to bang dishes on the table whenever a different young woman would pull up to Arrupe House to pick me up for a weekend. Bill Davis had, however, strongly recommended that I concentrate on just one woman, just to see what I thought about "that kind of lifestyle" before I decided to become an official Jesuit novice. He was therefore rather pleased to learn that I had resolved to direct my attention on Sara alone. Then I explained to Bill that I had not even spoken with her yet. He was surprised. This had the potential to become a significantly more serious challenge to my candidacy than he had planned.

One week later, I was delivering a seminar on the Nixon administration's draconian Senate Bill 1 at the National Council of Churches conference room in downtown Washington, D.C., when into the back of the room walked Sara Nelson.

I saw immediately that she was again carrying an armful of flyers and congressional reports. But I recognized, as well, a copy of the unmistakable, five-hundred-page Senate Bill 1, in which William Rehnquist, as a special assistant United States attorney general, had set forth an entire catalog of proposed reactionary amendments to the United States Criminal Code. I concentrated hard on the subject before me, however, so I wouldn't appear distracted in front of Sara. This turned out to be the right move. Sara Nelson, over and above being the executive director of Supporters of Silkwood, was the national labor secretary for the National Organization for Women. And she had come to the seminar to hear about provisions in the newly proposed Senate Bill 1 that directly adversely affected labor unions. My earnest attention to those specific provisions seriously impressed her. Somehow my trying like mad not to let myself get distracted by this gorgeous woman I only hoped to someday get to see again came off as passionate devotion to the cause of organized labor.

When I finished my presentation, I quickly gathered up my notes so I could catch her before she disappeared again. When I looked up to try to locate her in the back of the room, she was suddenly standing directly in front of me, a copy of Senate Bill 1 hugged firmly to her chest. I almost gasped out loud at the sight of her. I didn't know what to say, which is more than a bit remarkable for me. But I never got the chance to say anything— she spoke first.

"You are Danny Sheehan, aren't you? You're the lawyer that Patti Neighmond had come over to my presentation on the Silkwood case last week at IPS?"

"Ahh, yes . . . yes, I am!" I proclaimed, a bit too exuberantly. I was immediately stricken with the hope that I had not embarrassed myself by being so obvious. This was entirely new to me. I was never self-conscious around anyone, and certainly not around women . . . even very beautiful women. But I certainly was then.

"I didn't know that you were *religious*?" she half asked.

I told her that I was general counsel to the United States Jesuit headquarters. "That is sort of like being religious," I said only half-jokingly.

"Oh!" she said.

Was that a slight tone of disappointment in her voice?

"Does that mean that you are a priest?" she asked . . . a bit plaintively, I hoped.

"No, no!" I said, way too eagerly. "I mean," I said, calming myself, "No. I am not." I felt immediately like Peter denying that he even knew Jesus when confronted by the townspeople of Golgotha. When I recovered my courage, I said, "I am studying to *become* a priest."

"Oh?" she said coyly. "Then you are not a priest . . . yet?"

"That's right," I said "Not . . . yet."

Then she laughed, and I couldn't believe I was actually standing there, talking with her, after having thought about her every day since I had first seen her.

"Would you like to come to church with me this evening?" she asked straightforwardly.

"Absolutely!" I said, like I'd been asked if I wanted a big bowl of ice cream. I suddenly knew I was now sounding a bit overeager, but she didn't seem to notice. She was busy writing the address of a church on a corner of her copy of Senate Bill 1.

Then I realized that I already had a five o'clock appointment to meet with Jimmy Garrison, my staff assistant on nuclear disarmament policy in the Jesuit Social Ministry Office. I had no way to reach him to cancel it.

"I do have a meeting with one of my staff members at five o'clock," I had to tell Sara.

"That's OK," she said as she tore off the corner of her copy of Senate Bill 1 on which she had written the address of the church and handed it to me, already sweeping out of the room. She sang out over her shoulder as she walked away, "You can bring him with you!"

I was both ecstatic and disappointed: ecstatic because I would still get to see her, but disappointed because now I knew that it wouldn't be a date—even though it *was* at a church.

I left the United Methodist Building, met Jimmy Garrison directly across the street, and brought him with me to the church where I was to meet Sara, which turned out to be a fundamentalist Protestant church on the far side of D.C.

When Jimmy and I entered, I was a little shocked to see all the women seated on the left side of the church and all the men seated on the right side of the church. Everyone was between fifty and seventy, and all the women were wearing white gloves and long skirts that came almost down to their shoe tops.

And there was Sara, seated in the front row, in her floor-length blue jean skirt.

But there were no "men's seats" left in the church, so Jimmy Garrison and I each carefully leaned against the far right wall of the church and then sat down, cross-legged, on the floor.

I caught Sara's eye as she sang from a huge hardcover black hymnal. She smiled, casting her glance at the white gloves someone had obviously loaned to her and then back at me. I was delighted. Jimmy elbowed me lightly in the ribs.

An elderly, snow-white-haired minister clothed in bright red vestments ascended the pulpit and began a harangue against "loose morals" and "liberals." When he was done, he asked everyone to bow their heads and pray. He had just started to pray when he looked up and saw Jimmy Garrison and me seated cross-legged on the floor, eyes closed. Jimmy, who had been born in China, had his hands turned upward on his knees, with his thumbs and index fingers joined to form a circle in a classic Buddhist prayer position.

A look of sudden horror immediately flooded the features of the elderly minister, and he stopped abruptly in the midst of his prayer and shouted over at us, "You! You, over there! You can't sit like that in a house of God, in the presence of Our Lord!"

I had my eyes closed in prayer, and at first I didn't realize to whom he was speaking. Then he repeated himself, his loud booming voice clearly directed at us. "*You* there, over there sitting on the floor against the wall! You cannot sit like that in this church!"

I opened my eyes and saw the minister rushing down from the pulpit and coming across the chapel straight toward Jimmy and me.

"Get up, get up!" he shouted.

I slowly uncrossed my legs and rose to my feet.

"There were no more men's seats," I said, by way of defense.

"That's no excuse for your coming in here and sitting like heathens in the presence of Our Lord!"

Jimmy and I stood up against the wall, thinking that we would just stand there. But the white-haired minister wasn't having any of that. "Perhaps it would be best if you two gentlemen simply left, since, as you see, there are no more men's seats available."

So we shrugged and ambled out of the church. I figured that was it— Sara would probably never speak to me again. *And so what?* I thought, trying to rationalize my loss. *If she is into those kind of right-wing fundamentalist assholes, this was never going to work out anyhow.*

But, as Jimmy and I started to walk away from the church, Sara came rushing out, throwing her white gloves on the ground.

"Holy shit!" she declared. "What assholes! I can't believe that my brother wanted me to go to *that* fucking church!"

I was tremendously relieved that she was not one of those fundamentalists. Not only that, she could swear like a trooper—she also certainly had those people pegged.

Jimmy Garrison and I then took Sara to a local Thai restaurant, where Jimmy regaled both Sara and me with a litany of stories about his experience with fundamentalist Baptist services, both in California . . . and in China. As it turned out, both of Jimmy's parents were Southern Baptist missionaries. That was how they had met and that's why Jimmy had been born in China. Both Sara and I said almost nothing during the entire dinner together because Jimmy Garrison's stories were so damn interesting. Finally, Jimmy had to excuse himself to get to a meeting, and Sara and I were finally left alone.

Sara had been born the eldest child of a United States Marine officer in Quantico, Virginia, the home of the United States Marine Corps, at the height of World War II. She was raised, initially, by just her mother in the tiny North Dakota village of her father's family, with a population of only fifteen hundred people, until her father came back from the war, having fought in the Pacific. Her paternal grandfather had been A. H. Nelson, the founder and sole owner of the Scandia Bank, one of the original famous farmer cooperative banks in the Upper Midwest of Wisconsin and the Dakotas. So Sara, like me, had been a very large frog in a very tiny pond—that is, until she became an extremely precocious fourteen-year-old, finishing as the runner-up in the Miss Western North Dakota Beauty Contest, in which she won both the swimsuit competition and the talent contest by playing a Beethoven sonata on the piano. Fearing she would fall prey to the older boys in that tiny town, her grandparents had immediately shipped her off to Ferry Hall Academy, a high-toned all-girls prep school in Illinois.

She had blossomed at Ferry Hall, she said, where she was "free from being chased by boys." (*I can just imagine*, I said to myself.) Then she had gone to Cornell University, but she didn't like the elitist attitude there, so she transferred to UC Berkeley (because her cousin Connie had moved there). There she truly shined. She cofounded the first nonprofit public documentary film production and distribution company in the United States, then became a television news anchor in Santa Cruz, California. Because she had directed, filmed, produced, edited, and narrated the first major documentary film about women in labor unions in the United States, the president and the acting vice president of the National Organization for Women had then asked her to become the national labor secretary for NOW at its Washington, D.C., headquarters.

"And so, here I am!" she said breathlessly.

"Well, you certainly are!" I responded, and she laughed like chimes in springtime.

She then invited me to a birthday party that Friday evening for Bob Alvarez's and Kitty Tucker's little girl, Amber. Bob and Kitty were two of the founding members of SOS. "That way, you can tell me about *you*," she said.

Suddenly it dawned on me: this was the first time I had ever sat, perfectly silent, listening to someone else tell me *their* life story, without interrupting them to tell them mine. Even though Jimmy Garrison's life story had not deterred me from superimposing my own, I had been struck into utter silence in the face of Sara's origins. I was, for the very first time in my life, genuinely more interested in finding out about her than I was in telling her about me.

Needless to say, I immediately accepted her invitation to attend Amber's fourth birthday party, as well as the next Supporters of Silkwood meeting, to be held earlier on the same Friday afternoon as Amber's party.

At that next SOS meeting, Howard Kohn (a member of SOS and the Washington bureau chief of *Rolling Stone* magazine) set forth, largely for my benefit, I believe, the chronology of the Karen Silkwood case.

The Karen Silkwood case began at 7:30 PM Central Time on the evening of November 13, 1974.

It was a Tuesday night. Karen Silkwood, a twenty-eight-year-old health and safety organizer for the Oil, Chemical and Atomic Workers Union at the Kerr-McGee nuclear facility in Cimarron, Oklahoma, just north of Oklahoma City, left a 6:00 PM union meeting in her tiny white Honda Civic, headed down to Oklahoma City, where she was scheduled, at 8:00 PM, to meet with David Burnham, a prize-winning investigative reporter from *The New York Times*. Burnham was waiting at a Holiday Inn for Silkwood and several large envelopes of highly classified internal Kerr-McGee Nuclear Corporation documents that she was bringing with her. Those documents contained proof that the Kerr-McGee nuclear facility, the only nuclear waste reprocessing plant in the world, was missing more than forty pounds of 98 percent pure, bomb-grade plutonium that had been extracted from its waste materials—more than enough pure plutonium to make eight thermonuclear bombs the size of the ones that destroyed Hiroshima and Nagasaki, Japan.

But Karen Silkwood never arrived at that meeting. She was killed just two miles from the front gate of the Kerr-McGee nuclear facility when her tiny white Honda Civic was rammed twice from the rear and forced off the public highway into a concrete culvert. Her lightweight car rolled over in midair and landed, roof-down, in the bottom of the culvert, pinning her frail ninety-eight-pound body to the crushed ceiling, impaled by the steering wheel.

But her body then mysteriously disappeared from the wreckage. It was found forty-eight hours later with a "Jane Doe" tag on its toe in the

Oklahoma City General Hospital Morgue, many miles away—with all its soft tissue removed: her brain, heart, lungs, liver, kidneys, stomach, and intestines. Her crushed Honda Civic also mysteriously disappeared from the crash scene and was not taken, as was required by law, to the regional state highway patrol yard. It was found, instead, concealed in the garage of the Cimarron Ford dealership that serviced the Kerr-McGee Nuclear Corporation's vehicles.

Banner headlines went out around the world: "Nuclear Union Activist Killed in Mysterious One-Car Crash on Her Way to Meet with *The New York Times.*"

I saw the *ABC Evening News* account of Karen's death that night, after she had been killed, during a short break I was taking from an intense American Indian Movement meeting at the Pine Ridge Reservation in Wounded Knee in South Dakota.

I had made a quick trip from Boston back out to South Dakota to attend this meeting. I and the others present at the meeting were drawn like magnets to David Shumacher's November 14, 1974, account of Karen Silkwood's mysterious death and the disappearance of the documents she had shown to her coworkers just before departing from her last union meeting for her secret rendezvous with *New York Times* reporter David Burnham.

"Holy shit!" I had exclaimed. "Someone is going to kick their ass in court for that!"

Little did I know, at that moment, that that someone was going to include me.

Sara had become involved in the Karen Silkwood investigation seven months later, in late June of 1975. Kitty Tucker, a first-year law student at Antioch Law School and a member of the Washington, D.C., chapter of the National Organization for Women, had gathered a collection of published magazine articles about the Kerr-McGee Corporation and Karen Silkwood's mysterious death. She had also written up a prosecutor's memo synopsizing this information and delivered it to Sara in her capacity as the national labor secretary of NOW. Sara had not had time to read all the material until 2:00 AM that night. She sat alone on her bed, in a tiny makeshift attic bedroom in another NOW member's home, propped up against the wall with pillows.

(She later moved into the attic of the home of Kitty Tucker and Bob Alvarez on Butternut Street in Washington, D.C.) When Sara started reading, she became aware of Karen Silkwood's actual "presence" in her room, hovering immediately next to her small twin bed. Sara then "heard" Karen Silkwood say to her, "as clearly as I have ever heard any living person," "If you don't get the women to help me, no one is ever going to do anything about what they did to me."

Sara was stunned at the clarity of this experience.

The very next morning, she went directly to her Washington, D.C., office and called in all of the members of her National Labor Task Force. In that meeting, she informed the task force members that, among all the many other issues they had to work on that year, they were now going to have to address the additional issue of "the killing of Karen Silkwood." Sara explained to her staff that since NOW had been campaigning actively for more than two years to get women to play a more active role in the leadership of American national labor unions—and Karen Silkwood had so obviously been murdered because she was attempting to do just that at the Kerr-McGee nuclear facility—it was going to be the obligation of NOW's National Labor Department to take up Karen's cause and to generate a congressional investigation into what had happened to her and to her documents.

Sara immediately identified NOW's upcoming August 25, 1975, National Day Against Violence Against Women as the target of their organizing. She announced that she and her staff would make Karen Silkwood "the poster child" of that event and that Sara would personally get Karen Silkwood's mother, Merle Silkwood, to address the national NOW convention in August. Sara, Kitty Tucker, Bob Alvarez, and all seven of Sara's NOW National Labor Task Force members mobilized and set up a meeting with Attorney General Edward Levi for August 25 regarding the progress on the Karen Silkwood investigation. They also set about getting hundreds of thousands of NOW members from across the country to write letters to their respective congressmen and U.S. senators, demanding a congressional investigation into what had happened to Karen Silkwood—and what had happened to the documents in her car on the night she was killed.

As expected, the assistant United States attorney general and FBI officials informed Sara, Kitty, and NOW president Karen DeCrow, in that August 25 meeting, that the Karen Silkwood investigation had been "closed"—even though they had not answered a single one of the obvious outstanding questions in the case. FBI investigators and Justice Department attorneys simply assumed that the preliminary Oklahoma state highway patrol report filed on the night of November 13, 1974, had been correct when it simply stated— prior to any meaningful investigation—that "Karen Silkwood had probably fallen asleep at the wheel and accidently run off the highway into the concrete culvert." They had no explanation for how radioactive plutonium had contaminated food in Silkwood's home refrigerator prior to her death, and they had taken no steps whatsoever to determine from which lot number the radioactive contaminant found in Karen's home had come.[4] They also had no explanation as to where Karen Silkwood's documents had gone after her crash; nor did they provide any explanation as to what had happened to Karen Silkwood's body during the forty-eight-hour period immediately following her death. They also said they had discovered no evidence that the Kerr-McGee Nuclear Corporation was missing forty pounds of 98 percent pure bomb-grade plutonium. Despite these glaring, unanswered questions, they had officially "closed" the Karen Silkwood investigation.

In her press statement issued on the steps of the United States Justice Department following that meeting, Sara excoriated the FBI and the Justice Department for "their obvious participation in the cover-up taking place in the Karen Silkwood case." She publicly urged people from all across the nation to write and telephone their congressman and senators, demanding a full congressional hearing into "the killing of Karen Silkwood." It was on that date, August 25, 1975, that "The Killing of Karen Silkwood" became a national campaign slogan that found its way not only into the lexicon of our generation but also onto the subway walls and tenement halls of America.

NOW's public shaming of the Ford administration, the Justice Department, and the FBI resulted in the almost immediate scheduling of a joint House and Senate hearing into the Karen Silkwood matter. The Senate side of the hearing was to be chaired by Senator Lee Metcalf of Montana, chairman of the Senate Government Operations Subcommittee. The House side of the hearing was to be chaired by John Dingell, the fiery congressman from Detroit who chaired the House Energy Committee's Subcommittee on Energy and the Environment.

Sara and Kitty then successfully persuaded Merle Silkwood, a shy but immensely sincere and moving spokeswoman for her daughter, to make her first-ever public speech—to the entire assembled national NOW convention in September 1975.

Sara had become convinced, from discussions with Tony Mazzocchi, the Washington, D.C., legislative representative of the Oil, Chemical and Atomic Workers Union, that Karen Silkwood had indeed been murdered and that unless NOW took up the matter, nothing would ever be done about it. As a backup plan for *when* (not *if*) the Justice Department and Congress dropped the ball, Sara and SOS had resolved to file a federal civil rights lawsuit against the Kerr-McGee Corporation on behalf of Karen's children and family. That was where I came in.

I worked directly with Kitty Tucker to fine-tune her original conception of a draft federal civil rights complaint. Since Kitty was only a first-year law student at the time, she had not yet completed either her constitutional law course or her civil procedure course, so she had only a general idea about what to do—but her general idea was pretty damn good. For example, she didn't realize that one could not sue a *corporation* for conspiring to violate the civil rights of a private citizen. But I cured that difficulty by proposing that we name the *individuals* whom we reasonably determined had participated in the conspiracy to violate Karen's constitutional rights. In addition to Karen's First Amendment right to freedom of speech and freedom of the press, I included in the complaint Karen's Fourth Amendment right to be secure in her "person, property, papers, and effects against unreasonable searches and seizures," as well as her more esoteric First Amendment right to travel freely and safely on the public highways. We still needed to find some adequate degree of "state action" or federal government action to cojoin with the private action that had violated Karen's constitutional rights, which might be necessary to overcome the more conservative reading of the federal Civil Rights Act that required "government action" to generate an anti–civil rights conspiracy unless it was motivated by race.

I also explained to Kitty that we had to file our federal civil rights complaint before November 13 of 1976 because the federal district court in Oklahoma would almost certainly adopt the shortest possible statute of limitations applicable to civil assault claims under Oklahoma state law as the operational bar to any federal civil complaint that "sounded in" assault. And I assumed we would have a very adversarial federal judge on our case, since the judges had all been nominated for the federal bench by Robert S. Kerr, the four-term governor and then the three-term U.S. senator from Oklahoma who was the cofounder and de facto owner of the Kerr-McGee nuclear facility. That gave us only one year to complete our preliminary investigation before we had to file our complaint arising from the killing of Karen Silkwood.

I successfully persuaded both Kitty and Bob to file and litigate the case "right in the heart of Kerr-McGee country" rather than trying to bring the case in the District of Columbia. These were all subtle but important legal nuances that no first-year law student would have been reasonably expected to understand. But Kitty had all the basics very well in hand. She and I got along famously.

The presentation of my proposed federal civil complaint was met with uniform approval by members of SOS at our next meeting. Afterward, Sara invited me to spend the weekend with her at the Butternut Street house. We then spent the next three weekends together, because I had been able to persuade her to stop working by successfully finding a "politically relevant" movie to see each of those weekends.

Four weeks later, however, when I went directly from our weekly SOS meeting back to Arrupe House because it was my Friday to cook dinner for all of us there, I received a very distressed phone call from Sara.

"Are you coming over here to spend the weekend with me *or what?!*"

I immediately hung up the phone and asked Father Bill Davis, on my way out the door, to please serve the dinner that I had already cooked, because I had to "go do research on *that special project* that he had suggested I work on."

He laughed and said, "You had better get used to this." I could hear Father Jim Vizzard banging plates down on the table as I made a beeline

for the Blue Flame. From that weekend on, I spent my weekdays working sixteen-hour days at Jesuit national headquarters, attending all-evening
meetings with Catholic priests, Catholic nuns, Protestant ministers, and progressive religious political activists concerning various domestic and global
issues, and living with my Jesuit brothers at Aruppe House. And I spent
every weekend with Sara, preparing the Karen Silkwood case.

As the scheduled date of the joint hearing approached, Sara worked
on her and Karen DeCrow's public testimony to be presented to Congress
while Kitty Tucker and I completed the details of our draft federal civil rights
complaint to be filed as soon as Congress completed its final meeting without
discovering what had happened to Karen Silkwood and her documents.

In early April 1976, just days before the scheduled joint public hearing by
Congress, I was driving down Independence Avenue in the Blue Flame when
I heard a "special report" by Barbara Newman on NPR. She announced
that Senator Lee Metcalf had suddenly canceled the Karen Silkwood hearings "because Karen Silkwood's family has publicly announced that they are
entirely satisfied with the exhaustive investigation that has been conducted
by the FBI into this matter."

I had to pull off to the side of the highway to finish listening to the
report. When the report was over, I immediately turned around and drove
directly to the Rayburn House Office Building and marched into the office of
Peter Stockton, the chief investigator for Congressman John Dingell. When
I came through the office door, Stockton immediately leaped to his feet and
began to apologize profusely, informing me that he, too, was totally surprised by the unilateral announcement issued by Lee Metcalf's office. He
said that John Dingell had absolutely no plan to cancel his House side of
the public hearing. For the moment, I calmed down. But I insisted that Peter
take steps to find out who the hell had met with Lee Metcalf within the
past two days and persuaded Metcalf to call off his hearing by feeding him
that line of bullshit about the Silkwood family being satisfied with the FBI's
investigation. Stockton pushed back, accusing me of being a "conspiracy
theorist" . . . along with that "Afro-haired Tucker woman." He went on
to say that he had heard about our preparing a federal civil rights lawsuit
against the Kerr-McGee Corporation, and he warned me that if word got

out about it, it could stop any congressional investigation because "Congress cannot become involved in any matter that is under litigation between private parties."

"That's such an unmitigated crock of horseshit," I said. "You ought to be ashamed of yourself for even trying that one on me." I told him that I knew full well that the Democratic National Committee had been suing Nixon's Committee to Re-elect the President all through the Senate Select Committee public hearings on the Watergate burglary, and that neither Metcalf nor Dingell were going to get away with backing down on this investigation. Furious, I stomped out of his office.

I drove directly to Sara's office at NOW and confirmed that no such statement of any kind had ever been made by anyone in the Silkwood family. Then I met with Father Bill Davis and Terry Shea, the director of the Jesuit national headquarters, and updated them. Frankly, they were both rather excited to be in the middle of things rather than just sitting on the sidelines and attending meetings.

The very next day, Peter Stockton called me and asked me to come back to his office on Capitol Hill. When I arrived, he told me that he had discovered that Dean McGee himself had personally met with Lee Metcalf and claimed that the Silkwood family had stated that they were entirely satisfied with the FBI investigation. I told Stockton that was bullshit, because Dean McGee didn't have "the kind of juice" to get a Senate hearing stopped since the death of Robert S. Kerr at the end of the Kennedy administration. I demanded that Stockton get back in there and find out who else was in that meeting between Dean McGee and Lee Metcalf. Once again, Peter Stockton accused me of being "a conspiracy nut." But he agreed that he would look into it one last time. "But if you're wrong, Sheehan, your ass is grass over here on Capitol Hill, and I will be the lawn mower!" Stockton had such a colorful way of expressing himself.

When Stockton called two days later, I met him at his office and immediately asked what he had found out. "Not here," he said. "Let's take a walk." So we left his office and walked around the corner. When we were out on the public street, he suddenly turned to me and said, "Jeeeeezus H. Christ, Sheeeeehan! What the hell have you gotten me into here? You were right!

There *was* somebody else in that goddamned meeting with Dean McGee. But he wasn't signed in on the fucking official visitor log. It was Robert fucking Bennett! Robert F. Bennett! Do you know who the fuck *he* is?"

"Sure I do," I said. "He was the guy who took over as Howard Hughes's chief Washington, D.C., lobbyist right after Larry O'Brien got pushed out of the Hughes empire by the Mormons and Bob Maheu. He handled Howard Hughes's secret relationship between his Summa Corporation and the National Security Council. He went on to head up Mullen & Company, which employed E. Howard Hunt when Hunt became a member of the Plumbers Unit. I've always figured Mullen & Company as an agency proprietary. What do you think?"

Stockton, a former top-secret-clearance weapons analyst for the U.S. Defense Department, just stared at me, literally slack-jawed. He took a full step back, looked me up and down, and then said, "Just who the hell *are* you, anyhow?"

"I am the chief counsel to the United States Jesuit headquarters in Washington—and you don't get to that position from having fallen off some fucking melon wagon on the way into Washington, D.C.," I said.

"Well, well," he said. "You and I are going to have to have a few much more private conversations. But not in the company of those hair-on-fire radicals that you have been hanging out with. How the fuck did you ever get tied up with those loonies over there?"

I smiled. "Do you mean the Jesuits or the women in NOW?"

"Both!" he laughed. And we suddenly became good friends.

Stockton was now hooked. With Robert Bennett making an appearance in the Karen Silkwood case, Stockton was now convinced there was something much bigger going on "than just this Silkwood broad's having gotten herself bumped off for being a union organizer." There had to be something more in those documents than evidence simply proving that the Kerr-McGee Corporation was sloppy in its operations. "If Robert F. Bennett is involved in this, then 'the agency' might be involved in this. And if *that's* so, then Dingell is going to be pissed!"

From that point on, Peter Stockton and John Dingell were in it for the long haul.

Three days later, Stockton called me again to say that he wanted to meet me for lunch in the cafeteria of the Rayburn House Office Building. I was waiting at a small table when Pete arrived. He told me that he had just been visited at his office by a woman the previous afternoon. She had just walked in off the street and asked to see him. She told him her name was Jackie Srouji. She was an American married to a Middle Eastern man. She represented herself as being a reporter for the *Nashville Tennessean*, a prominent liberal Nashville newspaper run by John Seigenthaler, an old and trusted friend and aide of Bobby Kennedy's. So Pete had listened to her. Srouji had been asked to write a book about private nuclear power, she reported to Peter. But she wouldn't tell him who made that request. In the process of researching her book, it had been suggested that she might want to take a look at "the Silkwood matter." Again, she wouldn't say who had "suggested" that she do that. She had then come across information that revealed that Karen Silkwood "had been to bed with three different men—all inside of *one year!* And that she smoked marijuana!"

But she wouldn't say *how* she had "come across" this information.

When Peter challenged her and demanded to know from whom Srouji had gotten such information about Karen Silkwood, she reached for her briefcase and said, "Well, it's right here in the typed transcripts of her telephone conversations and the conversations in her house."

"Whoa there," Peter said to her, stopping her from pulling out the transcripts, which would have compromised him by putting him in a situation in which she could later testify that Congressman Dingell's professional staff investigator had made use of wiretapped telephone conversations and electronically recorded conversations in the home of Karen Silkwood.

"I don't want to see those! Where did you get those transcripts anyway?" he demanded.

"Why, I got them directly from James Reading, the chief of security for the Kerr-McGee Nuclear Corporation," she said, apparently naively.

"Holy shit!" Stockton exclaimed. "How did you get to talk with him? We have been trying to get a meeting with him for weeks!"

"Oh?" she said. "I was introduced to him by a friend I met when I was working for the *Nashville Banner* some years ago. He is now the FBI agent

in charge of protecting the security of the radioactive materials at the Kerr-
McGee Facility."

The *Nashville Banner* was the ultra-conservative daily newspaper in
Nashville. But Stockton let that go. "And how is it that you happened to
know that FBI agent in Nashville?" he asked her.

"Oops! I've probably said more than I should have," she said, ending
the conversation.

So that was my lead. Now I had to find out who had done the wiretapping and electronic surveillance against Silkwood. Whoever was doing that
might very well have been following Karen on the night she was killed. And
either those people had run her off the road or they would certainly have
seen who did.

CHAPTER *eighteen*

O NE AFTERNOON, AS I was giving a lecture on covert operations and illegal political surveillance at George Washington University Law School, a young woman raised her hand.

"Professor Sheehan, what is the LEIU?"

I was puzzled. I had heard a lot of acronyms in Washington, but I had never heard that particular set of letters.

"Do you mean LEAA?" I asked.

"No. Not the federal Law Enforcement Assistance Administration. The LEIU."

I confessed that I had never heard of anything called LEIU, so I asked her to come to see me at the end of class and give me more information so I could help her find out. Sheila O'Donnell, a tall, strong-shouldered woman of twenty-one, moved to the front of the room after class and waited for the group to thin out. Then she approached.

"So, what's the story? Where did you hear about this LEIU? Give me some context," I said.

"Well, I got a call last night from a guy I know up in Seabrook, New Hampshire. You remember the demonstrations there last year?"

"Sure I do, against the private nuclear plant in Seabrook."

"Right! Remember how the New Hampshire State Police arrested so many of the kids in those demonstrations that they ran out of jail space and had to warehouse them in the high school gymnasium and the fire station?"

"Yeah. I remember," I laughed.

She laughed too.

"Well, a friend of mine, who is an ACLU cooperating attorney up there in Seabrook, filed a federal civil rights lawsuit on behalf of the kids who were being held that way." She went on to tell me that the specific lawsuit had failed, but that her friend had run into the assistant U.S. attorney who had opposed her friend's motion demanding discovery of whatever evidence had been gathered by electronic surveillance and provided to the United States Attorney. That assistant U.S. attorney had chided her friend, saying, "There wasn't *that much* electronic surveillance information gathered on them anyhow." Her friend asked, as casually as he could, "Well, exactly *how much* such electronic surveillance was there?" The assistant U.S. attorney then told her friend that the only surveillance they had was some sort of newsletter, and he still had copies of it at his office. So her friend went over to the U.S. attorney's office and read the newsletter. It contained "dirt" on leaders and members of the New Hampshire Clamshell Alliance—information about their sexual relationships; about who was smoking dope, who was taking prescription drugs; things like that. What he couldn't figure out was where all the information was coming from. All the newsletter kept saying was "LEIU sources say . . . "

"So he called me this morning," Sheila said. "And he asked me, 'Who the hell is this LEIU?' I spent the whole morning calling around to see if I could figure it out. And nobody knows—*nobody*."

I asked if she knew anything else about this LEIU.

"That's about it," she said. "It seems to be some outfit that is gathering, or at least distributing, dirt on members of the antinuclear movement. The monthly newsletter was called *Information Digest*. It's put out by some guy who goes by the name of John Reese. Have you ever heard of this guy?"

I reflected. "No, I haven't. But I'll have one of my people look into this."

It was time to bring up the heavy artillery.

I called Sara and told the SOS group that I was not going to be party to filing any federal civil lawsuit without first being in direct possession of some reasonable amount of potentially admissible evidence demonstrating who had contaminated and killed Karen Silkwood and why. I explained that if Robert F. Bennett was involved in this case, we were going to be up against "the first string." We had better get a "first-string investigator" on our team. I told Sara that we would need at least $10,000 in cash to bring on board the man I had in mind.

Sara did it. She persuaded Barbara Marx Hubbard, one of the heiresses of the Marx toy company fortune, to donate $10,000 to the Supporters of Silkwood.

Since Bill Taylor and I had left Lee Bailey's firm two years earlier and had gone our separate ways back in the fall of 1973, Bill had founded the Florida Association of Professional Private Investigators. His William J. Taylor Agency office was below deck on the *My Sin*, a seventy-two-foot, teakwood, three-masted yacht that lay at bay at the Miami Yacht Club. *My Sin* was owned by one of F. Lee Bailey's not-so-lucky former clients who was, at that time, doing ten years in Leavenworth federal prison for federal income tax evasion. However, the man had this multimillion dollar yacht and a twenty-four-year-old mistress, both of which needed "looking after" by someone *completely reliable* for the years that the owner would be "away." That had been Bill Taylor's out from the Bailey firm, and Bill had taken it. The job was good for $50,000 a year, plus the right to pilot *My Sin*. All his expenses—and hers—were covered by a trust of which Bill Taylor was the sole trustee. It was a solid and cushy job. And since Bill Taylor was one of the very few security men Lee Bailey knew who could keep it in his pants around beautiful women who belonged to someone else—and also knew his way around sailing vessels of all sizes and descriptions—Bill Taylor had been the perfect man for the job. Besides, it gave Bill an opportunity to open his own PI firm with a fancy Miami Yacht Club address.

I drove to Union Station and took the escalator down into the domed reception area. I placed a call to Bill Taylor's beeper number on the public telephone inside the American Café. I then dutifully punched in the number of the public phone and a prearranged code number, hung up, and waited for Taylor's return call.

Within two minutes, the phone rang. I picked it up.

"Hey," I said.

"Hey. What ya got?" Bill Taylor's baritone "radio DJ voice" asked.

I filled him in on the details I knew about Karen Silkwood's death, and I told him what Peter Stockton had told me about Jackie Srouji. I also told him about Robert F. Bennett showing up, with Dean McGee, in Senator Lee

Metcalf's office and stopping the Senate investigation. Then I explained to Bill what Sheila O'Donnell had told me about the LEIU. I gave him the name John Reese and told him about the monthly newsletter *Information Digest*.

"We used to dig that shit up on the local ACLU hippies back in North Carolina around Lajeune all the time," Bill said.

"Yeah. Well they're at it again."

Bill said he would check it out. "But I can't do shit if I don't get ten grand up front. Annie isn't gonna let me outta town until I lay that in her pink little hand. I'll be lucky if I get one grand for expense money on the road."

Both of us laughed. Annie Taylor, Bill's *fourth* wife, was a pert and pretty model, right off the front cover of *Cosmopolitan*, but she neither understood nor cared about any issue that Bill or I might be interested in pursuing. What she cared about was a nice home, a nice car, and nice clothes for her and Alan, her young son from a previous marriage. As long as that was provided, she would provide Bill Taylor with everything he needed and a responsible administration of all the monthly bills. It was a perfect American marriage—from the 1950s. In exchange, Bill Taylor was free to travel on business as much as he liked and to be gone for as long as he needed to get any investigative job done.

I told him the money would be on its way the next day.

"OK," he said. "I'll call my guys, right after we ring off here, and get the ball rolling. When the ten arrives, I'll be on it. You get a discount flight to Disneyland, and we'll meet to put this operation on the road. Deal?"

"Deal."

"Keep your head down."

"It's down."

With this, we hung up.

I was sitting in my Capitol Hill office on North Capitol Street three days later when I heard the phone ring just once. I waited. After thirty seconds, it rang again, but just one ring. That was the signal from Bill Taylor. I knew it was time for a trip back to Miami.

The next morning, I descended the stairs in Miami National Airport from an Eastern Airlines flight directly from Washington, D.C. It was exactly twelve noon as I moved among the tourists and teeming children into the baggage claim area. There was Taylor, at the nearest newsstand, between the gate and the baggage area, "reading" the area from behind a copy of a Robert Ludlum novel. That was a small joke we shared, since neither one of us would ever read a Ludlum novel—in order to keep from confusing the fictional world of espionage with the strange reality that made up the world in which we worked.

I walked to the newsstand and purchased a pack of Dentyne gum—the sign to Bill that everything was okay. Taylor moved smoothly into a trailing position behind me as I walked to the luggage carousel. I feigned waiting for a bag while Taylor moved past me and proceeded out of the baggage area toward his waiting Land Rover. Now it was my turn to follow. We met at the Land Rover and drove away in silence.

After we had made our way onto the Tamiami Trail, Taylor spoke.

"We've got to stop and get a map of Georgia."

We stopped at a local gas station. After a few minutes, he came out, entered the vehicle, and drove away. We didn't talk. I was used to this. It was Taylor's style.

I waited. This, indeed, was one of the important features of my conduct that had caused Taylor to trust me. I was one of the rare men who was willing to give Taylor the space—and the unquestioning trust—that he needed to operate with another.

Taylor drove the rest of the way to the Miami Yacht Club in silence. He parked in a designated parking slot with the name John Stone on it. I followed Bill onto the white-painted walkway that led to the skiff he had tied at the end of the dock.

We boarded silently, and Bill piloted out to *My Sin,* which lay at anchor in the harbor, not too close to, yet not too far from, the other large yachts all around it.

He pulled alongside and motioned for me to mount the ladder that hung from the aft of *My Sin,* indicating that he would follow with my bag and briefcase. I climbed aboard.

It was gorgeous—all natural teak and bronze, polished and attended to in a manner that only experienced sailors or Marines knew how to do. It was a seventy-two-foot wonder.

As we walked along the port side walkway between the highly polished wood railing and the freshly scrubbed white-painted wall of the main living room, my eyes fell upon the nude body of a blond, twenty-four-year-old beauty lying on her stomach, adding to her already-considerable suntan. She did not stir as she heard us come aboard.

Bill gestured with a nod for me to enter the main door on my right, saying quietly, "Watch the step up," as I stepped over the six-inch riser at the bottom of the watertight doorway that stood open, awaiting our arrival. The living room was a luxuriously appointed layout that one would have expected to see on a Hollywood set. Bill gestured toward the couch as he entered a narrow door and went below to stow my gear in my state room. I went to the small refrigerator at the side bar and took out two bottles of Dr Pepper, which I knew would be there as long as Bill Taylor was the one in charge of stocking it. I put some ice into two large tumblers and poured the Dr Pepper over the cubes in both. I then sat down and waited for Bill to return.

He was back before I had finished half the Dr Pepper in my glass. He was carrying the map he had purchased on the way back from the airport. He opened the map and spread it on the bar.

I handed him his Dr Pepper. He took a long drink before scouring the map.

"I called Alpha," he said, as his steel-gray eyes moved methodically across the paper landscape of Georgia.

"I told him what we had. When he called back two days later, he said, 'Go to Georgia!' So I asked where in Georgia, but he said, 'That's all I can give you. Go to Georgia.' So here we are, and . . ." He bobbed his head toward the map and continued to search. "There is Georgia."

"What are we looking *for?*" I asked.

"I figure that we will know it when we see it," he said, still scouring the map.

Suddenly he moved his big ham-hand over the map and dropped his massive right index finger onto a point on the map. "*There,*" he said. He tapped his finger three more times on the spot. "There it is!"

I squinted my eyes and leaned toward the map to read the dark red letters: SAVANNAH RIVER NUCLEAR PLANT.

"It's a double-barreled nuke," he said. "I've heard about it."

"What about it?"

"It's in Georgia," he said. Then he started refolding the map.

"I don't want anybody else knowing about this information from our source. And I don't want any signals, either intentional or inadvertent, going out that we're looking at this place."

"*Are* we looking at this place?"

"You put the ten grand in my hand, and we're looking at this place within two day's time."

I reached inside my blue jean shirt and removed an envelope. I handed it to Taylor, and he smiled.

TWO DAYS LATER, Bill Taylor drove up to the large iron gate of the estate of Edward R. Garland Jr., just outside Atlanta, Georgia. Edward R. Garland Jr. was the lawyer son of Edward "Rubin" Garland Sr., the number 1 criminal defense attorney in Atlanta for the previous twenty-five years. Garland Sr. was now retired—was indeed at death's door. And his son Eddie Jr. was in the process of taking over his father's longtime law practice. So he was open to doing favors for his father's friends and legal associates.

It was just such a favor that brought Bill Taylor to his gate that evening. Taylor was there to ask Edward R. Garland Jr. what he knew about the Georgia Power Company's Savannah River nuclear facility and how to get a contact inside its nuclear division.

Edward Jr. gave Bill the address of a young woman by the name of Sally Williamson who worked in the payroll department of the facility's parent corporation, Georgia Power. The next day, Taylor tailed Sally Williamson, tracing her movements from a distance until she went into a local bar. He approached her there, and since she owed Edward Jr. a favor, she agreed to help him. She said the payroll department at the plant was switching over to a new printout system and that she could run some "test" printouts of the entire payroll for the company the following day. Taylor agreed to meet her for dinner the next night.

When he arrived for dinner, she was dressed for the occasion and greeted him with champagne and the promise of a Cornish game hen. Eventually, he got a look at that payroll list. And that's how he came across the name William Lovens.

Lovens had been a "dirty" U.S. Army CID (Criminal Investigation Division) type who ran with the agency guys in Southeast Asia between '68 and '70. Rumors had it that he was tied to one of the three major opium warlords in Thailand, and to missing U.S. weapons that had gone walkabout in Eye Corps. This was just the kind of guy that Taylor had been hoping might turn up in a list of Georgia Power employees.

In the computer entry next to Lovens's name, alongside his Social Security number and date of birth, was a three-digit number: 666. Sally Williamson told Taylor that the numbers represented Lovens's "unit designation." Unit 666 was the "Risk Management Unit." It was in the Public Relations Department.

"Cute," Bill said.

Bill then combed through the names and data of all the other employees of the Georgia Power Company with 666 next to their names. There were ten men in all. When he ran background checks on these ten men, he discovered a peculiar thing. Four of the ten had listed as one of their two previous employers the Boynton Beach Police Department in Florida. That was the kind of "coincidence" that Bill Taylor loved to find: something that didn't make any sense—because it almost always did.

Taylor made a call to a source to obtain the service record of a man whose name had caught his attention: Arthur Benson, the director of the Risk Management Unit of the Public Relations Department of the Georgia Power Company. Not only was he told that Benson's records were classified, but Taylor's source warned him that Benson was "a dangerous character who always carries a snub-nosed, silver-plated .357 magnum in his belt on the middle of his back and wears a skull and crossbones belt buckle. He was a 'wet operations man' in an outfit called the Phoenix Project in Vietnam."

There it was! The Phoenix Project! Vietnam!

Taylor then began to tail Bill Lovens. Though the man was heavier and going gray, Taylor recognized him immediately from their service together in Vietnam. Posing as another man the two of them had served with, Taylor approached Lovens at a bar after following him for a few days. Eager to impress an old service buddy, Lovens told Taylor where he worked and what the nature of his work was. He told Taylor that his Risk Management Unit had three cars, each equipped with a set of rotating headlights that, with a push of a button, you could switch from one configuration to another, so that if you were following someone at night, you could change the configuration, making the car look different. Each car was also equipped with long-range, telephoto-lensed video cameras with infrared photographing capacity. After several drinks, Lovens even offered to take Taylor out to the Georgia Power plant where the nuclear reactor was, boasting that it was the biggest in the country. It was there, he said, where the Risk Management unit did its real work.

Lovens was so tipsy when they arrived at his office that he punched in the entry code directly in front of Taylor; Taylor memorized the code, which gave access to the area that contained a cutting-edge UNIVAC computer. Once inside, Lovens showed off shelf after shelf of revolving files of index cards. Each card contained information on the sexual activities, drug use, and other sensitive behavior on the part of "potential enemies of the company," such as members of the local and state ACLU, those who had written letters to the editors of state and local newspapers criticizing private nuclear power—and even local members of the National Council of Churches.

Next Lovens showed Taylor a room full of two dozen telephones attached to voice-activated tape recorders. He said they had a contact at Southern Bell who would set up a direct tap to "monitor for suspected theft of services" on the phone numbers of anyone they wanted. The voice-activated tape recorders recorded every phone conversation of certain people, such as those whose names were on the cards in the UNIVAC. Taylor asked, out of genuine curiosity, "Can't you get your ass in a shitload of trouble if you get caught doin' that?" Lovens responded, "No way! We give everything to the LEIU!"

"Great, great!" exclaimed Taylor, even though he didn't have the slightest idea what the LEIU was.

Taylor then flew down to Boynton Beach, Florida, and started asking his sources about the Boynton Beach Police Department, where four of the members of Georgia Power's Risk Management Unit had been previously employed. He was told that the Boynton Beach Police Department had received a big grant from the Law Enforcement Assistance Administration of the Nixon administration's Justice Department. With that money, it had formed a Special Intelligence Unit and had purchased a helicopter. Every Tuesday afternoon, several members of the Boynton Beach Police Department's Special Intelligence Unit would get on that helicopter and fly away. They wouldn't come back until late Thursday night. Nobody Taylor talked to knew where they went.

After Bill Taylor relayed this information to me, I went directly to see a man I knew in Washington, D.C., named Robert (Bob) Fink. Bob was the chief investigator for Congresswoman Bella Abzug from New York City. She chaired the Individual Rights Subcommittee of the House Judiciary Committee. Bob Fink had been seconded from her investigative staff over to the Pike Committee of the House of Representatives, the corollary committee in the House to the Senate Select Committee on Government Operations Pertaining to Intelligence Activities, chaired by Senator Frank Church of Idaho.

Both of those committees were investigating the illegal foreign and domestic activities of the CIA and the FBI. These activities included drug smuggling and assassinations abroad, as well as the illegal domestic surveillance of organizations like the Black Panther Party, the American Indian Movement, the ACLU, the NAACP, and NOW. Bob Fink was a very well-informed man. When I had first come to Washington, D.C., I had met Bob and had told him what I had learned from my work on the Pentagon Papers case about the Central Intelligence Agency's smuggling of opium out of Southeast Asia and using money from the sale of that opium to finance a political assassination operation called the Phoenix Project. Bob had told me then, "Anybody who doesn't know that the CIA was smuggling opium and heroin in Southeast Asia is too ignorant to function effectively in Washington, D.C." But then he had added, "On the other hand, if anybody thinks that he can tell the American people about this, he is too naive ever to work effectively in Washington."

I went to talk to Bob because I knew he had become an expert on aviation matters while investigating the "cutout" aviation companies of the CIA, such as Evergreen Airlines, that the CIA used as proprietaries. I told Bob our problem: We had tracked this operation in the Karen Silkwood case down to the Boynton Beach Police Department. We knew that a Special Intelligence Unit, funded with an LEAA grant, flew off in a helicopter purchased with that LEAA grant every week for a few days. But we couldn't figure out where they were going. I asked his advice as to how we might find that out.

He suggested we check the LEAA grants and find the registration number of the helicopter purchased with their grant. Then we should get the tail number of that helicopter. With that, we could go to the Federal Aviation Administration and check flight records for that helicopter, since the pilots would be required to log in a flight plan as to where they were going each Tuesday. He agreed to do all that for us. It took him a while, but he found out that the helicopter had been flying from the Boynton Beach Police Department to the Fort Lauderdale/Hollywood Airport in South Florida. He even knew which helicopter pad, just off the tarmac at the Fort Lauderdale/ Hollywood Airport, it landed on.

Bill Taylor drove down to the airport in Fort Lauderdale to check out the landing pad. He stood on the pad and looked around in a 360-degree circle. And there it was! Just as big as life, way off to one side of the airport— a large building surrounded by an electrified metal fence with absolutely no signs or other forms of identification. It also had a conspicuous "no-man's-land" all around it. Bill recognized a "no-man's-land" when he saw one. Everything had been cut down for two hundred feet in every direction around this gigantic building. There were no brush, no trees, no high grass— nothing where anybody could hide to sneak up on the facility.

Bill asked around, but no one had any idea what that building was or what was going on inside it. Bill finally ended up talking to a former Marine Corps vet on the Boynton Beach Fire Department. The fire department was required to go in and check the fire extinguishers in all buildings in the county periodically, to make sure they were functioning properly. However, a special note had been inserted in the fire department's file regarding that building. It stated that fire officials could not go inside that facility "because it is a national security facility." One would have to secure a national security clearance to go in there.

Bill Taylor called me and told me what he had found. He said that the Boynton Beach Fire Department's file had the building registered as the National Intelligence Academy.

"What the hell is the National Intelligence Academy?" I asked.

Bill didn't know. He said he planned to stake out the building to see who came and went. So Bill rented an old rent-a-wreck and pulled it into the woods where he could maintain a full frontal view of the building. He actually cut down a bunch of little trees and packed the ground down firmly in a small area so he could get good traction out of there if he needed to leave quickly. He spent three days observing the facility through binoculars, and taking down license plate numbers of the vehicles coming and going, and taking long-range photographs of people entering and leaving the facility.

During his surveillance, Bill had discovered that behind the National Intelligence Academy was a small bay, where two large boats came and went twice every day. Each boat had a big satellite array on its top. Bill wanted me to authorize him to rent a boat so he could follow those boats.

I said, "OK, we can probably do that. Find out how much of the $10,000 it will cost. Let me check with Sara. I won't tell her what we need it for. But I'll tell her that we need to spend it."

Two days later, while I was waiting to hear back from Bill as to how much this boat was going to cost, I received a call at my office at the Jesuit headquarters from Tony Mazzocchi, the Washington, D.C., legislative representative of the Oil, Chemical and Atomic Workers Union (OCAW). Tony was running the investigation for the union on the Karen Silkwood case. Tony was the immediate supervisor of Steve Wodka, the OCAW field organizer who had been talking regularly with Karen on the telephone before she had been killed; and he had been at the Holiday Inn with David Burnham and Karen's boyfriend, Drew Stephens, on the night of November 13, 1974, waiting for Karen to arrive with her documents. Tony wanted me to come over to his office—right away.

CHAPTER *nineteen*

A FTER SPEAKING WITH Tony Mazzocchi, I drove over to the OCAW headquarters and went upstairs—and there were Steve Wodka and Tony waiting for me. We sat down, and Tony reached into the inside pocket of his sports jacket and removed an OCAW envelope. He emptied the contents of the envelope onto the small coffee table around which we were seated. There before us were dozens of tiny pieces of some kind of small electronic device. Tony asked me, "Do you know what this is?"

"Where did you get that?" I asked, staring at the pieces lying on the table.

Tony had recently been elected vice president of the Oil, Chemical and Atomic Workers Union and had been preparing to move out to the organization's national office in Denver. "I was taking the clock off the wall in our kitchen," he said, "when *this* thing fell out from behind the clock and onto the floor. It kind of fell apart like that. So I picked up the pieces and stuck them in this envelope. Do you have any idea what this is?"

I sat and stared at the pieces for a few seconds. Then I said, "Well, I've got a pretty damn good idea what it is. But I can find out for certain from a guy I know."

I put all the pieces of the device back into the envelope and took them with me. I drove a few blocks away and used a public telephone to call David Waters, an electronics expert who had been in the Research and Development Department of the Central Intelligence Agency for years. His specialty was electronic surveillance devices. David had become a "resource person" for my Washington Interreligious Task Force on Civil Rights.

"David, this is Danny Sheehan." He remembered me right away and seemed happy to hear from me. So I said, "I'd like to come out and see you, if I can. I have something I'd like to talk to you about. But I don't think we should talk about it over the phone."

He laughed. "I'm glad you remembered some of what I told you."

"Well, a lot of people might think I am being a bit paranoid. But you and I both know that I'm not."

David gave me his address and directions to his home. I drove out into the Virginia countryside, where David lived with his wife and daughter. I drove past his house and parked a few blocks away, around a corner and out of sight. I went to his back door and knocked. He came to the door in some kind of chef's outfit, with an apron and one of those puffy little white hats. He was cooking something in the kitchen.

We sat drinking tea for a few minutes, catching up on old times. Then, before I started talking about anything of substance, he said, "Wait here. Let me show you something I've been working on." He got up, wiped his hands on his apron, and walked over to a telephone on a small table on the other side of the living room. He punched into the phone a long number. Within seconds, the conversation we had just been having started playing loudly, in stereophonic surround sound.

"Isn't that great?" he said, beaming as he walked back to his seat across from me. "I can call in to that number from anywhere in the world at any time of the day or night and download any of the conversations that have taken place over the previous seventy-two hours on any of the phones in the house and any conversation that has taken place in any room."

I was amazed. Then I remembered what he had told me he had been working on when I had last spoken to him. "Your harmonica amplifier?"

"That's right! You remembered! I installed it because I've got a fourteen-year-old daughter, and this allows me to keep tabs on her."

I was offended. "Isn't that the very kind of thing that you were so worried about when you came to my task force last year and warned us about the capabilities that our intelligence agencies were developing to spy on citizens?"

He looked puzzled.

"That?" he said. "*That* was about the state spying on private citizens. That's horrible. This is just technology. As long as it is being used for something that is OK, it's fine with me. The state always abuses its power, and that is when it becomes dangerous."

I wasn't persuaded.

Then I remembered: David Waters was a die-hard libertarian. He was not opposed to anything that *private* people did. It was only "the state" that he feared. I knew I wouldn't further my objective by getting into a debate with him about those distinctions, so I turned to the matter at hand. I reached inside my sports jacket, removed the OCAW envelope from my inside pocket, and poured the contents onto the small coffee table between us.

David just stared at the dozen pieces of electronic equipment for several seconds. Then, without a world, he reached down and started to methodically reassemble the pieces into a working miniature electronic listening and recording device. After what seemed like only a handful of seconds, he held up the reassembled object between his thumb and index finger and said, "What have you been up to that the NSA is so interested in?"

"The NSA?" I asked.

"Yes," he said. "The National Security Agency."

"I know what the NSA is!" I said, a bit peeved. "I thought that the NSA was only operative on the international level, not on the domestic side."

I told him everything, giving him all the details as to what we were doing, concluding with an account of what Bill had discovered down at the National Intelligence Academy. I revealed to him that "my man in the field" (I did not give him Bill Taylor's name) had just called and said that he wanted to rent a boat.

Waters literally jumped up off the couch. "A *boat*? What does he want to do with a *boat*?"

"Well, I would guess it has something to do with those two boats he saw that have those big satellite dishes on top of them. He said he wanted to check out where they were going."

David became almost hysterical. He began talking very loudly and pacing back and forth. "Wait just a second. Wait just a second. You are getting in way over your head here. There is a guy I've got to call right away. You've *got* to have a meeting with this guy *before* you let your guy go anywhere near those boats!"

I was amazed. He seemed to know something that he was not going to tell me.

I told him that was OK with me, that this was why I had come to see him. "I figured you would know what to do about a thing like this," I said, gesturing toward the now reassembled object on the coffee table. It lay there looking like a large dead insect.

David went over to the telephone and called someone. I could hear him saying, in a low voice, "This is David. Is he there? Would you please try to find him right away? It's important. Very important. Please tell him to call me as soon as you can possibly find him. Tell him that I *need* him to call me, not that I just *want* him to call me. Do you understand? Good." Then he hung up. He poured us each another cup of hot tea and we settled back, waiting for his return phone call. Neither of us said another word.

I was about to tell him that I thought that he was being a bit overdramatic. And then the phone rang. He jumped up and dashed to the phone. It was his daughter, checking in. He was on his way back to sit down when the phone rang again.

"Yes . . . yes," I could hear him say into the receiver. Then he hung up. He came back, sat down, and told me that I would get a call within the next two days. "You will be asked whether you want to come to a beer and pretzels party. You will be 'the beer.' The man on the other end of that phone call will be 'the pretzels.' OK? Do you understand?"

"Sure I understand," I said. "I get invited to beer and pretzel parties all the time." He laughed. I thanked him and got up to leave. As I walked to the door, he reminded me again to be *very* careful.

That was a Friday afternoon. On Sunday morning, I was walking back from Mass with the Franciscan seminarians and some of the monks when Father Wally Kazubouski, a young Franciscan Capuchin priest and a law student of mine at Antioch School of Law, called out to me from the back porch of Arrupe House. There was a call for me. I didn't know whether it was Bill Taylor calling me back with a price quote for the boat or the invitation to the beer and pretzels party. I dashed up the back steps of Arrupe House and into the confessional phone booth.

"Hello, Dan. Do you know who this is?"

"Yes. Yes, I do."

"Would you like to come to a beer and pretzels party?"

"Sure," I said. "When and where?"

"Same place as Friday. One PM. And come alone."

I told him I would be there.

I drove back out to David Waters's house in Virginia in the Blue Flame. Again, I parked a few blocks away, but this time in a different location, taking greater care to park in a place that was very difficult to see. David answered the door and looked up and down the street, checking for the car that I had come in.

"Good," he said. "I like cautious men. Come in." David had barely poured tea for us when his other guest arrived. In fact, there were two of them. The man who had called me was strikingly handsome, about five foot eleven, in his early to mid-forties, and about 160 pounds. He was in good shape but not "Special Forces" shape. He was an office man. He wore dark-rimmed glasses; a short, close-to-his-face black beard; and a black, expensive-looking rolled-neck sweater. His "friend" was a no-neck, no-nonsense older military type, perhaps CIA or a "field man." But he was definitely not an office man. He was an "action officer." He never said a word, and no one made any effort to introduce him to me, but he was always there, never more than a step or two away from the Office Man.

The Office Man came in and sat down on the sofa next to the coffee table. David brought him a hot cup of tea. No-Neck stood at the end of the couch, periodically glancing out the window and constantly casing the place with his eyes. He reminded me of an older Bill Taylor.

"David, would you mind stepping out for a while? I am sure you have a few Sunday-morning errands to run. Is Gail home?"

"No," David said. His daughter had been up early and had gone over to her girlfriend's to do some homework.

"Fine. That's fine," said the Office Man. He waited until David had left the house.

I smiled to myself, remembering the phone system David had specially installed in his home to monitor his daughter's conversations and phone calls.

After No-Neck gave the Office Man a nod indicating that David had cleared the area, The Office Man turned to me, raised his teacup, and took a careful sip.

"David tells me that you have been involved in something that the NSA seems to have taken a special interest in?"

"*Am* involved in. I *am* involved in something that the NSA *is* taking a special interest in," I said, to make clear that I wasn't going to soft-shoe what we had come here to talk about.

"Very well. Something that you *are* involved in. Is this domestic or foreign, if I might ask?"

"Domestic," I said.

"Tell me more, if you would," the Office Man said.

So I laid it on him. Because the Office Man had come to me through David Waters, I figured that he was a friend rather than someone from "the other side," despite the presence of No-Neck. And, in my opinion, what I was doing was 100 percent red-blooded-American patriotic. So I didn't hold back anything—except for Bill Taylor's name and what he had done to protect his own life down in Fort Lauderdale. I laid out everything: about what had happened to Karen Silkwood; about the missing forty pounds of 98 percent pure bomb-grade plutonium; and about what "my man in the field" had discovered through our investigation down at the Georgia Power Company and at the National Intelligence Academy.

The Office Man sat quietly, sipping his tea, absorbing everything I was saying like a black hole. He said nothing until I got to the part about the boat.

"A *boat?*" he virtually shouted. No-Neck turned and instinctively assumed an "alert" posture. I was the one who now sat there calmly. For effect, I took a long slow sip of tea, even though mine was cold now. But the conversation was heating up.

"A boat?" the Office Man repeated. "What does your guy want to do with a boat?"

I told him that I assumed it had something to do with the two large boats that my man saw coming and going to and from the National Intelligence Academy. "I think he wants to know where they were coming from and where they were going."

"Jesus Christ!" the Office Man exploded. "You don't have any idea what you are dealing with here."

"Perhaps you want to enlighten me as to exactly what it is you think I am dealing with here," I said. The Office Man and No-Neck exchanged worried glances. I nodded at No-Neck. "Or perhaps your friend might wish to enlighten me as to what operational instructions I should give to my man in the field?"

No-Neck gave off a decidedly hostile vibe in response to my reference to him.

"Look, Dan," the Office Man said.

"You can call me Danny. All my friends do. Are we going to be friends, Mr. . . . ?"

"Allies, definitely. Friends? . . . maybe. Maybe someday." Then, as though he had resolved at least something, he said, "Look, Dan . . . Danny. You don't know us. But my friend here and I, together, have a list of security clearances as long as your arm. But that's all I can tell you right now. Perhaps I will be able to tell you more someday. What I can tell you is this: If your man in the field tries to go near that place where those two boats are coming from, he will be killed. And let me be as clear as possible about this: Nobody will do *anything* about it! He will be dead, and that will be that."

I let what he was saying sink in. It was not intended to be a threat. It was a genuine warning.

"OK," I said. "Let's assume that we are all serious men here, dedicated to trying to do the right thing. I am interested in knowing who placed electronic listening devices in Karen Silkwood's home in Oklahoma. I am going to find out who did that. I don't have to tear down the kingdom to do it—but I will if I have to. I am assuming that the two of you are capable of finding out who it was that did the Silkwood wiretapping. If you get me that information, then I—and my man in the field—will leave your island alone." The "island" part of that was a guess. I waited.

Both the Office Man and No-Neck reacted slightly at my mention of an island. I knew from their reaction that I had hit home. There was a brief moment of silent communication between the two men.

"Here is what I will do," the Office Man said, like a man who was used to making deals like this. "I will call you within two days. I will see what we can do to help you get what you are after. But you have to promise me that you will instruct your man to stand down, at least for three days, so I can be sure that he is not going to try to find out where those two boats are going. Will you promise me that?"

I knew that Bill was already at his "sanctuary" and that he needed a few days of medical attention anyhow. So I was able to make that agreement—to get something by giving up nothing.

And with that, the Office Man and I shook hands, warmly I felt, and he and No-Neck turned and left.

I drove back to Arrupe House and enjoyed the warm Sunday-afternoon sun.

On Monday morning, I spoke with Bill Taylor from a pay phone. I explained to him what had happened and what it was I had agreed to.

"Take three days off, my friend," I told him. "I think we are going to need it." Bill agreed to stand down for three days.

When Tuesday arrived, I made sure to be in my office, available for the call from the Office Man. The morning passed without any contact. Shortly after lunch, I received a call from David Waters.

"Hi, Dan. Have you heard from Terry yet?"

Ah, Terry, I thought to myself. *The Office Man.* I told David that I hadn't heard from him yet but that I was expecting his call by the end of the day.

"Yes. I know," David said, and we laughed, because we both knew how he knew this.

"I called over to the White House this morning and he was not available," David said. *The White House?* I exclaimed to myself. "I was told that he was in a very important meeting," David said. "So I'm assuming that it was about your matter."

"I hope so," I said. "I want to have as much assistance from Terry as I can get."

David asked me to let him know when I heard from Terry. And then he rang off.

It was almost 4:00 PM when I heard from Terry. I picked the phone up after the first ring.

"Sorry about it being so late in the day," he said. "Do you know who this is?

I said that I did.

"I am working on this as a top priority. But the information is not in place yet. I know that I am asking a lot, but could you have your man give me another day?"

Based on David's earlier report, I was convinced that Terry was telling me the truth and wasn't just stalling me. So I said, "I can do that. But I have people relying on me to get this information. So I cannot responsibly hold off much longer on an important lead like this."

"I appreciate that," Terry said. "I do. Be ready to come to a meeting tomorrow, if you would."

Wednesday morning, I was at my desk, in a suit and tie, waiting for Terry's call. The phone rang at 11:00 AM.

"Hello. Do you know who this is?" Terry asked. It was now clear that he was going to do this at the beginning of each of our phone calls.

"I do."

"Could you meet me for lunch today? Say at twelve noon?"

"I can," I said.

"Good. Go to George Washington University. You do seminars there, so your going there will not generate any suspicion. Go to the cafeteria, pick out a table in the center of the cafeteria, and I will be there soon after you are in place."

I agreed to do that, and he rang off.

I drove over to George Washington University, parked in my normal place, and walked to the cafeteria.

I brought only my daybook and a yellow pad and pen. After I bought an egg salad sandwich, I found a table in the middle of the cafeteria. Before I had finished the first half of the sandwich, I saw Terry and No-Neck come into the cafeteria and get in line. But there was a third man with them, a suit-and-tie type. He looked like a Capitol Hill staffer, younger than Terry and No-Neck.

I waited for them to come sit down at my table. Terry did all the talking, but he didn't really *say* anything. Then he turned to No-Neck. It was the first time I had heard him say anything, and I was surprised at how well-spoken he was. *Definitely former CIA,* I thought to myself. But No-Neck didn't have much to say either, just some "telephone security 101" and some personal security tips of a similar elementary nature. The entire meeting was turning out to be a total waste of time. I was beginning to change my mind about trusting Terry, so I started to get up to leave. I said as I rose, "I guess I was wrong in standing my man down, expecting something more from you than just a stall." But the moment the words were out of my mouth, the Third Man spoke for the first time.

"Dan—ahhh, I mean Danny, you mentioned that you were going to be going directly up to The Hill right after our lunch. I'm going that way. Why don't I give you a lift?"

This was the first interesting thing that had happened since they had sat down, because I hadn't said anything about going up to The Hill. So I viewed his invitation to give me a ride to be an invitation to come with him for a talk.

The Third Man and I got up and left together. We walked to his car, which turned out to be an unassuming Volkswagen Beetle—and not a new one at that. I scrunched into the tiny passenger seat, and we launched off toward The Hill. The Third Man immediately started grilling me about what exactly I was looking for. I essentially repeated the account I previously had given to David Waters and Terry. When I got to the part of the story in which my field man wanted to rent a boat, I half-expected him to have the same reaction that both David Waters and Terry had had. But the Third Man remained calm. This told me that Terry had already briefed him.

"What does your man want with a boat?" he calmly asked me.

"I think that he wants to go to the island where the two boats go from the National Intelligence Academy."

The Third Man's reaction to this offering—which now included "the island"—dwarfed the reactions I had gotten from David Waters and Terry. He actually temporarily lost control of his vehicle. Fortunately, there was not much traffic on Maryland Avenue at that moment, because his vehicle literally careened to the curbside and his front right wheel mounted the curb immediately adjacent to the United States Supreme Court.

When his car came to an abrupt stop, the Third Man popped the clutch and the car stalled.

"Wait!" he said. "We've got to get out of the car. Let's get out of the car." He pushed open his driver's side door, opening it right into Maryland Avenue without even looking back to see if any traffic was coming behind us. I immediately followed suit, climbing out onto the sidewalk beside the Supreme Court Building from my passenger side, since the front end of the tiny car was already partially up on the sidewalk.

"Wait!" he repeated. "Your man *can't* go to that island. He can't! They will kill him!"

Within seconds, the Third Man was literally on top of me, grabbing me by the lapels of my suit coat.

"You've got to listen to me! They will kill him. They killed an entire television news crew, just last year! And no one did a damn thing about it. An entire news crew!"

This was starting to get much more interesting. Although Bill and I were never able to verify his claim, the point was clear: Going to the island could be dangerous, if not fatal. At that moment, though, the Third Man certainly didn't strike me as the type I had to fear physically. There was a time when it would have been very dangerous for a man to grab me like that. But those days were in my past now. I simply grabbed his hands and firmly pulled them off my lapels.

Forcefully, I said, "Why don't we start by your telling me what is *really* going on at that 'National Intelligence Academy' and on that island?"

Fear surged back into his features. "I . . . can't. I've taken an oath. I would lose my security clearance."

"Well, you've got a choice. You either tell me what's going on on that island or I am going to release my field man from our pledge to hold off. And let me assure you that they—whoever they are—are not going to kill *this* guy. He is going to find out exactly what is going on, and you won't have any agreement from me—or from him—not to tell everybody about it."

His fear turned into genuine panic. "You can't do that! You don't understand!"

"Try me," I said. "I assure you that I will understand if there is a good enough reason for me not to tell everybody what is going on down there."

The Third Man grew calmer.

"Look," he said, his voice dropping to a whisper. "Under that island is the most secure underwater U.S. nuclear submarine refueling station on the planet. Our submarines go into that under-island base through a set of underwater gates so they will not be picked up by Soviet surveillance satellites, and they are refueled there. But, more importantly—" he hesitated for five or six long seconds, obviously reflecting on whether he dared to tell me. "But, more importantly, under that island is the computer center from which we retarget every American nuclear missile in the world *after it is airborne*, to compensate for any nuclear missiles that have been intercepted or that for any other reason have not reached their preassigned targets."

Holy shit! I said to myself. This was really something! After I had recovered from the shock of what he had told me, I said, "But that doesn't explain why those two boats from the National Intelligence Academy keep coming and going from there."

The Third Man looked crestfallen. He had assumed that what he had told me was enough to bring me into the club of "the men in the know" and that I would not ask any additional questions.

"Look! I don't know why they are coming from the National Intelligence Academy to that island," he said.

"Who are you guys, anyhow? How do I know that you guys are even capable of getting for me the information I want?"

"I'll ask Terry to contact you tomorrow. But, please, give us forty-eight more hours before you go near that island. Will you do that, please?"

He seemed to be entirely sincere. And he was genuinely frightened. I agreed to give him twenty-four more hours. "But if you can't tell me who the people are who tapped Silkwood's phone and bugged her home by this time tomorrow, I am sending my man to that island."

We had a deal. I told him I would take a cab back to GW so he could get started on his assignment. He didn't have a lot of time.

As he roared away in his Volkswagen Bettle, I crossed Maryland Avenue, went into Anne Zill's office at the Fund for Constitutional Government, and placed a call to Bill Taylor's beeper, inserting the prearranged phone number for a pay phone outside of the Dubliner Café. Then I took a cab to that phone and waited for Bill's call. I told him that we had agreed to stand down for twenty-four additional hours and that I was going to arrange for him to fly up to Washington to prepare him to "make the meet" with whomever we were going to be getting our information from.

Terry called my office at 10:00 AM the next morning and told me to have my man standing by at my office at this time the following morning. "You will receive a call telling him where to go for the information that you want." And then he hung up.

I let them have the additional time without protesting.

Bill flew in that night and was with me at my office the following morning at nine o'clock. My office phone rang on schedule at ten.

"Hello, Dan. Do you know who this is?"

"I do."

"Put your man on the phone, please."

I handed the phone to Bill. He put the phone to his ear and listened. After a full minute, he said, "That's a negative. I repeat. That is a negative. You will go, instead, to the Key Bridge Marriot in Rosslyn, arriving there at twelve noon today. You will find a pay phone immediately adjacent to the valet parking desk out front. That phone will ring at exactly 12:01 PM. You will answer it. And you will go directly to the address you are given at that time. You will be met there, at the exact location that will be described to you in that phone call. Repeat please!" After a few seconds, he said it again. "Repeat please!"

Then Bill smiled, as the voice on the other end of the line repeated his instructions verbatim.

Then Bill hung up.

"OK. We're on!" Bill pulled on his light jacket and went out the door. He got into the car we had rented for him and headed for the Virginia countryside.

Bill made the call to the pay phone at exactly 12:01 PM and gave directions to a small roadside diner a few miles outside of Rosslyn, Virginia, where he set up some friends to keep an eye out. When No-Neck entered the diner at 12:30 PM, he took the booth that Bill had described and sat down. Bill and his "friends" watched from a nearby hillside. Once Bill was satisfied that no one was accompanying No-Neck and no one else was conducting surveillance on the diner, he walked in.

No-Neck told Bill that the information we wanted was in "the June mail." "June mail" was a code name used in very high covert intelligence circles to refer to information obtained through *domestic* "black bag operations" conducted by the CIA. No-Neck had asked an associate who had another reason entirely to be in "the June mail room" to sneak a look and see whether there happened to be a Silkwood file there. And there was. In that file was a note saying that one of the operatives who was part of the Silkwood surveillance was a homosexual, that he was having a sexual affair with a male disc jockey at an Oklahoma City radio station, and that there was great worry that he might tell his paramour about the Silkwood matter. So the Oklahoma City PD had been directed to transfer him to a different region.

Before leaving, No-Neck turned to Bill and asked, "Can we assume that this is sufficient to cause you to stand down from . . . that other matter?"

Bill looked No-Neck squarely in the eye. "This is a need-to-know operation. I am not in that loop."

"Yeah, right! And I'm Whistler's mother!" No-Neck said.

Without hesitating, Bill replied, "I liked your son's book better than his painting."

No-Neck had no idea what that meant. James McNeill Whistler's book was entitled *The Gentle Art of Making Enemies*.

Bill and I flew immediately to Oklahoma and met with Sherri Ellis, Karen Silkwood's roommate. Sherri was bisexual, and it did not take Sherri and her gay and lesbian friends in the Oklahoma City area long to pinpoint a member of the Oklahoma City Police Department who was engaged in a homosexual relationship with a male disc jockey in the city and who had been transferred away shortly after Karen Silkwood's death in November 1974. The man's name was Harold Behrens.

While Bill and I worked on trying to figure out who had been engaged in the surveillance with Behrens, Sara, Kitty, and Bob Alvarez worked intensely on getting the Karen Silkwood hearing under way in Congress.

Sara, Tony Mazzocchi, and Kitty Tucker all testified at that hearing. John Dingell also issued a subpoena to Jackie Srouji to appear as a witness. In her testimony, Srouji struggled mightily to insert into the hearing record her conclusion that Karen Silkwood smoked pot and had "gone to bed with three different men inside of one year." But John Dingell kept cutting off Srouji's efforts to put these kinds of personal slurs against Silkwood into the Congressional Record. Then he had Mike Ward, legal counsel to the committee, confront Srouji with demands to answer specific questions about how she had gotten access to internal FBI files about the Silkwood case and whether she had been given any documents indicating that Kerr-McGee Security Department personnel had been engaging in illegal electronic surveillance against Karen Silkwood. Kitty Tucker also went after Srouji during the hearing, protesting Srouji's persistent efforts to cast aspersions on Karen Silkwood's character and insert those into the Congressional Record. Immediately after Srouji completed her testimony, Sara confronted her. "How *dare* you come here and try to say those things about Karen when she is not here to defend herself!"

The day after Srouji returned to Nashville, she was called into the publisher's office at the *Nashville Tennessean* by the editor in chief, John Seigenthaler. There Srouji admitted that when she had worked for the *Nashville Banner*, the conservative daily newspaper in Nashville, she had regularly used her news journalist's credentials to gain access to citizen's meetings of various student organizations, women's groups, antiwar groups, and other "activist" groups in the Nashville area for the FBI. She admitted that she had conducted "interviews" of members of those organizations, representing to them that she was preparing news stories sympathetic to their objectives, but that she had, instead, simply reported on the activities and plans of those organizations to the FBI. She tried to defend her actions to Seigenthaler by asserting that her editor at the *Nashville Banner* had introduced her to the agent in charge of the FBI Counter Intelligence Program (COINTELPRO) and that he had expressly approved of her engaging in those activities for the FBI. However, she refused to tell Seigenthaler who had suggested that she write a book about private nuclear power or to tell him who had suggested that she include a chapter about Karen Silkwood. So Seigenthaler fired her.

Shortly thereafter, a cadre of FBI agents descended on Nashville and began questioning John Seigenthaler's coworkers, friends, business associates, and neighbors "about John Seigenthaler's liking to have sexual

relations with little girls." In Detroit, Congressman John Dingell's home district, a prostitute then convened a public press conference at which she suddenly announced that her "favorite client" was John Dingell. It took Peter
Stockton less than two days to discover that that prostitute was a numbered
informant for the FBI.

John Dingell, furious at this attempted intimidation, immediately convened a second House hearing on the Karen Silkwood matter. In that hearing, he inserted into the public record his denial of ever having had any
relationship whatsoever with that woman. In that second hearing, John
Seigenthaler was also provided an opportunity to publicly denounce the FBI
for what it was trying to do to him. But that second hearing brought to an
end any further efforts on the part of Congress to try to determine what had
happened to Karen Silkwood . . . or to her documents.

At that point, it was then clear that the Silkwood family and NOW
would have to file and prosecute the contemplated federal civil rights lawsuit
against the Kerr-McGee Corporation if we were ever going to find out what
had happened to Karen—and her documents.

CHAPTER *twenty*

FLEW BACK FROM Oklahoma, where Bill Taylor and I had been investigating Harold Behrens, to Washington, D.C., to work with Kitty, Bob, and Sara to develop exactly what federal civil complaint we had to file in order to give us the breadth of discovery we would need to get to the bottom of these three mysteries: What had happened to Karen Silkwood? What had happened to her documents? And what had happened to the forty pounds of bomb-grade plutonium that had gone missing from the Kerr-McGee nuclear reprocessing plant? Our challenge was to not violate rule 11 of the federal rules of civil procedure, which required any licensed attorney who signed a given federal civil complaint to swear that he or she was in possession of adequately credible information (even if not yet in a technically court-admissible form) on the basis of which he or she had come to hold an *actual* "good faith belief" that each and every allegation set forth in the complaint was true and accurate—and had a reasonable chance of being proven to a reasonable jury to be "more likely than not" true.

Kitty Tucker, being only a first-year law student and not yet a licensed attorney, wanted me to "throw the kitchen sink" at everyone we could think of as a potential defendant. In support of her position, Kitty cited the typical plaintiff's tort complaint, in which the plaintiff's civil attorney sues everybody in sight, uses the civil discovery process to sort through all the named defendants, and then tosses out, one by one, the named defendants as they are each exonerated through the civil discovery process. For example, as Kitty argued, if a commercial airplane crashed into a private home, the plaintiff's attorney would usually sue the airline; the manufacturer of the airplane; the pilot and the crew of the plane; the company responsible for training the pilot and crew; the company in charge of maintaining the plane; the corporation that had manufactured the wheels for the airplane; and so on. This was typical "plaintiff's practice" as she understood it from law school.

I explained to Kitty that I was not a "typical private plaintiff's attorney." I was instead a people's advocate: a public interest civil prosecutor who would investigate and litigate cases that sought to effectuate the best interest of "the people" when the government's attorneys failed to do so or, more commonly, *refused* to do so for one political reason or another. I therefore insisted upon conducting myself just as though I were bound by the same constitutional constraints as were government prosecutors. I explained to Kitty that it was not my job to make all conceivable claims and then pick my way through them looking for the ones that were true. I had to personally believe that a *specific* accusation was true, *or else* I would not make it.

For that reason, I insisted that Bill Taylor and I be the sole arbiters as to what allegations would or would not be put into the Silkwood complaint—not the Silkwood family, not the National Organization for Women, and not anyone else. Moreover, I insisted that we adhere to the shortest possible statute of limitations when filing our lawsuit. That meant we would have to file our Silkwood federal civil lawsuit by November 13 of 1976, since it was conceivable that an overtly hostile federal district court judge in Oklahoma might deem Karen Silkwood's intentional contamination to be governed by the two-year Oklahoma statute of limitations, which would be applicable to a case of "simple common law assault" no matter what additional constitutional principles were violated by this same act.

Others thought we should file in Washington, D.C., because the FBI had so flagrantly participated in the cover-up of the killing of Karen, but I insisted upon filing the case in Oklahoma, in the very heart of Kerr-McGee territory. I agreed with including a count of FBI cover-up in the complaint, but I wanted to make the Kerr-McGee Nuclear Corporation the ultimate Bad Guy in the morality play that I intended to present to the jury—and to the nation. If we did everything right, we might even make the entire private nuclear industry the Bad Guy. But that was still no reason to file the case in Washington, D.C.

I proffered the following three-count federal civil complaint to be filed in the Karen Silkwood case.

- COUNT 1: Asserting that a number of specifically named private individuals had criminally conspired to violate the following fundamental constitutional rights of Karen Silkwood: (1) Karen Silkwood's First Amendment right to freedom of expression concerning her right to advocate for the establishment of a lawful labor union at the Kerr-McGee Nuclear Corporation; (2) Karen Silkwood's First Amendment right of association concerning her right to be a member of a lawful labor union; (3) Karen Silkwood's First Amendment right to freedom of speech and to freedom of the press concerning her right to meet with and to provide information to *The New York Times*; (4) Karen Silkwood's First Amendment right to travel freely and safely on American public highways; (5) Karen Silkwood's Fourth Amendment right to be secure in her person against physical assault and battery motivated by an animus toward her based upon her exercise of her First Amendment–protected rights to freedom of speech and freedom of the press; (6) Karen Silkwood's Fourth Amendment right to be secure in her home against unwarranted intrusion; (7) Karen Silkwood's Fourth Amendment right to be secure in her papers and effects against unwarranted search and seizure and against unlawful electronic eavesdropping on her private telephone conversations and her private conversations in her home; and (8) Karen Silkwood's fundamental Ninth Amendment right to life.

- COUNT 2: Asserting that agents and operatives of the Kerr-McGee Corporation and of the Kerr-McGee Nuclear Corporation had *intentionally* contaminated Karen Silkwood and Karen Silkwood's home with more than four hundred thousand disintegrations of radioactive plutonium per minute for the purpose of inflicting upon Karen Silkwood a full lifetime body burden of radioactive contamination so that the Kerr-McGee Nuclear Corporation could terminate the employment of Karen Silkwood, purportedly for her own personal safety but really to stop her from organizing a labor union at the plant and to destroy her credibility as a public critic of the health and safety procedures at the plant.

- COUNT 3: Asserting that agents and operatives of the Kerr-McGee Corporation and of the Kerr-McGee Nuclear Corporation had wantonly, recklessly, and *negligently* contaminated Karen Silkwood and Karen Silkwood's home with more than four hundred thousand disintegrations of radioactive plutonium per minute.

The specific persons that I proposed be named as defendants in count 1 were Dean McGee, president of the Kerr-McGee Corporation; R. T. Zitting, president of the Kerr-McGee Nuclear Corporation; James Reading, chief of security of the Kerr-McGee Corporation; Harold Behrens, an Oklahoma City police officer; two "John Doe" Oklahoma City Police Department detectives whom we suspected James Reading had hired to spy on Karen Silkwood with Behrens; Rick Fagan, the Oklahoma State Highway Patrol officer who supervised the site of Karen Silkwood's death; two "John Doe" members of the Oklahoma State Highway Patrol (one was the Oklahoma State Highway Patrol radio dispatcher who, on the night of November 13, 1974, expressly ordered licensed Oklahoma State Highway Patrol emergency vehicle driver George Martin to stand down from going to the crash scene of Karen Silkwood's death; Roy King, director of the Kerr-McGee Corporation personnel department; Larry Olson, the FBI agent assigned to protect the radioactive materials at the Kerr-McGee nuclear facility; and two additional "John Doe" agents of the FBI.

We filed the complaint in the United States District Court for the Western District of Oklahoma in Oklahoma City, literally in the shadow cast by the Kerr-McGee Tower across downtown Oklahoma City, on Tuesday, November 9, 1976, just four days short of expiration of the shortest possible applicable statute of limitations. The timing, a Tuesday morning, gave us the ideal news cycle to get the story picked up across the country.

The case was taken by the chief judge of the court, Judge Luther Bohannon. Thirty days later, we immediately filed dozens of "document demands" detailing the internal documents of the Kerr-McGee Nuclear Corporation and the Kerr-McGee Corporation that we reasonably believed had been taken from Karen Silkwood's car on the night she was murdered, and we demanded the right to review and copy those documents. But Judge Bohannon, a federal bench nominee of Senator Robert S. Kerr (the founder of the Kerr-McGee Corporation), sustained every even minor objection made to our discovery demands. So a major discovery battle began, with the Kerr-McGee Nuclear Corporation represented by William Paul, president of the Oklahoma State Bar Association and a partner in the largest law firm in the state, Crowe & Dunlevy.

For our Oklahoma local counsel, we secured the services of James Ikard, a six-foot-four former college basketball star at the University of Oklahoma and an ACLU cooperating attorney in Oklahoma City.

I effectively moved to Oklahoma City, with Father Bill Davis, to wage the discovery battle against the Crowe & Dunlevy firm, the Justice Department—and Judge Luther Bohannon. Sara, Kitty, and Bob continued, back in Washington, to build nationwide public support for our case. Sara recruited Bonnie Raitt, a native of Oklahoma, to put on a public benefit concert in Oklahoma to raise funds—and consciousness—for the case. Bonnie returned later with Jackson Browne for a second benefit concert. Then Bonnie and Jackson recruited David Crosby and Graham Nash to come on board to perform benefit concerts across the country with their partners Stephen Stills and Neil Young in their famous band Crosby, Stills, Nash & Young. These famous musicians joined forces with *Rolling Stone, The Nation,* and *Mother Jones,* as well as with National Public Radio, *The Village Voice,* and other progressive media throughout the country to inform all of the members of our generation about what had been done to one of our own by one of the most powerful corporations in America. I was thirty-one, and the Karen Silkwood case was beginning to feel like a generational culture war between our anti–Vietnam War/antinuclear generation and the World War II anticommunist/pro–nuclear power generation.

The Kerr-McGee Corporation—and the entire private nuclear power industry—struck back with a scurrilous multimillion-dollar personal smear campaign, accusing Karen Silkwood of being a lesbian, a bad mother, a drug addict, and a nymphomaniac who had sexual relations with "three different men all within one year"; of having intentionally contaminated herself to attract attention to her cause; and of having "accidentally contaminated herself while masturbating with a large salami from her refrigerator that had somehow become contaminated with radioactive plutonium."

The fight was on.

Even Judge Luther Bohanon got swept up into the battle. At one point in the midst of refusing to grant us one of our discovery demands, he exploded on the bench, calling Jim Ikard a "magpie" for his speaking with the media, and accusing me of "running off at both ends" (whatever *that* meant). He closed his verbal assault on us by declaring, "You should have already had all of your proof before you filed such an outrageous set of charges against some of the most outstanding men in our state!"

I immediately filed a motion to recuse him from the case, pointing out to the Tenth Circuit Federal Court of Appeals that Judge Bohanon had been nominated to the federal bench by Robert S. Kerr, the founder and first president of the Kerr-McGee Corporation—the very defendant that stood to potentially lose millions of dollars in the case before the court. Judge Bohanon quickly withdrew and transferred the case to Luther Eubanks, the worst judge in the entire federal district, who had a reputation for being seriously inebriated when he returned from his "long lunch" every weekday.

While this phase of the case was unfolding in Oklahoma, and while Sara, Kitty, and Bob were building support for our case out of Washington, D.C., Bill Taylor finally rented his boat. He used it to follow one of the satellite dish boats out of the bay behind the National Intelligence Academy at the Fort Lauderdale/Hollywood Airport. Bill trailed the boat to an island named Andros Island, located just off the east coast of Florida. Once he had discovered the island, Bill returned and got a friend to fly him, in his friend's personal helicopter, to within a few miles of the island, taking care to have the helicopter remain far enough from the island to not appear suspicious.

There, Bill roped down from the helicopter into the ocean and, using underwater aqualung gear, swam underwater to Andros Island.

Bill came ashore at a remote point on the island, stowed his diving gear in a secure place, changed into dry clothes and tennis shoes that he had carried with him in a waterproof backpack, and started to look around. He eventually came upon a compound where a dozen heavily armed men were speaking German. He took some photos and tried to record what they were saying. Then he returned to where he had stowed his aqualung and diving equipment. Redonning the scuba gear, Bill dove beneath the waves and explored the underwater terrain around Andros Island. As he was doing this, a huge Los Angeles–class U.S. nuclear submarine came cruising up out of the depths, moving directly toward what appeared to be a huge wall of land beneath the island. The submarine came to a virtual stop and hovered. Then, very slowly, a large section of the land mass under the island began to open. An entrance 25 percent larger than the width and height of the submarine slowly opened in the wall beneath the island. The submarine began to move forward at a very slow rate and disappeared beneath the island.

When Bill reported what he had found to Alpha, his highest-level source (whom I later learned was a liaison between the CIA and the Joint Special Operations Command of the Pentagon), Alpha told Bill that beneath that very island, inside that very facility, computers housed all of the secret LEIU and June mail "political intelligence," including data that had been gathered on Karen Silkwood.

Bill later briefed me on what he had found.

The LEIU, it turned out, was the Law Enforcement Intelligence Unit—a purportedly "private" U.S.-based "fraternal organization." To belong to this ostensibly private fraternity in one's "purely private capacity," however, one had to be an officially employed law enforcement officer in either a state bureau of criminal investigation or a "special intelligence unit" in a large metropolitan police department. Despite the "official-capacity law enforcement officer" requirement, each member belonged to this unique fraternity solely in his private capacity. That officer would gather private "political information" in his local area against union people, black civil rights workers, antiwar activists, women's groups, and other activists. Then that law enforcement officer, acting in his "purely private capacity," would forward this information to the LEIU—never using public postal services, electronic wire services, or any other form of interstate communication that was subject to federal government regulation or jurisdiction.

We discovered that the LEIU had what it referred to as a "pointer index switching system." If you were a private member of the LEIU and wanted "political information" on a particular citizen, you simply contacted the pointer index switching system facility, communicated your request, and were informed by that center which other "private" member of the LEIU possessed that specific political information. That pointer index switching system facility was hidden in Michigan, in the Upper Peninsula, in the same facility that housed the extra-low-frequency (ELF) communication system that our U.S. Naval Intelligence uses to communicate with our underwater nuclear submarine fleet. Nuclear submarines cannot come up to the surface to send communications, because if they do, they can be immediately located and identified by enemy satellites, which can then locate and monitor any broadcast to or from that submarine. So instead, our atomic submarines dive down to the bottom of the ocean and settle on the seabed. There, each submarine drives a long steel rod, or "antenna," *down* through the earthen seafloor, until the antenna contacts bedrock. Then the sub sends ELF pulse communication through bedrock, into which a receiving antenna is embedded at regional naval headquarters.

The members of the LEIU were therefore conducting a completely illegal domestic political surveillance operation in their allegedly "purely private capacity." And they were concealing this totally unconstitutional system of domestic political surveillance by embedding it inside the most sensitive national security facilities in our American arsenal. That way, if anybody tried to get near one of the facilities that was central to this illegal political intelligence-gathering and -dissemination system, that person would be subjected to the most summary type of punishment imaginable, and the rationalization would be made that such a summary punishment had been necessary to protect one of our most ultra-sensitive national security facilities.

Over the course of our investigation of the Karen Silkwood case, we discovered that our United States intelligence community was gathering domestic political intelligence information against people from all across the country, and that it was training both domestic law enforcement officers and agents of foreign domestic intelligence services, *together*, at the National Intelligence Academy in Florida. Heightening our concern, we also learned that foreign intelligence services—including Iran's dreaded SAVAK, South Africa's disgraced Bureau of Special Services, Chile's universally vilified DINA, and the internal security forces of numerous other ultra-right-wing military governments in South America—were also being trained, *directly beside domestic U.S. police officers*, at that academy to engage in this same conduct in nations where our American business interests ran. The illegal political intelligence information that was gathered through this process was being brought together and put into computers housed beneath Andros Island. This is where the information gathered against Karen Silkwood had been transferred in order to conceal it from the intense national investigation that had been triggered by her death.

In the midst of all of this, our Oklahoma City–based local counsel, Jim Ikard, received a call from an acquaintance who was a reporter for the *Oklahoma City Journal Record*, who wanted to talk to Jim right away. Jim went to the reporter's home in Oklahoma City. When Jim pulled up to the reporter's home, he saw a large Allied Van Lines truck parked in front. Allied Van Lines employees were loading all the reporter's furniture into the van. Jim went into the house to find the reporter sitting in a lone chair in the middle of his empty living room. The reporter told Jim that he had just resigned from the *Oklahoma City Journal Record* and was leaving Oklahoma City for good. He wanted to tell Jim, as a member of the Silkwood legal team, what had just happened.

The reporter said he had received a call several days earlier from a man he did not know, who wanted to meet him in a little bar in Oklahoma City. The caller claimed to have something important to tell him. The reporter went to meet the man, who turned out to be the husband of the executive secretary for the president of the Kerr-McGee Nuclear Corporation, R. T. Zitting. The man proceeded to tell the reporter that his wife had received a telephone call from the director of the Fast Flux Test Facility in Hanford, Washington, wanting to talk to the president of the Kerr-McGee Nuclear

Corporation right away. The director of the Fast Flux Test Facility told her that a very serious problem had arisen. The management of the Hanford facility had performed a quality-assurance test on one of the steel cylinder tubes that the Kerr-McGee Nuclear Corporation had forwarded to them, reportedly containing one hundred 98 percent pure, bomb-grade plutonium pellets. The problem was that two of the pellets were missing. They tested another fuel rod from the same shipment and discovered the same thing: that fuel rod, too, was missing two pellets. In fact, every one of the fuel rods tested from that shipment was found to contain only ninety-eight plutonium pellets instead of the officially reported one hundred.

When President Zitting of the Kerr-McGee Nuclear Corporation returned to the office, his secretary told him what the director of the Fast Flux Test Facility in Washington had reported. Zitting then turned to her and told her to "just go get the shipping invoice and change the number of plutonium pellets reported in each fuel rod from one hundred to ninety-eight." Shocked, the secretary refused to do this, so Zitting ordered her to just bring the file to him so that he could do it himself. And he did. The executive secretary was completely stunned.

A few months later, however, that same secretary got a second call from the director of the Hanford facility reporting that the exact same thing had occurred with another shipment of plutonium fuel rods sent from Kerr-McGee. Again, President Zitting of the Kerr-McGee Nuclear Corporation asked his secretary to bring him the pertinent shipping invoice, and he again changed the official records. The secretary was even more disturbed at this second incident. She went home and this time told her husband about it. Her husband decided to report this to a journalist at the *Oklahoma City Journal Record*.

The reporter drafted a news article reporting these bizarre events. But when his editor reviewed the story, he said they couldn't say these things about the most influential company in the state without first getting prior approval from the owner and publisher of the paper. So the editor took the reporter's draft of the story to the publisher, who said they couldn't run the story without first giving the Kerr-McGee Corporation a chance to counter the story, or at least to offer its own explanation of the events. As it turned out, the publisher sat on the board of directors of a local bank in Oklahoma

City with Dean McGee. He said that he would see McGee in a few days and show the story to him then. In the meantime, the reporter would have to sit on the story.

At the bank board of directors meeting a few days later, the publisher showed Dean McGee the draft of the story. McGee asked the *Oklahoma City Journal Record* publisher to hold off from publishing the story to give him a couple of days to check out what the problem might be. The publisher agreed to do that. When Dean McGee got back to the paper, he insisted that everything was fine, that he had determined that nothing was wrong with the fuel rod shipments. The publisher had the presence of mind to ask McGee what had happened. Dean McGee replied that the extra pellets had merely been "mis-shipped" to some other location.

"Really?" the publisher asked. "Where were they shipped to?"

"We found them in an airplane hangar down in San Diego, getting ready to be shipped off to some little nowhere dirt-water town in Mexico," Dean McGee had said. "But everything is OK. We found them all, and they will be sent to the Hanford facility in our next shipment."

The publisher accepted this story, went back to his editor, and ordered him to kill the story. The editor conveyed this message to the reporter, who got so angry that he resigned. But the reporter had decided to call Jim Ikard and tell him what had happened. When Ikard reported this to me, I filed it away as part of the growing body of "strange information" that we were encountering in the course of this investigation.

It was at that point that I subpoenaed Jackie Srouji to come to a sworn deposition.

Within days of her receipt of her deposition notice and subpoena, Srouji came to Washington, D.C., and sent word to me that she wanted to meet with me alone. I did not trust Srouji at all. So I had Father Bill Davis send word back to her: "Attorney Sheehan will not meet with you unless you are accompanied by your attorney." Srouji sent word back to us that she and her attorney would meet with me in Nashville, Tennessee, three days before her scheduled sworn deposition in Oklahoma City.

So Father Bill Davis and I went to Oklahoma City via Nashville to give Jackie Srouji an opportunity to talk with us before her deposition. The address that she sent for the meeting turned out to be a Cracker Barrel res-taurant that was closed between lunch and dinner. Bill and I pulled up and went to the door only to find it locked. But the manager, who peculiarly informed us that he was a fellow Catholic of Srouji's, invited us in. He told us that Srouji was in the lady's room and would be right out. Bill and I picked a table in the middle of the empty restaurant, sat down, and waited for her.

Within a few minutes, Srouji came out—almost certainly, I thought, after turning on an electronic body mic under her bulky clothes. But she had no lawyer with her. I immediately informed her that I was not going to allow her to manipulate me into a situation in which she could accuse me of having met with her without her lawyer. So I told her that either she get her lawyer to this meeting, right then, or else I was leaving. And I refused to talk to her anymore.

She started pleading. "They are going to kill me, just like they killed Karen! You've got to drop the subpoena! If they think I am going to testify, they are going to kill me!"

"Who's going to kill you?" I asked.

She didn't answer. She just looked pleased.

Then I said, "The safest way for you to protect yourself, if you think that someone wants to kill you, is for you to testify under oath as to what you know. That way, your sworn testimony will be officially preserved and could be introduced into evidence, no matter what happens to you later."

I realized suddenly that she was getting me to talk with her without her attorney being there. "No! Wait. Don't answer that! I am not going to talk with you until and unless you have your attorney with you."

She pouted. But she left and went back toward the restroom, giving the impression that she was going to call her attorney again. Father Davis and I waited, standing near a table in the middle of the restaurant. After sev-eral minutes, Srouji returned and said that her attorney had gotten lost but would be there in just a few minutes.

"Fine," I said. "Then let's wait until he gets here."

She waited only a few seconds before she started talking again. "Do you think they are going to try to kill me?"

I said, "Wait until your lawyer gets here."

After about fifteen minutes, a man drove into the Cracker Barrel parking lot, got out of his car, and knocked on the locked door. I went to the door and let him in, introducing myself as I led him into the restaurant. Then we all stood around a table in the middle of the restaurant. For some reason, none of us sat down. And none of us took off our coats.

I began the conversation. "I want to make it clear that I will not have any communication with Mrs. Srouji unless you consent to it and are present."

"You already have!" Srouji blurted out.

The man feigned shock.

"That is total bullshit," I said. "I have told you no less than three times that I am not going to talk to you unless and until your lawyer is here."

"Then why did you try to get me to tell you who it was that was going to kill me?"

I was shocked at her boldness. I turned to the man and said, "Are you Mrs. Srouji's attorney?"

"I represent Mrs. Srouji here in Nashville," he said. But he said it in a strange way.

"Are you an attorney?" I asked, point-blank.

"I represent Mrs. Srouji in business matters here in Nashville," he replied, ducking my direct question.

"Are you or are you not an attorney?" I said.

"No, I am not," he said. "I am a business consultant. Mrs. Srouji just called me about a half hour ago and asked me to come over here to represent her in this meeting. I thought it had something to do with business . . . about her book."

Srouji looked panicked. "It does have to do with my book! It does!"

That was it. I was out of there. I wasn't going to let her get away with this. I reached out and took Bill Davis by the arm and said, "We are out of here. This is bullshit!"

As we turned and were leaving, Srouji stopped us. "Why did you tell me that they were going to kill me unless I testified?" She turned desperately to her business consultant and shouted, "You are my witness! Attorney Sheehan told me that I was going to be killed unless I testified."

"That is total bullshit," I said to him. "She is the one who said that someone was threatening to kill her if she testified. I told her that we would not talk with her about this until her lawyer was here. She lied and said that you were her attorney and that you were going to be here in just a minute."

"He is my attorney—my attorney-in-fact!"

I was impressed. There are not many nonlawyers who know about an attorney-in-fact. This lady was a smoothie. She was not the bumbling dolt she pretended to be. But, fortunately, she was not that good at what she was trying to do either.

"You better be there on Monday. Or I will have you put in jail for contempt," I told her as Bill and I walked to the door.

"Did you hear that?" I heard her shout to the business consultant. "He threatened me! You heard him. You are my witness! He threatened me when I didn't have any lawyer with me!"

She was really something.

That day Bill and I drove from Nashville to Oklahoma City and went to Saint Anthony's, where we were staying with Father Paul Gallitan.

On Monday morning, at 9:30, Jim Ikard, Bill Davis, and I arrived at the Oklahoma City Federal Courthouse and set up for Srouji's deposition in the jury room, just off the courtroom. We wanted to have ready access to Judge Luther Eubanks, the federal district court judge who had replaced Luther Bohanon as the judge on our case, as soon as Srouji started refusing to answer questions that I put to her. William Paul, the president of the Oklahoma State Bar Association and a senior partner in the Crowe-Dunlevy law firm, would represent the Kerr-McGee Corporation at the deposition. Also present was Glenn Whitaker, a Justice Department attorney from Washington, D.C. He was representing the FBI defendants and, peculiarly, Oklahoma defendants such as Oklahoma highway patrolman Rick Fagan.

Srouji showed up one hour late, doing her helpless matron routine. She had with her some rumpled old Oklahoma state attorney in a $30 suit two sizes too big for him who looked like he was somewhere between ninety and dead. I told Srouji to "knock off the helpless matron routine" because she wasn't fooling anyone. She took great umbrage at my rudeness. But then we got down to business.

When the official court stenographer attempted to swear her in, Srouji tried to condition her oath by asserting, "There are some things that I cannot talk about because of certain agreements that I have made. And I will not answer any questions about those things." When I challenged her on this, right out of the box, she asserted that there were several different grounds on which she was going to refuse to answer certain questions. When I asked her what those grounds might be, she said, "My news journalist's privilege, my contract agreement with my publisher, and national security."

Glenn Whitaker, the Justice Department attorney, looked a bit shocked. I turned to him.

"Mr. Whitaker? To your knowledge, does Mrs. Srouji have any relationship with any United States intelligence agency that might conceivably entitle her to make a valid 'national security' objection to any question we might ask in her sworn deposition?"

Whitaker looked very uncomfortable. Before he could answer, Srouji jumped in. "I am a member of the United States Navy Reserve, and I hold a Q clearance that prohibits me from answering any questions concerning information I may have acquired in my capacity as a member of the United States Navy."

We all smiled. And Glenn Whitaker looked relieved.

"Are there any other capacities in which you have served as an operative or agent of any United States military unit, intelligence agency, or law enforcement agency, Mrs. Srouji, in which capacity you might wish to assert some 'national security' privilege in this deposition?" I asked.

Srouji looked very pleased at having been asked that question. "Yes, but I am not at liberty to discuss that!"

Whitaker slumped a bit in his chair.

"Really, Mrs. Srouji? And if you are not willing to identify what agency, or what capacity you might have had with any such an agency, with regard to which you might wish to assert such a 'national security' privilege—other than your status as a member of the United States Navy Reserve, that is— how is it that you might expect this court—or for that matter Mr. Whitaker here, who is representing the United States government in these hearings—to know whether your claim to such a privilege, in any given instance, is a valid one . . . or simply a bogus means by which you are attempting to deceive this court and the parties in this lawsuit so as to simply refuse to provide to us the information that you are required by law to provide in response to our questions?"

Srouji looked confused. "Could you repeat that question please?"

I had the court stenographer read the question back to her.

But Glenn Whitaker intervened. "I would like to have it made clear, on the record, that I do not represent the United States government in these hearings because the United States government is not a party to this lawsuit. And these are not 'hearings.' This is a simple federal civil deposition, like any other."

I smiled. "Then am I to take it from your testimony, Mr. Whitaker, that you will not be arguing, in this case or in this deposition proceeding, on behalf of or in support of any claim made by Mrs. Srouji to any 'national security' privilege?"

Glenn Whitaker turned red with anger. He had been trapped by his own arrogance into potentially excluding himself from being able to assist Jackie Srouji in any effort to avoid answering questions about her relationship with the FBI agent who we believed gave her copies of the illegal typed transcripts of Karen Silkwood's wiretapped telephone conversations and the typed transcripts of the illegally recorded conversations of Karen and her associates in her home.

"I did not say that!" Whitaker said. "I will address any given assertion on the part of Mrs. Srouji—if and when she might make any such assertion—as it arises."

"Does that mean, Mr. Whitaker, that you are going to be arguing on behalf of Mrs. Srouji in this proceeding if and when she asserts any claim of a 'national security' privilege?"

Srouji was loving this.

"I did not say that either! Why don't we just proceed and see what develops?" Whitaker said.

I said that would be fine. We then asked the old shaggy-looking lawyer who had come with Srouji to make his appearance on the record. He was nobody anybody had ever heard of. And he was very obviously way out of his league. Every time he wanted Jackie Srouji to not answer a question, he would drop his pen on the floor and disrupt the flow of the questioning. Actually, it wasn't even a pen. It was a cheap carpenter's nail punch that made a loud noise when it hit the floor. It was totally amateurish, and all the lawyers in the deposition smiled every time he did this.

Because of Srouji's late arrival, and her resistance to taking her oath without conditions, we didn't start her actual deposition until 11:30 in the morning. At exactly twelve noon, her lawyer dropped his nail punch on the floor and noted that it was time for lunch. He wanted to set the return time as 1:30 PM, but we all insisted that we be back in session by 1:00 PM. We realized that the long lunch was just a ploy on Srouji's part to delay any motions to compel testimony before Judge Luther Eubanks until after one of Eubanks's "long lunch breaks."

Srouji and her lawyer were late arriving back from lunch. When we recommenced her deposition at 1:20 PM, I started drilling in on Srouji right away.

"Who was it, Mrs. Srouji, who suggested that you might wish to write a book about the private nuclear power industry?"

"I refuse to answer that question because it would invade my right of privacy concerning my contract with my book publisher," Srouji said, obviously prepared to start asserting her panoply of alleged privileges now that Judge Eubanks had had a chance to go to lunch.

"Mrs. Srouji," I said. "There is no such privilege. I have not asked you any question about the particulars of your contract with your alleged publisher. I asked you who first suggested that you write a book about the private nuclear industry?"

"OK, then," she said. "Then I will assert my journalist's privilege. It is possible that the person who suggested this to me was a source of mine in my capacity as a journalist for the *Nashville Tennessean* newspaper."

"Mrs. Srouji. You are—or were—only a copy editor at the *Nashville Tennessean* newspaper, isn't that correct?"

She looked baffled. "Ah . . . I worked for the *Nashville Tennessean* newspaper. I had an ID card from the paper with my picture on it."

"Mrs. Srouji, that does not make you a newspaper reporter who is lawfully entitled to exercise the news journalist's privilege. That privilege is reserved to reporters who professionally gather news in the field from confidential sources. It does not apply to copy editors who merely sit in a newspaper office and edit copy sent to them."

"Well, I didn't know that!" she said. "So I may have relied upon that privilege when I was talking to that person."

"Well, *did* you rely on that privilege when you were talking to the person who suggested that you write a book about the private nuclear industry? Was that person conveying to you some confidential information that you intended to use in writing a news story for the *Nashville Tennessean* newspaper?"

Still she looked baffled.

"Let me try another question, Mrs. Srouji," I said. "When you were working for the *Nashville Banner*, a different newspaper in Nashville, did you, using your news journalist credentials as an actual reporter for the *Nashville Banner*, ever conduct a purported interview of any person solely for the purpose of gathering political intelligence data for the FBI?"

Glenn Whitaker rose from his chair and objected. "There has been no foundation laid for you to ask that kind of question. What evidence do you have to justify asking a question like that?"

I was more than a bit surprised, since it is absolutely unnecessary for an attorney to set forth his or her predicate evidence on the basis of which to ask a question in a sworn deposition.

"This is not a courtroom," I said. "And we are not on trial here. This is a deposition. I have no obligation whatsoever to provide to you, Mrs. Srouji, or her attorney the basis for my asking that question." I turned back to Srouji and repeated my question.

"What has that got to do with this case?" she demanded. "That was years ago."

"How many years ago?" I asked.

"I haven't worked for the *Nashville Banner* for over ten years," she said.

"And how long ago was the last time you used your news journalist credentials as an actual reporter for the *Nashville Banner*—or any other news outlet—to conduct a purported interview of any person solely for the purpose of gathering political intelligence data for the FBI?"

Whitaker jumped up from the table. "Don't answer that, Mrs. Srouji! Mr. Sheehan, if you have some specific question as to whether Mrs. Srouji was working as a journalist when she interviewed some specific person, about some specific subject, you can ask that. But you can't just go fishing, in general, about Mrs. Srouji's entire history."

"Oh? Really, Mr. Whitaker? And exactly when was it that you were put in charge of determining what questions I could or could not ask Mrs. Srouji? I will ask Mrs. Srouji any question I feel I am entitled, as a matter of law, to ask her. And she will answer it. If she—or you—wish to assert some specific privilege on the basis of which she is not required to answer that question, we will go before Judge Eubanks and will brief and argue that issue."

"Good! Then let's go," said Whitaker. And he pushed himself away from the deposition table and started to leave the room.

"Mr. Whitaker? Am I to assume that *you* are asserting some specific privilege on behalf of Mrs. Srouji on the basis of which she does not have to answer the last specific question I asked her? Or are you lodging a more general objection to some general line of questioning?"

"We'll take that question up, too, in front of Judge Eubanks." And he marched out of the deposition room and headed to Judge Eubanks's chambers.

It appeared that Judge Eubanks had been put on specific notice that we would be coming before him early that afternoon, because he was in his chambers—and in his judge's robe. I had notified him, the week before, that we wanted him standing by on the day of our deposition of Srouji. But I was sure that he had been contacted by Glenn Whitaker during the lunch hour and notified that we would be coming before him very shortly after the lunch break.

Immediately upon our walking into the judge's chambers, Glenn Whitaker began talking.

"Excuse me," I asserted. "Let's wait for the official court stenographer to set up before we begin these proceedings."

Judge Eubanks, whom we could all see was more than a little bit "in his cups," said, "I don't think that is going to be necessary. We handle things like this pretty informally around here."

"I'm afraid that I am going to have to insist, Your Honor. I believe that you will see why once we get into these proceedings."

Judge Eubanks shrugged and took his place behind his desk. The court stenographer set up her stenographic machine immediately next to Judge Eubanks, behind his desk, and got ready to type.

As soon as she signaled that she was ready, Glenn Whitaker began. "Glenn Whitaker, for the government, Your Honor."

I smiled at him, since he had just that morning expressly denied, on the record, that he was representing the U.S. government in these proceedings. But I said nothing.

"Your Honor, the witness in today's deposition is Mrs. Jackie Srouji. Mrs. Srouji is a longtime professional journalist from the state of Tennessee," Whitaker continued.

Eubanks turned to Srouji, scanned her up and down, and then said, with only a minor slur in his voice, "Welcome to Oklahoma, Mrs. . . . is it SA-ROOOO-JEE?"

"Srouji, Your Honor. It's Palestinian. My husband is Palestinian."

"Palestinian?" Eubanks exclaimed. "Aren't they those terrorists from the Middle East?"

Srouji and Whitaker were both taken aback. I could immediately see my opening here.

"Judge Eubanks. Daniel Sheehan, Your Honor, for the estate of Miss Karen Silkwood, the plaintiff in this civil litigation, Your Honor."

"Yes, Mr. Sheehan. You were the one that Judge Bohanon called a 'magpie,' aren't you?"

All the attorneys laughed along with Eubanks.

"Actually, Your Honor, that was Mr. Ikard, my associate and local counsel here from Oklahoma City. You remember Jim Ikard. He used to be the starting point guard for the OU basketball team a few years back."

"Oh, yeah," said Eubanks, softening considerably. "I remember him. He's the tall young fella with the white hair and the white beard now."

"That's right, Your Honor," I said. "This profession seems to make us all turn gray early."

He laughed. But the other lawyers didn't. They could see where this was going.

"Actually, Your Honor. I am the one that Judge Bohanon said was 'running off at both ends.'"

"Oh, yeah." Then, after a second, he asked, "What did that mean exactly? I don't know what that means."

Everybody could see now that he was quite drunk and not able to appreciate the seriousness of the issues that we were getting ready to put before him. So I moved in to take the initiative away from Whitaker.

"Your Honor. Mrs. Jackie Srouji is the witness in the deposition that, you will remember, we noticed for the courthouse here today, because we feared that she might refuse to answer questions—and we wanted you standing by in case we wanted to bring on a motion to compel."

The judge said yes, he remembered. "I assume that she has refused to answer some question that you have put to her?"

"Yes, Your Honor. In fact, she has refused to answer almost every question that we have asked her so far today, Your Honor."

Eubanks turned to Srouji and scowled at her. I didn't want him to get into some loose dialogue with her, so I immediately pushed forward to get to the issue we wanted him to address.

"Yes, Your Honor. Mrs. Srouji has been, for years, falsely using her credentials as an employee of one or another of the newspapers in Nashville as a cover for infiltrating American citizens' groups and spying on them, not for the purpose of writing any newspaper story about the groups, but solely to spy on them."

"Spy on them?" Eubanks exclaimed. "For who?"

Glenn Whitaker tried to intervene. "Your Honor, if I may be heard."

I cut Whitaker off. "This woman went to the Middle East because she is married to a Palestinian—and she infiltrated the Palestine Liberation Organization (PLO)!"

"The PLO?" Eubanks shouted. "The PLO? Isn't that that group that kidnapped that poor Hearst girl? That was a terrible thing. If this witness has had anything to do with that organization, she is going to have to answer any question that this young man wants to ask her! So that's my ruling. She's not going to be allowed to hide behind some claim that she is a reporter and therefore doesn't have to tell whatever she knows about. Now get out of here and get back to your deposition. And I don't want to see you back in here again on this issue. I have ruled on this."

Glenn Whitaker was shell-shocked. So was I, for that matter. But I jumped up immediately and pushed everyone back into the deposition, and I immediately started to drill down on Srouji, demanding that she answer my questions and threatening to take her back before Judge Eubanks and have him put her in jail for criminal contempt of court if she didn't answer my questions.

During the deposition, we learned that it had been "a friend in the FBI" who had suggested that she write a book about the private nuclear power industry. This "friend in the FBI" had directed Srouji to a specific publisher, and that publisher had suggested that Srouji might want to include in her book "a chapter on the Karen Silkwood matter." But when I asked her for the name of her "friend in the FBI" and of the publisher, Srouji refused to answer, again invoking her purported news journalist's privilege, her private contact agreement, and national security.

When I began to press her for answers, she *pretended to* cry, wailing that she was afraid she would be killed. "Just like Silkwood, just like you said I would be!"

Here we go again, I thought.

Sure enough, her shaggy old lawyer, right on an obviously prearranged cue, jumped up in his rumpled suit and proclaimed, in a saccharinely fake voice, "What? What did you say, Mrs. Srouji? When did Mr. Sheehan say that to you, Jackie? Did Mr. Sheehan meet with you at any time that you were represented by an attorney without that attorney being present or notified?"

Everyone in the room, except for Jackie Srouji and her poor excuse for a lawyer, was transparently embarrassed at this hokey charade.

Srouji's lawyer's phony display of surprise and indignation impressed no one.

I simply entered a statement into the record setting forth the details of my previous encounter, noting that Father Bill Davis, the director of the national Jesuit Office of Social Ministry in Washington, D.C., was present at all times during my encounter with Mrs. Srouji and was prepared to testify, under oath, as to the veracity of what I said had happened. But Srouji pretended to break down, allegedly out of fear of the death threats that had been made against her and reported to her by me.

Her frumpy old attorney thereupon melodramatically escorted her from the deposition room, stating, "This deposition will have to be continued at some other time. Mrs. Srouji is simply too distraught to continue today." Then he and Srouji simply got up and left. I didn't mind. That gave us more time to further investigate Srouji to find out the identities of her "friend in the FBI" and her "publisher."

I flew back to Washington, D.C., and was drafted by Sara to help her raise contributions to pay for a full investigation of all the crazy things that were going on in this case.

CHAPTER *twenty-one*

I N JUNE OF 1978, we were a full eighteen months into our investigation and discovery efforts against Kerr-McGee following the November 1976 filing of our civil complaint. But we were getting nowhere with our demands for discovery. Just as Judge Luther Bohanon had, Judge Luther Eubanks simply ignored all of our motions to compel discovery in the face of the stonewalling of our subpoenas on the part of Kerr-McGee and the state and federal agencies. So I filed a *second* motion to recuse the federal judge in the Silkwood case, this time against Luther Eubanks. Neither Glenn Whitaker, on behalf of the government, nor Bill Paul of Kerr-McGee opposed, since we all knew that Luther Eubanks would have been a disaster for all parties concerned in any trial. But I added to this second motion a demand that the Tenth Circuit Court of Appeals go out of state to find a highly competent federal district court trial judge to oversee the discovery process and trial of this case, since *all* the federal district court judges in Oklahoma had been nominated for their positions by former United States senator Robert S. Kerr, the owner and founder of the Kerr-McGee Corporation.

I was pleased when we received notice that the Tenth Circuit Court of Appeals had granted my motion and had appointed to supervise the discovery process and trial of the Karen Silkwood case the chief federal judge of the Federal District of Kansas, one Frank G. Theis. Theis was reputed to be a tough, smart, honest, even-handed federal trial judge who had three times turned down offers to be placed on the Tenth Circuit Court of Appeals "because he loved being a *trial* judge." And he was reported to have the best sense of humor of any federal trial judge west of the Mississippi.

Judge Theis flew into Oklahoma City and immediately notified all counsel that he wanted them before him the very next Monday morning.

We all arrived in the main courtroom in the federal courthouse in Oklahoma City. Bill Paul, the president of the Oklahoma State Bar Association, was there with his full staff of four trial attorneys from the Crowe & Dunlevy firm to represent the Kerr-McGee Corporation, the Kerr-McGee Nuclear Corporation, Kerr-McGee chief of security James Reading, and the Kerr-McGee Security Department "John Doe's." Glenn Whitaker was present, representing the FBI and the United States government for all "national security purposes." And I was there, with Jim Ikard, now joined by an additional young attorney named Arthur Angel, a bright young Harvard Law School graduate who had contacted my office in Washington, D.C., and had volunteered his services.

When Judge Theis entered the courtroom, his serious demeanor belied his reputation as a man of great humor. He took his place on the bench and prepared to address us. But Glenn Whitaker quickly rose to his feet and said, "Judge Theis, welcome to Oklahoma, Your Honor. My name is Glenn Whitaker. I am from the United States Department of Justice in Washington, D.C., and I am representing the United States government in this case."

Judge Theis leaned forward and looked over his rimless antique eyeglasses at Glenn Whitaker, sternly interrupting Whitaker. "Mr. . . ." He looked down at a name chart that he had obviously been reading. "Whitaker, is it? Sit down and *be quiet*, Mr. Whitaker!"

Whitaker shrank back and melted slowly down into his seat.

Judge Theis continued:

The way this case has been handled by the federal district court here in Oklahoma up to this point in time raises fundamental questions about the basic fairness of the entire federal judicial system in our country. I have been sent here by the Tenth Circuit Court of Appeals to give the family of Karen Silkwood—and these young lawyers here—a fair chance to obtain whatever evidence there is to prove that this young Karen Silkwood woman was killed in the course of her duties as a member of an American labor union while trying to protect the rights of workers in her plant. And, based upon whatever evidence they are able to find, we are going to either lay this young woman to rest, once and for all, or she is going to get up and walk in this courtroom.

Holy shit! I thought. *What do you know? What do you know? An honest judge!*

We then noticed up a second deposition of Jackie Srouji and set it to be held, once again, directly in the federal courthouse in Oklahoma City, this time requesting that Judge Theis be directly at this deposition to make any rulings that became necessary.

I put in a telephone call to Gerry Spence in Jackson Hole, Wyoming. Gerry was a well-known criminal defense attorney and plaintiff's attorney in the Rocky Mountain region. He had become a very wealthy man from his legal practice. I had spoken with Gerry a number of times by phone during my one-year tenure as chief trial counsel for the Rocky Mountain regional office of the American Civil Liberties Union—the region that included Gerry Spence's state of Wyoming. Most of these calls had concerned a case I had filed against the president of Wyoming State University, suing him under the federal Civil Rights Act for attempting to impose a system of prior censorship over the Friday-night movies that the WSU student government wanted to show to students. After I had filed that case, Gerry Spence had called and offered to try that case for us for free, "because this is my home state, and it embarrasses me to see things like this goin' on here," he had said.

I liked Gerry. And I think he liked me. So I called his office in Jackson Hole, intending to simply leave a message asking for a personal donation to help us finance our Karen Silkwood case. To my surprise, his assistant put him directly on the line, and Gerry was very interested in knowing more about the case. He had read about it and had heard a number of news reports about developments in the case. But he wanted to know more. He invited me to fly to Jackson Hole, to his home in Wyoming, to discuss the case with him. He said he might be interested in helping us on the case, since it was taking place in his neck of the woods. Gerry was obviously expanding his perception of his territory, but I was happy to go see him.

I flew to Jackson Hole. He and his wife picked me up at the small airport in his Land Rover and drove me to their ranch just outside of town. It was a grand place, more like a Spanish hacienda than a typical western ranch. Gerry was very gracious. And he began to ask some very insightful questions about our investigation. After a fairly expansive discussion of the case, Gerry said that he might be willing to conduct a few depositions for free, "just to get a feel for the case." I immediately thought about the second Srouji deposition and the deposition of her "friend in the FBI." Gerry was much more interested in count 2 of our case, the civil tort count. "That's where the money is going to be," he said. He said that "all of this conspiracy stuff" was interesting and that it certainly helped generate publicity. "That's good," he said, "because it will make the judge be much more attentive to the law than judges usually are. But the big money is going to be in count 2, the tort count."

Before I left Jackson Hole, we agreed to have Gerry Spence take the second deposition of Jackie Srouji, as well as the sworn deposition of her "friend in the FBI," as soon as we obtained his identity.

Gerry would conduct this deposition, with Jim Ikard second chairing, to keep Srouji from trying to disrupt the proceedings by claiming, again, that I had told her she was going to be murdered if she did not testify in the Silkwood case. And Judge Theis agreed to sit in on the deposition to be able to rule immediately on every objection that Srouji, her lawyer, the Kerr-McGee attorneys, or Glenn Whitaker might make to try to stop us from getting the information to which we were entitled as a matter of law.

Srouji refused, at first, to reveal who her publisher was. But she was ordered to answer the question by Judge Theis, who presided over the deposition from a raised table looming over Srouji. Upon being ordered by Judge Theis to answer the question, Srouji began her phony crying routine. In response, Judge Theis put on an equally inauthentic display of sympathy—and it worked. He persuaded Srouji not only to answer that the name of her publisher was Aurora Publications but to volunteer that she "did not know, at the time that [she] signed the contract with Aurora, that it was a CIA proprietary. I swear that I didn't, Your Honor."

This caused Judge Theis to stop and slide his rimless glasses down on his nose. Looking over his glasses at Gerry Spence, he said, "Well, Mr. Spence. It looks like you and I showed up in this case just in time to see it getting more and more interesting."

Gerry was baffled by Srouji's offering. He leaned over to me on his right, cupped his hand over his mouth, and whispered, "What the fuck does this mean?"

"I told you so," I whispered back.

Then Gerry started drilling in on Srouji about her "friend in the FBI" who had directed her to Aurora Publications to publish her book about the private nuclear industry. She again at first refused to answer any questions about this man, invoking her journalist's news privilege. Judge Theis was perplexed at this and asked her a number of questions designed to ascertain the potential applicability of the journalist's privilege. I intervened to explain to Judge Theis that I happened to be the attorney who had first asserted this particular testimonial privilege, first as coeditor of the *Harvard Civil Rights Law Review* and then as Supreme Court counsel for NBC, CBS, ABC, *The New York Times*, and *The Washington Post*. It was shameless. But Judge Theis loved it.

"Well, I am glad to see that we have the A-Team here to handle this case," Theis joked (obviously referring to Gerry Spence and me). Then he quickly turned to Bill Paul, Kerr-McGee's attorney and president of the Oklahoma State Bar Association, to add, "On both sides, Mr. Paul and Mr. Whitaker, on both sides." But it was clear to everyone present that he was referring to our side.

With Judge Theis's blessing, I then waged in on Srouji, hammering her with one question after another about her history with the *Nashville Banner* spying on private citizens' organizations in the Nashville area. But before I drilled down about the FBI agent who had served as her case officer coordinating her COINTELPRO activities in Nashville, I turned my attention to Srouji's activities in the Middle East, serving as a CIA covert operative. Srouji and Glenn Whitaker struggled strenuously to Judge Thies to order this area off limits in this deposition, on the grounds of both relevance and national security. But Judge Theis kept on saying, "No. No, I am finding this intriguing! I don't get to do cases like this in Kansas! Go ahead, Mr. Sheehan." He turned to Glenn Whitaker. "If anything pops out here that I think is in need of being protected because we end up looking up the skirt of the Statue of Liberty, I am sure we will be able to instruct counsel to keep that kind of information confidential."

Once again, I intervened to explain to Judge Theis that I was very familiar with such arrangements, since Floyd Abrams, Professor Bickel, and I had all reviewed highly classified information during the course of the Pentagon Papers case, in which I had also served as counsel before the United States Supreme Court.

"My, my, Mr. Sheehan. You get more and more interesting with every issue that comes up in this case." He was clearly ribbing me for being so shameless in my attempts to impress him.

Properly chastised, I returned to grilling Srouji. With Judge Theis's prodigious assistance, I extracted from Srouji that she had attended meetings with members of the Palestine Liberation Organization for the purpose of "reporting on the activities of those people to our government." When I pressed her to reveal to which agency of our government she was reporting, she balked again. When I chided her, suggesting that she was no more important than any other American tourist who might be asked by the State Department to be debriefed upon returning from a visit to "an area of interest," she took great umbrage and stated emphatically that it was *not* the State Department to whom she had been reporting. When she refused to tell me which agency it was, I asked her directly whether it was the CIA. She then claimed "national security privilege" as her grounds for not answering that question. Judge Theis intervened and asked her to tell *him* what agency it was so that we could get past this cat-and-mouse game. She told him that it was the CIA. "See, that wasn't so painful, was it?" Judge Theis said.

Having distracted Srouji with this CIA interrogation, and having gotten Judge Theis to order her to tell us that she had been spying on the Palestine Liberation Organization for the CIA, I immediately asked her, "Was Larry Olson the 'friend in the FBI' who suggested that you write the book about the private nuclear industry and include a chapter about Karen Silkwood?" Olson was the FBI agent in charge of the security of fissionable materials at the Kerr-McGee nuclear facility—and our investigation had revealed that he had, indeed, previously been assigned to the Nashville office of the FBI.

This caught her completely off guard, and she answered carelessly.

"He was not the one who suggested that I include a chapter about Karen Silkwood. That was the publisher."

Gerry Spence laughed out loud at how easily that ploy had worked on her.

"You mean the CIA man that was serving as your 'publisher' at Aurora Publications that you have already told us was a CIA proprietary?" I asked.

"That's right," she said. "It wasn't Larry!"

"You mean it wasn't Larry Olson who suggested that you include in your book about the private nuclear industry a chapter about Karen Silkwood, but it *was* Larry Olson who suggested that you write a book about the private nuclear industry . . . and it was the CIA man at Aurora Publications who suggested that you include in your book a chapter about Karen Silkwood?"

"I didn't know that he was a CIA man at the time that he suggested that. In fact, I don't even know now for an absolute fact that he was a CIA man."

"Well, you told us that you later learned that Aurora Publications was a CIA proprietary."

"Yes," she said. "Later. I only learned that later."

"Well, in any event, after you learned that Aurora Publications was a CIA front—"

"Proprietary!" she said indignantly.

"Proprietary," I said. "Excuse me."

"You're excused," she said.

Judge Theis laughed. "She's a tough one, all right!"

Everyone laughed, including Srouji, who seemed to be enjoying giving us all what she viewed to be a lesson on the proper lexicon to be employed when discussing CIA covert operations. But now she was rolling, so I pressed on, pretending to pay her respect for knowing all the proper terms for espionage activities.

"So, Mrs. Srouji, it is your testimony to this court that you were working directly with the CIA in the Middle East, infiltrating the PLO and reporting on the activities of the PLO directly to the CIA; that you were working with the COINTELPRO program of the FBI in Nashville, here in the United States, using your press credentials as a professional journalist for the *Nashville Banner* to gain access to private meetings of American citizens' groups and secretly reporting on their activities to Larry Olson of the FBI; that Larry Olson asked you to write a book about the private nuclear power industry and directed you to Aurora Publications, which you acknowledge was a CIA front organization; and that it was the CIA man inside Aurora Publications who asked you to include in your book a chapter about Karen Silkwood? Is that correct?"

"No. It is not!" she said.

"Oh. Really?" I asked. "What is it that is not correct about what I just asked you?"

"First of all, as I told you, Larry Olson did not ask me to write a book about the private nuclear industry. He just suggested it. And the man at Aurora Publications—whom I still do not *know* to have been a CIA man—he might have been simply working for a CIA proprietary and not even have known it, just like me. And he didn't ask me or assign me to include a chapter in my book about Karen Silkwood. He only suggested that I might do that, since Larry Olson was there at Kerr-McGee and I knew Larry. He said that might make it easier for me to get that kind of information about the case."

"And did it?" I asked.

"Oh! Oh!" she said, totally unconvincingly. "I think that I wasn't supposed to say that."

"That's OK, Mrs. Srouji. You don't have anything to worry about. You are required to answer these questions. No one is going to do anything to you because you answered these questions," I said.

This, however, opened a door for Srouji to get back into her phony damsel-in-distress mode. She immediately started her fake crying bit and shouted at me, "But you told me down in Nashville, before my last deposition, you told me that I would be killed if I testified about this!"

Judge Theis smiled his big bucktoothed smile directly at me, implying that I had walked right into that one. He had obviously read the transcript of Srouji's first deposition. I think he was actually enjoying watching how I was going to deal with this. Aware that Judge Theis was going to make me punch my way out of this clinch, I spoke calmly to Srouji.

"Now, Mrs. Srouji, does it make any sense to anyone that I would tell you *not* to testify or else someone was going to kill you when it was I who was *asking* you to testify?"

Srouji looked confused. Theis smiled. Gerry Spence looked like this was all some confusing waste of time, wrestling with an issue that he thought had nothing to do with how to make Kerr-McGee pay more money for contaminating Silkwood and her home.

She tried to wind her way out of her most recent lie. "Well, I think what you said was that *unless* I testified about this, I would be killed," Srouji said, reversing herself 180 degrees.

"Oh, really?" I said. "And why then did you tell me, 'They are going to kill me, just like they killed Karen'? Why would the same people who you think killed Karen Silkwood want to kill you *unless* you testified? Wouldn't they want you to *not* testify?"

Srouji now looked totally confused.

"Isn't it more logical, Mrs. Srouji, that if I said anything at all to you about testifying, that I would have said that the safest thing to do was *to* testify under oath about what you know, since if you thought you were in danger because of what you know, once you testified under oath about whatever it is you know, it wouldn't make sense for anybody to do anything to you . . . because you would have already testified, and your sworn deposition testimony could then be used, even if for any reason you weren't available to testify in person? It wouldn't do anybody any good to try to silence you."

Srouji simply stared at me in silence.

Judge Theis immediately broke into that big bucktoothed smile of his. He liked the way I had worked my way out of that one, so he finally spoke. "OK, Mrs. Srouji, why don't we just get past this issue of who wanted you to testify and who might not have wanted you to testify. You are here now. And you are testifying. So why don't we just get back to the issues in this case about which you *can* testify? Now, did you or did you not use your press credentials while you were working for the *Nashville Banner* to persuade people who were members of entirely lawful American citizens' groups to grant interviews to you, the content of which interviews you did not intend to use to write any news story for the *Banner*, but were instead intending to turn that information over directly to the FBI rather than to your newspaper?"

Srouji looked up at Judge Theis plaintively. "I *could have* used the content of those interviews to write stories for the *Banner*."

"*Did* you use the content of those interviews to write stories for the *Banner?*" Judge Theis repeated.

"I *could* have," Srouji repeated, obviously having plotted that dodge beforehand.

But it wasn't going to work on Frank Theis.

He started to get upset with her. "By 'I *could* have,' Mrs. Srouji, do you mean that maybe you *did* or maybe you *didn't* but you just can't remember whether you did or didn't write such a story? Or do you mean that you had the permission of the editor of the *Banner* to write a story if you had *wanted* to?"

"Both," Srouji said.

Judge Theis glared at her. "Mrs. Srouji! Can you point to a single story that you ever wrote using the content of an interview you conducted with a member of a citizens' group at the request of any agent of the FBI?"

"I can't think of any," Srouji said.

"And were there any interviews that you conducted of any member of any citizens' group that you secured by representing yourself as a journalist employed by the *Nashville Banner,* the content of which interview you turned over to any agent of the FBI and you did *not* use to write any story for the *Nashville Banner* or for any other newspaper of First Amendment–protected media?"

Srouji hesitated for a long moment. Then she said, "Only when I was asked to do that by my editor at the *Nashville Banner.*"

"Well, I don't think that that permission from your editor to do that entitles you to invoke any privilege reserved solely to bona fide news journalists, Mrs. Srouji," Judge Theis said.

"But I *was* a bona fide journalist, Your Honor!" Srouji proclaimed. "I wrote articles for the *Nashville Banner!*"

Judge Theis continued, "With regard to any of those articles, Mrs. Srouji, you would be entitled to invoke the news reporter's privilege. But, in light of the fact that you admit having used your press credentials to secure access to interviews and sources of information that were *not,* at any time, intended to be used in stories to be written for the *Nashville Banner* but were intended *instead* to be used as 'investigative information' to be supplied to an agent of the FBI, I am afraid that you are not going to be entitled to assert any First Amendment privilege in connection with your writing of the book that you were asked to write by the same FBI agent for whom you were gathering that prior investigative information when that book was being published by a CIA proprietary. You will be required to answer all of Mr. Spence's and Mr. Sheehan's questions as to your activities in connection with your investigation and writing that book. Mr. Spence, you may question the witness."

Gerry Spence thereupon systematically extracted from Jackie Srouji the fact that she had obtained numerous documents from Larry Olson, the FBI agent assigned by the United States government as the federal security officer responsible for safeguarding the highly fissionable materials at the Kerr-McGee nuclear facility; that FBI agent Larry Olson was, indeed, the FBI agent with whom Jackie Srouji had worked as a COINTELPRO operative in Nashville and for whom she had used her *Nashville Banner* press credentials to deceive members of American citizens' groups into granting her interviews; that Larry Olson was the FBI agent who had been communicating to her otherwise unattainable information about the FBI's investigation— not into Karen Silkwood's death or her contamination but instead into her union organizing and her sexual and drug activities, "efforts to smear her," as Srouji described them; and that the documents Srouji had obtained from Agent Olson "did pertain to the internal Kerr-McGee Corporation investigation of Karen Silkwood."

Srouji refused, however, to provide copies of any documents to us or to the court, despite Judge Theis's threat of a citation for contempt of court if she refused.

Gerry Spence, because of his appetite for exciting cases and his desire to "find out what the hell is going on in this case," decided to conduct the sworn deposition of FBI agent Larry Olson as well.

Despite the fact that Agent Olson bobbed and weaved and tried to evade answering Gerry Spence's questions about his relationship with Jackie Srouji and about Srouji's relationship with both the FBI and the CIA, Spence was able to secure from Olson valuable information as well. From Olson's testimony, Gerry Spence concluded that Jackie Srouji had been provided, by

Olson, copies of documents from inside the investigative files of both the FBI and the Kerr-McGee Nuclear Corporation that made it clear that neither Olson nor the FBI—nor for that matter the Oklahoma State Police—*had ever* been trying to investigate how Karen Silkwood had been mysteriously contaminated, how or by whom she had been run off the highway and killed, or what had happened to the documents that she had with her when she was killed. They were, instead, trying to investigate Silkwood herself—clearly in order to try to protect the Kerr-McGee Corporation and federal and state authorities from being exposed for what had been done to her.

That information caused Gerry Spence to consider joining our legal team. Gerry invited me back to his ranch in Jackson Hole. He told me that he was "contemplating becoming directly involved in the case, if I didn't mind." I told Gerry that I would be pleased if he were interested in litigating count 2. Gerry then monitored all the remaining depositions and discovery processes relating to counts 2 (the *intentional* contamination count) and 3 (the *negligent* contamination count), which were being expertly conducted by Jim Ikard and Arthur Angel. I returned to my investigation and litigation preparation of count 1, the anti–civil rights conspiracy count—and the murder count.

The next thing that Bill Taylor and I discovered was that the Office Man, the White House person to whom former CIA electronic surveillance specialist David Waters had introduced me, was none other than Terry Steichen, the director of the White House Office on Telecommunications Policy under Nixon, then under Ford, and then under Jimmy Carter. In that capacity, Terry had been directly responsible for putting up communications satellites and directing the installation of satellite surveillance around the world for the White House. Through these activities, Terry had come to realize that these surveillance satellites were capable of reading license plates from more than one hundred miles up in the sky and that our executive branch was in the process of attempting to identify *individual faces* from satellite range. He had become greatly distressed at the potential violations of personal privacy that this new technology portended. That was how Terry had met David Waters. Both Terry and David were ardent libertarians who were intensely worried about the privacy implications of these rapidly accelerating developments in the field of government surveillance and their potentially dangerous uses.

Bill Taylor and I then determined that we were going to conduct surveillance on Harold Behrens—the man whom, with the help of Terry Steichen, we had identified as someone who had been directly and personally engaged in the illegal electronic and physical surveillance of Karen Silkwood prior to her death. Bill Taylor hired one Joe Royer, a friend of Jim Ikard's, to watch Harold Behrens for us. Royer, whom we called "Clydie Joe," was a drummer in a local band, which meant that nobody would suspect him of being engaged in an activity like that. Bill and I put miniature tape recorders in both of Clydie Joe's cowboy boots and ran recording wires up his pants legs to tiny microphones in his jacket lapels. Clydie Joe physically tracked down Harold Behrens with the help of Sherri Ellis and her friends in the Oklahoma City gay community. Royer then followed Behrens around town for a couple of days before Bill had Royer move in on Behrens. After getting the go-ahead from Taylor, Clydie Joe followed Harold Behrens to a local Denny's restaurant. When Behrens got up to go into the men's room, Clydie Joe decided he would go to the men's room too. Clydie Joe walked up to the urinal immediately next to the one Behrens was using and started to take a leak. While they were standing there urinating, Clydie Joe casually looked over to Behrens and said, "Hey, aren't you Harold Behrens?"

Taken by surprise, Behrens replied, "Well, yes. Yes, I am."

"Well, my name is Joe Royer. I'm an investigator for the Karen Silkwood family, and I'd like to talk to you."

Harold Behrens turned around immediately and started running away, urinating on his pant leg in his rush to get out of the bathroom. Clydie Joe ran after him, slamming the bathroom door shut with his foot and shouting, "Look, I just want to talk to you!"

Behrens started crying, first denying that he knew anything about Silkwood. But when Royer confronted him with knowledge of his affair with the local male disc jockey and the fact that we *knew* he was part of the team of men who were surveilling Karen Silkwood for James Reading, Behrens blurted out on tape, "Look! We didn't mean to *kill* her! We were just trying to *stop* her, to get those damn documents from her. But she wouldn't stop!

She just wouldn't stop!" He kept saying that over and over. Clydie Joe tried to cut in, but Behrens went on. "I can't talk about this. They will kill me! I can't talk about this!"

When Clydie Joe told him that all he had to do was come clean about what was going on, Behrens said he couldn't. Then he pushed his way to the door and rushed out of the restaurant.

I then issued an immediate deposition subpoena for Harold Behrens, and Joe Royer reported that he had found Behrens in Las Vegas. We decided that Royer would be the best person to serve the subpoena. When Royer showed up on Behrens' doorstep, Behrens started crying again and telling Clydie Joe that he didn't want to testify, repeating that they would kill him. Royer reported that he served Behrens with the federal subpoena, filled out the return on the subpoena, and then had it notarized.[5]

We next subpoenaed Leo Goodwin Jr., the chairman of the board of the National Intelligence Academy. He was a private man, the major heir of the Geico insurance fortune. He was a spook aficionado and had decided to invest his fortune in creating a private facility at which to train men in the latest electronic surveillance techniques. Somehow one of Bill Taylor's sources ended up talking to Goodwin's son, with whom Bill Taylor then got in touch. Bill interviewed Goodwin's son, and the son set up a confidential meeting between Taylor and his father, Leo. Twenty-four hours before that scheduled meeting, Leo Goodwin Jr. suffered what was reported to be a "massive heart attack" and died at the age of fifty-eight, with absolutely no prior signs of any heart problems.

Next I prepared a subpoena duces tecum for Jack Holcomb, the executive director of the National Intelligence Academy. But when I filed it with the court clerk in Oklahoma City, an enterprising young reporter by the name of Gypsy Hogan snatched a copy from the court clerk's desk. She telephoned Jack Holcomb in Florida and asked him why the Silkwood family would be interested in subpoenaing him. Holcomb immediately fled the state of Florida, but not before he cleaned out the files of the National Intelligence Academy of all documents relating to Oklahoma City.

We then subpoenaed Jack Larson, Holcomb's number 2. He flatly told us that Jack Holcomb, after being notified by Gypsy Hogan that he had been subpoenaed by the Silkwood family, had removed a bunch of files from the central filing system and had taken them with him "to Europe somewhere."[6] We did learn from Larson's deposition that one J. D. Hand had sold to the Oklahoma City Police Department's Special Intelligence Unit several highly sensitive telephone wiretapping and electronic eavesdropping devices. We found this to be particularly interesting because Oklahoma had not enacted special legislation authorizing state law enforcement personnel to even possess such eavesdropping equipment. It was illegal to possess it in the state of Oklahoma.

Bill Taylor tracked J. D. Hand to a small town in Texas by the name of Flower Mound, just outside Dallas. I issued a subpoena duces tecum to Hand, demanding that he produce all of his records on the kind of electronic eavesdropping equipment he had sold to the Oklahoma City Police Department's Special Intelligence Unit, to whom that equipment had been delivered, and when it had been delivered.

I flew into Texas and met Joe Royer, who had flown in to serve the subpoena on Hand directly. Royer drove up to J. D. Hand's home and parked just up the street. I waited in the car while Joe walked up to the door, rang the bell, and announced who he was and why he was there. He heard Hand's wife turn from the door and talk to what sounded to Joe like a man. Then she told Joe that J. D. was not home. So Joe announced loudly to J. D. that he had heard Hand's voice in there, and he then slid the subpoena under the front door and walked back to the car.

As we drove away from J. D. Hand's house and turned the corner at the end of his street, a caravan of three police cars, red lights flashing and sirens screaming, came careening down the street.

"That would be us," I said. I told Joe to carefully take out his driver's license and identification, and I opened the glove compartment and removed the auto registration and insurance information. I then removed all my identification and stowed it under the passenger seat. I told Royer to drive—taking care to remain under the speed limit—back out onto the expressway and to head back to the hotel, where I was scheduled to take the sworn deposition of the director of Region VII of the National Labor Relations Board the next morning.

Only a short way onto the expressway, an unmarked car darted out of an on-ramp and accelerated rapidly toward us from behind. I saw it coming in the rearview mirror and let Royer know we were going to be pulled over. I saw the driver of the oncoming vehicle reach out of the driver's side window and plunk a small red flashing light onto the top of his car—and then the siren blared. I told Royer to slowly pull off onto the right shoulder, roll down his window, and be ready to present his driver's license, auto registration, and insurance verification. I told him to remain calm and not say anything that was untrue.

Within seconds, the civilian vehicle pulled in behind us, the siren dying to a drone as the car stopped. The driver thrust open the driver's side door, forgetting that he had pushed the flashing red light out through the open driver's side window, immediately dragging the light from his rooftop and entangling him in the electric cord. He had obviously plugged the electric cord of the siren into his cigarette lighter and then simply put the siren out his driver's side window and had forgotten that he couldn't open the door without dragging it down on top of himself. The man, dressed in a T-shirt, baggy shorts, tennis shoes, and a baseball cap, finally just threw the light and cord to the ground like a dead snake and tried to regain his composure before approaching the driver's side of our car.

Embarrassed and off his game, the man approached Joe's window and asked for his driver's license. He looked surprised when Royer simply handed it over to him.

"Registration!" the man demanded.

Royer immediately handed that to him too. Again the man looked surprised, and also a bit disappointed. He obviously wanted Royer or me to open the glove compartment and start to reach into it so he could use that as a pretext for pulling a weapon on us. But neither of us had given him the slightest provocation. When Royer was next asked for insurance verification, he immediately handed that over as well.

"What were you doing trespassing on Mr. Hand's property?"

"I was serving a duly issued federal subpoena duces tecum to Mr. J. D. Hand to testify in a sworn deposition forty-eight hours from today. I have a copy of the subpoena with me if you wish to see that and the notary form for certification of service."

The man glared at Royer. Then he looked past him to me.

"And you. Let's see some identification!"

"No, thank you," I said calmly.

"What?" he said. "Are you refusing to show a law enforcement officer of the state of Texas your personal identification?"

"I have no idea," I said. "I haven't seen any of your identification yet. And that's certainly not a standard Texas State Police vehicle that I see you driving there—or a regulation flashing red light, I might add. For all I know, you are just some friend of J. D. Hand's that has come running to his beck and call to interfere with the service of a duly issued federal subpoena in a murder case."

Rage surged from the man at the driver's side window, and he nearly came clambering over the hood of our car to get to my side of the vehicle. Before he could get around the hood, I reached up slowly and locked the passenger side door. He planted his feet on the ground, grabbed the door handle, and started yanking on it. I sat and stared straight ahead.

"Open this goddamned door!" he screamed, tearing at the door handle.

I rolled the window down less than an inch and waited for him to calm down. I told Royer to roll up his window and lock all the doors. After several seconds, I turned and looked over at the red-faced man standing beside my door, still pulling on the locked door handle, and I said, "Identification?"

He was stunned. "Identification?" he screamed.

"Yes," I said calmly. "I have no way to tell whether you are or you aren't a police officer. Show me some identification."

He proceeded to tell me, through the half-inch crack in the window, that he had been at a softball game when he had received the call from Hand and that he had left his ID in a jacket at the edge of the ball field. "But *you* are required by law to show me some form of official identification when I demand it of you," he said. "That's the law here in the state of Texas."

"No, it's not," I said. "And if it is, it's totally unconstitutional. So it's void. Totally void. Where the hell do you think we are here, in *Russia* or something?"

That genuinely stunned him, as if he had simply never thought about it like that. But he still insisted that that was the law in Texas. "Are you gonna open this goddamned door or aren't you?"

"Absolutely not," I said.

"Then you're under arrest!"

"Under arrest? For what?" I demanded. I was actually surprised. I didn't think he would have the balls to do that.

"For refusing to show proper official identification to a law enforcement officer of the state of Texas when it was demanded!" he declared.

Just then three police cars came over the horizon a mile away. So I unlocked the passenger side door and climbed out. The furious man immediately grabbed my right wrist and yanked on me. I instinctively turned away from him, just as I had been trained to do in Special Forces training, and he started trying to circle around me. He ran smack into the still-open car door, then fell backward and rolled down an embankment alongside the road. I didn't even do that on purpose; he was just a buffoon.

"You're resisting me!" he screamed as he tumbled, arms flailing like windmills, down the embankment.

I leaned over the embankment and shouted down to him. "Bullshit! If I were resisting you, you wouldn't be getting back up right now. So get your ass on up here if you're going to arrest me. I don't want any of your trigger-happy friends shooting me as some kind of cop killer!"

He clambered up the hill, hand-over-hand, not wanting to be found in that humiliating position by his friends when they arrived. He shouted at me to put my hands behind my back, which I did. I told him not to put the handcuffs on too tightly or I would tell his friends what an idiot he was. So he put the cuffs on fairly loosely and took me back toward his car. I told him that I would wait for the police officers to arrive before I got into any car, that I was *not* going to get into any *civilian* car under any circumstances. I would get into only a "regulation police vehicle." He laughed and said, "What do ya think we are, some kind of Ku Klux Klansmen *pretending* to be police officers?"

I considered my answer. Then I said, "Half the Klansmen in Mississippi *were* police officers!"

His friends rolled up right at that moment in three police cruisers, complete with uniforms and guns.

I was already "subdued," waiting to be escorted to a police cruiser. They dutifully pressed my head down to "force" me into the back of the cruiser, just to let me know that they could, and two deputy sheriffs drove me away to Flower Mound, Texas, to book me for refusing to provide official identification to a Texas police officer.

Meanwhile, the other two carloads of police and the John Doe who'd pulled us over stayed on "at the scene of the crime" and interrogated Joe Royer. When they were shown the copy of the subpoena duces tecum and the notary certification of service form, they released him. But they tossed the original subpoena that we had served on J. D. Hand onto the ground in front of Royer as they left and told him to "take that back to Oklahoma with you."

Royer drove immediately to a public phone and called Bill Taylor.

The deputy sheriff who was driving the police cruiser into which I had been put was a jovial kind of guy, obviously the good guy in the good guy/bad guy game that they were about to play. But neither one of them was very bright. Before we were even out of sight of the place where we'd been pulled over, he turned over his right shoulder and, through the wire grating separating me from the two deputies, asked, "What'd ya say your name was?"

The Bad Cop in the front passenger seat said, "He's that goddamned Jew lawyer from New York."

"Is that right?" the Good Cop asked, as if I were going to answer.

I just smiled.

It went on like that for the rest of the drive to the Denton County sheriff's office in Flower Mound, Texas, and then all through the booking and fingerprinting process. One deputy after another asked me my name, address, place of birth, and any other identifying information they thought they could get out of me. I didn't say a single word. So I was placed in a cell in the Denton County Jail.

One deputy went so far as to tell me, "If you don't give us your name, you ain't *ever* gonna get before any magistrate, because if we don't have a name, then we can't put you on the court calendar. So you'll just have ta sit here in jail until you give us your name."

I refused to eat the peanut butter sandwich they brought me for dinner. And I stayed up all night long simply sitting in a lotus position, meditating, going into that place that is no place, devoid of any time, place, or identity. The night passed without incident or distress.

The clerk of the Denton County Court arrived at 7:00 AM with a signed court order from the Denton County magistrate ordering the deputy sheriff to give me a phone call. I called Judge Frank Theis in Oklahoma and was pleasantly surprised to find that he was there. He had been contacted by a "Mr. Taylor" the night before and had been asked to go to the chambers of the Oklahoma City Federal Court for a telephone call from Attorney Sheehan from the Denton County Jail in Flower Mound, Texas, at 7:30 the following morning.

I apologized to Judge Theis for having to delay the deposition of the Region VII director of the National Labor Relations Board, which was scheduled for later that morning—but I told him that I had been "unavoidably detained."

We both laughed.

Judge Theis asked me what, if anything, I might want him to do for me. And he asked me if I believed that I was in any physical danger. I told him not to worry, that I would be out of there by noontime, but that I didn't think I would be able to make the 10:00 AM deposition. He laughed at that and agreed to delay it for as long as I thought was necessary. I told him to simply reschedule the deposition for the next morning at ten o'clock. I told him that I would have a funny story to tell about what had happened to me on the way to that deposition after the case was over. Then I told him that we had effectively served the subpoena on J. D. Hand. He told me that the subpoena had been returned to our process server, Mr. Royer, but after I told Judge Theis that the service had been "good service," he said he would consider the subpoena duly served and would expect Mr. Hand to appear for his deposition on the following Friday in Flower Mound, Texas. He wanted to know whether I wanted one of our other Silkwood attorneys to take Hand's sworn deposition. I said no, that I would enjoy taking it. He laughed and asked me to call his chambers as soon as I was released.

I went before the Denton County magistrate at 9:00 AM and told him exactly what had happened, blow by blow. Both deputy sheriffs who had officially arrested and booked me refused to come into the courtroom. And I could see the man (whose name I was never given) who had actually arrested me for "refusing to provide official identification to a Texas law enforcement

officer" watching the proceedings from the hallway, through a round port-
hole window in the courtroom door. The magistrate laughed out loud several times during the course of my presentation, after I announced who I was
and called myself as my first witness, since the district attorney had called
no one.

At the end of my testimony, the magistrate, trying to fight back laughter, said he was going to dismiss the charges against me. I, however, made a
motion for a judgment of acquittal, pointing out that, without such a final
judgment on the merits, the district attorney and the law enforcement officials of Denton County might conceivably attempt to recharge me with the
same crime based upon the same facts. So the magistrate, after giving the
district attorney the option of presenting additional evidence against me and
receiving no offer, entered a judgment of acquittal and apologized for the
rudeness that the law enforcement officials in Denton County had displayed
toward me. The magistrate also agreed to notify J. D. Hand that he had been
duly served with a subpoena duces tecum to appear in that same courtroom
for his sworn deposition on Friday morning at 10:00 AM, and the magistrate
told me that he would be proud to make his courtroom available to me for
that deposition. "It's the least I can do to try to make this up to you," he
said. I thanked him and got off the stand, then walked through the courtroom doors at the back of the court, past the glowering deputy sheriffs lining
the hallway walls.

However, on that Wednesday evening, J. D. Hand died of a massive
heart attack. He was therefore unable to appear for his deposition on Friday.

Bill Taylor decided that our next best move was to contact Leo
Goodwin III, the chairman of the board of the National Intelligence
Academy, and try to get the Goodwin family to agree to have an autopsy
done. They had buried him within twenty-four hours, believing that he
had died of a coronary, and they wouldn't allow an autopsy. All of this
was totally bizarre. We had Jack Holcomb at the National Intelligence
Academy, who had fled with documents to West Germany. Harold Behrens
had fled to Las Vegas. We had subpoenaed the chairman of the board, Leo
Goodwin Jr., and now he was dead, as was J. D. Hand. Although we felt
that Harold Behrens was directly involved in the killing of Karen Silkwood,

we believed he had had accomplices inside the Special Intelligence Unit of the Oklahoma City Police Department, which had been run by James Reading, the chief of security of the Kerr-McGee Corporation, at the time of Karen's murder. But the deaths presented significant challenges. The situation was beginning to spiral out of control. So I wrote an affidavit to Judge Theis outlining the recent events, detailing for him the number of suspicious deaths among our subpoenaed witnesses during this short period of time. Judge Theis was also becoming concerned, but we couldn't do much more than press ahead.

CHAPTER *twenty-two*

B Y NOVEMBER 1978, we had been working on the case for twenty-four months. Shortly after my second set of meetings with Gerry Spence, I received a telephone call from Barbara Newman. Newman had been working for National Public Radio when I had first gotten to know her. At the time of her call, however, she was working for ABC's show *20/20*. She called me in Oklahoma City and told me that one of her young reporters had just come in with a story that he saw on the AP wire. His name was Skip.

Skip came on the line. "Mr. Sheehan?"

"No. It's just Danny. I'm an old friend of Barbara's."

"I just brought this story to Barbara, and she said that I should call you right away because this might mean something to you."

"Go ahead," I said.

He told me that two middle-level executives of the Kerr-McGee Nuclear Corporation had just been detained down on the Mexican border. They had been caught trying to smuggle into Mexico some kind of sensitive plutonium weighing scale. He said they were on their way to some little nowhere town down in Mexico. "Does this mean anything to you?" he asked me.

The world suddenly shifted into sharp focus, and I was able to connect what Skip had told me with the story that I had gotten from Jim Ikard. I called Bill Taylor and told him we had to go to Washington, D.C., to meet with Pete Stockton.

Two days later, in Pete Stockton's office, I started to recount to him what had been reported to us. Suddenly, a look of shock, and some genuine fear, came over his features. "Not here! Don't talk about this here!" He immediately wrote down what turned out to be his private home address in Chevy Chase, Maryland where he wanted me to meet him. Just below the address on the note it said, "10:00 tonight."

Bill Taylor and I drove out to Chevy Chase that night at ten o'clock and went to Peter's home. He had six kids running all around, trying to avoid being corralled and taken off to bed. Looking harried, Peter invited us to go upstairs into his third-floor attic. There he had a specially built, completely soundproof "safe room," a large, stand-alone room with asbestos paneling on the inside and a plunger-operated door. We walked in and sat down, and he plunged the door closed.

I then proceeded to tell him the stories about the dozens of 98 percent pure plutonium pellets that had been intercepted, purportedly in the process of being "mis-shipped" down to some "little dirt-water town in Mexico" from the Kerr-McGee nuclear facility—pellets that the president of the Kerr-McGee nuclear facility had personally erased from the official shipping invoices. Then I told him about the report that I had just received from Barbara Newman's reporter.

"Jesus H. Christ," Peter exclaimed when I told him that. "I've got to report this to Dingell right away. I will brief him personally and privately about this, first thing in the morning. You both come back and see me, right here, tomorrow night, at the same time." We said OK and got up and left.

The following night at exactly 10:00 PM, Pete Stockton took us directly upstairs, and we closed ourselves into the secure room. Peter started talking immediately.

"Dingell almost shit! He sent an immediate priority memo over to Stansfield Turner, the director of the CIA, at Langley, reporting 'My top staff has come into possession of information causing us to suspect that plutonium may be being smuggled out of private nuclear facilities here in the United States with the knowledge of the high-level management of those facilities.' But nothing happened. He sent it over to Langley and nothing happened. We need more information!"

"What do you mean you need more information?" I said. "Holy shit! We are civilians. You're the government."

"Look, I'm just telling you the way it is," he said. "You seem to have better access to this sensitive kind of information than we do. You have to get more information if we are going to get the agency to cough up any information to us."

As Bill Taylor and I drove away, Bill said, "What the hell is going on here? *We're* supposed to be doing the investigation for the Congress?"

Bill called Alpha, his top source, and told him what we had. He also told Alpha who we were talking with and what it was we were trying to do. Bill asked Alpha to go to all his sources and get back to us within forty-eight hours if he could. Two days later, Bill received a message on his beeper and he went off to a pay phone to talk to Alpha. All that Alpha said to Bill was, "Israel, Iran, South Africa, and Brazil!"

"What about them?" Bill had demanded. But Alpha had said that was all we were going to get. Bill remembered that Alpha's earlier tip to "go to Georgia" had led us to the National Intelligence Academy.

Bill brought the new information back to me, and I called Peter Stockton.

"Same place? Same time? Tonight?" I asked.

"Yes," he said.

When the door to the secure room in Stockton's attic was sealed shut, Bill took out his pen and wrote down: "ISRAEL; IRAN; SOUTH AFRICA & BRAZIL." He turned the pad around and pushed it over to Stockton. After Stockton read it, he looked up at me and said, "Jesus Christ! My God, I've got to get this to Dingell right away." And he actually pushed his chair back from the table, got up, and left us sitting there. When he hadn't come back within fifteen minutes, we simply got up and showed ourselves out.

Stockton took the information directly to John Dingell. Dingell looked at the note, went directly to his office, and retrieved a copy of the priority memo that he had sent to Stansfield Turner three days earlier. On the front page of the memo, Dingell simply handwrote "ISRAEL; IRAN; SOUTH AFRICA & BRAZIL," and he then used a top-secret courier to send it directly over to Stansfield Turner at Langley at 8:30 the very next morning.

Within just two hours, CIA director Stansfield Turner was standing in John Dingell's office, priority memo in hand, pleading with Dingell to let Turner talk with him alone. At that point (and this is according to Pete Stockton, who gave Bill Taylor and me a complete blow-by-blow of exactly what happened after we gave him this extraordinary information), John Dingell had said to Stansfield Turner, "Fuck you, Stan! You had your chance to talk to me alone three days ago. And you didn't have jack shit to say to me. So you are going to talk to my entire committee now, and you're going to talk to us *under oath*. We are going downstairs into the secure room, and you are going to talk to all of us and tell us exactly what the hell this is all about!"

So John Dingell virtually dragged Stansfield Turner downstairs and into the secure room in the Rayburn House Office Building and put Turner under oath in front of the entire assembled Subcommittee on Energy and the Environment of the House of Representatives. He demanded that Turner explain the connection between the subject matter of Dingell's initial priority memo to Turner and the nations of Israel, Iran, South Africa, and Brazil.

Stansfield Turner had been caught with his pants down on this. So he said, "We at the agency had heard these rumors about potential smuggling going on of bomb-grade plutonium and highly enriched U-238 uranium to some of the countries on this list from private nuclear facilities here in our country. But our CIA has undertaken an official CIA Rumor Evaluation Report concerning these specific rumors. The results of those reports are highly classified, and even though we are here in a classified hearing, I am afraid that the members of this subcommittee do not have the requisite security clearances that would be required to have access to the result of those rumor evaluations." He went on to say that, in light of the seriousness of the implications of the memo that he had been sent by Congressman Dingell—and the degree of specificity that was contained in it—he had directed his staff to white out portions of the official CIA Rumor Evaluation Report that would rise above the top-secret classification so that committee members could see for themselves that the implications of the memo notations were not true.

According to Stockton, who was in the room when this all happened, there was then almost immediately a knock at the door of the secure room beneath the Rayburn House Office Building, and in came a top-secret courier from the CIA, who delivered to each subcommittee member a set of whited-out copies of the official CIA Rumor Evaluation Report that Stansfield Turner had referred to. The subcommittee members opened their packets to discover that, lo and behold, all the *wrong portions* of the report had been whited out—and what was visible showed that Dingell's priority memo was, in fact, absolutely correct—right down to the specific nations involved in receiving these materials. There it was, right in front of them![7] Dingell, who was well known for his hot temper, exploded at Turner and called him "a no-good lying son of a bitch." Dingell was so furious with Turner that he (and to this day I do not know exactly how he got this done) established contact with some of his people in the National Security Agency and arranged for an NSA satellite to be assigned to place real-time surveillance on the sister facility of the Kerr-McGee nuclear facility (since the Kerr-McGee nuclear facility had itself been shut down during the ongoing investigation of the Silkwood scandal). That sister plant was the NUMEC facility in Pennsylvania. NUMEC reprocessed spent enriched U-238, so it too had highly fissionable material. The NSA's real-time satellite surveillance caught personnel at NUMEC loading enriched U-238 into containers, taking those containers out to sea, and putting them on a Charter Oil Company vessel. The satellite then tracked this Charter Oil Company vessel out into the Atlantic Ocean, where the satellite photographed this vessel being boarded by crew members of an Israeli vessel. The NSA videotaped these activities and tracked these containers all the way to Israel. This was all accomplished within just three weeks.

I detailed all of this information in a sworn affidavit and submitted it directly to Judge Theis.

Within forty-eight hours, Judge Theis called me to notify me that he had felt compelled to share my sworn affidavit with the Kerr-McGee attorneys and with Glenn Whitaker, the attorney for the United States government defendants in the case. He told me that Glenn Whitaker had then asked for an in camera and ex parte meeting (that is, a meeting in the judge's private chambers and outside the presence of the other party, meaning me and the other Silkwood attorneys), at which Whitaker would be allowed to present to Judge Theis attorneys from the CIA. Judge Theis was calling to tell me about the meeting he had agreed to convene, even though Whitaker had expressly asked him not to inform me. In his call, Judge Theis said that he wanted me to come to his courtroom in the federal courthouse on Monday morning at 10:00 AM but that he was not going to let me attend the meeting. I told Judge Theis that I strongly objected to any such meeting from which I and the other Silkwood attorneys were to be excluded. Judge Theis noted my objection, but he stated that he was going to grant them the meeting anyhow.

On Monday, February 21, 1979, I was in Judge Theis's courtroom at 9:45 AM awaiting his entrance at 10:00.

At 9:55 AM Judge Theis entered the courtroom and took his place on the bench. He had an official court stenographer with him. On the record, Judge Theis noted my presence in the courtroom as well as my strong objection to his convening an in camera, ex parte meeting with government counsel and the CIA attorneys. Judge Theis and I and the official court stenographer were the only ones in the courtroom.

At 10:00 AM, Glenn Whitaker and two "suits" entered the courtroom from the public hallway. Glenn Whitaker was startled to see me in the courtroom, but the two CIA lawyers did not even look at me. When they were seated at the prosecution table, Judge Theis announced, on the record, the details as to how he had been contacted by Mr. Whitaker; how he had made his decision to grant Mr. Whitaker's request for the in camera, ex parte meeting; and how and why he had informed me of this meeting. He stated that he had agreed to exclude me from the meeting, noting my strong objection to its taking place. He then asked me, on the record, to remain in the courtroom while the meeting was taking place, and then he rose and went into his chambers with Whitaker and the CIA attorneys, taking the court stenographer with him.

Within minutes, in through the courtroom door from the public hallway came Seymour (Sy) Hersh, the well-known investigative reporter for *The New York Times*. I had met Sy on a number of prior occasions, but I had never gotten to know him well. I knew, however, that his primary sources were from dissenters *inside* the CIA. Sy came over to where I was sitting all alone at the counsel table, and we slid into one of the public pews in the courtroom.

"Danny!" he said. "What the hell's going on? I got word that two legal bigwigs from the CIA were leaving to fly out here to Oklahoma City to hold some supersecret meeting with the judge that had been assigned to the Karen Silkwood case. I dashed down to National Airport to fly out here—and there they were, right on the very same flight that I was on. What's going on here?"

I didn't ask him how he recognized, on sight, two legal bigwigs of the CIA. Instead, I told him all the pertinent details.

"Holy shit!" he said. "The source of the bomb-grade plutonium to Israel for Israel's atomic bomb! They will never let you get that story out. Hell, that's just as black as the truth behind the Kennedy assassination!"

I spent the rest of the hour briefing Sy on the full background of the Karen Silkwood case, suggesting that he talk directly with David Burnham to confirm most of the details that I was conveying to him. He took notes like mad. But we were finally interrupted by Judge Theis when he came back into the courtroom and ascended the bench.

Looking at me sympathetically, he announced,

> Well, Mr. Sheehan, you can be certain that it is sinister. But it is also most definitely secret. This is just "a glass mountain" that you and your young colleagues are simply not going to be allowed to climb in this case.
>
> I am, today, taking judicial notice of the fact that the federal Civil Rights Act, the specific federal statute under which you have filed count 1 of your federal civil complaint in this case, was enacted by Congress in 1868, immediately following the end of the American Civil War. And I am taking further judicial notice of the fact that the American Civil War was fought solely and exclusively for the purpose of freeing members of the Negro race from their previous condition of involuntary servitude, and that the federal Civil Rights Act was, therefore, in fact, enacted by the United States Congress solely and exclusively for the purpose of protecting the newly won federal rights of members of the Negro race.
>
> I am, therefore, ruling today that your cause of action number 1 is hereby officially dismissed—because I find that, nowhere within the four corners of the civil complaint that you have filed in this case, have you made any allegation that Miss Silkwood was a member of the Negro race, nor that she was deprived of the First Amendment rights and Fourth Amendment rights solely and exclusively because of her membership in the Negro race.

This court will, however, Mr. Sheehan, hear counts 2 and 3 contained in your civil complaint in this case—your claims that officials of the Kerr-McGee Nuclear Corporation in fact conducted their business activities here in the state of Oklahoma, at their Kerr-McGee Cimarron nuclear facility, in such a willfully and wantonly reckless manner that they are legally responsible for the contamination of Miss Silkwood, and that these officials either intentionally placed, or negligently allowed to be placed, four hundred thousand disintegrations per minute of deadly radioactive plutonium from their plant onto the food in the refrigerator of Miss Silkwood's private home in order to contaminate Miss Silkwood with a potentially lethal dose of radioactive contamination for the express purpose of enabling them to lawfully remove Miss Silkwood from their plant, where she was educating and organizing her fellow workers to protect themselves against the dangers of radioactive contamination.

And you will find, Mr. Sheehan, that this court will look very favorably upon all of the motions that you and your colleagues file in this case directed toward the objective of obtaining and submitting to this court all of the evidence that exists to support your second and third claims.

This case will therefore proceed to trial, two weeks from today, on March 6, 1979, solely on counts 2 and 3 of your complaint. I am perfectly aware of the fact that you disagree with my ruling as a matter of law.

"I certainly do, Your Honor. I strongly disagree," I said.

Your strong disagreement and objection are noted for the record. And I might say that I may even be wrong on this matter. So I am agreeing to sign an order requesting an expedited appeal of this ruling immediately to the Tenth Circuit Court of Appeals. And if the Tenth Circuit chooses to overturn my ruling on this matter, I will gladly reinsert count 1 back into your complaint, and we will proceed to trial on all three counts in your original complaint. But, until that occurs, we shall proceed to trial, in March, on counts 2 and 3 only. And you will be admonished by this court not to make any claims to the jury in this case about your allegations contained in count number 1. Do I make myself clear, Mr. Sheehan?

"Yes, Your Honor," I said. "May I ask the court stenographer for an official transcript of your ruling this morning, Your Honor? I am not sure that the Tenth Circuit would believe that you actually said that unless I have an official transcript of your statement."

Judge Theis smiled that big bucktoothed smile and said, "Of course, Mr. Sheehan. I would be glad to see that that happens. I will see you and Mr. Spence here, in this courtroom, two weeks from today."

And with that, the trial of the Karen Silkwood case was under way.

On March 6, 1979, we went to trial on counts 2 and 3, the contamination counts. The trial lasted for eleven straight weeks.

When the morning arrived for the closing arguments to the jury, all three national television networks were in the courtroom, as well as reporters for the Associated Press, United Press International, *The New York Times,* and *The Washington Post.* While being interviewed on the courthouse steps, Bill Paul, chief counsel for the defendants and president of the Oklahoma State Bar Association, was asked what it felt like going through this eleven-week trial. He said, "It felt like standing under a waterfall and having a waterfall pouring down on you all day long!"

When Bill Paul entered the courtroom with his entourage of "men in gray," he found Karen's three young children seated in the front row, immediately in front of the jury. When Judge Theis entered the courtroom and saw the children, he smiled his big toothy grin. Bill Paul leaped to his feet and asked to have a bench conference before the closing statements began. Judge Theis invited us to adjourn to his chambers but said that he didn't want to keep the jury waiting for very long.

When we were all seated in Judge Theis's chambers, Bill Paul rose and said, "Your Honor, when we arrived in the courtroom this morning, I was shocked to see who I assume to be Karen Silkwood's three infant children seated immediately in front of the jury. I wish to object! These children are not the plaintiffs in this case. The plaintiff in this case is the estate of Karen Silkwood. Well, I guess that the children are the heirs to the estate . . . I really don't know quite how to refer to these children."

Throughout this spiel, Judge Theis sat smiling at Bill Paul from behind his large Kerr-McGee jelly jar. Judge Theis broke into his full-toothed grin, reached up and slid his rimless spectacles down on his nose, and looked over them directly at Bill Paul.

"How about incipient millionaires?"

Then he continued:

And as long as I have you all in here before the closing statements, Mr. Paul, let me make something perfectly clear to you. If, in your closing statement, you so much as hint that Karen Silkwood did not have in her possession all of the internal Kerr-McGee documents that Mr. Spence has informed this jury that Ms. Silkwood had, I am going to immediately stop your closing statement, and I am going to reopen this case and allow Mr. Sheehan to put before this jury all of the evidence that he has to support his count number 1. And let me advise you, Mr. Paul, that, based upon my having served as a trial judge for over forty years, if Mr. Sheehan presents the evidence that he has to support his count number 1 to this jury, this jury is going to conclude that the Kerr-McGee Corporation murdered Karen Silkwood! So be warned, Mr. Paul. I mean what I say.

Based on that remark from Judge Theis, I genuinely believe that we would have been able to have successfully convinced the Karen Silkwood jury in Oklahoma that agents of the Kerr-McGee Corporation had in fact murdered Karen Silkwood if we had just been given the chance to put our entirely admissible evidence before that jury. But, as Judge Theis made clear, we were never provided that opportunity.

Gerry Spence delivered the closing argument that we had prepared, and he tap-danced on the grave of the Kerr-McGee Corporation. The following are the highlights of the case that we put before that jury:

We outlined the long chain of intentional disregard for the health and safety of the mostly young workers recruited by Kerr-McGee to work at its nuclear facility. Gerry highlighted this by hauling before the jury large graphic blowups of pages from the Kerr-McGee–authored *Health and Safety Manual,* which he posted next to pages of a *Scientific American* magazine article from which entire paragraphs had been transparently plagiarized— except for yellow-highlighted sentences in the original article that plainly stated that exposure to plutonium would cause cancer. All those sentences had been intentionally deleted from the health manual into which that article had been plagiarized by Kerr-McGee.

We reviewed, in detail, that when a fifty-gallon drum filled with highly radioactive wastewater had ruptured on the back of a Kerr-McGee Corporation truck and spilled into the bed of that truck, the management of the Kerr-McGee nuclear facility had ordered that highly contaminated truck to be simply taken down to the local public car wash and washed down, so that all of the contamination went into the public sewage system of Cimarron, Oklahoma.

We reviewed the testimony of our expert witness, Dr. John Gofman, who testified that the management of the Kerr-McGee Corporation had knowingly exposed its workers to multiple times the level of radiation that was known throughout the scientific community to cause cancer.

We reviewed how we had proven beyond any contested opposition that the radioactive plutonium on all of the home furnishings and possessions of Karen Silkwood (that the Kerr-McGee Corporation had buried) had come from Lot 29, an experimental batch of plutonium produced at the Kerr-McGee nuclear facility two years before Karen Silkwood had even been employed at the facility. Not one single speck of Lot 29 plutonium had been anywhere in the plant during any time that Karen Silkwood had ever been present or employed there. The only sample of that plutonium was under lock and key in the exclusive custody and possession of the management of the Kerr-McGee Corporation—and its Security Department.

We reviewed how independent witnesses and workers for the Kerr-McGee Corporation had testified that the company's upper-level management had ordered employees to don fishing waders and wade into the Cimarron River, in the dead of night, to secretly scoop up and bury thousands of fish that had been killed by the accidental release of deadly radioactive plutonium wastewater into the public river, so as to conceal this release from both the public and from the Atomic Energy Commission.

We reviewed how Robert S. Kerr, the owner and founder of the Kerr-McGee Nuclear Corporation, in his capacity as chairman of the all-powerful United States Senate Armed Services Committee, had insisted on building his private plutonium reprocessing plant directly in the center of "Tornado Alley"—every year the site of more than a dozen major tornados, including one that had touched down within just one mile of the Kerr-McGee nuclear facility on the very evening following the testimony of the Kerr-McGee Corporation's chief engineer, in which he had sworn that *such tornadoes* never came near the plant.

We reviewed how the Kerr-McGee legal team—when confronted with our expert witnesses from Los Alamos National Laboratory, who had taken nasal swabs and sputum samples from Karen Silkwood following the discovery of the deadly radioactive contamination of her home and food in her refrigerator—had suddenly produced slices of Karen Silkwood's actual lung tissue that bore lower levels of radioactive contamination than what had been projected by our experts. This evidence of course had compelled us, and Judge Theis, to demand to know how the Kerr-McGee Corporation had come into possession of these actual slices of Karen Silkwood's lungs. We then were allowed by Judge Theis to present to the jury how Karen Silkwood's entire body had gone missing for forty-eight full hours after her death on the highway and how her body had simply and mysteriously reappeared as an unidentified Jane Doe in the Oklahoma City Hospital Morgue with all of her internal organs missing. Judge Theis thereupon ordered the Kerr-McGee legal team to turn over to us, right there in front of the jury, all the slices of Karen Silkwood's lungs and tissue that Kerr-McGee had stolen. This led to a disclosure that Karen Silkwood had, in fact, been exposed to three times the amount of radiation that we had even projected and *ten* times the amount the Kerr-McGee legal team had tried to deceive the jury into falsely believing had been deposited into her lungs.

We then reminded the jury of how it had been proven by direct internal Kerr-McGee classified documents—copies of which Karen Silkwood had had with her on the night she was killed while on her way to deliver those documents to David Burnham of *The New York Times*—that the Kerr-McGee Nuclear Corporation was "missing" over forty pounds of 98 percent pure, bomb-grade plutonium capable of creating four atomic bombs twice the size of the bombs that totally destroyed Hiroshima and Nagasaki, Japan, in August 1945.

Finally, we reminded the jury how the final expert for Kerr-McGee had testified that the Kerr-McGee nuclear facility was "as safe and secure as" the Three Mile Island facility in Pennsylvania—right at the very moment when the Three Mile Island facility was actually melting down.

The jury laughed out loud for one final time, and we rested our case.

The first bombshell from Judge Theis came when, in his jury instructions, he pointed out that the estate of Karen Silkwood had asked for $11 million in damages. He specifically instructed jury members that they were constitutionally authorized to give the plaintiff that full amount if they deemed the evidence to warrant such an award—despite the Price-Anderson Act, which Congress had passed on behalf of the private petroleum and nuclear industries, purporting to limit damages in civil cases to $10 million, but which Theis then expressly ruled to be unconstitutional. Judge Theis then agreed to place before the jury a set of specific interrogatories that we had requested and drafted, which greatly reduced any chance of a pro-plaintiff's judgment being reversed by an appellate court based upon "conflicting conclusions of fact obviously reached by a jury."

Finally, Judge Theis expressly authorized the jury to consider imposing punitive damages not only on the Kerr-McGee Nuclear Corporation (Karen Silkwood's employer) but also directly on the Kerr-McGee Corporation itself (the "mother ship" corporation), which housed the corporate treasure—the size of which he instructed the jury they were entitled to take into consideration in determining how large a punitive judgment to impose on that defendant as punishment for the grievous wrongdoing (if any) the defendant was determined by the jury to have engaged in. Then Judge Theis gave the jury a series of specific factual determinations that they would have to arrive at by a unanimous verdict in order to "penetrate the corporate veil" that had been erected between the Kerr-McGee Corporation and the smaller and less financially capable Kerr-McGee Nuclear Corporation and to use the net assets of the more prosperous Kerr-McGee Corporation, as the corpus against which the jury could assess punitive damages.

This was the opening we had been hoping for—one that could carry us beyond the damages limit that Congress had tried to impose upon awards assessed against private nuclear facilities by American juries with its enactment of the Price-Anderson Act. Judge Theis had unlocked the door—but that door would have to be opened and walked through by the jury. If it did walk through, that would sound the death knell for the private nuclear industry in America.

On the morning of June 4th, 1979, eleven weeks after the beginning of the trial of the Karen Silkwood case, the clerk asked the jury to answer "special interrogatory number 1": "Do you find by a preponderance of the evidence that Karen Silkwood intentionally—that is, knowingly and consciously—carried from work to her apartment the plutonium that caused her contamination?"

We had stared the Kerr-McGee Corporation and its high-paid attorneys squarely in the eye and had put directly to the jury the very issue of fact that was the Kerr-McGee Corporation's factual theory of the case. We knew that if we defeated this contention on the part of the Kerr-McGee Corporation, the rest of the verdicts would all go our way, leaving as the only remaining question the *amount* of damages to be assessed.

"No. We do not," the foreman of the jury announced in a loud voice.

Cheers went up in the courtroom. Judge Theis looked over at us and smiled. Then he gestured cheerfully to the assembled throng in the courtroom to contain themselves. And they did. He then asked the court clerk to go on.

The clerk then read "special interrogatory number 2" to the jury. This was the count 3 "fallback position" advocated by Gerry Spence as the alternative to our count 2 theory, that Karen had been intentionally contaminated with plutonium from Lot 29. However, when our count 1 was dismissed by Judge Theis, Gerry Spence and Bill Silkwood (Karen's father) determined that just as much money could be made from Kerr-McGee by proving "willful, wanton, reckless disregard for the health and safety" of Karen Silkwood as could be made from proving that she had been contaminated intentionally.

"Do you find that the Kerr-McGee Nuclear Corporation was negligent in its operation of the Cimarron nuclear facility so as to allow the escape of the plutonium from the facility and proximately cause the contamination of Karen Silkwood?"

The foreman of the jury announced, "Yes! We do!"

Further cheers broke out, and the wire reporters dashed out of the courtroom to file what they thought would be *the* story of the Karen Silkwood Case: "Kerr-McGee Nuclear Corporation Found to Be Negligent in Contamination of Silkwood." But the real headline was yet to come.

Judge Theis then calmed the uproar in the courtroom with a smile and directed the court clerk to continue.

"Please enter the amount of actual damages suffered by Karen Silkwood as defined in the court's earlier instructions."

The foreman of the jury delivered the award.

"Five hundred and five thousand dollars." Gasps went up in the courtroom.

This was still the age of fairly limited money damages against large corporations, since public interest law firms were just beginning then.

"And do you find by a preponderance of the evidence that the Kerr-McGee Nuclear Corporation is a 'mere instrumentality' of the parent Kerr-McGee Corporation?" the court clerk read aloud. The foreman of the jury hesitated, aware of the import of his upcoming announcement.

Then he lifted his chest and declared, "Yes! We do!"

Even more pandemonium broke out in the courtroom. Now everybody knew what was coming. They just didn't know how big it was going to be. Above the din (which Judge Theis wasn't even trying to stop), the voice of the court clerk could be heard reading the final, all-important "special interrogatory number 5":

"If you find by a preponderance of the evidence presented in this case that exemplary damages—or punitive damages—are appropriate, as defined by this court's instructions, please enter the amount."

The foreman turned to his fellow jurors and smiled. Then he turned to the young Silkwood children sitting directly before the jury and smiled. He delivered the announcement to them:

"Ten million dollars!"

It was the largest civil damages money award ever awarded in the entire history of the American judicial system!

What was important to us, however—and to the literally millions of Silkwood supporters around the world—was that this jury had openly defied the combined power of the private petroleum industry and had effectively broken through the glass ceiling of the amount of private money damages that could be lawfully awarded by any future American jury for a single nuclear incident, which the petroleum industry (and its lobbyists in Congress) had tried to cap at $10 million.

This meant that no private insurance company in the world would be willing to provide an insurance policy to any future private nuclear power plant in the United States. And, as a result of this decision, not one new private nuclear power plant was ordered or built in the United States from the date of the ruling in the Karen Silkwood case (June 4th, 1979) until 2012—when (of all people) Barack Obama authorized the licensing and building of a new private nuclear power plant in Savannah, Georgia. That authorization included the promise of federal subsidization of any insurance policy needed to construct and operate that plant. But the members of the Karen Silkwood team will make certain that that plant is never built.

We went up to the Tenth Circuit Court of Appeals, which bounced the case around and made a number of reactionary rulings; the principal one was quickly overruled by the United States Supreme Court. When the Supreme Court sent the case back down to Judge Theis to allow us to retry *not* the question of the legal liability of the Kerr-McGee Corporation (which had been affirmed by the Supreme Court) but just what the total amount of damages could be, we immediately raised our punitive damages demand to $70 million. Because the Tenth Circuit Court of Appeals noted that the jury in the Silkwood trial had not distinguished between the medical damages inflicted by the Kerr-McGee Corporation on Karen Silkwood's body and the property damages inflicted by the Kerr-McGee Corporation on Karen Silkwood's personal property in her home, the Silkwood estate was provided a second opportunity to litigate the amount of punitive damages that could be awarded by the jury. We then filed a motion to Judge Theis to reconsider his March 1979 ruling dismissing count 1.

The Tenth Circuit Court of Appeals took eighteen weeks to rule on the emergency appeal that I had lodged against Judge Theis's dismissal of count 1 in our complaint—the longest period for an emergency appeal in the history of the Tenth Circuit Court of Appeals. By the time the Tenth Circuit Court of Appeals ruled, we had already won the largest civil judgment in the entire history of the United States. So the issues that I had raised in our emergency appeal were, in effect, moot.

Immediately after receiving our motions to reinstate count 1 and to increase our demand for punitive damages from $10 million to $70 million, Bill Paul and the Kerr-McGee Corporation reached out to Gerry Spence and Bill Silkwood—without ever notifying me—and offered to immediately pay $1.38 million in cash to the Silkwood children and to waive any right Kerr-McGee had to appeal. Bill Silkwood accepted this offer because he had contracted cancer and thought that he might not live long enough to win reinstatement of the full punitive damages award. He wanted to pass from this world knowing that he had secured a "million-dollar judgment" against the Kerr-McGee Corporation, which would enable Karen's children to attend college and be taken care of after he died.

I would like to add the following, by way of mere observation.

Our United States Congress never told the American people about the smuggling of plutonium to Israel by the Kerr-McGee Corporation; by Robert S. Kerr, the chairman of the U.S. Senate Armed Services Committee; and by the CIA. Until this publication, no national news medium has dared to reveal this dark secret. Even Seymour Hersh, the usually heroic and esteemed American investigative journalist, as well as The New York Times, deemed this extraordinary fact to be "news not fit to print." Nor has anyone publicly revealed the fact that the CIA was responsible for smuggling 98 percent bomb-grade plutonium to the shah of Iran, even in the face of the recent twenty-first-century turmoil surrounding Iran's attempt to develop a nuclear weapon.

This important aspect of the Karen Silkwood case has, until now, remained a complete secret. We only discovered all this nationally critical information over the course of our investigation following Karen Silkwood's death. We tried to tell the world in open court, but we were not allowed to do so, even by a liberal Democratic judge.

I have two principal reasons for revealing these previously secret details about this famous case now. The first is that these facts explain how Israel obtained its nuclear weapons, which have so radically destabilized the entire Middle East. It is important for our citizens to know that it was the Central Intelligence Agency that did this and that its actions had to have been approved by Richard Nixon.

My second reason for revealing the above facts is to demonstrate why it is so important to eliminate private nuclear power plants in the United States. There are presently 103 such private nuclear power plants, and every one of them is approaching the end of its safe life expectancy. The private companies that own these nuclear power plants are growing desperate, because the nuclear waste materials from these facilities have completely filled their onsite nuclear storage capacity. These facilities will, therefore, soon have to stop operating if they cannot obtain permission to move all these highly radioactive materials to some remote location. Moreover, the operating licenses of many of these facilities will expire at the end of 2014. To renew those licenses beyond those plants' "safe life expectancy," the private companies will have to dispose of the special nuclear materials that are buried on the property surrounding those facilities.

We, as citizens of the United States, ought not allow this to happen. These radioactive materials have a five-hundred-thousand-year half-life. They will exist, for all practical purposes for our human family, forever. We cannot risk allowing these highly radioactive waste materials to enter our water table and oceans in the event of earthquakes, floods, and other natural disasters. Private nuclear power is one of the key industries that our two largest generations, the baby boomers and the millennialist generation, have to bring to a stop right now.

The story of the Karen Silkwood case was an adventure saga in many ways. But, more importantly, it's an important lesson regarding some of the darker events that have transpired in our country during our lifetimes—operations undertaken in blatant defiance of the promises that our government has made to our people. We must mobilize Americans of every generation to refuse to tolerate such self-destructive and selfish policies that endanger our families, our future, and, indeed, our very planet.

CHAPTER *twenty-three*

THE MORNING AFTER the announcement of the Silkwood verdict, I was contacted by telephone by Ed Lawrence, executive director of the Veatch Foundation of the Unitarian Universalist Church. Ed asked me to fly the Silkwood team immediately to Three Mile Island in Pennsylvania. It had been only four days since the Three Mile Island nuclear facility, owned by the General Public Utilities Corporation and Metropolitan Edison in Pennsylvania, had partially melted down, releasing radiation into the neighborhoods surrounding the facility. Within those four days, the industry-friendly Nuclear Regulatory Commission had already declared that there had been no melting of any kind of the fuel in the reactor's core, and it had therefore issued a license authorizing the Three Mile Island nuclear facility to vent coolant water from the damaged reactor into the Susquehanna River. The NRC was totally wrong in that determination. In fact, more than half of the nuclear fuel in one of the two reactors had melted, releasing substantial radiation into the coolant water, which would have been discharged directly into the Susquehanna. If the radiation safety experts who testified in our Karen Silkwood case were accurate in their assessments of the damage that would be caused by exposure to those levels of radiation, that water release would have generated as many as fifty thousand cases of cancer downriver from the Three Mile Island plant.

Ed Lawrence was asking us to fly into Three Mile Island to educate and to rally the local population to litigate to stop the pumping of radioactive effluents into the Susquehanna River. The Veatch Foundation board of directors had convened an emergency meeting and had voted unanimously to fund whatever our Silkwood team could possibly do to stop that from taking place. So, while others in the Silkwood community across the country were celebrating our victory in Oklahoma, and while national news media were lining up to interview us to explain the full implications of the largest civil judgment ever awarded in American history, I was on a plane to Three Mile Island in Pennsylvania with two of our Silkwood team attorneys, Lewis Pitts and Rob Hager.

As we approached the town of Three Mile Island in the early morning light, we saw the iconic cone-shaped cooling tower looming over the community, spewing clouds of vapor into the air. Emergency vehicles of all sorts careened through the streets. Facility managers were still unable to shut the valve that was stuck open, still releasing radioactive gases into the area. The volunteer fireman who picked us up at the airport drove us directly to the local high school, where the local townspeople were gathered, waiting for us to arrive.

What we encountered was a scene right out of a Norman Rockwell cover of the *Saturday Evening Post*. There was the captain of the Dauphin County Volunteer Fire Department in a red-and-black-checked hunting jacket and hunting boots; the Middletown High School football coach in a sweatshirt and sneakers; several teachers from a local elementary school; the local Catholic priest with women from the local Altar Rosary Society; the local Methodist minister; a number of couples ranging from their mid-twenties to their mid-sixties; and the mayor and members of the town council.

They didn't know what to do. "How do we know whether there was a meltdown of any of the fuel in the core and a potential breach of the containment vessel?" asked a local high school science teacher. The mayor confirmed that the Nuclear Regulatory Commission had already issued the plant a license to pump all the water out of the damaged core into the river. "How do we stop them if the federal government has already authorized them to do this?" the Catholic priest wanted to know.

I calmed them down and told them that we were going to file an immediate appeal of the NRC licensing decision and demand emergency access to the data on which the NRC had issued its initial license. I knew the NRC would be familiar with such a challenge and believed the challenge alone would cause the NRC to reconsider its issuance of the license long enough for us to demonstrate that there had in fact been a meltdown in the core.

We immediately won the right to an emergency NRC hearing and made our arguments. Fortunately, we held up the actual dumping of the contaminated water into the Susquehanna River long enough for the NRC to more seriously evaluate the data. When it did, the NRC "discovered" the partial meltdown of the fuel in the core of the reactor and the compromised integrity of the containment vessel, verifying that significant amounts of radioactive nucleoids had in fact escaped into the coolant waters that the NRC had previously authorized to be vented into the river. Radioactive material would have been vented directly into the public river had the citizens of the area not organized and intervened. As a consequence, the NRC "voluntarily" reversed its original license, and a catastrophe was prevented by the heroic actions of the everyday citizens of the community of Three Mile Island.

When our Silkwood team returned, one by one, to Washington, D.C., after many weeks—in my case many months—away from Arrupe House, we were besieged with requests to stay together. We had become the champions of our generation. We had successfully welded together a unique and historic alliance among several important constituencies and movements: the American civil rights and civil liberties community; the antinuclear community (both antinuclear weapons and antinuclear power); the American labor union movement; the American feminist movement; the antiwar movement; the environmental movement; and the American Trial Lawyers Association. Uniting them all were fifty-four of the major religious denominations in America, their progressive Washington Interreligious Staff Council, and its social justice lobbying arm, IMPACT.

The question we had to answer was, were we going to make our new organization permanent or was it time for each of us to go our separate way? These had been heady days together, bringing to heel one of the most powerful and dangerous industries in history; discovering the murderers of one of the bravest members of our young generation; uncovering a shadowy private association of public law enforcement officers who gathered and shared constitutionally forbidden political intelligence data against our own citizens, and revealing to Congress the ultra-secret, behind-the-scenes alliance between the CIA and secret corporate "security officials" who had attempted to supply bomb-grade plutonium to several of the most unstable governments in the world. How could we possibly let this all go on and simply return to the way we were before? Some of us could not—would not.

However, Sara and I first had to adjust to our life as a mother and a father. Danny-Paul, our first son, had been born just four months before the commencement of the Silkwood trial.

I was in the midst of preparing the briefs in an emergency appeal when Sara had gotten a sudden urge to return to Arrupe House to clean up the attic for Kidlette (the name we had taken to calling our little baby prior to his arrival). When Sara told me that she was on her way back to Arrupe House, I knew it was time for me to fly home too.

We were in the upstairs shower together, just a few days later, when Danny-Paul decided it was time to come out into the world on the morning of December 12, 1978. We had arranged for a natural childbirth—no drugs, no anesthetic—in the natural birthing room at Washington, D.C., Memorial Hospital, just a mile away from Arrupe House. We had sacred Buddhist spiritual chants playing in the background, and we videotaped the entire day, including Danny-Paul's actual birth. I "interviewed" Danny-Paul the moment he came out into the world, and when I introduced him to Sara, she greeted him with, "Oh! It's a *baby!*"

I brought Danny-Paul to sit with me at the counsel table during preparation of the proposed jury instructions for the Silkwood jury, and I took him with us into chambers for meetings with Judge Theis. The Kerr-McGee lawyers were being so roundly beaten up that they did not even dare protest my bringing Danny-Paul into chambers. I explained to Judge Theis that Sara was busy attending to all the press surrounding the trial, so I was on baby duty. "Actually," I told Judge Theis, "I *want* to have Danny-Paul with me. He is going to be an attorney too when he gets a little older, so I want him to get started early." Judge Theis laughed and said he was glad to have a budding attorney sit in on our deliberations. Bill Paul and the other Kerr-McGee lawyers just hung their heads and let it all go on around them.

Now we were all back in Washington, D.C., and warmly ensconced back in Arrupe House.

Sara and Danny-Paul moved in with Father Davis and me and the other "cool" Jesuits. Sara and I were demonstrating to these progressive Jesuit priests what it looked like to be a loving couple working together on social justice issues and *not* disowning the mate you loved or the child who was the fruit of your love for that mate. It was all actually quite remarkable. Sara and I made the entire attic into a baby's room and our new home together. Father Wally Kazubouski, a thirty-year old Franciscan Capuchin monk, sawed out window openings in the attic and installed windows in the turrets of the old Victorian house, a long-abandoned convent. He converted the downstairs former confessional into a private, soundproof phone booth. Everyone was delighted to be back home with two wonderful legal victories under our belt—and a brand new "Silkwood baby" in the family. It filled the old convent with life. We liked to refer to it as our version of "the right to life."

Visitor after visitor came to Arrupe House to pay their respects to Danny-Paul—and no doubt to marvel at the manner in which Sara and Danny-Paul and I had been openly welcomed into the Jesuit community as full members. I remained an official candidate for the Jesuit order, continuing my lengthy discussions with Father Davis and my other Jesuit superiors concerning changes that the Society of Jesus would be well-advised to make to attract and *keep* "wonderful prospects like Danny Sheehan." Sara wanted to become a Catholic—not because she had to (the old rule in the Catholic Church when a Catholic man and a Protestant woman mated) but because she viewed Danny-Paul to be a gift from Mother Mary, since on the night of his conception she had seen and heard Mother Mary clearly telling her, "Nothing matters other than our relationship with God."

It never even occurred to either Sara or me, for a single microsecond, *not* to have Danny-Paul, just as it never occurred to either of us that we would not be together for the rest of our lives to raise him and continue working together for social justice. Our union and our parenthood were absolutely natural, even though neither of us had had any such thing in mind as we had gone about our respective NOW and Jesuit business. The progressive Jesuits were absolutely mesmerized by the smooth progression of it all. It was so totally different from all the hiding, cheating, and concealment of the love relationships that many Jesuits wanted to integrate into their lives as "men for others." They had been forced to choose between two different lives, yet here they saw Sara and me successfully integrating both our spiritually motivated lives of social justice activism *and* our perfectly healthy and happy love relationship with each other, and with our new baby.

Arrupe House was a wonderful place to be in those halcyon days following the birth of Danny-Paul and the victories in the Karen Silkwood case and the Three Mile Island case. All our religious friends, as well as all our progressive secular political activist friends, gathered at Arrupe House for Danny-Paul's baptism and the celebration of Sara's and my decision to mate for life. Priests sprinkled holy water on the three of us. Our closest priest and nun friends became the godparents of Danny-Paul, and our medievalist friends played harps and flutes and gave us amulets. The health food and fruit drinks flowed. And all was blessed.

In that same week after we returned to D.C., after all of the ceremonies had concluded, we gathered at Arrupe House for a "summit conference." It was at this weekend gathering that the Christic Institute was born.

Sara sat in the big overstuffed armchair in the bay window of the living room of Arrupe House, with Danny-Paul bubbling happily on her green-skirted lap, the fall sun bathing them in golden light. I sat at their feet in faded blue jeans and a cream-colored chemise shirt and bare feet. It was Labor Day weekend of September 1979. Father Bill Davis sat across from us on the couch next to Wally Kazubouski, who looked just like a young version of the Marlboro Man. Rob Hager, a Harvard Law School friend and classmate who had decided to specialize in environmental law (especially antinuclear and antichemical pollutant law), sat in the middle of the living room, legs crossed, on a big couch pillow. Also present were Justin Zinn, our computer specialist and my dear friend; Artie Burns, a friend from my days at Cahill-Gordon; Patti Austin, my long-trusted personal secretary who had been with me since my days at the Rocky Mountain regional office of the ACLU back in 1974; Bill Taylor, who had flown up from Florida with his third wife, "Little Annie Fanny"; and Lewis Pitts, a lanky, bearded South Carolinian public interest lawyer who had been part of the Silkwood team.

Jimmy Garrison had been in our earlier meetings, but he had to leave to return to Cambridge, England, to complete his PhD in theology and to determine how to get the Soviet Union to join with our government to stop the production of nuclear weapons. But he was with us in spirit. Bob Alvarez and Kitty Tucker, who were integral members of the Silkwood team, had returned to the Environmental Policy Institute and to Antioch Law School, respectively. They would remain close allies of whatever organization we created out of this meeting, but they would not become active members. The same was true of Howard Kohn, who would remain as the Washington, D.C., bureau chief of *Rolling Stone* magazine; Howard Rosenberg, who would remain as the chief researcher for Dan Rather at *CBS Evening News*; Bob Fink, who would remain with New York congresswoman Bella Abzug as the chief investigator for her judiciary subcommittee on individual rights; and the other journalists from NPR, *20/20*, NBC News, and *The New York Times* who had been integral members of the Silkwood team but stayed in their professional positions.

It was at this meeting that we resolved to form a permanent organization. I would be our president and general counsel; Sara would be our vice president and executive director; and Father Bill Davis would be our secretary-treasurer. Bill Taylor would be our chief of security. We would become "the people's advocates" for those who had long been denied justice. We would function out of a tiny cobbler shop at the base of Capitol Hill. We would serve as "the people's Justice Department," taking on cases that extended well beyond nuclear power and nuclear weapons issues. Our de facto client would be not just the U.S. Jesuit order but the entire Washington Interreligious Staff Council, thereby allowing our new organization to represent the collective religious social ministry community in the United States. We decided to call ourselves the Christic Institute. "Christic" was the designation given by Pierre Teilhard de Chardin, a famous Jesuit theologian and philosopher, and a paleontologist who had discovered Peking Man, to "that binding force that binds every ultimately non-divisible integer of matter in the entire physical Universe together into one, single, harmonic whole . . . and that engines the upward evolution of spirit and matter into an ever-increasing degree of complexity that will ultimately bring each member of our entire human species to that same state of consciousness that was manifested by Jesus and by the other Prophets of our human family's great religions."

In short, we would be the law firm representing the ascending spirit within our human family—the better angels of our nature.

In that incarnation, we were considered by the Washington religious community to be the most political *religious* organization in Washington and we were at the same time considered by the Washington political community to be the most religious *political* organization in Washington. The Christic Institute had been born coincident with the birth of the first baby in our community.

We treated the board of directors of the Washington Interreligious Staff Council as our de facto board of directors. Our office had a Litigation Department that I headed up as general counsel; an Investigation and Research Department headed up by Bill Taylor (though he continued living in Florida, so Father Bill Davis was the "resident head" of our Investigation Department); a Grassroots Organizing Department headed up by Mary Cassell, a graduate of Cornell University's famous Labor Department; a Press Office headed up by Peter Dykstra, the former press director for Greenpeace; a Development (fund-raising) Department headed up by Steve Deal; and an Administration Department headed up by Sara. Our office manager was Claudia Gibson, a 300-pound "strong-arm specialist" who could keep us all in line. Our "inside board," which met every Monday morning, was comprised of the six department directors plus Patti Austin, Lewis Pitts, and Rob Hager.

The little cobbler shop we worked out of was at a terrific location, with the U.S. Capitol Building dome visible from every window of our office. But it was also in the middle of "the Combat Zone": one of the most crime-ridden public housing projects in the city. There were drug deals going down in the alley behind our office for the first four weeks we were there, as well as two fatal shootings on the sidewalk directly in front of our office. But it was free. So we took possession of the office and began cleaning up the place, painting and fixing up the old building while residents stood at either end of the block watching us warily, wondering whether our presence in the neighborhood was going to ruin their drug business.

On a Thursday morning soon after we had dug a twelve-foot-deep basement, Rob Hager, Lewis Pitts, and I were sitting in my top-floor front office exchanging war stories about the Silkwood and Three Mile Island cases. We were in the process of reviewing the various priorities of the Washington

Interreligious Staff Council to determine what initial major litigation we should design and mount, when the next case walked into our office.

A young man in a blue hardhat from the Chesapeake and Potomac (C&P) Telephone Company came in and began crawling around my office floor, installing wiring for our new telephone system. He was down on his knees screwing in the telephone lines, listening to our stories, when he suddenly turned, looked up, and asked, "Hey, are you guys the lawyers that just did that Karen Silkwood case out in Oklahoma?" We said that we were, and he became very serious. He took off his hardhat and gloves and then sat down with us. "I am a member of the UE," he said, referring to the United Electrical Workers, one of the most progressive labor unions in the nation. "I am also a member of a group by the name of the Workers Viewpoint Organization." None of us had ever heard of it.

"Did you guys hear about what just happened over the weekend down in Greensboro?"

I had seen Dan Rather on the *CBS Evening News* do a short report about the Ku Klux Klan having shot down a number of young demonstrators on the streets of Greensboro, North Carolina. But we had all been so preoccupied with fixing up our new office building that we had not gotten the full story. The telephone man proceeded to explain that North Carolina ranked dead last in the nation for organized labor because the state was so radically opposed to any organized unions. The owners and management of the textile mills in North Carolina had executed a very effective propaganda campaign that led most North Carolinians to view labor organizers as communists. Meanwhile, workers in textile mills in North Carolina were suffering from a virtual epidemic of brown lung disease from inhaling cotton dust, which resulted in a disease very similar in its symptoms to tuberculosis. In response to this ongoing situation, eight young medical doctors from New York City had gone down to Greensboro and opened clinics to provide free medical treatment to workers. They had also tried to get workers to organize to put a stop to the epidemic, but they couldn't get enough people to come to their meetings.

So the eight doctors went in individually and applied for low-skilled positions in the textile mills. They simply refrained from stating that they were college graduates with degrees from medical schools. Once they had gotten hired by the plants, they realized that the only way to effectively remedy the situation was to organize a labor union that would educate workers on ways to clean up the plants. They had then created the Workers Viewpoint Organization (WVO) and began to hold organizing meetings, but the companies hired goons to come in and physically break up their meetings. Eventually the Ku Klux Klan began to picket the plants because the young doctors and their supporters were organizing black and white people together. Then members of the American Nazi Party joined the Klan in the demonstrations.

In response, the doctors organized a big anti-Klan rally, and on Saturday, November 3, 1979, the workers gathered in Five Points, a black neighborhood in Greensboro. Local television stations were on hand with cameras rolling when, all of a sudden, a caravan of a dozen cars was spotted heading their way. Without explanation, Greensboro police officers immediately started getting into their cars and quietly driving away. The caravan rolled in, and Klansmen and Nazi Party members leaned out of the vehicle windows and started shouting racist epithets at the gathering demonstrators.

One of the demonstrators thereupon walked over to a Klan car and kicked the front bumper. As if on cue, all dozen cars immediately stopped, and the Klansmen and Nazi Party members jumped out. They waded into the marchers and started punching and kicking them and beating them with billy clubs and baseball bats. After the demonstrators overcame the initial shock of the flagrant attack, they realized they outnumbered the Klansmen and Nazis about one hundred to forty, so they turned on their attackers. Seeing that his group was starting to lose the fight, a man who had remained in the lead car of the Klan caravan fired a black powder pistol into the air. The Klansmen and Nazis immediately withdrew from the fight, walked calmly back to their cars, opened the trunks, and started handing out handguns and rifles. They then waded back into the crowd and started gunning people down. All of this was being broadcast on live television *and videotaped.* The gunmen shot and killed five of the principal leaders of the WVO. After two long minutes of killing, the Klansmen and Nazis turned around, simply walked back to their cars, and drove away.

After the Klansmen and Nazis had apparently fled, members of the Greensboro Police Department slowly started returning to the scene. Nelson Johnson, one of the surviving WVO organizers, shouted at the police for allowing the Klan to come in and shoot his people. The police immediately surrounded Johnson and arrested him for "disturbing the peace."

Meanwhile, dozens of townspeople who had witnessed the attack started shouting to the police and pointing toward a yellow van that was parked only a block away. The police officers finally went over to the van, where they discovered six Klansmen just sitting in the back with their guns still smoking. The police were basically forced to arrest them, but they then also immediately arrested six march organizers. The Greensboro district attorney then charged the six shooters and the six arrested march organizers equally with public rioting.

After hearing this account from the telephone man, we decided to help. Lewis Pitts, Bill Davis, Rob Hager, and I flew to Greensboro on that Saturday morning, when the funeral for the slain marchers was taking place. The funeral procession marched all the way from downtown Greensboro to the cemetery, where twenty-one WVO marchers waited with rifles, lined up to stage a twenty-one-gun salute for their arriving fallen comrades. Bill Davis and I couldn't help but notice the careless regard they all displayed for gun safety. These young people did not appear to know the first thing about how to safely handle loaded firearms; the guns were more of a symbol of their willingness to openly defy armed unjust authority than they were an actual means of effective armed self-protection.

After the funeral, we met with the group's remaining leaders. We learned that the doctors and principal organizers of the Workers Viewpoint Organization had previously all been members of the Communist Party in New York City. They began the meeting with a doctrinaire speech, which went on for hours before I finally told them, "I didn't come down here to be inducted into your organization and listen to this propaganda. Let's sit down and figure out what the defense is going to be against these charges of public rioting and start designing our affirmative federal Civil Rights Act civil complaint." We agreed that I would go immediately to the Civil Rights

Division of the federal Justice Department and try to initiate a *criminal* Civil Rights Act investigation of those responsible for the killings.

We flew back up to Washington, D.C., and I went directly to see Drew Days III, the assistant United States attorney general in charge of the Civil Rights Division of the Justice Department. Drew told me that he had to wait for completion of the city and state criminal investigations, since murder charges might well be brought by the city against the shooters, and he did not want to interfere with the investigation. Ultimately, the six Klan and Nazi Party members were tried by the Greensboro district attorney before an all-white jury. But just getting that case to trial took a full year, and they were all acquitted on the grounds of self-defense.

Immediately after the acquittal, we returned to meet with Drew Days in November 1980. By then, however, Jimmy Carter had been defeated by Ronald Reagan in the presidential election; we wanted the criminal civil rights investigation officially started before Days and his staff were moved out. Sure enough, as soon as the Reagan–Bush administration appointees came on board to run the Civil Rights Division of the Justice Department, they publicly announced, "The only theory pursuant to which we can or will federally prosecute any member of the Ku Klux Klan or the American Nazi Party under the federal Civil Rights Act will be on the basis of a finding that that person shot and killed a member of the Negro race . . . and that he did so solely and exclusively because that person was a member of the Negro race." With this obvious defense in place, all six members of the Klan and the Nazi Party were acquitted for a second time in 1984—this time by a *federally* selected all-white jury.

However, while the federal jury had been deliberating the fate of the Klansmen and Nazis, I had learned through a friend of Bill's that the entire Greensboro incident, as it was referred to within the Justice Department, had been instigated by law enforcement. Bernard Butkovich, an ATF agent from Cleveland, Ohio, had infiltrated the American Nazi Party in Greensboro to investigate a report that the Klan might have acquired fully automatic weapons from the Hells Angels—who had been provided those illegal weapons by the 2506 Brigade in Miami, Florida (a radical right-wing anti-Castro group of Cuban exiles). Our investigation led me to believe that when Butkovich saw what was going on between the WVO activists and the Klan in Greensboro, he worked directly with the Greensboro Police Department and FBI informant Eddie Dawson to organize a coalition among the Klan, the Hells Angels, and the American Nazi Party, and then actively instigated the physical attack on the anti-Klan rally. That way, if the Klan or the Nazi Party members had come into possession of fully automatic rifles, and went to retrieve those weapons to use them against the demonstrators, Butkovich could then call in ATF agents to swoop in and arrest any Klan or Nazi Party member who retrieved such a weapon to use in the assault.

However, Butkovich had apparently come to the conclusion that the Klan and Nazi Party members did not have any such automatic weapons, so he and his superiors in the ATF took no action whatsoever to try to stop the attack that he and Dawson had actively instigated. In fact, we secured a copy of a handwritten report from Butkovich detailing to his ATF superiors how he had walked over to the demonstration—having warned no one what was about to happen—and had simply watched the Klan and Nazi Party members drive in and gun down the demonstrators, and then had simply returned to his apartment, telling no one what he knew.

In our subsequent federal civil rights complaint, we named not only all forty members of the Ku Klux Klan and the American Nazi Party who had directly participated in the attack on the WVO anti-Klan march but also Butkovich, Dawson, and two members of the Greensboro Police Department who had directly supervised Dawson in his instigation of the attack. I am certain I could have convinced the jury that Butkovich and his superiors refrained from stopping the attack on the demonstrators because of the "class-based, invidious discriminatory animus" they harbored against the targeted demonstrators based on their political beliefs and their effort to support black workers. But to do that successfully, I would have needed the full support of the clients in setting forth my theory. But they were having none of that theory—they were convinced they had been intentionally targeted by the U.S. government for assassination because they were "the vanguard of the working class." To make matters even more difficult, shortly before the trial, the Workers Viewpoint Organization formally changed its

name to the Communist Workers' Party, which resulted in a public relations nightmare for Sara—who was trying to raise money from our former
Silkwood supporters and church people to defray the expenses of the trial.

Since I was unable to persuade the WVO plaintiffs to permit me to
present my proposed theory of the case to the jury, I felt like I was trapped
in a bad dream. In September 1982, after conducting virtually all of the
depositions in the Greensboro civil rights case, I decided that the best course
of action was for me to turn the case over to Lewis Pitts, who was much
more in sympathy with the clients' theory of the case. I then flew back to
Washington, D.C., to focus on other matters.

In 1985, the Christic Institute eventually secured a federal jury verdict
finding the Klansmen and Nazi Party members to be civilly liable for the
killing of the demonstrators *and* finding the city of Greensboro and members of the Greensboro Police Department to be legally responsible for the
deaths as well. However, when the plaintiffs refused to allow me to put forth
the "reckless endangerment" theory of the case against Butkovich and his
ATF superiors based on the "class-based discriminatory animus" identified
above—and when the plaintiffs insisted on putting to the jury their theory of
having been intentionally targeted for assassination by the U.S. government
because they were "the vanguard of the working class"—the jury recoiled
and refused to acknowledge the existence of *any* civil rights conspiracy at all,
instead entering a verdict of a simple civil assault against only those specific
Ku Klux Klan and American Nazi Party members who had personally shot
one or more of the victims, and against the two Greensboro police detectives
who had supervised Eddie Dawson.

Upon my return to Washington in 1982, I found a man waiting for me
on the back porch of Arrupe House. His name was Arnett Lewis. He was a
huge black man, weighing maybe 250 pounds, and looked to be in his early
thirties. He was a very charming, intelligent, and articulate guy, dressed in
denim overalls and orange leather work shoes. He wanted our help.

Arnett was from a tiny town deep in the Mississippi Delta called Tchula,
located in Holmes County, the tenth poorest county in the entire United States.
Even though 86 percent of the Holmes County population was black, the
area had been historically governed solely by local white plantation owners.

A railroad track ran straight through the middle of Tchula, Mississippi, and one side of the town was completely black and the other side was completely white. Three large plantations just outside the town were owned by rich white families, and those plantations provided virtually the only source of employment for the black people in the county. Arnett had a friend from Ole Miss named Eddie Carthan who had returned home after his first year of law school following his father's death. Carthan and Lewis had organized the black citizens of Holmes County to register to vote, and in 1978, Carthan had been elected mayor of Tchula. In that same election, the first four black members of the Tchula Town Council were also elected.

The former mayor of the town, John Edgar Hayes, had previously appointed his white brother-in-law as the chief of police. Carthan replaced Hayes's brother-in-law with a black man named Howard Huggins. However, the first time Carthan left town, the former police chief gathered together a posse of white men, made up largely of his former deputies, and stormed the Tchula Police Station. They grabbed Howard Huggins, dragged him out of the office, and threw him into the street. The white posse then took over the Tchula Police Station.

When Carthan returned, he and Arnett Lewis gathered eight deputy police officers (all black men), and with Howard Huggins they returned to the police station, threw out the former chief of police, and took back the police station. Frank Carleton, the white district attorney, charged Carthan with "assaulting a police officer," but Carthan was found not guilty, as the man was no longer a police officer.

Four years later, on a hot Sunday night in July of 1982, one Roosevelt Granderson, a black man, was closing his shift at a convenience store called the Jitney Junior. Granderson worked there during summers and coached the all-black high school boys' basketball team during the school year. He was one of the four black town council members who had been elected in 1978, and he also directed the town's volunteer fire department. Just before midnight, Granderson ran out to respond to a fire alarm, leaving his two female coworkers to close up the store. When Granderson returned to the Jitney Junior a short while later, one of the women opened the door for him. Suddenly, two black men carrying guns appeared behind Granderson, shoving him and the two women inside. The intruders then robbed the store and dragged Granderson to the back, where they shot him in the head. They left, yelling at the women to stay on the floor and not to look up or they would be dead.

The women lay on the floor crying hysterically for forty minutes before some people noticed that the lights were still on in the Jitney Junior. They went in and found the women—and Granderson. They called the police, and Howard Huggins arrived with two deputies. But the former mayor, John Edgar Hayes, also arrived on the scene, loudly proclaiming, "This was the work of Eddie Carthan!" Hayes claimed that Carthan wanted Granderson dead because white plantation owners were financing Granderson's campaign against Carthan in the next mayoral election. Howard Huggins, however, refused to arrest Carthan because he had no evidence to support Hayes's theory.

The white town council members and Hayes decided to organize a large funeral ceremony for Granderson, spreading the rumor that Eddie Carthan had killed Granderson and would probably try to disrupt the funeral with violence. As a result, a dozen Mississippi State Police cars had been sent to guard the funeral. During the ceremony, Police Chief Huggins noticed a pickup truck with suspiciously dressed passengers drive by. He confirmed that the pickup had been stolen that morning, and his pursuit of that truck turned into a multicar chase in which three of the four suspects escaped. The fourth turned up two days later and was arrested. When the police got that man back to Tchula, District Attorney Frank Carleton went into the man's cell and started interrogating him, asking whether he was part of "Carthan's gang." The man—Vincent Bohlen—insisted that he had never heard of Carthan. Carleton then said that he just wanted Bohlen to say that he and his associates had been retained by Carthan to murder Roosevelt Granderson. If Bohlen would just "admit" this, Carleton offered to dismiss many of the more serious potential charges against him. Finally, Bohlen said, "Well, sure, yeah! Whadda ya want me to say?" So he signed a confession entirely drafted up for him by District Attorney Carleton.

This entire exchange took place in Bohlen's jail cell. Directly across from Bohlen's cell, a young man who had been arrested for stealing a pair of socks witnessed the entire process. Three Catholic nuns who visited the jail every few days talked with him and learned what had taken place between Carleton and Bohlen. The nuns then told Arnett Lewis and told him about the Christic Institute, because they knew that we were conducting the case against the Klan in Greensboro. That was how Arnett Lewis arrived at Arrupe House asking for our help.

I thought it sounded ridiculous. "This is 1982," I told him, "They are not going to indict the mayor just because he's black."

"This is Tchula, Mississippi," Arnett replied. "You don't know what you dealing with here." I said we were very busy with the Greensboro case, but I told him that if Mayor Carthan were indicted, we would go to Tchula and help. Within a week, I received a frantic call from Arnett—Eddie Carthan had just been indicted for the first-degree murder of Roosevelt Granderson.

I immediately flew down to Jacksonville and called for the rest of our team members—including Sara—to meet me in Mississippi. We all moved into an old farmhouse that belonged to a local professor who was gone for the summer. One night—it was actually the night that Sara's and my second baby, Daegan, took his first steps in that farmhouse—we heard a commotion outside. Twenty carloads of Klansmen had shown up, driving around the house, flashing their headlights, and shouting racial epithets at us. My people were frightened and very upset. So I telephoned Bill Taylor, even though he was in the hospital at the time, and asked him what he thought we should do. He told us to lock the doors and stay inside, so we did.

After a few hours, the cars began to disappear. When we peeked out the next morning, we discovered Bob Haid and eight other "friends" of Bill Taylor's, in full camouflage, with M-16 rifles, lying in the fields surrounding the house. Bill had sent them in.

The next day, I went to the Tchula courthouse to meet and interview Eddie Carthan in the Holmes County Jail. Howard Huggins met me in the door, however, and informed me that I couldn't see him. "Nobody can see him," Huggins said. "He's under protective custody." I told Huggins that I was Carthan's attorney and that if he didn't let me in to see Carthan, I would file a federal criminal charge against him and everybody on the town council who had approved the order keeping Carthan from meeting even with his attorney for conspiracy to violate Carthan's civil rights. Huggins didn't want trouble like that. So he brought Carthan up and told me we could meet right there in the courtroom.

Eddie Carthan was a very intelligent and articulate man of thirty-three, and he had no idea what had happened to Roosevelt Granderson. All he knew was that he didn't kill him. So I was going to have to figure out what had happened for myself.

I called Mel Gibbs, a former New York City police detective who had been shot and had retired early after he had helped organize an all-black police union in New York City. His retirement package had enabled him to go to law school at Antioch, where I had met him in the constitutional law course that I taught there. I asked Mel to come down and help me investigate the case, partly because Bill Taylor was still in the hospital and partly because I needed an investigator who could move around more easily in Holmes County's black community. While Mel started his investigation, I interviewed the two women who had been at the Jitney Junior with Granderson on the night of his murder. The first woman, Rosie, told me that when Granderson had returned from responding to the fire alarm, she had playfully locked the door and wouldn't let him in at first. But she said that Granderson had seemed a little exasperated, so she opened the door.

Then it struck me. "When you first saw him through the glass door," I asked, "he wasn't afraid, was he?"

"Actually," she said, a little puzzled, "he wasn't."

"Yet there were these two masked men who had to be standing right behind him with guns in his back?"

"Yeah, they must have been," she said. She started to speed through the rest of the events. I asked her to slow down so she could recount every possible detail. She then went carefully through the whole account and came to the moment when the two men were about to leave the store—when Granderson, from the floor beside the other woman, mumbled something to them.

Rosie didn't know what he had said. She had been too far away to hear him clearly. So I talked to the second woman. She said, "Granderson said, 'It's in the other safe, over under the cash register.'"

She said that the store put most of its money in a floor safe beneath the front counter, not in the safe in the back room to which Rosie had guided the robbers when they had demanded the money. Granderson was supposed to take the money from the floor safe each night and deposit it into the bank. But he hadn't done that all weekend, so there had been a lot more money than usual in the floor safe. Granderson had told the robbers where all that money was, and after that they dragged him into the back and killed him.

Something wasn't adding up.

Then Mel Gibbs told me that he had picked up on a rumor that Joe Carthan, Eddie's somewhat ne'er-do-well half brother, knew someone who might have been involved with the chase Howard Huggins had engaged in at Granderson's funeral. We clearly needed to talk to Joe Carthan.

He was hiding in some kind of ranger's cabin in a state park. When I confronted him, Joe told me that the summer before, he had met a man named David Hester, a gangster from East St. Louis, Illinois. Joe began bragging about his own "business" in Holmes County and told Hester that he ought to talk to a guy by the name of Roosevelt Granderson.

It quickly emerged that Granderson was part of a countywide drug racket. Mel Gibbs discovered that when the cotton market had plummeted years before, the white plantation owners in the Tchula area had decided to start growing marijuana instead. The entire economy of this poor little county became totally dependent on the growing and selling of marijuana. The plantation owners used Granderson as a distributor into the black community, and Granderson used the young black boys on his high school basketball team to deal this marijuana for him.

Hester, it seems, tracked down Granderson and explained that he headed up a large gang in East St. Louis that sold cocaine. Hester wanted Granderson to use his marijuana network to distribute Hester Gang cocaine as well. And Roosevelt had agreed to do this.

This operation had been going smoothly for everyone—including the black people who now had steady work on the plantations again—when, suddenly, John Edgar Hayes was ousted from local political power by the surprise election of Eddie Carthan, who immediately shut down the illegal marijuana-smuggling network.

Recently, something had suddenly gone terribly wrong with Granderson's scheme of using his young black basketball players to deal drugs in the black community. One boy refused to participate in the operation. At one basketball practice, Granderson became so enraged at the boy's refusal that he tied a rope around the boy's ankles and hung him upside down in the gymnasium. Then Granderson lost control of himself and smashed the boy in the head with a baseball bat. The other boys cut him down and had brought him to the hospital, where he had to undergo a number of major operations to save his life. He survived but was left with severe brain damage. Granderson panicked, fearing that some of the other basketball players would start to talk. So Granderson began skimming money off the cocaine profits of the Hester Gang so he could buy expensive gifts for his basketball players, essentially trying to buy their silence.

But it wasn't long before Hester realized that Granderson was holding out on him.

When Hester had caught Granderson skimming, Granderson had arranged to let Hester and Bohlen rob the Jitney Junior to repay the Hester Gang. However, after recovering his money, Hester had murdered Granderson in cold blood, punishing him for stealing from the gang.

No one was willing to talk about Roosevelt Granderson's marijuana dealing because the public revelation threatened to reveal the dark southern secret that bound the seemingly disparate white and black cultures of the Mississippi Delta. This was the fact that they were all deeply involved in growing and smuggling-marijuana in their county. It was Mel Gibbs who finally broke the case by persuading a courageous young black basketball player to defy the century-old "Delta factor" and to refuse to allow the black community of Holmes County to surrender its first black mayor. Ultimately, this was only possible because that young basketball player was willing to risk his basketball scholarship to Ole Miss (*his* only way out of the Delta) by confessing his participation in the marijuana smuggling operation run by Coach Granderson, thereby revealing what Granderson had done to the boy who had refused to deal drugs.

With that tangible witness available, I called Bill Taylor and told him that we were getting ready to begin the trial in a few days. We needed to find David Hester and put him on the stand. Bill said he would see what he could do.

Within just the first few days of the trial, we faced a number of obstacles. First the clerk of the court tried to rig the jury selection to produce an all-white panel in a country where 86 percent of the registered voters were black. Once we were able to secure the first all-black jury in the state of Mississippi, we had to deal with District Attorney Frank Carleton blatantly leading Bohlen on the witness stand. Bohlen's testimony was rendered moot when it became clear that he had no idea who Eddie Carthan was, even though his signed statement (drafted by District Attorney Carleton) named Carthan as the man who had ordered Granderson's murder.

In the pandemonium that followed this revelation, I asked the judge if I could take a witness out of order, even though it was the prosecution's turn to put on its witnesses. I told the judge that the witness I wanted to call would be available for only a very limited period of time.

"Who is it?" the judge asked, without saying that I actually could call the witness.

"He's right here, Your Honor." I had Lewis Pitts dramatically open the door at the back of the courtroom, and in walked David Hester, with an armed U.S. marshal on each side of him. He was in chains. There had been an old federal warrant outstanding for David Hester for interstate hijacking. Bill Taylor's friends in the U.S. Marshals Service had put out an all-points bulletin on him, and when they tracked him down up in Alaska, they arrested him and brought him back to East St. Louis through Tchula. We put him up on the stand, and I gladly stood aside and asked Johnny Walls, a black former law school classmate of Eddie Carthan's, to defend his friend.

Johnny then asked Hester what his occupation was.

"I am the head of the Hester Gang in East St. Louis," Hester said.

"What's the Hester Gang do, exactly, *Reverend* Hester?" Johnny asked after Hester insisted that he was also a licensed minister.

"We do primarily interstate hijacking, and we sell cocaine mostly."

I, along with everybody else in the courtroom, was stunned.

"Well, *Reverend* Hester," Johnny Walls asked sarcastically over the loud laughter of the jury, "can you tell us what you know about this case?"

David Hester then proceeded to explain that the only contact he'd ever had with Tchula was when he had met a guy named Roosevelt Granderson, who was bragging about his marijuana distribution.

District Attorney Carleton immediately leaped to his feet to object, saying that this information had nothing to do with the case.

"Shut up and sit down," I said. "You know that it has *everything* to do with this case."

The judge said, "I'm afraid . . . uh . . . sit down and be quiet, Mr. Carleton. Let's see where this goes."

So Johnny Walls continued with his questions. "So, *Reverend*, you went into the business of distributing marijuana with this Mr. Granderson?"

"No. No," Hester said. "We don't do marijuana. We distribute cocaine. I got this Granderson fella to distribute our cocaine from East St. Louis. I got him to distribute it through the same network that he used to distribute his marijuana that was grown around here."

Suddenly the entire courtroom grew tense. No one wanted this secret out.

So Johnny Walls went straight to the heart of the issue: "And you became angry at Roosevelt Granderson because he had been taking your money. He was burning you by skimming money from his cocaine sales for you, wasn't he?"

"You're damn right he was."

"He was burning you, and you couldn't stop him, *could you?*"

"Oh, I stopped him alright," Hester shouted. "I goddamn *killed* him!"

And the courtroom was suddenly silent.

After a long minute, Frank Carleton rose to his feet and said, "Your Honor, the state would request a brief adjournment while it has an opportunity to interview this witness. We have not been afforded an opportunity to interview this surprise witness."

The judge immediately adjourned the case and instructed the jury not to talk to anybody. After three days, the judge called to say that he was ready to reconvene the following morning.

David Hester returned to the stand. Frank Carleton stood up and said that he wanted to cross-examine immediately. I protested, saying that we hadn't finished the direct examination of our own witness, but the judge ruled in favor of the DA. So Carleton turned to Hester and asked, "Mr. Hester, can you tell us anything else that you didn't get to testify about three days ago?"

"Oh, yes," Hester said. "We killed Roosevelt Granderson because Mayor Eddie Carthan hired us to do it."

Everybody in the courtroom, which was now almost full of black people, looked at each other and started laughing. The judge held his head in his hands.

I was in disbelief myself, but I maintained my cool and said, "Your Honor, may Mr. Walls ask him a question or two, in light of this rather extraordinary testimony—after three days of Mr. Carleton's having had this witness entirely to himself?"

And the judge said Mr. Walls could.

So Johnny Walls asked, "*Reverend* Hester, between the time that you were on the stand last and the point when you came here to testify this morning, did you have any conversations with the district attorney?"

District Attorney Carleton objected, claiming this was privileged information.

"No, it's not privileged," I said. "We have a right to know if he's spoken with the district attorney."

"Yes. Yes, I have," said Hester, volunteering the information over the objection of the district attorney.

Johnny Walls asked, "In his conversations with you, did the district attorney make any offers or promises to you in exchange for the testimony that you have just given here today?"

Again the district attorney jumped to his feet and objected, but the judge let Johnny Walls continue. Hester told the court that DA Carleton had offered to drop the charges against him for conspiracy to commit bank robbery, which, as it turned out, was what had been going on when Hester and his gang drove into Tchula during Granderson's funeral.

"What about the murder?" Johnny asked.

"Oh, right, that too. He was going to dismiss the first-degree murder charge against me if I would testify that Mayor Carthan hired us to kill Roosevelt Granderson."

He had his deal officially in place, and he *had* testified that Mayor Carthan had hired him to kill Roosevelt Granderson. He therefore had iron-clad immunity for any truthful testimony thereafter. So he just came straight out and said it. Frank Carleton sat at the prosecution table, immobile and stone-faced.

Everyone in the courtroom was astonished.

Johnny Walls turned to the jury and said, "Your Honor, the defense rests!"

The jury took only forty-five minutes to come back and declare Mayor Eddie Carthan innocent—not simply *not guilty* but *innocent*—and the whole courtroom erupted in cheers. Everybody started jumping up and down and cheering. The judge, the district attorney, and the assistant district attorney—all white—rushed out of the courtroom, back through the judge's chambers.

CHAPTER *twenty-four*

FATHER PHILIP WHEATON's call to me came in April 1984. He was an Episcopal priest I had known since June 1975, when I arrived in Washington to take up my post as chief counsel to the national headquarters of the United States Jesuit order. I loved Phil Wheaton. He had been thrown out of every South American and Central American country to which he had ever been posted by his Episcopal church, asked to leave not by his religious superiors but instead by the authoritarian regimes that had seized control of those nations from the peasants who lived there.

Phil was calling in his capacity as a member of the national board of directors of the American Sanctuary Movement, the grassroots movement organized by priests, women religious, and Protestant clergymen active in mission work in Central and South America. Their work included attempting to protect villagers and peasants from death squads that had been organized by right-wing military governments that the American government not only supported but indeed had actively put into power in many small nations, providing them with funding, military equipment, and special operations training, all as "a bulwark against communism in Latin America."

The call came on a quiet Sunday morning. Sara and I, Father Bill Davis, and Father Wally Kazubouski had just returned from Sunday-morning Mass at the U.S. Catholic Cathedral just one block from Arrupe House.

We were arrayed around the long dining table in Arrupe House that Father Kazubouski had built out of two doors on sawhorses. We were quietly exchanging sections of the Sunday *New York Times* and *The Washington Post* and making periodic comments on the perspectives of both papers when the phone rang. Sara rose and went to answer it.

"It's Phil Wheaton," Sara said. "It's for you, Danny."

Father Bill Davis knew Phil Wheaton better than I, because the two priests had been stationed together in the Dominican Republic several years earlier. Phil had been serving there as a missionary when Bill Davis was sent on assignment for *American* magazine, the monthly magazine of the Jesuit order, for which he was an official photographer. However, this job was a means by which Davis performed certain intelligence-gathering duties for his immediate Jesuit superior, Father Pedro Arrupe, the superior general of all Jesuits throughout the world.

I got up, tossed my section of *The Washington Post* onto the terry-cloth-covered table, and took the call.

Father Wheaton said that he had, just the night before, received a telephone call from John Fitzpatrick, the Catholic archbishop of South Texas, who was stationed in Brownsville, Texas, directly across the border from Matamoras, Mexico. Archbishop Fitzpatrick wanted to know if Father Wheaton knew the people from the Christic Institute—the ones who had handled the Karen Silkwood and Three Mile Island cases.

A Catholic lay social worker, a young woman named Stacy Lynn Merkt, and a professed woman religious, Catholic sister Diane Mullencamp, who both worked directly for Archbishop Fitzpatrick at his Casa Oscar Romero, a sanctuary in Brownsville, had been arrested by "the Migra" (the U.S. immigration police) the previous evening while driving two Salvadorian political refugees from Brownsville to San Antonio, Texas. A local Methodist pastor in San Antonio was going to help the refugees file applications for political asylum under the 1980 Refugee Act, signed into law by President Jimmy Carter just before he lost the 1980 presidential race to Ronald Reagan. In addition to the refugees, Merkt and Mullencamp had been driving with Jack Fisher, a young reporter from the *Dallas Times Herald*. They had been driving in Archbishop Fitzpatrick's private automobile.

Archbishop Fitzpatrick wanted to know if the Christic Institute lawyers might be able to come down to Texas and help them.

Ultimately, what would become our most controversial case, the Iran-Contra case, started not with a bang but with a simple phone call from one of the Lord's servants to another, asking for help for the poor and the powerless.

Father Wally Kazubouski and I suited up and flew down to Brownsville the following morning. It was a Monday. To our surprise, we were met at the Brownsville Regional Airport by the vicar general of the Archdiocese of South Texas. He picked us up in his long black limousine. Wally and I eyed each other as we climbed into the back and took our places on the dark blue velvet seat, directly across from the vicar general.

During the short ride from the Brownsville Regional Airport to his official residence, the vicar general of South Texas explained the case to us. Then, in a lowered voice, he leaned over and quietly said to me, "It has been arranged for Judge Felimone Vela to attend the 6:00 AM morning Mass tomorrow, and he will be available to speak with you—privately, of course—in the vestry following Mass about a possible quiet disposition of the case, should you wish to discuss that with him." I knew that Vela, a federal district court judge, had already assigned the case to himself. I learned only later that he had received his presidential appointment to be a federal judge from President Jimmy Carter at the direct recommendation of Archbishop Fitzpatrick.

Why was I not surprised by this, after having served for nine years as chief counsel to the United States Jesuit order in Washington, D.C.?

Upon arriving at the vicar general's official residence, Father Kazubouski and I were shown to our respective quarters. We were later treated to a servant-attended dinner with the vicar general and Archbishop Fitzpatrick himself. At this dinner, Archbishop Fitzpatrick explained how he and other Catholic leaders, along with various Protestant clergy, had created the American Sanctuary Movement in response to the governments of Guatemala and El Salvador, whose death squads, comprised of off-duty military men and national police, were systematically kidnapping and "disappearing" peasants, union organizers, university students, professors, priests, and Catholic nuns who tried to organize and challenge the power of wealthy landowners and the oligarchs. A number of Catholic and Protestant churches in the United States (and a few synagogues) had established themselves as an underground railroad to help people on the "death lists" escape and be brought to the United States. There they were given sanctuary in a growing number of American churches. By providing political refugees with the historical common law "right of sanctuary," church leaders could keep American law enforcement personnel and immigration agents from entering their churches to arrest the refugees and deport them.

According to the 1980 Refugee Act,

> If any person from any foreign nation finds himself or herself here in the United States—and he or she, at that time, harbors a good-faith belief that, if they return to their native country, they will be persecuted by their own government because of their religious beliefs or because of their political beliefs—those persons are hereby granted, by this statute, a federally guaranteed right to go to the nearest American Embassy or to the nearest U.S. Immigration Office and file an Application to be declared a "Political Refugee."

Those who met the criteria established by the statute were legally authorized to remain in the United States until they could be given full administrative hearings or until it was officially determined that it was safe for them to return to their countries of origin.

All through 1980, up until Ronald Reagan's inauguration in January 1981, many Latin American refugees went to Casa Oscar Romero in Brownsville, where Archbishop Fitzpatrick had assembled a staff of kind and considerate people, including Sister Diane Mullencamp and Stacy Lynn Merkt. All of a sudden, immediately after January 21, 1981—after several Latin American dictators had literally danced at Reagan's inaugural ball—U.S. Immigration Department officials in Brownsville adopted a new policy. Political refugees whom Casa Oscar Romero–sanctuary movement workers had brought to the U.S. immigration office in Brownsville started being arrested and imprisoned in a large wooden stockade called La Cordeleon. They were held there until they were deported back to the countries from which they had just escaped, often with advance notice given to the deadly security forces that would receive them upon their arrival.

The deportations occurred only a few times before Archbishop Fitzpatrick's staff got the message that it was no longer a good idea to deliver political refugees to the U.S. immigration office in Brownsville. The staff quickly determined that it was better to drive the political refugees from Brownsville up to San Antonio—a four-hour drive—and to have them apply for political asylum at the San Antonio immigration office.

On the night of their arrest, Sister Diane Mullencamp and Stacy Lynn Merkt were simply bringing two Central American political refugees to San Antonio to lawfully apply for political asylum. But they were arrested. And now they were being criminally prosecuted.

What was going on here?

In my capacity as general counsel to U.S. Jesuit headquarters in Washington, of course I was familiar with the sanctuary churches. I knew many young Jesuit priests and Catholic women religious in South and Central America who had been engaged in helping political refugees. But our office was not directly involved in any of these activities until Archbishop Fitzpatrick called and asked us to go to Texas.

During that first dinner with Archbishop Fitzpatrick and the vicar general, nothing at all was said about the private arrangement with the judge that had been communicated to me by the vicar general during our short drive from the airport. After dinner, however, as Archbishop Fitzpatrick was entering his private limousine to leave, he turned casually to me and asked, "Will I be seeing you and Father Kazubouski at the 6:00 AM morning Mass tomorrow morning, Danny?"

I nodded, without a word. He smiled, bent his six-foot frame down to duck into his limousine, and was driven away.

The following morning, Father Kazubouski and I attended the 6:00 AM Mass. It was celebrated by the archbishop himself, with the vicar general con-celebrating. As I approached the communion rail to receive Holy Communion from the archbishop, I was surprised to find myself joined, immediately on my right, by Judge Vela. As Archbishop Fitzpatrick approached us, host raised in hand, Judge Vela leaned over to me and whispered, "Might I have a private word with you after Mass, Mr. Sheehan?" I nodded, turned, and immediately received the host from the smiling archbishop. Judge Vela did the same. It felt like the baptism scene from The Godfather.

As Mass ended and the faithful were filing out, I rose, crossed the altar alone, and went into the vestry immediately behind the altar. Archbishop

Fitzpatrick and the vicar general changed into their black-and-white street clothes silently, carefully kissing and folding each vestment as they removed it and put it away. I sat silently observing. Then they left without saying a word.

Within minutes, Judge Vela entered. No one else was present; it was just the two of us.

"Thank you for agreeing to see me, Mr. Sheehan. I would like to discuss a rather delicate matter with you, here in private. His holiness was kind enough to provide a venue for us to meet discreetly."

"You are most welcome, Your Honor. I must admit that I was a bit surprised to receive your invitation . . . I mean, so early in the proceedings."

"That is exactly why I wanted to have this opportunity to speak with you in private, Mr. Sheehan. It is *Mr.* Sheehan, is it not? Not *Father* Sheehan?"

"Mr. Sheehan will be fine, Your Honor. But you can call me Danny. All my friends do."

"Ah. Then, Danny, what I have in mind—and I have reason to believe that this arrangement would meet with the approval of his eminence—is that when you appear in my courtroom tomorrow morning at the arraignment, you simply enter a plea of guilty on behalf of your clients to the felony charge of unlawfully transporting undocumented aliens. I will agree to reserve any strictly technical legal arguments you might wish to preserve on behalf of your clients, and I will agree to sign an immediate expedited appeal to the Fifth Circuit Federal Court of Appeals. In this way, everyone involved will be able to avoid any embarrassing public trial in which, for example, it might be publicly revealed that the illegal aliens were being transported in . . . ahh . . . in the archbishop's private automobile."

I was amazed, frankly—not so much at his approach to me (though it certainly was inappropriate) but more by the substance of what Judge Vela perceived to be a real offer.

I waited a moment, trying to determine how I could refuse Judge Vela's offer without alienating him for the trial—a trial I had every intention of forcing him to provide us, even though he clearly did not want to do so. Through the trial, I intended to reveal to the world the illegality of what it was that the Reagan–Bush administration was now doing in Brownsville.

I told Judge Vela that I would, of course, have to discuss his offer with my clients—whom I had not yet even had an opportunity to meet.

He seemed distressed that I was not willing to simply inform my clients of how it was going to be. But he said nothing more. I told him that I would get back to him with the answer from my clients as soon as I'd had a chance to speak directly with them.

Later that same Tuesday morning, I met directly with Sister Diane Mullencamp and Stacy Lynn Merkt, who had been released on their own recognizance. The two Salvadorian refugees, however, remained in the custody of the Migra as "illegal aliens." In that first meeting with Stacy and Sister Diane, I said it would be a bad idea to accept the offer being made by Judge Vela, and they agreed. I then sent word to Judge Vela that my clients had respectfully declined his offer.

The next morning, Wednesday, we all went to the preliminary hearing. Both of the "illegal aliens" were brought to the courthouse by U.S. immigration police. When the preliminary hearing commenced, the U.S. attorney put on the stand two uniformed Migra officers, complete with dark sunglasses (which they wore even inside the courtroom) and huge .357 magnums on their hips. The first Migra officer took the stand and testified that they had arrested the defendants based upon a tip they had received from an anonymous source.

I didn't cross-examine either of the two officers because I didn't want to provide any basis on which Judge Vela might simply dismiss all the charges against Sister Diane or Stacy. We wanted a trial. Instead of putting forward any witnesses in the preliminary hearing, we simply demanded that a speedy trial be scheduled as soon as Judge Vela's trial calendar was clear. Then he knew what was coming.

Sister Diane and Stacy were officially bound over for trial, but Judge Vela ordered them both to remain released on their own recognizance. He did state on the record, though, that he assumed that Archbishop Fitzpatrick would keep an eye on them and make sure they would be available for trial.

I then rose and made a specific motion that the court instruct the U.S. attorney not to extradite Maria or Mauricio, the Salvadorian refugees, back to El Salvador before the trial. Judge Vela frowned down at me, as though that should have gone without saying.

However, the U.S. attorney rose and objected. "It has been clearly established that these two people are illegal aliens, and therefore they have no right to remain here in this country."

Judge Vela looked surprised. He turned his frown on the U.S. attorney. "Mr. C——! I had thought, for a moment, that Mr. Sheehan's motion was a bit out of line, fully expecting that there would be no question but that both of these people from El Salvador would remain available for trial, since they are clearly material witnesses."

"That was the basis of my motion, Your Honor," I said.

Again Judge Vela frowned down at me, as if to say, "Let me handle this."

The judge affirmed that both witnesses would remain in the country and be available for trial. Then he thought for a moment and said, almost as an afterthought, "In fact, I think that I will order the release of both of these young Salvadorian citizens and place them in the custody of Archbishop Fitzpatrick, personally."

"I can personally assure the court that Archbishop Fitzpatrick will agree to these terms, Your Honor," I said.

The U.S. attorney rose again to object but then thought better of it and sank slowly back down into his chair.

Judge Vela entered those orders and announced that the trial in this case would begin in just two weeks, noting that the defendants had expressly refused to waive their right to a speedy trial and had indeed expressly demanded an immediate jury trial.

The next morning, Archbishop Fitzpatrick came to the vicar general's residence and met with Wally and me for breakfast. He announced that there was somebody he wanted me to meet after we had finished eating. When that time came, Archbishop Fitzpatrick escorted Father Kazubouski and me to a private office in the vicar general's official residence. There sat a distinguished-looking man of about sixty-five, waiting patiently for us.

Archbishop Fitzpatrick introduced the man as the bishop of the Methodist Church in Brownsville.

"I have a problem," the Methodist bishop said. "I have been asked
by Archbishop Fitzpatrick to have my Methodist congregation vote as to
whether they wish to become a sanctuary church. And, quite frankly, I was
quite favorably disposed toward that idea. However, a member of my congregation—who as it turns out is the special agent in charge of the FBI office
here in Brownsville—approached me this past Sunday morning after our
service and asked to have a private word with me. I met with him three
days ago, and he told me that he had come into possession of information
that made it clear that I, and our congregation, should have nothing to
do with the American Sanctuary Movement. I asked him what made him
think I was even entertaining the idea of having anything to do with that
movement. And he said, 'We know that Archbishop Fitzpatrick is trying
to get you to have our church become a sanctuary church, bishop. But you
should have nothing to do with them—because the Catholic Church and
the American Sanctuary Movement are smuggling known communist terrorists into the United States under the guise of being political refugees from
Central America.'"

The FBI man had gone on to say that the administration in Washington
had very reliable intelligence confirming that in the event that President
Reagan and Vice President Bush were compelled to send U.S. military troops
into El Salvador or Guatemala—or into Nicaragua—to protect those anti-
communist governments from falling into the hands of the communists, the
five hundred thousand undocumented Central Americans illegally in the
United States were going to be organized into military cadres to attack U.S.
military bases and police stations, sabotage our power grids, and poison our
public reservoirs.

Wally Kazubouski and I couldn't help but laugh, though we tried not
to be impolite to the bishop. Our reaction seemed to distress the Methodist
bishop rather than set his mind at ease.

Earlier, Archbishop Fitzpatrick had told the Methodist bishop that if
anything like what this FBI man was talking about was in fact going on,
"the Jesuits would certainly know about it." Then Archbishop Fitzpatrick
had said, "We just happen to have the general counsel for the Jesuit order
in the United States staying here at the vicar general's residence, helping us

on the trial of Sister Mullencamp and Stacy Merkt. Why don't we just ask him about this?"

So the Methodist bishop was waiting for me to actually answer his question. I said, "Are you really asking me whether known communist terrorists are being smuggled into the United States by the Catholic Church and the American Sanctuary Movement to train Central American aliens to attack U.S. military bases and our reservoirs here if Reagan and Bush order U.S. military troops into El Salvador, Guatemala, or Nicaragua?"

"Yes," he said. "Yes, I am asking you: Are they doing that?"

"Absolutely not!" I said. Then I reflected for a moment and for effect said, "And Archbishop Fitzpatrick is absolutely right. If there were anything like that going on, then let me personally assure you, bishop, the Jesuits absolutely *would* know about that. And if they knew about it, then I, as their chief legal counsel, would certainly know about it. And I am telling you that it's just not true."

That finally seemed to relieve him. But his question only served to add to my uncertainty about everything that was happening with this case. So I told the bishop that I would have Jesuit headquarters in Washington conduct an investigation but that I was sure they would find that nothing like that was going on. I promised to let him know the results of that investigation.

"Let me personally assure you, bishop," I said, shaking his hand as he rose to leave. "I wouldn't be down here doing this trial if I thought, for a single minute, that anything like that was even possibly going on."

After he left, I went to my room and telephoned Bill Taylor. I explained to Bill what I had been told by the Methodist bishop in Brownsville, and I asked Bill to look into the situation. As cofounder of the National Association of Former Federal Investigators, Bill Taylor was as well positioned as anyone I knew to find out if the idea was actually being bandied around by state and federal law enforcement officials or by people in the intelligence community.

I also called Howard Rosenberg, Dan Rather's chief researcher at *CBS Evening News* in Washington and asked him to do the same. Then I called Howard Kohn, Washington bureau chief of *Rolling Stone* magazine, and then Bob Fink, chief congressional investigator for New York City congresswoman Bella Abzug, chairwoman of the House Judiciary Committee's

Subcommittee on Individual Rights. Bob had been seconded by Abzug to work for the House Select Committee on Governmental Operations with Respect to Intelligence Activities, directly under the select committee chair, Democratic congressman Otis Pike from the First District of New York. Since the House select committee was the direct partner of the Senate select committee investigating that same issue, which had thoroughly investigated the illegal covert operations of the CIA during the postwar period, Fink was also perfectly positioned to find out whether this rumor was being circulated within the intelligence community.

I then turned my full attention back to preparing for the American Sanctuary Movement trial.

In our pretrial discovery motions, we demanded, among other things, a copy of the executive order that I was confident had been issued by someone high up in the Reagan–Bush administration in order for U.S. immigration officials in Brownsville to have been doing what they were doing. And over a vigorous (and typically spurious) "national security" protest lodged by the U.S. attorney, Judge Vela ordered the White House to turn over to us a copy of "whatever such executive order—if any—had been issued on this specific subject." And we got it.

We then proceeded to trial. We based our defense strategy squarely on the Constitution—on the illegality of this executive order attempting to override an express act of Congress on the basis of some bogus "national security" consideration. It was my intention to put this central legal issue squarely to the jury as a question of fact, legally obligating Judge Vela to instruct the jury that they were required, as a matter of law, to acquit all our defendants if we were able to prove that the Reagan–Bush administration had, indeed, issued such an entirely unconstitutional executive order. I also planned to place directly before the jury, and the country, the detailed stories of what Maria and Mauricio had experienced in El Salvador. And indeed they each had a terrible story to tell.

I picked as close to an all-Catholic jury as I could, which was not difficult to do in Brownsville, and one with as many women on it as possible.

The trial was called to order two weeks later in a standard federal courtroom: bare walls, no frills, a large round metal official seal of the United

States hanging on an otherwise blank wall behind a blond wooden judge's bench. The jury box stood on the left side of the courtroom. Two wooden tables with chairs faced the front of the courtroom. Prosecution attorneys were always allowed to sit on the side of the courtroom nearest to the jury, reflecting the structural bias favoring government attorneys built into our national legal system. The defense table was on the other side of the room, in this case on the far right.

The prosecution opened, as we expected, with the newly appointed Reagan–Bush administration Republican United States attorney for South Texas delivering a xenophobic, fear-mongering criticism of the policy of the Carter administration, which he claimed virtually invited dangerous illegal aliens to flood into our country. His opening statement was tempered only by an attempt to show some consideration for Sister Mullencamp and Stacy Lynn Merkt, whom he said had been "misled by their superiors in the Catholic Church to believe that it was OK to violate the law if one simply disagreed with the policy of our country." He called upon the jury to do their duty to protect the rule of law in our nation by rejecting the theory that anybody was free to defy any law they wish, simply because they disagreed with the policy on which it was based. He demanded that the jurors convict these people "who certainly knew that they were violating the law of our country." He went to great lengths, at the conclusion of his opening statement, to point out that "It will be up to Judge Vela—a fair man and a good Catholic—to determine what the sentence should be for these people, who we, the government, are not saying are bad people. We are simply saying that it is clear that they have violated the law and that they knew they were violating the law. But you can assume that Judge Vela will be lenient in his sentencing of them. It is your responsibility solely to determine, as a matter of fact, that they did, in fact, violate our laws prohibiting private citizens from taking it upon themselves to smuggle people into our country when they know that that is expressly prohibited by our laws."

He must have expected me to rise and strenuously object to his remarks about what Judge Vela would do when it came time to sentence my defendants if the jurors convicted them. Even Judge Vela looked my way when the U.S. attorney said this. But I let it pass, knowing that sooner or later Judge Vela would make him pay for having said that in the course of the trial.

I then rose to make my opening statement. I told the jury that there was a technical legal term that described what the U.S. attorney had just told them in his opening statement. "It was," I said, pausing for effect, "a big fat lie." I told them that this trial was going to be very easy for them. I told them, "The people who are violating the law in this case are not Sister Diane Mullencamp, Stacy Lynn Merkt, or this young Salvadorian girl Maria or this older Salvadorian man Mauricio . . . or Archbishop Fitzpatrick or your Catholic Church."

The U.S. attorney leaped to his feet and tried to object. I simply ignored him and pressed forward, waiting to see when, or if, Judge Vela was going to stop me. He didn't. It was payback time for the U.S. attorney.

"It is Ronald Reagan and George Bush and U.S. attorney C——!" I said. "They are the ones who are violating the laws of our country. You will see that in this case. That's all I have to say." Then I sat down while the U.S. attorney was still on his feet, trying to complete his objection. Judge Vela, who had not had a chance to rule on it, looked down on the U.S. attorney and simply shrugged. He was indicating that he was going to let the two sides have at each other—and may the best man win!

The prosecution followed, predictably, by putting the two U.S. immigration police officers on the stand. This time they appeared in neat business suits and ties, without their sidearms. The first Migra officer covered the tracks of his partner by fixing the errors in his partner's testimony during the arraignment.

I let it go. I did not want to confuse the jury by putting too many issues of fact before them. I would focus solely on the big issue. If I analyzed a case carefully enough, there was always one big factual truth on our side. American juries don't do well at remembering, or strictly applying, the law. What they are very good at, however, is searching out lies. The key is to figure out how to get the entire case to turn on which of the two sides is telling the jury the truth on one very big and important fact. American juries can tell that better than anyone would ever expect.

In my cross-examination of the Migra officers, I asked whether they were familiar with the content of the Refugee Act of 1980. Both of them professed to be aware of it, but neither was able to quote any aspect of it or answer any of the questions I asked them about it. The U.S. attorney was obviously relying on the good faith of the Migra officers in following orders from above to arrest these people. This was perfect for us because it was "the orders from above" that I was after in this case, not these two Migra officers. After I had adequately demonstrated their comparative ignorance of the provisions of the Refugee Act of 1980 (and, through my questioning, educated the jury as to the clear provisions of that act), I said, "Officer, let me ask you this: Isn't it in fact true that you and every other U.S. immigration agent and officer in the Brownsville office of the U.S. immigration office have been under a direct order from the Reagan–Bush administration to *not* enforce any provision of the 1980 Refugee Act since about February of 1981?"

"Your Honor, I object!" the U.S. attorney shouted.

Judge Vela smiled. "I'll bet you do, Mr. C——. But your objection is overruled. The witness will answer the question, if he can."

"I . . . I don't recall any such specific order at this time. No," the Migra officer said.

"Oh, really?" I said. "Then I would like to introduce into evidence and ask you to examine defense exhibit A, a February 1981 executive order signed by Ronald Reagan, expressly ordering the Brownsville office of the United States Immigration and Naturalization Service to disregard all mandates of the Refugee Act of 1980 and to arrest, detain, and deport back to their countries of origin any and all applicants for political asylum who are citizens of either El Salvador or Guatemala, citing 'a national security concern' about maintaining 'positive diplomatic relations' with those Central American nations 'in our mutual fight against communism.'"

I took the exhibit from Wally and handed it to the Migra officer on the stand.

Judge Vela said sarcastically, "Mr. Sheehan, I don't think that it is necessary for you to characterize, much less quote verbatim from, the exhibit. Just have the witness examine it and have him tell you whether or not he is familiar with the exhibit. If he is, then it will be made available for the jury to read. If he is not, then the exhibit will not be introduced through this witness and will not be read by this jury."

Judge Vela had all but coached the witness as to how to keep the exhibit from being admitted into evidence. After allowing the Migra officer to read the exhibit, I asked him whether he had ever seen or read the document that we had extracted from the government during the discovery proceedings prior to the trial. Reluctantly, after a few feeble efforts to pretend that he couldn't quite remember having actually read it, he admitted that he had either read it or been told about it.

Then I had the jury read it, slowly and thoroughly, as the Migra officer sat silently, absorbing the glowering stares from one juror after another as each finished reading the document.

I left the Migra officer sitting there on the stand, absorbing every one of these hostile stares for as long as I could before saying, "No more questions, Your Honor."

On redirect examination, the U.S. attorney did his best to try to resuscitate his witness. But it was to no avail. The Migra officer kept asserting that he and his partner had arrested these defendants in good faith—once they had established that they were citizens of El Salvador, that they had entered the United States by swimming across the Rio Grande, and that they had not immediately turned themselves in to the nearest available U.S. Immigration and Naturalization Service office, which would have been in Brownsville.

On my very brief re-cross-examination, I simply asked, step by step, what the Migra officer knew about the unlawful order received by his INS office in February 1981. And I asked him how many citizens of El Salvador and Guatemala he personally knew to have been deported after filing for political asylum *at the Brownsville INS office* during the previous three-year period. I had reserved this line of questioning for the re-cross, since I knew what the U.S. attorney was going to do on his redirect. The Migra officer's position was that none of the people had been deported after *applying for* political asylum because they had not even been allowed to fill out applications in light of the order received from Washington.

That testimony did not go over well with the jury. The government rested after presenting just those two witnesses. It was going to get worse for the prosecution—much worse—before this trial was over.

Judge Vela pointedly inquired as to whether the defense wished to make a motion for a directed verdict (a judgment of acquittal) or even to go directly to closing arguments. He assumed we were not going to put our own defendants on the stand.

Oh! Quite the contrary, Your Honor," I said to him. "We intend to put both of our defendants on the stand, as well as both of the refugees who were arrested with them, as well as a few other witnesses who are personally familiar with the facts of this case. The defense has nothing whatsoever to hide from this jury in this case, Your Honor."

Judge Vela immediately called both attorneys to the bench and assured me that if he happened to deny any motion that the defense might proffer for a judgment of acquittal or a directed verdict, he would agree to specially reserve any technical legal defense I might wish to make for an expedited appeal, which he would immediately forward to the Fifth Circuit Court of Appeals. He was, in effect, simply reiterating his original offer to me.

I thanked him politely for his offer, but I told him, at the bench, that all four of my clients had insisted upon testifying and that both of the refugees wanted to tell their story to the jury so the American people would know what their government had been doing since the Reagan–Bush administration had come into office.

Judge Vela growled his disapproval, warning me quietly, "I have found it to be unwise for a criminal defense attorney to put his criminal defendant on the stand in his own defense. You can never tell what might come out on cross-examination that will cause a jury to punish your client."

"Thank you, Your Honor. Thank you for the advice. I will keep that in mind when they are testifying tomorrow."

At my request, Judge Vela adjourned the case until the following morning.

On the following morning, we led off with Maria, a sixteen-year-old Salvadorian refugee who had fled to the United States with her six-month-old baby. In her testimony, Maria said that she was a high school–educated doctor's assistant in El Salvador. The doctor for whom she worked had provided medical assistance to a young member of a radical group of college students who were opposed to the Salvadorian government. The student had been shot by Salvadorian government troops during an antigovernment demonstration. The young man had been brought to Maria's doctor in very serious shape. The doctor operated on the young man and saved his life. The Salvadorian military soon found out that the doctor had saved this young man's life. Soldiers then came to the doctor's tiny clinic and warned him that if anybody he suspected was supportive of a revolutionary movement against the Salvadorian government ever came to his office again, for *anything*, he was forbidden to provide any medical services to such a person—or else the soldiers would come back and kill the doctor and all of his medical staff. Then they left.

However, something like that *did* happen again. A teenage boy was brought to Maria's doctor with a bullet wound in his shoulder. The boy's mother told the doctor that he had been merely an innocent bystander, watching a public demonstration against the government of El Salvador on his way home from school. The boy had been shot in the shoulder by a stray bullet fired by Salvadorian troops who had arrived in army trucks to quell the demonstration. So the doctor removed the bullet from the boy's shoulder and gave him some antibiotics to take to keep the wound from becoming infected.

The military arrived the very next morning at the clinic and took the doctor away. Soldiers brought him to nearby police headquarters and tortured him in the basement. They wired his thumbs together behind his back and then wired his wrists together. They then tied a rope around the wires holding his wrists together and threw one end of the rope over a beam on the ceiling of the basement. They then hoisted the doctor off the ground, tearing his shoulders from their sockets until both shoulder blades tore all the way out through the skin of his back. He hung like that for two full days. But he did not die. After two days, they cut him down to make room for another torture victim and tossed him out into the street, directly in front of police headquarters, so that everyone would know who had done this to him.

The doctor's friends rushed to recover the doctor and brought him back to his clinic. Doctors who admired his courage came from far and near and performed four separate operations on his back and shoulders. After many months of recovery, the doctor reopened his little medical clinic. He, Maria, and an older female medical assistant then began once again to provide basic medical assistance to the poor people in their village.

Soon, though, a five-year-old boy was brought into the clinic. He had been shot by soldiers breaking up another demonstration against the government. The doctor, thinking the military would certainly understand that a boy of only five years old had not been involved in any revolutionary movement against the government, treated the boy and saved his life.

However, he had been wrong about the military. Soldiers came back to his clinic, murdered him, and threw his body into the street directly in front of his clinic. Then they returned in the middle of that night and dragged his older medical assistant out into the courtyard. She was eight months pregnant. This death squad then lit torches and fired their rifles into the air to wake up the neighbors, so they could witness what would be done to people who defied the military or the government.

They then cut off all her clothes with their bayonets and tied her, naked, to a wooden post in the middle of the courtyard. They then cut off both of her breasts with their bayonets and sliced her open, removing the almost fully formed baby from her womb. They impaled the eight-month-old fetus on a bayonet and paraded it around the courtyard in the torchlight. The mother was forced to watch her dead baby paraded around as she bled to death hanging on the wooden post.

Maria testified that she had become terrified witnessing all of this from the window of her tiny bedroom above the courtyard, where she had hidden, crouching in terror, sheltering her then five-month-old baby in her arms. Without stopping to take anything to care for her baby or herself, Maria had fled with her baby in her arms, the baby folded in a blanket. She had found her way, in the depths of the night, to the nearby Catholic church. Pounding on the door and crying out to the Virgin Mary to save her and her baby, she had been let into the church by a Catholic nun, whom she begged for protection for her child and herself.

The local Catholic priest put Maria and her baby into the underground railroad of the American Sanctuary Movement. The priests, nuns,
and Protestant ministers together brought Maria and her baby, one church
at a time, up out of El Salvador, through Mexico, up to the Rio Grande,
and immediately across from Brownsville. There, Maria waded into the Rio
Grande with her baby in her arms. But she couldn't make it across. As she
was struggling and in danger of drowning, an older man—Mauricio, our
other defendant—came to the aid of her and her baby. Mauricio helped
Maria and her baby to the opposite shore, in Brownsville, where Archbishop
Fitzpatrick was waiting with his people to help them from the river and
to a new life of freedom. Archbishop Fitzpatrick brought them to Casa
Oscar Romero. There, Maria was told, "You cannot go to the local U.S.
Immigration Service office here in Brownsville to apply for political asylum
because you will be arrested and sent back to El Salvador. You need to come
with us to San Antonio."

Sister Diane Mullencamp then borrowed Archbishop Fitzpatrick's car,
and she and Stacy Lynn Merkt, along with *Dallas Times Herald* reporter Jack
Fisher, who was in Brownsville interviewing staff members of Casa Romero
for a "local color" story on the American Sanctuary Movement, headed for
San Antonio with Maria, her baby, and Mauricio. They were driving north
in the night, recounting their personal stories to Fisher, when the Migra officers pulled up behind them and turned on their red lights and siren.

They told the immigration officers who they were and that they were
on their way to San Antonio to apply for political asylum, but they were all
arrested, including Fisher. The Migra officers said, "We have our orders. We
have to arrest you and take you back to Brownsville."

The U.S. attorney agreed to dismiss the charges against Jack Fisher. But
he had insisted on prosecuting Sister Mullencamp and Stacy Lynn Merkt and
on deporting Maria and Mauricio back to El Salvador.

Just minutes into Maria's testimony, every member of the jury was crying. I was crying. Judge Vela was crying. Even the U.S. attorney had to turn
his face away to hide his tears from the jury. This was exactly what I wanted.

After Maria was helped from the stand, weeping and calling out to the
jury to help her and to save her and her baby from being sent back to El

Salvador, where they both would be killed by the military police, we presented Mauricio's story.

As Mauricio took the stand and fixed his gaze on the jurors, the U.S. attorney tried desperately to ingratiate himself to the jurors by asking for a fifteen-minute break so they could recompose themselves. I objected. I said that these defendants and refugees had a right to tell their stories and to be released from the threat of death hanging over them as soon as possible. Judge Vela was astonished, but he let us put Mauricio on the stand immediately following Maria's devastating testimony, with no break.

Mauricio testified that he had been on his way home from his job in a large town in El Salvador when he had come upon a public demonstration against the government. Mothers whose sons and daughters had been "disappeared" by Salvadorian police and soldiers had gathered in the public square and were banging loudly on pots and pans, shouting for the government to return their children or to tell them where they were buried. Each mother carried in her hand or wore on a string around her neck a soiled and wrinkled photograph of a child or grandchild who had been disappeared.

The U.S. attorney objected, claiming that Mauricio was presenting hearsay evidence to the jury in an attempt to prejudice them against the Reagan–Bush administration, which had officially denied all such stories.

Judge Vela scowled at him. "This is direct eyewitness testimony from a man who saw this with his own eyes. He is not asking the jury to believe these mothers and grandmothers. He is asking them to believe *him*. Sit down, Mr. C——!"

Mauricio went on. He explained to the jury how he had stopped to watch what was going on when two truckloads of Salvadorian military troops entered the square, followed by a small armored vehicle that he referred to as a tank. It was actually a mechanized half-track with a mounted .50-caliber machine gun—the kind that Salvadorian security forces obtained only from the United States military. The troops jumped out of the back of the trucks and began beating the women with their rifle butts and driving people from the square. From somewhere, a shot rang out, and the troops began firing indiscriminately into the crowd of women. Suddenly, the half-track began firing into the crowd as well.

"It was horrible," Mauricio said. "It was like the women were being struck with small bombs. Whole pieces of them flew off, and they were thrown into the air and fell, far away, in small piles, like ragdolls, obviously dead." He said that he had fled in terror, not knowing in what direction to run. He could still hear the firing going on behind him as he ran down a side street leading out of the square.

After he had run for several blocks, he turned down another side street and joined a group of people who had also fled from the square and were searching for someplace to hide. A young man came out of a house on that side street and waved wildly for them to come into a garage beneath his house. The group surged toward the open door, and Mauricio followed them into the garage. He wound up pushed into the very back of the garage as they all packed into the tiny space. Mauricio said that there must have been about forty or fifty people: men and women, young and old, even several small children. When they were all packed into the garage and the garage could hold no more, the young man lowered the garage door and locked it so that the people would be safe. The people who could not fit into the garage then fled, seeking another hiding place.

After several minutes, total silence filled the garage. Then the sound of the half-track's metal treads could be heard on the cement street, coming in their direction. Mauricio could feel the terror surging through the tiny huddled mass of people crouching in the darkness. The mechanized vehicle was obviously hunting for people who had fled from the square.

Suddenly, the sound of the clanking metal treads stopped—directly in front of the closed garage door.

A soldier, apparently an officer, shouted for the people to come out, promising that they would not be harmed if they came out. But nobody believed him. The sounds of crying from the children inside the garage began to increase, as did the sounds of mothers trying to silence them.

"Come out! Come out, and you will not be harmed," the Salvadorian officer shouted again. "If you don't, you will be fired on."

The people in the garage did not know what to do. Mauricio was certain that if they opened the garage door, they would all be killed. He was frozen in terror, he told the jury.

People inside the garage began to crowd toward the back of the garage, crushing Mauricio against the back wall as they tried to get as far away as they possibly could from the bullets they feared would be tearing through the closed garage door at any moment. Mauricio felt himself being smothered.

At that point in his testimony, Mauricio began to cry openly on the witness stand, apologizing to the jury for his cowardice. He admitted to them that he had fallen to his hands and knees and had begun to crawl under as many of the bodies pressing against him as he could, attempting to shelter himself from the bullets that he knew would soon be coming.

Then, without further warning, the explosion of the machine gun filled the garage. He could hear the .50-caliber bullets tearing through the flesh of people all around him as he crawled beneath their bodies. He could even feel the physical concussion of the bullets compressing the air in the cramped space. Screams and cries of agony became his entire world for what seemed an eternity. Mauricio prayed to Mother Mary that she would spare him so that he could tell the world what was happening to his people, there in his tiny country. In his terror, he swore an oath to the Blessed Virgin that if she would intercede with Her Son and spare his life amid this torrent of hot metal tearing through this mass of flesh all around him, he would live a life dedicated to Her Son and, with his life that had been spared, he would help every mother and child whom she put in his path in need of help.

He was convinced, he told the jury, that it was the Virgin Mary who had brought him to the banks of the Rio Grande that day to help Maria and her child make it into that courtroom, so she could tell her story to this jury.

When the thunder of the machine gun fire finally stopped, Mauricio lay still, uncertain whether he was alive or dead. "As I lay there, in total silence, the smell of gunpowder filling the tiny garage, a strange sound suddenly surrounded me. It was like a quiet wind, I thought at first. No, it was more like a quiet gentle stream, on a sunlit day. Then I smelled that unmistakable metallic smell, which, if you have ever smelled it, you will never forget. It was the smell of human blood. And the sound of the gentle wind, of the gentle stream, was the sound of human blood streaming down through the pile of torn bodies all above me. It poured down into my mouth. My world was filled with the acrid taste of metal on my tongue. It poured down into my eyes. My eyes burned with my tears and the blood of my fellow country-men in death. It poured down into my hair, into my heart." He began to cry uncontrollably on the witness stand

The jury convulsed with tears. Women in the jury turned to each other and clung to one another. The men in the jury put their arms around the women to try to comfort them, but they too were crying. They all knew that this was the truth.

Judge Vela asked me whether we wished to take a break, to allow the witness to compose himself.

"No, Your Honor. I have no more questions for this witness."

The U.S. attorney had no questions.

Next we called to the witness stand the two Catholic priests from El Salvador to whom Maria and Mauricio had respectively fled for help. They corroborated each story in every detail known to them. They swore that the stories both refugees had told the jury were, word for word, the exact stories that they had told in the heat of their escape, making them "excited utter-ances" that were, by their nature, more reliable than accounts composed after people have had time to alter and amend their accounts of what they have seen and experienced.

We then called to the stand the Methodist minister who had been stand-ing by in San Antonio, awaiting Maria's and Mauricio's arrival to assist them in filing their official applications for political asylum. This witness con-firmed that everyone involved with Maria and Mauricio had done everything humanly possible to comply with the U.S. laws that provided a clear and specific way for them to obtain political refugee status in the United States.

Then we rested.

In my closing argument, I implored the jury, "Look at the facts that have been presented to you. A sixteen-year-old girl named Maria, escaping from Herod's men with her infant child in her arms, both of whom would be sent back to the slaughter if they were caught. And this older man, the man who was not the father of the child but who took it upon himself to help them flee from Herod's men. Does this story not sound familiar to you? We have all heard it before!"

Everybody on the jury, most of whom were Catholics, froze when I said this. The U.S. attorney jumped to his feet and started shouting. "I object! I object! Your Honor, this is an outrage!"

"You are absolutely right," I shouted to the jury. "This *is* an outrage. The U.S. attorney and these two immigration officers—and this entire administration—should be ashamed of themselves! Our whole country should be ashamed of ourselves for allowing this to happen, in our name, to these two innocent people. These men," I said, gesturing toward the prosecution table. "These 'Herod's men,' should be ashamed of themselves for trying to draw you twelve good Americans on this jury into this dirty business against these two innocent victims, pursuant to which this administration would have you send them back to their certain deaths. Then the wrong that they have attempted to commit will become the wrong that you *have* committed. I do not believe that you will do this. Do *not* do this."

The U.S. attorney jumped up. "I object! I object!"

But I pressed on. "Let these people go! These men," I said, turning toward the assistant U.S. attorney, "are 'Herod's men.' But you have a choice, a choice that none of us were alive to make two thousand years ago when our human family was confronted with this exact same choice before. You and I are privileged to have been given the opportunity to make this choice, this choice that we have all, as Americans, been asked to make in this case. Will you let these people go? The choice is up to you, my fellow Americans. The choice is up to you."

The jury was in tears. Judge Vela was in tears. I was in tears. Archbishop Fitzpatrick was in shock.

"Objection overruled!" Judge Vela started shouting. "Your objection is overruled. Sit down, Mr. C——."

When order was restored to the courtroom, Judge Vela continued with his ruling against the U.S. attorney's objections. "While considerably more colorful than I might have recommended, what Mr. Sheehan has said in his closing remarks does state what he quite obviously sincerely believes, I am sure in good faith, to be the import of the evidence that he has presented to this jury. And as you know, great leeway is accorded to attorneys in their closing remarks. I will instruct the jury at the appropriate time that what the attorneys say in their closing arguments is not to be considered as evidence. And they, not me . . . nor you Mr. C—— . . . will determine whether what attorney Sheehan has said in his closing remarks to this jury is or is not, in the jury's opinion, an accurate portrayal of what the evidence has been in this courtroom."

I later persuaded Judge Vela to give a specific instruction to the jurors, directing them, "If you are convinced, by the evidence presented to you in this courtroom, that the defendants were, in all good faith, attempting to comply with the word and the spirit of the Refugee Act of 1980 when they were arrested; And if you find, from the evidence that was presented to you here in this courtroom, that the leaders of our government, specifically President Ronald Reagan or Vice President George Bush, issued an executive order directly commanding, or even authorizing, officials of the U.S. immigration office here in Brownsville, Texas, to refuse to accept applications for political asylum from any citizens from the nation of El Salvador; then you will be required by law to find the defendants before you in this case to be not guilty because I am instructing you, at this time, that such an executive order, even if personally signed by the president himself, would be unlawful and would be null and void as a matter of law."

As soon as that instruction number 1 was given to the jury, I knew that we would win.

The jury was out for two full days, however. Shouting and crying could be heard coming from the jury room. The jury twice asked Judge Vela to send in, in writing, instruction number 1. It was clear that someone was hanging the jury, so I convinced Judge Vela to add an instruction 1-B, which stated even more clearly that the jury was required to find our defendants not guilty if they found, based on the evidence presented to them, that President Reagan or Vice President Bush had issued an executive order directly commanding, or even authorizing, officials of the U.S. immigration office in Brownsville, Texas, to refuse to accept applications for political asylum from any citizens from the nation of El Salvador.

"You should be satisfied with that," Judge Vela had said to me pointedly when I tried to get him to be even more specific. We all knew what the jury's question meant: Somebody on the jury had been convinced by the U.S. attorney's argument that the defendants had avoided complying with the clear letter of the law because, by going to San Antonio instead of Brownsville, they did not turn themselves in to "the nearest available office of the U.S. Immigration Services."

On the morning of the third day, I received a telephone call at the vicar general's residence. I assumed at first that the jury must have come in with its verdict. But it wasn't that. It was Bill Taylor.

Bill insisted that I fly to Florida right away to speak with him in person. He said that he had an answer to the question I had assigned to him, but he would not talk with me about it over the telephone under any circumstances. "You will understand why and you will agree with me when you hear what it is. You're not gonna believe this, Major," he said. Bill called me "the Major," the code-name used by Cliff Robertson in *Three Days of the Condor*, only when something very serious was happening.

I told Bill that I would fly directly to Florida to meet with him the morning after we received the verdict. I hung up the phone wondering what could possibly require me to fly to Florida on such an immediate basis.

I received the phone call from Judge Vela's chambers on the morning of the fourth day of jury deliberations. Judge Vela had just received a note from the jury. He wanted all counsel to come to his courtroom immediately to be informed about the content of this communication.

The vicar general's driver got us to the courthouse within minutes. Judge Vela took the bench and read us the note from the jury, which said, "We are hopelessly deadlocked in our effort to reach a verdict." Judge Vela hesitated and looked up from the note to tell us that it also revealed what the split in the jury was—and what the single issue that was splitting the jury was—something that he was not at liberty to share with counsel. Then he said, "I am not going to dismiss this jury after all the time and emotion that has been put into presenting this case to this jury. What I am going to do is, I am going to send a note in to the jury informing them that I am withdrawing instruction 1 and instruction 1-B and ordering them to return a unanimous verdict to this court without giving any consideration whatsoever to those two instructions."

I, of course, leaped to my feet and lodged my most strenuous possible objection to his doing that. But he replied that his decision would give my clients the clearest possible record on this issue to the Fifth Circuit Court of Appeals if for any reason the jury were to convict the defendants after the instructions were withdrawn. And then he withdrew them.

Within one hour of his having sent his note into the jury room, the jury returned. They entered a verdict of guilty.

We, of course, immediately filed a motion for an expedited appeal, which Judge Vela immediately signed—just as he had offered to do when I first met with him at the archbishop's Mass three weeks earlier.

Within a matter of days, the Fifth Circuit Court of Appeals unanimously reversed the verdict on the face of the record submitted to it and entered an order directing Judge Vela to summarily dismiss all charges against the defendants—and to allow Maria and Mauricio to be transported to San Antonio, where they were to be allowed to lawfully apply for political refugee status.

This order was accompanied by an additional Fifth Circuit Court of Appeals order enjoining any further federal criminal prosecutions of any persons aiding Salvadorian or Guatemalan refugees in the federal Southern District of Texas on the grounds that they were transporting said refugees to apply for political asylum outside of that district. So we had not only won our clients' acquittal in a public trial, but we had secured a victory that affected political refugees entering into the entire Southern District of Texas.

I saw Judge Vela one more time after the ruling from the federal court of appeals. It was at communion at the six o'clock Mass celebrated by Archbishop Fitzpatrick, welcoming Maria and Mauricio into his parish. Judge Vela and I took communion together, side by side for a second—and final—time. Nothing was said. But as he left the church, he turned to me and smiled. I nodded goodbye to him and returned to the vicar general's residence. There I began to pack to fly to Florida.

PART IV

CHAPTER *twenty-five*

B ILL TAYLOR MET me at the airport in Orlando, where we went into the Delta Crown Room (Bill being a Delta million-mile member). Sitting at a corner table, we ordered our traditional ginger ales, and he began to tell me what he had found out about the FBI man's reports of "known communist terrorists" in Brownsville. Like most of Bill's hot tips, he had gotten this from an old friend from the Marine Corps, one who was now the commander of the Louisiana State National Guard.

Bill had flown to New Orleans to meet with this old Marine Corps buddy and had learned that something very weird was going on. According to Bill's friend, the Reagan–Bush administration had held a "national readiness exercise" in April of that year (1984) to practice a potential invasion of Nicaragua or El Salvador. The army had rehearsed airlifting the entire Eighty-second Airborne Division—ten to fifteen thousand troops—out of Fort Bragg, North Carolina, under the cover of night, and flying them into either El Salvador or Nicaragua to enforce a state of martial law. The operation had been code-named Operation Night Train. The overall readiness exercise was code-named REX 84, or Readiness Exercise 1984.

However, the new director of the Federal Emergency Management Agency (FEMA) under Ronald Reagan and George H. W. Bush, Louis Giuffrida, had gotten wind of the readiness exercise and had confronted Edwin Meese, chief of staff of the White House, about FEMA's not having been included in the exercise. Meese had brought Giuffrida in from California with him to run FEMA, the brand-new federal agency that Jimmy Carter had started for natural domestic disaster response. Before being tapped for the FEMA post, Giuffrida had been commandant of the California Specialized Training Institute in San Luis Obispo, California, an antiterrorist training center for California State Police. After Giuffrida showed up in Washington, he was dissatisfied with FEMA's limited mission; he wanted Meese to persuade Reagan to expand FEMA into a full-blown antiterrorist force.

When Giuffrida learned of the 1984 readiness exercise, he asked Meese, "What happens if Reagan and Bush launch this invasion into El Salvador or Nicaragua and all of these five hundred thousand undocumented Central American aliens here unlawfully inside our country all organize themselves into military cadres and attack our military bases or try to poison our reservoirs?" It was Giuffrida, then, who had come up with this cockamamie theory that the American Sanctuary Movement was somehow smuggling "known communist terrorists" into the country.

Giuffrida sold this bizarre scenario to Meese, who then sold it to Reagan, and they ended up creating REX 84 BRAVO, pursuant to which Giuffrida had been tasked with practicing rounding up all five hundred thousand undocumented Central American immigrants and putting them into twelve military stockades. On top of this, Giuffrida requested access to the ADEX list—the names of some four thousand U.S. citizens whom the attorney general of the United States had designated to be "potential threats to the national security of the United States in the event that the president of the United States determines it to be necessary to declare a state of national emergency." This list had been developed through the secret Continuity of Government program. Meese gave Giuffrida permission to go to Attorney General William French Smith and demand a copy of the ADEX list. But Smith had refused to give it to him, even after Giuffrida threw a fit and got Ronald Reagan to directly order Smith to give it to him. Not only did William French Smith refuse to obey Ronald Reagan, he refused when Meese demanded his resignation for failing to obey a direct order from the president. But Meese and Reagan couldn't do anything about it because William French Smith swore that if he were fired, he would publicly reveal why.

Ultimately, Giuffrida went forward without the ADEX list. His principal challenge, however, had been the Posse Comitatus Act, which Congress passed in 1878, which expressly prohibits deploying U.S. military forces inside the United States to enforce civilian laws against the civilian population. Because of that statute, Giuffrida was not allowed to employ any U.S. military personnel to help him round up civilians—even "undocumented" civilians. His solution was to start looking for *civilian* recruits who could be deputized to carry out his plan of rounding up five hundred thousand aliens in the event of a state of emergency. He proposed the creation of *civilian* "state defense forces," which would be made up of private paramilitary zealots—the kind of men who spent their weekends playing war games, hiding in the woods from each other, wearing camouflage clothes, and shooting at each other with paintball guns. These were the kind of men who subscribed to *Soldier of Fortune* magazine, which was exactly where Giuffrida advertised for them.

Giuffrida then persuaded Meese to get various right-wing state legislatures to pass statutes creating civilian "state defense forces," which were to be like the old Civil Air Patrol, whose members, at the height of the second Red Scare in the mid-1950s, scanned America's skies for potential invading Russian airplanes. Giuffrida had all his recruits volunteer for these civilian state defense forces. Meese secured permission for these units to be provided with millions of dollars of U.S. military equipment, directly from the Pentagon, to be used during the REX 84 BRAVO readiness exercise scheduled for April 1984.

So that answered the question that had been posed to me by the Methodist bishop of Brownsville during the American Sanctuary Movement case.

However, Bill Taylor's former Marine Corps buddy told him that there was something else that was really strange about the entire project, at least in Louisiana. As commander of the Louisiana State National Guard, he had been ordered, directly by the Defense Department, to hand out military equipment directly from the Pentagon to the civilian defense forces in Louisiana. But after that equipment had been distributed, his office had been ordered by the Pentagon to revalue all of that equipment, with each weapon assigned a new, and much higher, "replacement value." For example, say $3 million in U.S. military equipment from the Pentagon had been distributed to the civilian defense forces in Louisiana; it was to be revalued at $6 million. Then, at the conclusion of the REX 84 readiness exercise, the commander had been ordered to gather back only $3 million in weapons (using the new valuations)—thereby leaving half of the brand-new Pentagon-issued U.S. military weapons in the hands of *private* members of these radically right-wing civilian defense forces.

Bill Taylor, upon hearing this, had only half-jokingly asked his friend if the wackos were secretly being organized and armed to stage or support some kind of right-wing military takeover of the country—similar to what had been attempted in the 1964 film *Seven Days in May,* in which the American Joint Chiefs of Staff attempt a military coup against an unpopular American president who is trying to eliminate all nuclear weapons through a treaty with the Soviet Union.

Bill's friend, the commander of the Louisiana State National Guard, had told him, "Hell no. They are planning to smuggle all of those weapons to the Contras down in Central America." He knew that much, but he didn't know why.

In March 1984, Congress had passed the Boland Amendment, expressly prohibiting, by federal law, the granting of any military aid, either direct or indirect, to the Contras of Central America by any intelligence agency of the United States. The Contras had been found by the International Court of Justice in Geneva, Switzerland, to be guilty of international war crimes for their having planted explosive mines in the international harbors of Nicaragua, thereby threatening international commercial shipping lanes.

The Reagan–Bush administration's attempt to supply arms to the Contras through this indirect method was, therefore, as Bill and I immediately realized, a directly *impeachable* offense. That was why Bill Taylor had wanted to talk to me in person and not over any telephone.

There I was, just back from successfully completing the American Sanctuary Movement case, and we had walked straight into the middle of proof that the Reagan–Bush administration was not only knowingly unconstitutionally arresting legitimate political refugees and Americans who were trying to help them comply with the American law but was also criminally smuggling U.S. military equipment to the Contras in Central America—in direct and flagrant defiance of an express act of Congress. It had been a productive month, indeed, for the Christic Institute.

We returned to Washington and focused on investigating these highly explosive activities.

I began my investigation by moving around Washington, asking certain people what they had heard about what we had uncovered. I told Bob Fink, Howard Rosenberg, and Howard Kohn. I also tried to determine who might make the most appropriate plaintiffs in a litigation that our office might initiate to stop this. In other words, who would have "standing" to bring such a case before a federal court of justice?

One of Father Bill Davis's contacts told him there was going to be an article in *The Washington Post* related to this issue. Leafing through *The Washington Post* after Sunday Mass, I found a long story by Brian Barger, the young man I had defended back in 1975 in the big final anti–Vietnam War demonstration at the White House. Barger was now an AP reporter. He had undertaken an investigation of a group of former U.S. military men in Florida who were smuggling weapons to the Contras. In the early summer of 1984, he wrote a long story in *The Washington Post* about what he had learned.

A journalist friend of Brian's had told him that a former U.S. military man she had known in high school had told her that he and some other former U.S. military men were training Contras from Nicaragua in military tactics in a swamp in the Everglades. She told Brian that these men were securing U.S. weapons, ammunition, and explosives from some mysterious source that her friend would not reveal. Being the industrious—and adventurous—young investigative journalist that he was, Brian Barger had gone to the Everglades and had found their encampment. He just walked right in, and since he spoke fluent Spanish, he sat down and started talking with these U.S. military veterans. They eventually told Brian that some of them were preparing for a meeting with like-minded U.S. military veterans at a hotel in Honduras. Brian flew back to Washington and told his AP supervisor what he had learned, and he asked for permission to follow up on the story. However, his boss at AP told him to stop. He said, "If some red-blooded American veterans have taken it upon themselves, as private citizens, to try to help the Contras—since the administration was forbidden from helping them—well, the Associated Press doesn't think that one of our reporters should be going around telling everyone what they're doing." The Associated Press was pushing Brian to drop this story.

So Brian took a week of vacation time and, on his own dime, flew to Honduras and went directly to the hotel where these "patriots" had told him they planned to meet. He sat in the lobby of the hotel pretending to read a Spanish-language newspaper while he watched these guys, decked out in store-bought camouflage clothes, as they came and went. Finally, a man walked over and sat down next to Brian. His name was Tom Posey, the self-appointed commander of the small Civilian Military Assistance Group, the Alabama State Legislature–created civilian defense force. Brian leaned over to him and said, "Jeez, there sure are a lot of American-lookin' guys around here. And all in camouflage. What's going on around here anyhow?"

"These guys are all patriots," Posey had said, and he then proceeded to tell Brian about the communists who were trying to take over Central American governments. He said the American veterans at the hotel were meeting to help the Contras throw the communists out of Central America. When Brian mentioned that he was a journalist, making it sound as if he was just a stringer instead of a full-time Associated Press correspondent, Posey asked whether Brian might be interested in doing a story about all of this.

Posey thereupon invited Brian to come with him into the meetings. So Brian sat right next to Posey in all of the meetings of these former U.S. military men sitting around in mufti in this Honduras hotel. As it turned out, some of the members of the Alabama State National Guard had been stealing weapons from the National Guard Armory in Alabama and giving them to Posey to take to Florida. The weapons were then being flown from the Fort Lauderdale/Hollywood Airport directly into El Salvador, to a place called Ilopango.

Brian stayed with these men for several days and then flew back and wrote up their entire story. It was basically a glowing account of those men who perceived themselves to be true American patriots helping democracy in South America. From the point of view of those men, Brian's article was a total puff piece. In that sense, it was a work of genius. Tom Posey and all the men named in the article just loved it; it said exactly what they wanted the world to hear about them. However, everyone in Washington, D.C., was completely horrified. The Republicans were absolutely freaked out that this operation had been so publicly exposed. And the Democratic congressmen who had voted to enact the Boland Amendment were equally horrified—but for exactly the opposite reason. It was a great scoop for *The Washington Post*—and a great day for Brian Barger. But it was also a great day for us.

After I read the article that early summer day in 1984, I drove over to check data at the Associated Press office and found Brian, whose telephone was ringing off the hook. I explained to him what we had found out about where the weapons, ammunition, and explosives were coming from. He explained to me, in much more detail, the information he had gotten from the men in Honduras. So we agreed to work together on a case that I could bring before a federal court. I wanted to get a judicial declaration that what the Reagan–Bush administration was doing in Central America was in direct violation of the Boland Amendment and was, therefore, an impeachable offense. Brian would write news articles about this investigation as we developed the evidence. He was already deep inside with these men, and I had a number of well-connected professional investigators digging with all their sources.

Months later, in 1985, Brian called and told me that we had to meet—but away from the AP office. In this meeting, Brian explained that a group of "*Soldier of Fortune* types," working with the Contras from secret bases in Costa Rica, directly across the border from Nicaragua along the Rio San Juan, had blown up a press conference in Costa Rica in May of the previous year—on May 30, 1984. They had been attempting to assassinate Edén Pastora, "Commandante Zero" of the Sandinista government. Six international journalists had been killed in the explosion of a bomb placed in a metal suitcase at the foot of a makeshift podium where Pastora had been scheduled to publicly denounce the Contras, who were attempting to recruit Pastora into their ranks against the new Sandinista government in Nicaragua. Pastora had almost been killed in this explosion, but the podium had shielded him from much of the blast.

Brian told me that there was dramatic footage of this explosion and its immediate aftermath because so many professional news journalists and television crews had been at the scene. There was footage of one particular man coming into the press conference, casually placing that metal suitcase at the foot of the podium, and skulking out of the rear door of the small room just as Pastora began to speak. Seconds later, as Pastora began his remarks, the videotape captured a blinding flash of light and the sound of a huge explosion. The entire room was destroyed, and the roof was blown off the tiny building in which the press conference was being held.

A portion of the floor also collapsed, and through the smoke and debris, bloody bodies could be seen strewn all around the room from the perspective of a camera that was now lying on its side on the floor, but still filming.

One young man lying on the floor of the destroyed room, but still moving, was a tall, gangly, freelance television cameraman with ABC News. His name was Tony Avirgan. Brian explained that Avirgan, an American, had survived the bomb blast and that he and his professional journalist wife, Martha Honey, had immediately begun an investigation to identify the mystery man who had placed the metal suitcase containing the bomb at the foot of the podium. Avirgan and Honey started their investigation by tracking his movements. They then identified him as a man who had been using the false name "Per Anker Hansen," portraying himself as a freelance professional journalist from Scandinavia. After further investigation, they had tracked that man to meetings with an ultra-right-wing American expatriot in Costa Rica by the name of John Hull. John Hull, it turned out, was hosting a number of *Soldier of Fortune*–type Americans—just like the ones Brian Barger had seen coming and going from that meeting in Honduras a few weeks prior to that bombing. Finally, Avirgan's and Honey's investigation had led them to the conclusion that John Hull and a group of pro-Contra, anti-Castro, Miami-based Cuban exiles and American *Soldier of Fortune* types had hired and paid Per Anker Hansen to blow up Edén Pastora's public press conference. They wanted to kill Pastora to stop him from publicly condemning the Contra movement and publicly revealing that the American CIA was secretly financing, training, and supplying the Contra movement with weapons, ammunition, and explosives—all in violation of the Boland Amendment enacted by Congress.

Avirgan and Honey had written a small, self-published booklet in Costa Rica, explicitly naming John Hull and several of the men Hull was "hosting" on his Costa Rican ranch as the people who had hired Per Anker Hansen to blow up the Pastora press conference.

Brian wanted to know whether any of the independent investigations that my professional investigators and I had been engaged in had revealed any connection between John Hull in Costa Rica and the provision of illegal weapons to the Contras by the Reagan–Bush administration. If such a connection could be made, Brian and I reasoned together, it might be important for me to speak directly with Avirgan and Honey.

When I expressed a willingness to meet with them, Brian only then revealed to me that John Hull had in fact filed a federal criminal complaint against Avirgan and Honey in the Costa Rican federal court, charging them both with criminal libel, for which they could be sentenced to years in federal prison in Costa Rica if they were convicted. Avirgan and Honey had hired a well-known and allegedly respected criminal defense attorney in Costa Rica, but that attorney had advised them to simply play games with the court by refusing to explain which parts of the booklet each one of them had personally written. That lawyer kept emphasizing to Avirgan and Honey that it was difficult to defend a criminal libel case in Costa Rica because, in the Costa Rican culture, it was considered to be a grave offense against a person's entire family to publicly accuse that person of a crime—even if the accusation was true!

"Tony Avirgan and Martha Honey need legal help," Brian told me. "Do you think you could help them?"

I was a bit taken aback. What had started out as a conversation about a potential source of important information for our investigation had suddenly been transformed into a request for legal assistance from our office.

But, being the public interest lawyer that I am, I ended up flying down to Costa Rica with Father Bill Davis in the fall of 1985 to meet with Tony Avirgan and Martha Honey.

When I arrived at their home in San José, Costa Rica, I found them in a state of near despair. It was literally the very last day they had to file any discovery demands that they wished to file demanding that the federal prosecutor turn over to their attorney whatever discovery they required to defend themselves in court. Their lawyer had told them, however, that it was best not to ask for any discovery—"because that would only irritate the prosecutor and would motivate him to demand more discovery from them."

Their lawyer's defense plan (if one could call it that) was to simply do the best that he could to keep the prosecution from finding out which one of them had written which parts of the book. "If you can keep the prosecution from finding that out," he argued, "you will have a good technical defense on appeal because the prosecution could not have proven that either of you had personally libeled John Hull." This approach assumed that they were both going to be convicted, which their lawyer apparently thought was a forgone conclusion.

This was, of course, utter incompetence. I spent my first hour with them passionately explaining that they *had to* radically change their entire defense strategy and go on the attack against John Hull to prove, in court, that what they had said about Hull in their book was in fact true. They were immediately enthusiastic about that idea. So we had to scramble like mad to write up some two dozen discovery demands and an official notice to be filed with the Costa Rican federal court *that very afternoon,* informing the court that they intended to change their legal counsel and that they *did* want certain documents in discovery. Then we literally raced for the courthouse to get there in time to file the documents by five o'clock. However, when we arrived at the courthouse at 4:45 PM, we discovered that the court closed on Fridays at 4:30.

Avirgan and Honey were technically no worse off than they would have been had I not even made it to Costa Rica; however, it was certainly not a way to ingratiate myself to them as their potential lawyer. I felt terrible, and embarrassed. My mistake made Honey feel that she should be the person, henceforth, to make all future decisions in her husband's case.

We then met with a well-respected, progressive union attorney, Oto Castro, the very next day, and laid out the plan for our attack strategy. Attorney Castro informed us that our aggressive approach had never been tried before in a Costa Rican court because of the low regard in which the courts and the culture viewed people who publicly besmirched the family name of another. But we were collectively able to persuade Attorney Castro that Avirgan and Honey did, in fact, possess enough direct, court-admissible evidence at the time of publishing their book to support a good-faith belief that what they had written about John Hull was in fact true—and that such a showing in court would require a judgment in their favor.

So that is exactly what we did. In October of 1985, Tony Avirgan, Martha Honey, and their courageous Costa Rican attorney Oto Castro crushed John Hull in their four-day Costa Rican federal libel case in federal court. In fact, shortly after Avirgan's and Honey's victory over John Hull, the attorney general of Costa Rica returned first-degree murder indictments against Hull and four anti-Castro Cuban exile guests whom Hull was "hosting" on his ranch at the time of the Pastora press conference bombing. In response to these federal criminal indictments, John Hull and all four of his Cuban exile "guests" immediately fled Costa Rica. Hull was airlifted out of Costa Rica in a CIA plane provided by Dewey Clarridge, the CIA station chief in Central America, and flown by an American CIA pilot. This information was established through a later investigation of the Senate Select Committee on Narcotics and Terrorism. John Hull and his four anti-Castro Cuban exile "guests" were then all placed on Interpol's Ten Most Wanted list.

Between October 1985 and April 1986, Father Bill Davis and I turned the attention of our entire Christic Institute staff and the attention of all of our field investigators to the task of linking up John Hull and his covert weapons- and explosives-smuggling operation on his ranch in Costa Rica with the flights into and out of the Fort Lauderdale/Hollywood Airport about which Tom Posey had told Brian Barger.

Tony Avirgan had volunteered to be a plaintiff in any federal civil lawsuit that our office wished to file in the United States against Hull and his associates in the criminal weapons- and explosives-smuggling operation. I took great pains to explain to Tony—and to his wife, Martha—that now that they had been officially acquitted, they were entirely free and clear from their previous threat of federal imprisonment in Costa Rica and they were not required to do anything more. "You can just walk away from this case, and away from this entire issue, if you choose to do so." But I told them that the Christic Institute and the people we represented were planning to dig out evidence that would allow us to file a federal legal action in the United States against the men who were smuggling the weapons and the explosives to the Contras, through Costa Rica, in clear violation of the Boland Amendment. I warned them, however, that the case was much, *much* bigger than just their single bombing case and that it might go all the way up to the impeachment of the president and the vice president of the United States for their active involvement in authorizing this activity in direct defiance of Congress. "If you become a plaintiff in *that* case, you will be in a position similar to the individual schoolchildren who were technical plaintiffs in the famous *Brown v. Board of Education* school desegregation case that was brought all the way to the United States Supreme Court back in 1954. Those students were, as you might imagine, not in charge of deciding what was to be done in that case. Nor were their parents. They were just the individuals who had the official "standing" to sue for what was being done to literally hundreds of thousands of other people as well as to them. I told them that I and the Christic Institute, not they, would be in charge of deciding what was to be done in such a case.

I asked Tony if he clearly understood and agreed to that. He said that he did. Then I told him that he had better explain that to his wife and get her to consent to that as well.

Tony thereupon looked very uncomfortable. "I will *explain that part* to her later, after she has told me that she agrees with my being a plaintiff."

We both laughed. "Well, you know how to get her to agree with this better than anyone else. So I will leave that up to you. But I want to know that she agrees with this principle before we agree to have you be one of the plaintiffs."

"Good. We'll do that," Tony agreed.

Now that we had a potential client on board with very real standing to sue these men, Brian and I—and then Tony Avirgan and I—continued our respective but closely coordinated investigations of these men. Tony Avirgan and Martha Honey continued to investigate and gather evidence of the criminal activities of Per Anker Hansen, John Hull, Hull's "guests," and any others who were operative in Costa Rica. The Christic Institute investigated and gathered evidence of the criminal activities of members of this enterprise outside Costa Rica and the connection between them and members of the executive branch of the Reagan–Bush administration who were involved in this criminal enterprise. And Brian Barger and his Associated Press partner Robert Parry continued their AP investigation, trying to track down as many

450 THE PEOPLE'S ADVOCATE

direct eyewitnesses as they could to prove that John Hull and the guests on his ranch were directly receiving weapons and explosives from the United States and distributing them to the Contras. Those weapons included the very rare type of C-4 explosive that was used by Per Anker Hansen to blow up the Edén Pastora press conference.

Tony Avirgan's and Martha Honey's investigation brought us four direct eyewitnesses, whose testimony proved that John Hull and the guests on his ranch had in fact directly planned and assisted Per Anker Hansen in his carrying out the May 30, 1984, bombing of Edén Pastora's press conference.

The first of these four witnesses was Carlos Rojas Chinchilla, a young Costa Rican man who had been approached by one of the "guests" on John Hull's ranch, a man named David. David had tried to get Carlos to help him escape, because although he had participated in planning and carrying out the press conference bombing, the group was now planning to assassinate the American ambassador to Costa Rica, Lewis Tambs, with a bomb just like the one the group had used to blow up the Pastora press conference. David was opposed to this being done and did not want to participate in that action. The plan was to blame this assassination on the new Sandinista government in Nicaragua. Carlos provided a sworn deposition to our office, in person, explaining how he and David had gotten caught trying to effectuate David's escape plan from Hull's ranch and how both he and David had been kidnapped by several of John Hull's men and locked in a shed on Hull's ranch. Carlos explained in his sworn deposition how he had escaped from the shed during the night and had sought out Tony Avirgan and Martha Honey when he heard about their victory in court over John Hull.

The second eyewitness was D——, John Hull's personal driver. He provided our office with a sworn deposition swearing that he had driven John Hull, sometime shortly before May 30, 1984, to a private meeting with Per Anker Hansen (whom he identified out of a photo lineup) at a small house near Hull's ranch. D—— swore that he had personally witnessed this meeting and that, during the meeting, he had personally witnessed John Hull hand Per Anker Hansen a small manila envelope that appeared to be filled with currency, based on the way the man had opened it and counted what looked like bills inside. After this meeting, D—— testified that he had driven John Hull back to the ranch.

The third direct eyewitness was Sheila Ugalde, John Hull's personal secretary. She provided our office with a sworn deposition stating that, sometime shortly before May 30, 1984, Hull had directed her to go to his bank, withdraw $50,000 in cash, put it into an envelope, and bring it to him. She also swore that there was no bill or any other transaction of which she, as his personal secretary, was aware that required Hull to deliver $50,000 in cash to anyone. But she had no idea to whom John Hull had delivered the money. She knew only that it was never redeposited into his bank.

The fourth direct eyewitness was Albert Guevara Bonilla, who stated in a sworn deposition that he had personally witnessed John Hull meeting with Per Anker Hansen at a site directly across the Rio San Juan from the tiny hamlet of La Penca, where Edén Pastora's press conference was later blown up. Bonilla swore that he had rented John Hull and this man a boat and had personally watched them ride together in that boat across the Rio San Juan directly to La Penca. He swore that he had witnessed the two men doing this about twenty-two days before the May 30, 1984, bombing of Edén Pastora's press conference at La Penca. He, too, picked this man's photograph out of a photo lineup of eight different men.

A fifth eyewitness, Jack Terrell, was provided by Brian Barger. Terrell was an associate of Tom Posey's in the Civilian Military Assistance Group out of Alabama. Terrell swore under oath that he had been contacted by one Felipe Vidal, an anti-Castro Cuban exile. Vidal had told Terrell that he and five other anti-Castro Cuban exiles were guests on John Hull's ranch in Costa Rica. Terrell testified that the men were Felipe Vidal, Rene Corvo, Alvero Cruz, Frederico Saenz, and Raul and Jorge Villeverde. Terrell swore under oath that he had attended a meeting with Vidal, Hull, and these five other anti-Castro Cuban exiles and that in this meeting the men had specifically tried to hire him to kill Edén Pastora. Vidal, gesturing to the other men in the meeting, had told Terrell, "We are the ones who put the bomb under Edén Pastora at his press conference. But it didn't kill him. So we want to hire you to kill Pastora for us." Terrell, under intense questioning at his deposition, held fast to his sworn statement, asserting emphatically that he was absolutely certain that all of the men in that meeting—including John Hull—could hear perfectly well what Vidal had said and that not a single one of them offered any sign of protest.

Finally there was a sixth witness, Jorge Chavarria Guzman, the attorney general of Costa Rica, who swore under oath that it was Per Anker Hansen, with direct assistance and support from John Hull and these six specific Miami-based anti-Castro Cuban exiles, who had blown up the Pastora press conference at La Penca, killing the journalists present. Guzman testified under oath for two entire days in a Costa Rican courtroom, in a sworn deposition taken by our office. In his sworn testimony, Guzman provided a step-by-step blueprint of the Costa Rican federal government's criminal murder investigation against Per Anker Hansen, John Hull, and the six anti-Castro Cuban exiles named above. He provided official government-certified documentation detailing each step of the Costa Rican criminal investigation, complete with official forensic scientific evidence. Moreover, in his sworn testimony, the Costa Rican attorney general provided the names of, the official government identification numbers for, and the means of contacting each and every Costa Rican government investigator who had been responsible for certifying and cataloging each piece of evidence in the case. He also provided the names and contact information of every forensic scientist who had performed each test for the investigation. We agreed to call every one of these investigators and scientific experts in our civil case.

With this aspect of our case secured, we turned to Brian Barger to assist us in connecting John Hull and the men indicted for this bombing in Costa Rica to the illegal weapons- and explosive-smuggling operation being conducted out of the Fort Lauderdale/Hollywood Airport in South Florida. This would help us ascertain the appropriate venue in which to file our federal Racketeer Influenced and Corrupt Organizations (RICO) case now that we had a plaintiff with secure standing to complain against this RICO organization.

Brian was able to provide critical witnesses to our office. These eyewitnesses included two American pilots who had flown weapons and explosives into the Ilopango Airport in El Salvador, which was administered jointly by the United States military and the Salvadorian government. These pilots had watched the weapons, ammunition, and explosives being loaded onto smaller planes, which they then piloted to John Hull's ranch. One of these pilots, Gary Betzner, provided our office with maps with inked-in flight routes from the Fort Lauderdale/Hollywood Airport to the Ilopango Airport, and from the Ilopango Airport to John Hull's ranch, complete with code-words that had to be radioed to Hull to authorize the landing of the weapons and explosives on his dirt landing strip. Betzner also provided an affidavit swearing that he had personally delivered at least two shipments of weapons and explosives from the Fort Lauderdale/Hollywood Airport directly to John Hull, who had met the pilot's plane on the airstrip. He swore that Hull had personally supervised the unloading of the weapons and explosives into small trucks.

The second pilot, Michael Tolliver, shocked us all by testifying that he had waited on John Hull's dirt airstrip as Hull personally supervised the loading of hundreds of pounds of cocaine to be carried on the plane's return flight back to South Florida. Tolliver explained how the airplane in which he flew the cocaine into the United States was equipped with a radio transmitter that emitted his call sign to all air traffic controllers along his planned route over U.S. territory. His call sign, he explained, told air traffic controllers that his plane was engaged in an official U.S. government intelligence mission and was not to be inspected or in any other way interfered with by U.S. law enforcement agents. Hull and his associates knew they could load the plane with cocaine and have it flown back into the United States without any fear of interference. This process required that the cocaine be transferred from small planes onto larger planes at the Ilopango Airport, which was under direct U.S.–Salvadorian government control.

Brian put me into direct touch with Celerino Castillio, an agent with the U.S. Drug Enforcement Agency stationed at the Ilopango Airport. Castillio briefed me in detail about witnessing the transfer of hundreds of pounds of cocaine at a time from small planes returning to the Ilopango Airport from Costa Rica onto larger planes bound for South Florida. He confirmed that all this took place on a section of Ilopango Airport grounds that was under direct U.S. government control. Castillio told me that he had filed official report after official report about this activity directly to his DEA superiors, both in El Salvador and in the United States, pleading for additional DEA agents to be sent to El Salvador to assist him in arresting the people responsible. But he had been told, "Stay out of this, Cele. This is an authorized U.S. government covert operation."

With this surprising turn of events, we pressed forward in Washington, D.C., to determine how high up this operation went, how widespread operations like this were inside the Reagan–Bush administration, and who knew about what was going on. Our objective was to trigger a genuine investigation of these activities by Congress, which had forbidden such activity in the Boland Amendment. Everything in Washington is political, but we hoped to present enough objective and indisputable factual evidence in our civil case to keep any congressional investigation from being totally politicized. To get a set of hearings, it would be necessary for our case to generate so much unavoidable publicity that Congress *had* to investigate the activities and the larger problem they represented: the fact that the CIA and the entire government intelligence community created by the National Security Act of 1947 had, in effect, gone "renegade" and was defying the Congress of the United States.

By this time, I was caught up in a quest to publicly expose not only these operations in Central America but also the fundamental contradiction that the Reagan–Bush administration and intelligence community represented in a constitutional democracy. I did not feel the least bit self-conscious about doing this, though I guess that many people would have felt daunted. Frankly, it felt no more challenging than taking on a major rival in a high school football game in Warrensburg or an opponent in one of the many federal civil rights cases I had conducted as chief trial counsel for the ACLU for the Rocky Mountain region. I was used to being a key player in these scenarios rather than a mere spectator or a person who felt overwhelmed by the circumstances.

It was like being *in* a movie. The correct *moral* action to be taken was perfectly clear. The Good Guys and the Bad Guys were all perfectly clearly identified to me. With adequate hard work and constant attention to maintaining an honest and straightforward position, justice would prevail, as it almost always had for me before—and as it did in the movies.

CHAPTER *twenty-six*

I WAS IN THE midst of discovering the Reagan–Bush administration's involvement in embezzling Pentagon-issued rifles, handguns, ammunition, explosives, and shoulder-fired weapons to be smuggled to the Contras when I was contacted by Paul Hoven, whom I had previously met while I was chairing an organization in Washington, D.C., named the Fund for Constitutional Government.

The Fund for Constitutional Government was the first national organization to dig out whistleblowers, encourage them to speak out, and legally protect them through litigation. The Fund for Constitutional Government also founded and financed the Project on Military Procurement, the organization that blew the whistle on gross Pentagon misspending, and the Fund for Investigative Journalism, which identified potential news stories, searched out qualified and enterprising young investigative journalists to uncover the facts of such stories, and then funded the legwork and research necessary to get those stories published. We also paid for attorneys to protect the whistleblowers whom our journalists needed to provide the detailed inside information often necessary to make a story a real exposé.

Because of this vast responsibility, the Fund for Constitutional Government had representatives from the entire spread of the Washington political spectrum on our board of directors. We had Ernie Fitzgerald, the Defense Department specialist who had blown the whistle on the C5-A cargo plane cost overruns. We had Indie Badwar, one of Jack Anderson's top investigative researchers. The chairman of our board of directors, prior to me serving in that capacity, was Russell Hemenway, a tall, strikingly handsome, liberal New York City patrician who had been a close personal friend of Jack Kennedy's in the U.S. Navy during World War II. South Dakota senator James Abourezk, chairman of the American Indian Policy Review

Commission and the inaugural chairman of the Senate Select Committee on Indian Affairs, was also on our board. The spark plug of the entire organization was Anne Zill, a forty-year-old red-headed fireball who was the closest thing that 1970s' Washington had to a classic Washington, D.C., political salon hostess. Anne would invite politically eclectic groups of bright and well-informed "insiders" to her Capitol Hill home and ply them with champagne and great food. Then they would all become personal friends who could rely upon each other. Very importantly, Anne had direct access to Stewart Mott, the liberal heir to the Mott applesauce fortune. She was able to convince Stewart to contribute more and more of his significant fortune to the organization each year.

It was through my service as chairman of the board of the Fund for Constitutional Government that I met Paul Hoven, a weapons specialist and a consultant for our Project on Military Procurement. Hoven was a classic *Soldier of Fortune* type: a huge guy, ruggedly handsome, and barrel-chested. He would swagger into our meetings, proudly wearing his large belt buckle with the crossed swords of the First Air Cavalry. He was a former helicopter jock in Vietnam, a member of a class of men who were to be respected, and in Vietnam he had become familiar with various weapons and weapons systems.

Paul liked to make a big show of not liking or respecting liberals, which he at first assumed all of us to be. But over the months, Hoven and I ended up getting along with each other, especially after he found out that I had a couple years of training in the U.S. Special Forces. Hoven was fascinated by the fact that my chief investigator was a former Marine Corps CID man and that virtually all of my other investigators were former military criminal investigators. I think Hoven fancied himself a potential intelligence agent in addition to fancying himself a "snake-eater" (as we called special operations guys because we had all been trained to eat snakes in the jungle if necessary to survive behind enemy lines).

Hoven called me six months after we had begun our Iran-Contra investigation, around November of 1985.

"Do you got a minute to meet at the gook place?" he had asked. This was how Hoven identified the Vietnamese restaurant on the north side of Capitol Hill where we used to meet.

"Sure," I said. "What's up?"

"I'll tell ya about it when I see ya."

"OK," I said. I looked down at my watch. "It's 11:45 AM. What time do you want to meet?"

"How 'bout twelve?"

"Sure," I said, realizing that whatever he had to tell me, he thought it was important. "I'll see you there."

When I arrived, Hoven was already seated and in his usual fog bank of Camel smoke.

"This is gonna kill you, Hoven," I laughed, waving my way through the cloud of smoke.

"Yeah. Well, nobody gets outta life alive, pal." He rose and stuck out his big ham-sized right hand, seizing mine with his considerable strength.

"I always said that you missed your calling, Hoss. You shoulda been a professional wrestler."

He frowned. He preferred it when I called him a snake-eater. But then he laughed. "You sure are an asshole, Shee-han."

"Well. That's one of the reasons you love me, Hoss. It takes one to . . . *be* one."

He struggled, momentarily, with the implication of this surprise ending, turning it over a bit too slowly in his brain, trying to determine whether the switch implied some insult to him. Of course it did not. And once he'd determined this, his face filled with happy surprise and he laughed again and pulled me toward the empty seat at his table.

"I ordered the usual for us," he said. "Let's get down to it."

"Shoot."

"Last night I went over to one a those shirt 'n' tie affairs that the Heritage Foundation puts on."

I groaned.

He smiled. "Look, some of us gotta keep an eye on what those other guys are doin'."

"Whattaya mean *other guys,* white man?" I quipped, referencing the old kid's joke about the Lone Ranger and Tonto. Again, Hoven blinked. But he did not wait this time to translate my joke. Instead, he pressed on, acting on faith that I was not "harpooning" him, as he liked to say (by which he meant *lam*pooning).

"Well, while I'm there, there was this old guy, he musta been sixty, maybe sixty-five. Anyway, this guy is really sockin' 'em down. It was an open bar, and he was standin' right next ta the bar all night, putting away one after another. He was all by himself. An every time I went back for another beer, he would look at me and mumble sumthin', like he was talking ta me. But I wasn't sure. So the first few times I ignore the guy. You know. Ya never know about these Washington, D.C., types."

"Yeah," I shrugged, urging him to go on.

"Like the third or fourth time this guy does this, I kinda catch his eye, an' he gestures ta me to come over to talk ta him. And he asks me, he says, 'Hey, pal. You been in The Nam?' Surprised, I said, 'Yeah. Eye Corps. Two tours.' So then this guy lights up and throws his arm around me and drags me over to da bar an' says, 'Give my ole Vietnam buddy here another beer . . . and give me one more too.' Anyway, this guy takes me out onto the back porch, an' he starts ta cry on my shoulder about how some guy dat he was in business with, shipping 'humanitarian goods' down to Nicaragua ta da refugees fleein' from da comminists, had screwed him over, had lost one of his planes, an' how he was all pissed off an' such. Finally, I realize dat this guy seems ta know what the hell he's talking about. All the names were right. All the places he named were right. An', as he realized that I was listenin', he started ta get more an' more sober. Finally, dis guy is layin' dis story on me that was, well, it was sure as hell over my head. Then I remembered you! So I listen ta dis guy for a few more minutes, an' then I says ta him, 'Listen. I got this friend. He's kinda a brain, went ta Haavad, an' he can figure out what ya need ta do.'"

"What did he need to do?" I asked.

"What did he need ta do? Dey lost his plane!" he said.

"They lost his plane?"

Now Hoven was getting a little pissed off. "Yeah! I jus *told* ya. Dey lost his plane. An' I couldn't figure out what it wus he wus fuckin' talkin' about. But I knew you would. I wus jus' thinking, since you been looking for someone ta be a plaintiff for ya in dat lawsuit dat you wanna file against George

Bush and his pals down in Nicaragua. I wus figurin', dat maybe, jus' maybe, dis guy wus your guy. Ya know—loss of business property an' all dat shit."

I was genuinely impressed. Hoven had remembered everything that I had told him about how I was looking for a client to serve as a plaintiff in the federal civil Racketeering Act lawsuit I wanted to file against the former CIA associates of George Bush. Now here it was: another potential client.

Hoven set up a meet for me with this guy. The meet was to be at "a friend's place" out in Virginia. I didn't know whose friend, but it didn't make any difference to me, so I said yes.

Two days after my lunch with Hoven, I drove out to Virginia and met him at a roadside restaurant. He was waiting for me across the street from the restaurant in a borrowed car with cigarette smoke pouring out of the driver's side window. I parked Father Davis's Blue Flame in the parking lot behind the restaurant and waited. I knew Hoven was there from the smoke, but I humored him and waited for him to make his presence known. After several minutes, he knocked on my window, looking around and over his shoulder. I rolled down the old hand-cranked window of the Blue Flame.

"Coast is clear. Get out an' follow me."

We got into his cigarette-smoke-filled car and headed into the hills. We arrived at the meet at dusk. There were no other cars in sight. We got out and entered a nondescript house. It was unlocked. As we entered the small living room, I could see, in the growing darkness, the outline of a man sitting in a large overstuffed chair. A bottle of beer sat on the table to his right.

I sat on the end of the couch, facing the man. Even though it was growing steadily darker, neither Hoven nor the man made any move to turn on a light. I sat waiting. Hoven left and went into the kitchen. I heard him open the refrigerator and take out a bottle of beer. The sound of him opening the bottle filled the silence. Then he came back into the small living room and leaned silently against the doorjamb.

I said nothing. The man in the dark said nothing. He reached to his right and picked up his bottle of beer.

"You don't drink?" he asked into the darkness between us.

"The Brits invented whiskey to keep the Irish from taking over the world," I replied flatly.

He laughed, despite his obvious preparations to emphasize the solem-
nity of the moment. Then it was silent again. He would try to reestablish
the mood.

Then, "Hoss tells me that you're a pretty bright guy."

"He's confused because he thinks I'm a Jesuit."

Again the man laughed, despite himself. "And you're not?"

"No. Not yet. But I'm a candidate for the Jesuits. Right now I'm just
their lawyer."

"Worse yet," he drawled.

I recognized the accent.

"Oklahoma . . . " I said. "Up around Tulsa." Silence filled the room.

"Pretty bright boy," he said finally. "Even if you're not a Jesuit."

"Yet," I added.

"Yet," he replied. Finally, after a long minute, he spoke again. "Hoss
tell you what is going on?"

"Something about your losing one of your planes." Silence again. After
a long moment I decided to risk it. "You want to tell me about it?"

"Why should I?"

"Why shouldn't you?"

He laughed again. Hoven laughed too, somewhere behind me.

"I don't even know who you are," the man answered.

"You know more about me than I know about you," I said.

"Well, just what do you know about me?" he asked.

"Well, I know you come from Oklahoma. You probably served in the
air force." I guessed, since I knew that he owned a plane. And I also guessed
that he was OSI (Office of Special Investigations) because I knew that Hoven
had met him at the Heritage Foundation, which was involved in the higher
end of right-wing activities, but I didn't mention that part.

Silence. Then, "Even Hoss here didn't get that. So I guess he didn't tell
you that."

"You just did," I said, trying to draw him out.

"A wise man never gives away his tradecraft," he offered.

"I never said I was wise."

"Just smart."

"Let's say 'well educated'."

"By the Jesuits?"

"No, by Henry Kissinger, Edwin Reischauer, James Schlesinger, and John Kenneth Galbraith," I stated.

"Well, three out of four ain't bad."

Now I laughed. Then he laughed too. Hoven joined in from behind, and the ice was broken. I suspected that Hoven didn't know what we were talking about or why it was so funny.

The man in the shadows then pulled himself forward onto the front edge of the cushion of the large overstuffed armchair that had held him in its folds until that moment.

"Hoss told you that I had lost a plane," he said.

"And that you had been fucked over by the guy that had talked you into letting him use your plane to ship weapons down to the Contras." I ventured the latter based upon what little Hoven had told me.

The man stiffened, his head snapping back in the shadows. "What makes you say that?"

"Well, I know that you weren't flying humanitarian goods to any refugees from the communists in Nicaragua because there aren't any refugees from the communists in Nicaragua—except the Contras, and they're not interested in humanitarian goods. They're interested in guns, and ammunition, and explosives."

"And what else?"

Ah, here it comes, I thought. "And cocaine," I said, surprised at how simply it had come out.

"Bingo!" he said. "These men lost one of my planes after I had agreed to let them use it. Actually, I was letting them use twenty."

I was a little shocked and showed it. Did he mean twenty planes?

"Yeah," he said, noting my surprise. "Twenty of them little mini C-130s, drop-tails, like the big C-130 but smaller. Smaller payloads but easier to move around. Civilian jobs. Not military."

"Oh?" I said, not bothering to disguise my ignorance. I had already stretched what I knew and what I had only guessed to the limit. And it had worked. So I wanted to proceed from this point on on as solid a footing as

I could. It was clear that this guy knew a bunch, and I didn't want to say something wrong now that he was talking that might make him stop.

"After I had let them use the planes to fly humanitarian supplies to the Contras"—he was not going to admit that his planes had been flying weapons and explosives—"those bastards loaded one of my planes up with cocaine on its way back from El Salvador. It went down in the Caribbean on its way back into the States. They told me that I couldn't file any insurance claim because if I did, insurance investigators might go looking for it to confirm that it had really been lost—and they might discover it lying there under shallow water filled with cocaine. So I'm supposed to eat it. That's a one-million-dollar aircraft!"

"That's pretty steep," I said, trying to encourage him to continue with his story.

And he did. He proceeded to tell me that he had been contacted by a man he had known in the Marine Corps in Vietnam. He clarified here that he'd been in the air force—OSI, just like I'd thought. But he was in the Marine Corps before that, back in the '60s. He went into the air force in the '70s and had been security chief at Khe Sanh when he was in the Marines.

"Holy Shit!" I exclaimed without thinking. "What the fuck was *second* prize?"

"No shit, Sherlock," he replied, now realizing that I did know what I was talking about.

My years with Bill Taylor were paying off here, big-time. That was how I knew about Khe Sanh. It had been the American Dien Bien Phu, a reference to the decisive battle in which the French had been surrounded and defeated by General Giáp of the Vietnamese army, forcing France to withdraw from Vietnam back in 1954. Khe Sanh had been one of the historic nightmares of the United States Marine Corps, right alongside the Inchon Reservoir in Korea, at which seventeen thousand Marines had been slaughtered by the Chinese back in 1950. I was sitting across the room from the chief of security for the U.S. Marine Corps at Khe Sanh. *Holy shit!* I exclaimed to myself. *This guy is part of the woodwork.*

"In the OSI, I was in charge of the criminal investigation of Dick Secord when he was deputy comptroller to the Defense Security Assistance Agency

(DSAA) under Howard Fish. That was when Secord was suspected of skimming monies from DSAA military contracts between the Pentagon and the shah of Iran and the House of Saud in Saudi Arabia."

Holy shit, I thought to myself again. *This guy* is *the woodwork!*

"Yeah, go on," I said, as gently as I could. I didn't want to do anything to stop this guy from talking. He was a gold mine.

"When majors Turner and Schaffer were both murdered during our investigation of Secord, I knew that something was dirty as shit. So when OSI called off the investigation, under pressure from above, I kept on investigating Secord until I figured out what was happening." He stopped.

I waited. I worried that if I tried to push him to give me more information, or more detail than he was willing to give at any given moment, that this meeting would come to an abrupt end, just like that, and I would probably never get to see him again. So I waited.

And waited.

He was waiting me out, to see if I was going to pry. I wasn't. After a full two minutes, he asked me the first serious question he had asked since I had come into the house.

"So what is it that you're after or whoever you're working for is after?"

This caught me off guard. It hadn't dawned on me that he would have thought that I was working *for* anyone. Then I realized . . . Hoven. Hoven thought that I could be working for someone, and he must have put this idea into the man's head. Now I had to decide whether it was to the advantage of this project or not to let him continue to believe that I was working *for* somebody or to tell him the flat truth: that I was doing this for myself, or, more accurately, that I was doing this for everybody—for everybody who believed in our Constitution, for everybody who believed in the rule of law, for everybody who believed in democracy, for everybody who believed in our country.

But I didn't believe that would sell. So I decided to let this play out a bit more before I answered.

"Working for?" I asked.

"Yeah. Like whoever is paying your bills, whoever is paying your salary."

"Oh, *that* somebody." I breathed, relieved that this was all he was looking for. "Actually, I don't get paid shit. And I don't know who is going to pay for this investigation. I'm not even sure exactly what 'this investigation' is . . . yet."

The man in the shadows laughed.

"I sure as shit know what that's all about," he said. "I've been carrying on this investigation for almost fifteen years now, and I haven't gotten paid a fucking dime."

This was my opening. Something about the way that he had said that led me to believe that he was looking for a *financial* partner to help cover the expenses of what he clearly viewed to be *his* investigation.

"And what, exactly, is 'this' investigation?" I asked.

He laughed. "It's one hell of a lot more than a few weapons being shipped to Nicaragua, son. I can goddamn guarantee that! And it's about one whole hell of a lot more than just one fucking press conference getting blown up and a bunch of commie reporters getting blown up! "

I wasn't going to take that bait.

And I had to tread lightly here. He obviously wanted to know the financial and political sponsor of *my* investigation. I did not want to lie to this man. Not only was I opposed to doing that for ethical and metaphysical reasons, I was also opposed to lying to him for practical reasons. I had no way of knowing what the right answer was. I knew, of course, that if I had been working for the KGB or for some South American communist movement, I would certainly not be acceptable to this guy. He had been at the Heritage Foundation, for Pete's sake. But I didn't know whether he was merely a conservative or if he was a reactionary—or CIA or DIA or DEA—or what.

"Ah, exactly how much do you think this investigation might cost if it were going to be done in a completely professional and competent manner?" I asked. "And how long do you think it will take?"

The man lit up. I could see that even in the darkness of the room. And it was now fully night. He pulled himself up to the edge of the cushion of his seat again and stared through the darkness at me. I could feel his glare. This was the moment this meet had been all about.

Then he settled back into his big overstuffed chair and said, "OK, Hoss. You can turn the lights on now."

When the lights came on, I was sitting across from Gene Wheaton: the sixty-five-year-old former chief of security for the United States Marine Corps at Khe Sanh; a former master sergeant in the United States Marine Corps CID; the former chief OSI investigator for the United States Air Force assigned to investigate Major General Richard V. Secord; and the former U.S. Army Chief of Security for the United States military mission in Tehran, Iran. It was through his last assignment that he came to know the key to the Iran-Contra investigation.

"Do you have a pencil and paper, son?" he asked. "This is gonna be a long, long story."

"Go ahead, Sir. I have a good memory."

"So do I, son. So do I."

Over a series of several long face-to-face meetings between November 1985 and May 1986, Eugene Wheaton revealed more to me about his experience at the U.S. military mission in Tehran. Gene knew everybody who was anybody in Iran. He knew officials in the SAVAK, Iran's secret military police. He spoke fluent Farsi; and he knew the shah of Iran personally. In fact, he knew the entire Pahlavi family. Eventually he started to tell me how he had come to own a private commercial air cargo operation and how he had been approached by a man (whose name he wouldn't give me at first) who asked if he would consider making his planes available to fly "civilian humanitarian goods" to the poor refugees in Nicaragua who had been displaced by those nasty Sandinistas. But there were no such refugees. In fact, they were actually flying boots, clothing, and equipment to the Contras . . . at first. He had agreed to do that. And ultimately that had led to his plane going down in the Caribbean with cocaine in it, after he had graduated to allowing his planes to fly military equipment and weapons to the Contras.

Angry about this, Wheaton had started to investigate to see how that had happened to his plane. Pursuant to that investigation, he was introduced to Rob Owen, who turned out to be the former Latin American staff person to Senator Dan Quayle of Indiana. When Owen realized that Gene Wheaton was experienced with smuggling weapons to the Contras in Central America and to the Mujahedeen in Afghanistan, Owen introduced Gene directly to United States Marine Corps lieutenant colonel Oliver North, the deputy director of the Reagan–Bush administration's National Security Council in Charge of Anti-Terrorism.

I started to get the sense that the reason Gene Wheaton wanted to keep talking to me had to do with more than just the fact that he was pissed off about losing some of one of his planes. After several more meetings with him, I discovered that the same people involved in directing the smuggling of weapons to the Contras had been directly involved in directing the covert political assassination operations of our clandestine services. Wheaton then told me about that. He had been preparing to retire as the chief of security of the U.S. military mission in Tehran and had been offered a job as chief of security for a private over-the-horizon radar operation in the Middle East. While Gene was literally waiting for the CEO of that private American corporation to arrive at Gene's final interview for the position, that CEO had been assassinated. Wheaton had undertaken an independent investigation (using all the resources at his disposal) to determine who had assassinated his prospective CEO and why. That investigation had led him to the conclusion that the assassination group had been led by one Edwin P. Wilson, an American CIA "retiree" who was, in fact, working for Moamar Kadafi in Libya. Wilson, after allegedly "retiring" from the CIA, had built a "clean room" for Kadafi in Libya and was providing sophisticated, radio-activated triggers for bombing devices, which Kadafi was providing to Middle Eastern "freedom fighters," along with training in how to use them.

Gene Wheaton and I formed a positive working relationship, pursuant to which he would communicate his information to me. I would then investigate it, confirm it to my independent satisfaction, and then come back and gather more information from him. Wheaton's information was specific and detailed, and that made it easier for my professional investigators to confirm. These investigators were headed up by Bill Taylor (and all of his extraordinary sources), and included Bob Fink, Howard Rosenberg, Howard Kohn, and of course Father Bill Davis, who gave me access to the information gathered by over ten thousand Jesuit missionaries around the world.

As I began to confirm the validity of Wheaton's information, Bill Taylor and our team of investigators began to assemble a basic blueprint of what the entire operation of "the enterprise" looked like. The man who had approached Gene to make his twenty mini C-130 airplanes available for the Contras had been one Carl Jenkins. Jenkins had been the CIA liaison officer between Theodore G. Shackley, chief of station of the CIA in Saigon (and earlier in Laos), and Vang Pao, a Laotian opium warlord. As the CIA station chief in Laos, Shackley wanted to institute a major political assassination program that was going to require a lot of money. Shackley decided to make an offer to one of the three Laotian opium warlords to eliminate that man's two principal opium competitors. In exchange, the now-monopoly-controlling warlord would give Shackley an agreed-upon percentage of the profits from his then-increased opium sales. This was the deal that Shackley had cut with Vang Pao back in 1967. Gene Wheaton knew about this because Carl Jenkins had explained it to him.

Carl Jenkins was also a former U.S. Marine who had been transferred to the U.S. Army Special Forces at its very birth and who had been brought on to train elite covert operatives for the Bay of Pigs invasion in the Miami station back in the early '60s. Jenkins had been deeply involved in training the Miami-based anti-Castro Cuban exiles. As it turned out, Carl Jenkins was the chief trainer of the S-Force, put together at the direct request of Richard Nixon in July 1960, and trained in Oaxaca, Mexico, to assassinate Fidel Castro, Raúl Castro, Che Guevara, and five other leaders of the Cuban revolutionary government. Jenkins had also been the chief trainer and CIA case officer of the top two men in the Ilopango military weapons–supply operation to the Contras, Felix Rodriguez and Rafael "Chi Chi" Quintero. With this connection to Jenkins, Bill Taylor and I had struck a gold mine of information. Not only did we have Gene Wheaton, who seemed to know all about the very things we needed to know, but Wheaton was also in regular communication with Jenkins, to whom he eventually agreed to introduce me. Jenkins knew *everything* . . . and I mean *everything!*

I drove out of Washington, D.C., crossed the Key Bridge into Virginia, and drove to a safe house to meet Carl Jenkins. Gene picked me up one block from the U.S. Conference of Catholic Bishops headquarters on Massachusetts Avenue, literally in the shadow of the large statue of "Jesus hailing a cab" on Embassy Row. I had arranged for Gene to pick me up there to continue the mystique that I had allowed to persist regarding the mysterious alliance that was "sponsoring" me. No matter how many times I tried to convince Gene that I was an independent like him, he refused to believe me. So I started having him meet me a short distance from various locations where I actually did have some "connections." The U.S. Conference of Catholic Bishops was one such place. Wheaton smiled as he leaned across the front seat and swung open the passenger side door of his beige Mercedes station wagon.

"Are you ready to meet the big man?" Gene asked as he wheeled the big station wagon out into Mass Ave traffic. As of that point, he hadn't told me who we were going to meet.

I looked at him quizzically. "Shackley?"

Gene laughed out loud. "Yeah. Well, right. But . . . who below that?"

I thought about it. "Vernon Walters?"

"Well, I guess, yeah." Wheaton wrestled the big steering wheel of the Mercedes from Mass Ave into Dupont Circle, around the circle, and down Fourteenth Street toward downtown Washington. He seemed impressed with my guesses, but it was clear that that was not who he had in mind. "But who below that?"

I realized that he was thinking of the big man from his bottom up, not from the top down. "Oh, Carl!"

"Right!"

Wheaton turned right and headed toward Georgetown.

We drove in silence, driving through Georgetown, slowly passing wealthy women shoppers, university students, tourists, and lobbyists. Gene turned left and crossed the Potomac. The rapids were off to our right, and Washington, D.C., lay off to our left. As we approached the Key Bridge Marriott, Wheaton seemed to concentrate on staring straight ahead a little too intensely I thought.

"Ah, the Key Bridge Marriott," I said.

Gene looked suddenly surprised—and nervous. "Why would you say that?"

From Bill Taylor's source Alpha, Bill had learned that many highly secret meetings among spooks took place at the Key Bridge Marriott. But this was known only by "inside men." I had inadvertently revealed to Wheaton that I knew this. I was caught in a strange game, having to pretend to know more than I knew one day and less than I knew the next. I was used to telling the truth, flat out, and then challenging others to do the same, assuming that whomever I was talking with would want to achieve the same end as I. However, that was not the case with men like Gene Wheaton—and, I guessed, like Carl Jenkins.

I tried to gloss over this slip. "I don't know. It just occurred to me that that might be where we were going."

After a long moment, he said, "No. It's somewhere else. Someplace more . . . private."

After more long moments of driving in silence, Gene said to me, still looking straight ahead, "It will be important for you to level with this guy. He's pretty much a straight-from-the-shoulder type of guy. Just level with him."

"OK," I said.

"If Carl gets up and leaves the room and comes back in with Elizabeth, his wife, then you will have passed your first test with him. But then you will have to deal with Elizabeth. Then you will be dealing with the *real* agency."

"I thought you said that Carl *was* the agency."

"*Was* agency. Carl is retired from the agency now. Elizabeth is still active." He hesitated for effect. "She is a full colonel in the agency, a G-14. She is the head of psychological evaluation."

"Holy shit," I exclaimed. Wheaton loved surprising me. I think it was part of his effort to figure out who I was.

"You'll have to be very careful of her. She'll have to tell the agency everything she does, even when she is moonlighting for Carl. You know, the monthly polygraph."

"Polygraph?" I asked. "I would think that, at her level, they would use the Psychological Stress Evaluator (PSE)."

Wheaton was shocked again. He actually pulled the big Mercedes over to the side of the road and stopped in the breakdown lane. He turned off the ignition, turned, and looked directly at me with the most serious expression that I had seen on his face to date.

"Look, my young Irish friend, you had better not fuck with this guy. This guy makes people dead. D-E-A-D *dead!* If you're working for some kind of intel outfit—either one of ours or one of theirs—you had better god-damn level with me, right now, before we get to Carl's, or at least before we get to Elizabeth." Again he invoked the name of Elizabeth as though he were invoking a demon. "Now I want you to tell me exactly who you are working for, or working with, or who you're reporting to, before we go any farther on this thing."

I didn't know whether Wheaton was bluffing or telling the truth. Hell, I didn't even know if we were, in fact, on the way to meet with Carl Jenkins. This could all have been a simple ruse on the part of Wheaton to get me to tell him what he had been trying to figure out for the past two months. But I actually had nothing to hide, even if I had allowed Wheaton to draw a series of less-than-entirely-correct conclusions about me. So I told him the following:

> When we were investigating and litigating the Karen Silkwood case, the Kerr-McGee Corporation attorneys and investigators had spent half of their time and energy trying to figure out who we *really* were and who we were working *for* instead of focusing on what we were actually saying and doing. They couldn't believe that we were just a bunch American citizens who were pissed off that they had killed one of our generation and that nobody was going to do anything about it. However, because *they* were representing people and forces behind the scenes, and they were lying about it, they simply assumed that we were too. It reminds me of what an old CIA friend of mine told me once. He said, "These are the kind of guys who will climb up a tree to tell a lie, even when it would be in their best interest to simply stand flat on the ground and tell the truth."

Wheaton just stared at me. Then he calmly reached up, turned on the ignition, and quietly guided the Mercedes back out onto the roadway. After driving a few more miles, he negotiated several suburban side streets and gestured to a small, tan-shingled home in a quiet Virginia suburb. He drove past the house to the end of the block, turned around, and parked the big Mercedes on a side street, out of sight.

We walked the length of the block back to the house. It was a small house with dark-green shutters, a freshly mowed front lawn, and off-white stucco walls with some brown shingles. Gene led the way up the short side-walk to the house. But rather than go to the front door, he led me around to the back. He rang the bit-too-loud doorbell twice. He waited a few seconds. Then he rang it three times more.

A quiet buzz released the lock. He turned the knob and walked in, with me closely behind. As we entered through a small kitchen and into the small living room, Carl Jenkins rose from the couch and rolled from side to side, like an old sailor, as he glided across the tiny living room toward Gene. He held out his large right hand at the end of a short, muscled forearm. I saw the way he held his right elbow tightly to his side so he would draw Gene closer in to shake his hand—within his area of control, like a skilled wrestler. He was a short, burly, barrel-chested man of unascertainable age. His hair was dark black and cut in a military-style, flattop crew cut. His face was surprisingly open, though deeply tanned and leathery. He was wearing a red-and-black plaid flannel hunting shirt, tucked in at the waist, dark work pants, and a pair of dark work shoes. He reminded me immediately of the actor Fred Ward from *Tremors*.

The room was stark—masculine and cold. There were no pictures on the walls. I was suddenly aware that there was some kind of covering on the windows, between the venetian blinds and the windowpanes. All that was in the room were three wooden chairs and a big overstuffed couch against the far right wall, from which he had risen to greet us. The room was bathed in an eerie deep-yellow golden light with an off-orange tint, like an old tintype Western photo. This effect, I noticed, was caused by the venetian blinds being pulled against the bright outside sunlight, along with whatever was covering the windows. I got the distinct feeling that no one really lived here. It was a safe house.

"Carl Jenkins . . . Danny Sheehan," Gene said, introducing us. He turned back toward Carl and added, "The leprechaun that I've been telling you about."

Jenkins extended his big leathery hand toward mine, and I seized it, giving him the old Bill Taylor vise grip. I could tell that a solid handshake was going to be important to a man like this. Our eyes locked. His were battleship gray with a memory of blue in tiny crystal circles surrounding his pupils. The color of mercury came to mind. I looked down into the man, through those mercury windows of his soul, for several long seconds, and he looked up into mine. Our handshake remained tight and locked.

He smiled a smile that I had never seen before—at the same time sinister and sincere, warm and threatening, chilling, yet setting me at ease. I remember thinking that it was truly a unique moment. This was Carl Jenkins, the trainer of men who killed other men for a living.

Finally he broke eye contact and gestured toward one of the wooden chairs. I moved past him and took a place at the right end of the overstuffed sofa. He bristled, but only for a microsecond, before sliding onto the extreme other end of the couch. Gene awkwardly turned and surveyed all three of the still-empty wooden chairs before deciding to sit on the center chair.

"So," Carl growled. "Gene here tells me that you and your friends are interested in suing somebody down in Central America for *allegedly* shipping weapons and explosives to the Contras from here in the U.S.?"

"Not exactly, Sir," I said, fully aware of the importance of the first impression I would make. "Not my friends. *I* am going to sue John Hull, Adolfo Calero, and their associates in the Nicaraguan Democratic Force (FDN) Contra organization for violating the federal civil Racketeering Act. And I am going to sue them not only for shipping weapons and explosives to the Contras in and around Nicaragua, in direct violation of the Boland Amendment, but also for smuggling cocaine back into the United States, which is a violation of the federal Controlled Substances Act."

"Well, that's pretty tough talk for a one-eyed fat man," he stated drolly, making an oblique reference to a famous line uttered to John Wayne playing Marshal Rooster Cogburn in *True Grit*.

"Well, Sir. Those sons of bitches had better fill their hands, because I'm comin' after 'em," I said, quoting John Wayne's reply in the film.

The barrel-chested man threw back his head and bellowed a loud laugh to the ceiling. He laughed for a full ten seconds before he composed himself again.

"Well, I like your spirit, son," he managed to say. "And just what's in this for you?" He was good. He had slipped in one of his most important questions, almost as a point of humor.

But I wasn't going to respond to it as a humorous question. My stare grew serious. "I uncovered this operation while I was defending a young sixteen-year-old girl and her six-month-old baby from El Salvador, Sir. She had swum across the Rio Grande with her baby in her arms, after seeing the doctor she worked for as a medical assistant in El Salvador murdered right in front of her, and seeing her associate medical assistant wired to a pole in the center of her town and having her eight-month-old fetus cut from her womb and run through with a bayonet and paraded through her town for their having provided medical assistance to a child who had been shot by a right-wing death squad."

A thick and ominous silence fell over the room. I waited for a long moment before I continued.

"I don't pretend to have seen the kind of horror that you have seen, Sir. Both of you, I imagine," I added, looking at Gene. "I refused to stay in the Green Berets after being instructed to kill women and children if they saw me HALO into their hometown behind enemy lines in Vietnam. I never saw the horrors of war. My father did, on the beach at Salerno. And I know that you two men have as well. I'm not telling you anything that you don't know even better than I. So, are you going to help me stop these bastards, or are you going to oppose me and become my enemies?"

The two men stirred uncomfortably.

Then I said, "I certainly wouldn't want that. But I'm hoping that you are better men than Ted Shackley and that bastard Otto Skorzeny who trained him."

"Ah . . . just a minute, son," Jenkins said. "I want ta go git my Mrs." He pulled himself from the couch and, almost as if he were in pain, started his slow rolling motion toward a side room that I judged to be a small bedroom.

"Could I get you something to drink? A Coke, a beer?" he asked over his shoulder.

"He doesn't drink alcohol, Carl. He says it's because the Brits invented whiskey to keep the Irish from takin' over the world." He laughed his way through the final words of the quote.

"So, a Coke, then?"

"A Coke would be fine, Sir." I hated Coke. I remembered the story about how a copper penny would completely dissolve in a glass of Coke if it were left submerged overnight. But I didn't want to get too far out of line with these men if I was going to have any hope of securing their trust and cooperation in helping me get to the bottom of this investigation.

I could hear a brief and muffled conversation with a woman after Carl went into the other room. Then he came out and went directly into the tiny kitchen. Within a minute, Elizabeth Jenkins emerged from the side room. She was big. Bigger than Carl in a way. She was taller and heavier—at least broader. She was big-shouldered, big-chested, big-bottomed, and, as it turned out, big-voiced.

She moved smoothly across the living room, her right hand extended. I rose in a self-conscious effort to be a gentleman. She appreciated the gesture. Gene smirked and rolled his eyes at me over the move. As she approached, I reached out and shook her hand. Firm, but not forced. She smiled, seemingly genuinely.

I offered her my seat and took one of the wooden chairs immediately across from her. She sat comfortably, allowing the silence. She was waiting to see if I was going to speak. I didn't.

Within a few moments Carl came back with a tray holding four water glasses filled to the brim with Coke and ice. He held out the tray, first to Elizabeth, then to me, and finally to Gene. Then he settled onto the cushion on the far end of the couch where he had been seated earlier.

"Gene tells us that you're interested in stopping the flow of weapons to the Contras in Central America?" Elizabeth half-asked and half-stated.

"And the supply of cocaine back into the States," I added.

"And the cocaine back into the United States," she echoed, casting a quick half-glance at Carl. I waited. "Gene seems to think that you believe that we can be of some assistance?"

"I do," I said.

"And what makes you think that?"

I smiled. "Well that depends entirely upon how much you are willing to acknowledge that you know about this operation." Then I quickly corrected myself, "About operations *like* this."

"And exactly what is 'this operation' *like?*" she asked with a Cheshire cat smile.

"Well, that's the question I think we're here to discuss. Aren't we?" I turned slowly from Elizabeth to Carl to Gene.

"What do you mean by that?" she pressed.

I moved forward slightly, to the edge of my chair. *Here it goes,* I thought.

"If this is just a straightforward covert operation of the CIA Operations Directorate, being undertaken pursuant to the express authorization of the president—the written authorization, that is, in light of new amendments to the National Security Act passed last year—then this is a simple impeachment case. The president will be impeached. The vice president will be impeached. Bill Casey will be impeached. And probably several other men, such as Elliott Abrams and Dewey Clarridge. And my federal civil lawsuit will be dismissed, pursuant to rule 12(b)(6) of the federal rules of civil procedure, in the face of the invocation, by the president, of the doctrine of sovereign immunity."

A cold chill descended over the room. I moved quickly to my major point.

"On the other hand, if this is an off-the-shelf operation being conducted by *former* CIA operatives like Ted Shackley—and this operation has not been expressly authorized by the president in writing—and these people are smuggling cocaine into the United States to finance the purchase of the weapons being shipped down to the Contras through John Hull's ranch in Costa Rica and by Woody Jenkins and Adolfo Calero's brother down in New Orleans . . . " Both Gene Wheaton and Carl Jenkins went rigid at my identification of these two specific locations and two specific individuals. I pressed forward, " . . . then this would be a classic federal criminal racketeering enterprise, devoid of any sovereign immunity, and those men will go to prison, just as they should."

I stopped. *Prison?* I could see them all asking themselves.

"Is there anything that you believe I've left out?" I asked. "You see, this is the moment you've all been waiting for. The moment when the chickens come home to roost. These guys have just stepped so far outside the lines that they are now vulnerable. The question is, how vulnerable?"

After a long pause, Carl spoke. "And that depends on what?"

"That depends on you," I said.

His head jerked back slightly.

And I turned to Elizabeth. "And you, too, I would judge. Because there is going to have to be some decision on the part of the agency as to how much protection these guys are going to be given, both inside and outside of the administration."

"I spoke with Sporkin last week," Carl said, turning to Gene. Stanley Sporkin was general counsel for the Central Intelligence Agency. "Sporkin said, 'Shackley's operation is not ours.' He was emphatic about it. 'Shackley's operation is not ours.'"

"Just what is motivating you to do this?" Elizabeth asked me. "Who are you working with? Who is funding you?"

That question again. These people had lived their entire professional lives in the shadows, working in clandestine operations for the CIA. It was in their blood. I had to be working *for* somebody. Things couldn't be as simple as they were professed to be.

"Look," I said. "I didn't even plan to be doing this kind of thing. I was planning to become an astronaut!"

Then I told Elizabeth Jenkins, the chief of psychological evaluation of the CIA, my story. I told her about my childhood. I told her about my father. I told her about what I used to imagine when I stared up into the stars at night. And I told her about missing out on the Air Force Academy and going to Harvard and everything leading up to the Karen Silkwood case and the American Sanctuary Movement.

"I'm not a complicated person, Mrs. Jenkins." I was determined to tell them the truth—the whole truth.

I was convinced that if they only understood, they would help me. Not because it was me who wanted to do this but because it was all of us who wanted to do this—because my story was not my story alone. It was the story of our country. It was the story of our time. It was the story of our reason to bring this whole set of practices to a stop.

I told them that I was doing this for my father, whom I really never knew. I was doing this for the tiny woman and her child in Vietnam whom I did *not* kill but who were killed by some other young American in my stead, a young American who had not known enough *not* to go. And I was doing this because my country had *asked* me to do this, in everything that it had ever taught to me and in everything that I had ever read about what it is that we were doing here together—as Americans.

I finished by saying, "Look, we only get a short time to be here on this earth. Eighty maybe ninety years. We are part of a long line of other people who have come and gone. Some have made our world a better place while they were here. Others have made it worse. I intend to make it a better place than it was when I arrived. I think you do too. I hope we can find a way to work together and make this happen."

Elizabeth turned to Carl, and Carl turned to Elizabeth. Both had tears in their eyes. I had tears in my eyes.

"Let's do this!" Elizabeth said.

Carl growled his consent. "Let's do it."

Carl Jenkins, as it turned out, had been interested in blowing the whistle on this operation because he had become truly upset that these men were smuggling cocaine into our country, just as he had been upset about these same men smuggling opium out of Southeast Asia and heroin into the United States years before. This was a man who did not mind killing innocent Asian civilians in the Phoenix Project. But the smuggling of heroin into the United States upset him. Gene Wheaton was the opposite: He didn't mind the smuggling of the cocaine all that much, but having people he knew being assassinated—Americans getting assassinated by other Americans—*that* bothered him.

I spent weeks getting to know these two men and trying to determine where they were coming from, what was actually going on inside their minds, constantly aware of the possibility that they were trying to play me. I came to the conclusion that they were upset about the excesses of the Central Intelligence Agency. They were not in any way opposed to the basic mission of the CIA or to the agency's covert operations. They weren't opposed to espionage. But they didn't like these "excesses." They didn't like the heroin and the cocaine smuggling and the assassination of Americans. So we worked out a deal. Carl Jenkins and Gene Wheaton would funnel information directly to me, and I agreed that I would not go after the CIA as such but would focus only on knocking out these "excesses."

The deal had been struck. I *hoped* that it had not been a deal made with the devil.

CHAPTER *twenty-seven*

BEGAN TO PIECE together the very top of the "strategic" structure of "the enterprise." I narrowed in quickly on Rafael "Chi Chi" Quintero, whom Jenkins had overseen as his former CIA case officer. Chi Chi Quintero had been recruited into the S-Force. After the overthrow of the fascist dictatorship of Anastasio Somoza in Nicaragua in July 1979, Chi Chi had become part of the operation headed up by Edwin P. Wilson to transfer illegal weapons, ammunition, and explosives to former Nicaraguan National Guard troops who had fled Nicaragua with Somoza. Then, when Ronald Reagan and George H. W. Bush had been elected in November 1980, Chi Chi had become the number 2 man at the Ilopango Airport in El Salvador, overseeing the smuggling of arms flown in from the United States and distributed to the Contras by the Reagan–Bush administration. Quintero, who was in regular communication with Carl Jenkins, sat immediately under Felix Rodriguez, a.k.a. Max Gomez, the chief operations officer for the whole Contra weapons-supply and cocaine-smuggling operation.

Chi Chi had been reporting all of these activities, in detail, to his former CIA case officer, Carl Jenkins. I had hit the the mother lode.

The entire off-the-shelf enterprise had been created by Theodore G. Shackley, the Deputy Director of Covert Operations when George H. W. Bush directed the agency from 1976 to 1977. Jenkins explained that Shackley had started creating "the enterprise" as far back as 1974, when Shackley was director of Far East operations for the agency in the closing months of the Vietnam War. He had created it to be a self-financing, private, covert operations organization, complete with its own air force under the command of retired U.S. Air Force major general Richard V. Secord; its own army under the command of retired U.S. Army major general John K. Singlaub, the former commander of all Western ground forces in South Korea, who, after having been fired by Jimmy Carter, had become worldwide president of the World Anti-Communist League, a group of out-and-out fascists; and its own navy, operating under the auspices of a private maritime company named ANV, Inc., based on the peninsula of Jupiter, Florida.

Shackley had begun to plan "the enterprise" as soon as he realized that Richard Nixon was going to withdraw from Southeast Asia and "abandon" the anticommunist crusade that Nixon and others had recruited and trained Shackley and his covert operations specialists to prosecute for them starting in the waning months of World War II. Shackley viewed this withdrawal to be an act of political cowardice on the part of Nixon, and a personal betrayal of him, his men, and the anticommunist allies whom Shackley had been ordered to support and sustain in power from South America through Central America to the Middle East and Southeast Asia. So, beginning in 1974, Shackley, from his postition as the director of Far East operations for the CIA, had begun to coordinate the theft of literally thousands of tons of U.S. arms, military equipment, explosives, and ammunition, which he had his operatives in the field falsely report as having been "lost to the Viet Cong" during the closing months of the Vietnam War. Shackley had had the arms, military equipment, explosives, and ammunition secretly transported to several huge airplane hangars that he had had constructed at the Udorne Air Base in Thailand and secreted them there until the end of the war. Then, between 1976 and 1977, when he was Deputy Director of Covert Operations of the Central Intelligence Agency under George H. W. Bush, with the direct assistance of Edwin P. Wilson, Shackley had created a parent corporation for a number of private covert operations companies to carry out the equivalent functions of the Covert Operations Directorate of the CIA and its Joint Special Operations Command ally inside the Pentagon. This private parent corporation was the Egyptian American Transport and Service Company (EATSCO).

As Carl Jenkins and Gene Wheaton provided this strategic information to me, I brought it directly to Bill Taylor, Howard Rosenberg, Howard Kohn, and Bob Fink, who then proceeded to independently verify it. Since we knew ahead of time exactly what we were looking for, that made it far easier to confirm from independent sources exactly what was going on—while protecting the identity of our confidential source, who was none other than Rafael "Chi Chi" Quintero, the number 2 man in the entire Contra weapons supply operation.

Immediately below that top "strategic" level of the operation, I had sources that Brian Barger and Robert Parry were developing to explicate the "tactical" level of the operations of "the enterprise." Brian had acquired access to these sources through Tom Posey, who described to him the *tactical* details as to how "the enterprise" smuggled weapons out of the Fort Lauderdale/Hollywood Airport, through Ilopango Airport, onto John Hull's ranch in Costa Rica, and then to the Contras. Through Bill Taylor, we then had access to the Louisiana State National Guard commander, who could recount to us the logistics of the transfer of United States government weapons to civilian defense forces on the ground, who then moved these weapons and explosives to the Fort Lauderdale/Hollywood Airport.

I was therefore able to draft a federal civil complaint that named all of these men, at the strategic, tactical, and logistical level of the enterprise, describing in detail the specific violations of the Neutrality Act; the illegal weapons-supply operations; the violation of end-user certification rules; and the violations of customs regulations that each of these operatives were committing.

To safely file within the statute of limitations period, we had a filing deadline of May 28, 1986. I drafted the complaint and took it to Scott Armstrong, executive director of the National Security Archive, in early May of 1986. Armstrong had been an investigator on the staff of Peter Rodino, the chairman of the House Judiciary Committee, during the Watergate burglary hearings. Indeed, it had been Scott Armstrong who had gotten Alexander Butterfield, one of Nixon's chief administrative assistants, to admit in an interview with Armstrong that there was an electronic tape-recording system set up in the Oval Office. This then enabled Armstrong to subpoena the tapes of Richard Nixon and prove that Nixon had almost certainly ordered the Watergate burglary and that he had definitely directed the cover-up. Because of the central role that Scott Armstrong had played in bringing down Richard Nixon, he had become a rather famous celebrity in Washington, D.C. circles and had been made director of the National

Security Archive. I walked over to the archive from our Jesuit headquarters office just up the street on Massachusetts Avenue and asked Scott to read the draft of our federal civil complaint and to let me know what kind of documentation he might have at the National Security Archive that might help officially document our case before we filed it.

Scott read through the complaint slowly, flipping through one page after another, a few times looking back onto the previous page to reconfirm a name. When he completed his reading, he looked up and said, "This isn't true. Secord is a Middle East guy. He's got nothing to do with South America. And Richard Armitage, he's got nothing to do with this. He was just a lawyer in Iran. Someone has been feeding you a line of bullshit. If this were true, then I would know it."

I looked at him calmly. "Well, the fact is, this is true. And you don't know it . . . yet." I asked him to go talk to whomever he had to go talk with to confirm that what I was saying here was true, and I told him that I would come back after he had done that.

Two days later, Scott called me, totally excited. "Come on over," he said. "We need to talk." I went back to the National Security Archive, and Scott said, "I took your draft complaint to Sy Hersh and a couple of other guys. And I'll be a son of a bitch if this isn't true. I was shocked. You were right and I was wrong. It takes a big man to admit when he was wrong."

His tone had changed completely from two days earlier, when he had assumed automatically that he knew more than I did. But I let it go. He continued, "I am going to go over this afternoon and talk directly with Peter Rodino, the chairman of the House Judiciary Committee, and I am going to lay this all out in front of him, telling him that this has been confirmed by Sy Hersch. He is going to want to put together a special select committee with staff," he said.

I had actually told him that this was exactly what we should do when I had first showed him the complaint. Now he was presenting it as his own idea. "And I'll be the chief of staff of that select committee. And we'll impeach these bastards." That was fine with me. I didn't care who got the credit for the idea—as long as it got done.

Two days went by, and I heard nothing. Then three days. On the fourth day, I called over to the National Security Archive and got ahold of Tom Blanton, Scott's deputy director. I told him that I had expected to hear from Scott by now. "Ah, yeah," Blanton said. "Come on over, I've got to talk to you."

So I went back over to the archives on Massachusetts Avenue and went straight into Tom's office.

"Look, Dan," he said. "Scott went over and talked directly with Rodino about what you told him. Rodino listened to it all, then read your complaint, and then said, 'My god, this is horrible!'"

I thought, *Great, Rodino is going to do something about this.*

Then Blanton went on. "Rodino said that he had been telling people, for years, that if they didn't like the way that the United States was being run, they should write to their congressman. And if he didn't do anything about it, then they should vote for someone else and throw him out of office. But, if what you are telling me here is true, why, then . . . we haven't even been in charge! I'm not going to have Congress investigate anything *like that*."

"What? Wait a second!" I said. I was completely floored. "What is Scott saying here? These are clearly directly impeachable offenses, and Peter Rodino is the chairman of the House Judiciary Committee. That is the only committee that has the authority to do what Congress is legally and constitutionally required to do."

"Scott feels like shit about this, Dan," Tom said.

"Scott feels like shit about this? *That's* supposed to make me feel better, that Scott feels like shit about this? I have been busting my ass getting this information together for over *two years*! And I'm supposed to feel sorry for Scott because he won't get to be the chief of staff of a special select committee to investigate this for the House Judiciary Committee?"

Tom Blanton just hung his head and said, "I feel like shit too."

"Oh!" I said. "That makes me feel a *lot* better! You feel like shit too! Great! I'm glad that you guys both feel like shit about this. I'm glad that you could both be of so much help on this." And with that, I turned and left his office.

As I walked back to my office, I considered once again the chasm between what really went on in Washington and what the general public was told. Then I remembered what Gary Sick had written in his book *October Surprise: America's Hostages in Iran and the Election of Ronald Reagan,* which analyzed what had happened to President Jimmy Carter in 1980. Sick was the National Security Council liaison to President Carter during Carter's 1980 negotiations with Hezbollah during the American hostage negotiations. Investigating the claim that William Casey, the Republican presidential campaign director for Ronald Reagan and George H. W. Bush, had secretly met with members of Hezbollah and had struck a deal with them, promising that the Reagan–Bush Administration, if it were elected to replace Jimmy Carter, would provide TOW missiles and valuable military materials to Hezbollah if Hezbollah would see to it that our fifty-two American hostages were held in captivity until *after* the 1980 presidential election, to weaken Jimmy Carter in the eyes of the American voters, Gary Sick had said this:

> We in Washington are accustomed to the petty scandals of Washington politics. . . .
>
> However, there is another category of offenses, described by the French poet Andre Chenier as *"les crimes puissants qui font trembler les lois,"* crimes so great that they make the laws themselves tremble. We know what to do with someone caught misappropriating funds. But, when we are confronted with evidence of a systematic attempt to undermine the very political system itself, we recoil in a general failure of imagination and nerve. . . . We know that certain individuals and certain groups covet such immense power for either personal or ideological reasons. But we somehow suppose that those ambitions will be pursued within the confines of our laws and within the confines of the values of our society and our democratic political system. . . .
>
> However, if those who operate politically beyond the law are deft enough and determined enough, they can learn to benefit from our often false sense of confidence in this regard. For there is a

natural presumption on the part of those of us who deem ourselves to be politically sophisticated that "no one would actually dare to do such a thing." Most mere observers are, therefore, very much disposed toward misbelief and are, therefore, willing to disregard evidence that is directly presented to them . . . and even to construct alternative explanations for events that seem just too distasteful to want to believe. This all-too-human propensity provides just the margin of safety that is needed by those who would dare to undertake what would otherwise be regarded as just too immensely a risky undertaking to attempt. . . .

For example, when the Iran-Contra scandal exploded in 1986, both the Congress and the national mainstream media pulled up short. . . . The laws trembled at the prospect of a political trial that threatened to shatter the compact of trust between the rulers and the ruled, a compact that was the foundation upon which the very law itself rested. The lesson was clear: accountability declines as the magnitude of the crime and the power of those charged increase.

I got back to my office, finished putting together the final complaint, and delivered copies to Bill Taylor, Wally Kazubouski, and Father Bill Davis. Copies were also served on more than two dozen defendants. On May 28, 1986, just two days short of the expiration of the two-year statute of limitations for assault, Bill Taylor filed the complaint at 4:30 PM in the Southern District of Florida in Miami.

On the following Monday morning, May 31, I received a telephone call at my office on North Capitol Street. When I picked up the phone, my secretary, Patti Austin, told me, "There's a call for you from the chief judge of the United States District Court for the Southern District of Florida in Miami, a James Lawrence King." I took the call.

"I have here before me your civil complaint," the judge said. "I have decided to take this case myself, in light of the importance of the allegations that you have made in your complaint. And I would just like to let you know that I am entertaining a motion for an order of summary judgment against your complaint at this time."

"On the Monday morning after a Friday 4:30 PM filing?" I asked. "Don't you mean a rule 12(b)(6) motion to dismiss as matter of law—not a rule 56 order of summary judgment? There hasn't even been any discovery in the case so far."

"I am only calling you, Mr. Sheehan, to inform you that I have before me a motion to enter an order of summary judgment, and I will be granting that motion unless you are personally in my courtroom, here in Miami, by 2:00 PM this afternoon. I expect to see you here, Mr. Sheehan, or I will summarily dismiss your complaint. Good day."

And with that he hung up.

I was more than a bit flabbergasted. It wasn't even conceivable that a federal judge could enter a rule 56 order of summary judgment one business day after the filing of a federal civil complaint. It didn't make any sense legally.

But I hung up the phone and jumped into my suit, which I kept in the closet of my office in case I had to dash over to The Hill on short notice. Then I rushed off to National Airport by cab and flew to Miami. When I came hook sliding into the federal courtroom of James Lawrence King at about ten minutes before 2:00 PM, there was Judge King, sitting up on the bench in his robe. There were also some two dozen lawyers just sitting there waiting. This was Monday afternoon, less than five business hours after the filing of our complaint.

"Mr. Sheehan, I've called you here to introduce you to the counsel who will be representing the defendants whom you have named in this complaint. This is Mr. Anthony Lapham, who will be serving as the chief attorney for the defendants in this case. Mr. Lapham will be representing Mr. Adolfo Calero, the man whom you accuse in your complaint with being the head of the FDN Contras."

Anthony Lapham? I asked myself. *Where do I recognize that name from?* And then it dawned on me: Anthony Lapham was chief counsel for the United States Central Intelligence Agency when George H. W. Bush was director of the CIA, from 1976 to 1977. And now here he was, showing up as chief attorney for all these guys who, during the vice presidency of George Bush, were running guns and explosives to the Contras in direct violation of the Boland Amendment. This meant that Bush had to be up to his armpits in this operation and that his former CIA legal counsel was showing up here only with his blessing, if not at his express direction. The introduction of Anthony Lapham was actually very helpful. It meant that Bush's vice presidential national security adviser, Donald P. Gregg, one of Bush's most senior field officers in the CIA, would have to be the action officer on this operation. That would mean, in turn, that we should be looking for Felix Rodriguez, the "special operations golden boy" for Donald P. Gregg.

"Well, hello, Mr. Lapham," I said. "Fancy meeting you here."

He said nothing. He just smiled and nodded.

Judge King continued. "And, here we have Mr. F——. He is going to be representing Mr. Ronald Joseph Martin Sr., the owner of the Tamiami Gun Shop, whom you have accused in your complaint of providing the illegal end-user certificates for the weapons you allege are being smuggled out of the Fort Lauderdale/Hollywood Airport in this federal district down to . . . where is it?" He started leafing through the complaint, which he had placed in front of him on the bench.

"Ilopango, Your Honor," I said.

"Oh, yes . . . Ilopango." Then he added, "You may recognize Mr. F——'s name because Mr. F—— was the chief assistant United States attorney here in the Southern District of Florida, in charge of the criminal division, until last Friday night at 5:00 PM. But he has decided to retire to go into private practice to defend, ah, to defend . . . "

"*Professional criminals,* I think is the term that you are looking for, Your Honor," I said a little too pointedly.

"Now, Mr. Sheehan, I don't want to have any of that here in my courtroom. I have heard about you. This matter is going to be handled like gentlemen. And while we are on this subject, let me inform you that I am hereby notifying you, on the record, that I have exercised my discretion to place your complaint under seal, and if you so much as tell another person that this complaint has been filed or you reveal to anyone anything that is contained in this complaint, I will personally hold you in immediate direct criminal contempt of court and put you in federal prison for six months."

"Well, Your Honor. Might I inquire as to what your rationale is for such an order?"

"Well, Mr. Sheehan, you may not be familiar with the local rules of this court here in the Southern District of Florida, but down here, if a jury trial is requested—and I see that you have asked for a jury trial in this matter—I have the right to determine how best to keep a jury from becoming biased. I don't want you saying anything to anybody about the existence of this case as it could conceivably get back to potential jurors and make it more difficult for this court to pick an objective jury in this case. That is why I wanted to make certain that you were directly in front of me, in my courtroom, so you could be informed of this in person, so there would be absolutely no doubt that you knew this constraint."

I was shocked.

"And on exactly what legal authority do you purport to be basing such an . . . an unconstitutional order, Your Honor?"

"Well, Mr. Sheehan, you may not be familiar with our local rules down here in the Southern District of Florida . . ." he began again.

"Well, Your Honor, I assume that they are the same as federal rules of civil procedure that my professor of civil procedure at Harvard Law School, David Shapiro, actually supervised the writing of for the federal judicial conference and that are in effect in every federal court in the United States."

He was furious. He started to speak, but I interrupted.

"I assume, Your Honor, that you are purporting to base your order on the provision that grants some degree of discretion to a federal district court trial judge to fashion a fair but constitutional order facilitating his ability to oversee the obtaining of a fair and impartial jury in cases in which a jury has been requested by a complainant."

Judge King scowled at me and then continued with his prepared script. "Our local rules of civil procedure accord our trial court judges down here a high degree of discretion," he said, misquoting the provision, "in fashioning orders to facilitate the ability of the court to oversee the seating of a fair and impartial jury in cases in which a plaintiff has requested a trial by jury."

Now it was my turn to smile. He didn't. He repeated his order, then turned to the entire courtroom. "Gentlemen, this case will be tried only on the evidence presented in this courtroom. It will not be tried in the newspapers or on the evening news shows! Do I make myself clear?"

"Yes, Your Honor," came murmurs from around the courtroom.

"Are we through here, Your Honor?" I asked a little too loudly.

Judge James Lawrence King scowled at me and said, "Yes. We are through here, Mr. Sheehan. But don't forget what I have said here in this courtroom today."

"Your Honor, I will not forget it. But I want to make it clear, on the record, that I consider your order to be entirely overbroad and considerably outside of the reasonable discretion that a federal district court judge has been granted by the new federal rules of civil procedure. And I do not intend to be bound by it. Just so we are perfectly clear.'"

Judge King glowered down at me from the bench. "Well, it isn't necessary for you to agree with my order, Mr. Sheehan. It is only necessary for you to understand what it is and obey it. I have given you fair warning as to what I will do to you if you do not."

With that, he gathered up his papers and exited the door behind his bench.

I left the courthouse and flew back to Washington thinking, *What a beginning . . . this is gonna be a beaut!*

When I returned, I explained to Sara, Bill Davis, and everybody else on our board what had happened. I told them that I had made it clear that I didn't agree with Judge King's gag order and that I wasn't intending to abide by it. But we had to be careful.

The next morning, Tuesday, June 1, 1986, I called Russell Hemenway, former chairman of the Fund for Constitutional Government and director of the Fund for an Effective Congress, and asked him to set up a meeting for me, as soon as possible, with Tip O'Neill, the Speaker of the House, which was under control of the Democratic Party. He called me back within the hour and said that he had set up a meeting for later that very morning. I went directly over to meet with Tip O'Neill at his office on The Hill.

In the meeting, I gave Tip O'Neill and his chief of staff a copy of the complaint that we had filed the previous Friday afternoon. I explained in detail the charges in the complaint and the evidence we had to back them up. I also told them about Judge King's gag order and about the presence of Anthony Lapham as chief counsel for the defense.

Tip O'Neill explained that even though the House was under control of the Democratic Party, the United States Senate, as of that June 1 morning of 1986, was still under control of a Republican majority. He said that it was clear to him, as the Speaker of the House, that what we had discovered was indeed a direct and serious violation of the Boland Amendment and that it was therefore impeachable conduct on the part of any high-level officials we could prove knew about and had authorized these activities. But he said that it would be futile for the Democrat-controlled House of Representatives to return a bill of impeachment against any of the Reagan–Bush administration higher-ups because the Republican-controlled Senate would never convict any of them of this conduct, no matter how much direct proof we presented. However, he said if the Democrats could win back the Senate in the upcoming midterm elections that November, the House could then return a bill of impeachment and put the Reagan–Bush administration men responsible for these "impeachable offenses" on trial before a Democratic Senate.

"Let's have you go see Claiborne Pell," Tip O'Neill said. "He's the ranking Democrat on the Senate Foreign Relations Committee. You go see him and show him what you have. Ask him if he will agree to set up a special select committee in the Senate to investigate your charges if the Democrats retake the Senate in November. He will ask who you think should chair this special select committee, and you should tell him John Kerry of Massachusetts. Claiborne loves John Kerry. He wants him to be president. We all kid that John Kerry must be his illegitimate son, he loves him so much. But you just tell him that you want John Kerry to chair the special select committee that you want him to set up. And you watch—he'll jump at it."

So I did just that. And Claiborne Pell did exactly what Tip O'Neill said he would.

We now had in place an agreement from the Speaker of the House of Representatives and the ranking Democrat on the Senate Foreign Relations Committee that a special select committee, chaired by Massachusetts Democratic senator John Kerry, would be immediately established by the

United States Senate Foreign Relations Committee as soon as the U.S. Senate reconvened in January 1987—as long as the Democratic Party retook the U.S. Senate in the November 1986 midterm elections. A good morning's work done—the very day after returning from Miami and being threatened with federal prison by Judge King.

When I arrived back at the Christic Institute, Patti Austin told me there was an older gentleman waiting for me in my office.

"Who is it?" I asked.

"He didn't say," Patti replied. This was a little peculiar. I gave her a curious look. "It seemed that he might be important. But he definitely didn't want to tell me who he was."

I found the man sitting quietly in my office. He was in his late fifties but seemed, somehow, much older in his light-tan African safari–like jacket and tan cargo pants. He was carrying a U.S. Army hemp briefcase.

"Hello," he said. "I'd like to talk with you about the federal complaint that you filed down in Miami last Friday afternoon."

I was surprised—and a little leery about a potential setup. There had not yet been any publicity about the filing, and it had been expressly placed under seal by Judge King, who had ordered me not to talk about the complaint with anyone.

"I have a copy of your complaint here," the man said, bending down and removing a copy from his khaki-colored World War II–vintage carrying bag. I noted that it did not have a file stamp or a certification stamped on it. That made me even more suspicious. The complaint had been filed at 4:30 on Friday afternoon, and it must have been put under seal by Judge King by no later than 5:00 PM. I couldn't figure out how this man could possibly have gotten an uncertified copy of the complaint in such a short period, though it was possible.

He seemed to notice my skeptical look. "Look, I have the complaint here. You don't know who I am yet and . . ."

I interrupted. "Yes, I noticed that you have not introduced yourself yet."

"Just give me a moment of your time, and if you will just bear with me and let me ask you a couple of questions, I will tell you who I am, and I might be able to help you on this matter."

I wasn't certain what the older man meant by "this matter." But I had one of those feelings that good trial lawyers have to have to know how to take advantage of an opportunity that might come and go in the blink of an eye—and make all the difference between success and failure in a case.

So I said, "OK, what?"

The man smiled as if I had passed some secret test. Then he held out the complaint to me. "There's a list here of your defendants. Can you tell me who you think the most important of all of these twenty-six defendants is, and why?"

"That's easy," I said without hesitation. "He's right here. Theodore Shackley."

I waited.

He looked at me and said, "Really? And why is that exactly?"

"Well, a lot of people would say it's because Shackley was the Deputy Director of Covert Operations for George Bush and because Donald P. Gregg—who is now his vice presidential national security adviser—is actually running the Ilopango air operation through Felix Rodriguez. Shackley was Gregg's boss at one time. A lot of people would think that's the reason why Shackley is the most important name on that list."

He stared at me. "But what is the real reason you say he is the most important defendant?"

"Because he was the chief of the Miami CIA station on November 22, 1963," I said.

He looked stunned for an instant. Then tears actually began to form in his eyes. He rose from his seat, painfully it seemed, haltingly took the few short steps across the room, and stood in front of my desk. He leaned over my desk toward me, and through tear-filled eyes, he said, "There are not five men alive today who would have answered that question that way." He held out his old and cramped right hand and said, "Mr. Sheehan, my name is Dick Billings. I was the chief staff writer for the House Select Committee on Assassinations. I think that you and I might be able to help each other out, if you will let me volunteer to help you on this case."

I smiled broadly. "That's far-out!" I pulled my chair out from behind the desk, and we both sat down and exchanged our stories.

After some time, Billings said, "Look, Dan. There's a guy that you have to meet. He has some information that you should have if you are going to do this case." He asked me to meet him for lunch the following day. He asked where I'd like to meet. I picked the Dubliner Café at the foot of Capitol Hill, just across from Union Station.

The next day at noon, I walked down from my office to the Dubliner Café. Dick was already there, standing out front. I walked up to him, and we shook hands. As we walked inside, I saw an older man sitting alone at a table in the middle of the room. He was about seventy. Dick led me over to the man's table. "Joe, this is Dan Sheehan. Dan, this is Joe Smith."

"Yeah, right!" I said.

"Yeah, I get that a lot," the older man said. "But that is my real name, Joseph Burkholder Smith. Dick thought that you and I ought to talk about some information that I have."

"Fine. Let's do that. Would you like me to order you some fish and chips or something?"

"No, thank you. I'm fine." The older man smiled and gestured for me to sit down, and then he began, "I was the deputy CIA station chief in Mexico City in 1973 when Theodore Shackley came on board as director of Western Hemisphere operations for the agency. He had just been taken out of Vietnam . . ."

"Yes. I know," I said.

"Do you?"

"Yes."

"Well, do you know *why* he was taken out?" the old man asked.

"I do," I said, then waited.

He waited too, testing me to see if I really did know.

So I began, "It was because Shackley had come under direct investigation by General Creighton Abrams, the U.S. Army chief of staff in Vietnam. I know this because Jerry Zeifman, who was chief counsel for the House Judiciary Committee, called me one morning and invited me to come to a meeting, much like this one that we're having now. I got Sara Nelson, our executive director, and we went over and sat down with him in a restaurant, much like this one, except that it was a Chinese restaurant up on The Hill."

Smith told me the whole story. He said that Peter Rodino, chairman of the House Judiciary Committee, had approached him and had said, "Look, there have been five U.S. Special Forces guys indicted for first-degree murder over in Vietnam. One of them was Colonel Reaux. And they've been charged with murdering this young South Vietnamese CIA agent." He continued:

> Peter Rodino wanted Jerry Zeifman to get ahold of the five congressmen from the home districts of these five guys, assemble them into a task force, and mobilize political support to get the indictments dismissed against these guys. Richard Nixon had called Rodino personally and had asked this as a favor for him. So Jerry got assigned the job of working on that project, and he succeeded in getting all the charges dismissed. The five men were all so happy about this that they invited Jerry Zeifman to meet with them in a city somewhere, which he did. When they were celebrating, they all got drunk and started bragging to Zeifman about what they were actually doing over there: They were *assassinating* people for Theodore Shackley. Shackley, as the CIA station chief in Saigon, had decided that he wanted to assassinate the neutralist prince Souvanna Phuma of Indonesia, and he had put together this team of five Special Forces guys from the Phoenix Project to assassinate him. One of the guys they worked with peripherally was a young CIA guy from South Vietnam. They discovered that his mistress was also the mistress of a North Vietnamese general. Shackley got so worried that this guy might have somehow gotten wind of their plan to assassinate Prince Souvanna Phuma that he wanted this Vietnamese CIA guy killed to eliminate him as a potential leak. The difficulty was that one of the five American men in that unit was the best friend of this Vietnamese guy, and Shackley had ordered that *that* man had to pull the trigger and kill him so there would be no chance that he would rat them out. So they kidnapped the young Vietnamese CIA guy, tied him up, and took him out on a boat into a deep lake, and his best friend put three slugs into his head. They then tied a bag of rocks to him and dropped him into the lake. However, after a few weeks, the

young American who had killed him felt so guilty about what he had done that he went directly to the headquarters of General Creighton Abrams, the commanding officer in Vietnam, and confessed what he had done. He ratted them all out, despite the preventative measures that Shackley had taken, and Creighton Abrams had all five of the men indicted for that murder. In the face of the investigation that Creighton Abrams had ordered into the activities of Shackley, the CIA pulled Shackley out of Vietnam and brought him back stateside. There he served, for a very short period of time, as the Israeli desk man for the agency. At that post, he authorized the smuggling of 98 percent pure bomb-grade plutonium out of the Kerr-McGee nuclear facility in Cimarron, Oklahoma, to Israel, as well as to the shah of Iran, to South Africa, and to Brazil. After that, Shackley was made head of Western Hemisphere operations for the agency.

"I guess that's where you come in, right?" I asked the old man.

He looked dumbfounded. "Well, I'll be damned. You certainly *do* know why Shackley was taken out of Vietnam. After he was assigned to be director of Western Hemisphere operations for the agency, Shackley argued that Philip Agee, who was known to be writing a book entitled *Inside the Company: CIA Diary*, was threatening to compromise the agency. Agee might have known the names of all the CIA station chiefs throughout Central America and South America, so Shackley used this as an excuse to remove them and replace them with his own hand-picked men. He removed the station chief in Mexico City, who shall remain nameless, and put in a new guy . . ."

"Yeah, Tom Polgar," I said.

Again the old man was surprised. "Yeah, Polgar. So when Tom Polgar first arrived, he came directly to my office and said, 'Joe, I'm Tom Polgar. I'm the new station chief here, and I don't know whether I'm going to be keeping you on as my deputy. There will be a guy that's going to come in tomorrow morning, at about ten, to your office. You'll recognize him when you see him. And he's going to ask you a few questions. He may even want you to go with him somewhere to introduce you to some people who may have some more questions for you. And, depending on how you answer those questions, that'll determine whether you're going to be kept on here as my deputy.' So I agreed to meet with whoever that guy was. So the next morning, at about ten, into my office walks Nassar Harro. Do you know who Nassar Harro is, Dan?"

"All I know is that he is the head of XXX (DFS) in Mexico," I said.

"Very good! Very good."

"But that's all I know," I hastened to say, not wanting to discourage the old man from telling me all he knew. He continued:

Well, the DFS in Mexico is like the combined CIA and FBI. This Nassar Harro was—is—a very nefarious guy, a Lebanese-Mexican and a total right-wing cretin actually. He led me downstairs and we got into this black Suburban with the classic smoked windows, and he drove me to the Mexico City Airport. We got out and went completely around all the security at the airport, and we boarded a private jet and flew away. Finally we landed, and I discovered that we were in Buenos Aires, Argentina. We got out of the jet, and again we didn't go through any customs or security. We simply crossed the tarmac, got into a private helicopter, and flew away. We flew way up to the northwesternmost tip of Argentina, and we landed at a place that I later came to find out was called Salta. The helicopter landed on what looked like a soccer field, and I followed Nassar Harro across the field to a big embankment. I looked down over the edge, and it looked like we were in Bavaria! There was this German town down there. We walked down the hill, and this Nassar Harro led me over to this Bavarian inn. We walked inside, and there were six men sitting at this big dark oak table directly in front of this huge natural stone fireplace. And above the fireplace, above the mantle, was a huge swastika flag, right out of the Third Reich. I looked up at this flag, and my eyes must have gotten big. The man in the middle of the six men, on the opposite side of the table from me, beckoned for me to come over and sit down. There was just one chair on my side of the table. So I sat down. And the guy opposite me said, "Joe, we understand that there is some question as to whether you are going to be asked to stay on as the deputy station chief for the agency in Mexico City. We'd like to tell you that we have just spent a long time, and a lot of money and effort, putting together a major cocaine cartel down in Colombia. A portion of the profits generated by that cartel from the sale of cocaine is going to be used to help finance the 'war without boundaries' being fought against our common enemies—yours and ours. We want your assurance that if you are asked to stay on as the deputy station chief in Mexico City, you will do nothing, at any time, to interfere with the flow of this cocaine."

Joseph Burkholder Smith interrupted his story to look directly at me and say, "I swear to God, Dan, I don't know of anything I had ever done in my entire life that would have led them to believe I would have gone along with an agreement like that."

"How about being the deputy CIA station chief in Mexico City, for a start!" I said rather matter-of-factly.

The old man took immediate umbrage at that and turned to Dick Billings. "I thought that he was going to cooperate with us on this?"

Dick Billings shrugged. "Hey, look. I just met the guy. You asked him, and he told you."

The old man immediately pushed his chair back from the table with the backs of his legs and rose from his seat. "OK. Alright. Now I have told you. I've told you the story." He walked around the table and stood next to me, looking down at me. Then he reached out his right hand, waiting for me to shake it. So I reached up and took his hand. He squeezed my hand firmly, and, drawing me up toward him, he leaned down so that his face was no more than a foot from mine. He looked me straight in the eye and said, "I just wanted to make sure that you knew exactly who you were dealing with, if you are going to go forward with this case."

Then he shook my hand, released it, and turned to leave. After taking just a few steps, however, he stopped, turned back to me, and smiled warmly. "I'm a Harvard man, too, Dan. And I wish you all the luck in the world on this. I hope that your generation can stop these bastards. Because ours never did."

To APPRECIATE THE deeper context in which the Iran-Contra scandal arose, as I saw it from the inside, one must harken back to the period immediately following the return of the articles of impeachment against and the resignation of President Richard Nixon in August of 1974.

The impetus for that was, of course, the infamous Watergate burglary, which took place on the night of June 17, 1972, two years earlier, when Richard Nixon was in the midst of his presidential reelection campaign. However, it was not until July 27, 1974, almost two full years after Nixon had been reelected, that the Judiciary Committee of the House of Representatives voted out articles of impeachment against Richard Nixon. Almost immediately, on August 9, 1974, Nixon resigned and Gerald Ford was installed as president. Virtually the first act of Gerald Ford's presidency was to issue a full presidential pardon to Richard Nixon for any crime that he may have "or may not have" committed while president. That act on the part of Gerald Ford generated a huge popular uproar and a political backlash that fatally undermined the potential for Ford's reelection when he ran for the presidency in 1976.

The change from the Richard Nixon–Gerald Ford administration to the administration of Jimmy Carter was then a transition of power from a publicly disgraced administration to an idealistic one. The former's disgrace deeply involved the activities of the Central Intelligence Agency, particularly concerning the deep, behind-the-scenes events that gave rise to the Watergate burglary. For that reason, in 1976, Gerald Ford selected George H. W. Bush to become his new director of the Central Intelligence Agency and delegated to him the task of diverting and deflecting any effective investigation of the CIA by the United States Senate Select Committee on Intelligence Abuse pertaining to the Watergate burglary. It was during Bush's tenure as head of the CIA that certain extremely aggressive, antiterrorist, and reactionary covert operations specialists within the CIA ascended to ultimate power. That very group of men was at the heart of the Iran-Contra scandal. During the ten-year period over which the Iran-Contra scandal played itself out, these men struggled to remain in the shadows.

The head of this group was Theodore G. Shackley, who at that time was virtually unknown both in and outside of Washington. One of George H. W.

Bush's very first acts as CIA director was to appoint Shackley to be Deputy Director of Covert Operations. These two men, unknown to the outside world, represented a very specific element within the covert political world.

George Herbert Walker Bush's family had a long history, through Bush's maternal grandfather, George Herbert Walker, of pursuing private business profit by intervening in and manipulating American foreign affairs. George Herbert Walker's private investment firm, Brown Brothers Investment Group, had funded and supervised private, behind-the-scenes covert activities that had caused the United States government, in 1909, to send a foreign military expeditionary force into Central America to overthrow the democratically elected government of the nation of Nicaragua and to put into place Anastasio Somoza Sr. This event constitutes the actual origin of the "Contra" half of the Iran-Contra scandal. In 1977, Anastasio Somoza III, the grandson of Anastasio Somoza Sr., created the Contras, made up of fascist national guard troops and officers of his La Guardia.

Theodore Shackley also had a long history of employing torture, political assassination, and any other means necessary to accomplish his covert objectives within the Covert Operations Directorate of the CIA. These activities included partnering with a specific Laotian warlord in heroin smuggling and the mass extermination of even suspected sympathizers of the Viet Cong in Vietnam: his infamous Phoenix Project, which he founded and directed from his position as CIA station chief first in Laos, then in Saigon.

George Herbert Walker Bush and Theodore Shackley rose to power at the heads of the CIA virtually coincident with my arrival in Washington, D.C.—which was also marked by the assassination of Sam Giancana, the don of the Mafia in Chicago, who at the time of his murder, in June of 1975, was being actively sought by the Senate Select Committee on Governmental Operations with Respect to Intelligence Activities (the famous Church Committee chaired by Senator Frank Church of Idaho), which was investigating potential CIA involvement in covert assassinations, which was somehow apparently connected to the Watergate break-in. I remember being amazed at the vast difference between what was really going on "behind the scenes" and what was being presented to the American public as "the truth" by the Nixon–Ford administration, by Congress, and by the American news media.

I was meeting one afternoon with Bob Fink, who had served on the investigative staff of the Pike Committee (the House side of the Senate Select Committee on Government Operations investigation), about this bizarre disconnect between the deep background of American history reflected by the assassination of Sam Giancana and the deception that was being foisted upon the American public by public officials and the mainstream news media. We talked, for example, about the fact that since the end of World War II, the CIA had been directly involved in smuggling thousands of tons of heroin from Southeast Asia into the United States through Cuba to help fund, first the Nationalist Chinese in Formosa and more recently the CIA's criminal covert operations in Southeast Asia. The fact was that even with all of these Senate Select Committee hearings and Pike Committee investigations, no one in official circles was making any effort whatsoever to tell the American public a word about what was actually being discovered. They were all consciously and cooperatively concealing this massive criminality on the part of the Central Intelligence Agency and our other covert operations agencies—all in the name of "national security."

As I recounted earlier, Bob said to me, "Look Danny, if anyone is so ignorant that he doesn't know that the Central Intelligence Agency has been smuggling heroin from Southeast Asia through Cuba into the United States for decades to secretly finance first the Nationalist Chinese and later their covert operations in Southeast Asia, then that person is too ignorant to function effectively in Washington, D.C. On the other hand, if that person were so naive as to try to tell the American public that the Central Intelligence Agency was smuggling heroin into the United States, that person would be too naive to ever be able to function effectively in Washington."

That was what I had been told, almost immediately upon my arrival in Washington, by a professional investigator for the United States House of Representatives, who took me under his wing and tried to reveal to me "the facts of life in Washington."

"Don't make the foolish mistake of trying to tell the American people about the secret history of the United States," Bob advised me. "Instead, use whatever information you learn to make your way into 'the inner circle of power' in Washington. And from there you can try to do some small amount of good 'from the inside.'"

I had resolved, very soon after arriving in Washington, D.C., that I was going to do everything I could to change that operating principle in Washington. I was not only going to uncover what was really going on inside that darker history of the United States but I was going to communicate that reality as effectively as I possibly could to the people of our country so that we could, together, remedy the very serious problems that this secret history had generated for us throughout the world rather than allowing those problems to fester in secret, causing one "surprise" after another, such as we experienced in Vietnam . . . and that we would experience again in September of 2001.

That became my "mission" in Washington. So when I discovered what was secretly being done by the Reagan–Bush administration and "the enterprise," I resolved that I was going to reveal this information to the American public. And I would do so by generating a major public "show trial" in federal court.

CHAPTER *twenty-eight*

I N THE FIRST week of July 1986, thirty days after filing our civil complaint in the Iran-Contra case, I began to serve document demands on the defendants and their attorneys, demanding flight records, daily schedule-book entries, correspondence between the defendants, and copies of their correspondence with members of the administration. But by the end of the thirty-day period that each defendant was accorded by the federal rules of civil procedure to respond to those official demands, no response whatsoever had been forthcoming. So I began to file one motion to compel after another, petitioning Judge James Lawrence King in Miami to compel each defendant to comply with the federal rules of civil procedure that required the defendants to provide discovery materials to us or to seek some kind of protective order from the court authorizing them not to provide these records. But nothing happened in response to any of these motions. Judge King simply ignored them, letting our discovery demands—and our motions to compel compliance with them, filed with him—stack up.

Then I began to issue deposition subpoenas. No response came back for those either; the defendants simply ignored them. So I filed motions to compel the defendants to respond to these deposition notices. But James Lawrence King did not respond. He simply stonewalled us—almost as though he were part of their defense team.

Then Bill Taylor produced a letter that had been written by defendant John Hull's attorney to John Hull. It said, "We have been informed by trusted sources that Judge King is on our side. All you have to do is make any kind of motion, asking for a protective order against discovery, and he will grant it."

I attached a copy of this letter to yet another motion to compel discovery and filed it directly with Judge King. Suddenly a raft of sworn affidavits came flooding into our office, one from each defendant. They said nothing more than "I did not personally participate in placing the bomb at the La Penca press conference of Edén Pastora. I deny any responsibility for that act. So I therefore am planning to move for an order of summary judgment against the complaint filed in this case."

In short, as an answer to our complaint, every defendant (except for John Hull and the six Miami-based anti-Castro Cuban exiles whom we had specifically named as being directly and personally involved in planning and assisting Per Anker Hansen in bombing Edén Pastora's press conference) simply denied having participated in *that one specific* act. They did nothing to deny their involvement in any other overt acts specifically charged against them in the complaint. From a legal point of view, those sworn affidavits were totally meaningless. I had accused them of being direct participants in a major federal criminal racketeering enterprise, individual members of which had personally committed various statutorily prohibited overt acts for the purpose of effectuating the criminal objectives of that enterprise. It was transparently *not* required that every individual active participant in that criminal racketeering enterprise be personally and directly involved in carrying out each and every one of the unlawful overt acts that had been conducted by other members of that unitary enterprise to carry out and effectuate its criminal objectives. That was the entire point of RICO. The federal Racketeer-Influenced Corrupt Organization Act had been enacted by Congress for the express purpose of designating *every* active member of an "ongoing federal criminal racketeering enterprise" to be a coconspirator of *every other* active member of that enterprise.

From a strictly legal perspective, that response on the part of each of the defendants was totally meaningless. And "legal" was all that counted, since we were, after all, in a court of "law."

I moved for an order of summary judgment against each of them in August 1986 on the grounds that their failure to deny any of the relevant charges filed against them in our complaint within the required thirty-day period (indeed, I had given them ninety days) required the entrance of an order of summary judgment against each one of them. But Judge King simply ignored that motion as well. This was getting to be preposterous.

So, in early September 1986, I began to take official sworn depositions from *our own* witnesses, a step that was absolutely unheard of for a plaintiff's lawyer in a federal civil action.

I did this to establish an uncontestable public record of the massive amount of evidence that our investigators had compiled against those defendants—even if Judge King was not going to abide by the federal rules of civil procedure.

The defendants and their lawyers simply ignored these depositions, with the exception of the sworn deposition of Carlos Rojas Chinchilla, which we took in Canada, where Carlos was hiding. The defendants sent Chi Chi Quintero, the known anti-Castro CIA-trained assassin, to sit and glower at Carlos during his deposition. However, because Quintero showed up to do this, I was able to personally serve him with a deposition subpoena. He could not deny that he had received that subpoena, since my service of him was recorded on videotape officially on the record of Carlos's sworn deposition.

I then issued federal subpoenas to Felix Rodriguez and Donald P. Gregg. But they just flat-out refused to appear for their noticed depositions. Meanwhile, my motions to compel were still getting absolutely no response from Judge King. It went on and on like this until it became absolutely incontrovertible that Judge James Lawrence King was actively refusing to comply with the law. So I asked my investigators to *diplomatically* undertake a background investigation of James Lawrence King. It turned out that King had been appointed by Richard Nixon at the direct recommendation of Nixon's close personal friend Bebe Rebozo, a known Mafia associate. Moreover, King, prior to being appointed by Richard Nixon, had been a member of the national board of directors of Meyer Lansky's Miami National Bank—the very bank through which Carlos Marcello and Santo Trafficante had laundered the skim off the cash proceeds of Mafia-controlled casinos in Las Vegas, a portion of which had been used to finance the training of the S-Force down in Oaxaca, Mexico.

Mitchell Rogovin, former special counsel to the CIA, indeed personally attended a set of legal seminars for incoming CIA lawyers, and James Lawrence King had been in those seminars, being trained as a "CIA attorney." If we had known that at the time, we would have moved to have him recuse himself or we would have filed a motion with the Eleventh Circuit Court of Appeals to have him forcibly removed from the case.

Failing to do that proved to be a fatal error on my part.

Our decision to take the fully noticed, sworn, videotaped depositions of our own plaintiff witnesses, thereby setting forth our affirmative evidence for full public view, paralyzed Judge King. He didn't know what to do about this. He clearly wanted to enter some kind of a dismissal or summary judgment against our complaint to stop it from going forward because he was functioning as a direct surrogate of the Central Intelligence Agency rather than as an honest and objective judge. But I kept submitting, on the official record, one piece of overwhelming direct evidence after another. I finally wrote a fifty-page sworn affidavit summarizing the evidence that we had. I laid out, for Judge King and for the world, the entire chronology of our case, listing one source after another and setting forth the information that each witness had conveyed to me or to one of our investigators. I submitted this to the court as a "supplement" to our complaint—a conditional supplement in case Judge King or the defendants attempted to assert that there was inadequate factual information set forth in our original complaint to fend off a summary dismissal.

So even though James Lawrence King would not help us by enforcing the federal rules of civil procedure that were expressly designed to assist plaintiffs in assembling information to prove their cases by court-admissible evidence, this affidavit blocked King from being able to grant any motions to dismiss our case. Ultimately, this caused Judge King to hate that affidavit and to hate me for having filed it.

During my many conversations with Gene Wheaton and Carl Jenkins, I came to learn that Edwin P. Wilson was one of five members of the board of directors of EATSCO (the Egyptian American Transport and Service Company), the "mother ship" corporation of "the enterprise." The other members of the board of directors were Theodore Shackley, the de facto chairman of the board; Richard V. Secord; Tom Clines; Erich von Mar Bod; and Albert Hakim. Edwin P. Wilson was the business mind behind the organizational structure of this parent company to "the enterprise." However, Wilson had been indicted and charged with illegally supplying weapons to

Moamar Kadafi of Libya. In 1984, he had been sentenced to fifty-five years in the maximum-security federal prison in Marion, Illinois, making it difficult (intentionally) for anyone to interview him.

I was finally able to get an interview with Wilson at Marion Prison. I had to go through four different belowground levels of deadlock to get to Wilson, who was on twenty-three-hour-a-day confinement. It took me three or four different interviews, telling him who I was and basically leveling with him so that he would trust me. It worked. I got him to talk, and he ended up giving me a two-volume sworn deposition that went on for two days. In it he laid out, in detail, the entire founding of the enterprise and the founding of EATSCO, and he outlined incriminating information against all the defendants involved. I submitted his deposition to Judge King, who immediately sent it back to me. So I brought it down to Miami personally, gave it to the clerk of the court, and got it stamped as officially received by the court.

On the evening of October 6, 1986, I was sitting on the couch in the private home of John Mattes, the chief federal public defender in Miami, preparing to watch a rerun of *Miami Vice* with him, when Mattes's home telephone rang. It would prove to be a significant breakthrough. On the phone was a Nicaraguan Catholic priest, Father Miguel D'Escoto, the foreign minister of the new Nicaraguan Sandinista government. He was calling to speak with "Señor Daniel Sheehan." Father D'Escoto informed me that on Sunday afternoon, October 5, a young Nicaraguan Sandinista soldier had shot down over Nicaragua a U.S. military surplus C-123 cargo transport plane carrying weapons and explosives to Contra forces. The pilot and copilot, William H. Cooper and Wallace B. Sawyer Jr., had been killed in the crash. But the load master, one Eugene Hasenfus, had been captured and was being held by the Sandinista government for questioning. Father D'Escoto wanted me to send Father Bill Davis down to Nicaragua to interview Gene Hasenfus—because Hasenfus was terrified and too incoherent to be of any intelligence value unless he could be calmed down. Father D'Escoto felt that Gene Hasenfus might be more cooperative talking to an American Catholic priest.

I immediately agreed to send Father Davis right away but asked Father D'Escoto to agree not to allow any Sandinista government officials to speak to Hasenfus until Father Davis arrived to question him. Bill was on his way to Nicaragua early the following morning, October 7.

Bill Davis found Gene Hasenfus to be as Father D'Escoto had described. He had "drunk the Kool-Aid" served up by Samoza's Contras and their right-wing allies in the Reagan–Bush administration and was terrified that he would be tortured and spend the rest of his life in some communist gulag. Father Davis, in full Jesuit collar and black suit, put Hasenfus at ease right away. Bill then went over the massive amount of information that we at the Christic Institute already knew about the Contra air operations from Gary Betzner, Michael Tolliver, Geraldo Duran, and others and about the cocaine trafficking going on in conjunction with it.

Hasenfus was totally surprised that we at Jesuit headquarters knew the Contra weapons-supply operation in such detail. Father Davis made Hasenfus a deal: If Hasenfus would come clean and state, on the record, what he knew about this operation (virtually all of which, Father Davis convinced him, we already knew), then Davis would intervene with Father D'Escoto, a fellow Catholic priest, and ask that Hasenfus be set free. That was too good an offer to refuse. So Hasenfus went on camera and spilled the beans on the Contra movement and the American network that was supplying the Contras with arms and explosives.

When the videotaped confession was played on Nicaraguan television on October 8, an enterprising young United Press International reporter in Nicaragua copied down the address of the safe house that Hasenfus had identified in his press conference, located the house, and actually went inside. He copied down the number off the telephone in the house, went down to the local telephone company, and obtained a printout of the telephone bill. Right on the phone bill, dating back four months, were the private, unlisted home telephone numbers of eleven of the twenty-six defendants named in our federal civil complaint. Also discovered, on a tiny slip of paper in the wallet of William H. Cooper, the dead pilot of the C-123 air cargo plane, was the private, unlisted home telephone number of Donald P. Gregg, the national security adviser to Vice President George H. W. Bush.

This headline about Hasenfus's sworn testimony hit the American newspapers like a proverbial bombshell the following Thursday morning,

October 9, 1986. About one hundred activists, led by a courageous young man named Brian Willson (who was later run over and had his legs cut off by a train in the San Francisco Bay Area while protesting the movement of nuclear warheads), immediately occupied the public steps of the House Side of the U.S. Capitol in Washington, D.C., demanding that the Democratic-controlled U.S. House of Representatives convene an immediate emergency session to hold public hearings into this impeachable offense.

After two days of this embarrassing public protest, Michael Barnes, a moderate Democrat from the state of Maryland who chaired the House Subcommittee on Latin American Affairs, came out to speak with the demonstrators. Willson told Barnes that the demonstrators would not leave the Capitol steps until Barnes convened an emergency session of the House Subcommittee on Latin American Affairs and "took the testimony of Daniel Sheehan of the Christic Institute, who has all of the evidence supporting the public claims of this Eugene Hasenfus guy that are in all of the newspapers."

Barnes immediately telephoned me and implored me not to make him convene such a hearing on the eve of the midterm elections. He then asked me, "You don't really want to testify about this matter, do you?"

"Of course I do," I said.

He was crestfallen. But I insisted. He then asked me whom else he should subpoena to testify at this special hearing.

I told him to get Robert White, the former United States ambassador to El Salvador under Jimmy Carter, who could testify to his own personal knowledge that it was absolutely impossible for these weapons and explosives to be transported from South Florida through the Ilopango Airport and then on to John Hull's ranch in Costa Rica without the U.S. administration being directly involved. I also told him to get Elliott Abrams, the administration's assistant secretary of state for Latin America. Abrams would either have to perjure himself or try to cover for what they were doing.

I appeared before that subcommittee of the House Foreign Affairs Committee on October 15, 1986, ten days after Eugene Hasenfus, William Cooper, and Wally Sawyer had been shot down over Nicaragua, and four and a half months after we had filed our federal civil Racketeering Act complaint.

Former ambassador Robert White testified first and established that the U.S. administration had, necessarily, been directly involved in the transfer of weapons and explosives from South Florida to John Hull's ranch in Costa Rica—directly in violation of the Boland Amendment enacted by Congress, which expressly prohibited that conduct.

Then it was my turn. I began by handing up a court-stamped, certi-fied copy of the complaint that we had filed against the twenty-six named defendants. I then went through the complaint, paragraph by paragraph, explaining to the subcommittee members what specific charges we had made against these defendants. When I started to outline the direct evidence we had against individuals within the Reagan–Bush administration, Henry Hyde, the congressman from the Sixth District of Illinois, who was on the subcommittee, leaped to his feet and began to shout, "This is an outrage! You are publicly disclosing sensitive, classified national security information of the utmost secrecy here in these public hearings! You should know bet-ter. And, moreover, this complaint has been placed under seal by the United States district court in Florida. I am insisting that these C-SPAN cameras be turned off immediately and that all the public and media persons in this hearing room be ordered to leave at once. I am demanding that this hearing be discontinued until this room is cleared and that we then reconvene in a closed session at which you, Mr. Sheehan, will be required to provide to this subcommittee your sources for this information—"

I stood up and interrupted his tirade. "I am not going to present any of the sources of this information to any committee of which you are a part, Congressman Hyde. Both you and Bill McCollum here, from the Fifth District of Florida, ought to be in federal prison, because we have direct proof that both of you have been in repeated meetings directly with Rob Owen, the liai-son for Lieutenant Colonel Oliver North directly to the Contras, and that, in these meetings, both you and Congressman McCollum were aware of this criminal operation to smuggle weapons and explosives from this administra-tion to the Contras in direct violation of the Boland Amendment passed by this Congress. I wouldn't give the names of our sources to you in a hundred years. They would be dead within a week!"

The hearing room was stunned. Hyde was completely flabbergasted. Bill McCollum just cowered in his seat. Mike Barnes was at a total loss as to what to do. But everybody in the public audience started to get up and leave, and the C-SPAN cameras were immediately turned off—leaving the entire country in the dark as to what was going on in the hearing.

Chaos reigned in the hearing room.

I walked from the witness table directly up to Mike Barnes and advised him to send aides to round up all the Democratic members of the subcommittee and the full committee they could find (since full committee members had the right to sit in on any hearing of the subcommittee), and to then get them to take a vote on Hyde's motion and vote it down.

When Hyde realized what was happening, he started calling for an immediate vote on his motion. Fortunately, he had not taken the time to count heads, and the Democrats by that time had two more votes than the Republicans. His motion was defeated. But by then the hearing was breaking down and everyone from the public had left. So I got up and walked out too.

As I was walking out, I saw Elliott Abrams, who had been sitting just behind me, in front of the public audience. As I passed, he glowered up at me and said, "You little prick, Sheehan. You're going to pay for this!"

I went back to my office, and first thing the next morning, I received a faxed order from James Lawrence King. It was an order to show cause as to why I should not be held in immediate direct criminal contempt of court for revealing to the United States Congress the existence of our complaint and its content. I was perfectly happy to respond, so I went into my office, sat down, and started to draft my response, arguing that I had revealed this information, under subpoena, to the United States Congress, which had direct jurisdiction over the subject matter of this affair. Moreover, I argued that Judge King's gag order was unquestionably unconstitutional and that I had expressly informed him, on the record, that I had no intention of abiding by it.

As I was sitting at my desk writing this response, my secretary, Patti Austin, came in and announced that a man on the phone wanted to talk to me right away. I told her that I was pretty busy at the moment.

Patti said, "I think it's pretty important. He wanted me to tell you that his name is Ross Perot."

When I picked up the phone, his distinctive Texas twang came over the line.

"Hello, Dan! Ross Perot here."

"Well, hello, Mr. Perot. How are you? What can I do for you today?"

"You may not know this, Dan, but I'm on President Reagan's National Security Advisory Committee, and I've got the brief on the POWs over in Southeast Asia."

"Yes," I said. "I'm aware of that, Sir."

He went on to tell me that he had, over the course of his years of investigation of that issue, constantly run across three names in connection with the disappearance of our POWs—three names that I had mentioned in my testimony before Congress the previous day: Theodore Shackley, Tom Clines, and Richard V. Secord. "I've been trying to figure out why all of our MIAs were left in Vietnam when our troops were pulled out, and everybody keeps telling me that these same three men have the answer and that I should contact Dan Sheehan over at U.S. Jesuit headquarters in Washington. He seems to know a lot about these guys." He said that a staff person of his had called yesterday and had told him to turn on C-SPAN "because that Sheehan fella is on testifying about the guys that you are interested in." He had therefore been watching the hearing on C-SPAN when Congressman Hyde had jumped up and demanded that they turn off all the C-SPAN cameras. Perot was calling because he wanted to know what I had said that had made them turn off the cameras.

After I explained that to him, he said, "You know, Dan, as long as these guys are in operation, no man can truly call himself president."

Then I told him what Elliott Abrams had said to me as I was leaving the hearing room. And I told him what James Lawrence King was doing, as we spoke, to try to silence me. In response, Perot told me that he was going to be flying in to Annapolis, Maryland, on November 12 to deliver the Forrestal Lecture to midshipmen at the U.S. Naval Academy. He invited me to be his guest at the lecture and then fly with him back to Texas to brief him in more detail on this matter.

I said, "OK, I will be there."

I brought Brian Barger with me to the Naval Academy. I thought that would be a great story for Brian to tell the *Soldier of Fortune* types with whom he was speaking. They all loved Ross Perot because he was the main person trying to recover the Vietnam vets who had been "left behind in The Nam" when the Nixon–Ford Administration had pulled everybody out. Brian and I were the only guys in civvies in the whole place—except for Perot. All the midshipmen were in their dress whites. In his lecture, Perot recounted the operation that he had personally financed and put together as a private extraction team to go into Iran, right after Ayatollah Khoumani had taken over, and to pull his corporate people out and carry them to safety.

When he finished his presentation, Perot came straight down from the stage and walked directly over to me. He stopped and reached out his hand. "Ross Perot, Dan." I introduced Brian Barger and told Ross what an important and courageous role Brian had been playing in digging into the information that I had told Ross in our initial phone call.

"I've got to go and stand in this long line and shake hands with everybody and meet all the brass hats," Perot said. "But we're going to jump on the Lear as soon as I get done here and hop back down to Texas. We can talk on the plane."

But before he left us, there were two people he wanted to introduce to me. They were William Stevenson, who had written *A Man Called Intrepid*, and Monika Jensen, a former producer for *60 Minutes* on CBS. They were researching a book to be entitled *Kiss the Boys Goodbye*, about our MIAs left behind in Vietnam. Their thesis was that a sizable number of American military men had worked directly with Theodore Shackley in Saigon, guarding and actively participating in the illegal covert heroin-smuggling operation with Shackley's associate Vang Pao, and that many of these U.S. military men who were deep into this covert CIA operation had been left behind because they were simply too far off the communication lines to get the word when U.S. forces were pulled out of Vietnam so precipitously. That was the same thesis Ross Perot had been investigating. He wanted me to brief them on what I knew about Shackley's involvement with Vang Pao.

So while Ross stood in the reception line, shaking hands with the top brass of the Naval Academy, I met with Stevenson and Jensen and passed on to them what I had been told by Carl Jenkins and Gene Wheaton about Shackley's heroin-smuggling operation in Southeast Asia:

Theodore Shackley, who had been the CIA's Miami station chief between mid-1962 and mid-1965, had been transferred to Laos in late 1965 (after a brief stint as the acting chief of station in Rome) to serve as the deputy CIA station chief in Laos. There in Laos, Shackley had come up with the idea of tapping off some of the opium the CIA had been participating in smuggling out of the Golden Triangle of Southeast Asia since the end of World War II. Shackley knew about that operation because opium from the Green Gang, the top opium-smuggling gang in Southeast Asia, which was processed into marketable heroin by the Corsican Mafia, had been smuggled into the United States between 1947 and 1959 through Cuba. This was the operation in which Santo Trafficante had partnered with Cuban dictator Fulgencio Batista. Shackley had learned of that during his time as Miami station chief, when he had overseen covert operations against Cuba.

The front organization through which this heroin was smuggled into and out of Cuba was a CIA proprietary company named the Southeast Asia (SEA) Supply Corporation. The director of the SEA Supply Corporation was one Paul Helliwell, a full-time, officially employed agent of the CIA. A portion of the profits generated by the sale of this heroin in the United States was being used to purchase weapons and explosives for the Nationalist Chinese under the command of Chiang Kai-shek, based in Formosa. Paul Helliwell was a close associate—indeed, a business partner—of Fulgencio Batista, the ultra-right-wing, anticommunist dictator of Cuba, who was in turn business partners with one William D. Pawley, an American businessman who personally owned Cuba's only public transportation company, which ran the busses and trolleys in Havana and throughout Cuba. Pawley was a central figure, along with Henry Luce, Clare Booth Luce, and Heinie Aderholt (a Richard V. Secord associate), in the founding and directing of Flying Tigers Airways, a private company that flew SEA Supply Corporation–purchased weapons and explosives into China in support of the Nationalist Chinese effort to combat Mao Zedong.

When Shackley arrived in Laos in the fall of 1965, he immediately reached out to Vang Pao, one of three major opium warlords competing against one another for control of the opium trade in Laos. As I briefly touched upon earlier, what Theodore Shackley did was ingenious.

In his capacity as CIA station chief in waiting in Laos, Shackley organized an opium irradiation project, directing Major Richard V. Secord's unit of the U.S. Air Force to fly sorties over the opium caravans of Vang Pao's two competitors and to drop incendiary ordnance on those caravans. In this way, Shackley had eliminated Vang Pao's only two opium-producing competitors, thereby giving Vang Pao a virtual monopoly over opium production in Laos.

It was a classic Shackley operation. In exchange for the elimination of his rivals, Vang Pao agreed to provide Shackley with a percentage of his newly increased opium profits. Thus Shackley's operation was completely invisible to the outside world, which was led to believe that opium production in Laos had simply been reduced by a third, which it technically had been. Indeed, Shackley actually had the gall to accept an award for his suppression of the opium trade in Laos. I knew all of this because the man who had negotiated Shackley's deal with Vang Pao had been Carl Jenkins.

Indeed, Carl Jenkins and Richard V. Secord had traveled together to Sydney, Australia, to set up Shackley's own bank, the Nugan Hand Bank, where Shackley could deposit millions of dollars in opium profits. Out of these illegal funds, Shackley then withdrew millions of dollars to create and secretly fund his infamous Phoenix Project, a covert political assassination project deployed throughout Southeast Asia between 1965 and 1974. The Phoenix Project was responsible for assassinating more than two hundred thousand civilians in Southeast Asia who Shackley and his associates arbitrarily and sometimes capriciously designated to be enemies of the West.

I explained all this to Bill Stevenson and Monika Jensen at the U.S. Naval Academy and gave them contact information for Gene Wheaton. I of course did not tell them about Carl Jenkins. After Ross finished "pressing the flesh," as he phrased it, he and his personal secretary, Susan, whisked me off to his private Learjet at Butler Aviation at National Airport in Washington, D.C. We boarded the jet and took off for Texas.

During the flight, Ross asked me to brief him in full about Shackley's entire operation. I named all the principal operatives in "the enterprise" and told him who had primary responsibility for which aspect of the operations. Richard V. Secord was in charge of air operations, which were coordinated out of a site in Mena, Arkansas. Ground operations were under the command of John K. Singlaub, the former commander of all U.S. forces in South Korea—until he was relieved of his command by President Jimmy Carter for insubordinately refusing to obey a direct presidential order to stop making public speeches intensely critical of the Carter administration's less-militaristic foreign policy in Korea. Those ground operations were based out of Belize. Singlaub was at that time the president of the World Anti-Communist League, a group of out-and-out fascists. Naval operations of "the enterprise" were coordinated on a large peninsula jutting into the Atlantic Ocean off Florida, out of a private company named ANV, Inc. (named for *acta non verba,* the Latin motto of the U.S. Coast Guard Academy in New London, Connecticut). I explained to Perot how this organization had been conceived and set up by Theodore Shackley.

When I finished my briefing, Ross exclaimed, "This is terrible, Dan! We have got to tell somebody about this."

"I've been trying to tell everybody," I said. "I told Congress last week. I told Tip O'Neill about it all, right after I filed the complaint. I told Claiborne Pell all about it immediately after that. He's the ranking Democrat on the Senate Foreign Relations Committee. And I told Scott Armstrong, who's a close associate of Peter Rodino, chair of the House Judiciary Committee, which has jurisdiction over impeachments."

I then told Ross what I had been told that Peter Rodino had said about not wanting the House Judiciary Committee to investigate "anything like that!"

"This is terrible!" Perot repeated. "Maybe I should tell George Bush about this. I know George. He's just like a Boy Scout in all of this."

I hesitated. "Well, Ross, if you want to tell somebody who doesn't already know about this, I would suggest that we talk to somebody other than George Bush. Bush's vice presidential national security adviser, Donald P. Gregg, is the former CIA case officer of Felix Rodriguez, the Miami-based anti-Castro Cuban exile who is running the entire weapons- and explosives-supply operation to the Contras out of Ilopango. If you want to tell someone who doesn't already know about this operation, I would propose someone like Bill Webster, the director of the FBI. After all, this is a criminal enterprise, and that should place this investigation squarely within the jurisdiction of the FBI, directly under Bill Webster."

"I know Bill Webster," Perot said. "I'll call him. You do a wire diagram for me, Dan, of this entire bunch. And write me up a little memo, explaining who all these guys are and where they all come from, and I'll give him a call." He leaned back into his chair and lit up with a big smile that somehow made his ears look even bigger than they usually did. "You know, Dan, that's one of the advantages of being a billionaire. They'll always take your call!"

We agreed that I would draft this memo for him, along with a wire diagram graphically displaying how each one of these men and each one of these departments of "the enterprise" related to the whole. Then Ross would call FBI director Bill Webster and expressly ask him to investigate this crowd.

We flew into Dallas and landed at Butler Aviation, on the private side of the airport. Ross drove me in his big white Cadillac to one of the most expensive hotels in Dallas, where he had already reserved one of the best rooms for me. Then he drove away, telling me to send the memo and the wire diagram to him from Washington as soon as I had them ready. I went to the desk, registered, and let the expensively dressed bellhop carry my shabby-looking overnight bag up to the room.

I worked on the memo and the wire diagram late into the night. Then I remembered that I had no flight reservation back to Washington. So I called the Dallas Airport and got a ticket back to Washington for $500, because it was on such short notice. The hotel had no shuttle service to the airport, so I had to call a cab, which cost me an additional $30. And when I went to the front desk to check out, I only then learned that Ross had reserved the room for me but that no one had paid for it. I had to pay the entire $300 room cost for one night! I never did tell Ross about this. I guess a billionaire just doesn't think that $300 for one night at a hotel and $500 for a flight to Washington is such a big deal. Hell, the $30 for just the cab ride to the airport was beyond my daily budget.

Back in Washington, I told Bob Fink what I was doing, and he insisted upon reviewing both the memo and the wire diagram before I delivered it to Ross. I remember that he threw a veritable fit over the fact that I had used commas where I should have used semicolons and that I had capitalized over half a dozen words that he thought I should not have. To say that Bob Fink was meticulous about detail is like saying that Michelangelo was an OK ceiling painter.

"What did you think of the *substance* of the memo and the diagram?" I asked him.

"Oh, the substance is fine. Fine. But it was so sloppy with the poor punctuation and the misuse of all those capitals."

When I completed the memo and the wire diagram, I decided it would be good to have someone reliable know that I was delivering these important documents directly to Ross Perot for FBI director Webster. So I had Bob Fink himself, Bella Abzug's chief congressional investigator, personally hand-deliver the package directly to Ross Perot. Ross was in Washington attending a session of Ronald Reagan's National Security Advisory Committee. Bob was thrilled to meet Ross in person, and Ross spoke freely with Bob about the contents of the package and what Ross was going to do with it.

So, as of November 15 of 1986, the fat was in the fire, and the Iran-Contra scandal was about to explode.

Ross Perot went directly to Bill Webster and hand-delivered the documents. Webster opened the package in Perot's presence, read the memo carefully, reviewed the wire diagram—and went through the roof.

Webster immediately assigned his top FBI investigator, one Danny Coulson, to this vital matter. I spoke directly with Danny a number of times between mid-November and mid-December of 1986. I communicated one lead after another to him, giving him names of pilots, names of people who were smuggling cocaine into the United States, and everything else he asked for. I was completely confident that Danny Coulson was on the job and was sincerely going after these guys. And I am sure, to this day, that he was intending to get them.

A few days later, Gene Wheaton came to my office at the Christic Institute—which was a rare thing for him to have done—and he asked me, to my surprise, if it would be all right if he agreed to Oliver North's request that Gene fly over to Pakistan and meet with Pakistani president Mohammad Zia ul-Haq. North wanted Gene to negotiate a truce between Zia and North in a conflict over Zia's having stolen a portion of the weapons that North had been secretly shipping to the Mujahedeen in Afghanistan through Zia's "good offices" in Pakistan. It turned out that when North had found out that Zia was doing this, North had called Zia "a fucking thief." Zia had responded by flatly refusing to act any longer as the go-between for North and the Mujahedeen in the CIA's arms-smuggling operation to arm Afghan rebels in their fight against the Soviet invasion of their country. Since Gene had known Zia personally for many years, North wanted Gene to fly to Pakistan to extend North's personal apology to Zia so that Zia would once again agree to serve as the "cutout" for U.S.-supplied arms to the Mujahedeen. Wheaton wanted to know if it was alright with me if he did this for North.

I had never personally disliked North or held it against him that, as deputy director of Reagan's National Security Council, he had carried out direct orders to assist the Contras—orders that no doubt were given to him directly by Admiral John Poindexter, Ronald Reagan's national security adviser. And North was doing one hell of a job at assisting the Contras, I thought. It was just that what he was doing was absolutely unconstitutional—and criminal to boot—which was why I was going to have to put him in federal prison for his having done it.

But as far as the Mujahedeen were concerned, I told Wheaton that I had absolutely no personal objection to his helping North by flying to Pakistan and delivering North's personal apology to Zia, though I told Wheaton that I thought that Zia was a total fascist—and a very weird person as well.

Gene checked in with me as soon as he returned to Washington from Pakistan. When he did, he told me the weirdest story: It seems that Gene had been instructed by North to fly back from Pakistan through Rome after he had completed his mission. He was instructed by North to go directly to a particular address in Rome. There, Gene would be told what to do. The address turned out to be international headquarters of the Knights of Malta, an extremely conservative fraternal order of ultra-right-wing Catholic men. The Knights of Malta has included such luminaries as Italy's Benito Mussolini; the Third Reich's anti-Soviet and anti–Eastern Bloc Nazi intelligence chief Reinhard Gehlen (Theodore Shackley's immediate superior in Berlin for twelve years); Otto von Habsburg; Archduke Carl Ludwig of

Austria; Franz von Papen; Juan Perón of Argentina; and such American co-luminaries as William F. Buckley Jr., William "Wild Bill" Donovan, James Jesus Angleton, Patrick Buchanan, John Raskob, Robert Abplanalp, Joseph P. Kennedy, John A. McCone, J. Peter Grace, Rick Santorum, and Cardinal Francis Spellman.

When he arrived and announced himself, Gene was immediately shown to a private room, where he was then given a slip of paper with a telephone number handwritten on it. He dialed the number. It was the private, unlisted home telephone number of William Casey, Ronald Reagan's CIA director. Gene presented his oral report directly to Casey himself, then hung up and flew home to Washington. Once back in Washington, he came straight to me and reported in.

At the end of the third week of November 1986, I received another telephone call from Gene Wheaton. He wanted me to come to his office on K Street, right next door to the Audubon Society headquarters in downtown Washington, D.C. I was a bit puzzled. I had not known that Gene Wheaton even had an office in downtown Washington—or anywhere else for that matter.

I drove in the Blue Flame to the address he had given me. It was a small townhouse. I walked up to the second floor, and there he was in a full suit and tie. It was the first time I had ever seen Gene in a suit.

I looked around the office. There were little fighter planes, tanks, armored personnel carriers, and other miniature military vehicles everywhere. Then I saw, sitting on Gene's desk, a personally signed photograph of Bashir Gemayel, the assassinated president of Lebanon, and his brother Amine, who had replaced him as president of Lebanon the month after Bashir's assassination in 1982. I knew that Gene had been the chief of security for the U.S. military mission in Tehran and that he spoke fluent Farsi. But I had not known that he knew, or had had anything to do with, the Gemayel brothers or the Lebanese Christian militia.

I asked him about the picture as I sat down across from him at his desk.

"Oh, yeah. That!" he said with a smile. "Just a token of their affection, for a favor that I did for them once, before Bashir was killed."

"Oh!" I said, as if that was just an everyday occurrence.

Without any further explanation of the photograph or the various min-iature military vehicles appointing his office, Gene announced, "A Lebanese magazine by the name of *Ash-Shiraa*, which I happen to subscribe to, this morning published a story reporting that Oliver North has arranged to sell a number of TOW missiles to Hezbollah in Iran and to transfer a portion of the profits from the sale of those missiles to the off-shore bank account in the Bahamas of Adolfo Calero of the FDN Contras. I thought you would want to know."

I did.

Gene then went on to suggest that I tell Bill Casey at the CIA that I knew this before he learned how I found out, "since it will take the assholes in the agency a week to get the news." Gene told me that he just happened to know Ed Hymoff, the author who was working with Casey on his autobiography. Gene could set up a lunch meeting for me with Hymoff the very next day, where I could communicate to Casey, through him, that I knew about this. "It will drive Casey crazy," Gene said, "especially if you meet Hymoff here, in this office!"

I agreed to do that, though I couldn't quite figure out what Gene was up to.

The next day I had lunch, right there in Gene Wheaton's K Street office, with Hymoff. As recommended by Gene, I explained to Hymoff that I knew all about North's sale of TOW missiles to Hezbollah and about the deposit of a portion of the funds generated from that sale into the Caribbean bank account of Adolfo Calero. Hymoff almost shit! That evening Hymoff duti-fully reported to Casey what I had told him.

The very next day, Oliver North and his secretary, Fawn Hall, started their famous "shredding party," during which they shredded hundreds of secret documents from North's files at his NSC office. North had his secre-tary smuggle dozens of other documents out of his office in her underclothes. These were delivered directly to Tom Green, an attorney in Washington, D.C., who was representing Richard V. Secord, Rafael "Chi Chi" Quintero, Tom Clines, and Middle Eastern businessman Albert Hakim in our civil racketeering case.

On November 25th, Gene called me back to his office on K Street, saying that some kind of announcement was being prepared, right at that moment, by the White House. He wanted us to find a local bar or restaurant at which to watch the upcoming announcement together, live.

I drove over to Gene's office, and we quickly left to find a sports bar where we could see any televised announcement the White House might make.

We hadn't been there for more than five minutes when a special bulletin came on the television. Edwin Meese, Reagan's and Bush's attorney general, was scheduled to hold a press conference within minutes. None of the news staff on the network had any idea about the subject of the press conference. But they didn't have to wait long. Meese came to the podium at the Justice Department and announced,

> The Justice Department has just learned that a young lieutenant colonel in the Marine Corps has, without any authorization whatsoever, personally organized a number of retired U.S. military personnel and intelligence agents into an off-the-shelf, private, covert operations enterprise that appears to have been responsible for obtaining and distributing surplus American arms to members of the former National Guard forces of Nicaraguan president Anastasio Somoza, which might possibly be considered, by some, to constitute a violation of the recently enacted Boland Amendment.

He went on to say that this lieutenant colonel appeared to have somehow secured American-made TOW missiles, sold them to the Hezbollah of Iran, and then deposited a portion of the profits generated by this sale into a bank account in the name of an organization supporting the Nicaraguan Contras. Meese announced that the young Marine Corps lieutenant colonel in question had been immediately suspended from his duties, without pay, and that Meese was drafting, for submission to the Special Panel of the United States Court of Appeals for the District of Columbia for the Appointment of Special Counsels, a petition for the appointment of a special counsel to investigate whether these activities had been authorized, in writing, by the president of the United States.

"What bullshit!" I exclaimed. "That's *not* the right question! There are literally dozens of potentially impeachable officials in the Reagan–Bush administration who have committed criminal acts who need to be investigated and officially impeached if there is going to be any effective solution of this problem."

Wheaton grunted his agreement. And we got up from the table at the sports bar and went back to his office to plan our response to this turn of events.

Later that afternoon, when I had returned to my office, I received a telephone call from Danny Coulson. He told me that in light of the request for the appointment of a special prosecutor by Attorney General Meese, he had been told by Director Webster that he would have to stand down from his previous investigation. He wanted to assure me, however, that he would turn over everything that I had given to him to the special prosecutor to be appointed by the U.S. District Court of Appeals. He said that he would call me as soon as he knew who that was going to be.

Meese, in his official request for the appointment of a special counsel, requested that the special counsel investigate only the very narrowest possible question: whether the president of the United States ever expressly authorized, in writing, the sale of American TOW missiles to members of Hezbollah . . . and then expressly authorized, again in writing, the transfer of any portion of the profits generated by that sale to Contra forces in Central America—and whether that, even if proven, would constitute an impeachable offense, in light of the fact that the Boland Amendment had been only a "resolution" of Congress and not a *law* as such.

Danny Coulson called around Christmastime and told me that the special counsel who had been appointed by the court of appeals was one Lawrence Walsh, a senior partner in the Oklahoma City law firm of Crowe & Dunlevy, the very law firm that had represented the Kerr-McGee Nuclear Corporation in the Karen Silkwood case against us back in 1977.

This was not an auspicious start.

In early January 1987, Danny Coulson called me again to tell me that he was, at that very moment, leaving his office at the Justice Department to drive to National Airport to pick up former Republican federal judge

Lawrence Walsh when he arrived to begin his investigation. Coulson said that FBI director Webster was making a specific request to have Coulson assigned as one of Special Prosecutor Walsh's staff investigators. This was good. I had developed confidence in Danny Coulson, from the questions he had asked in our telephone conversations and from the follow-up questions he had asked soon thereafter, making it clear to me that he understood what I was telling him and that he was actively investigating what I was telling him.

Coulson wanted to know if I could go with him, right then, to immediately meet Judge Walsh and to brief Walsh directly on what I had discovered, to date, in my investigation of "the enterprise."

However, I could not meet with Judge Walsh right at that moment because I was expected momentarily to meet directly with Joe Biden, the new chairman of the U.S. Senate Foreign Relations Committee in the new Democratic-controlled Senate. I was scheduled to brief chairman Biden at 10:00 AM.

That was the second serious mistake I made in the Iran-Contra case; the first was my *not* making a motion to the Eleventh Circuit Court of Appeals to have James Lawrence King forcibly removed as our judge. In retrospect, I should have called Joe Biden immediately and postponed my appointment with him so I could have met directly with Judge Walsh and made certain that he fully understood the exact details of "the enterprise" and the seriousness of its constitutional implications. I thought I would be able to meet with him the very next day, or even later that afternoon. But that did not happen.

The next day, one Victor O'Korn, the chief investigator assigned by Walsh to investigate "the enterprise," came to my office at the Christic Institute on North Capitol Street to interview me. I was disappointed that Danny Coulson was not with him and that I had not been asked again to meet directly with Judge Walsh himself. Coulson knew the lay of the land in this investigation. I would have to bring Victor up to speed on all the facts, which were not simple.

As I laid out the contours and personnel of "the enterprise" to Victor O'Korn, I could tell by his expressions and demeanor that he was growing more and more shocked with each revelation. In fact, it became increasingly apparent that O'Korn really did not *want* to hear what I was telling him. I noted that, after just a few minutes, he was no longer taking notes. He just fixed his gaze on me and nodded at various points.

It was the third mistake on my part in this case to *not* insist that that meeting be tape-recorded so there would be a verifiable record that Judge Walsh and his staff were indeed fully informed about every key fact concerning "the enterprise" and its relationship to George H. W. Bush, Theodore Shackley, and the CIA.

It was clear to me that Victor O'Korn had made a conscious decision only partway into my presentation that much of what I was telling him was somehow "beyond the very narrow scope of what Special Prosecutor Walsh had been expressly authorized by the court of appeals to investigate." So he simply refused to memorialize that information in any manner.

I explained to O' Korn, in that first special prosecutor interview, that their investigation had to focus in on the kidnapping and torture of CIA Beirut station chief William Buckley back in March 1984. "You have to understand the centrality of that specific event in order to truly understand what 'the enterprise' is all about," I told him. "William Buckley was not kidnapped and tortured simply because he was the Beirut station chief for the CIA. CIA station chiefs come and go, in Beirut and in other places. But they don't get kidnapped, tortured, or assassinated."

I asked O' Korn if he knew the last previous CIA station chief to be assassinated.

He did not know.

"It was Richard Welch," I explained to him, "the CIA station chief in Athens. But he, too, was not assassinated simply because he was the CIA station chief in Athens." I let a moment of suspense pass while O' Korn sat there, puzzled. He was still not taking any notes.

"They both worked directly under Theodore Shackley, coordinating tactical assassination projects in the Middle East!" I told him.

He shuddered for the briefest moment, then simply stared at me. He asked, "Who is Theodore Shackley?"

"Theodore Shackley," I said, "is the former Deputy Director of Covert Operations of the CIA who was hand-picked for that position by George

Bush when Bush was appointed by Gerald Ford to be director of the CIA, just before Welch was assassinated. Shackley is the *actual* creator and director of the 'off-the-shelf enterprise.' It is not Oliver North."

"It's not?" O'Korn exclaimed.

"No," I said. "It is not. It is Theodore Shackley." I then explained to O'Korn what I had learned from Carl Jenkins and Chi Chi Quintero—everything from the Phoenix Project to the opium warlords in Southeast Asia to the smuggling of weapons through the Ilopango Airport to the Contras. "This is all about terrorism, Victor. Shackley is assassinating people all over the world whom he designates to be 'terrorists.' And he is branding everyone who opposes his rabidly anticommunist policies, with any resort to arms, as a 'terrorist.' And he is *systematically exterminating* them, Victor. That's what this is all about."

O'Korn almost shit!

I gave him all the names and all the contacts who could confirm this information for Judge Walsh. But O'Korn would not write them down. Instead, he was overwhelmed by how far above his pay grade this conversation had gone. So he clambered out of his chair and gathered his materials to get out of my office as quickly as he could. The information had simply overloaded the circuits of his belief system, almost certainly causing him to categorize me as a "conspiracy theorist."

I telephoned Danny Coulson numerous times, trying to explain that I was certain that this Victor O'Korn character whom Judge Walsh had assigned to be the chief investigator of the Iran-Contra scandal was *not* up to the task at hand. I needed to get Coulson to sit down with me, face-to-face, so I could explain what I could not safely communicate to him over the telephone. But he stopped answering my calls. He never called me back after my single interview with O'Korn.

A short time later, I received a phone call from Ross Perot. I drove over to National Airport to pick him up at Butler Aviation and showed up in a little blue Volkswagen Squareback that had been donated to the Christic Institute. I drove away, with Ross Perot, the billionaire, in the passenger seat of this old blue Volkswagen. I drove across the Key Bridge and out to the Virginia safe house where I always met with Carl Jenkins. I wanted to introduce Ross directly to Jenkins, whom I considered "the mother lode" of inside information about Theodore Shackley and "the enterprise"—information that was coming directly from Chi Chi Quintero, the number 2 man at Ilopango.

Gene Wheaton had arranged for me to bring Ross to meet directly with Carl, but when we arrived, only Gene was there in the living room. Gene told Ross, "Carl and Elizabeth are on their way here. They will be here in a minute."

Then Gene did something very strange. He pulled me aside and asked me to leave so that he could talk with Ross alone and so that Ross could talk alone with Carl and Elizabeth. I agreed, knowing that they would probably talk more freely without me in the room. I was to call in to the safe house in two hours and be prepared to come pick up Ross or to wait for any additional length of time that they needed to finish their meeting. It took two such calls for Ross to complete his first meeting with Carl and Elizabeth.

When I picked Ross up, he asked me to drive him to Georgetown. He did not say what for, but I remember him saying that he had to make "an important phone call." I was happy to do whatever I could to help Ross help us get to the bottom of what was going on. When we got to Georgetown, he asked me to park the Volkswagen and walk with him to where he was going to make the call. So I did. When he came back from making his call, he was in great spirits and began to explain that the General Motors board of directors (which had recently made him a member upon his having purchased a major percentage of GM shares to help the company out of a tight financial spot) had just bought back all of his shares, at a huge profit to Ross. GM wanted him off its board of directors because, at every meeting, he told them exactly what he thought they had to do to put the company back into proper business shape. "So I just made a huge profit with just one phone call!" he told me. "That's how business gets done in America, Dan! Ain't it great to be an American?" And he *meant* it.

I wasn't accustomed to discussing multimillion-dollar stock sales with billionaires, but I walked jauntily down the street in Georgetown with Ross Perot, perfectly happy to share his obvious joy at having gotten the best of the General Motors board.

I drove Ross back to Butler Aviation, and he turned to shake my hand as he climbed aboard his private Learjet to return to Texas.

"You're a good man, Dan. You are a real patriot," he said. And then he climbed aboard and the door closed.

I stood there on the tarmac as night fell over Washington, next to the beat-up little blue Volkswagen Squareback, and I couldn't help but feel like the beneficiary of the afterglow of a successful deal closed by one of America's top businessmen. But I wasn't sure whether it was the deal with Carl Jenkins or the deal Ross Perot had just closed with General Motors that excited him more. Perhaps it was both. I guess that is how business is done in America. "What's good for General Motors is good for America."

The Iran-Contra affair was soon going to unravel in full public view. The question was, would anyone understand what it was truly all about? Or would it be just like the Watergate burglary—and the Kennedy assassination—just too complicated to ever *really* understand?

CHAPTER *twenty-nine*

A S OF JANUARY 21 of 1987, Congress was finally back under the full control of the Democrats, and they created a *joint* House and Senate select committee to investigate and hold hearings on the Iran-Contra affair. And, true to his word, Rhode Island Democratic senator Claiborne Pell, the ranking Democrat on the Senate Foreign Relations Committee, took all the steps necessary to establish a separate and independent select committee in the Senate to investigate the Christic Institute's charges against "the enterprise" and the Reagan–Bush administration. It was to be called the Senate Select Committee on Narcotics and Terrorism, and it was, indeed, to be chaired by Massachusetts senator John Kerry, just as I had requested. The second investigation, entirely separate, was the criminal investigation by Judge Walsh, the court-appointed special prosecutor of the Iran-Contra scandal.

And, of course, there was the third investigation: our civil prosecution that we were attempting to wage in the Southern District of Florida, if we could ever figure out how to get around James Lawrence King's efforts to block our every move in court.

My hopes were not high for what was going to be done by the House and Senate joint select committee on Iran-Contra, in either the House or the Senate, since three out of every four members of the committee, appointed by the Democratic House and Senate leadership, were ardent active supporters of the Contras and had actually voted, in 1985, to give $100 million in aid to the Contras for "humanitarian assistance" as a sop to the right-wing anticommunists in the House and Senate. Worse yet, the Republican Senate leadership had succeeded in getting Tom Polgar named to be the chief Senate investigator for the joint select committee. He was the career CIA agent hand-picked in 1973 by Theodore Shackley to become the new CIA station chief in Mexico City, and he was the man who had dismissed Joseph Burkholder Smith as his deputy.

When I heard that Tom Polgar was being considered to be the chief investigator for the joint select committee, I immediately approached ranking Republican senator Warren Rudman in a meeting set up by Carl Jenkins and warned him about Polgar. Rudman literally exploded at me, shouting and turning red in the face. He jumped up and down in his office and declared what a good man Tom Polgar was and how unpatriotic "all of your types" were. It was truly one of the most remarkable displays of infantile behavior on the part of an elected official that I had ever seen in all of my years in Washington—and I had seen more than a few. Bill Taylor had accompanied me to the meeting, but Rudman had wanted to meet with me in private. When he exploded, Bill was able to hear him all the way in the waiting area.

"What an unmitigated asshole!" I proclaimed to Bill Taylor—and to everyone else within earshot—as I walked out of Rudman's office, with him still shouting and stomping around behind me, apparently unaware of the fact that I had walked out on him.

With Tom Polgar in place as chief investigator for the joint select committee, the following people served on committees to investigate the Iran-Contra affair:

HOUSE SELECT COMMITTEE TO INVESTIGATE COVERT ARMS TRANSACTIONS WITH IRAN:
> Representative Lee Hamilton (D-IN), chairman
> Representative Thomas Foley (D-WA)
> Representative Peter Rodino Jr. (D-NJ)
> Representative Jack Brooks (D-TX)
> Representative Louis Stokes (D-OH)
> Representative Les Aspin (D-WI)
> Representative Edward Boland (D-MA)
> Representative Ed Jenkins (D-GA)
> Representative Dante Fascell (R-FL), vice chairman
> Representative Dick Cheney (R-WY), ranking member
> Representative William Broomfield (R-MI)

Representative Henry Hyde (R-IL)

Representative Jim Courter (R-NJ)

Representative Bill McCollum (R-FL)

Representative Michael DeWine (R-OH)

John Nields Jr., chief counsel

George Van Cleve, chief minority counsel

SENATE SELECT COMMITTEE ON SECRET MILITARY ASSISTANCE
TO IRAN AND THE NICARAGUAN OPPOSITION:

Senator Daniel Inouye (D-HI), chairman

Senator George Mitchell (D-ME)

Senator Sam Nunn (D-GA)

Senator Paul Sarbanes (D-MD)

Senator Howell Heflin (D-AL)

Senator David Boren (D-OK)

Senator Warren Rudman (R-NH), vice chairman

Senator James McClure (R-ID)

Senator Orrin Hatch (R-UT)

Senator William Cohen (R-ME)

Senator Paul Trible (R-VA)

Arthur Liman, chief counsel

As the House and Senate joint select committee plodded forward as slowly as it possibly could without risking a public outcry, we were making significant headway, behind the scenes, with the Kerry Committee, as it came to be called. John Kerry's chief investigator, Jack Blum, was aggressively seeking information from us, from Brian Barger and Robert Parry, and from eyewitness after eyewitness whom we, together, provided to him. Blum and his assistants on the Senate Select Committee on Terrorism and Narcotics went so far as to prepare an initial draft of a report of the select committee, a copy of which he provided to us for review and comment. That initial draft expressly concluded that those in charge of the illegal weapons- and explosives-supply operation to the Contras were directly involved in *knowingly* smuggling cocaine into the United States on aircraft that were being used to smuggle the arms and explosives into Central America, as well as on specific shrimp company boats that were going into and out of Miami.

Matters were definitely looking up. We had John Kerry, Claiborne Pell's "future Democratic Party star," leading the Senate investigation. Jack Blum was accepting all of our recommendations as to whom he should subpoena and question. And all of those interviews were providing Blum and Kerry with totally credible, directly admissible evidence proving, beyond any reasonable doubt, exactly what we were asserting in our civil complaint. Kerry's committee had even put it in writing, flatly accusing the Reagan–Bush administration of consciously and willfully sanctioning massive cocaine smuggling into the United States to secretly finance a right-wing war against Nicaragua, with whom our nation had open diplomatic relations—actions that had been expressly prohibited by Congress through its enactment of two Boland amendments.

A significant negative development was getting ready to take place, however, when Marine Corps lieutenant Oliver North refused to fall on his sword and take the rap for allegedly having created the off-the-shelf enterprise on his own, as Reagan–Bush attorney general Edwin Meese had charged in his November 25 press announcement. Instead, North testified before the joint House and Senate select committee that he had been doing nothing but following direct orders from Admiral John Poindexter, president Reagan's national security adviser. North testified, with regard to those orders, "I had every reason to believe [they] came directly from the president." The administration's proffered fall guy had shockingly refused to take the fall. He was pushing back.

We were, at first, delighted.

Strangely, Oliver North was not denying what he had done. He was, indeed, proud of what he had done. He effectively wrapped himself in the American flag, pressed out his chest full of medals, and spit directly in the eye of Congress, stating, "Certainly, I lied to you! This was a covert operation!" North championed fighting "terrorists," which he branded the entire Sandinista government, despite the fact that the Sandinista government had been expressly recognized as the legitimate government of Nicaragua by the Democratic administration of Jimmy Carter. North also was totally unapologetic about having diverted profits from selling what he professed to be defective TOW missiles to Hezbollah terrorists in the Middle East and channeling those funds to the Nicaraguan Contras . . . even though Congress had expressly and publicly prohibited the administration from giving them any aid, direct or indirect. "I thought that it was a neat idea," North proclaimed proudly to Congress and to the American people, who were glued to their television sets across America, hanging on his every word.

Oliver North basically "faced down" the purely politically motivated members of Congress, playing both the old anticommunist card and the new antiterrorist card simultaneously against the Democratic Congress on behalf of the Republican administration. He refused to apologize, but at the same time he refused to shelter the president or the president's national security adviser, Admiral John Poindexter. Instead, he stood them up and championed their cause, effectively challenging them to join him in his confrontation of the Democratic Congress and pushing them into the fight, offering to hold their coat—but *not* offering to fall on his sword as they had hoped he would.

Oliver North actually declared in his testimony that the executive branch of our federal government possessed the unilateral authority to make war on any country that the president deemed appropriate—even if the Congress of the United States had expressly prohibited him from doing so. North argued that all that the Constitution provides is that Congress shall "control the purse strings" with regard to paying for such a war. But Congress could not stop the president from making war on any country or group he chose if he could get the money to finance such military action from some source other than Congress. In this instance, Reagan, Poindexter, and North's "other source of funding" had come from such foreign sources as the sultan of Brunei. North, of course, did not reveal the fact that one of the principal sources of funding for the off-the-shelf, self-financing, *private* covert operations enterprise was a percentage of the profits being generated by the Medillian Colombian cocaine cartel. And not one of the select joint committee members deigned to ask him anything about that. Though North's bold assertion as to the limited constitutional authority Congress had over the war-making power of the United States government was an absolutely sophomoric misconstruing of the constitutional structure of our United States government, it certainly was a pure and bold idea.

And, when pitted directly against nothing more than the aimlessly relative values harbored by almost every professional politician in the Congress, such a "pure and bold idea" had a distinct advantage. And North impressively—and successfully—pressed that advantage over members of Congress on national television during his testimony before the joint select committee.

The testimony of North and the frankly politically cowardly response to that testimony on the part of Democrats on the joint select committee constituted a turning point in the Iran-Contra investigation *away* from the positive direction in which it had been heading. To make matters even worse, the joint House and Senate select committee granted prosecutorial immunity to most of the principal participants in the Iran-Contra weapons supply operation, thereby making it functionally impossible to effectively criminally prosecute those individuals after they had testified. It was becoming clear to me that members of Congress did not *want* to get to the bottom of the Iran-Contra scandal because they knew what lay there, waiting to explode.

However, things then got even worse. We were able to take the sworn deposition of the personal secretary of Vice President George H. W. Bush. She provided to us certified copies of internal White House talking-point notes pertaining to two key meetings. The participants in those meetings were Vice President George H. W. Bush himself; Donald P. Gregg, Bush's vice presidential national security adviser; and Felix Rodriguez. The talking-point notes from those meetings expressly stated that on two separate and distinct occasions, Bush, Gregg, and Rodriguez had met personally to discuss "the military resupply of the Contras," an act that was expressly forbidden by Congress pursuant to its passage of the Boland Amendment.

When I subpoenaed and cross-examined Donald P. Gregg on this matter, he blatantly perjured himself, swearing that both written records contained identical "typographical errors" that *should have* read "the military resupply of the copters" that had been provided by the administration to the Salvadorian government.

Despite reluctance on the part of members of the joint select committee to press members of "the enterprise" to reveal their criminal conduct,

Iran-Contra special prosecutor Lawrence Walsh returned his first set of federal criminal indictments against Richard V. Secord, Rafael "Chi Chi" Quintero, Theodore Shackley's immediate deputy Tom Clines, and Middle Eastern businessman Albert Hakim.

When Secord, Hakim, and Quintero appeared at their federal criminal arraignment before Judge Gerhard Gesell in the United States District Court for the District of Columbia, attorney Tom Green (who had helped Oliver North and Fawn Hall unlawfully remove and destroy secret government documents from North's office) made a motion to postpone any further proceedings in the criminal case, informing Judge Gesell, "There is a federal *civil* case going on down in Florida that has made the exact same charges against all of the people named as coconspirators with us in this indictment, and it would be unduly burdensome for these defendants to have to try to defend themselves in this new criminal case while we are still trying to defend them against these same charges in that civil case. So we would therefore request that this criminal court agree to postpone all further proceedings in this criminal case until the civil case mounted by the Christic Institute in Florida is completed."

Judge Gesell was totally shocked at that request. "Excuse me, Mr. Green. I think that you have a very serious misunderstanding of what is to be done under such circumstances. You have it completely backward. When a civil case is under way and a criminal indictment is brought arising out of the same facts and circumstances as underlie that earlier civil case, all the proceedings, including civil discovery, in that previously filed civil case are to be put on hold until the *criminal* case is disposed of. So if you will just tell me who the judge is on that federal civil case down in Florida, I will immediately contact him personally, and I will have him postpone all further proceedings in that civil case. Who is the judge in that case, Mr. Green?"

"The judge in that case, Your Honor, is Judge James Lawrence King," Tom Green said.

After we saw the report of these proceedings on the national news, we expected to hear, very quickly, from Judge King. Indeed, on the very following morning, I received a telephone call from King's law clerk from Miami, asking me to come before Judge King the following Friday morning at ten o'clock. The conference was scheduled to take place in the ceremonial courtroom in the federal courthouse in Miami.

Lewis Pitts, Rob Hager, and I flew down to Miami Thursday night and went to the federal courthouse on Friday morning. We were in the ceremonial courtroom at about 9:30 AM when Judge King's law clerk entered the courtroom. He was younger than we, so we were all chatting with him, putting him at ease, asking him what this conference was going to be about. Judge King's law clerk informed us that Judge Gesell had indeed called Judge King on Tuesday afternoon and that Judge King had immediately asked the clerk to set up this conference. So he assumed that that was what this was about.

"That's good," I said. "We have been having a very difficult time getting Judge King to rule on our numerous motions to compel a response to our discovery demands issued to the defendants."

Judge King's law clerk looked a little embarrassed. He was actually sitting in the witness box in the courtroom. We were the only ones there, so to break the tension, Lewis Pitts started clowning around with him. Lewis approached the witness box and, with artificial drama, leaned on the witness stand like a defense attorney in a movie. He said dramatically, "And just where were you, Mr. Witness, on the night in question, at the time of this heinous crime?"

Realizing the humor of the moment, Judge King's young law clerk played the caricatured "lying witness" role, answering with the classic dodge answer. "Ah, I have no specific recollection of the events of that night as I sit here right now."

All of us in the room were having a great laugh at this skit when, suddenly, Judge King entered the courtroom from the judge's chambers. We all scurried to our respective places. Judge King then took the bench and made an immediate announcement.

"I have decided that we have spent enough time wrangling over discovery questions in this case. So I have decided that we are going to move this case immediately to trial one week from next Monday." Without any hesitation, he started to lay out logistical rulings as to where each of the parties would sit in the courtroom and how many reserved seats each side would be allotted. He obviously intended to drone on, delivering more such minutiae as a means of filibustering the conference.

I stood up and interrupted him. "Your Honor, I must frankly state that this comes as a total shock. The plaintiffs still have over two dozen outstanding discovery motions pending, ranging from motions to compel to motions for more specific production. We also still have over one dozen already-scheduled sworn depositions officially noticed that have not yet been conducted."

Judge King looked up from his notes and said, "Mr. Sheehan, you know my opinion of most of your discovery efforts in this case to date. I think the plaintiffs have had ample time to complete whatever discovery to which you were entitled. You delayed your discovery in this case for almost an entire year!"

"Your Honor! There was an outstanding rule 12(b)(6) motion to dismiss our complaint as a matter of law and a motion to dismiss our complaint on the grounds that it failed to state adequate facts to support reasonable notice to the defendants as to what we were specifically charging each of them with having done. So we devoted the early stages of this case to the preparation of a lengthy affidavit, which we submitted to the court as an attachment to our opposition to the defendant's motion to dismiss and our legal briefs, Your Honor. And the court, with all due respect, Your Honor, has not ruled on any of our plaintiffs' motions to compel discovery or on any of our responses to any of the defendants' motions. It seems hardly appropriate, with this being the status of the discovery process in this case, to move this case to trial, Your Honor, with all due respect." The sarcasm of my emphasis on the "all due respect" portion of my remarks was not lost on Judge King.

"I know your tactics, Mr. Sheehan. I have read about you! I know that you are just attempting to make me angry, so I will say something inappropriate, so you can move to have me recused from this case. But that is not going to happen in this case, Mr. Sheehan! I am in charge of how this case will be handled in this court, not you. It is my ruling that the plaintiffs in this case will be provided one more month, from this date, within which to complete all further discovery in this case. It is not this court's fault that the plaintiffs in this case spent one whole year running around holding press conferences and holding fund-raisers instead of conducting proper discovery in this case. I am ruling that this case will proceed to trial one month from today, in this courtroom!"

He started to get up and leave the bench. But Lewis Pitts rose to speak.

"Your Honor? Lewis Pitts for the plaintiffs." Lewis brought up Judge Gesell's ruling that all further proceedings in the civil case should be postponed pending the conclusion of the criminal case. "Your Honor, we frankly expected you to inform us that you had granted Judge Gesell's request."

There was a long pause as Judge King glowered down on Lewis from the bench. Then Judge King replied, "I am not responsible for what you assumed, Mr. Pitts! And I have no idea whatsoever as to what you are talking about concerning any proceedings that took place up in Washington, D.C., in some other courtroom. I received no call from Judge Gesell! The men you have accused in this case are entitled to a speedy trial. This case will proceed to trial, in this courtroom, one month from today!"

But Lewis was not to be put off so easily. "Your Honor, your law clerk announced to all of us lawyers assembled here this morning, no less than five minutes ago, that you did, indeed, receive a telephone call directly from Judge Gerhard Gesell—on Tuesday afternoon of this very week."

James Lawrence King filled with rage. He rose up out of his chair behind the bench and menaced Lewis Pitts from on high.

"Are you calling me a *liar*, Mr. Pitts?"

"I am only telling you, Your Honor, what your own law clerk told all of us no more than five minutes ago, sitting directly in that witness box," Lewis responded, rather calmly under the circumstances.

Judge King then turned on his law clerk. But as his eyes fell upon the witness stand to which Lewis Pitts had just referred, an obvious idea seemed to come to him.

"You!" Judge King exploded turning toward the young law clerk. "You will take a seat in that witness box, and you will raise your right hand and take an oath subjecting you to the potential punishment of perjury, for which I can personally imprison you for up to six months in federal prison.

And you will tell these lawyers that I never received any such call from Judge Gerhard Gesell or any other person from Washington telling me to postpone the proceedings in this case!"

The poor young law clerk was paralyzed with fear. "Ah, right now, Your Honor?"

"Right now, right here!" King said, pointing like the Grim Reaper to the witness box in the ceremonial courtroom of the Miami federal courthouse.

Trembling visibly with fear, the young law clerk moved into the witness box. Once he was seated, Judge King, who had not sat back down since he had risen from his chair in rage, literally roared at the young man, "Raise your right hand!"

The young man responded by timidly raising his right hand.

"You *do* swear to tell the truth, the whole truth, and nothing but the truth, do you not?"

"I do. I do," the law clerk squeaked.

Then Judge King, looming over him from the bench, said, "Now, you never received any telephone call from Judge Gerhard Gesell from Washington, and you never transferred any such telephone call to me in my chambers last Tuesday, or at any other time, did you?"

The poor young man looked desperately around the room at each of us, knowing that each and every one of us—his peers—knew perfectly well that he had, in fact, taken that call and had transferred it to Judge King in his chambers, just as he had told us minutes before. His eyes seemed to plead with us to release him from his loyalty to us to spare him the wrath of this tyrant. But each of us returned his glance with a cold hard stare. He knew what the truth was. It was his obligation—to us, to his generation, to his country, to his Constitution—to tell the truth, the whole truth, and nothing but the truth.

But instead he said, staring me directly in the eye, "Ah, I have no specific recollection of those events as I sit here right now."

Judge King, expecting his young law clerk to deny the existence of the phone call, was a bit puzzled at his response. To make absolutely clear that he wanted the young man to definitively lie, he put the demand to the young law clerk once again.

"Your Honor?" Lewis Pitts interjected. "If I might object. You are plainly leading your own witness."

Judge King turned on Lewis and raged at him some more. "I will question him in any way I please!" He turned back to the young man in the witness box and repeated the patently leading question for a third time.

When he was finished, the young man looked up at Judge King and, fixing his jaw, said, "I have no specific recollection of those events as I sit here right now."

Enraged, but seeing his only opportunity to claim victory, Judge King said, "There you have it! He does not confirm your story, Mr. Pitts. You be here, with Mr. Sheehan, when it comes time to try this case." He then turned and lumbered down from the bench. But when he reached the door to the chambers, he turned and said, "You have only two weeks, however, within which to submit to this court the names and the testimony of each witness that the plaintiffs wish to call, and a certified copy of every exhibit that the plaintiffs intend to submit in support of their case to this court." Then he turned and left.

The young law clerk just sat there in the witness box and hung his head. Lewis Pitts walked over to him and gave him an affectionate pat on the shoulder, letting him know that we were grateful to him for at least not affirming James Lawrence King.

Judge Gesell simply went forward with the criminal cases presented to him by Special Prosecutor Lawrence Walsh. Even with the extra three weeks gained by arguing with Judge King, we had to scramble like mad to get all of our documents and witnesses ready to begin trial in one month.

I contacted Philip Hirschkop, an old friend who was an experienced trial attorney and a member of the national board of directors of the ACLU, to help Lewis, Rob, and me review all the evidence in our case—to let us know how persuasive this evidence appeared to him to be, from an outside perspective. After reviewing the evidence, he agreed to second chair the case.

I wanted Philip's more cynical and less idealistic perspective on how we should approach a trial with such an obviously hostile and overtly prejudiced judge.

During a month-long marathon, Phil confirmed virtually all my legal and evidentiary judgments about the case. But he was still astonished that a case with such profound national security implications could actually have gotten all the way to trial. Phil said that he assumed that a man like James Lawrence King, with his relationship to the CIA, would have pulled a fast one to have gotten rid of this case, forcing us to then get past the Eleventh Circuit Court of Appeals before we would be allowed to put our case before a jury.

In preparation for trial, I explained virtually every step of the investigative, public education, and litigation strategy that had checkmated James Lawrence King at every critical juncture of the case.

We gathered up our hundreds of boxes of investigative files, sworn depositions, exhibits, and legal briefs; loaded them and all of our computers into a rented eighteen-wheel tractor-trailer truck; and drove down to Florida to try the Iran-Contra case.

We set up offices at Florida International University, where the Miami Dolphins were practicing.

CBS's *60 Minutes* was scheduled to go on the air on Sunday, June 26, 1988, and prepare the country for the Monday-morning start of the trial.

On June 23, at about one in the afternoon, I received a telephone call from the Associated Press. A young AP reporter was on the line.

"I just received a personal telephone call from James Lawrence King, the chief judge of the federal court in Miami," the reporter said. "He told me there is going to be a very important announcement about this Iran-Contra case today at 5:00 PM. Today. He asked me to come over to his chambers to personally pick up a copy of a filing that he is making. Do you know what this thing is about?"

We had no idea what this could be about. We knew all the journalists covering this case, because it was journalists who had been killed in the bombing at La Penca at which our plaintiff Tony Avirgan had been seriously injured. And the press was all over this case because it was the hottest news in the country. But none of them had heard anything about an upcoming announcement.

So Lewis, Rob Hager, and I drove over to the federal courthouse and took the elevator up to Judge King's chambers. It must have been about 3:00 PM when we got there. When we walked in, the judge's secretary saw us and her eyes got as big as saucers. She jumped up and literally ran out of the room into Judge King's personal office. Judge King then came out just a few seconds later and literally shouted at us. "Get out! Get out of my office right now!"

"Excuse me, Your Honor," I said. "We have been told that there is going to be some important announcement about our case. We'd like to know what that is."

"I told you to get out of my office, and that's an order! Or I will call the U.S. marshals and have you arrested!"

We walked out and sat down in the hall immediately across from his office. His secretary came out, slammed the door, and lowered a set of venetian blinds over his office windows.

We were still sitting there at 4:00 PM when Judge King's secretary came walking out of his chambers with three dozen copies of an official document to be filed. We got up, walked over to her, and asked if the document was for filing in the Iran-Contra case.

"I have been instructed by Judge King not to speak to you at all," she said.

"We're supposed to be served with an official copy of any filing in our case," I said.

"I have been instructed not to talk to you. You will receive your copy of the filing by mail, at your office up in Washington, D.C." She just kept walking to the elevator.

We entered the elevator with her, to her great discomfort, and rode with her down to the first floor, where the office of the clerk of the court was located. She walked straight to the court clerk's office and filed the required number of copies with the clerk of the court. We heard her explicitly tell the clerk of the court *not* to provide our plaintiffs' copy of the filing to us but to *mail* it to our office in Washington, D.C.

I stepped up to the court clerk's window as soon as Judge King's secretary had turned and walked away. I introduced myself to the clerk of the court, showing him my identification and D.C. Bar card. I then directed his attention to the address on our plaintiffs' copy of the filing and insisted that he hand-deliver our copy right then. The clerk of the court leaned out of the filing window, watched Judge King's secretary get into the elevator, and waited for the door to close. Then he smiled at me.

"I can't say as I've ever received an order quite like that from any judge's secretary. But I think that it will be perfectly fine for me to hand-deliver your copy of the filing to you here." And he did so.

Lewis, Rob, and I found three seats along the wall, sat down, and immediately began reading what Judge King had filed.

In eight distinct steps, James Lawrence King, in effect summarily dismissed our entire case—without any trial—just as he had threatened to do the very business day after our having filed it.

As step 1, King bifurcated our civil complaint.

King identified count 1 of our complaint, filed against two dozen alleged public and private associates of Oliver North and Theodore Shackley's off-the-shelf, self-financing, stand-alone, private covert operations enterprise, as the federal criminal racketeering count.

King identified count 2 of our complaint, filed against a dozen men we charged with directly and personally participating in the planning and execution of the La Penca bombing, as the common law tort count.

However, Judge King expressly refused to acknowledge that we had categorized the assassination attempt as just one overt act—of the dozens that we had specifically identified—of the *ongoing* federal criminal racketeering enterprise, thereby making each member of that unitary enterprise equally civilly responsible for each such action.

As step 2, King ruled that to have personal standing to bring a federal criminal Racketeering Act civil suit pursuant to count 1, a private citizen had to plead and prove that he or she had suffered a direct business loss as a direct and proximate result of one of the overt acts intentionally undertaken by a conscious participant in the ongoing federal criminal racketeering enterprise alleged in the complaint, and that that act had to have been undertaken to effectuate the unlawful criminal objectives of that ongoing federal criminal racketeering enterprise.

As step 3, King ruled that the specific direct business loss that our plaintiff, Tony Avirgan, had suffered was the destruction of his privately owned television camera and recording equipment in the La Penca bombing; physical injury was not a claim that would fall under RICO.

As step 4, King ruled that for Tony Avirgan to have standing to bring his count 1 RICO cause of action against the named associates of Oliver North and Theodore Shackley's enterprise, we would have to provide court-admissible evidence directly linking a proven member of the enterprise named in our complaint with the planning and commission of the common law tort identified in count 2 as having been committed against Tony Avirgan and the other journalists killed and maimed in the La Penca bombing as an overt act of that count 1 racketeering enterprise conspiracy

Each of those four rulings was entirely correct. So we could tell that he knew what the law was.

However, in step 5 of his ruling, without any legitimate legal support whatsoever, Judge James Lawrence King then excluded every piece of court-admissible evidence with which we had clearly and directly linked defendant John Hull and six of the other expressly proven members of the ongoing federal criminal racketeering enterprise to the planning and execution of the May 30, 1984, La Penca bombing.

Judge King erroneously ruled to be hearsay the direct eyewitness testimony of Jack Terrell (a proven participant in the Alabama-based Contra weapons supply operation run by Tom Posey), in which Terrell swore, in an official noticed, videotaped sworn deposition in our case, that he had been physically present in a secret meeting with John Hull and several other of the named defendants in our complaint and that in that meeting, he had personally witnessed and heard named defendant Felipe Vidal state, in the physical presence and hearing of each of the three other named defendants, the following direct criminal admission: "We are the ones who put the bomb under Edén Pastora at La Penca, but we missed him. And we want to hire you to kill Edén Pastora for us."

Any first-year law student familiar with the federal rules of evidence knows that such a direct criminal admission uttered by a specifically named defendant against his own criminal interests in the physical presence and hearing of others is an express exception to the hearsay rule and is directly admissible against the speaker of that direct criminal admission against interests. Such a direct criminal admission is deemed to be inherently believable because no one would be likely to make such a direct criminal admission against his or her own interests unless it were true. Moreover, a direct criminal admission against the interests of the speaker that directly criminally implicates others who are physically present when that statement is made within their plain hearing is directly admissible against every one of those listeners if they do and say nothing to try to disassociate themselves from that statement. That is a further direct exception to the rule against hearsay, which every law student knows.

Judge King then excluded the sworn deposition testimony of John Hull's private secretary, who testified to withdrawing $50,000 in cash for Hull, Judge King claiming that the events she testified about were "too far removed from the time of the La Penca bombing."

For that same reason, Judge King excluded the testimony of John Hull's professional driver, who swore that he personally drove Hull to a secret meeting with Per Anker Hansen, the man who stood criminally indicted as the perpetrator of the La Penca bombing, and that he saw Hull give Hansen an envelope filled with cash shortly after Hull's secretary had delivered the cash to Hull.

Judge King also excluded the testimony of the proprietor of a small boat rental hut on the Rio San Juan who had rented a boat to John Hull and Per Anker Hansen twenty-two days before the La Penca bombing and who had personally witnessed Hull and Hansen traveling in that rented boat directly across the Rio San Juan to the La Penca site, where the bombing was perpetrated by Hansen twenty-two days later. This testimony was excluded by Judge King, again on the grounds that it was "too far removed in time from the bombing" and that "to allow this testimony to be presented to a jury would be highly prejudicial to the defendants, since the jury might mistakenly confuse the date of the sighting with the date of the bombing and, therefore, mistakenly believe that John Hull was with Per Anker Hansen on the day of the bombing.

Judge King then excluded, again as hearsay, the direct sworn testimony of Carlos Rojas Chinchilla, who had sworn, in a videotaped deposition, that John Hull and the other named defendants in the bombing against Edén Pastora were planning to blow up a portion of the U.S. Embassy in San José, Costa Rica, thereby assassinating United States ambassador Lewis Tambs and planning to blame that bombing on the Sandinistas. After hearing of this plot, Carlos had volunteered to help a man named David escape from Hull's ranch. Judge King excluded Carlos's sworn testimony as inadmissible hearsay because David was not a named coconspirator in our civil complaint—only because David had been murdered by John Hull's men.

Finally, Judge King excluded from our case the entire two-day sworn videotaped deposition of the attorney general of Costa Rica, who had given a step-by-step presentation of every piece of directly court-admissible evidence that the government of Costa Rica had compiled that had established, beyond any reasonable doubt, that Per Anker Hansen had in fact placed and detonated the La Penca bomb in an attempt to assassinate Edén Pastora.

Upon having stricken the testimony of all six of those key plaintiff witnesses, Judge King (as step 7) ruled that

> The plaintiffs will, therefore, not be able, at trial, to produce adequate court-admissible evidence to prove that Per Anker Hansen was, in fact, the La Penca bomber or that named defendants John Hull, Felipe Vidal, or the five other named Costa Rican–based defendants had any direct or indirect contact or relationship with this Per Anker Hansen. And for that reason, the plaintiff's count 2 common law civil tort claim against John Hull and the other six named defendants is hereby dismissed as lacking adequately probative *admissible* evidence to justify that count being presented to a jury.

And once that nexus between the La Penca bombing and the more extended activities of "the enterprise" of which John Hull and his associates had been a part had been severed by Judge King, King then undertook step 8 in his ruling and declared "plaintiff Tony Avirgan therefore to be 'without standing' to pursue any claim against the enterprise described in count 1 of this complaint."

So, on June 23, 1988, Judge James Lawrence King thereupon entered a rule 56 order of summary judgment against us on count 1 of our complaint in favor of all twenty-six of the named defendants.

Lewis Pitts, Rob Hager, and I simply stared at Judge King's order of summary judgment in utter disbelief.

It was only then, standing there in the office of the clerk of the court in the Miami courthouse, that Lewis Pitts revealed to me that he had been confidentially informed by Mitchell Rogovin, special counsel to the U.S. Central Intelligence Agency under President Jimmy Carter, that Rogovin had personally attended a training for "CIA legal counsels" *with Judge James Lawrence King.* If I had known that earlier, I would definitely have filed a motion to recuse Judge King from presiding over our case, since numerous interests of the CIA and a number of active CIA agents were certainly "at issue" in our case. Lewis had not told me of this earlier because he had personally promised Mitchell Rogovin that he would never reveal what Rogovin had confided to him. But since Rogovin had then recently passed away, this information could be publicly revealed.

I was shocked, to say the least. Perhaps it was my own fault for not discovering that fact for myself. I knew that James Lawrence King had been nominated by Richard Nixon—and that he had indeed served as a member of the board of directors of Meyer Lansky's Miami National Bank. It was now perfectly clear that James Lawrence King had been actively litigating against us, since the very inception of our case, as an active and conscious operative of the CIA.

However, King did not stop there. Immediately after entering his order of summary judgment against our complaint, King instantly transferred back to us all of our exhibits and affidavits, thereby attempting to foreclose our ability to appeal his ruling. I immediately sent the exhibits and affidavits back to him, informing him, in a letter, that we anticipated seeking an immediate appeal from his "transparently erroneous" ruling. He sent a message back to me informing me that if I sought to appeal his ruling against our complaint, he would immediately entertain a rule 11 order of sanctions from the defendants against me, against the Christic Institute, and even directly against Tony Avirgan if he allowed his attorneys to undertake a "frivolous appeal" in the case. Rule 11 of the federal rules of civil procedure authorizes a federal judge to impose a monetary fine against an attorney who files a bad-faith complaint or appeal while knowing that he or she has no legal or factual support for the claims or assertions made in the filing.

When I sent back the two-volume sworn affidavit of Edwin P. Wilson, one of the creators of "the enterprise," King made good on his threat. Terrified that Wilson's sworn deposition would attract widespread national attention if included in the record forwarded to the Eleventh Circuit Court of Appeals, Judge King immediately entered a rule 11 order of sanction against me, against the Christic Institute, and directly against Tony Avirgan, assessing us a total of $1.6 million, which Judge King demanded be posted *in cash within one week's time* as a "*pre*appeal bond" and as a prior condition to his agreeing to forward the record of this case to the court of appeals. Should we still insist upon filing an appeal from his ruling, he ruled, this cash bond would be automatically paid over to the defendants if we did not prevail on our appeal.

Nothing like that had ever been seen in the entire history of our federal court system. No one had ever been assessed a rule 11 sanction that amounted to even 1 percent of what Judge King had assessed against us. Moreover, a losing *plaintiff* had never been personally assessed the total amount of the claimed attorney fees of the defendants. Those fees are always understood to be vastly inflated when submitted to a court. But King actively solicited the highest possible attorney fees from the defendant's attorneys and ordered us to pay every single penny of them—unless we agreed to withdraw our appeal of his rule 56 order of summary judgment.

King clearly assumed that *that* would finally stop us.

However, I couldn't conceive of our not prevailing on this appeal. A rule 56 order of summary judgment is an extraordinarily rare order to be granted by a federal court. Such an order is to be issued by a court only when there is absolutely no disputable question of fact left to be resolved by a jury. Such a situation is almost impossible to conceive of after a reasonable period of civil discovery. But, of course, King had avoided such reasonable civil discovery by simply sitting on all of our motions to compel discovery. Then King had arbitrarily and capriciously excluded the key nexus evidence linking plaintiff Tony Avirgan's business injury to the broader activities of "the enterprise." Now he was engaged in an active campaign to misrepresent our federal civil complaint as not only "without merit" but also as a case that "we should have known" would never have been allowed to go to a jury.

I thought that James Lawrence King's legal arguments against the admissibility of our sworn evidence were so transparently arbitrary and erroneous that any first-year law student familiar with the federal rules of evidence would vote against sustaining King's rule 56 order of summary judgment against us. So I took the bit in my teeth, raised the $1.6 million in one week ($1 million was posted as a "conditional loan" from Los Angeles human rights legend Aris Anagnos), and filed our appeal to Judge King's order of summary judgment.

CHAPTER *thirty*

REMAINED HOPEFUL FOR success before the Eleventh Circuit Court of Appeals when we drew a three-judge panel that was to be chaired by Judge Robert Smith Vance, a well-known civil rights attorney who had been nominated to the court of appeals by President Jimmy Carter. A second member of the panel was Judge Joseph Hatchett, also a Carter nominee. So even though the third member of the panel was Judge Paul Roney, who was appointed by Richard Nixon, I thought we would win a two-to-one reversal of Judge King's ludicrous rule 56 order of summary judgment.

Therefore, while we prepared our appeal to the Eleventh Circuit Court of Appeals, we were optimistically gearing up for the trial of our case. We mounted a full-scale nationwide public education campaign, publicly emphasizing the direct correlation between the evidence in our civil case and the investigative revelations flowing steadily from the Iran-Contra special prosecutor's investigation and indictments.

However, after Oliver North cowed the already heavily pro-Contra members of the joint House and Senate select committee, the congressional committee began to waffle in its purported resolve to hold the participants in "the enterprise" responsible for their unconstitutional conduct. The targets of our investigation, then buoyed by the growing public sympathy for North and the waning courage of Congress, suddenly began receiving aid from their national security reporter allies embedded in the American news media,[8] who began a transparent counterattack against Iran-Contra special prosecutor Lawrence Walsh and his staff.

As Robert Parry, Brian Barger's investigative partner at the Associated Press, reported,

For Walsh, a lifelong Republican who shared the foreign policy views of the Reagan administration, the Iran-Contra experience was a life-changing one, as his investigation penetrated one wall of lies only to be confronted with another and another—and not just lies from Oliver North and his cohorts but lies from nearly every senior administration official who spoke with investigators. . . . Walsh's investigation was hampered from the start by congressional rashness and hostility from key elements of the media.

Soon thereafter, in 1990, I received a telephone call from Russell Hemenway, director of the New York City–based Committee for an Effective Congress and an old friend of Jack Kennedy's. The Committee for an Effective Congress raised literally millions of dollars every year from wealthy liberal Americans and distributed these millions of dollars to liberal candidates, "whether Democrats or Republicans," Russ used to joke. Russ had become a dear friend of mine, even though I didn't get to see him as often as I would have liked. I had gotten to know him well during my tenure as the chairman of the board of directors of the Washington, D.C.–based Fund for Constitutional Government. Russ had been chairman before me and remained on my board.

I received Russ's call just as Lawrence Walsh was giving out signals of getting ready to throw in the towel.

"Danny! I've got to tell you something," he said. "I just left a meeting with John Kerry in his office, not three minutes ago. When I was meeting with John, in walked Don Riegle." Riegle was a Democratic senator from Michigan, and he apparently had rushed in to speak with Kerry privately about something urgent. Kerry had told Riegle that he trusted Russ, so he said that Russ could stay in the room. Riegle then told Kerry that the leadership of the Democratic Party had just been contacted by the Republican leadership, who said they were willing to withdraw their outstanding official request for $100 million in military aid to the Contras from Congress and to support a covert CIA operation to fund Violeta Chamorro in the Nicaraguan election against the Sandinista government—if Kerry would stop his investigation into the narcotics-smuggling and assassination program being directed by the Iran-Contra enterprise. Riegle emphasized that it was entirely up to Kerry but that the Democratic leadership wanted this to happen and that if Kerry agreed to drop his investigation, "the party leadership will be very, very grateful to you, personally, in the very near future."

I asked Russ, "What the hell does *that* mean?

He said, "That means the Democratic nomination for vice president in the year 2000."

I was stunned. At that point in 1990, Bill Clinton and Al Gore hadn't even been *nominated* to run in 1992 against Bush. Russ seemed to suggest that things were already being planned out another eight years down the road.

"How the hell do you know that from just what Riegle said?" I asked.

Russ laughed and said, "Look, Danny. I've been around this town, and around the Democratic Party leaders, for a long, long time now. And I'm telling you, that's what they were saying to him."

"Well, that sure as hell throws a wrench into our expectations from Kerry," I said. "Do you think there is any chance that Kerry will turn them down and stick to his guns on this?"

Russ laughed out loud on the other end of the phone line. "This is John Kerry that we are talking about here! He has wanted to be president since he was a freshman at Yale."

I laughed, too, because I knew John Kerry as well.

The very next morning, almost immediately after 9:00 AM, I got a telephone call from Jonathan Wiener, chief legal counsel to John Kerry's Senate staff. Jonathan was very excited and wanted to talk with me right away. I told him I would be right over to see him in the Senate office building. "No, no! Not in the office," he said. He gave me the name and address of a Chinese restaurant on The Hill.

I jumped in the Blue Flame and drove directly to the restaurant. Jonathan was sitting at a small table when I walked in. I sat down across from him. It was early, way before lunchtime, so we were pretty much all alone in the restaurant. He had already ordered tea for us, and as soon as the waitress left, Jonathan leaned over the table and whispered to me, "Something really important has just happened!"

He waited a moment, probably to see if I was going to ask him if it was some development in the select committee investigation, so he could surprise me with much different news.

After a long moment, I scowled at him. "You aren't going to try to tell me about the Riegle meeting yesterday, are you?"

He sank back, crestfallen. But within a second or two, he perked up again. "How the hell did you know about *that*?"

"How the hell do I know *anything* that I know, Jonathan?" I said, feigning exasperation. "I have had to spend the better part of a year telling all of you what the hell has been going on in Central America, and you are the fucking *government!*" I was letting my anger out at what I knew Kerry was getting ready to do. So I calmed down and took a drink of tea.

Wiener also took a sip of tea and regathered himself. He could not be certain that I knew exactly what Don Riegle had said to Kerry. After all, as far as Wiener knew, Riegle had been alone in the room with Kerry when Riegle had made Kerry the offer.

"The leadership of the party said that they would be very, very grateful to John in the very near future," he said, "if he would drop his investigation of the drug smuggling and the assassinations of 'the enterprise.'"

"I know, I know," I said. "And just what the hell does that mean anyhow?"

"That means the vice presidential nomination in 2000!"

I'll be damned, I thought to myself. *Russ was right on the money.*

"The vice presidential nomination, Dan!" Wiener repeated. Then he leaned over to me and grasped my left forearm. "And we'll be there, Dan. You and I, we'll be there!"

A feeling of revulsion immediately welled up in me. I couldn't believe that I was sitting there, in a Chinese restaurant on Capitol Hill, having some weasel like Jonathan Wiener ask me to go along with such a profoundly immoral sellout just to secure a position on the staff of the vice president.

I couldn't help it. I reached out and pried Wiener's fatuous hand off my arm and pushed it away. Then I rose and leaned over into Wiener's face.

"Fuck you, Jonathan! *Fuck you!* . . . If I had wanted to be on the vice president's staff, I would have gone there directly from Harvard Law School!

I wouldn't have had to spend seven fucking years conducting a criminal investigation against these assholes that you and John are now planning to get into bed with, just to get John the vice presidential nomination! *Fuck you!* . . . And fuck John Kerry if he takes that deal! And you can tell him that I said that!"

And with that, I got up and stomped out of the Chinese restaurant—and effectively out of political life in Washington, D.C.

By the time I got back to my office on North Capitol Street, John Kerry's chief of staff was on the telephone, waiting for me to return. When I got on the line (with Sara listening in on a second phone), the chief of staff proceeded to rant and rage at me, saying, "Your political life in this town is over! You will never be given any position in this town! John has said that you are never to mention your name or the name of the Christic Institute in the same sentence with his name again!"

I waited for her to finish and then said, "If John takes that deal offered to him by Riegle and the party leadership, then neither John nor you are going to have to worry about anyone ever mentioning John Kerry's name in connection with any of the church groups or in connection with any of the Central American human rights organizations in this town again!"

And I hung up on her.

From that point on, a withering assault began against the Christic Institute: from James Lawrence King, from John K. Singlaub and the World Anti-Communist League, from Henry Hyde, from George H. W. Bush, and directly from Theodore Shackley himself—who surfaced from the shadows for the first time in his professional life and went around, from door to door in Washington, D.C., personally denouncing the Christic Institute as "an agent of the DGI."

I didn't even know what the DGI was. I learned only later that it was the Cuban intelligence service. And I couldn't have even ordered a glass of water in Spanish.

The national security reporters embedded in the various national news outlets then began to parrot "the line" asserted by James Lawrence King: "Oh, *that* civil lawsuit that was thrown out by a federal judge down in Florida, who said that the Christic Institute and its lawyer, Dan Sheehan, lied by "making up nonexistent sources" to support their false claims made against dozens of patriotic Americans."

That charge came from Judge King's rule 11 order of sanctions. He based that bogus charge solely on the fact that, among the "numbered sources" that I had cited for specific information to evidence charges that I had made against the Iran-Contra "enterprise" defendants, I had assigned two different numbers to Gene Wheaton. He had given me two distinct pieces of information, and the attribution of *both* of those pieces of information to the same numbered source would have enabled the defendants (and the CIA) to have triangulated in on Wheaton's identity, thereby exposing him to potential retaliation.

Special Prosecutor Lawrence Walsh's investigation continued from 1987 through 1990. Walsh eventually returned felony criminal indictments against the first five people our office had publicly named as criminal coconspirators with Colonel Oliver North in Shackley's enterprise. But Walsh effectively had a war waged against him in 1990 when he submitted to the federal court of appeals his preliminary report outlining how numerous members of the Reagan–Bush administration were clearly criminally involved in the Iran-Contra scandal. However, all three federal judges on the Special Panel for Appointing Independent Counsel had been appointed by Ronald Reagan or George Bush, and they delayed and then officially placed under seal Walsh's final report. While his final report was being embargoed by the panel, those judges contacted every person named as a criminal conspirator in Walsh's report and provided them the opportunity to submit, through their lawyers, an opposition report. Nothing like that had ever been done before in the entire history of the special prosecutor statute.

The Special Panel for Appointing Independent Counsel then spent federal tax dollars to publish all of the opposition reports, which totaled three times the number of pages as the actual special prosecutor's report.

Reagan–Bush administration allies simply buried Special Prosecutor Walsh. Then George H. W. Bush issued presidential pardons to all of the defendants Walsh indicted. Every one of the Reagan–Bush-appointed members of the U.S. District of Columbia Court of Appeals voted to reverse and set aside all but one of Special Prosecutor Walsh's convictions of Iran-Contra enterprise participants. In light of those actions, Walsh simply threw in the towel and filed a final report, declaring that it was, in effect, pointless for him to continue his investigation and prosecutions. "There is simply no political will on the part of either the Republican or the Democratic Party to really get to the bottom of this," his final report said.

Despite Special Prosecutor Walsh's frustration with the entire process, it is important to note that, as a consequence of his investigation, the following people were charged:

- Caspar Weinberger, secretary of defense, was indicted on two counts of perjury and one count of obstruction of justice on June 16, 1992. President George H. W. Bush pardoned him on December 24, 1992, before he was tried.

- William Casey, head of the CIA, was stricken ill hours before he would testify.

- Robert C. McFarlane, national security adviser, was convicted of withholding evidence, but after a plea bargain, he received only two years' probation. He was later pardoned by President Bush.

- Elliott Abrams, assistant secretary of state, was convicted of withholding evidence and agreed to a plea bargain for two years' probation. He was later pardoned by President Bush.

- Alan D. Fiers, chief of the CIA's Central American Task Force, was convicted of withholding evidence and sentenced to one year of probation. He was later pardoned by President Bush.

- Clair George, chief of covert CIA operations, was convicted of two charges of perjury but was pardoned by President Bush before sentencing.

- Oliver North, a member of the National Security Council, was convicted of accepting an illegal gratuity, obstruction of a congressional inquiry, and destruction of documents. However, the ruling was overturned because he had been granted immunity.

- Fawn Hall, Oliver North's secretary, received immunity from charges of conspiracy and destroying documents in exchange for her testimony.

- Jonathan Scott Royster, liaison to Oliver North, testified in exchange for immunity from prosecution on charges of conspiracy and destroying documents.

- John Poindexter, national security adviser, was convicted of five counts of conspiracy, obstruction of justice, perjury, defrauding the government, and the alteration and destruction of evidence. The Supreme Court upheld a lower court ruling that overturned these convictions.

- Duane (Dewey) Clarridge, an ex-CIA senior official, was indicted in November 1991 on seven counts of perjury and false statements relating to a November 1985 shipment to Iran. He was pardoned before trial by President Bush.

- Richard V. Secord, the ex–major general in the Air Force who organized the Iran arms sales and Contra aid, pleaded guilty in November 1989 to making false statements to Congress. He was sentenced to two years' probation.

- Albert Hakim, a businessman, pleaded guilty in November 1989 to supplementing the salary of North by buying a $13,800 fence for North with money from a set of foreign companies that Hakim used in Iran-Contra. Hakim received two years' probation and a $5,000 fine.

- Tom Clines, deputy to Theodore Shackley and the only Iran-Contra participant who did not receive a pardon from Bush or an overturned verdict, was convicted of four counts of income tax evasion. He served eight months in federal prison and was fined $40,000.

Despite the dramatic difference between the public version of events that I had seen consistently presented by our government officials and our mainstream news media, and the behind-the-scenes reality that I had discovered, I was still comparatively confident that the Eleventh Circuit Court of Appeals would have to reverse Judge King's transparently erroneous hearsay rulings, pursuant to which he had so artificially excluded the reliable and clearly admissible testimony of the six key witnesses in our case. However, this confidence was based solely on the fact that two of the three federal judges on the panel that had been assigned to hear our appeal had been appointed by Democratic president Jimmy Carter and that only one of those judges had been appointed by Richard Nixon. That was, I admit, a sad commentary on the totally "politicized" nature of our American judicial system at that time. However, twenty years into my legal career, I had come to realize that this was just a simple fact of life in our country.

Therefore, despite the fact that the joint House and Senate select committee had literally turned off the television cameras and shut down the hearings within just three minutes of Admiral John Poindexter's transparently perjured testimony; despite the fact that the members of the Court of Appeals Special Panel for Appointing Independent Counsel had narrowly crafted their order appointing Lawrence Walsh to limit his authority to answering only the question of whether Ronald Reagan had authorized the unlawful acts at issue *in writing*; and despite all of the forces arrayed against us, I still felt that there was enough integrity remaining in the American judicial system that Judge King's rule 56 order of summary judgment entered against our case would simply *have to* be reversed and that I would ultimately be allowed to present our clearly admissible evidence to an American jury.

However, all of that had changed on the morning of December 16, 1989. Just one week before our appeal was scheduled to be heard by the three-judge panel of the Eleventh Circuit Court of Appeals, Judge Robert Smith Vance was assassinated by a letter bomb in a package delivered to his home that morning. While that assassination was unrelated to our case,[9] Judge Vance's murder provided an opportunity for then President George H. W. Bush to replace Judge Vance on our Eleventh Circuit Court of Appeals panel with Stanley Birch, a major financial contributor to Bush's

1988 presidential campaign. Stanley Birch had never served a single day as a judge, not even as a traffic court judge, prior to receiving that appointment to the federal court of appeals, positioned just one step below the U.S. Supreme Court. Stanley Birch had been nothing more than the very wealthy patent lawyer for the Cabbage Patch Kids. The oral argument of our case was postponed until June 1991, allowing time for Stanley Birch to take his place on the court and then be appointed to *chair* the three-judge panel that was to hear our appeal.

On the morning of June 8, 1991, Stanley Birch virtually leaped off the bench within seconds of the commencement of our oral argument. He excoriated us for "attempting to usurp the exclusive jurisdiction of the Justice Department, which has, for whatever reason it has deemed to be adequate, decided, in its unreviewable discretion, *not* to investigate or criminally prosecute those responsible for creating the so-called enterprise." His thorough ignorance of the legislative intent of Congress in enacting the federal Racketeering Act was shocking and embarrassing to everyone in the courtroom, for that act had been expressly enacted by Congress to empower private attorneys to act as private attorney generals when the federal Justice Department and state and local prosecuting authorities chose, for whatever reason, to abstain from prosecuting an ongoing federal criminal racketeering enterprise.

Even worse, Stanley Birch went on to declare, "Because you were so inappropriately attempting to usurp the exclusive jurisdiction of the Justice Department, you must have *known* that you would never be allowed to present such a case to a jury." So, on that basis, he declared—before even listening to our appeal—that we must have been pursuing our Iran-Contra case in bad faith. He therefore announced that he was going to affirm Judge James Lawrence King's rule 11 order of sanctions against us.

And, of course, he knew he was able to rely upon the vote of the second Republican member of that panel, Paul Roney, the presiding judge of the U.S. Foreign Intelligence Surveillance Court in Washington, D.C., who had been "specially designated" to sit on the Eleventh Circuit Court of Appeals just in time to hear our case. That gave James Lawrence King the two votes that he needed to sustain both his rule 56 order of summary judgment and his rule 11 order of sanctions entered against us.

So that ended the last remaining chance that the American people had of getting to the bottom of the Iran-Contra scandal—and our ability to expose the truth about the world that lay hidden behind it.

That, of course, had always been the objective of both the Reagan–Bush administration and the Bush–Quayle administration. (Remember that Rob Owen, Oliver North's proven liaison to the Contras, had been Indiana senator Dan Quayle's Latin American legislative aide immediately prior to Quayle's being selected [apparently "out of the blue"] by George Bush to serve as his vice president—and Dan Quayle's grandfather had been the cofounder of the John Birch Society in the state of Indiana *with the father of John Hull, the principal defendant in our Iran-Contra civil lawsuit.*)

But, to our surprise, it turned out that that had also been the shared objective of the leadership of *both* the Republican Party *and the Democratic Party.* Neither organization wanted the dirty laundry of our covert operations during the Cold War to be publicly aired in the closing months of the Cold War.[10]

I thought that the Iran-Contra scandal presented a golden opportunity for our country to put the dark practices of the Cold War behind us and to distance ourselves from them, to prepare for a new era of cooperation and peaceful relations among nation-states now that the Cold War was coming to a close. But Theodore Shackley and his reactionary cohorts were having none of that.

Then Tom Spencer, attorney for John K. Singlaub, submitted a motion to Judge King, inviting him to enter an order confiscating all of the files of the Christic Institute, purportedly to sell them for their scrap paper value to cover the defendants' attorney fees and costs. The real reason for this motion was, of course, that the Iran-Contra defendants still desperately wanted to ascertain the identities of our sources.

In the face of this motion—before Judge King had time to rule on it—I ordered our entire set of files to be loaded onto a large U-Haul truck and transported to California, where they were deposited in Jackson Browne's home at the Hollister Ranch outside of Santa Barbara. I then ordered our office in Washington, D.C., to be sold, including all of our office equipment and furniture, and we used the proceeds to pay off the entire $1.6 million

rule 11 order of sanctions entered by Judge King to cover the Iran-Contra
defendants' attorney fees and costs.

In the face of the public relations assault mounted against the Christic
Institute and Special Prosecutor Walsh, the national security reporters publicly declared the Iran-Contra affair to be "too complicated to really understand." And Walsh, after being subjected to this withering attack, simply
gave up on his effort to hold the participants in "the enterprise" criminally
responsible for their activities.

Special Prosecutor Walsh thereupon, in his final report to the court, and
publicly warned the nation that because our legal and political leaders—of
both parties—had so steadfastly and *consciously refused* to confront and
punish the men who were responsible for the constitutional violations of
the off-the-shelf enterprise that had led to the Iran-Contra affair, our nation
would, sooner rather than later, be confronted by a powerful National
Security State infrastructure that would engage in violations of our individual constitutional rights in a way that had had not been experienced since
the Civil War under the guise of anti*terrorism*. That dire warning turned
out to be entirely accurate, of course, his prediction taking the form of the
Patriot Act and the National Defense Authorization Act, the powers of
which were aggressively demanded by the George W. Bush administration
immediately following September 11, 2001, less than one decade after the
Cold War warriors had lost communism as the ultimate "other" that they
had used for a full century to justify their reactionary National Security State
measures. They now had "terrorism" as their new nemesis.

As if all this wasn't enough, I also received a telephone call from the
director of the Washington, D.C., and Virginia regional office of the Internal
Revenue Service. He wanted to come to our office to discuss an important
matter. Sara and I met with him the following morning at ten o'clock. He sat
down and gravely informed us that his regional office had received numerous complaints that our Christic Institute, as a 501(c)(3) tax-exempt public
interest organization, had been issuing public statements critical of the policies of one or more candidates for elective office—or candidates for reelection to public office. This, he said, was expressly forbidden to 501(c)(3)
tax-exempt organizations.

"Really?" I said. "Do you have any idea which elected officials we are charged with talking about?"

"Uh, I can't remember exactly who it was," he said. "But the accusations are that you've been saying unfavorable things about elected members of political office who are candidates for reelection."

"Could it possibly be George H. W. Bush, your boss, that we are talking about here?"

He snapped his fingers, as though he had just recalled it. "Ah! That's right. Now that you mention it, it *was* George Bush. You've been saying negative things about him."

"Allegedly!" I said.

"Certainly. Allegedly, I mean. That's what the complaints allege."

"He's the president of the United States! Are you saying that a 501(c)(3) public interest and public policy organization is not allowed to publicly criticize the policies of a sitting president just because he has decided to run for reelection?"

"Well, yes. You can't publicly criticize his policies or his conduct if he is a candidate for reelection. Our rules and regulations make no exception for the president. A 501(c)(3) public interest organization is expressly forbidden from making negative or critical public comments about candidates for elective public office. That is considered by our office to be "engaging in political activity." I just wanted to extend the courtesy of notifying you personally that your organization is under active IRS investigation."

From that moment on, the IRS went after us with a vengeance. It sent teams of agents into our office on repeated occasions, digging through all of our records and all of our public statements.

The IRS agents demanded videos of our television interviews, listened to recordings of our radio appearances, and reviewed our published statements. Then they began to dig into our internal communications, asserting that they were entitled to review them to see if we were discussing, even among ourselves within our office, the "political implications" of the public statements that we were making about Republican candidates. And, of course, they combed through our financial records to see if they could find any conceivable financial irregularities, since they had the right, at any time, to inspect our books and records. The IRS agents were looking for anything they could use to revoke our 501(c)(3) tax-exempt charter to stop us from raising any further contributions from tax-exempt organizations or foundations to prosecute our appeal. But they were unable to find a single thing.

Nevertheless, shortly after Special Prosecutor Lawrence Walsh officially dropped his final case and we had paid the final installment of the $1.6 million in attorney fees and costs to the Iran-Contra defendants, the IRS regional director officially notified us that the IRS was revoking our 501(c)(3) tax-exempt charter on the grounds that the Christic Institute had engaged in political activity by filing and prosecuting a "meritless case" against associates of the administration. Because both the Reagan–Bush and the Bush–Quayle administrations maintained that there was never anything to the charges we had filed, the IRS claimed that the only reason we might have had for filing those "false charges" was that we were functioning as a direct operative of the Democratic Party and were therefore engaging in political activity.

After Special Prosecutor Walsh filed his final report with the Circuit Court of Appeals for the District of Columbia in August 1993, I was immediately invited to deliver the Cesar Chavez Memorial Lecture at the University of California, Santa Barbara, to compare and contrast Walsh's findings and the charges that we had originally filed in our Iran-Contra federal civil racketeering case. In that ninety-minute presentation, I explicated, step-by-step how, despite the fact that Walsh had pursued a criminal fraud theory of his case and we had pursued a federal criminal racketeering theory, Walsh had determined that the same men we had named in our complaint were engaged in exactly the same conduct with which we had originally charged them.

Moreover, Lawrence Walsh had gone to great lengths to explain that, to understand the potential gravity of letting these men get away with what they had been caught doing, it was necessary to go back to the Watergate burglary and the series of congressional investigations and hearings that had flowed from that scandal. Walsh pointed out that the unlawful, unethical, and unconstitutional conduct undertaken by CIA operatives and other covert operations agencies of our executive branch in the name of "anticommunism" between 1947 and 1977 (uncovered by congressional investigators in the aftermath of the Watergate burglary) had been repeated by the men who had created and operated the off-the-shelf enterprise—but this time they had committed their illegal acts in the name of "anti*terrorism*." Walsh warned the American public that if our political leaders did not shut down and criminally punish those men, they were the kind of zealots who would, in fact, rant and rave about terrorists just as they had ranted and raved against communists, and that these men would suppress constitutional rights, invade privacy, and go on witch hunts to throw out of office people they deemed to be "soft on terrorism."

Walsh essentially warned that these covert operations, and the zealots who ran them, constituted a clear and present danger to the constitutional order of our democracy. That was his final verdict on the Iran-Contra case. And he then folded his tent and left the field of combat.

But we did not.

Immediately after the IRS issued the order revoking our 501(c)(3) tax-exempt charter, Sara, Father Bill Davis, and I were contacted by the Oscar Romero Foundation, a twenty-year-old 501(c)(3) tax-exempt public interest organization in Los Angeles. The leaders of that organization told us that the actions that the Christic Institute had been engaged in were very important. After learning that the IRS had officially revoked our 501(c)(3) tax-exempt charter, the directors of the Oscar Romero Foundation convened an emergency meeting and elected me as their new president and general counsel. They also elected Sara as their new vice president and executive director and Father Bill Davis as their secretary-treasurer. Then the entire board of directors resigned and forwarded all of their official documents to us.

We therefore were able to recommence our public interest activities as the Romero Institute after only minor amendments to the articles of incorporation of the Oscar Romero Foundation.

MANY OF THE same men who were in charge of the off-the-shelf enterprise are the ones who began to move the new antiterrorism regime into place during the administration of George W. Bush. That is why the pardons issued by George H. W. Bush in December 1992 are, in a sense, the end of a chapter that opened with Gerald Ford's pardon of Richard Nixon. From 1972 to 1992, all of these scandals involved the exact same men and the exact same kind of covert criminal activities that underlay not only the Watergate burglary but also the Iran-Contra scandal. The real truth of each event was consciously and assiduously concealed from the American public by our political and legal leaders. These scandals continue to be viewed by our American public as "deep political mysteries" that befuddle the collective public mind of America, preventing our American public from realizing the full implications of these events.

William Brennan, a justice of the United States Supreme Court, stated in an address to Georgetown Law School in 1992 that if one truly understood the full implications of the Iran-Contra scandal, one would see that it constituted the most serious threat to the constitutional order of our nation since the American Civil War. Yet nothing was done to effectively rid us of the threat posed by these men, so that threat still lingers today, confronting us, just below the surface of our constitutional democracy.

CHAPTER *thirty-one*

N OT LONG AFTER I received word that the Eleventh Circuit Court of Appeals had officially affirmed both Judge James Lawrence King's rule 56 order of summary judgment and his rule 11 order of sanctions, I found Sara sitting in our North Capitol Street Christic Institute office with her head in her hands.

When I walked in, she looked up and said plaintively,

I am totally disillusioned ... not by the actions of the Reagan–Bush or the Bush–Quayle administrations or by the Republican Party leadership—their actions were entirely to be expected—but by the conduct of John Kerry and the leadership of the *Democratic* Party, the national news media, and the "hard left," who so aggressively criticized us for not suing Ronald Reagan, John Poindexter, George Bush, Donald P. Gregg, Bill Casey, Oliver North, and all the other Reagan–Bush administration officials *personally* for so clearly facilitating and protecting the off-the-shelf enterprise. The hard left also criticized us for using, as our investigators, men like Bill Taylor, because he was a three-tour Vietnam Marine Corps combat veteran; Gene Wheaton, because he had been the former chief of security for the U.S. military mission in Tehran; and Bill McCoy, because he was commander of the U.S. Army's Criminal Investigation Division. Because we wouldn't sue those officials in their official capacities, the hard left publicly accused us of allowing ourselves to be duped by "the ruling class," insisting that we *must* have known that we were predestined to fail in our mission—that we were guilty of misleading an entire generation into believing

that things can be changed by working within this corrupt system.
I am now wondering whether they might have been right and we
were wrong.

I smiled and told Sara, "It is a lot better to be *dis*illusioned than to continue to be illusioned."

Suddenly it dawned on both Sara and me that our disillusionment
through the attempt to prosecute the Iran-Contra case entirely within the
rules of law was not entirely a bad thing, as painful as it had been for
us to have our prior illusions—first about John Kerry, second about the
Democratic Party, third about the United States Congress, and fourth about
the major corporate news media—dispelled. What was necessary to remember, we told each other, was that virtually every one of the social ministry
offices of all of the major Christian and Jewish denominations in our country had aggressively supported us, all the way to the end, in our effort to
prosecute and publicly expose the participants in the off-the-shelf enterprise
and to make public the shortcomings of the fundamentally flawed American
intelligence system. They also stood by us in our efforts to expose the much
deeper alliance that our American military, our intelligence community,
and even our two major national political parties had consciously (though
covertly) established to serve as a "bulwark against communism" throughout the Cold War, both in Europe and Latin America.

With all of our research and investigative files loaded aboard three
U-Haul rental trucks, and with the Christic Institute office and all of our
office equipment sold to pay the defendants' attorney fees—*and* with Arrupe
House and Sara's and my personal house sold to make sure that Tony Avirgan
and Martha Honey did not have to pay a single penny of the rule 11 order of
sanctions imposed against us by Judge King—Sara, Father Bill Davis, and I
packed up Danny-Paul and Daegan (and our Great Pyrenees puppy Sophie)
and drove to California on the morning immediately after George H. W.
Bush had been defeated for a second term in office. He had been defeated
not just by Bill Clinton and the Democratic Party but indeed by Ross Perot,
who had decided to run against Bush and had succeeded in taking away 19
percent of the vote from Bush. As Ross explained to me, he did this because

Bush had lied to him when Perot had asked him, straight out, man-to-man, Texan to Texan, whether Bush and his people in the administration were providing weapons to the Contras. "A man like that cannot be allowed to remain as the president of the United States," Perot said.

So while we had not won our federal Racketeering Act civil lawsuit, we *had* played a significant role in stopping George H. W. Bush from securing a second term in office by successfully persuading Ross Perot, a true patriot, to take a stand for his principles and help save America from Bush's "New World Order."

As I drove away from Washington, D.C., one last time, I looked in the rearview mirror of the rented U-Haul truck and thought that I could almost see Ross Perot walking jauntily down the main street of Georgetown, reliving that moment, back in 1987, when I had walked down that same street with him, on the night he was informed that the board of directors of General Motors had voted to purchase back all of his shares of GM stock at twice the price he had paid for them, just to get Ross off the board—because the management of General Motors didn't want to listen to his recommendations as to how they could save General Motors from bankruptcy.

I couldn't help telling myself, as Washington, D.C. faded from view in the rearview mirror, one last time, *I guess it's true: What was good for General Motors was good for America.*

When we arrived in California, we were greeted as conquering heroes by a wide array of ardent Christic Institute supporters, ranging from film producer Paul Haggis, who invited us to stay in his summer home in Lake Arrowhead, California, until Sara and I had finalized arrangements to teach at the University of California in Santa Barbara, to Jackson Browne, who invited us to then live in his seldom-used, seaside second home on the beautiful Hollister Ranch just north of Santa Barbara. There, famous *Endless Summer* surfer/producer Bruce Brown's son Wade taught both Danny-Paul and Daegan how to surf, while Sara and I made the daily trip into Santa Barbara to teach a course of our own creation at the University of California entitled The Hidden History of America: The History of CIA Covert Operations from World War II to the Present. It became the most popular course in the history of the university; we had to teach the course from the

campus television studio as a live broadcast to multiple classrooms because
there was no single room or auditorium on campus large enough to accommodate all the students and professors who wished to attend. During that
time, over a dozen major Hollywood producers and directors approached
Sara and me, asking to make a movie out of our experience during the
Iran-Contra affair. But they insisted on fictionalizing the story so as not to
make the CIA out to be "the bad guys." We of course passed on every one
of those offers to be able to preserve the true story on a high-quality video
that was broadcast from the campus television studio out to the students of
a new generation.

Sara and I spent our days teaching at UC Santa Barbara, and I spent
the evening hours upstairs in Jackson Browne's home beside the sea with
the sound of the waves of the Pacific breaking along two miles of deserted
beachfront, typing up the notes of our experiences into an early-era desktop
computer. I worked at a small table immediately next to Jackson's piano, on
which he had written "Lives in the Balance":

I've been waiting for something to happen
For a week or a month or a year
With the blood in the ink of the headlines
And the sound of the crowd in my ear
You might ask what it takes to remember
When you know that you've seen it before
Where a government lies to a people
And a country is drifting to war

And there's a shadow on the faces
Of the men who send the guns
To the wars that are fought in places
Where their business interest runs

On the radio talk shows and TV
You hear one thing again and again
How the USA stands for freedom

And we come to the aid of a friend
But who are the ones that we call our friends—
These governments killing their own?
Or the people who finally can't take anymore
And they pick up a gun or a brick or a stone
There are lives in the balance
There are people under fire
There are children at the cannons
And there is blood on the wire

There's a shadow on the faces
Of the men who fan the flames
Of the wars that are fought in places
Where we can't even say the names

They sell us the president the same way
They sell us our clothes and our cars
They sell us everything from youth to religion
The same time they sell us our wars
I want to know who the men in the shadows are
I want to hear somebody asking them why
They can be counted on to tell us who our enemies are
But they're never the ones to fight or to die

And there are lives in the balance
There are people under fire
There are children at the cannons
And there is blood on the wire

Jackson Browne wrote those lines of "Lives in the Balance" to be played at public concerts across the country that he put on along with Bonnie Raitt; Crosby, Stills, and Nash; Kris Kristofferson; and many others from our generation to raise funds to help defray the costs of investigating and prosecuting the Iran-Contra case.

WHILE SARA AND I were teaching at UC Santa Barbara, Russian president Mikhail Gorbachev was formulating his follow-up to having carefully guided his people through glasnost and perestroika to the voluntary dissolution of the Soviet Union. A Christic Institute confidant and my best friend from Harvard Divinity School, Jimmy Garrison, was at Gorbachev's side throughout that process as president of the post–Cold War Gorbachev Foundation. In early 1993, Jimmy asked me to participate in the State of the World Forum, an organization that he and Gorbachev had founded in San Francisco. The mission of the State of the World Forum was, in the immediate aftermath of the Cold War, to convene a series of entirely off-the-record meetings and discussions among former presidents, vice presidents, secretaries of state, secretaries of defense, and economic ministers of all of the major nation-states of our world. We also brought together with these leaders officials of the United Nations, our world's economic leaders, the CEOs of the world's major business corporations, the leaders of our world's major religious communities, and the CEOs of major public interest and nongovernmental organizations recognized by the United Nations. The purpose of these off-the-record meetings was to attempt to identify the principles and policies pursuant to which we, as one human family, might all come together to create a more peaceful, cooperative, and mutually prosperous world now that the Cold War was over. Gorbachev identified this mission as "our common enterprise."

I traveled to San Francisco and participated as a member of these extraordinary discussions between 1995 and 1998. Then Garrison asked me to become director of the State of the World Forum's principal Strategic Initiative to Identify the New Paradigm. Sara became the executive director of the State of the World Forum, while Jimmy served as its president and Gorbachev served as its principal driving force. With $1 million in donations from CNN founder Ted Turner, Men's Wearhouse owner George Zimmer, and U.S. Internet entrepreneur Joseph Firmage (and smaller though substantial donations from other well-known persons), Jim, Sara, and I established our base on the grounds of the Presidio, the first major U.S. military facility to be decommissioned at the close of the Cold War. Our office was immediately beside the Golden Gate Bridge. From there we convened annual gatherings of these world leaders at the Fairmont Hotel in San Francisco—in the exact same rooms in which the founding meetings of the United Nations had been held in the immediate aftermath of World War II. In those meetings, we set about collectively discerning and identifying the operating principles and policies of a New Paradigm worldview to replace the dialectical and confrontational worldview that had so dominated and disrupted the entire twentieth century and had degenerated into the almost fatal Cold War that had brought our human family to the very brink of nuclear self-destruction.

Teaching at the University of California in Santa Barbara and participating in the State of the World Forum in San Francisco occupied a significant portion of Sara's and my time and attention following the refusal of our nation's leaders to address the post–Cold War manifestation of the National Security State.

Rather than taking time to reflect philosophically on my thoughts and feelings in the immediate aftermath of the collapse of the Iran-Contra investigations and the Christic Institute, I turned my attention instead to attempting to understand, politically and sociologically, what was taking place in our country, and what Sara and I could do to keep the forces of reaction from reasserting themselves in some dangerous replacement of the Cold War.

I believe that this entirely rational, seemingly emotionless response on my part was the function of two factors in my life. The first was the development, during my early childhood in Warrensburg, of a strong psychological self-defense mechanism against becoming overwhelmed by circumstances that were potentially traumatic from an objective standpoint but over which I had only a very limited degree of personal control. Similar circumstances might well have emotionally overwhelmed other young children, but I had developed a mechanism to steel myself against such a response. The second factor was the training that I was privileged to have received throughout my schooling—first from Coach George Khoury in Warrensburg, in how to mobilize my full emotional, intellectual, and physical energies and direct them toward calmly identifying the concrete steps necessary and available to me for me to recover from temporary setbacks and immediately press forward; and then from Harvard University in how to intellectualize every potentially paralyzing experience and to then chart out a strictly logical course of action.

It was through my studies and direct conversations with various world leaders—both political and economic—at the State of the World Forum that I came to recognize the existence and activities of a self-conscious alliance dating all the way back to the period immediately preceding World War I. This alliance began among men like George Herbert Walker, a number of major industrialist clients of Brown Brothers-Harriman, and other radical right-wing elements in Europe. These parties united not only against every form of socialism or communism but also, more importantly, in active affirmative support of a specific authoritarian, racist, *state*-capitalist model of government that advocated the subsidizing of privately owned, capitalist corporations through the collection of tax monies from the common people, and the subsidizing of the buildup of a massive and aggressive national military that could project national military power into every area of the world for the purpose of protecting the business interests of the owners of those private business corporations. President George H. W. Bush, the grandson of George Herbert Walker, had ordered U.S. military forces into the Middle East, with the direct support of the House of Saud, to occupy Middle Eastern oil fields on behalf of the private owners of the seven major oil companies of the Arabian American Oil Company, and to secure these oil reserves to fuel the largest military machine in the history of our human family. There was, in fact, a deep alliance between the Bush family and the House of Saud going all the way back to 1924.

On January 6, 1992, the Monday morning after the Soviet Union voluntarily dissolved itself, Paul Wolfowitz, the assistant secretary of defense under Dick Cheney at that time, gathered a team in the West Wing of the White House. He declared, "Now that the Soviet Union has collapsed, we are faced with an entirely different world configuration. We are now the sole remaining superpower in the world. So we are going to reconfigure the entire strategic military plan and foreign policy of the United States to seize the advantage presented by this unique situation." He thereupon assembled Douglas Feith, Scooter Libby, and William Kristol, who would later become the editor in chief of the *Weekly Standard*, a right-wing newspaper in Washington, D.C. This team was secretly financed by Richard Mellon Scaife, the wealthy scion of the Mellon family.

That week the group drafted the initial iteration of the 1992 *United States Defense Department Policy Planning Guidance Document*. In that document, they asserted, under the leadership of Secretary of Defense Dick Cheney, that the United States would immediately adopt a radically different foreign policy and military policy to stop any government or group *anywhere in the world* from developing adequate military strength to effectively resist the unilateral assertion of U.S. military power, even inside a country's own territory. If any government so much as attempted to create a military that might have the ability to resist unilateral U.S. military power, the United States would assert its unilateral right to strike militarily against that government to stop it from developing such a military capacity. Wolfowitz and his cohorts were effectively declaring that the United States no longer needed to abide by the traditional international rules of warfare governing the conduct of nations because we were now "the sole remaining superpower in the world." They viewed the United Nations to be a toothless tiger—an outdated remnant of the Cold War—and asserted the United States now to be the unilateral "police power" of the world. Not only did they assert the U.S. right to act unilaterally on behalf of its own narrow, selfish national interests, but they also asserted the right of the United States to engage in preemptive warfare against any nation-state or group that attempted to challenge the United States. In short, they wanted to assert U.S. military, economic, political, and cultural hegemony over the entire world.

Wolfowitz and his confederates submitted the 1992 *United States Defense Department Policy Planning Guidance Document* to Dick Cheney, who was delighted with the policy and the plan and immediately signed off on it. Then Cheney and Wolfowitz submitted the document to George H. W. Bush for his approval. Bush accepted it as well.

The policy reflected in that document was nothing short of a bald reiteration of the same white-superiority, state-capitalist, imperialist thesis that had been actively in practice by virtually every Western nation-state throughout the latter half of the nineteenth century and the first decade of the twentieth century as Manifest Destiny. In a way, Cheney's and Wolfowitz's action was entirely predictable and made perfect sense. After all, why *wouldn't* the Western powers simply *return* to those exact same principles and policies as soon as their only effective "opposition" voluntarily withdrew from the field? The Western powers had not abandoned those principles simply voluntarily; the people of various regions of the world had organized and fought back against their efforts, usually armed and trained by socialist and communist forces financed by the Soviet Union.

On February 18, 1992, George H. W. Bush circulated the 1992 *United States Defense Department Policy Planning Guidance Document* to certain "select members" of both his cabinet and his Joint Chiefs of Staff in the Pentagon.

However, someone provided a copy of that document to *The Washington Post*, which published a scathing editorial just two days later, denouncing that new policy. The editorial declared that new policy to be nothing short of a return to nineteenth-century "gunboat diplomacy" and "imperialism" on the part of the United States now that the Soviet Union was no longer present as a deterrent. The following Sunday morning, *The New York Times* followed suit with a similarly scathing editorial aggressively denouncing that document.

George H. W. Bush, embarrassed by this public disclosure, issued a rare public statement pertaining to such a highly classified internal executive branch document. In the fourth week of February 1992, Bush stated that the document being criticized by *The Washington Post* and *The Times*—without either admitting or denying that any such classified document actually existed—was "just a draft." He asserted that any such policy being proposed had not yet been accepted or adopted. Bush said that his administration was in the process of drafting an alternative policy planning document that would, of course, also have to remain classified—so the world would not be allowed to see it. "However," Bush said, "you can take my word that the final policy will be very different from that attributed to any such draft critiqued by *The Washington Post* and *The New York Times*."

Thereupon, George H. W. Bush and Theodore Shackley coauthored, with General Colin Powell, the head of the Joint Chiefs of Staff at the Pentagon, a second version of the document, which they entitled *The Projection of U.S.*

Military Power into the Twenty-First Century and Beyond. In that version of the Department of Defense policy planning document, Bush, Powell, and Shackley set forth a new post–Cold War U.S. military and foreign policy doctrine. They proposed the creation of a "New World Order" to be established in the wake of the collapse of the Soviet Union. In this new document, Bush expressly rejected the doctrine of United States unilateralism that had been the core of the Wolfowitz draft of the 1992 document. In its stead, he proposed pursuing the exact same *strategic* objective of military, economic, and cultural world domination by the United States, but not through *unilateral* action on the part of the United States alone. Instead he proposed the undertaking of cooperative, multilateral actions on the part of all the Caucasian nation-states of the Northern Hemisphere: the United States, Canada, Mexico (under the political control *not* of the indigenous mestizo people of Mexico but instead the Castilian Spanish), the United Kingdom, France, Spain, the new reunified Germany—and Russia (now that Russia had spun off all of its "ethnic"—that is, its non-Caucasian—provinces). Bush identified this alliance as the New Northern Industrial Alliance.

The mission of the New Northern Industrial Alliance, as stated in Bush's classified 1992 *Projection of U.S. Military Power into the Twenty-First Century and Beyond,* was "to make certain that we continue to maintain our present 'privileged access' to the strategic raw materials that are needed by the member-states of this New Northern Industrial Alliance."

In that document, Bush proposed that the military arm of the New Northern Industrial Alliance be NATO, and that the United States agree to supply all of the military equipment needed by NATO so that all member-states would have the same rifles, ammunition, military aircraft, tanks, anti-aircraft weapons, and so on. The U.S. military-industrial complex would produce all of these military materials *for purchase* by the other member-states. However, the United States would retain and exercise exclusive control over all of the highly technically sophisticated military equipment needed by the combined military forces of the New Northern Industrial Alliance, such as intercontinental ballistic missiles and antiballistic missiles. But the other member-states would have to supply all of the military ground forces to the alliance because, since Vietnam, U.S. citizens had become increasingly upset about U.S. military personnel being engaged in foreign military operations in other parts of the world.

Bush went on, in this second "more moderate" version of the first post–Cold War Defense Department policy planning document, to propose that the member-states of this New Northern Industrial Alliance should immediately develop a much stronger economic alliance by establishing, first among the United States, Canada, and Mexico, a North American Free Trade Agreement (NAFTA). Coincidentally he proposed that the European member-states of the alliance should enter into a General Agreement on Tariffs and Trade (GATT) to constitute the first step toward the formation of one large new European Union, similar to the United States of America. Then the two major continental economic alliances, NAFTA and GATT, could join together into one new grand international economic alliance. That economic alliance would then develop a common parliament that would be authorized to enact legislation enforceable within all member-countries. There would then be in place a military alliance, an economic alliance, and a common parliament.

Thus as of April of 1992, George H. W. Bush was secretly proposing the gradual formation of one transatlantic unified nation-state, much like the original United States, to be made up of only semi-independent nation-states under a centralized government called the New Northern Industrial Alliance. This would enable the Western powers to more effectively compete with and ultimately confront the New Asian Empire of China. That was indeed a very different set of principles and policies than the unilaterally nationalistic proposals made by Dick Cheney, Paul Wolfowitz, Elliott Abrams, Douglas Feith, and the other men who had advocated what would later come to become known as the Project for a New American Century.

If one were able to obtain access to these two different 1992 classified documents of the Bush administration, one would see that, at the immediate end of the Cold War, there arose the assertion of two very different worldviews: the "reactionary" worldview that was being proposed by the advocates of the Project for a New American Century, and the merely conservative worldview manifested by President George H. W. Bush, Major General Colin Powell, and former Bush CIA covert operations director Theodore

Shackley in their second version of that document, which proposed the pursuit of the same long-range *strategic* objective of world military, economic, and cultural domination by the Caucasian race, but not through the unilateral action of the United States alone but instead through the multilateral creation of a New Northern Industrial Alliance to confront the coming New Asian Empire under the growing hegemony of China. This was the situation that confronted us as we approached the November 1992 presidential election with the then-anticipated victory of George H. W. Bush. As the presumed winner, George H. W. Bush would have been the first president of the United States elected after the Cold War, thereby enabling him to implement his plan for the New World Order secretly identified in his classified 1992 *Projection of U.S. Military Power into the Twenty-First Century and Beyond.*

IN 1991, I had arranged for Gene Wheaton to meet directly with Bill Clinton, the Democratic governor of Arkansas, to provide to Clinton information that our Christic Institute had uncovered at the Mena Airport in Mena, Arkansas. We had uncovered dispositive proof that "the enterprise" were smuggling weapons to the Contras from the Mena Airport and were smuggling cocaine back into the United States also through that airport.

I had contacted Ross Perot and—remembering his statement, "That is one of the advantages in being a billionaire, they will always take your call"—had asked Ross to set up that meeting for Gene with then Governor Bill Clinton.

However, Bill Clinton had taken that information that we (the Christic Institute, Ross Perot, and Carl Jenkins) had given to him and, rather than exposing and prosecuting those responsible, had instead decided that the time had arrived for him to run for the Democratic Party nomination and against George Bush in the 1992 presidential election. However, instead of the traditional dialectical contest taking place between just Clinton and George H. W. Bush, Ross Perot had surprised the world by entering the race. Perot was upset with Clinton for not having taken the proper steps to reveal and prosecute the information that we had given to him. But Ross was even more upset because George H. W. Bush had lied directly to him when Ross had asked Bush, back in 1986, whether Bush and his accomplices in the Reagan–Bush administration were supplying the Contras in Central America with arms in direct violation of the Boland Amendment. So Ross had decided to run for the presidency against both of them as a third-party candidate.

In 1992, we therefore witnessed the first genuine three-way race for the American presidency in our lifetimes. George H. W. Bush did not in fact lose the 1992 presidential election because he had said, "Read my lips: no new taxes," and had then raised taxes—as was the rap put on him by his detractors inside the Republican Party. He lost the election, in fact, because Ross Perot had run against him, thereby enabling Bill Clinton to win the presidency with only 43 percent of the votes cast that year to George H. W. Bush's 38 percent—because Ross Perot had won 19 percent of the votes— which every expert acknowledges came directly out of those that would have otherwise gone to Bush.

Then two very peculiar events occurred.

First, as soon as Bill Clinton was shown the classified second version of the 1992 United States Defense Department policy planning document drafted by George H. W. Bush, he eagerly embraced that "conservative" U.S. foreign and military policy and immediately began to push against his own Democratic Party to aggressively advocate the creation of the North American Free Trade Agreement, which he knew full well was the initial step toward implementing Bush's New World Order and his New Northern Industrial Alliance.

The second peculiar thing that happened was that Republican Henry Hyde of the Sixth District of Illinois and Republican Bill McCollum of the Fifth District of Florida immediately began to dig into every aspect of Clinton's background in an unrelenting effort to *impeach* Bill Clinton. These efforts included Whitewater, "Travel Gate," the death of Vince Foster, alleged murders committed in Arkansas at the purported order of Clinton, and several different sexual affairs that Bill Clinton was purported to have had with several different women. Hyde and McCollum were outraged because they had been directly involved in meeting with Oliver North and Rob Owen, and were aware of the illegal smuggling of weapons to the Contras. And they felt that the Democratic Party had somehow *allowed* the Iran-Contra case to go forward, with Democrat Michael Barnes of Maryland actually having invited former ambassador Robert White and me to testify before the House Foreign Affairs Committee's Subcommittee on Latin American Affairs, of which both Hyde and McCollum were members.

Hyde and McCollum felt that *that* was what had actually instigated the appointment of a special prosecutor, which had in turn threatened the entire Republican administration of Ronald Reagan and George Bush and had eventually unseated George Bush and the Republican Party from power in Washington. Hyde and McCollum viewed Ross Perot to have been directly involved with the Christic Institute in the entire operation to oust the Republican Party from power. Hyde, McCollum, and their reactionary cohorts in the House of Representatives wanted to retaliate against the Democratic Party for its not having adequately controlled its own forces— that is, the Christic Institute and the progressive community that had somehow effectively pushed George Bush and the Republican Party from power. The reactionaries within the Republican Party therefore spent the entire first term of Clinton's administration trying to devise a way to punish the Democratic Party.

The Project for a New American Century advocates from within the former Bush administration began to publicly espouse the line that Bush had lost the election in 1992 because he was too soft and had not been *far enough right*—that is, that George Bush had lost the 1992 presidential election because he had adopted too conciliatory a *merely* "conservative" model for the projection of U.S. military power into the twenty-first century rather than having embraced the neoconservative (that is, *reactionary*) worldview tendered to him by the advocates of a Project for a New American Century. So all the Project for a New American Century advocates within the former Bush administration (including Dick Cheney, Paul Wolfowitz, Elliott Abrams, Scooter Libby, and Doug Feith) mobilized and mounted an aggressive public education campaign (financed largely by Richard Mellon Scaife) to drive the American public farther and farther to the right, to try to get the public to embrace the principles and policies of the extreme right-wing

Project for a New American Century, and to utilize that worldview to drive the Democrats from power.

That effort, subjecting Bill Clinton and his wife, Hillary, to an ever-ascending (or descending) campaign of scathing attacks from the far right, caused Bill Clinton to move further and further to the right to try to survive politically. Eventually Clinton, the first president of the post–Cold War era, was forced to become a virtual "Republi-Crat," differing only slightly in his policies and principles from a 1960s' moderate Republican such as John Lindsay of New York City, Nelson Rockefeller of New York State, or Lowell Weicker of Connecticut.

Indeed, from the midway point of his first term as president in 1994 to the end of his eight-year term in office, over half of all Bill Clinton's nominees—for example, to the federal bench—were Republicans. Bill Clinton not only advocated the NAFTA proposal of George Bush; he also actually started aggressively pushing for the creation of NAFTA, knowing full well that that was the critical first step toward establishing the conservative New World Order of Bush's *Projection of U.S. Military Power into the Twenty-First Century and Beyond* document, which was directly contrary to the historical interests of all the major constituencies within the Democratic Party.

These public events took place directly in the public eye. However, what was going on behind the scenes was an ever-deepening and much more profound discussion of the different worldviews reflected in the two different versions of the 1992 Defense Department policy planning document. This deeper and more profound discussion constituted a clash of worldviews in determining the principles pursuant to which world order would be remade in the immediate aftermath of the Cold War.

Since the morning of January 1, 1992, following the exhilarating night of the sudden and dramatic voluntary dissolution of the Soviet Union and the end of the Cold War, there has been a secret global policy debate taking place among the elite leaders of Western civilization. This secret policy debate concerns the structure and content of the specific new worldview that will be adopted by the leaders of our world human family following the Cold War: the organizing principle with which leaders of the post–Cold War Western world will undertake to comport their conduct.

The details of this still largely secret global policy debate must be brought to our public's attention and self-consciously examined—both here in the United States and around the world—if we are to make certain, as informed citizens, that all public and private policy options that are available to us are honestly presented for collective consideration in the face of the recent, disturbingly restricted national public policy debate that has been allowed to take place between the Republican and Democratic parties during the 2000, 2004, 2008, and 2012 presidential elections.

Since arriving in California in the fall of 1992, a significant percentage of my time has been spent researching and drafting a philosophically intensive twelve-hundred-page monograph setting forth my analysis of the strategic, tactical, and logistical state of affairs in which I believe our nation finds itself here at the end of the almost century-long struggle between capitalism and communism. In the appendix, I present a brief, distilled outline of the major conclusions to which I have come regarding this important issue, and I set forth there the steps that I believe that we need to take as a human family to effectively address and solve the serious public policy problems that confront us in the twenty-first century. My limited point here, however, is that Sara and I have not simply "folded our tent" and retired from public interest work following the shutting down of the Iran-Contra investigation by the forces of reaction and the revocation of the 501(c)(3) tax-exempt charter of the Christic Institute by George Bush in retaliation for our having helped oust him from office. I have spent many long days and nights reading and continuing the research and writing that I began at Harvard Divinity School in the fall of 1973, after just three short years of experiencing deep concern in the face of the deep gap that I discovered between the *ideal* American reality as we had been promised it was and the *real* America and the real international reality.

When the Iran-Contra investigation came to an end, I took full advantage of whatever position I had achieved through my first twenty-five years of practice as a lawyer, and over the next years, as a member of Gorbachev's State of the World Forum, to affirmatively develop a concrete alternative progressive worldview, and its agenda, to replace the dialectical organizing principle of the Cold War era with a New Paradigm worldview. So while it may *have appeared* that I had merely suppressed my emotional trauma engendered by the unraveling of the Iran-Contra case and the closing of the Christic Institute by George Bush and his reactionary allies, I was in fact responding entirely rationally in light of the specific training I was fortunate enough to have received earlier in my life. I felt it to be my duty to provide the best possible advice that I could to my fellow citizens to help them cope with the legal and political challenges with which we found ourselves confronted by that failure—indeed *refusal*—on the part of our Democratic and Republican Party leaders to address the critical constitutional issues presented to us by the Iran-Contra scandal.

For the last ten years, I have been busy and productive trying to reach, and sometimes succeeding in reaching, these goals. Sara and I are happy and healthy, teaching now at UC Santa Cruz, living on beautiful Monterey Bay. We have remained deeply engaged in public interest litigation. Most recently, we have been occupied preparing a major federal civil rights litigation to be filed on behalf of the great Sioux Nation (the Oceti Sakowin Oyate) against the South Dakota Department of Social Services and its Child Protection Division for their seizure and removal of more than five thousand Lakota children from their parents, families, and tribe during the eight-year reign of George W. Bush. These Lakota children were involuntarily placed in large group homes (resembling the former boarding schools into which literally tens of thousands of Lakota and other Native American children were forcibly placed during the late nineteenth and early twentieth century) and, between 2001 and 2009, were then adopted out or involuntarily placed in white foster care homes. As a result, over 63 percent of the children who have aged out of those placements have been found, within two years, to be either homeless and on the streets, in prison, or dead. Peabody Award–winning radio journalist Laura Sullivan has reported on this issue over National Public Radio.[11]

This project takes Sara and me from California to South Dakota for ten days every month and has cost us our life savings to date. But the world is generous to those who serve their fellow human beings. So we enjoy the assistance of several extremely generous supporters, who provide us with small salaries that allow us to live in a modest rented home on Monterey

Bay and to continue our work. Sara and I now direct the Romero Institute, a 501(c)(3) public interest law office and public policy center in downtown Santa Cruz. Danny-Paul, our "Silkwood baby," is now happily graduated from Harvard University in the field of political philosophy and political theory, and is presently engaged in his graduate work in those two fields, and in theology, at the University of Chicago. Daegan, our "Equal Rights Amendment baby," has just finished producing, editing, and mixing his fourth CD of spiritual hip-hop songs under his performing name, Stepworthy the Freedom-Dweller. He is planning to enroll in Full Sail University in Florida this fall.

Sara and I are also busy with other endeavors. In 2015, we will found and direct the New Paradigm Academy in Lucerne, California. We also have plans to work in Los Angeles as script consultants on an HBO series based on our experiences. By that time, we intend to have returned the three thousand Lakota children who still remain in the unlawful custody of the state of South Dakota to their homes in South Dakota. We will then establish an all-Lakota-staffed Lakota People's Law Office in Rapid City, South Dakota.

APPENDIX

A S EARLY AS the age of the Greek Stoics, in the fourth century BC, a number of political, economic, intellectual, and cultural thinkers and leaders in Western civilization discerned that each ultimately nondivisible integer of matter in the entire universe (whether this unit be designated an atom, a quark, a neutrino, or something else) is physically attracted to every other such irreducible integer of matter in the universe, no matter what distance exists between them. Greek Stoics thought that each and every such interaction was governed by universal laws that function, always and everywhere within our universe, in exactly the same manner at all times. These immutable laws pursuant to which these physical integers of matter consistently interact were deemed to constitute "the natural laws of the universe." It was a principal tenet of this "natural law theory" that these natural laws bound every integer of matter into one single, internally harmonious unit: the cosmos.

Since these integers of matter went into making up everything, including human beings, all such things were deemed to be governed, if you will, by these same natural laws. Thus the belief was that our human family had simply to determine what specific human conduct, both individual and collective, was harmonious with these physical natural laws and *dis*harmonious with these natural laws in order to determine what specific forms of human conduct were right or wrong—for every human community everywhere and at all times. Thus originated, in Western civilization, the idea of some absolute referent for human conduct. Indeed, this is the specific belief that lies at the very heart of the entire ethical system known today as Greek philosophy. It is this essential belief that underlies all of Western civilization's historical quest for a system of moral valuation. Importantly, for our present analysis, this belief undergirds the political philosophy that was developed by Socrates in his famous *Dialogues*, which in turn constitutes the basis of the philosophy of all Western government set forth in the writings of Socrates's most famous student, Plato.

Most important for my purposes in this short essay is the fact that our United States Constitution was consciously founded on an eighteenth-century version of this very "natural law philosophy." And it was this very natural law worldview that the ruling classes of Western civilization attempted to push aside in the early nineteenth century, in the immediate aftermath of the French Revolution in Europe, and to replace with the 1824 "alternative theory of right" developed by Georg Wilhelm Friedrich Hegel: the philosophy of dialectical materialism. This attempt to substitute this new, strictly materialist and dialectical worldview for the more traditional natural law worldview occurred when leaders of the ruling classes in Europe and leaders of the Roman Catholic Church became seized with fear that the peasants and the unlanded might come to fully understand this natural law theory and invoke it to provide a rationale for a successful revolution—which had been lacking in the unsuccessful French Revolution in Europe in 1789.

However, such a philosophical natural law rationale was *not* lacking in our American Revolution in that same decade. This natural law worldview therefore proved to be successful as a means of rationalizing (that is, rendering more rational) our American Revolution against the domination of our common people by this same ruling class (both royalist and clerical), which had historically claimed a unique access to such "natural laws" as the source of its alleged superior power and authority.

The scientific validity of these subtle and intuitive natural law insights was shockingly established between 1923 and 1926 by scientific discoveries made in the new field of quantum physics. However, despite those extraordinary (and now virtually undisputed) scientific discoveries, the leaders of Western civilization continued to function as if the earlier theories underlying the utterly different Newtonian/Cartesian *materialist* worldview were still valid, declaring that our universe functions entirely separately and independently from our human intentions—and that we, as human beings, function entirely separately and independently from our universe and the physical world that surrounds us. This strange disconnect from now scientifically proven reality continues to hold true today, even in many fields of the "hard sciences" such as cosmology, astronomy, physics, medicine, biology, and molecular psychology, all of which are based directly on a specific understanding of the underlying laws of physics. It should be obvious to all members of Western civilization that all people of the twenty-first century should become educated so as to understand exactly why these important 1923-to-1926 physical discoveries ought to be employed to amend our human understanding in these important fields of the hard sciences. This task has been undertaken systematically by such scientists as William A. Tiller of Stanford University, who in 2001 published *Conscious Acts of Creation: The Emergence of a New Physics.*[12]

However, while most well-educated people realize that citizens of the twenty-first century should and must be educated to adequately understand the importance of these early twentieth-century discoveries as they apply to the physical (or hard) sciences, most people (even the very best-educated among us) do not as readily grasp the fact that the same truth holds for all of the nonphysical fields of human knowledge as well—because the data in these fields are also fundamentally embedded directly in our factual presumptions regarding the underlying physical laws of natural science. These latter fields of human knowledge are commonly referred to as the humanities and include such disparate fields as philosophy, theology, psychology, history, and political philosophy. By this time, the physical discoveries made between 1923 and 1926 in the field of quantum physics should logically have been thoroughly intregrated into the field of, for example, epistemology (the study of how we, as human beings, are able to ascertain the reality around us), having generated by now a dramatically increased recognition of the physical reality of the human faculty of intuition as an *additional* means by which we human beings are capable of directly obtaining objectively reliable data to answer the ultimate cosmic questions of fact that underlie our philosophy, our political philosophy, our theory of human psychology, our mode of spiritual expression, and the other derivative beliefs that make up the worldview that undergirds the Western humanities.

However, this recognition has not yet occurred. Indeed, the same scientific discoveries that were made between 1923 and 1926 should have, by this time, resulted in a dramatic increase in and endorsement of the central role that the human faculty of intuition plays in the construction and function of the ethical reasoning that we employ to determine what is right and what is wrong. This recognition should therefore by now be employed by the leaders of Western civilization to a much greater extent to supplement the now proven-unsound mode of ethical reasoning—grounded in the purely materialist assumptions of scientific materialism and scientific logical positivism—that is presently being subconsciously employed in the making of our most important ethical decisions, including those pertaining to fields of public policy, both domestic and international. This is indeed ironic, since this idea of having human intuition play a central role in the mode of ethical reasoning that we employ as human beings was the most important intent of adherents of the Stoical school of philosophy in ancient Greece—an idea that is taught in virtually all Western colleges and schools of law.

The answer to the present progressive dilemma in seeking to identify a new progressive human worldview to replace the now-discredited worldview of secular socialism lies, therefore, in the effective restructuring of the classical fields of human knowledge in Western civilization that constitute the traditional academic curriculum of the modern Western college and university system—including the field of political philosophy—to bring the content of these classical fields of human knowledge into full comportment with the content of the extraordinary scientific discoveries made in the twentieth century in the fields of quantum physics, human biological energy, and modern cosmology. I believe that the "freeze" imposed by the Cold War upon truly creative ideological thinking—both by direct Eastern authoritarian thinking and, less coercively but often equally effectively, Western cultural censorship, because such new discoveries so profoundly threatened the underlying dialectical materialist worldview that was ironically accepted in both the East and the West during the seventy-five-year period of the Cold War—prevented this creative integrative process from taking place.

In this context, in June 1989, almost three years prior to the end of the Cold War, a global worldview debate began. It was sparked by University of Chicago political science professor Francis Fukuyama through the publication of his article "The End of History" in *The National Interest*. The article proposed that, after the dissolution of the Soviet Union, there would be a brief window in which Western society could reset the political landscape. After the end of the Cold War, the debate sparked by this article grew into a full-fledged conflagration. It quickly drew into its flames spokespersons of the numerous reactionary and conservative think tanks throughout America, as well as those of the fewer moderate and the still-fewer liberal think tanks that existed in the country in 1992. Those spokespersons have now become participants in an intense global public policy debate as to which worldview should govern the post–Cold War era. However, only two very narrow questions seem to be being debated. These are:

1. Which *capitalist* worldview should all major American economic, political, academic, cultural, and business leaders operatively embrace and then deploy in the twenty-first century to guide the political, economic, and military decisions of our nation and of other Western nations: (a) the reactionary capitalist worldview; (b) the conservative capitalist worldview; or (c) the moderate capitalist worldview?

2. Once the chosen *capitalist* worldview is agreed upon, should this one worldview then be imposed upon the rest of the nations of our planet (a) unilaterally by the United States, acting alone as the sole remaining superpower after its victory in its protracted seventy-five-year Cold War against world communism; or (b) by a New Northern Industrial Alliance to be formed among the eight major North Atlantic industrial powers: the United States, Canada, Mexico (the three nations of NAFTA), the United Kingdom, Germany, France, Spain, Italy (the major signatory nations to GATT), and Russia?

There are, however, additional worldview offerings presently available to us. We must ask ourselves, has the brief window of opportunity to deliver the long-promised gifts of constitutional democracy and economic prosperity that Dr. Francis Fukuyama identified in his famous 1989 essay now closed? And if it has not, what can we do now, twenty-two years after the end of the Cold War, to successfully facilitate a New Paradigm worldview that will appeal to and be peacefully accepted by all the other cultures of our world? And if we believe that we should try to do this, exactly what should we present to the world as our highest ideals? Do these ideals truly mandate that all nations and cultures adopt capitalism or the free-market model as their sole mode of economic development? Do these ideals mandate that all nations and cultures adopt parliamentary representative democracy as the sole mechanism by which democracy must be implemented? Precisely which individual rights do we deem to be truly indispensable to a system of ordered liberty and to be therefore universal in nature? And which other individual rights might we be willing to concede to be merely cultural beliefs of the West and therefore potentially dispensable in other nations?

There are at least two additional options beyond the reactionary, conservative, and moderate capitalist worldviews that should be considered. The first is liberal capitalism, and the second is a genuinely progressive worldview that proffers a mixed array of potential economic modes of development and distribution of resources.

In June 1992, Dr. Zbigniew Brzezinski, of the Council on Foreign Relations, published a short monograph entitled *Out of Control: Global Turmoil on the Eve of the Twenty-First Century*. In this monograph, Brzezinski declared that our post–Cold War world was on the verge of imminent global chaos as early as 1993 within a specific thirty-two-nation region that he identified as "the Eurasian Oblong." This area stretched from the Adriatic Sea (the Balkans) eastward to the westernmost border of China's Xinjiang Province, and from the southernmost Russian frontier to the Persian Gulf.

Brzezinski predicted that this state of global chaos would be generated by the immediate geopolitical power vacuum created in that area of the world by the sudden and unanticipated collapse of the Russian Empire as a world power. As a result of this power vacuum, Brzezinski asserted, there would no longer be any chance of developing, within the foreseeable future, a stable Russian–Chinese–Middle Eastern alliance that would be culturally capable of peacefully governing that region in accordance with a clearly defined set of political, economic, social, business, and cultural principles that might have previously been agreed upon among those cultural powers. Brzezinski predicted that the United States would be sorely tempted to intervene in that part of the world, to attempt to police the region and to undertake the superficially appealing task of stopping what many would perceive to be an unacceptably dangerous threat to world stability. Indeed, Brzezinski predicted that many nation-states would actively implore the United States to *unilaterally* intervene in that part of the world in the face of the potentially soul-shattering examples of human torture and racial genocide that would be forthcoming in the immediate aftermath of the sudden end of the Cold War. However, Brzezinski sternly warned the leaders of the United States to resist yielding to this strong temptation and instead to consciously endure this temporary horror to engage in the task of reconfiguring the nations of the post–Cold War world into a new global confederal structure—separate and distinct from the United Nations—which the United States could then lead in projecting *collective* power into this dangerously unstable region of the world in the form of a multilateral alliance.

Brzezinski asserted that for this to happen, it would be absolutely necessary for the leaders of the United States and other Western world leaders to become the moral leaders of this New World Order. To earn this unique status, Brzezinski argued, U.S. leaders had to (a) publicly identify and (b) publicly commit themselves to voluntarily comporting their conduct—both individually and collectively—in strict accordance with a specific set of ethical principles, ultimately moral in their nature. Brzezinski argued that a voluntary comportment of conduct in accordance with a commonly agreed-upon set of essentially moral principles would, in practice, lead the nations of the West away from what he called the pursuit of permissive cornucopia, or the "actual ideal" of Western civilization. He identified this pursuit of permissive cornucopia as greed and the pursuit of material wealth on the part of individual private American citizens; corporate greed on the part of managers of private American business corporations; and the overt and conscious pursuit of the accumulation of unilateral American political, military, and economic power and control over the natural resources of the rest of the world on the part of leaders in both the Republican and Democratic parties.

A voluntary comportment of our leaders' conduct would not only lead the nations of the West away from the exclusive pursuit of permissive cornucopia but would also lead us *toward* the more successful accommodation of "the general social needs of the people of the world": (1) the pursuit of more effective alleviation of global poverty; (2) the preservation of our natural environment; and (3) the protection of the authenticity of each individual human identity in the face of the growing threat posed by technology in the fields of human genetic engineering, cloning, and the development of deadly weaponry. Brzezinski argued that only with this described cooperation of our leaders would the United States be able to successfully earn—rather than unilaterally claim—the role of moral leader of a new global confederation, guided by democratic principles and free-market values but voluntarily self-restrained from the exclusive pursuit of permissive cornucopia.

Brzezinski identified the achievement of these two specific tasks as "the challenge that confronts the political, economic, intellectual, cultural and business leaders of the United States and the Western World" in the aftermath of the Cold War. When analyzed objectively, Zbigniew Brzezinski's 1992 "moral challenge" can be seen as nothing more radical or novel than a simple rearticulation of the advice that the chairman of Harvard University's Department of Philosophy, John Rawls, gave to Western leaders in his famous 1972 *A Theory of Justice*. In that historic treatise on moral ethics, Rawls advocated that Western policy makers, in search of a truly effective and morally defensible standard of justice, should self-consciously amend any standard public policy choice they might otherwise be motivated to make strictly in accordance with a wooden application to the classical utilitarian mode of ethical reasoning, thereby selecting the public policy choice that, more or less mechanically, would generate "the greatest good for the greatest number." Rawls suggested that U.S. and Western leaders should instead employ an alternative mode of ethical reasoning that would cause them to select an alternative public policy choice that would also provide at least *something* for the least well-off. Rawls argued in his 1972 work that the adoption and employment of such a self-consciously alternative mode of ethical reasoning on the part of Western policy makers would generate an ethical compromise between (a) the adoption and merely wooden application of a strictly classical utilitarian mode of ethical reasoning in the field of public policy making and (b) the adoption and employment of the mode of ethical reasoning advocated by adherents of what Rawls identified as the Intuitionist School of Justice, which is given to uttering such seemingly impenetrable declarations as "All men are created equal [and] are endowed by their Creator with certain inalienable Rights . . . among these are Life, Liberty and the pursuit of Happiness."

This compromise mode of ethical reasoning was, of course, just a more philosophically sophisticated restatement of the classic Western liberal ethic.

Brzezinski's 1992 recommendation that this specific liberal compromise be utilized by Western leaders to arrive at their post–Cold War public policy positions was concretely translated into his advocacy of U.S. domestic and foreign policies. American leaders would dictate the public policy choices of our post–Cold War order *primarily* by the operation of the unregulated play of capitalist market forces, but consciously tempered by national leaders through their self-conscious act of supplementing choices by simultaneously providing at least some minimum guarantee of individual well-being to those "least well-off."

Thus both John Rawls and Zbigniew Brzezinski proposed, as a guide for immediate American post–Cold War policies, nothing more than a simple rearticulation of the classical liberal ethic publicly advocated in 1955 by Professor Louis Hartz of Harvard University in his famous work *The Liberal Tradition in America.*

Unfortunately, the progressive community within Western civilization did not respond to Professor Fukuyama's 1989 challenge because it failed to take seriously his prediction of the imminent demise of the Soviet Union. Unlike adherents to other systemic worldviews, members of the progressive community in the United States remained intellectually and philosophically paralyzed following the collapse of the Soviet Union. The progressive community throughout Western civilization stood like the proverbial deer in the headlights of the onrushing truck of reactionary worldview advocates, because its members were simply stunned by the sudden and unexpected collapse of the nation-state that had led the worldwide secular socialist movement for the duration of their lifetimes.

While adherents to the progressive worldview consider Brzezinski's merely liberal call for a more balanced organizing principle to be entirely inadequate, progressives *did* endorse his call for the public identification of a set of ethical principles in accordance with which leaders should comport their conduct. However, adherents to the progressive worldview believe it to be the duty of a democratic government to make adherence to such ethical principles concretely enforceable public legislation.

Twenty-two years after the end of the Cold War, the leadership of the American liberal community still has not deigned to identify such a set of ethical principles. Instead, they have virtually abandoned the field now that the threat of communism has disappeared. This is the tragic scope of the post–Cold War failure on the part of the leadership of the American liberal community—and the American Democratic Party—especially on the part of President Barack Obama, Secretary of State John Kerry, and former secretary of state and senator Hillary Clinton, any one of whom might have effectively offered himself or herself to the American public as such a post–Cold War leader of the American liberal community. Indeed, Hillary Clinton and John Kerry both expressly disassociated themselves from the principles, policies, and programs of the liberal worldview during the 2004 and 2008 Democratic presidential campaigns. And Barack Obama's actual conduct, as distinguished from his mere rhetoric, belies his commitment even to true liberal ethics.

Until this task has been faced and effectively completed by the leadership of the liberal community in the United States, that community will remain disconnected from its true source of ethical and moral authority. Consequently, it will not be asked by the American people to govern. More importantly, until this task has been effectively performed, the liberal community in the United States will not even have a concrete idea as to how to lead the American people or the Western world.

The true tragedy of our present post–Cold War situation is that this task could be quite easily performed by the liberal and progressive communities if we would simply engage in the classically understood discipline of consciously discerning and publicly identifying a commonly agreed-upon set of four pillar beliefs[13] that underlie our respective worldviews (an idea that has long been academically recognized in the field of comparative social ethics); have each community translate those specific pillar beliefs—through the derivation, from these strategic assumptions, of pertinent "middle axioms"; and then translate these respective middle axioms into concrete policies and programs.[14]

Unfortunately, the performing of that task within the liberal community since the end of the Cold War has been left to members of the liberal community who are satisfied with seeking the minimalist objective of identifying principles and policies that will do nothing more than "more effectively *address*" (rather than solve) our major public policy problems, while placing primary emphasis on safeguarding and preserving the continued "pursuit of permissive cornucopia" by stubbornly adhering to transnational corporate capitalism as the sole acceptable mode of economic development.

Since members of the progressive community believe that this classic liberal strategic goal is morally inadequate, we progressives must then direct our efforts to identifying underlying pillar beliefs of a genuinely progressive worldview that consciously seeks to solve the life-threatening global public policy problems of massive global climate change, the potential global collapse of an economic system rooted in the open-ended exploitation of our inevitably limited natural resources, potential thermonuclear war between a potential New Northern Industrial Alliance and the newly emerging New Asian Empire led by China, and the maintenance of human integrity in the face of rapidly developing technology both in the area of weapons of mass destruction and in the field of human genetic engineering—whether the pillar beliefs of this worldview require a transnational corporate capitalist mode of economic development and distribution of natural resources or some additional choices.

That is the task that is now before the progressive community.

NOTES

1   I will set forth the full details of that account—and those of my future investigation of that information—in the full book that will follow the publication of this legal memoir.

2   Jesuit Conference, Documents of the Thirty-second General Congregation of the Society of Jesus (Washington, D.C.: The Jesuit Conference, 1975).

3   Ibid.

4   Each unit of plutonium recovered from nuclear waste materials generated by a specific private nuclear power plant bore an absolutely unmistakable "radiological fingerprint" consisting of unique isotopic readings that could be ascertained by means of a simple examination.

5   In 1991, Harold Behrens was convicted of first-degree murder of another person. He died in prison in Springfield, Missouri, in 2004.

6   We later traced Jack Holcomb to a tiny town in West Germany, home to one of the major Bohnner-Meinhoff antiterrorist training centers in Europe, at which "antiterrorists" are trained to jump out of trees onto each other.

7   Stansfield Turner, the CIA director appointed by Jimmy Carter, was so hated by his colleagues at the CIA—for firing more than 420 members of the CIA's Covert Operations Division in the famous October 1977 "Halloween Massacre" and for cutting off all military aid to both Manuel Noriega of Nicaragua and the shah of Iran (both CIA favorites)—that his CIA colleagues had intentionally sandbagged Turner by whiting out the wrong sections of the report to humiliate him before this committee.

8   A 1976 investigation by the Senate Select Committee to Governmental Operations with Respect to Intelligence Activities (the Church Committee) verified that at least forty-two such former or active employees of the Central Intelligence Agency were "embedded" inside major American news agencies, including *Time* magazine, *Life*, *Newsweek*, all three national television news networks, and almost every major metropolitan newsroom in the country. See United States Senate, Final Report of the Select Committee to Study Governmental Operations with Respect to Intelligence Activities (Washington, D.C.: U.S. Government Printing Office, 1976).

9   Walter Leroy Moody was convicted of murdering Judge Vance in retaliation for an
    adverse decision entered against Moody in a case before the Eleventh Circuit Court
    of Appeals, even though Judge Vance had nothing whatsoever to do with considering
    or ruling on Moody's case.

10 See Seymour Hersh, "The Iran-Contra Committees: Did They Protect Reagan?" *The
    New York Times Magazine*, April 29, 1990.

11 See National Public Radio, "Native Foster Care: Lost Children, Shattered
    Families," October 25, 2011, www.npr.org/2011/10/25/141672992/native
    -foster-care-lost-children-shattered-families (accessed April 24, 2013).

12 See also Tiller's *Science and Human Transformation: Subtle Energies, Intentionality,
    and Consciousness*; and David Bohm's *The Undivided Universe* and *Wholeness and
    the Implicate Order*. This suspicion is further supported by the works of Saul-Paul
    Sirag of the University of California, Berkeley. See his "A Combinational Derivation
    of the Proton-Electron Mass Ratio," *Nature* 268 (July 1977), 254; his more exten-
    sive "Physical Constraints as Cosmological Constraints," *International Journal of
    Theoretical Physics* 22 (1983), 1067–89; and his "Consciousness: A Hyperspace
    View," in Jeffrey Mishlove, *The Roots of Consciousness* (Oakland, CA: Council
    Oak Books, 1993), 327–65.

13 These beliefs are (1) cosmology (the theory as to how our physical universe came into
    being and pursuant to what eternally consistent operating principles our universe
    operates); (2) teleology (the theory as to whether our physical universe is "unfold-
    ing," or evolving, pursuant to some discernable teleological pattern or algorithm
    that enables us to ascertain toward what end—if any—our universe is evolving; (3)
    ontology (the theory as to how consciousness—especially human consciousness—
    came into being, or whether it has always existed and will continue to exist eternally;
    and (4) epistemology (the theory as to what means we as human beings have at our
    disposal to ascertain, or discern, the answers to such "cosmic questions" as numbers
    1, 2, and 3).

14 For an explication as to how this process is performed, see John A. Coleman, *An
    American Strategic Theology* (New York: Paulist Press, 1982).

SOURCES AND BIBLIOGRAPHY

Abell, Aaron I. *American Catholic Thought on Social Questions*. New York: Bobbs Merrill Co., Inc., 1968.

Ammermman, Robert. *Belief, Knowledge, and Truth: Readings in the Theory of Knowledge*. New York: Charles Scribner's and Sons, 1970.

Anderson, Scott and John Lee Anderson. *Inside the League*. New York: Dodd, Meade and Co. 1986.

Anderson, Sherry and Paul H. Ray. *The Cultural Creative: How 50 Million People are Changing the World*. New York: Harmony Books, 2000.

Ardrey, Robert. *The Territorial Imperative: The Animal Origins and the Property of Nations*. New York: Atheneum, 1966.

Aronson, Elliot. *The Social Animal*. 6th ed. New York: WH Freeman & Co, 1954.

Bailey, Charles and Fletcher Krebal. *Seven Days in May*. New York: Bantam Books, 1962.

Bennett, J.G. *The Dramatic Universe, Vol. 4: History*. Charlestown, West Virginia: Claymont Communications Co., 1966.

Berger, John J. *Nuclear Power: The Unviable Option*. New York: Dell Publishing Co. 1977.

Blada, H.E. *The Warrior Culture and the Ecological Crisis*. Hanover, Massachusetts: Christopher Publishing, 1991.

Bonhoeffer, Dietrich. *Letters and Papers from Prison*. New York: MacMillan Co. 1953

Braden, Gregg. *The Divine Matrix: Bridging Time, Space, Miracles, and Belief*. New York: Hay House Inc., 2007.

Brisard, Jean-Charles and Guillaume Dasquie. *Forbidden Truth: US0-Taliban Secret Oil Diplomacy*. New York: Thoires Mountain Press, 2002.

Brownstein, Ronald and Nina Easton. *Reagan's Ruling Class*. New York: Pantheon Books, 1982.

Capra, Fritjof. *The Tao of Physics*. New York: Bantam Books, 1976.

Capra, Fritjof. *The Turning Point: Science, Society, and the Rising Culture*. New York: Bantam Books, 1982.

Carson, Rachael. *Silent Spring*. Greenwich, Connecticut: Fawcett Publications, 1962.

Churchill, Ward. *Agents of Repression: the FBI's Secret War Against the Black Panther Party and the American Indian Movement*. Cambridge: South End Press, 1988.

Cockburn, Leslie. *Out of Control*. New York : Atlantic Monthly Press, 1987

Cohen, Lee and Steven Avner. *Nuclear Weapons and the Future of Humanity: The Fundamental Questions*. Rowman & Allanheld Publishers, 1986.

Colfax, J. David and Jack Roach. *Radical Sociology*. New York: Basic Books Inc., 1971.

Collins, Larry and Dominique Lapierre. *Freedom at Midnight*. Avon Books, 1975.

Derrett, Daniel C. *Darwin's Dangerous Idea: Evolution and the Meaninglessness of Life*. New York: Simon & Schuster, 1995.

Drinan, Robert F. *Cry of the Oppressed: The History and Hope of the Human Rights Revolution*. San Francisco: Harper & Row Publishers, 1987.

Elanet, Ivan. *The Empire Has No Clothes: US Foreign Policy Exposed*. Oakland, CA: The Independent Institute, 2004.

Feldbaum, Carl and Ronald Bee. *Looking the Tiger in the Eye: Confronting the Nuclear Threat*. New York: Harper & Row, 1985.

Freire, Paulo. *Pedagogy of Freedom: Ethics, Democracy, and Courage*. New York: Roman & Littlefield Publishers, 1998.

Freire, Paulo. *The Pedagogy of the Oppressed*. New York: Continuum & Seabury Press, 1973.

Fuller, Buckminster R. *Critical Path*. New York: St Martin's Press, 1981.

Garrison, James. *The Plutonium Culture: From Hiroshima to Harrisburg*. New York: Continuum, 1981.

Gelbspan, Ross. *Break-ins, Death Threats and the FBI*. Boston: South End Press, 1991.

Gerzon, Mark. *A House Divided: Six Belief Systems Struggling for America's Soul*. New York: Jeremy Tarcher & Putnam Books, 1996.

Golden, Remmy and Michael Connell. *Sanctuary: The New Underground Railroad*. New York: Orbis Books, 1986.

Gore, Al. *Earth in the Balance: Ecology and the Human Spirit*. New York: Plume Books, Penguin Group, 1993.

Goulden, Joseph. *The Death Merchant: The Rise and Fall of Edwin P. Wilson*. New York: Simon & Schuster, 1984.

Greider, William. *Secrets of the Temple*. New York: Simon & Schuster, 1987.

Griffin, David Ray. *Reenchantment without Supernaturalism: A Process Philosophy of Religion*. Ithaca, New York: Cromwell University Press, 2001.

Halberstam, David. *The Best and the Brightest*. New York: Penguin Books, 1972.

Harrington, Michael. *Politics at God's Funeral: The Spiritual Crisis of Western Civilization*. New York: Penguin Books, 1983.

Harrington, Michael. *Socialism, Past and Future*. New York: Arcade Publishing, 1989.

Hendricks, Steve. *The Unquiet Grave: The FBI and the Struggle for the Soul of the Indian Country*. New York: Thunder's Mouth Press, 2006.

Herbert, Frank. *Dune*. New York: The Berkeley Publishing Group, 1965.

Hilgartner, Stephen, et al. *Nuke Speak: The Selling of Nuclear Technology in America*. New York: Penguin Books, 1982.

Holleman, Edith and Andrew Love. *Inside the Shadow Government; Declaration of Plaintiffs' Counsel, Filed by the Christic Institute*. United States District Court: Miami, Florida, 31 March 1988.

James, William. *The Varieties of Religious Experience*. Middlesex, England: Penguin Classics, 1902.

Jewett, Robert. *The Captain America Complex: The Dilemma of Zealous Nationalism*. Santa Fe, New Mexico: Bear & Co., 1991.

John, Da Free. *Scientific Proof of the Existence of God Will Soon Be Announced by the White House*. Middletown, CA: Dawn Horse Press, 1980.

Karp, Walter. *Indispensable Enemies: The Politics of Misrule in America*. New York: Franklin Square Press, 1993.

King, Martin Luther, Jr. *Why We Can't Wait*. New York: Signet Books, 1964.

Kingsley, Peter. *Reality*. Inverness, CA: The Golden Sufi Center, 2003.

Kohn, Havard. *Who Killed Karen Silkwood?* New York: Summit Books, Simon & Schuster, 1981.

Kuhn, Thomas. *The Structure of Scientific Revolutions*. Chicago: University of Chicago Press, 1962.

Kwitney, Jonathan. *Crimes of Patriots*. New York: W.W. Norton & Co. 1987.

Lapham, Lewis. *The Wish for Kings*. New York: Grove Press, 1993.

Lee, Martin and Bruce Schlain. *Acid Dreams: The CIA, LSD, and the Sixties Rebellion*. New York: Grove Press, 1980.

Leigh, David. *The Wilson Plot*. New York: Pantheon Books, 1988.

Maas, Peter. *Manhunt*. New York: Random House, 1986.

Manchester, William. *The Glory and the Dream.* New York: Bantam Books, 1974.

Martin, Malachi. *The Final Conclave.* New York: Simon & Schuster Pocket Books, 1978.

Martin, Malachi. *The Jesuits: The Society of Jesus and the Betrayal of the Roman Catholic Church.* New York: Simon & Schuster, 1987.

McCoy, Alfred. *The Politics of Heroin.* New York: Lawrence Hill Books, 1991.

Muck, Otto and Karl Rahner. *The Transcendental Method.* New York: Herder and Herder, 1968.

O'Brien, David and Thomas Shannon. *Renewing the Earth: Catholic Documents on Peace, Justice, and Liberation.* New York: Image Books, Doubleday and Co., 1966.

Obst, David. *Too Good To Be Forgotten: The 60s and 70s.* New York: John Wiley and Sons, Inc., 1998.

Ore, Tracey. *The Social Construction of Difference and Inequality: Race, Class, Gender, and Sexuality.* Boston: McGraw Hill, 2003.

Parent, Michael. *Democracy for the Few.* 5th ed. New York: Sr. Martins Press, 1988.

Parry, Robert. *Fooling American.* New York: William Morrow, 1992.

Parry, Robert. *Lost History: Contras, Cocaine, the Press and 'Project Truth.'* Arlington, Virginia: The Media Consortium, 1999.

Peck, Scott M. *People of the Lie: The Hope for Healing Human Evil.* New York: Simon & Schuster, 1983.

Perkins, John. *Confessions of an Economic Hit Man.* New York: A Plume Book & Penguin Group, 2004.

Pilger, John. *The New Rulers of the World.* London and New York: Verso, 2002.

Pringle, Peter and James Spigleman. *The Nuclear Barons.* New York: Avon Books, 1981.

Quigley, Carroll. *Tragedy and Hope: A History of the World In Our Time.* New York: McMillian & Co., 1966.

Rashke, Richard. *The Killing of Karen Silkwood.* Boston: Houghton Mifflin Co., 1981.

Rawls, John. *A Theory of Justice.* Cambridge, Massachusetts: Harvard University Press, 1971.

Reich, Charles A. *The Greening of America.* New York: Bantam Books, 1970.

Reiser, Oliver. *Cosmic Humanism: A Theory of the Eight-Dimensional Universe.* Cambridge, Massachusetts: Schenkman Publishing Co., 1966.

Roof, Wade Clark. *A Generation of Seekers: The Spiritual Journey of the Baby Boom Generation.* San Francisco: Harper, 1993.

Roszak, Theodore. *Where the Wasteland Ends: Politics and Transcendence in Post-Industrial Society*. New York: Anchor Books, 1973.

Roszak, Thodore. *The Making of a Counter Culture: Reflections in the Technocratic Society of Its Youthful Opposition*. New York: Anchor Books & Doubleday & Co. Inc., 1969.

Rothenberg, Paul S. *White Privilege: Essential Readings on the Other Side of Racism*. New York: Worth Publishers, 2002.

Savage, David. *Turning Right: The Making of the Rehnquist Supreme Court*. New York: John Wiley and Sons, Inc, 1992.

Schell, Jonathan. *The Fate of the Earth*. New York: Alfred A Knopf, 1982.

Schultz, Bud and Ruth Schultz. *It Did Happen Here*. Berkeley: University of California Press, 1993.

Schwartz, Herman. *Right Wing Justice: The Conservative Campaign to Take Over the Courts*. New York: Nation Books, 2004.

Scott, Peter Dale and Jonathan Marshall. *Cocaine Politics*. Berkeley: University of California Press, 1991.

Scott, Peter Dale and Jonathan Marshall. *Obstruction of Justice: The Reagan-Bush Cover Up of the Contra Drug Connection*. Berkeley: University of California Press, 1990.

Sharp, Gene. *The Politics of Non-Violent Action*. Vol I, II, III. Boston: Extended Horizons Books, 1973.

Sheehan, Neil. *The Pentagon Papers: The Secret History of the Vietnam War*. New York: Butterfield, Fox, Bantam Books, 1971.

Sick, Gary. *October Surprise*. Toronto: Time Books, Random House, 1991.

Simpson, Christopher. *Blowback*. New York: Weisenfield & Nicholson, 1988.

Smith, Houston. *Beyond the Post-Modern Mind*. Revised edition. New York: Crossroads Publishing Co., 1992.

Spring, Joel H. *Education and the Rise of the Corporate State*. Boston: Beacon Press, 1972.

Stevens, Franklin. *If This Be Treason: Your Sons Tell Their Stories of Why They Won't Fight*. New York: Peter H. Wyden, Inc., 1970.

Stevenson, Leslie. *The Study of Human Nature*. Oxford: Oxford University Press, 1981.

Stevenson, William. *Kiss the Boys Goodbye*. New York: Time Warner, 1992.

Strauss, William and Neil Howe. *Generations: The history of America's Future*. New York: William Morrow, 1991.

Sun Tzu. *The Art of War,* in *Classics of Strategy and Counsel,* Boston: Thomas Cleary, ed., Shambala, 2000.

Tarnas, Richard. *Cosmos and Psyche: Intricacies of a New Worldview.* New York: Viking Press, 2006.

Tarnas, Richard. *The Passion of the Western Mind: Understanding Ideas That Have Shaped Our World View.* New York: Ballantine Books, 1991.

The Christic Institute. *Inside the Shadow Government.* Washington DC: 1988.

Tiller, William. *Science and Human Transformation: Subtle Energies, Intentionality, and Consciousness.* Walnut Creek, CA: Quality Books, 1997.

Timms, Moira. *Beyond Prophecies and Predictions: A Guide to the Coming Changes.* New York: Ballantine Books, 1980.

Unger, Craig. *House of Bush, House of Saud: The Secret Relationship Between the World's Two Most Powerful Dynasties.* New York: Scribner, 2004.

Vankin, Jonathan. *Conspiracies, Coverups and Crimes.* New York: Paragon House, 1991.

Vidal, Gore. *Imperial American.* New York: Nation Books, 2004.

Walsh, Lawrence E. *Final Report of the Independent Counsel for Iran/Contra Matters; Vol. 1 Investigations and Prosecutions,* United States Court of Appeals for the District of Columbia Circuit, 4 August 1993.

Walsh, Lawrence E. *Firewall; the Iran Contra Conspiracy and cover-up.* W.W. Norton & Co. 1997.

Wheaton, Philip. *Flowering of the Prophetic Word in the Americas: Unmasking US Imperialism and Religious Fundamentalism.* Washington DC: Epica Books, 2009.

Whitehead, Alfred N. *Process and Reality: An Essay on Cosmology.* Macmillan & Co., 1929.

Yergin, Daniel. *The Shattered Peace: The Origins of the Cold War and the National Security State.* Boston: Houghton Mifflin Co., 1977.

Young, Arthur M. *The Reflexive Universe: The Evolution of Consciousness.* Cambria, CA: Anodos Publications, 1976.

Zweig, Connie. *Meeting the Shadow: The Hidden Power of the Dark Side of Human Nature.* Los Angeles: Jeremy Tarcher, Inc., 1991.

INDEX

1980 Refugee Act, 411, 413, 423, 434

1992 United States Defense Department Policy Planning Guidance Document, 573–574

20/20, 368, 392

2506 Brigade, 397

5412 Committee of the National Security Council, 213

60 Minutes, 512

9/11, 4, 560

A

A&P, 174–176, 178

ABC, 350, 368

ABC Evening News, 285

ABC News, 112, 445

Abernathy, Rev. Ralph David, 270, 272

Abourezk, James, 455–456

Abplanalp, Robert, 519

Abrams, Creighton, 493, 495

Abrams, Elliott, 475, 508, 510, 511, 555, 576, 579

Abrams, Floyd, 108, 112, 114, 124, 127, 128, 129, 130, 141, 142–144, 146, 147, 148, 152, 155, 157–161, 164–173, 176, 178, 179, 180, 351

Abzug, Bella, 304, 392, 419, 517

ACLU, 114, 115, 116, 122, 195, 197, 217, 224–227, 238–242, 251, 260, 303, 304, 327, 391, 454, 539, 295298

Actors Studio, 124

Aderholt, Heinie, 513

ADEX list, 439

Adirondack Mountains, 8, 20, 37, 44, 45

Afghanistan, 465, 518

Agee, Philip, 495; Inside the Company: CIA Diary, 495

AIM, 195–197, 217, 224, 251, 252, 254, 285, 304

Alabama, 443, 451, 530

Alabama State National Guard, 443

Alamogordo (NM), 21

Alch, Gerald L. (Gerry), 92, 183, 208, 209

Allied powers, 2, 3, 18

Alvarez, Bob, 283, 286, 289, 323, 327, 328, 391

American Catholic Church, 48, 258, 260, 261, 263, 266, 390, 412, 418, 419, 421, 585. See also Catholicism

American Civil Liberties Union (ACLU). See ACLU

American Federation of Teachers, 225, 226, 227

American Indian Movement (AIM). See AIM

American Indian Policy Review Commission, 455–456

American Nazi Party, 395, 397, 398, 399

American Revolution, 585

American Sanctuary Movement, 410–414, 418–420, 428, 439–441, 476

American Trial Lawyers Association, 388

Amsterdam, Tony, 111–113, 173

Anagnos, Aris, 548

Anderson, Jack, 455

Andros Island (FL), 328, 329

Angel, Arthur, 347, 357

Angiulo Brothers, 211

Angleton, James Jesus, 519

Anhoui, Jean, 64; Un Chant d'Amour, 64, 65

Annapolis (MD), 14, 15, 511

Antioch Law School, 285, 310, 392, 403

ANV, Inc., 480, 515

Anzio (IT), 21

AP. See Associated Press (AP)

Arabian American Oil Company, 572

Archdiocese of Boston (MA), 48

Argentina, 496, 519

Arizona, 214, 215, 225

Arkansas, 514, 577

Armitage, Richard, 482

Armstrong, Michael, 107, 108, 117–118, 119, 128

Armstrong, Scott, 481–482, 483, 515

Arrupe House, 30, 278, 289, 310, 314, 388, 389, 391, 399, 402, 410, 566

Arrupe, Fr. Pedro, 257–259

Ash-Shiraa, 520

Asoin, Les, 529

Associated Press (AP), 275, 368, 376, 442–443, 444, 449, 540, 549

ATF, 195, 196, 217, 397, 398, 399

Athens, 523

Atlanta, 301

Atomic Age, 12, 21

Attica Correctional Facility (NY), 30

Aurora Publications, 350, 352, 353, 354, 355, 356

Austin, Patti, 390, 393, 485, 491, 510

Australia, 514

Avirgan, Tony, 445–450, 540, 543, 545–546, 547, 548, 566

Axis powers, 3

B

Baba Muktananda, 253

Baba Ram Dass, 254

Badwar, Indie, 455

Bailey, Alch & Gillis, 183, 220, 261, 297

Bailey, F. Lee (Lee), 90–93, 130, 180–196, 207–211, 217–220, 261, 297

Bailey, Lynda, 184, 186

Baird, William (Bill), 98–99, 100, 102

Ballero, Joe, 97, 98, 99–100

Banco Internationale (MX), 215

Bancroft, Harding, 111

Barger, Brian, 268–275, 442, 444, 445, 448, 449, 451, 452, 481, 511, 512, 530, 549

Barker, Bernard, 207, 211, 212, 215, 216

Barnes, Michael (Mike), 508, 510, 579

Bates, John, 111

Batista, Fulgencio, 513

Battle of Midway, 2

Bay of Pigs, 216, 467

Beck, Gary, 63

Behrens, Harold, 320, 323, 326, 358, 359, 366

Beirut, 523

Belize, 515

Bellecourt, Clyde, 197, 224